Ancestral House

ANCESTRAL HOUSE

The Black Short Story
in the Americas
and Europe

edited by

CHARLES H. ROWELL

WestviewPress

A Division of HarperCollinsPublishers

Copyright © 1995 by Westview Press, Inc., A Division of HarperCollins Publishers, Inc.

Published in 1995 in the United States of America by Westview Press, Inc., 5500 Central Avenue, Boulder, Colorado 80301-2877, and in the United Kingdom by Westview Press, 12 Hid's Copse Road, Cumnor Hill, Oxford OX2 9JJ

Library of Congress Cataloging-in-Publication Data
Ancestral house : the Black short story in the Americas and Europe /
    edited by Charles H. Rowell.
        p.   cm.
    A collection of short stories.
    ISBN 0-8133-2028-3. — ISBN 0-8133-2029-1 (pbk.)
    1. Short stories—Black authors. I. Rowell, Charles H.
PN6120. 92. B45A53   1995
808. 83'108896—dc20   95-15429
                                                                                          CIP

Printed and bound in the United States of America

The paper used in this publication meets the requirements of the American National Standard for Permanence of Paper for Printed Library Materials Z39.48-1984.

10   9   8   7   6   5   4   3   2   1

To the memory of
BESSIE WASHINGTON JONES
(1932–1995),
my first writing teacher
—C.H.R.

Contents

Foreword, JOHN EDGAR WIDEMAN   xiii
Introduction, CHARLES H. ROWELL   xv
Acknowledgments   xxix

AI, *United States*
    Absolution   1

JOSÉ ALCÁNTARA ALMÁNZAR, *Dominican Republic*
    My Singular Irene   8

TINA MCELROY ANSA, *United States*
    Willie Bea and Jaybird   14

TONI CADE BAMBARA, *United States*
    The Organizer's Wife   21

AMIRI BARAKA, *United States*
    Words   34

HAL BENNETT, *United States/Mexico*
    Miss Askew on Ice   36

DIONNE BRAND, *Trinidad/Canada*
    I Used to Like the Dallas Cowboys   50

OCTAVIA E. BUTLER, *United States*
    The Evening and the Morning and the Night   59

OSWALDO DE CAMARGO, *Brazil*
    Civilization   78

AÍDA CARTAGENA PORTALATÍN, *Dominican Republic*
    They Called Her Aurora (The Love of Donna Summer)   84

MAXINE CLAIR, *United States*
    Cherry Bomb   87

AUSTIN C. CLARKE, *Barbados/Canada*
    Griff   95

MICHELLE CLIFF, *Jamaica/United States*
    Columba   110

MERLE COLLINS, *Grenada/England/United States*
The Visit   117

CHRISTINE CRAIG, *Jamaica*
Night Thoughts   125

LUIZ SILVA "CUTI," *Brazil*
Avenues   129

SAMUEL R. DELANY, *United States*
Tapestry   131

RENÉ DEPESTRE, *Haiti/France*
Rosena on the Mountain   135

RITA DOVE, *United States*
Under the Rose   151

SUZANNE DRACIUS-PINALIE, *Martinique*
Sweat, Sugar, and Blood   156

HENRY DUMAS, *United States*
Ark of Bones   164

QUINCE DUNCAN, *Costa Rica*
A Letter   174

NELSON ESTUPIÑÁN BASS, *Ecuador*
The Miracle   179

PERCIVAL EVERETT, *United States*
Randall Randall   188

GUY-MARK FOSTER, *United States*
This Man and Me   199

ERNEST J. GAINES, *United States*
Three Men   205

THOMAS GLAVE, *Jamaica/United States*
Accidents   227

LORNA GOODISON, *Jamaica*
By Love Possessed   241

CLAIRE HARRIS, *Trinidad/Canada*
She Wakes   246

WILSON HARRIS, *Guyana/England*
Kanaima   256

JOHN HOLMAN, *United States*
Presence   262

KELVIN CHRISTOPHER JAMES, *Trinidad/United States*
Circle of Shade — 265

CHARLES JOHNSON, *United States*
Alēthia — 274

EDWARD P. JONES, *United States*
The First Day — 281

GAYL JONES, *United States*
The Fisherman's House — 285

JOHN R. KEENE, *United States*
Transits — 292

WILLIAM MELVIN KELLEY, *United States*
My Next-to-Last Hit — 300

RANDALL KENAN, *United States*
The Origin of Whales — 309

JAMAICA KINCAID, *Antigua/United States*
Song of Roland — 317

YANICK LAHENS, *Haiti*
The Blue Room — 324

HELEN ELAINE LEE, *United States*
Marriage Bones — 328

EARL LOVELACE, *Trinidad*
Shoemaker Arnold — 334

CLARENCE MAJOR, *United States*
City Flesh and Country Manners — 340

PAULE MARSHALL, *United States*
Some Get Wasted — 346

JOHN McCLUSKEY JR., *United States*
Specimen — 354

REGINALD McKNIGHT, *United States*
The More I Like Flies — 362

TERRY McMILLAN, *United States*
Quilting on the Rebound — 374

MARK McMORRIS, *Jamaica/United States*
Black Pieces — 385

JAMES ALAN McPHERSON, *United States*
The Story of a Scar — 392

PAULINE MELVILLE, *Guyana/England*
  I Do Not Take Messages from Dead People   402

OPAL MOORE, *United States*
  A Happy Story   413

TONI MORRISON, *United States*
  Recitatif   422

BRUCE MORROW, *United States*
  A Play   437

WALTER MOSLEY, *United States*
  Voodoo   448

ADALBERTO ORTIZ, *Ecuador*
  Bewitched   452

STANLEY PÉAN, *Haiti/Canada*
  The Devil's Maw   456

RICHARD PERRY, *United States*
  Juby's Morning   463

M. NOURBESE PHILIP, *Tobago/Canada*
  Stop Frame   471

ALIX RENAUD, *Haiti/Canada*
  Yawetir   480

JEWELL PARKER RHODES, *United States*
  Enough Rides   489

ESMERALDA RIBEIRO, *Brazil*
  Keep a Secret   498

ASTRID ROEMER, *Surinam/Holland*
  The Inheritance of My Father: A Story for Listening   503

ELIO RUIZ, *Cuba/Mexico*
  The Little White Girl   515

DARIECK SCOTT, *United States*
  This City of Men   524

OLIVE SENIOR, *Jamaica*
  You Think I Mad, Miss?   541

MAKEDA SILVERA, *Jamaica/Canada*
  Her Head a Village   546

CARLOS ARTURO TRUQUE, *Colombia*
    Sonatina for Two Drums   551

ANA LYDIA VEGA, *Puerto Rico*
    Kembé   557

ALICE WALKER, *United States*
    Nineteen Fifty-Five   562

JOHN EDGAR WIDEMAN, *United States*
    Fever   573

    About the Book and Editor   593
    Notes on Contributors   595

Foreword

JOHN EDGAR WIDEMAN

As EDITOR OF *Callaloo,* Charles H. Rowell has developed that scholarly journal into a major vehicle for discussion and dissemination of African American arts and culture. *Callaloo*'s perspective is international, multidisciplinary, and multimedia; it introduces new talent, showcases established artists, and features retrospective analysis and celebration of major figures. Literature is presented in the context of the African Diaspora, the history of Pan-African political and aesthetic consciousness. All voices are welcome and form, as one turns from page to page, from volume to volume of the journal, a background against which works of art, especially literary works of art, can be viewed in terms of their implications for communal survival, the collective imagination, their potential for social and personal identity. In short *Callaloo* is doing good work—unique, invaluable.

Thus I was excited by the prospect of an anthology of fiction gathered by Charles Rowell. And sure enough, as the project reaches its final stages, I find the selections for this book represent the abiding strengths of *Callaloo,* the perspective that has proved indispensable for serious students of the cultures of people of color.

The editor's informed eye has ranged thoughtfully, imaginatively, far and wide to the many regions of the globe where African-descended peoples have touched down or settled. Which is to say, everywhere. One beauty of the anthology is how it dispels indisputably various narrow, tenacious stereotypes of what African American literature could or should be. This collection demonstrates that we can write, and write well, about everybody, everything, everywhere.

African Diasporic writers have enlarged and refined the parameters of the medium of narrative fiction. This anthology is not a record of voices at the margin reporting to the mainstream but rather a documentation of how African Diasporic voices have both subverted and expanded fundamental premises of written literature.

Herein can be viewed not only a striking variety of styles, themes, settings, and subjects but also a fusion of these simplistic categories into cohesive, unique cultural statements. The fictions are abundant proof of African continuities; of cultural exchange among Europe, Africa, Asia, the Americas; of shared literary traditions and oral traditions among countries, continents, and epochs. The writers represented here are enmeshed in their cultures, they are producing their cultures, and we have to hustle to try and keep up with the kinds of fascinating inter-relationships that are evolving—mulatto, syncretic, creolized, imitation, parody, deconstruction, integration, separation, radical displacement, just to name a few.

Clearly no easy definitions, no catch-all categories can tame the energy and variety in the texts Rowell has collected. Rather, reader and critic are confronted by material that should spur redefinition and reevaluation of what fiction means, what forces are unleashed when imaginative writers of African descent put pen to paper.

Read on. This is an entertaining, evocative, thought-provoking mix. Not a new kid on the block, but a mature presence, and we should wonder why we always take so long to notice and appreciate it.

Introduction

CHARLES H. ROWELL

Jesús, Estrella, Esperanza, Mercy:

> *Sails flashing to the wind like weapons,*
> *sharks following the moans the fever and the dying:*
> *horror the corposant and compass rose.*

Middle Passage:
> *voyage through death*
> *to life upon these shores*
>> **—Robert Hayden, "Middle Passage"**

i have a daughter/mozambique
i have a son/angola
our twins
salvador & johannesburg/cannot speak
but we fight the same old men/in the world . . .

i have a daughter/la habana
i have a son guyana
our twins
santiago & brixton/cannot speak
the same language
yet we fight the same old men.
> **—Ntozake Shange, "Bocas: A Daughter's Geography"**

We're the first potential parents who can contain the ancestral house.
> **—Wilson Harris, *The Whole Armour***

᳀   ᳀   ᳀

When Gordon Massman of Westview Press first asked me to assemble this anthology of short stories, I had no problem with the idea of gathering texts written by authors who are part of what is called the African Diaspora. Actually, I reveled in the idea of mounting such a collection and immediately began a call for original manuscripts in English and for translations of texts from other languages. After all, gathering and editing manuscripts from various corners of the African Diaspora is part of what I have been doing, as editor of *Callaloo,* for almost twenty years; in this short fiction anthology I would attempt—as I have tried in the journal—to represent some of the contemporary literary and cultural practices of the peoples of the African Diaspora. This project then, I thought, would be problem-free. And, until after I had selected almost all of the texts, it was. Suddenly, or so it seemed at the time, there was the question of a title for the project: What was the volume to be called? When I attempted to create or identify a line or phrase commensurate with the various contributions in this international anthology, I encountered my first problem.

Naming or creating titles has never been—and I say so politely—a problem for me. In fact, I have always considered the process fun, a delightful self-test of poetic skills. But giving this anthology a title proved for me to be a very serious problem. For three months I struggled; I found no satisfaction in what my creative imagination offered. Neither did my recollections of the lyricism of our rich vernacular traditions bridge the distance between Salvador da Bahia and Oscar, Louisiana, between London, England, and Port-au-Prince, Haiti, or between Quito, Ecuador, and Nova Scotia, Canada. And when I began to review memorable passages from vernacular texts and from fiction by such writers as Toni Morrison, Ralph Ellison, or Jean Toomer, my intellect and imagination failed me again; I could not even recall from all that lyricism or eloquence a phrase or clause that would connect blacks in Amsterdam, Holland, to blacks in Boston, Massachusetts, or the writing community in Kingston, Jamaica, to its black counterpart in Montevideo, Uruguay. This problem troubled me deeply, and I began to view my lack of what VèVè Clark calls "diaspora literacy"[1] as a serious personal problem. But now I know that the problem of diaspora *illiteracy* is not mine alone; it is pervasive: In the United States a great number of us who share the heritage that is a result of the Middle Passage suffer from "diaspora illiteracy." We cannot read beyond ourselves—what for the boundaries imposed by the European languages we were forced to speak, by "the alien language of another tribe," to use Amiri Baraka's description in "Words." We cannot read ourselves beyond ourselves—what for the geographic boundaries imposed by European enslavement, colonization, and racism, by circumstances "making strangers out of people who are not."[2] It was this inability to read the African Diaspora that prevented me from creating or locating, with facility, a title for this short story anthology.

My failure to create or locate a title for this volume was not only personal; it was also collective. It is symptomatic, to use a phrase from Carter G. Woodson, of "the mis-education of the Negro"[3]—a mis-education that is a persistent contributor to "the crisis of the Negro intellectual."[4] In spite of our glib references to the African Diaspora and of the invaluable comparative work that Paul Gilroy, Carol Boyce Davies, and Tejumala Olaniyan,[5] for example, continue to contribute toward the development of an African Diasporic discourse, we, in literary and cultural studies in the United States, have been negligent: We have not adequately extended our discursive practices to address the phenomenon we call the African Diaspora. To the universal literary and cultural practices of the African Diaspora, are black scholars who work in African American literary studies "black toubobs"?[6]

As a matter of fact, our current African Americanist literary and cultural discourse is insular; it is limited to the United States. At intervals, we, however, give some cursory attention to Africa, but our failure to examine, in a thoroughgoing comparative way, our relationship, for example, to peoples of African descent in Colombia, in Venezuela, in Mexico, in Costa Rica, in Peru, has perpetuated an insular discourse. We hardly even give any attention to writers in the English-speaking Caribbean—not to mention those in or from the Dutch-, French-, or Spanish-speaking islands. In other words, my inability to create a title for this anthology was not only a sign of my failure to develop "diaspora literacy," it was also a statement about our collective failure to position the phenomenon of the African Diaspora as "a centerpiece" in our discourse on *Blackness*.

Our failure to develop an African Diasporic discourse is an indirect identification of a condition we share with European Americans: xenophobia. And that xenophobia, which encourages North American imperialism, contributes to our isolationist efforts to construct and reconstruct, within the confines of the United States exclusively, a collective black identity, with instant, unexamined, and mythologized references to Africa. We seem to be so desperate to forge an identity that we continue to ignore the lives, histories, and cultures of other peoples whose ancestors—and they are ours too—also experienced and witnessed the Middle Passage and its consequences.

Here in the United States we seem to forget that those other heirs of the Middle Passage might very well—and I am convinced that they do, as do we—carry in their bodies histories that will not only help illuminate our past but will also inform us about our contemporary selves. The presence and uses (spiritual and aesthetic) of the black cat's bone in Mr. LeRoy's brief account to his son Martin in Walter Mosley's "Voodoo" and Headeye's "little mojo bone" in Henry Dumas's "Ark of Bones" are not unrelated to the spirit worlds of African-derived religious culture in various regions of the Americas. Although they are not sacred or religious objects, the *figa* in Brazil is as powerful as the rabbit's foot of the rural Black South[7]—and their presence in the African Diaspora illustrates the persistence and relevance of the power of "the spirit" and its ability to inhabit certain inanimate objects and from them serve human beings. Divine figures in Brazilian Candomblé, Cuban Santaría, and Haitian Vodun also serve human beings. The Orisha in Luiz Silva Cuti's "Avenues" and Elio Ruiz's "The Little White Girl," the Loas in Ana Lydia Vega's "Kembé," along with the West African religious imperatives and the spirit worlds they reference—these divine figures, and the cultural patterns and practices associated with them, help me account for the "spirit," sacred (and "spirits," secular), in traditional religious belief and cultural practices in the Black South of the United States. In spite of numerous European interventions in the religious practices and spirit worlds of the enslaved Africans in the

Americas, these spirits, and the Loas and Orisha, along with obeah and voodoo—all of which share a common ancestry in West Africa—have persisted throughout the Americas into the twentieth century.[8]

In the Deep South of the United States, various forms of African spiritualism, which also manifest themselves in different ways in diasporic religious cultures in South America and the Caribbean, persist in the black church. Nowhere in this anthology is this cultural survival better illustrated than in Henry Dumas's "Ark of Bones," Fish-hound's narrative about how young Headeye is "called" and anointed to go forth and minister to the political, as well as spiritual, needs of black people. In an intense spiritualized moment, both Headeye and Fish-hound, his young practical friend, participate in and witness, respectively, the workings of the spirit in a vision on a river—an instant during which Headeye is made prophet, preacher, liberator. Unlike the religious patterns found in Europeanized Christianity, but like the spiritualism found in African-derived religious practices in the Americas, the workings of the spirit that Fish-hound—and the reader—witness are a coherent relationship of cooperation between the spirit and the human being. The collaboration of spirit and human being aboard the "ark of bones," the "soul-house," on the river in Henry Dumas's narrative is an instance of the spirit serving the human being, and the human being serving the spirit by accepting its charge.

The cultural syncretism in "Ark of Bones" is, however indirect, a profound revelation of one of the consequences of the Middle Passage. Embedded in the visionary moment of "Ark of Bones" is the meeting and merger of two cultural imperatives that result in what we now call African American. There is the one culture we call European, which handed down the biblical story of Ezekiel's Valley of Dry Bones, another visionary moment that Fish-hound references more than once in Dumas's narrative. There is also the other culture we call African, which does not separate the spirit world from our physical sphere; the two sites are inter-dependent, and the initiate moves in and out of them at the appropriate time. In the Black South's Africanization of Christianity, Africa and Europe meet, and as a result of that meeting the Black South created religious practices that are both spiritual and liberatory. From the combination of these and other cultural practices, which were ultimately informed by enslaved and post-enslaved circumstances and experiences, emerges the identity we describe as African American—and diasporic. It is not surprising, then, that Henry Dumas is able to invoke the African Diaspora with his ancestral house, the ark or "soul boat," when the old man "dressed in skins" tells Headeye:

> Son, you are in the house of generations. Every African who lives in America [read *in the Americas*] has a part of his [or her] soul in this ark. God has called you, and I shall anoint you.

The question for us here in the United States is whether we can read this text, however different its form or representation, when it presents itself in varied, yet related, communities in the African Diaspora.

In her essay on Maryse Condé's novel *Hérémakhonon*, VèVè Clark speaks of "diaspora literacy" as

> the ability to read and comprehend the discourses of Africa, Afro-America, and the Caribbean from an informed, indigenous perspective. In such an environment, names such as *Sundiata, Bigger Thomas,* and *Marie Chauvet* represent mnemonic devices releasing learned traditions. The protagonist of [Maryse Condé's] *Hérémakhonon* demonstrates that Diaspora literacy is more than an intellectual exercise. It is a skill that requires social and political development generated by lived experiences.[9]

Clark goes on to tell us that Europe—along with Africa, the Caribbean, and Black America—is the fourth region that figures into her concept of "diaspora literacy." I view the geographics and demographics of the Diaspora in slightly different terms: When I speak of the geography of the African Diaspora, I am referring mainly to the Americas (the land, including the islands, from Alaska, in the north, to Cape Horn, Chile, in the south), the United Kingdom, and Europe—that is, wherever people of African descent were scattered, as a result of the Middle Passage, and were forced to live. The continent of Africa, then, is not part of the Diaspora; it is instead a common ancestral reference point, the original homeland, however far removed in time and place.

As early as the sixteenth century, the Portuguese, and then the Spanish, began transporting captured Africans from the West Coast of Africa to certain parts of the Americas, to what we now refer to as South America and the Caribbean. Shortly after the Spanish and Portuguese began their trans-Atlantic traffic in African peoples as chattel, the Dutch, the British, and the French followed their example, as they too began a campaign of genocide against indigenous populations and the establishment of colonies for the good of their respective European homelands. The African peoples, whom these different European nationals and settlers enslaved and transported from Africa across the Atlantic, would later constitute the African Diaspora, and their passage from their indigenous continent to the Americas would come to be known as the Middle Passage—the "Voyage through death / to life upon these shores," says Robert Hayden, in his ironic representation of that horrific experience in his poem of that title.

But the people of the African Diaspora are not only situated in the Americas; they are also located in Europe. For political and economic reasons since the abolition of chattel slavery, followed by colonization and "decolonization," people of African descent in the Caribbean, for instance, have found it necessary to migrate to Britain and to other European nations, countries that, in the not so distant past, controlled them, first as enslaved and then as colonized people. Jamaicans, for example, migrated to England; Surinamese, to Holland; and Haitians, to France. But the contemporary "French West Indies" has its own peculiar form of migration: Believing themselves to be citizens of France, a great number of people of these francophone islands either remove themselves to the metropole, or they move back and forth to metropole, while others remain in these dispossessed

islands imagining "social and economic progress."[10] Whether they are active participants in the French game of departmentalization or not, Martinicans, in Fort-
de-France and in Paris, are still part of the African Diaspora. So too are the exiles
and migrants (in England and Holland)—and their descendants—from
Trinidad, Guyana, Surinam, Barbados, Curaçao, St. Kitts, and Grenada. So too are
their counterparts who migrated to the United States and Canada. For all of his
desire to think of himself as an Englishman and deny his blackness, and for all his
pretensions toward superiority, the protagonist in Austin C. Clarke's "Griff," who
migrated from Barbados to England and then to Canada, is a member of the
African Diaspora. That is, migrants of African descent from the Caribbean in
Canada and the United States, as well as in the United Kingdom and Europe, are
also part of the African Diaspora.

What is the African Diaspora? Who are the people of the African Diaspora?
Where do they live? These basic questions of historical circumstances and issues
of geographics and demographics I had to address before I could assemble this
volume of short stories. Having done so, I still had not become highly lettered in
matters African Diasporic; I had not completely solved my problem of "diaspora
illiteracy," a condition that prevented me from creating or discovering a title for
this fiction anthology.

ii

So long,
So far away
Is Africa's
Dark face.
—Langston Hughes, "Afro-American Fragment"

There is a difference between the transplanting (by exile or dispersion) of a peo-
ple who continue to survive elsewhere and the transfer (by the slave trade) of a
population to another place where they change into something different, into a
new set of possibilities.
—Edouard Glissant, *Caribbean Discourse*

Whatever decision you make, I think that your canvassing of writers in search
of a title for this collection captures the spirit of the work itself. It is the writing
of the story of a book.
—Opal Moore, Letter

In my search for a title for this anthology, I moved, as a second stage toward
discovery, from African American vernacular and literary traditions to texts by
Caribbean writers. I have, over the past decade, come to depend on Edward
Brathwaite, Aimé Césaire, Wilson Harris, Maryse Condé, Edouard Glissant, and

Derek Walcott. The timing of the second stage of my quest for a title was propitious. After all, I had recently finished reading and evaluating the final manuscripts for the special Wilson Harris issue of *Callaloo* (Winter 1995), a project Nathaniel Mackey was guest-editing. I had also just finished reading the extensive revisions of the transcript Wilson Harris himself had made of an interview I had conducted with him at his home in England in May 1992. I needed, of course, to speak with him about our interview—and about the special issue of *Callaloo* we were assembling on his work and career. During our trans-Atlantic telephone conversation, I asked Wilson Harris, whose "Kanaima" is included in this anthology, whether he thought there was any passage or phrase in his oeuvre that would suggest a title for my anthology. He responded with a polite and cautious, "I don't think so, Charles." And after I told him what problems I had encountered, I boldly asked him whether he would be willing to write a statement that would assist me in solving my problem. He said, "Yes," and he kindly accommodated me.

Within a few days, Wilson Harris telephoned that he had composed a statement (see Appendix A) about the African Diaspora. As he read his occasional commentary aloud to me over the telephone, I immediately identified the phrase—"the waters of the maelstrom"—that might have served as my title, but which I thought would not wear well on the North American, the immediate audience of this volume. I realized, too, that Wilson Harris's provocative statement is an interrogation and a reading of the African presence in the White West. Wherever those African peoples, with their multifarious linguistic backgrounds and disparate cultural practices, were transported, by force, into the Americas, they necessarily changed, Edouard Glissant writes, "into something different, into a new set of possibilities," some few of which are represented by and in the short stories assembled in this anthology. In the Americas, these changed and changing Africans were a major presence that made an indelible impact on the Europeans who enslaved them. As Wilson Harris wrote for me, the "consequences of the African Diaspora have left their sign or mark upon an entire civilization."

Contrary to what the architects, advocates, and consumers of "white mythologies"[11] contend, European peoples have been (and continue to be) profoundly influenced by the consequences of the African Diaspora. The African presence in the Americas and other parts of the West has not only affected Western political and intellectual traditions; populations of African ancestry have also created universal cultural practices and informed cultural productions throughout the Americas and Europe. One need not invoke over and over—and then again—the subject of music (and dance) in the Americas. But during these final years of the twentieth century, one ought to begin, at least, teaching the White West lessons in intellectual honesty by (dis)forming white patterns of domination and exploitation, and by (re)naming those forms and practices whose names camouflage their African and African Diasporic derivations and dimensions. I think immediately of so-called Latin music. The "Latin music" of that culturally—and racially—black nation called Brazil is African Diasporic. The "Latin music" of that cultur-

ally—and racially—black nation called Cuba is African Diasporic. When one
carefully examines literary production in the United States, one discovers, in spite
of the white Americanist's impulse toward denial and camouflage, the informing
and transforming imprint of the African Diasporic presence. I do not refer here
to white writers' attempts at using black figures as characters in their texts. Rather,
I am talking about how, for example, the "slave" narrative, as an aesthetic construct and a sociopolitical text, informs and/or (dis)forms Thomas Nelson Page's
In Ole Virginia, Harriet Beecher Stowe's *Uncle Tom's Cabin,* and Mark Twain's *The
Adventures of Huckleberry Finn.* The short stories collected in this anthology are
likewise a testament to the presence and imprints of African Diasporic peoples on
the European-derived genre called *the short story.* When the heirs of the victims
of the Middle Passage first directed their voices to the printed page in the
Americas, they entered a space that was once reserved for whites, and on that site
called the printed page African Diasporic peoples inscribed their voices for all the
world to read. And when they spoke in their own voices and from their own collective or individual worldviews and memories, they transformed and extended
the possibilities of that former all-white space. In other words, those slave ships
crossing the Atlantic for the Americas would not only transform their human
cargo of enslaved Africans; the descendants of those Africans would in turn
change Europeans and their literary and other cultural productions into "a new
set of possibilities."

With his emphasized reference to those fateful ships on "the waters of the
maelstrom," Wilson Harris directed my attention to the centrality of the Middle
Passage in the formation of the African Diaspora. In fact, the Middle Passage is a
defining moment; it was, as Glissant argues in *Caribbean Discourse,* transformative and transforming. The Middle Passage was the beginning of the process
through which the diverse ethnic groups became one people upon specific sites—
Recife, Savannah, Paramaribo, or Puerto Plata—in the Americas: Haitians in
Haiti, African Americans in the United States, Afro-Brazilians in Brazil, Bajuns in
Barbados, Black Brits in England—all of them being African Diasporic peoples in
the context of this anthology. "During the process of their becoming a single people," Sterling Stuckey writes,

> Yorubas, Akans, Ibos, Angolans, and others were present on slave ships to America
> and experienced a common horror—unearthly moans and piercing shrieks, the
> smell of filth and the stench of death, all during the violent rhythms and quiet cours-
> ings of ships at sea. As such, slave ships were the first real incubators of slave unity
> across cultural lines, cruelly revealing irreducible links from one ethnic group to the
> other, fostering resistance thousands of miles before the shores of the new land ap-
> peared on the horizon—before there was mention of natural rights in North
> America.[12]

It is the experience of the Middle Passage, not the illusive and relative constructions of race,[13] that we must turn to in our efforts to identify those peoples in
Europe and the Americas as members of the African Diaspora. For it is the legacy of that horrific experience called the Middle Passage that, first and foremost,

these peoples of African descent in Europe and the Americas share in common. That is, they are all heirs of the heritage of the Middle Passage; each one of them descends from one or more victim of that historic transfer, and each one of them, at some moment in his or her life, has been subjected to the violence of white mythologies.

My emphasis on the Middle Passage, as opposed to race, is neither to deny the white racism that has worked against people of African descent nor to gloss over the racialization of the African presence in Europe and the Americas. There are short stories aplenty in this anthology that direct our attention to the violence of racism. The founder of the African Methodist Church, Richard Allen,[14] is fictionalized as a narrator in John Edgar Wideman's "Fever," which recounts the horrors of the plague that struck the city of Philadelphia during the eighteenth century. In his recollection, the fictionalized Richard Allen does not forget the whites' uses of race during that pestilence:

> Despair was in my heart. The fiction of our immunity had been exposed for the vicious lie it was, a not so subtle device for wresting us from our homes, our loved ones, the afflicted among us, and sending us to aid strangers. First they blamed us, called the sickness Barbados fever, a contagion from those blood-soaked islands, brought to these shores by refugees from the fighting in Santo Domingo. We were not welcome anywhere. A dark skin was seen not only as a badge of shame for its wearer. Now we were evil incarnate, the mask of long agony and violent death. . . .
>
> We were proclaimed carriers of the fever and treated as pariahs, but when it became expedient to command our services to nurse the sick and bury the dead, the previous allegations were no longer mentioned. Urged on by desperate counselors, the mayor granted us a blessed immunity. We were ordered to save the city.

The uses of race are no less conspicuous in Ernest J. Gaines's "Three Men," a narrative set in twentieth-century Louisiana. White Roger Medlow and the white law officers support and defend a system that racializes human interaction, a social structure that whites use to dominate and manipulate Proctor Lewis, "Hattie" Brown, Munford Bazille, and other black people in Gaines's mythological St. Raphael Parish. As Munford Bazille demonstrates in his deconstruction of "the system," it is through their victimizing ritual of dependency on the Other that the white men (who construct themselves as superior to the racial Other) and the black men (who are forced into a self-internalizing position of inferiority) define themselves as human entities. Munford Bazille's discourse on difference is emancipatory—but liberatory only if "Hattie" and Proctor follow Munford's implied charge:

> They need me to prove they human—just like they need that thing over there [*meaning Hattie who is, ironically, objectified by a fellow victim of the same kind of process*]. They need us. Because without us, they don't know what they is—they don't know what they is out there [*the white officers working in the jail*]. With us around, they can see us and they know what they ain't. They ain't us. Do you see? Do you see how they think? . . .

> But I got news for them. They us. I never tell them that but inside I know it. They
> us, just like we is ourselves. Cut any of them open and you see if you don't find
> Munford Bazille or Hattie Brown there. You know what I mean?

It is not so much that the black victim of racism cannot forget race; it is that the
white racist—as Oswaldo de Camargo reminds us in "Civilization"—forever
reminds the victim of the fiction of race as difference. The successful struggle
against these and other forms of racism is what Wilson Harris was telling me
when he wrote that the "slave-ship that crossed the Atlantic has been profoundly
re-oriented in the waters of the maelstrom of history. . . ." Unlike the shifting concept of race, the Middle Passage is no fiction; the Middle Passage, only one part
of whose heritage is the struggle against racism, is a fixed moment in the past that
African Diasporic people share.

It is the idea of sharing a legacy, not a single race or racial construct, that I
wanted the title for this anthology to reflect. Because the work of Wilson Harris
is filled with infinite ideas about the peoples of the Americas, I knew that a sentence or a phrase suggesting a common heritage for African Diasporic peoples
was embedded somewhere in one of his novels or essays. So when Nathaniel
Mackey suggested I consider a statement by Cristo, Megda's "epic son," in Wilson
Harris's *The Whole Armour,* I was relieved. Near the end of "All the Aeons," the
final book of the novel, Cristo proclaims to Sharon that *"We are the first potential
parents who can contain the ancestral house."* A major claim indeed, but one in
which he articulates two reasons: (1) He and Sharon, like the peoples of the
African Diaspora, represent "every race under the sun," and (2) they, unlike the
other people of Guyana who are still "the first aliens and arrivals," have come to a
crucial moment of self-knowledge, self-conquest, in relation to the land. In other
words, Cristo and Sharon, who also embody the past, represent new possibilities:

> All the restless wayward spirits of all the aeons (who it was thought had been em-
> balmed for good) are returning to roost in our blood. And we have to start all over
> again where they began to explore. We've got to pick up the seeds again where they
> left off.

When he journeys into the underworld of the bush in Books Two and Three of
the novel, Cristo recovers that which was lost, and as a result he undergoes a
metamorphosis. In the person and experience of Cristo, an African Diasporic figure, Wilson Harris brings together all the warring peoples, ancient and modern,
in one person who represents new possibilities in the Americas.[15] Like the majority of the people of the African Diaspora, Cristo is both "multi-racial" and "multicultural"; he is a "new world" of infinite possibilities. Cristo is indeed an "ancestral house." And Nathaniel Mackey led me there, to the title of this anthology,
"ancestral house"—resonating words, Opal Moore, the author of "A Happy
Story," would later declare to me in a letter (see Appendix B).

Once I had re-examined Wilson Harris's novel *The Whole Armour,* I was immediately convinced that "ancestral house" should be the title of this anthology, for

the words not only evoke kinship, family, origins, forebears; the phrase also suggests a commonness of values and ideas, bound together by spiritual and cultural ties. The past in time present and future. Collectivity. Similarities. Connections. Continuums. Community. Legacies. But also diversity. And individuality reflecting and demonstrating more than the particularity of its *self*. *Ancestral House. Ancestral House.* The texts in this volume, like other cultural productions in the African Diaspora, contain the ancestral house.

Salvador, Bahia
Charlottesville, Virginia

Notes

1. VèVè A. Clark, "Developing Diaspora Literacy: Allusion in Maryse Condé's *Hérémakhonon*," in *Out of the Kumbla: Caribbean Women and Literature*, eds. Carole Boyce Davies and Elaine Savory Fido (Trenton, N.J.: Africa World Press, Inc., 1990), 303–319.

2. Edouard Glissant, *Caribbean Discourse: Selected Essays*, trans. J. Michael Dash (Charlottesville: University Press of Virginia, 1989), 5. Describing how the people in the Caribbean are still separated from one another in spite of "modern means of communication," Glissant writes that "colonization has divided into English, Dutch, Spanish territories a region where the majority of the population is African: making strangers out of people who are not."

3. Carter Godwin Woodson, *The Mis-Education of the Negro* (Washington, D.C.: The Associated Publishers, Inc., 1933).

4. Harold Cruse, *The Crisis of the Negro Intellectual* (New York: William Morrow & Co., 1967).

5. See their most recent contributions to this subject: Paul Gilroy, *The Black Atlantic: Modernity and Double Consciousness* (Cambridge: Harvard University Press, 1993); Carole Boyce Davies, *Black Women, Writing and Identity: Migrations of the Subject* (New York: Routledge, 1994); and Tejumala Olaniyan, *Scars of Conquest/Masks of Resistance: The Invention of Cultural Identities in African, African-American, and Caribbean Drama* (New York: Oxford University Press, 1995).

6. In Reginald McKnight's "Palm Wine" (*Callaloo* 18.2, Spring 1995: 219–230), Doudou, a Senegalese who speaks Wolof and French, refers to McKnight's narrator, a visiting African American anthropologist, as "a black toubob." "'How does it feel,' he said, 'to be a black toubob?' I felt my face suddenly grow hot. My guts felt as if they were in a slow meltdown. I took a large draft of the wine and disgust made me wince. 'By "toubob,"' I asked, 'do you mean "stranger" or white? I understand it can be used both ways.'" Of course, in West Africa, a *toubob* is a white person, *a stranger, a foreigner*—all equal terms.

7. The *figa*, often worn on a small chain as a bracelet or necklace, is a small carving of a tight fist with the thumb jutting upward between the index and middle fingers. Like the dried rabbit's foot that is carried in one's pocket or purse, the Brazilian *figa* is a good luck charm.

8. For an illuminating discussion of spiritual traditions in the African Diaspora, see Joseph M. Murphy's *Working the Spirit: Ceremonies of the African Diaspora* (Boston: Beacon, 1994).

9. Clark, "Developing Diaspora Literacy," 304.

10. Glissant, *Caribbean Discourse,* 12.

11. When Jacques Derrida speaks of "white mythology," he is referring to "Metaphysics—the white mythology which reassembles and reflects the culture of the West: the white man takes his own mythology, Indo-European mythology, his own *logos,* that is, the *mythos* of his idiom, for the universal form of that he must still call Reason." "White mythology—metaphysics has erased within itself the fabulous scene that has produced it," Derrida continues, "the scene that nevertheless remains active and stirring, inscribed in white ink, an invisible design covered over in the palimpsest." See "White Mythology: Metaphor in the Text of Philosophy" in Derrida's *Margins of Philosophy,* trans. Alan Bass (Chicago: University of Chicago Press, 1986), 213. In his examination of Eurocentric theories of history, Robert Young uses the term "white mythologies." See his provocative and illuminating book, *White Mythologies: Writing History and the West* (New York: Routledge, 1990).

12. Sterling Stuckey, *Slave Culture: Nationalist Theory and the Foundations of Black America* (New York: Oxford University Press, 1987), 3.

13. Racial constructions in the African Diaspora vary from country to country. For example, in the United Kingdom, those individuals who are not of "pure" Anglo-Saxon or some other "pure" European ancestry are *black;* in England, Asian and Arab peoples, as well as peoples of African ancestry, are black people. In many parts of the Caribbean the mulatto is not a black person, but in the United States the mulatto (a person with very light to white skin) or anyone with a "drop of black blood" is black. In Latin America, especially in Brazil, many of the people who are considered to be white are black in the United States. And some black people in the United States would be considered white in Brazil.

14. Co-founders of the Free African Society in 1787 in Philadelphia, Richard Allen and Absalom Jones described the white racism directed against black people during the 1793 yellow fever epidemic in *A Narrative of the Proceedings of the Black People During the Late Awful Calamity in Philadelphia: And a Refutation of Some Censures Thrown Upon Them in Some Late Publications,* a pamphlet they co-authored and published in 1794. Born into slavery in Philadelphia in 1760, Richard Allen, who purchased his liberty in 1783, founded the Bethel Church of Philadelphia on July 17, 1794; this was the first African Methodist Episcopal church.

15. Of himself as a "racial composition," Derek Walcott's narrator in "The Schooner *Flight*" says:

> *I'm just a red nigger who love the sea,*
> *I had a sound colonial education,*
> *I have Dutch, nigger, and English in me,*
> *And either I'm nobody, or I'm a nation. . . .*

In Walcott's *Star-Apple Kingdom* (New York: Farrar, Straus and Giroux, 1979), 4. Walcott's description of his narrator and Wilson Harris's characterization of Cristo also imply the cross-cultural dimensions of their heritage.

APPENDIX A

The consequences of the African Diaspora have left their sign or mark upon an entire civilization. Europe, Asia, but above all throughout the Americas, North America, Central America, South America, and the Caribbean.

As the twentieth century draws to a close, it is possible to begin to weigh the diverse and significant works that black men and women are creating in music, in the arts, in scholarship, and in the sciences.

The slave-ship that crossed the Atlantic has been profoundly re-oriented in the waters of the maelstrom of history and new pilots are coming to the helm in the name of bitter, hard-won freedoms.

The short passage quoted hereunder from *Resurrection at Sorrow Hill* may embody perhaps a quintessential summation of transition from victim and captive to pioneer and steersman. "The stake or the cross or the noose or the electric devastation of the eyes and the nerves was older than one could ever imagine but it had begun to cool in the waters of the maelstrom . . . into healing Shadow . . . in the steersman of the globe."

Wilson Harris

APPENDIX B

11 October 1994

Dear Charles:

It is eleven thirty-five P.M. and I am thinking about the two titles you've proposed for the short story collection now subtitled: "The Short Story in the African Diaspora."

"Mirrors" or "The Ancestral House."

Well, it seems to me there is no contest. "Mirrors" is too empty. A reflection is nothing but an illusion; it has no substance of its own and the reflection is not always true. The mirror is so often a symbol of distortion or of distorted feelings. The mirror is flat, two dimensional. Upon its surface, the three dimensional world is made flat, the real transformed to illusory shadow. I do not like this title, "Mirrors." It is too thin. I look past the mirror and there is nothing but cardboard backing a silvered sheet of glass. It is one of the gimmicks that Europe traded for a foothold in Africa. It is the trick that keeps Marlena Shaw's good man from putting his hand to the work that might feed them both, feed us all.

I think you are right in considering the title "The Ancestral House" from the work of Wilson Harris. But I think you don't need the article. It diminishes. I write this title, "Ancestral House" on a slip of paper as you tell it to me and the "A", capital, is like a shelter. Visually, it speaks to me.

"Ancestral House" evokes past. Place. Presences. It is the house of story where we kept our place, history, self, presence and Presences. The Ancestor stands its two legs upon the page, a doorway.

I can understand why some of the people you interviewed on this question might find "mirrors" appealing. It has a contemporary feel. Slick. New. Cliche-Pop. Skinny. Mini-skirted. People are tired of being reminded of the ponderous past. The Ancestral House does not flicker, shimmy, or shift in the light. It does not cast a pinkish glow to soften the creases of age or our interesting dissipations. It is not nouveau. But I like the sturdiness of "House."

You may be laughing by now at the extensiveness of my argument for the name of a book. But perhaps this will suggest how such a collection of stories can resonate into the imagination. How stories of the African diaspora have the capacity to bring out our desires, to articulate what we wanted to rescue out of our ancient and transformative story. What we wanted from the past for the people that we are right now. How story can remind us that we have always been talking to each other across artificial divides of space, separation, death, and loss.

Whatever decision you make, I think that your canvassing of writers in search of a title for this collection captures the spirit of the work itself. It is the writing of the story of a book.

It is midnight. Goodnight!

Opal [Moore]

Acknowledgments

I am grateful to Dean Raymond Nelson and Patricia Meyer Spacks of the University of Virginia and to the many other individuals who gave me assistance in one way or another when I was assembling this anthology. It is impossible to include all of their names, but I would be remiss if I did not mention the following: Kathleen Balutansky, Carol Beane, Effie J. Boldridge, Carrol F. Coates, Rhonda Cobham-Sander, Finnie Coleman, James Davis, Carolyn Richardson Durham, Percival Everett, Eric Ashley Hairston, Trudier Harris, Marvin Lewis, and Bruce Morrow. For their invaluable support, I am indeed grateful.

"Absolution" by Ai. Printed by permission of the author.

"My Singular Irene" by José Alcántara Almánzar. Translated by Joe F. Scott. First published in English in *Callaloo* 12.1 (Winter 1989).

"Willie Bea and Jaybird" by Tina McElroy Ansa. First published in *Callaloo* 13.2 (Spring 1990).

"The Organizer's Wife," reprinted on pp. 21–33, from *The Sea Birds Are Still Alive* by Toni Cade Bambara (New York: Vintage/Random House, 1982). Copyright © 1974, 1976, 1977 by Toni Cade Bambara. First published by The Women's Press Ltd, 1982, 34 Great Sutton Street, London EC1V 0DX. Reprinted by permission of Random House, Inc., and The Women's Press Ltd.

"Words" from *Tales* by LeRoi Jones (Amiri Baraka) (New York: Grove Press, 1967). Copyright © 1967 by Amiri Baraka. Reprinted by permission of Sterling Lord Literistic, Inc.

"Miss Askew on Ice" by Hal Bennett. First published in *Callaloo* 10.1 (Winter 1987).

"I Used to Like the Dallas Cowboys" from *Sans Souci and Other Stories* by Dionne Brand (Stratford, Ontario: Williams-Wallace, 1988). Copyright © 1988 by Dionne Brand. Reprinted by permission of the author.

"The Evening and the Morning and the Night" by Octavia E. Butler. First published by Omni Publications International, Ltd. Copyright © 1987 Omni Publications International. Reprinted by permission from the author and publisher.

"Civilization" by Oswaldo de Camargo. Translated by Carolyn Richardson Durham. Printed by permission of the author and translator.

"They Called Her Aurora (The Love of Donna Summer)" by Aída Cartagena Portalatín. First published in Spanish in *Tablero: doce cuentos de lo popular a lo culto* by Aída Cartagena Portalatín (Dominican Republic: Taller, 1978). Translated by James J. Davis and Terry L. Collier.

"Cherry Bomb" from *Rattlebone* by Maxine Clair (New York: Farrar, Straus & Giroux, 1994). Copyright © 1994 by Maxine Clair. Reprinted by permission of Farrar, Straus & Giroux, Inc., and the author.

"Griff" by Austin C. Clarke. First published in *Savacou*. Reprinted by permission of the author.

"Columba" from *Bodies of Water* by Michelle Cliff (London: Methuen, 1990). Copyright © 1990 by Michelle Cliff. Reprinted with the permission of Michelle Cliff.

"The Visit," reprinted on pp. 117–124, from *Rain Darling* by Merle Collins, first published by The Women's Press Ltd, 1990, 34 Great Sutton Street, London EC1V 0DX, is used by permission of The Women's Press Ltd.

"Night Thoughts" from *Mint Tea and Other Stories* by Christine Craig (Oxford: Heinemann, 1993). Reprinted by permission of Heinemann Publishers (Oxford) Ltd.

"Avenues" by Luiz Silva "Cuti." Translated by Carolyn Richardson Durham. Used by permission of the author and translator.

"Tapestry" by Samuel R. Delany. Copyright © 1994 by Samuel R. Delany. Reprinted by permission of the author and his agents, Henry Morrison, Inc. First published in *New American Review* 9 (1973).

"Rosena on the Mountain" by René Depestre. First published in French in *Alléluia pour une femme-jardin* by René Depestre (Paris: Gallimard, 1981). Copyright © 1981 by Editions Gallimard. Translated by Carrol F. Coates. Used by permission of the publisher and translator.

"Under the Rose" by Rita Dove. Copyright © 1995 by Rita Dove. Printed by permission of the author.

"Sweat, Sugar, and Blood" by Suzanne Dracius-Pinalie. First published in French in *Le Serpent a Plumes,* no. 15 (Spring 1992). *De sueur, de sucre et de sang* copyright © 1992 by Suzanne Dracius-Pinalie. Translated by Doris Y. Kadish. Used by permission of the author and translator.

"Ark of Bones" from *Goodbye, Sweetwater: New and Collected Stories* by Henry Dumas, ed. Eugene B. Redmond (New York: Thunder's Mouth Press, 1988). Copyright © 1988 by Henry Dumas. Used by permission of the publisher, Thunder's Mouth Press.

"A Letter" by Quince Duncan. Translated by Dellita Martin-Ogunsola. Used by permission of the author and translator.

"The Miracle" by Nelson Estupiñán Bass. Translated by Ann Venture Young. Reprinted by permission of the author.

"Randall Randall" by Percival Everett. Copyright © 1995 by Percival Everett. Printed by permission of the author.

"This Man and Me" by Guy-Mark Foster. First published in *The Portable Lower East Side* 8.2 (1991). Reprinted by permission of the author.

"Three Men" from *Bloodline* by Ernest J. Gaines (New York: W. W. Norton, 1976). Copyright © 1968, 1976 by Ernest J. Gaines. Used by permission of Doubleday, a division of Bantam Doubleday Dell Publishing Group, Inc., and JCA Literary Agency.

"Accidents" by Thomas Glave. First published in *Callaloo* 15.4 (Fall 1992).

"By Love Possessed" by Lorna Goodison. First published in *Callaloo* 11.2 (Spring 1988).

"She Wakes" from *Drawing Down a Daughter* by Claire Harris (Fredericton, New Brunswick: Goose Lane, 1992). Copyright © 1992 by Claire Harris. Reprinted by permission of Goose Lane Editions.

"Kanaima" by Wilson Harris. First published in *Facing the Sea*, ed. Ann Walmsley and Nick Caistor (London: Heinemann, 1986). Reprinted by permission of the author.

"Presence" from *Squabble and Other Stories* by John Holman (New York: Ticknor & Fields, 1990). Copyright © 1989, 1990 by John Holman. Reprinted by permission of Wylie, Aitken & Stone, Inc. and Ticknor & Fields/Houghton Mifflin Co. All rights reserved.

"Circle of Shade" from *Jumping Ship and Other Stories* by Kelvin Christopher James (New York: Villard Books, 1992). Copyright © 1992 by Kelvin Christopher James. Reprinted by permission of the author and Villard Books, a division of Random House, Inc.

"Alēthia" from *The Sorcerer's Apprentice* by Charles Johnson (New York: Atheneum, 1986). Copyright © 1977, 1979, 1981,1982, 1983, 1984, 1985, 1986 by Charles Johnson. Reprinted with the permission of Scribner, an imprint of Simon & Schuster, Inc., and Georges Borchardt, Inc. for the author. Originally published in *Antæus*.

"The First Day" from *Lost in the City* by Edward P. Jones. Copyright © 1992 by Edward P. Jones. Reprinted by permission of William Morrow & Company, Inc.

"The Fisherman's House" by Gayl Jones. Copyright © 1995 by Gayl Jones. Printed by permission of the author.

"Transits" by John R. Keene. First published in *Callaloo* 16.3 (Summer 1993).

"My Next-to-Last Hit" by William Melvin Kelley. Copyright © 1995 by William Melvin Kelley.

"The Origin of Whales" from *Let the Dead Bury Their Dead and Other Stories* by Randall Kenan (New York: Harcourt Brace, 1992). Copyright © 1992 by Randall Kenan. Reprinted by permission of Harcourt Brace & Company.

"Song of Roland" by Jamaica Kincaid. Copyright © 1993 by Jamaica Kincaid, first published in *The New Yorker*, reprinted with the permission of Wylie, Aitken & Stone, Inc.

"The Blue Room" by Yanick Lahens. First published in French in *Tante Résia et les Dieux* by Yanick Lahens (Paris: l'Harmattan, 1994). Translated by Kathleen M. Balutansky.

"Marriage Bones" by Helen Elaine Lee. Copyright © 1995 by Helen Elaine Lee. Printed with the permission of Helen Elaine Lee.

"Shoemaker Arnold" from *A Brief Conversation and Other Stories* by Earl Lovelace (Portsmouth, N.H.: Heinemann, 1988). Copyright © 1982, 1988 by Earl Lovelace.

"City Flesh and Country Manners" by Clarence Major. First published in *Callaloo* 14.1 (Winter 1991).

"Some Get Wasted" by Paule Marshall. First published in *Harlem, U.S.A.*, ed. John Henrik Clarke (Berlin: Seven Seas, 1971). Reprinted by permission of the author.

"Specimen" by John McCluskey Jr. Copyright © 1995 by John McCluskey Jr. Printed by permission of the author.

"The More I Like Flies" by Reginald McKnight. Copyright © 1995 by Reginald McKnight.

"Quilting on the Rebound" from *Voices Louder Than Words* by Terry McMillan (New York: Random House, 1991). Copyright © 1991 by Terry McMillan. Reprinted by permission of the author.

"Black Pieces" by Mark McMorris. First published in *Hambone* (1994). Reprinted by permission of the author.

"The Story of a Scar" from *Elbow Room* by James Alan McPherson (Boston: Little, Brown, 1977). Copyright © 1973 by James Alan McPherson. First published by *Atlantic Monthly*. Reprinted by permission of Little, Brown and Company and Brandt & Brandt Literary Agents, Inc.

"I Do Not Take Messages from Dead People" from *Shape-Shifter* by Pauline Melville, first published by The Women's Press Ltd, 1990, 34 Great Sutton Street, London EC1V 0DX. Copyright © 1990 by Pauline Melville.

"A Happy Story" by Opal Moore. First published in *Callaloo* 12.2 (Spring 1989).

"Recitatif" by Toni Morrison. First published in *Confirmations: Stories by Black Women* (New York: William Morrow, 1983). Reprinted by permission of International Creative Management, Inc. Copyright © 1983 by Toni Morrison.

"A Play" by Bruce Morrow. First published in *Callaloo* 16.2 (Spring 1993).

"Voodoo" by Walter Mosley. First published in *Callaloo* 12.1 (Winter 1989).

"Bewitched" by Adalberto Ortiz. Translated by Teresa Labarta de Chaves. First published in *Afro-Hispanic Review* (May 1983).

"The Devil's Maw" by Stanley Péan. First published in French in *La Plage des songes et autres récits d'exil* by Stanley Péan (Montreal: Les Éditions du CHDIHCA, 1988). Translated by Carrol F. Coates. Reprinted by permission of the publisher.

"Juby's Morning" by Richard Perry. Copyright © 1995 by Richard Perry. Printed by permission of the author.

"Stop Frame" by M. Nourbese Philip. First published in *Prairie Schooner* 67.4 (Winter 1993). Reprinted from *Prairie Schooner* by permission of the author and the University of Nebraska Press. Copyright © 1993 by University of Nebraska Press.

"Yawetir" by Alix Renaud. Translated by Carrol F. Coates. Printed by permission of the author and translator.

"Enough Rides" by Jewell Parker Rhodes. First published in *Callaloo* 14.1 (Winter 1991).

"Keep a Secret" by Esmeralda Ribeiro. Translated by Carolyn Richardson Durham. Printed by permission of the author and translator.

"The Inheritance of My Father: A Story for Listening" by Astrid Roemer. First published in Dutch in *Niets wat pijn doet* by Astrid Roemer (Amsterdam: In de Knipscheer, 1985). Copyright © 1985, 1992, 1993 by Astrid H. Roemer. Translated by Hilda van Neck-Yoder. Reprinted by permission of the author and translator.

"The Little White Girl" by Elio Ruiz. Translated by Sandra L. Dixon. First published in *Afro-Hispanic Review* 13.1. Reprinted with permission.

"This City of Men" by Darieck Scott. First published in *Callaloo* 17.4 (Fall 1994).

"You Think I Mad, Miss?" from *Discerner of Hearts* by Olive Senior. Used by permission of the Canadian publishers, McClelland & Stewart, Toronto.

"Her Head a Village" from *Her Head a Village* by Makeda Silvera (Vancouver: Press Gang Publishers, 1994). Reprinted with permission.

"Sonatina for Two Drums" by Carlos Arturo Truque. Translated by Elizabeth M. Allen.

"Kembé" by Ana Lydia Vega. Translated by Mark McCaffrey. Printed by permission of the author and translator.

"Nineteen Fifty-Five" from *You Can't Keep a Good Woman Down* by Alice Walker (New York and London: Harcourt Brace Jovanovich, 1981). Copyright © 1981 by Alice Walker, reprinted by permission of Harcourt Brace & Company and David Higham Associates.

"Fever" from *Fever: Twelve Stories* by John Edgar Wideman (New York: Henry Holt and Co., 1989). Copyright © 1989 by John Edgar Wideman. Reprinted by permission of Henry Holt and Co., Inc.

Ancestral House

ABSOLUTION

I FIRST MET Minnie in 1955, when our driver, Sam Earl, brought her to the house one Sunday after lunch. Sam was a thin, stooped man of indeterminate age with straight black hair and was so light skinned and "white" featured that he'd often be taken for a white man. It became a joke around the house. My father, Judge Poole, often spoke of the time a white lady from Atlanta had tried to make Sam sit down beside her on the bus. She made such a fuss that, finally, Sam Earl had to tell her he was colored. The white riders laughed so hard that the driver threatened to put them off the bus if they didn't quiet down and let him drive.

"Ain't I colored?" Sam asked the impassive faces back of the bus, as a hush fell over everyone. "I'm colored," he said to the white folks.

"Go on, boy," said Bud, the driver, finally. "That's right, ma'am, he's a nigger and he's got a nigger's disposition too. Who do you think you are, boy? Git on back before I call the sheriff on you."

"Yas suh. Yas suh," said Sam.

"Sam was meek as a little black sheep," my father would say, barely keeping a straight face when he told the story.

When Sam brought Minnie to the house, she was a cause for conversation too, for she was blue-black and her hair looked like a tight cap of crinkly black wool. Folks said he'd got her off a wild girl, who lived by the river, but they were wrong. The girl would do it for a mirror, a piece of wood, or even string. It seems she was off in her mind, and after each time she'd start screaming and scratching and the boy would be catching more hell than it was worth, unless it was his first time, of course. We were sitting on the porch. My mother and my father were in the old swing and I was straddling the railing, a ten-year-old with red hair and freckles everywhere. I had a keen interest in hunting cats with a slingshot, model airplanes, and banana popsicles.

"Lordy, looka there," I said.

"Hush, Sonny," said my mother.

Sam Earl stopped at a respectful distance, hat in one hand and Minnie's hand in the other.

"Who you got there, Sam?" asked my father.

"My daughter, suh."

"I wouldn't want to speculate about that."

"Naw, suh, you ain't have to do that. I just the only one willing to take her in. Ain't got no kin I knows of. Her mama drowned. I had a dream last night. Her mama kep' pointing at me, saying, 'I lost something.' Today, I gone on out there to the shack and this little 'un sitting in a pile of her own waste. 'Scuse me, missus. It ain't right to leave her like that, so I taken her over to the church and let Reverend Williams' wife clean her up for me, but she don't know nobody go out of their way for a orphan. So I guess she stay with me, if it's all right with you."

My father took out his handkerchief and blew his nose like he trying to decide one of those cases of public drunkenness that gave him so much distress, because he did not care to punish anyone really. He did his duty because he had to, having earned the mayor's gratitude for some discrete service. He just wanted to sit in the sun and rock. He wanted hot toddies before he went to bed, not the discomfort of administering justice.

He was already sixty-five when his first wife died, leaving him to inherit her house and fifty thousand dollars, which he invested and made for himself even more money.

He met my mother at a literary salon. She was thirty-five and there was talk of her "getting caught," but after awhile, even that stopped. Now she was admired and respected by the ladies in her circle. She'd earned that respect mainly because she had a good eye for fashion and also excelled as a peacemaker. She knew how to turn an unkind remark into a compliment. In her circle, her talent was in constant demand, for the ladies were a nasty bunch, and my father would complain to her that she was wasting herself. Emma Poole, my mother, would only smile and say there was some good in everybody. I think she truly believed it. I loved her and she loved me, but a girl would have been more to her liking, so she left me in my father's care and when he wasn't there, I had Sam Earl to teach me how to chunk rocks, fish, and pitch baseballs. Once when I was angry at her, because she locked me out of the house, so she could nap "in peace," I hurled the baseball as hard as I could and hit Sam in the head. He said it didn't hurt, but he just stood there shaking himself.

"Dumb nigger," I said. "You can't catch nothing."

"Naw, son, I expect I can't," he said.

I ran out back and lay down in the grass and blew on milkweed, watching it float past my eyes, until the sky got dark. We never played baseball again and whenever I insisted, he'd say I'd learned all he could teach me.

"Where you going to keep her?" I asked. "Up there with you?"

Sam lived in a room above the garage. Sometimes the gas fumes were so strong, I wondered how he could stand it. Now the two of them would climb the stairs to lay them down to sleep.

"What's her name?" I asked.

"Why, I hadn't thought of that," he said. "Goodness me. My mama's name was Minnie. It's not so bad to call her that, is it?"

"Yeah, I guess it's okay. You want to play, Minnie?"

I'd always been solitary, but once Minnie settled in, I knew the joy of torment-ing another child and I became more interested in playing games for two *and* since I controlled whatever we would do, it was still I who chose the winner and the loser, who usually skinned of knee and out of breath let out a wail that would get me a mild scolding from Lucielle, the cook, who took to ignoring Minnie's cries after awhile. Eventually, we learned to settle our own disputes. When I was fourteen and Minnie was twelve, after I hauled off and punched her in her breast, Minnie chased me and fell on a broken bottle. A piece of glass stuck in her thigh and there was blood all over her Sunday dress. When they finally let me visit her, I found her lying on her back, looking at the ceiling.

"Feeling all right?"

"Yeah," she said, "why you want to know?"

"You mad?"

"No!"

"Are too."

"I got a secret," she said. "Bet you can't guess what it is."

"Can too."

"What is it then?" She laughed. "No, it's girl stuff and you don't know nothing 'bout girls, do you?"

"Do you know anything about boys?"

"Yes, 'cause I'm grown."

"No, you aren't."

"Am. Looka here," she said, sitting up and rolling the sheet down to her feet.

When she raised her gown, I leaned down to look. What I saw shook me. Jammed between her legs was a bloodstained rag. "I thought you were better," I said.

"I am. This my ministration, fool." She lowered her gown and I sat beside her on the bed. "I bleed now, just like your mama do. I got to use Kotex too, soon as Daddy Sam work up the nerve to buy me some."

"My mother doesn't bleed. Why would she?"

"Got to. The Lord cursed women, 'cause we all whores and it's a sign of our wickedness."

"Who told you that?"

"Sam."

"He never told me."

"Ask him. You'll see."

I sat there a little longer, telling her about my first week of high school, then I left her to her newly acquired wickedness.

I saw Minnie less and less. Lucielle taught her how to cook and eventually, she took over some of the kitchen duties. She also cleaned the house. She even shined my father's shoes, when he'd forgotten to have it done at the courthouse. I joined the chess club, which bored me. I joined the science club, too. I ran for sophomore class president and lost. My junior year, my father enrolled me in the Fathers and Sons gun club competition. I took first prize in that. That year, Minnie and Sam moved into a rundown cottage my father owned. Our old gardener, who'd died, had lived there rent free, but you might say my father got it back by charging Sam rent.

The day I went away to college, Sam and Minnie were sitting on the cottage steps when I stopped to say goodbye.

"Didn't think you was going to come see us before you left," said Sam. "Glad to see you going off to get your education."

"Libel to get himself a wife, too," said Minnie. I thought she was making fun of me, but I didn't see any reason to let her know it.

"Hush, Minnie, he just a boy," said Sam.

"Boys grow up, daddy."

"He doesn't have time for girls," said Sam. He didn't realize I thought about them constantly. I mean I thought about sex. I dreamed about sex too. Sometimes Minnie was in those dreams. I was ashamed to think of her naked and writhing beneath me, but I couldn't stop myself. Just the day before, I'd caught her at the shallow stream way out back of the cottage. She'd taken off her blouse, and when she unfastened her brassiere she must have heard me because she half turned and I caught just a glimpse of one of her breasts. It was a large, swollen looking thing and when she faced me fully, her black nipples seemed to spin like rings of even blacker smoke.

"See," she said.

I turned my head quickly. "Cover up, cover on up," I hissed, though I wished she would come and hold my head against her breasts, so I could kiss and lick and suck them, and when she passed close to me, I could have touched her, but I did not.

"Look good, don't they?" she asked, as she grabbed my belt buckle.

I knocked her hand away.

"You'll pay for that. I'm not twelve no more."

When she tried to kick me, I grabbed her foot and pulled her to the ground, then I threw myself on top of her, as if I could press my whole body into her, as if I could erase my longing by disappearing inside her.

"Let go, you bastard."

When I managed to get my mouth on hers, she tasted like licorice. I gagged, because I'd always hated licorice.

"Had enough, white boy?"

I got off her. "You going to tell?" I asked.

"Shoot. You didn't do nothing."

"I could, if you didn't taste so bad."

"And stink too, I reckon."

"Yeah, that too."

"Stay away from me, Sonny," she said.

"You can't kiss anyway," I said.

"I kissed plenty boys. Men, too, and they all love it. Sam tries to keep me from learning anything, but I learn lotsa stuff and I could teach you something."

She started to walk away, but came back and stood close to me. "Since you think I'm a whore, you get to pay me for my service."

"How much?"

"One hundred dollars."

"For what?"

"Everything."

"But I don't have that kind of money."

"How much you want it?"

"Enough," I said, "enough."

"Aw, go on, hot stuff," she said. "Some other time, okay? Put them thoughts out of your mind."

I did, until they were joined by thoughts of another kind. In them, Sam's body hangs from the tree where he once taught me how to climb by locking my knees to its trunk and inching up. I still ask myself how such a thing could happen, but I know what came to pass was no accident of fate, but the outcome of hatred that found in the face of one old man false evidence of guilt.

Now as the past unravels, I travel back along the railroad tracks that run past a shack hidden behind some shrubs and junked cars. A search party stumbles on the body of Nancy Pierce, a white girl, who used to twirl baton for the high school football team. Her hair is strawberry blonde and she is bound to a chair with a pair of nylon stockings. She had been strangled, and tangled in her hair are bits of wood that could be shavings. They smell like cedar and Pete, my best friend, says, "Sam Earl makes his canes out of cedar, doesn't he?"

I protest, but it does no good. After all, it couldn't have been one of us who did it, could it? Easier to think the beast is colored, for who else would murder such a peach blossom and go and have possum stew and sweet potatoes for dinner and be sleeping soundly when we find him and drag him from his bed. I lead them to him. I admit it.

"Let's get the nigger," says the captain of the football team, a mean son of a bitch, built like a fire hydrant with a pug face and acne. He has beady, watery, blue eyes and thighs as round as pickle barrels, but he sings Christmas carols with the sweetest voice. We call him Roy, short for Royce, and when he looks at you, you have no choice but to do what he wants, or he'll take your head off with one twist like a bottle cap. I'm not afraid of him. I'm afraid of what my friends will say, if I don't go along. I just don't have the guts to tell them they are nuts and that Sam wouldn't give a dime for any girl, colored or white, except for Minnie, who is off on a trip to Atlanta.

Sam has sent her to buy some clothes for school, because he's been fool enough to pay for her education at some colored college, where they teach colored people just enough to let them know what they are missing. My father says it will be all for nothing. Minnie will end up stuffing her head with dreams she can't ever realize, but Sam keeps pushing her in that direction until finally she agrees. She can always teach school, she says. Maybe then she can impress upon another poor colored girl the need for an education because the seed of freedom resides there.

The night before she left, when I wandered by, the cottage was filled with the scent of pine, for she'd been cleaning. Its pungency sent a thrill through me. Sam caught me watching her, as she set about making dinner.

"Now boy, don't lose your head. My girl is not for anybody but herself, as I have taught her. You oughta find yourself a nice white girl, who'll help you maintain your position, same as your mama do for your daddy. It's plain as day to me you're seeing more in Minnie than is decent. I speak to you like a father would, if he knew."

"I don't know what you are talking about," I said, turned and left. I ran down the path to the stream, where I had seen Minnie that time, cleaning herself like some water sprite. Is it to break the spell that I hold Sam up to the tree and let him go, when the noose is slipped over his head? I stand back to gaze upon his face, but find it covered by a flour sack. I think I hear Sam ask for water, before they kick the stool out from under him. I am relieved it's over. We leave him hanging. Some drift off in pairs, others alone. I stay behind. I try to find the part of me I thought was honorable and decent. In the rubble of myself is a twin, a double, who has given in to murder, just the same as that girl's killer. Yet I know no one will question what we've done. The colored folks will bury Sam and go on and keep their thoughts to themselves. The rest of us will dwell inside the gate that says, "White Only."

Minnie never came back. I went to her. It took fifteen years to find her. She worked on the assembly line at a Ford plant in Detroit. I suppose she'd given up her dreams because she had two sons to support. When she opened the door, I thought she'd slam it in my face, but she only stepped aside to let me enter. I tried to speak, but she cut me off.

"Now I see you for what you are," she said. "I didn't back when, but then I was a foolish girl. I thought the world was different than it is. You got nothing to give me but excuses. I know you want forgiveness, but you get that somewhere else, not here, from me. You see, don't you? We're enemies. We always were. It's just you proved it first."

"You haven't changed enough," I said.

"And you still want me, don't you?" she asked. I felt a thirst so great I wanted to take a bite out of her throat and drink her until I choked. As in a trance, I moved toward her, but she hauled off and hit me with her fist.

Finally, I said, "What do I do?"

"You wipe your mouth. It's bleeding," she said, handing me a cloth.

When I gave it back to her, she held it up for me to see.

"Remember?" she asked.

Yes. I did remember the day so long ago, when love began and ended with the ebb and flow of blood.

JOSÉ ALCÁNTARA ALMÁNZAR

MY SINGULAR IRENE

L IFE IS UNJUST and treacherous this way. One makes an effort to walk a clear
and straight path, to work like an animal much more than eight hours—which is
the usual, to study vehemently, to have a job that will permit one to live decently,
to respect the law, to marry as God commands, to be, in short, an honorable citizen, and when one begins to establish himself, to progress, with a house although
bought on credit and the car almost paid for, one starts wondering why things
like this are not happening to others. I'm not saying it because of the manner in
which Irene went away (it is still hard to believe it and I have only returned to the
scene of the events because it seems a lie to me that she has left the comfort of her
house without any regrets), but it is rather because of what occurs to one on the
day least expected.

Irene had asked me to take her on an outing in the country. The trips along the
Mirador and a few beers in the restaurant at the lake no longer satisfied her; she
wanted to see the countryside in full daylight, put her bare feet in the water of a
stream, climb a mountain to feel like an amateur mountain-climber, and to catch
butterflies. Since women have their whims and poor Irene very seldom asked me
for things and, except for when she visited her mother, she spent weeks and
months tied to the house taking care that everything was in order on my return
from a trip, it seemed not a bad idea to appease her. A little peaceful trip to the
country was not bad for me either. The idea was for us to go to Cibao; there the
vegetation is pure and one feels transplanted to a so-called "nice" place. But as I
was not completely recuperated from my last attack of bronchitis and the coolness

---

Translated by Joe F. Scott.

that makes one sick still is found in those hills in March, I told Irene that we would go to the south. Perhaps we would arrive in Barahona and on our return we would pass through Ocoa, where my wife's family lives. It seemed incredible to her that I myself would propose a route and carefully plan the trip. It had to be that way. As a professional traveler I did not like improvisations; I take care to plan my trips, make a list of the participants, gather the backlogged invoices, and make a little map of the places where I am going to stop. If any one of those clients who talk up a storm detains me more than necessary, I have a devil of a remedy to put things back into perspective again. But to start out without a plan, never.

I began to pack the clothes and to wonder about what we would do. I saw her so full of anticipation that I began to think of my luck in having married her. When we got married I thought she was so unwilling to fulfill her duties as a wife that I would never have believed then that we would become a perfect pair. The only point on which we did not agree was the matter of being in the street, walking about, or visiting. I had to be firm and demand more attachment to the household. At first she accepted my imposition unwillingly. Then she demonstrated how much she was assimilating my way of thinking and accepted that I was right. I was not going to permit my wife to run around as if she had no one to protect her. Not that. And no visitors either. Sisters and mothers who are the only ones that I trust were allowed in my house. Friends in the street, the cafeterias, the stadium. In an instant she packed the suitcase and made the necessary arrangements for the trip while I took the car to the station to have them fill it and give it a wash, all because in the south there is such a drought and such dust at the beginning of Lent, and anyway the car was going to come back a complete wreck. Upon my arrival at the house, she was already at the door, dressed in white pants and a bluish green little blouse—as she would say—that I had brought her from abroad. She was wearing a scarf that covered her ears and made her face an adorned melon, a puppet doll. To me she seemed happy, spontaneous, prepared to go with me to the end of the world. When I saw her smiling face I thought she was a happily married woman, and I threw my arm around her shoulder. She leaned against my chest for a moment, holding me with both hands.

It was the end of March, a clear day like today, exactly the same; therefore I believe I am going to come across her at any moment, that she is going to tell me to forgive her for the foolishness she did, that we should go back to the way it was before, to our lives of mutual understanding. The first thing I did was not to leave the house immediately. We took a turn around the area and went back to the gas station to have the boys check the oil and to take a look at the water in the radiator. My car was OK, but it is always better to be sure, when in doubt. Irene started to become impatient: she lowered the window, put the package of novels that she was carrying in her hand on the back seat, looking around everywhere. I knew that she was nervous and that she would have gladly smoked a cigarette, but I had forbidden her to do it and out of consideration she didn't dare. We went back to the house again, only to be sure that no one was lurking around it. I didn't want them to rob me of the stereo equipment I had just bought or the shotgun that my uncle had given me.

At times Irene did not comprehend my reasons and I can understand that because the poor girl never had much sense. It is regrettable to say that at this moment, but it is true. I had chosen her for that, and that is the way I want her. A woman who thinks too much can become dangerous. She will invent things, she will plot, live discontentedly; in short, she will ruin her husband's life. Irene was almost perfect; she didn't think too much, although she often showed signs of weariness, of wanting to escape. That's why I bought her the television, for her to entertain herself at home. I bought her the best brand, ceasing to bet on the horses for weeks. My trips kept me from taking her to the movies frequently. After we moved to the suburbs, downtown was too far away. I generally felt tired and fell asleep with the newspaper on my knees before nine in the evening. I didn't want her to feel restless; therefore, I bought the television and everything that she ever needed. I satisfied her whims as much as possible, as I also did during the trip. I have no regrets at all.

After we passed the distillery we headed toward the south. On that side of the city it seemed that we were going to run into Haina, with those massive construction projects. I have taken the precaution of saving, getting a plot from the State, and requesting a loan from the bank to build my house with the comforts that I have always dreamed of. In my profession (I am an accountant, but I have my own business: the promotion and sales of home appliances) one cannot afford the luxury of chance. Irene observed everything with the curiosity of a lepidoptera: her big eyes, from which two large mascaraed eyelashes emerged, attentive to the changes of the highway. Her antennae stuck out of the window and were examining pieces of recently painted buildings, weeds growing in the road, naked children at the doors of the ranches. She was enjoying the outing, sucking in the hint of aridity that was now being announced on both sides of the highway. Upon passing the bridge she wanted me to let her get out to look over the river. I said no. I had seen the road, the bridge, the highway, the tollbooth so many times that her interest meant very little to me. Everything touched her, made her sit up in the seat, carelessly stick her head out the window and say goodbye to a stranger who greeted her, or burst into a flurry of innocent words of satisfaction.

Before reaching San Cristobal I knew that the outing was not going to come out all good. She insisted on getting out to see the little hill where there were wild daisies. We were enjoying ourselves, I shouldn't be so selfish; I stopped the car and waited for her to cut some daisies. In San Cristobal we stopped to have breakfast. Irene was hungry. The diner was a typical one for a village: four or five tables with checkered tablecloths and a fat cook dispatching orders from behind the counter. I had planned to go to a more expensive place but in a town everything is the same and in the diners one has to wait less. Ten minutes after being in the place, the fat lady came with two steaming dishes and large cups of coffee with cream. Irene stirred the sugar slowly, smiling at me after each stir she made in her cup.

Since she didn't like hot dishes I thought she was cooling the coffee. Two little "tigers" came and stopped in the entrance to the business and were taking us in with their eyes. Irene smiled at them, winked, and they covered their bashful faces. The fat lady yelled three expletives at them, frightening them away immediately. After a short while they were watching us again. I tried to finish quickly and I told Irene to hurry, but the "pushover" took the plate and the cup, got up and went to give them to the little tykes. They swallowed everything in a gulp and the fat lady took the dishes from them because she assured us that they were capable of walking away with them in the wink of an eye.

"Don't bother the young lady," the fat lady said to me in nice words. "If that pleases her, let her do it. Apparently she is even pregnant."

I thought it was not worth the trouble to tell her that it would have pleased me very much to entrust her with a girdle for her to hold in that immense stomach. Irene was content. It was a crime to spoil a moment for her. Between San Cristobal and Bani I punished her a little to make her aware of her immaturity; I kept quiet. Irene was most aloof from the hassle, playing with the daisies. The south was now being noticed in the dust on the highway, the hovels on the hills, the dry shell on the roads. Some cows crossed the road and I was obliged to put on the brakes. With that Irene got out of the car and ran toward one side of the road, in the direction of the hill. She ran, shouting and jumping. I rolled up the window, moved the car toward the emergency lane and struck out after her on foot. In view of the fact that lately I am a little stout—not a little, very stout—the race took quite a bit of my breath away and I could not catch her except upon reaching the top of the hill. The poor fool opened her arms, spinning around screaming, forgetting about the cliff.

"Irene, you must be losing your mind."

Almost without paying me any attention, lost in a different world, unknown to me, Irene came down. In the car she continued with her stupidity and opened the window. I felt like going back, to leave her at home and go out with my friends. That did not resolve the problem. On the other hand, the fact that Irene was behaving like an idiot pricked my curiosity and moreover she didn't even give an explanation. I felt hot when we reached Bani. We were no longer speaking: she being stupid, with her foolishness; I paying attention to the road. The car filled up with tension. I took off my jacket and loosened my tie. Irene smiled, took the jacket and put it without folding it on the seat. The car bounced like a frog each time it would hit a pothole in the road. No sooner than the car had come to a halt, Irene rushed to the edge of the bridge, applauding like a child for God knows what new foolish reason. She began to undress: she took off her shoes, and seated on a rock, she put her feet in the current of the river. Worst of all the water wet her pants and she seemed not to be aware of anything. She yelled for me to accompany her. It was a relief for me to discover that she was still conscious of my existence, but a moment later she seemed to lose awareness of everything around her. She took off her pants and blouse, preparing to throw herself into the water.

"IRENE!"

She didn't even look at me. Nor did I know if she still heard my shouts. With an insane happiness she splashed in the water; she was not the Irene that I had known, the one that had brought peace to my life as a bachelor. I didn't recognize her. From then on everything got worse. I feared that she would drown and went to rescue her.

"Irene, have you gone crazy?"

Between her whoops and uncontainable laughter I took her out of the water. She was almost in the raw because her underwear had stuck to her body in such a way that anyone would need no other encouragement to attack her. We ended up taking our clothes off near the car. I rubbed her with a towel and took the clothes from the suitcase. In the car, Irene made no response to my chastisements. Her naked body awakened old anxieties in me, sweet moments not experienced for many days. Her fresh skin, the cologne discreetly rubbed on alluring spots, made me forget the anger that I was feeling because of so many strange events. The road continued to be solitary, perturbed only by the chatter of water in the river and the cicadas. There was a way to calm that sudden anxiety and no man can escape it. Irene did not react; my caresses became violent without results, and she gave in disinterestedly. It was the first time that had occurred in our married life; it was a defeat on my own turf, but that was not my fault. Irene was going to form part of a different world and she was being transformed.

Unfortunately, that day the butterflies were gathering. The butterflies were the seducers that stole her from my life. Very near Bani thousands of butterflies came out of the side roads and smashed against the windshield or instinctively avoided the glass. Irene participated in the simple grace of the insects. Her eyes bugged out, she followed each precipitous flight, her hands made deceptive attempts to capture them and she gave confusing calls, invitations in code, greetings of an old friend. My patience reached its limit. That trip could not continue. Nevertheless, life has its arbitrariness and I kept my foot on the accelerator. The butterflies increased in number, the colors were multiplied; they came from the trees, they invaded the highway, they darted about crazily, wrapped in the warm breeze. Irene rolled down the window and by accident some butterflies got inside and were trapped. She knelt on the front seat and bent over to try to capture them, leaving her backside well exposed. It was useless to struggle with that little girl. I went on a short way and stopped the car next to a clearing where thousands were fluttering about. It was too late to arrive at Azua before the sun would begin to set. It was a harsh time of day, and the heat was intense. Irene had taken off her blouse and she formed a net like those used by collectors. There was something of a ritual in her actions. To see them fly produced a pleasure in her that increased with the quantity of them. Now half naked, the blouse-net was not enough and she pulled off her shirt. I told myself that it was too much, my wife had lost her senses. I ran after her: Irene was spinning with her butterflies and I, with a devil of a panting spell, was trying to grab her so that nobody would see her that way. I don't know where so much agility and quickness came from; my efforts were in vain. A foolishness was trapping me, the butterflies were multiplying, they pursued me, I wanted to free myself and it was impossible; thousands of butterflies were leaving their cocoons and coming out to join Irene, who ran about happily, completely nude. She had taken off all her clothes and ran about impatiently among the multicolored insects. She was no longer pursuing or catching them, it was enough to run about with her friends and dance to the beat of their dance. I collapsed almost in a faint. I got up to continue my race after Mary Irene; now everything was totally confused, terribly confused: I saw a woman who was divided into others, they were several Irene-butterflies who were merging and separating. I had to rest quite awhile on the grass and wait until the insanity should pass from my wife. But she started to be transformed; an arm changed into an enormous wing, yellow, with black eye-like spots, and then the other arm did the same. She made four turns and then two big antennae came out that moved to each side. The friend-butterflies were celebrating the enrollment of my wife into the butterfly order, of which she would be, undoubtedly, an important member. Her thorax changed into an ashen trunk, covered with small hairs, her legs were converted into two twisted feet. Horrifying! Irene changed into a horrendous butterfly! I stood up and fell again, powerless now. She would leave me, she would take flight and leave me. The gigantic Irene Butterfly smiled at me, diminished, and disappeared with the others.

I am at the site of the events, waiting for Irene's return. She has to return. She cannot deny me the peace that her company always offered me.

TINA McELROY ANSA

WILLIE BEA AND JAYBIRD

WHEN WILLIE BEA first saw Jaybird in The Place, she couldn't help herself. She wanted him so bad she sucked in her bottom lip, cracked with the cold, then she ran her tongue so slowly over her top lip that she could taste the red Maybelline lipstick she had put on hours before. He looked like something that would be good to eat, like peach cobbler or a hot piece of buttered cornbread.

She had just entered the bar clutching her black purse under her arm and smiling to try to make herself look attractive among the 6 o'clock crowd of drinkers and dancers and socializers, every one of them glad to be done with work for the day. He was there at the end of the bar in his golden Schlitz uniform sharing a quart of Miller High Life beer with a buddy. Willie Bea noticed right away how he leaned his long frame clear across the bar, bent at the waist, his elbows resting easily on the Formica counter. There didn't seem to be a tense bone in his lean efficient body.

"He look like he could go anywhere in the world," Willie Bea thought as she followed her big-butt friend Patricia as she weaved her way to a nearby table already jammed with four of her friends, two men, two women. "If somebody put him in a white jacket and a flower in his buttonhole, he could pass for an actor in a Technicolor movie."

As the juke box started up again, playing a driving Sam and Dave number, he looked around the bar, picked up his glass of beer and headed toward her table with his chin held high over the other patrons. When he smoothly pulled up a chair to her table and straddled it backwards, Willie Bea crossed her stick legs and pinched her friend Pat's thigh under the table to give her some Sen-Sen for her breath.

"Hey, Little Mama, you got time for a tired working man?"

14

She had to remember to wipe the uncomfortable moisture from the corners of her mouth with her fingertips before she could respond to him.

She still felt that way, four years after they had started going together, when she looked at him.

Nothing gave her more pleasure than to be asked her marital status with Jaybird around.

"Willie Bea, girl, where you been keeping yourself?" some big-mouthed woman would shout at her over the din of the jukebox at The Place. "I ain't seen you in a month of Sundays. You still living with your aunt, ain't you?" This last expectantly with pity.

Willie Bea would roll her shoulders and dip her ears from side to side a couple of times in feigned modesty.

"Naw, girl, I *been* moved out of my aunt's," Willie Bea would answer. "I'm married now. I live with my . . . *husband.*"

The old horse's big mouth would fall open, then close, then open as if she were having trouble chewing this information.

"Husband? Married??!!"

"Uh-huh. That's my *husband* over there by the juke box. Naw, not him. My Jay is the tall light-skinned one, the one with the head full of curly hair."

Willie Bea never even bothered to look at her inquisitor when she pointed out Jay. She could hear the effect the weight of the revelation had had on the woman. And Willie Bea only glanced smugly at the old cow as she raced around the bar nearly knocking over a chair to ask her friends and companions why no one told her that skinny little shiny-faced Willie Bea had a man.

"I thought she was sitting there mighty sassy looking."

Even Willie Bea would have admitted it: Most days, she did feel sassy, and it was Jaybird who made her so. He burst into the bathroom while she was in the bathtub and pretended to take pictures of her with an imaginary camera. He teased her about flirting with Mr. Maurice who owned the store on the corner near their boardinghouse when the merchant sliced her baloney especially thin, the way she liked it.

Now, she really thought she was cute, with her little square monkey face and eager-to-please grin, a cheap jet black Prince Valiant wig set on the top of her head like a wool cap with her short hair plaited underneath and a pair of black eyeglasses so thick that her eyes looked as if they were in fish bowls.

Jaybird had done that to her. He even called her "fine," an appellation that actually brought tears to her eyes made huge and outlandish by the Coke-bottle-thick glasses.

"Fine." It was the one thing in life Willie Bea longed to be. She had no shape to speak of. She was just five feet tall and weighed about 90 pounds. But she did her best to throw that thing even though she had very little to throw.

"If I had me a big old butt like you, Pat," she would say to her friend, "ya'll couldn't stand me."

The pitiful little knot of an ass that she had was her sorrow, especially after noticing from Jaybird's gaze that he appreciated a full ass. His favorite seemed to be the big heart-shaped ones that started real low and hung and swayed like a bustle when the woman walked. Many mornings, Jay lay in bed watching Bea move around the room getting dressed and thought, "Her behind ain't no bigger than my fist." But he didn't dare say anything, even as a joke. He knew it would break her heart.

But since she knew she didn't have a big ass, she did what she had done since she was a child when someone told her what she was lacking: She pretended she did and acted as if her ass was the prize one in town. The one men in jukejoints talked about.

Wherever she went—to the market, to work cleaning houses, to The Place, downtown to shop—she dressed as if she had that ass to show off.

She wore tight little straight skirts that she made herself on her landlady's sewing machine. Skirts of cotton or wool or taffeta no wider than 12 inches across. Not that wide, really, because she wanted the skirt to "cup," if possible, under the pones of her behind and to wrinkle across her crotch in front. Using less than a yard of material and a Simplicity quickie pattern she had bought years before and worked away to tatters, she took no more than an hour to produce one of her miniature skirts.

On Sundays, when the house was empty of other boarders or quiet from their sleep, Willie Bea used her landlady's sewing machine that she kept in the parlor. The steady growl of the old foot-pedal-run Singer disturbed no one. In fact, on those Sundays she and Jaybird went out and she did no sewing, the other tenants of the large white wooden house felt an unidentified longing and found themselves on the verge of complaining about the silence.

Willie Bea looked on the ancient sewing machine, kept in mint condition by the genial landlady who always wore plaid housedresses and her thin crimpy red hair in six skinny braids, as a blessing. She didn't mind that the machine was a foot-propelled model rather than an electric one. It never occurred to her to expect anything as extravagant as that. For her, the old machine was a step up from the tedious hand-sewing that she had learned and relied on as a child. With the waist bands neatly attached and the short zippers eased into place by machine, her skirts had a finished look that would have taken her all night to accomplish by hand.

Many times, she felt herself rocking gently to the rhythm she set with her bare feet on the cold iron treadle to ease a crick in her stiff back before she realized that she had been at the job non-stop all afternoon. Just using the machine made her happy, made her think of men watching her at the bus stops in her new tight skirt and later, maybe, these same men letting some sly comment drop in front of Jaybird about her shore looking good.

She imagined Jaybird jumping in the men's faces, half-angry, half-proud, to let them know that was his *wife* they were talking about. Just thinking of Jaybird saying, "my wife" made her almost as happy as her being able to say "my husband."

She loved to go over in her head how it had come to pass, their marriage. They had been living together in one room of the boardinghouse at the top of Pleasant Hill for nearly three years, with him seeming to take for granted that they would be together for eternity and with her hardly daring to believe that he really wanted her, afraid to ask him why he picked her to love.

As with most of his decisions, movements, he surprised her.

One evening in August, he walked into their room and said, "Let's get married." As if the idea had just come to him, his and original. She responded in kind.

"Married? Married, Jay?" she said, pretending to roll the idea around in her head a while. Then, "Okay, if you want."

It was her heart's desire, the play-pretty of her dreams, being this man's wife.

She bought stiff white lace from Newberry's department store to make a loose cropped sleeveless overblouse and a yard of white polished cotton and sewed a tight straight skirt for the ceremony at the courthouse.

When they returned to their room for the honeymoon, Willie Bea thought as she watched him take off his wedding suit that no other man could be so handsome, so charming, so full of self-assured cockiness . . . and still love her.

He was tall and slender in that way that made her know that he would be lean all his life, never going sway-backed and to fat around his middle like a pregnant woman. He was lithe and strong from lifting cases and kegs of Schlitz beer all day long, graceful from leaping on and off the running board of the moving delivery truck as it made its rounds of bars and stores.

Once when he had not seen her, Willie Bea had spied him hanging fearlessly off the back of the beer truck like a prince, face directly into the wind, his eyes blinking back the wind tears, a vacant look on his face. His head full of curly hair quivering in the wind. The setting sunlight gleamed off the chrome and steel of the truck, giving a golden-orange color to the aura that Willie Bea felt surrounded him all the time.

Overcome by the sight, Willie Bea had had to turn away into an empty doorway to silently weep over the beauty of her Jaybird.

Jaybird even made love the way she knew this man would—sweet and demanding. When her friend Pat complained about her own man's harsh unfeeling fucking, Willie Bea joined in and talked about men like dogs. But first, in her own mind, she placed Jaybird outside the dog pack.

"Girl, just thank your lucky stars that you ain't hooked up with a man like Henry," Pat told her. "Although God knows they all alike. You may as well put 'em all in a crocker sack and pick one out. They all the same. One just as good as the other. Just take your pick."

"Uh-huh, girl, you know you telling the truth," Willie Bea would answer.

"Why, that old dog of mine will just wake any time of the night and go to grabbing me and sticking his hand up my nightdress. He don't say nothing, just grunt. He just goes and do his business. I could be anything, a sack of flour, that chair you sitting on."

"What you be doing?" Willie Bea asked in her soft sing-song voice even though she already knew because Pat always complained about the same thing. But she asked because she and Pat had grown up together, she had been Pat's friend longer than anyone outside of her family. And Willie Bea knew what a friend was for.

"Shoot, sometimes I just lay there like I *am* a sack of flour. I thought that would make him see I wasn't getting nothing out of his humping. Then, I saw it didn't make no difference to him whether I was having a good time or not. So, now, sometimes I push him off me just before he come. That makes him real mad. Or I tell him I got my period.

"Some nights, we just lay there jostling each other like little children jostling over a ball. I won't turn over or open up my legs and he won't stop tugging on me."

"Girl, both of ya'll crazy. That way, don't neither of you get a piece. That's too hard," Willie Bea said sincerely.

"Shoot, girl, some nights we tussle all night." Pat gave a hot dry laugh. "Henry thinks too much of hisself to fight me for it, really hit me up side my head or yell and scream 'cause with those little paper sheer walls, everybody next door would know our business. So while we fighting, it's real quiet except for some grunts and the bed squeaking."

Then, she laughed again.

"I guess that's all you'd be hearing anyway."

Willie Bea tried to laugh in acknowledgment. Once Pat told her, "Shoot, girl, I've gotten to liking the scuffling we do in bed better than I ever liked the screwing."

That made Willie Bea feel cold all over.

"It's like it make it more important," Pat continued. "Something worth fighting for. Some nights when he just reach for me like that, it's like he calling me out my name. And I turn over ready to fight.

"I would get somebody else, but they all the same, you may as well pick one from the sack as another. But look at you, Bea. You just agreeing to be nice. You don't believe that, do you?"

"I didn't say nothing," Willie Bea would rush to say. "I believe what you say about you and Henry. I believe you."

"That ain't what I mean and you know it. I'm talking about mens period."

"I know what you saying about men."

"Yeah, but you don't think they all alike, do you?" Pat asked.

Willie Bea would start dipping her head from side to side and grinning her sheepish closed-mouth grin.

"Go on and admit it, girl," Pat would prod.

After a moment, Willie Bea would admit it. "I don't know why he love me so good."

Then, Pat would sigh and urge her friend to tell her how sweet Jay was to her . . . in bed, at the table, after work. Especially in bed.

Willie Bea balked at first, each time the subject came up. But she always gave in, too. She was just dying to talk about Jaybird.

Most women she knew held the same beliefs that Pat did about men. They sure as hell didn't want to hear about her and the bliss her man brought her. She had found they may want to hear about you "can't do with him and can't do without him" or how bad he treat you and you still can't let him go. All of that. But don't be coming around them with those thick windowpane eyes of hers all bright and enlarged with stories of happiness and fulfillment. Those stories cut her other girl-friends and their lives to the quick.

But her friend Pat, big-butt Pat, urged Bea to share her stories with her. Sometimes, these reminiscences made Pat smile and glow as if she were there in Willie Bea's place. But sometimes, they left her morose.

Willie Bea, noticing this at first, began leaving out details that she thought made Pat's love pale in comparison. But Pat, alert to nuances in the tales, caught on and insisted that Willie Bea never leave stuff out again if she was going to tell it.

And Willie Bea, eager to tell it all, felt as if she were pleasing her friend as much as herself. So, she continued telling stories of love and dipping her ear down toward her shoulder in a gay little shy gesture.

"When Jaybird and me doing it, he has this little gruff-like voice he uses when he talks to me."

"Talk to you? What ya'll be doing, screwing or talking?" Pat would interrupt, but not seriously.

"He says things like, 'Is that all? That ain't all. I want it all. Uh-huh.'"

At first, Willie Bea was embarrassed disclosing these secrets of her and Jaybird's passionate and tender lovemaking. But Pat seemed so enthralled by her stories that Willie Bea finally stopped fighting it and gave herself over to the joy of recounting how Jaybird loved her.

Pat never told Willie Bea that many of the women at The Place talked under their breaths when Jaybird and Willie Bea came in together.

"He may sleep in the same bed with her, but I heard he put an ironing board between 'em first," some said.

"He can't really want that little old black gal. He just like her worshipping the ground he walk on," another would add.

Pat knew Willie Bea would have tried to kill whoever said such things. But even Pat found it hard to believe sometimes that her little friend had attracted Jaybird.

Mornings, Pat watched Willie Bea step off the city bus they both took to their jobs, her too-pale dimestore stockings shining in the early light, her narrow shoulders rotating like bicycle pedals in the direction opposite the one she sent her snake hips inside her straight skirt and thought how changed her friend was by the love of Jaybird. Now, that walk is something new, Pat thought as the bus pulled away from the curb.

Willie Bea, who lived two blocks above Pat, got on the bus first, then alit first when she got near the white woman's house she cleaned five days a week. Pat stayed on until the bus reached downtown near the box factory where she worked. They rode to and from work together nearly every day.

So, one evening when Pat wasn't on the bus when she got on returning home, Willie Bea began to worry about her. All that one of Pat's co-workers on the bus said when Willie Bea asked was, "She left work early."

"I wonder if she's sick," Willie Bea thought.

She was still thinking about her friend when the bus began making its climb up Pleasant Hill. "I better stop and see 'bout her," Willie Bea thought.

She was still standing with her hand near the signal wire when the bus slowed to a stop in front of the cinder block duplex where Pat lived, and Willie Bea saw the gold of a Schlitz beer uniform slip back inside the dusty screen door of her friend's house.

The bus driver paused a good while with the bus door open waiting for Willie Bea to leave. Then, he finally hollered toward the back of the bus, "You getting off or not?"

Willie Bea turned around to the driver's back and tried to smile as she took her regular seat again. When she reached her boardinghouse, she was anxious to see Jaybird and ask him who the new man was working on the beer truck. But he wasn't home.

She sat up alone on the bed in the boardinghouse room long after it grew dark.

Willie Bea didn't know how long she had been asleep when she heard the rusty door knob turn and felt a sliver of light from the hall fall across her face. Jaybird almost never stayed out late without her or telling her beforehand.

"You okay, Jay?" she asked sleepily.

He only grunted and rubbed her back softly. "Go back to sleep, Bea," he said. "I'm coming to bed now."

Willie Bea lay waiting for Jaybird to say something more, to say where he had been, to say he saw her friend Pat that day. But he said nothing.

And when he did finally slip into bed, it felt as if an ironing board was between them.

TONI CADE BAMBARA

THE ORGANIZER'S WIFE

The men from the co-op school were squatting in her garden. Jake, who taught the day students and hassled the town school board, was swiping at the bushy greens with his cap, dislodging slugs, raising dust. The tall gent who ran the graphics workshop was pulling a penknife open with his teeth, scraping rust from the rake she hadn't touched in weeks. Old Man Boone was up and down. Couldn't squat too long of account of the ankle broken in last spring's demonstration when the tobacco weights showed funny. Jack-in-the-box up, Boone snatched at a branch or two and stuffed his pipe—crumblings of dry leaf, bits of twig. Down, he eased string from the seams of his overalls, up again, thrumbling up tobacco from the depths of his pockets.

She couldn't hear them. They were silent. The whole morning stock-still, nothing stirring. The baby quiet too, drowsing his head back in the crook of her arm as she stepped out into the sun already up and blistering. The men began to unbend, shifting weight to one leg then the other, watching her move about the jumbled yard. But no one spoke.

She bathed the baby with the little dew that had gathered on what few leaves were left on the branches crackling, shredding into the empty rain barrels. The baby gurgled, pinching her arms. Virginia had no energy for a smile or a wince. All energy summoned up at rising was focused tightly on her two errands of the day. She took her time going back in, seeing the men shift around in the heaps of tomatoes, in the snarl of the strawberry runners. Stamped her shoe against each step, carrying the baby back in. Still no one spoke, though clearly, farmers all their lives, they surely had some one thing to say about the disarray of her garden.

The young one, whose voice she well knew from the sound truck, had his mouth open and his arm outstretched as though to speak on the good sense of

21

turning every inch of ground to food, or maybe to rant against the crime of letting it just go. He bent and fingered the brown of the poke salad that bordered the dry cabbages, his mouth closing again. Jake rose suddenly and cleared his throat, but turned away to light Old Man Boone's pipe, lending a shoulder for the old one to hunch against, cupping the bowl and holding the match, taking a long lingering time, his back to her. She sucked her teeth and went in.

When she came out again, banding the baby's carry straps around her waist, she moved quickly, stepping into the radishes, crushing unidentifiable shoots underfoot. Jake stepped back out of the way and caught his cuffs in the rake. Jake was the first in a long line to lose his land to unpaid taxes. The bogus receipts were pinned prominently as always to his jacket pocket. Signed by someone the county said did not exist, but who'd managed nonetheless to buy up Jake's farm at auction and turn it over swiftly to the granite company. She looked from the huge safety pin to the hot, brown eyes that quickly dropped. The other men rose up around her, none taller than she, though all taller than the corn bent now, grit-laden with neglect. Out of the corner of her eye, she saw a white worm work its way into the once-silky tufts turned straw, then disappear.

"Mornin," she said, stretching out her hand.

The men mumbled quickly, clearing their throats again. Boone offering a hand in greeting, then realizing she was extending not her hand but the small, round tobacco tin in it. Graham's red tobacco tin with the boy in shiny green astride an iron horse. It was Graham's habit, when offering a smoke, to spin some tale or other about the boy on the indestructible horse, a tale the smoker would finish. The point always the same—the courage of the youth, the hope of the future. Boone drew his hand back quickly as though the red tin was aflame. She curled her hand closed and went out the gate, slowly, deliberately, fixing her tall, heavy image indelibly on their eyes.

"Good-for-nuthin."

They thought that's what they heard drift back over her shoulder. Them? The tin? The young one thought he saw her pitch it into the clump of tomatoes hanging on by the gate. But no one posed the question.

"Why didn't you say somethin?" Jake demanded of his star pupil, the orator, whose poems and tales and speeches delivered from the sound truck had done more to pull the districts together, the women all said, than all the leaflets the kids cluttered the fields with, than all the posters from the co-op's graphic workshop masking the road signs, than all the meetings which not all the folk could get to.

"Why didn't you speak?" Jake shoved the young one, and for a minute they were all stumbling, dancing nimbly to avoid destroying food that could still be salvaged.

"Watch it, watch it now," Old Boone saying, checking his foot brace and grabbing the young one up, a fistful of sleeve.

"You shoulda said somethin," the tall gent spat.

"Why me?" The young one whined—not in the voice he'd cultivated for the sound truck. "I don't know her no better than yawl do."

"One of the women shoulda come," said the tall gent.

The men looked at each other, then stared down the road. It was clear that no one knew any more how to talk to the bristling girl-woman, if ever any had.

It wasn't a shift in breeze that made the women look up, faces stuck out as if to catch the rain. 'Cause there was no breeze and there'd been no rain. And look like, one of them said, there'd be no bus either. The strained necks had more to do with sound than weather. Someone coming. A quick check said all who worked in town were already gathered at the bus stop. Someone coming could only mean trouble—fire broke out somewhere, riot in town, one of the children hurt, market closed down, or maybe another farm posted. The women standing over their vegetable baskets huddled together for conference, then broke apart to jut their bodies out over the road for a look-see. The women seated atop the bags of rags or uniforms, clustered to question each other, then scattered, some standing tip-toe, others merely leaning up from the rocks to question the market women. And in that brief second, as bodies pulled upward, the rocks blotted up more sun to sear them, sting them, sicken them with. These stones, stacked generations ago to keep the rain from washing the road away, banked higher and broader by the young folk now to keep the baking earth from breaking apart.

Virginia nodded to the women, her earrings tinkling against her neck. The "Mornins" and "How do's" came scraggly across the distance. The bus-stop plot was like an island separated from the mainland road by shimmering sheets of heat, by arid moats and gullies that had once been the drainage system, dried-out craters now misshapen, as though pitted and gouged by war.

One clear voice rising above the scattered sopranos, calling her by name, slowed Virginia down. Frankie Lee Taylor, the lead alto in the choir, was standing on the rocks waving, out of her choir robes and barely recognizable but for that red-and-yellow jumper, the obligatory ugly dress just right for the kitchens in town. "Everything all right?" the woman asked for everyone there. And not waiting for a word once Virginia's face could be read by all, she continued: "Bus comin at all, ever?"

Virginia shrugged and picked up her pace. If the six-thirty bus was this late coming, she thought, she could make the first call and be back on the road in time for the next bus to town. She wouldn't have to borrow the church station wagon after all. She didn't want to have to ask for nothing. When she saw Graham that afternoon she wanted the thing stitched up, trimmed, neat, finished. Wanted to be able to say she asked for "nuthin from nobody and didn't nobody offer up nuthin." It'd be over with. They'd set bail and she'd pay it with the money with-held from the seed and the fertilizer, the wages not paid to the two students who used to help in the garden, the money saved 'cause she was too cranky to eat, to care. Pay the bail and unhook them both from this place. Let some other damn fool break his health on this place, the troubles.

She'd been leaving since the first day coming, the day her sister came home to cough herself to death and leave her there with nobody to look out for her 'cept some hinkty cousins in town and Miz Mama Mae, who shook her head sadly whenever the girl spoke of this place and these troubles and these people and one day soon leaving for some other place. She'd be going now for sure. Virginia was smiling now and covering a whole lotta ground.

Someone was coming up behind her, churning up the loose layers of clay, the red-and-yellow jumper a mere blur in the haze of red dust. Everyone these dry, hot days looked like they'd been bashed with a giant powder puff of henna. Virginia examined her own hands, pottery-red like the hands of her cousins seen through the beauty-parlor windows in town, hands sunk deep in the pots, working up the mud packs for the white women lounging in the chairs. She looked at her arms, her clothes, and slowed down. Not even well into the morning and already her skimpy bath ruined. The lime-boiled blouse no longer white but pink.

"Here, Gin," the woman was saying. "He a good man, your man. He share our hardships, we bear his troubles, our troubles." She was stuffing money in between the carry straps, patting the chubby legs as the baby lolled in his cloth carriage. "You tell Graham we don't forget that he came back. Lots of the others didn't, forgot. You know, Gin, that you and me and the rest of the women . . ." She was going to say more but didn't. Was turning with her mouth still open, already trotting up the road, puffs of red swirling about her feet and legs, dusting a line in that red-and-yellow jumper the way Miz Mama Mae might do making hems in the shop.

Virginia hoisted the baby higher on her back and rewound the straps, clutching the money tight, flat in her fist. She thought about Miz Mama Mae, pins in her mouth, fussing at her. "What's them hanky-type hems you doin, Gin?" she'd say, leaning over her apprentice. "When ya sew for the white folks you roll them kinda stingy hems. And you use this here oldish thread to insure a quick inheritance. But when you sew for us folks, them things got to last season in and season out and many a go-round exchange. Make some hefty hems, girl, hefty."

And Virginia had come to measure her imprisonment by how many times that same red-and-yellow jumper met her on the road, faded and fading some more, but the fairly bright hem getting wider and wider, the telltale rim recording the seasons past, the owners grown. While she herself kept busting out of her clothes, straining against the good thread, outdistancing the hefty hems. Growing so fast from babe to child to girl to someone, folks were always introducing and reintroducing themselves to her. It seemed at times that the walls wouldn't contain her, the roof wouldn't stop her. Busting out of childhood, busting out her clothes, but never busting out the place.

And now the choir woman had given her the money like that and spoken, trying to attach her all over again, root her, ground her in the place. Just when there was a chance to get free. Virginia clamped her jaws tight and tried to go blank. Tried to blot out all feelings and things—the farms, the co-op sheds, the lone gas pump, a shoe left in the road, the posters promising victory over the troubles. She never wanted these pictures called up on some future hot, dry day in some other place. She squinted, closed her eyes even, 'less the pictures cling to her eyes, store in the brain, to roll out later and crush her future with the weight of this place and its troubles.

Years before when there'd been rain and ways to hold it, she'd trotted along this road not seeing too much, trotting and daydreaming, delivering parcels to and from Miz Mama Mae's shop. She could remember that one time, ducking and dodging the clods of earth chucked up by the horse's hooves. Clods spinning wet and heavy against her skirts, her legs, as she followed behind, seeing nothing outside her own pictures but that horse and rider. Trying to keep up, keep hold of the parcel slipping all out of shape in the drizzle, trying to piece together the things she would say to him when he finally turned round and saw her. She had lived the scene often enough in bed to know she'd have to speak, say something to make him hoist her up behind him in the saddle, to make him gallop her off to the new place. She so busy dreaming, she let the curve of the road swerve her off toward the edge. Mouthing the things to say and even talking out loud with her hands and almost losing the slippery bundle, not paying good enough attention. And a ball of earth shot up and hit her square in the chest and sent her stumbling over the edge into the gully. The choir organist's robe asprawl in the current that flushed the garbage down from the hill where the townies lived, to the bottom where the folks lived, to the pit where the co-op brigade made compost heaps for independence, laughing.

Graham had pulled her up and out by the wrists, pulled her against him and looked right at her. Not at the cabbage leaves or chicory on her arms, a mango sucked hairy to its pit clinging to her clothes. But looked at her. And no screen door between them now. No glass or curtain, or shrub peeked through.

"You followin me." He grinned. And she felt herself swimming through the gap in his teeth.

And now she would have to tell him. 'Cause she had lost three times to the coin flipped on yesterday morning. Had lost to the icepick pitched in the afternoon in the dare-I-don't-I boxes her toe had sketched in the yard. Had lost at supper to the shadow slanting across the tablecloth that reached her wrist before Miz Mama Mae finished off the corn relish. Had lost that dawn to the lazy lizard, suddenly quickened in his journey on the ceiling when the sun came up. Lost against doing what she'd struggled against doing in order to win one more day of girlhood before she jumped into her womanstride and stalked out on the world. I want to come to you. I want to come to you and be with you. I want to be your woman, she did not say after all.

"I want to come to the co-op school," she said. "I want to learn to read better and type and figure and keep accounts so I can get out of . . ."—this place, she didn't say—"my situation."

He kept holding her and she kept wanting and not wanting to ease out of his grip and rescue the choir robe before it washed away.

"I had five years schooling 'fore I came here," she said, talking way too loud. "Been two years off and on at the church school . . . before you came."

"You do most of Miz Mama Mae's cipherin I hear? Heard you reading the newspapers to folks in the tobacco shed. You read well."

She tried to pull away then, thinking he was calling her a liar or poking fun some way. "Cipherin" wasn't how he talked. But he didn't let go. She expected to see her skin twisted and puckered when she looked at where he was holding her. But his grip was soft. Still she could not step back.

"You been watchin me," he said with the grin again. And looking into his face, she realized he wasn't at all like she'd thought. Was older, heavier, taller, smoother somehow. But then looking close up was not like sneaking a look from the toolshed as he'd come loping across the fields with his pigeontoed self and in them soft leather boots she kept waiting to see fall apart from rough wear till she finally decided he must own pairs and pairs of all the same kind. Yes, she'd watched him on his rounds, in and out of the houses, the drying sheds, down at the docks, after fellowship in the square. Talking, laughing, teaching, always moving. Had watched him from the trees, through windows as he banged tables, arguing about deeds, urging, coaxing, pleading, hollering, apologizing, laughing again. In the early mornings, before Miz Mama Mae called the girls to sew, she had watched him chinning on the bar he'd slammed between the portals of the co-op school door. Huffing, puffing, cheeks like chipmunks. The dark circle of his gut sucking in purple, panting out blue. Yes, she watched him. But she said none of this or of the other either. Not then.

"I want to come to night school" was how she put it. "I don't know yet what kinda work I can do for the co-op. But I can learn."

"That's the most I ever heard you talk," he was saying, laughing so hard, he loosened his grip. "In the whole three years I've been back, that's the most—" He was laughing again. And he was talking way too loud himself.

She hadn't felt the least bit foolish standing there in the drizzle, in the garbage, tall up and full out of her clothes nearly, and Graham laughing at her. Not the least bit foolish 'cause he was talking too loud and laughing too hard. And she was going to go to his school. And whether he knew it or not, he was going to take her away from this place.

Wasn't but a piece of room the school, with a shed tacked on in back for storage and sudden meetings. The furniture was bandaged but brightly painted. The chemistry equipment was old but worked well enough. The best thing was the posters. About the co-op, about Malcolm and Harriet and Fannie Lou, about Guinea-Bissau and Vietnam. And the posters done by the children, the pictures cut from magazines, the maps—all slapped up as though to hold the place together, to give an identity to the building so squat upon the land. The identity of the place for her was smells. The smell of mortar vibrating from the walls that were only wood. The smell of loam that curled up from the sink, mostly rusted metal. The green-and-brown smell rising up over heads sunk deep into palms as folks leaned over their papers, bearing down on stumps of pencil or hunks of charcoal, determined to get now and to be what they'd been taught was privilege impossible, what they now knew was their right, their destiny.

"Season after season," Graham was dictating that first night, leaning up against the maps with the ruler, "we have pulled gardens out of stones, creating something from nothing—creators."

Sweat beading on a nose to her left, a temple to her right. Now and then a face she knew from fellowship looking up as Graham intoned the statements, tapping the ruler against the table to signal punctuation traps. And she working hard, harder than some, though she never ever did learn to speak her speak as most folks finally did. But grateful just to be there, and up in front, unlike the past when, condemned by her size, she's been always exiled in the rear with the gold-fish tanks or the rabbits that always died, giving her a suspect reputation.

"The first step toward getting the irrigation plant," he continued, crashing the ruler down, "is to organize."

"Amen," said one lady by the window, never looking up from her paper, certain she would finally train herself and be selected secretary of the church board. "That way us folks can keep track of them folks" was how she'd said it when she rose to speak her speak one summer night.

"What can defeat greed, technological superiority, and legal lawlessness," Graham had finished up, "is discipline, consciousness, and unity."

Always three sentences that folks would take home for discussion, for transformation into well-ordered paragraphs that wound up, some of them, in the co-op newsletter or on the posters or in the church's bulletin. Many became primers for the children.

Graham had been wearing the denim suit with the leather buckles the first night in class. Same fancy suit she'd caught sight of through the screen door when he'd come calling on Miz Mama Mae to buy the horse. A denim suit not country-cut at all—in fact, so *not* she was sure he would be leaving. Dudes in well-cut denim'd been coming and leaving since the days she wore but one yard of cloth. It was his would-be-moving-on clothes that had pulled her to him. But then the pull had become too strong to push against once his staying-on became clear.

She often fixed him supper in a metal cake tin once used for buttons. And Miz Mama Mae joked with the pin cushion, saying the girl weren't fooling nobody but herself sneaking around silly out there in the pantry with the button box. Telling the bobbins it was time certain folk grew up to match they size. And into the night, treadling away on the machine, the woman addressed the dress form, saying a strong, serious-type schoolteacher man had strong, serious work to do. Cutting out the paper patterns, the woman told the scissors that visiting a man in his rooms at night could mean disaster or jubilee one. And Virginia understood she would not be stopped by the woman. But some felt she was taking up too much of his time, their time. He was no longer where they could find him for homework checks or questions about the law. And Jake and Old Man Boone sullen, nervous that the midnight strategy meetings were too few now and far between. The women of the nearby district would knock and enter with trapped firefly lanterns, would shove these on the table between the couple, and make their point as Graham nodded and Virginia giggled or was silent, one.

His quilt, Graham explained, leaving the earrings on the table for her to find, was made from patches from his daddy's overalls, and scraps from Boone's wedding cutaway, white remnants from his mother's shroud, some blue from a sister's graduation, and khaki, too, snatched from the uniform he'd been proud of killing in in Korea a hundred lives ago. The day students had stitched a liberation flag in one corner. The night students had restuffed it and made a new border. She and Miz Mama Mae had stitched it and aired it. And Virginia had brought it back to him, wrapped in it. She had rolled herself all in it, to hide from him in her new earrings, childish. But he never teased that she was too big for games, and she liked that. He found her in it, his tongue finding the earrings first. Careful, girl, she'd warned herself. This could be a trap, she murmured under him.

"Be my woman," he whispered into her throat.

You don't have time for me, she didn't say, lifting his tikis and medallions up over his head. And there'd never be enough time here with so many people, so much land to work, so much to do, and the wells not even dug, she thought, draping the chains around his bedpost.

"Be my woman, Gin," he said again. And she buried her fingers in his hair and he buried his hair inside her clothes and she pulled the quilt close and closed him in, crying.

She was leaking. The earrings tinkling against her neck. The medallions clinking against the bedpost in her mind. Gray splotches stiffened in her new pink blouse, rubbing her nipples raw. But other than a dribble that oozed momentarily down her back, there was no sign of the baby aroused and hungry. If the baby slept on, she'd keep on. She wanted to reach Revun Michaels before the white men came. Came this time brazenly with the surveyors and the diggers, greedy for the granite under the earth. Wanted to catch Revun Michaels before he showed them his teeth and wouldn't hear her, couldn't, too much smiling. Wanted to hear him say it—the land's been sold. The largest passel of land in the district, the church holdings where the co-op school stood, where two storage sheds of the co-op stood, where the graphics workshop stood, where four families had lived for generations working the land. The church had sold the land. He'd say it, she'd hear it, and it'd be over with. She and Graham could go.

She was turning the bend now, forgetting to not look, and the mural the co-op had painted in eye-stinging colors topped her. FACE UP TO WHAT'S KILLING YOU, it demanded. Below the statement a huge triangle that from a distance was just a triangle, but on approaching, as one muttered "how deadly can a triangle be?" turned into bodies on bodies. At the top, fat, fanged beasts in smart clothes, like the ones beneath it laughing, drinking, eating, bombing, raping, shooting, lounging on the backs of, feeding off the backs of, the folks at the base, crushed almost flat but struggling to get up and getting up, topple the structure. She passed it quickly. All she wanted to think about was getting to Revun Michaels quick to hear it. Sold the land. Then she'd be free to string together the bits and scraps of things for so long bobbing about in her head. Things that had to be pieced together well, with strong thread so she'd have a whole thing to shove through the mesh at Graham that afternoon.

And would have to shove hard or he'd want to stay, convinced that folks would battle for his release, would battle for themselves, the children, the future, would keep on no matter how powerful the thief, no matter how little the rain, how exhausted the soil, 'cause this was home. Not a plot of earth for digging in or weeping over or crawling into, but home. Near the Ethiopic where the ancestral bones spoke their speak on certain nights if folks tamped hard enough, sang long enough, shouted. Home. Where "America" was sung but meant something altogether else than it had at the old school. Home in the future. The future here now developing. Home liberated soon. And the earth would recover. The rain would come. The ancient wisdoms would be revived. The energy released. Home a human place once more. The bones spoke it. The spirit spoke, too, through flesh when the women gathered at the altar, the ancient orishas still vibrant beneath the ghostly patinas some thought right to pray to, but connected in spite of themselves to the spirits under the plaster.

WE CANNOT LOSE, the wall outside the church said. She paused at the bulletin board, the call-for-meeting flyers limp in the heat. She bent to spit but couldn't raise it. She saw Revun Michaels in the schoolhouse window watching her. He'd say it. Sold the land.

Virginia wondered what the men in her ruined garden were telling themselves now about land as power and land and man tied to the future, not the past. And what would they tell the women when the bulldozers came to claim the earth, to maim it, rape it, plunder it all with that bone-deep hatred for all things natural? And what would the women tell the children dangling in the tires waiting for Jake to ring the bell? Shouting from the clubhouses built in the trees? The slashed trees oozing out money into the white man's pails, squeezing hard to prolong a tree life, forestalling the brutal cut down to stump. Then stump wasting, no more money to give, blown up out of the earth, the iron claw digging deep and merciless to rip out the taproots, leaving for the children their legacy, an open grave, gouged out by a gene-deep hatred for all things natural, for all things natural that couldn't turn a quick penny quick enough to dollar. She spit.

Revun Michaels, small and balding, was visible in the schoolhouse window. His expression carried clear out the window to her, watching her coming fast, kicking himself for getting caught in there and only one door, now that the shed was nailed on fast in back.

"Did you sell the land as well?" she heard herself saying, rushing in the doorway much too fast. "You might have waited like folks asked you. You didn't have to. Enough granite under this schoolhouse alone"—she stamped, frightening him—"to carry both the districts for years and years, if we developed it ourselves." She heard the "we ourselves" explode against her teeth and she fell back.

"Wasn't me," he stammered. "The church board saw fit to—"

"Fit!" She was advancing now, propelled by something she had no time to understand. "Wasn't nuthin fitten about it." She had snatched the ruler from its hook. The first slam hard against the chair he swerved around, fleeing. The next cracked hard against his teeth. His legs buckled under and he slid down, his face frozen in disbelief. But nothing like the disbelief that swept through her the moment "we ourselves" pushed past clenched teeth and nailed her to the place, a woman unknown. She saw the scene detached, poster figures animated: a hefty woman pursuing a scrambling man in and out among the tables and chairs in frantic games before Jake rang the bell for lessons to commence.

"And what did the white folks pay you to turn Graham in and clear the way? Disturber of the peace. What peace? Racist trying to incite a riot. Ain't that how they said it? Outside agitator, as you said. And his roots put down here long before you ever came. When you were just a twinkle in Darwin's eye." Virginia heard herself laughing. It was a good, throaty laugh and big. The man was turning round now on the floor, staring at her in amazement.

"Thirty pieces of silver, maybe? That's what you preach, tradition. Thirty pieces 'bout as traditional as—"

"Just hold on. It wasn't me that— The board of trustees advised me that this property could not be used for—"

The ruler came down on the stiff of his arm and broke. Michaels dropped between two rickety chairs that came apart on top of him. The baby cried, the woman shushed, as much to quiet the woman that was her. Calm now, she watched the man try to get up, groping the chairs the folks had put together from cast-offs for the school. Her shoe caught him at the side of his head and he went under.

The station wagon was pulling up as she was coming out, flinging the piece of ruler into the bushes. She realized then that the men had come in it, that the station wagon had been sitting all morning in her garden. That they had come to take her to see Graham. She bit her lip. She never gave folk a chance, just like Miz Mama Mae always fussed. Never gave them or herself a chance to speak the speak.

"We'll take you to him," Jake was saying, holding the door open and easing the baby off her back.

The young one shoved over. "Mother Lee who's secretarying for the board has held up the papers for the sale. We came to tell you that." He waited till she smiled to laugh. "We're the delegation that's going to confront the board this evening. Us and Frankie Lee Taylor and—"

"Don't talk the woman to death," said Boone, turning in his seat and noting her daze. He was going to say more, but the motor drowned him out. Virginia hugged the baby close and unbuttoned her blouse.

"That's one sorry piece of man," drawled Boone as they pulled out. All heads swung to the right to see the short, fat, balding preacher darting in and out among the gravestones for the sanctuary of the church. To the phone, Virginia figured. And would they jail her too, she and the baby?

Then everyone was silent before the naked breast and the sucking. Silence was what she needed. And time, to draw together tight what she'd say to Graham. How blood had spurted from Revun Michael's ear, for one thing. Graham might not want to hear it, but there was no one else to tell it to, to explain how it was when all she thought she wanted was to hear it said flat out—land's been sold, school's no more. Not that a school's a building, she argued with herself, watching the baby, playing with the image of herself speaking her speak finally in the classroom, then realizing that she already had. By tomorrow the women would have burrowed beneath the tale of some swinging door or however Revun Michaels would choose to tell it. But would the women be able to probe and sift and explain it to her? Who could explain her to her?

And how to explain to Graham so many things. About this new growth she was experiencing, was thinking on at night wrapped in his quilt. Not like the dread growing up out of her clothes as though she'd never stop 'fore she be freak, 'cause she had stopped. And not like the new growth that was the baby, for she'd expected that, had been prepared. More like the toenail smashed the day the work brigade had stacked the stones to keep the road from splitting apart. The way the new nail pushed up against the old turning blue, against the gauze and the tape, stubborn to establish itself. A chick pecking through the shell, hard-headed and hasty and wobbly. She might talk of it this time. She was convinced she could get hold of it this time.

She recalled that last visiting time trying to speak on what was happening to her coming through the shell. But had trouble stringing her feelings about so many things together, words to drape around him, to smother all those other things, things she had said, hurled unstrung, flung out with tantrum heat at a time when she thought there would always be time enough to coolly take them back, be woman warm in some elsewhere place and make those hurtful words forgettable. But then they had come for him in the afternoon, came and got him, took him from the schoolhouse in handcuffs. And when she had visited him in the jail, leaning into the mesh, trying to push past the barrier, she could tell the way the guards hovered around her and baby that clearly they thought she could do, would do, what they had obviously tried over and over to do, till Graham was ashy and slow, his grin lax. Then she could break him open so they could break him down. She almost had, not knowing it, leaking from the breast as she always did, not keeping track of the time. Stuttering, whining, babbling, hanging on to the mesh with one hand, the other stuffed in her mouth, her fingers ensnarled in the skein of words coming out all tangled, knotted.

"I don't mind this so much," he'd cut in. "Time to think."

And when she pulled her fingers from her mouth, the thread broke and all her words came bounding out in a hopeless scatter of tears and wails until something—her impatience with her own childishness, or maybe it was the obvious pleasure of the guards—made her grab herself up. She grabbed herself up abrupt, feeling in that moment what it was she wanted to say about her nights wrapped up in the quilt smelling him in it, hugging herself, grabbing herself up and trying to get to that place that was beginning to seem more of a when than a where. And the when seemed to be inside her if she could only connect.

"I kinda like the quiet," he had said. "Been a while since I've had so much time to think." And then he grinned and was ugly. Was that supposed to make her hate him? To hate and let go? That had occurred to her on the bus home. But roaming around the house, tripping on the edges of the quilt, she had rejected it. That was not the meaning of his words or that smile that had torn his face. She'd slumped in the rocking chair feeding the baby, examining her toenail for such a time.

"They never intended to dig the wells, that's clear," Old Man Boone was saying. "That was just to get into the district, get into our business, check out our strength. I was a fool," he muttered, banging his pipe against his leg remembering his hopefulness, his hospitality even. "A fool."

"Well, gaddamn, Boone," the tall gent sputtered. "Can't you read? That's what our flyers been saying all along. Don't you read the stuff we put out? Gaddamnit, Boone."

"If you don't read the flyers, you leastways knows history," the young one was saying. "When we ever invited the beast to dinner he didn't come in and swipe the napkins and start taking notes on the tablecloth 'bout how to take over the whole house?"

"Now that's the truth," Jake said, laughing. His laughter pulled Virginia forward, and she touched his arm, moved. That he could laugh. His farm stolen and he could laugh. But that was one of the three most moving things about Jake, she was thinking. The way he laughed. The way he sweated. The way he made his body comfy for the children to lean against.

"Yeh, they sat right down to table and stole the chicken," said Jake.

"And took the table. And the deed." The tall gent smacked Jake on his cap.

"Yeh," Old Man Boone muttered, thinking of Graham.

"We ain't nowhere's licked yet though, huhn?"

The men looked quickly at Virginia, Jake turning clear around, so that Boone leaned over to catch the steering wheel.

"Watch it, watch it now, young feller."

"There's still Mama Mae's farm," Virginia continued, patting the baby. "Enough granite under there even if the church do—"

"But they ain't," said the young one. "Listen, we got it all figured out. We're going to bypass the robbers and deal directly with the tenant councils in the cities, and we're—"

"Don't talk the woman to death," soothed Boone. "You just tell Graham his landlady up there in the North won't have to eat dog food no more. No more in life. New day coming."

"And you tell him . . ."—Jake was turning around again—"just tell him to take his care."

By the time the bolt had lifted and she was standing by the chair, the baby fed and alert now in her arms, she had done with all the threads and bits and shards of the morning. She knew exactly what to tell him, coming through the steel door now, reaching for the baby he had not held yet, could not hold now, screened off from his father. All she wished to tell him was the bail'd been paid, her strength was back, and she sure as hell was going to keep up the garden. How else to feed the people?

WORDS

Now that the old world has crashed around me, and it's raining in early summer. I live in Harlem with a baby shrew and suffer for my decadence which kept me away so long. When I walk in the streets, the streets don't yet claim me, and people look at me, knowing the strangeness of my manner, and the objective stance from which I attempt to "love" them. It was always predicted this way. This is what my body told me always. When the child leaves, and the window goes on looking out on empty walls, you will sit and dream of old things, and things that could never happen. You will be alone, and ponder on your learning. You will think of old facts, and sudden seeings which made you more than you had bargained for, yet a coward on the earth, unless you claim it, unless you step upon it with your heavy feet, and feel actual hardness.

Last night in a bar a plump black girl sd, "OK, be intellectual, go write some more of them jivey books," and it could have been anywhere, a thousand years ago, she sd "Why're you so cold," and I wasn't even thinking coldness. Just tired and a little weary of myself. Not even wanting to hear me thinking up things to say.

But the attention. To be always looking, and thinking. To be always under so many things' gaze, the pressure of such attention. I wanted something, want it now. But don't know what it is, except words. I cd say anything. But what would be left, what would I have made? Who would love me for it? Nothing. No one. Alone, I will sit and watch the sun die, the moon fly out in space, the earth wither, and dead men stand in line, to rot away and never exist.

Finally, to have passed away, and be an old hermit in love with silence. To have the thing I left, and found. To be older than I am, and with the young animals marching through the trees. To want what is natural, and strong.

Today is more of the same. In the closed circle I have fashioned. In the alien language of another tribe. I make these documents for some heart who will recognize me truthfully. Who will know what I am and what I wanted beneath the maze of meanings and attitudes that shape the reality of everything. Beneath the necessity of talking or the necessity for being angry or beneath the actual core of life we make reference to digging deep into some young woman, and listening to her come.

Selves fly away in madness. Liquid self shoots out of the joint. Lives which are salty and sticky. Why does everyone live in a closet, and hope no one will understand how badly they need to grow? How many errors they canonize or justify, or kill behind? I need to be an old monk and not feel sorry or happy for people. I need to be a billion years old with a white beard and all of ASIA to walk around.

The purpose of myself, has not yet been fulfilled. Perhaps it will never be. Just these stammerings and poses. Just this need to reach into myself, and feel something wince and love to be touched.

The dialogue exists. Magic and ghosts are a dialogue, and the body bodies of material, invisible sound vibrations, humming in emptyness, and ideas less than humming, humming, images collide in empty ness, and we build our emotions into blank invisible structures which never exist, and are not there, and are illusion and pain and madness. Dead whiteness.

We turn white when we are afraid.

We are going to try to be happy.

We do not need to be fucked with.

We can be quiet and think and love the silence.

We need to look at trees more closely.

We need to listen.

Harlem 1965

HAL BENNETT

MISS ASKEW ON ICE

FIRST OF ALL, it is important to pronounce her name correctly: *Askew*, like ask you, more or less. The other way, a*skew*, meaning out of line, awry, would certainly describe Cousinsville in those candy-striped days. But never Miss Dorothea Askew, although she weighed over three hundred pounds and stood taller than six feet when she fell on the ice that winter in the 1930s and couldn't get up for the life of her.

You would have known that Miss Askew was always together, so to speak, by the fact that thirteen years' worth of extraordinarily horny students in her seventh-grade English classes at Oakwood Avenue School had never been able to catch her with her big fine legs sufficiently open to look up her dress. When Miss Askew hit the sidewalk, bells from Catholic churches near and far began throwing their tintinnabulations all over town hilariously, like colorful confetti thrown at carnivals.

What the bells meant, of course, was that old Irish and Italian women wearing somber kerchiefs, and most of them with a sprig of beard, were piling into Cousinsville's churches just at the moment of Miss Askew's impact, to suck and gnaw over the blood and body of Christ at that hour of the evening. It is probably safe to say that none of this consuming of the Deity really affected Miss Askew, who was Baptist, like all the other colored people in Cousinsville. While our stern and frowning red brick church did have a handsome bell, it was almost never rung and had probably become glued by cobwebs in its decrepit roost, while Catholics preempted the airwaves at practically every hour to announce the eating of their god.

Still, it did seem somewhat prophetic that the Catholic bells began their clamoring at the precise moment that Miss Askew fell, which was at six o'clock in the evening of the second Saturday in February of 1939. Miss Askew, like myself, was part of that era's audience—when life was fairly uncomplicated, or gave the sly appearance of being so—with World War II standing not far offstage to perform in the coming tragedy. The Depression was winding down, and the war in Europe was bringing prosperity to America before we ourselves entered the conflict on two fronts and the prosperity was unexpectedly stained with American blood.

Nevertheless, those were good, bright, and golden days in Cousinsville. I was nineteen going on twenty, in my second year at Newark Rutgers, on the outs with what had been the current girl friend and leisurely looking around for a new victim. If I did not have the world precisely by the balls, I felt that I certainly had a fair handful of its crotch hair, which was the correct way for a Rutgers sophomore to feel in those days. Even that winter behaved herself and carried a definite promise of spring about her, and it had been unseasonably warm all that Saturday up until Miss Askew fell, as though we had skipped a whole season and were waiting for the fires of summer rather than the robins of spring.

The main activity of Cousinsville, away from its commercial center, went on around a small park with a raised band-stand in its middle, which politicians had erected to excite rallies and to make their speeches from. This was in the Decatur section of Cousinsville, where the colored people lived, along with a sprinkling of Irish and Italians and a few Jews who had stayed behind. One of those Jews was Miss Miriam Finkelstein, who had recently converted to the Catholic faith, and soon thereafter became very friendly with Miss Dorothea Askew.

When Miss Askew fell on the ice, shortly before sunset, Miss Finkelstein was in the park trying to scrape up other candidates for Holy Mother Church. There was also bare-chested Wilson Brown—decidedly a 97-pound weakling—practicing his Charles Atlas exercises over near the bandstand where red, white, and blue bunting was being raised for the beginning of Brotherhood Week tomorrow, when the politicians would come to speak and bring along colored preachers and "civic" leaders to satisfy the spirit if not exactly the substance of brotherhood.

And there was Harry Claiborne, who was extraordinarily black, having the usual discussion about his manhood with Nancy O'Reilly, the white woman who had renounced her race and religion in order to live with Harry's impotence. Just before Miss Askew fell, Nancy O'Reilly was telling Harry Claiborne in her delicious brogue: "But you can't get it up, Harry me lad. How do you expect me to treat you like a colored stud when you can't get it up?"

Beyond them, behind some gardenia bushes which would burst into startling white bloom even earlier this year than usual, two winos shared a purple bottle and confessed their real love for one another, since there was no one else that either of them had to love. Which would have pleased Miss Edwina Robinson enormously. A scrawny black woman who drooped like a damp crow, Miss Edwina was known in Cousinsville as the woman who weeded out fags.

According to Miss Edwina's own estimation of herself, any male who had sex with her was a hundred percent normal; those unwilling or unable to were immediately branded the other thing and more often than not intimidated into the baptismal juices of Miss Edwina's vagina, or frightened into disastrous marriages, or skipped town altogether in order to escape the devastation of Miss Edwina's daily muster: "Billy Smith is a fag. Stanley Jackson is a fag. Carl Edison is a fag . . ." —which she read from a rolled list that looked suspiciously like parchment, as though she were the king's crier, full of high-sounding oyezes and ringing denunciations. I had managed to avoid Miss Edwina's list by having sweaty sex with her from time to time always in the very darkest rooms and when I was pissy drunk; by her own admission, I was her youngest, her biggest, and her best, which seemed to me the only honest thing she'd ever said.

Beyond Miss Edwina on the other side of the park was the woman who was said to be mad, up in her second-story window, moaning "I'm a nigger. I'm a nigger," in a hurt indignant wail, as though the revelation had come to her late on in life, bringing irreparable damage.

"I can too get it up," Harry Claiborne whined, as Nancy O'Reilly shook her head with marvelous disbelief. As I have said, winter had been unusually benign, and the afternoon sky that day was a bright gay blue adorned with scattered twists of clouds. Japanese cherry trees in the park had already developed small furry breasts on their branches. Clusters of forsythia ejaculated the first traces of tiny yellow blossoms, like caught butterflies, and bushes of pussy willows put forth their silken catkins. "I have been too long without love, and it naturally makes me nervous," Nancy O'Reilly complained. "It's the wine that keeps you down, Harry me boy."

"Don't you call me boy." Harry cried, and fell into her waiting arms.

Children suddenly appeared in the park on roller skates, whirling expertly around patches of ice and snow in a mad, noisy ballet, while Miss Edwina intoned her barbarisms to the dull cadence of hammer strokes where bunting was being raised for the rally: "Thurston Morton is a fag. Louis Reynolds is a fag. Robert Williams is a fag. . . ." Above all of this, Mr. Giottio's hurdy-gurdy wheezed out strident tunes like breathless metal birds with colorful strands of emphysema. And from Mr. Giottio's brawny shoulder, a wizened monkey wearing red fez and yellow vest, sprang forth with a tin cup to beg.

As for me, I was wandering around in this circus, pulling slyly on myself through a torn pocket in my dungarees, until Miss Miriam Finkelstein, the Jew converted to Catholicism, waylaid me near the bandstand. Squinting at me down the slope of her nose, she tried to sign me up for catechism at St. Philip Neri's.

"I'm a Baptist, Miss Finkelstein." I felt very good pulling my pud without Miss Finkelstein even realizing it. "I've already been saved." She shook her mane of flaming red hair disdainfully, as though I had committed an indecency by confessing to be Baptist. "No one is saved except by Holy Mother Church," she snorted.

She went on like that, trying to break my balls; so I was glad when I saw Miss Dorothea Askew coming our way down Central Place. And even Miss Finkelstein stopped harassing me to watch Miss Askew, who had unaccountably become her best friend since Miss Finkelstein had abandoned the synagogue for Holy Mother Church.

It was always an exciting event to watch Miss Askew walk, as though one of those lovely old houses along Central Place had uprooted itself to go for a stroll. If I had known them then, I certainly would have thought of all the grand marches from the great opera literature: *Aida, The Prophet,* the entrance of the apprentices in *Die Meistersinger,* to mention a few—horns and trumpets blaring, the stringed instruments sturdy but muted, as though being lightly walked upon by the footsteps of greatness.

Miss Askew was tall; heavy in the arms, legs and butt, the breasts as well; but carrying all that meat with a kind of incongruous supple grace that could well have belonged in a carnival. Except that Miss Askew was certainly not a freak. Unusual, yes, but beautiful in large portions. Handsome face shaped like a nut-brown heart; cupid's-bow lips painted bright red; hair impeccably straightened in a page boy cut; well shod in black patent leather pumps with reinforced heels.

She was wearing a small navy blue straw hat in the shape of a shallow pot, with plastic flowers sewn around the brim. Her favorite color was navy blue, which might have been a mistake on another woman her size—the danger that you'd meet this block of blue coming at you and panic—but Miss Askew was always preceded by an ineffable smell of clean washed flesh tempered by a dab of subtle perfume, the odors going before her like celebrant heralds announcing the coming of Miss Askew contained, an army bottled up inside of itself.

"She is absolutely beautiful," Miss Finkelstein breathed beside me. "I certainly wish I could be that beautiful."

Fat chance of that, I thought, without taking my eyes from Miss Askew. There were patches of stubborn ice on the sidewalk, which Miss Askew gracefully avoided. She wore white gloves and white piping at the collar of her dress. And to further break up what might have been an indistinguishable mass, she had pinned a corsage of fresh flowers in the area of her left breast.

She was grand and she had style. But the most exciting thing about her was the quiet swish of silk always underneath her dress when she walked, where her thighs rubbed together against her silk stockings. It was a sound that had sent many of her students, myself among them, off into spasms of masturbation, shooting sperm like uncontrolled garden hoses as we thought of Miss Askew's big fine legs encased in shining silk, but held forever tightly together underneath the opening of her specially built desk.

Now, everyone in the park had stopped to watch her. But I think that the most affected of us all was Miss Finkelstein, standing next to me. Suddenly, she raised her hands and began to applaud. Which did not seem especially out of place, since Miss Askew was a performance all in herself. The woman in the window sang: *I'm a nigger, I'm a nigger,* with jubilation now, as though it was not an especially terrible thing to be. The hurdy-gurdy soared, and the children on skates screamed louder and went around and around faster in an ever-widening circle. I started clapping, and other people did, too. It is a telling point that Miss Edwina Robinson also applauded, without stopping once in her repetition of the names of our alleged fags. Mr. Giottio pumped his barrel organ even harder, and the day was filled with music as the wrinkled monkey skinned its lips back and began to dance.

And we all applauded enthusiastically because the coming of Miss Askew was an apt addition to the day's ending, its appropriate coda, like Beethoven's barroom carousing at the very end of the *Ninth.* Even the winos drinking behind the gardenia bush laid aside their bottle and clapped.

But the unexpected greeting obviously caught Miss Askew by surprise. I saw her head jerk up, then to one side and the other. And I saw her foot reaching out tentatively to where a thin sliver of ice lay almost invisibly on the sidewalk. Before I could cry out to warn her, Miss Askew's foot hit the ice.

Her arms and legs shot out at crazy angles. She hung poised in the air for a split second, looking somewhat like a pretty surprised elephant about to dance. Then she hit the ground. In her blue costume, it was like watching the collapse of a dismal spring before it had ever begun.

It was exactly six o'clock in the evening, the sun flaming red and gold as it went down behind the wooden houses, seeming to burn them. And the church bells set up their clamoring as we all raced to Miss Askew floundering on the sidewalk on her back.

In those days, it was said that a fear of falling is the only fear that a child is born with. Christine Barnhill told me that. She was a very pretty and light-skinned colored girl who read books on psychology while she studied voice in order to be an opera singer. She was the last girl I had gone steady with before Miss Askew's fall. But I had not been too upset about our breaking up. I came from a clean, decent family, while Christine's father was our local undertaker. Whenever we kissed, I always had a mild sense of distaste that I was sucking on the slimy sweet tongue of a girl whose father trafficked in death.

Christine claimed to be as squeamish about her father's calling as I was; but the truth would out later on, when she came back from college with a degree in what was unctuously called the mortuary sciences and moved into her father's business. With all her phony opera training—surely a cover-up to keep decent people from knowing what macabre desires really delighted her heart—I could picture her vigorously singing the bell song from *Lakme* as she briskly hacked out some poor dead black bastard's heart.

So I was glad that our affair hadn't worked out, although I had been walking around with pain in my own heart and feeling lost and alone most of the time since we had broke up. Seeing Miss Askew fall made me think again of Christine and the night we went to Branchbrook Park, which is down in Newark near the Cathedral of the Sacred Heart, to make love in a Tarzan tree. The trees were called that because they were easy and pleasant to climb, with abundant old branches that you could sit on and read a book, or do your homework, or just sit there and moon at the stars if you wanted to. They were very comfortable, like crazily shaped armchairs growing out of the ground.

Christine and I went there on the trolley car down to Orange Street and then walked over to the Tarzan trees while we talked about the Cathedral of the Sacred Heart, which loomed like a small Gibraltar against the deep blue backdrop of the sky. A million stars shone like bright measles at a distance from a nearly full moon; and while it was the end of January, it was by no means as cold as it usually was at that time of year.

In fact, a lot of strange things had been happening recently: like the Orson Welles radio program about the Martians supposedly landing in the Jersey meadows, when people went wild and some even committed suicide; and those weird flashes at night against the sky, caused by the northern lights. And the winter not seeming to be winter at all, which caused some people to say that the world was coming to an end.

Which I suppose was really true—not actually the apocalypse that the Bible talks about, but a very real ending to the world as we knew it back in the bubble gum Thirties—more properly put, an end to innocence and the taking up of fear and cynicism—after the Great Depression had drawn us all together around the radio, at least in Cousinsville, in perhaps the most genuine humanity that has ever existed in modern America. "They brought that cathedral here from Europe, brick by brick," Christine said, leaning against me. "The Italians paid to have it done. They took up collections."

I loved the fresh smell of her hair, which was not straightened or curled, but was fine and almost silky. "Yeah. They also have priests' babies buried down in the basement there somewhere."

"That's not true," Christine said, laughing nervously. "That's just anti-Catholic propaganda."

"So what? You planning on becoming a Catholic or something?"

"Maybe I will." She sounded oddly absent-minded, almost wistful. "Daddy says it would be very good for business. We might be able to attract some of the Catholic trade."

I nuzzled my nose into her neck. "Let's go to the Tarzan trees," I murmured. And I felt her body heat all over.

"Not just yet," she said. "Is it true that boys and girls do nasty things there?"

She had a lovely, clear voice; she would have made a very good opera singer if she hadn't got sidetracked by embalming.

"What do you mean by nasty?" I said. And I took her hand and swooshed it to my swollen pants. Quickly, secretly, her fingers clawed my John Henry like heated crustaceans; then she pulled away. "You know exactly what I mean," she said.

"So what's nasty about making love?" I took her hand again and gave her another good feel. "Oh, you," she said, pretending exasperation. But her breath was coming fast, and she started walking towards the Tarzan trees, acting non-chalant.

Christine and I had never made love before, and the idea of doing so excited and frightened me at the same time. Suppose I knocked her up? That was the very worst thing you could do to a nice girl in those days. But to wear one of those thick innertube rubbers was as uncomfortable to contemplate as the possible consequences of sending John Henry naked into the play. And if Christine did get pregnant from my going bare-backed, she would be ostracized in Cousinsville, and so would I. Sliced to death by the community's tongue and by our own unforgiving consciences—which would never let us leave the nest of Cousinsville, no matter what—we would definitely have to give up our dreams of being journalist and opera singer and settle down to the drudgery of a love-less marriage.

It was something to think about as we moved to the Tarzan trees, all solid trunks and branches underneath the waning moon, casting dark shadows on the ground. It had turned somewhat chilly, but the whole northern sky was lighted with colors fanning out like the gaudy tails of glass peacocks. "Look," Christine said softly. And we stood there like the children we were and admired the north-ern lights, which were caused by the sun reflecting on the great snow masses of the Arctic.

"They're beautiful," I finally said, tugging her towards the trees. She took a last look and came with me.

"How do we get up them?" she said stupidly.

"We climb."

"I can't climb a tree. I've never climbed a tree in my life."

"I'll help you."

I could see large dark shadows moving in the trees. People making love, some carrying their portable Philco radios. I suppose all of us could have found more reasonable places to make love in. On the ground, for example. Or inside of cars. Or even in beds, I suppose. But the Tarzan trees had become a kind of institution among black people, perhaps even a symbol of defiance to all the politician's hol-low promises, and probably helped satisfy the ape in us that some white people swear is a part of all niggers.

"Be careful where you put your hands," Christine Barnhill whispered indig-nantly, as I tried to boost her up the tree.

"I got to put them somewhere," I said. I couldn't believe she'd never climbed a tree before. Dumb shit. "Or maybe you'd just like to levitate," I said nastily.

"To *what?*"

"Forget it," I whispered, for it was obvious that the apes had paused in their coupling and were watching us with chuckles and sniggers. "You got to help, you know," I said, huffing and puffing like a damned fool.

"I am helping," she snapped, with heavy irritation. She was heavy herself; it had never occurred to me that a girl who looked like her could weigh so much. She was wearing a dress made of something soft and slippery, like synthetic silk, and her ass and tits felt good against my wrestling hands. But every time I got her halfway up the tree, she slid down again, as though the trunk was greased. It was the most exciting thing I'd ever done in my life.

"Here," I panted. "Let's try again."

"I'm really very disappointed," Christine Barnhill said coldly, as though her lips had turned to ice.

"Let's do it here on the ground, then. I'll use my jacket for a blanket."

"I will not!" she said, with the greatest determination, stamping her foot. "What kind of girl do you think I am? Besides, you promised. I want to do it in the tree."

Titters were all around us now, falling like dryly amused leaves from the occupied trees. From one of them, the golden voice of Kate Smith singing *God Bless America* came muted from the radio.

"I can't get you up the fucking tree!" I groaned, and tried again. And failed as Christine slid down past me, her butt hard and solid, as though it alone weighed a hundred pounds.

"Well, I'm certainly sorry that I came here with you," Christine said. She sounded on the verge of tears.

My heart filled with panic; she was about to give up. And she'd tell everybody and I'd be the laughingstock of Cousinsville.

"Never say die," I said gamely, and I boosted her again. But she came down *smack* again, like an elevator that has slipped its cables.

She landed right on my John Henry, to say it indecently, as she had done every time. It was getting quite a beating and obviously enjoying it.

For I felt that sledge hammer hit the back of my brain and then the familiar tightening of the butt that happens just before John Henry comes. And then the dirty deed was done.

"God*aaaam!*" I muttered, halfway between pleasure and disappointment. But I dared not tell Christine what had happened. "Let's go," I said.

"What's the *matter*?" she cried. "*Why?*" She sounded absolutely furious.

"Come on," I said. "Don't ask questions. Don't you feel dumb any way, wanting to get fucked in a tree? What are you, some kind of ape or something?"

Her eyes were drawn into sharp slits; her cheekbones looked like the cutting edge of hatchets. "Well, Miss Edwina Robinson is going to be tickled pink to hear about this," she said bitterly.

"You trying to say I'm a fag? You dumb shit." It was too much to take, me with my drawers all turned to jism just from touching her. "Why don't you just go and fuck yourself?" I said, and I walked away.

When I looked back once, she was standing there hugging that tree like it was the real John Henry shaft, hard come to life. And she was crying softly while soft moaning fell from the trees where the other apes were copulating successfully.

Somebody had turned up the radio, and Ella Fitzgerald was singing *A Tisket, A Tasket*. I went out and caught the trolley car home. And that was the end of my love affair with Christine Barnhill, the undertaker's daughter.

Miss Askew was a considerable handful where she sprawled on her back like a very large and topsy-turvy tumblebug. The sheer weight of her pulled us down on her when we tried to pick her up, as though she had become imbedded in the cement. But as we huffed and puffed over her with no success at all, it soon became apparent that only a few of the smirking on-lookers were really unhappy to see Miss Askew down and helpless. In the circus that was Cousinsville in those days, Miss Askew stood out as someone quite different from the usual performer and commanded a dignified response when standing on her own two feet. But flat on her back, she was especially vulnerable, and the whispered comments about her dripped with slander:

"She thinks she *somebody*."

"Yeah. Fat bitch. Just because she graduated college."

"Yeah. Shit. She think she *white*."

Like an impassive brown sphinx, Miss Askew maintained her composure throughout the malice and all of our efforts. Not a hair that we could see had come out of place in her page boy cut; the small navy blue hat with the plastic flowers had not moved a fraction from its sculptured slant. Indeed, Miss Askew managed to give the impression that we were the fallen rather than she, as though she had confronted a primordial fear and conquered it, going back to the position that best suited her, while the rest of us were out of place in our awkward uprightness.

For some, such an attitude was clearly disconcerting: the woman moaning her woes as a nigger out the window, withdrew her head like a disgruntled turtle and slammed the window after her; the winos, who had been steadily kissing behind the gardenia bush before Miss Askew's fall, examined her through grape-flavored giggles and tottered away among the skating children, who had also lost interest.

Except for the chimes at St. Philip Neri's, to announce the angelus, church bells would not ring over Cousinsville again until dawn; and night closed around us quietly, like spurted ink. Gas street lamps flared somewhat brightly for a while, the ones nearest Miss Askew finally settling down to blinking at us wearily like the sleepy eyes of alligators.

Very soon after Miss Askew's impact, Miss Miriam Finkelstein had hustled off with red hair waving like a danger signal as she flung over her shoulder that she was going to call an ambulance. So, after our fruitless efforts with Miss Askew, Harry Claiborne suddenly stiffened and cackled: "I ain't going to call no ambulance. I'm going to knock me off a piece of this Irish bitch. Then I'm going to call the *crane*."

He sniggered, and grabbed himself so that Nancy O'Reilly could see. What she saw, what we all saw, caused her to dance a happy jig. "Harry, me lad, you did get it up!" She fell into Harry's arms, fondling him with open lasciviousness, until they stumbled together across the park with Harry's restored virility preceding them in the gloom like a procession of proud pickaninnies.

Indeed, Miss Askew's falling seemed to have the same effect on several other men, including five or six on Miss Edwina Robinson's selected fag list. Heated now, they rung in Miss Edwina like bristling spears as she twirled in the center of them. "I declare! I certainly do declare!" she cried delightedly. Wearing broad grins, the men rushed her off into the darkness, apparently to expunge their names from her obnoxious list.

So Mr. Giottio and I, urged on by the squealing monkey, tried to get Miss Askew to her feet. Even with our efforts to raise her, she still managed to keep her legs glued together. "Goddamn it, somebody give us a hand!" I groaned, thinking vividly of Christine Barnhill and the Tarzan tree.

But nobody helped; the women swallowed giggles and the men stood around enjoying the spectacle, obviously hoping that Miss Askew's big fine legs would somehow fall open. Until Miss Askew herself put an end to it. "Let's wait until the crane gets here," she said calmly. "I certainly don't want anybody to injure himself trying to get me off the ground."

Muttering in Italian, Mr. Giottio trudged away with his hurdy-gurdy, the excited monkey chastising him shrilly. Soon the other people left, and I was alone with Miss Askew. I told her a carefully edited version of my encounter with Christine Barnhill and the Tarzan trees, to entertain her until the crane came. But Miss Askew was no dummy; she could read between the lines. And she laughed merrily after I finished the story.

"Imagine somebody trying to get me up one of those trees," she chuckled. Although she had been my seventh grade English teacher, it was the first time I had talked to her as one adult to another. She was really very pleasant and I liked her a lot.

"You ought not to pay attention to all those dirty things they said," I began, determined to apologize for the evil of our community. But Miss Askew cut in gently: "I was not offended by their comments. They're not to be blamed for what they say."

She made me feel good all over; certainly she represented all that was best and noble about us: our lives, our laws and our religions; and even our oppression, which was a burden that would remain stubbornly unlifted in Miss Askew's time, and in mine. I remembered how we had watched slyly in school with a sense of throbbing expectation for her legs to fall open so that we could look up her dress. Thinking about it, I felt intensely ashamed.

"Can I get you something?" I said. Her house was right down the block; she'd been lying on the ground for nearly an hour by then, and I thought that she might need a blanket or something.

"No. I don't need anything," she said. "Thank you just the same. Although I do wish they'd hurry and come. You can imagine how I feel lying here. But you're very kind to stay with me. And I want you to know how pleased I am that you are in college, and studying journalism. I remember what a devil you were in grade school, but you were always excellent in English."

"Yes, ma'am." It probably seemed a stupid thing to say, after her generous compliment; but I was feeling strange and excited, as though a meteorite had fallen intact from the sky and was talking to me. That idea was not as farfetched as it might sound, for the northern sky had been steadily brightening, and the dazzling display of colored light fanned out now like rhinestone rainbows. Miss Askew and I watched them awhile in silence. Then she said, "Haven't you wondered where I was on my way to when I fell? It seems that a journalist—and you're going to be a fine journalist, I promise you—a journalist would want to know the answer to that."

What a splendid person she was! It seemed impossible that anybody could be so pleasant and polite, considering the position she was in. Years later, when I had indeed become a fine journalist—and that by many accounts other than my own—I would remember Miss Askew sprawling on her back on the sidewalk, but still taking the time to urge me gently towards my goal. "Where were you going?" I said.

"I was to be baptized a Catholic at St. Philip Neri's," she said. "I've been taking catechism from Father McGarrity. It seemed to me that the Baptist Church had become somewhat unserious—silly, if you'd like; grotesque—and was producing silly, grotesque people."

She reached down to arrange her dress, which was already perfectly in place, her legs nailed together as usual. "My father died when we were very poor," she went on. "They buried him in a coffin that was too narrow and too short. It was obvious that the undertaker had broken his arms and probably cut off a part of his legs to make him fit in that ugly pine box." From the uneven way she sighed, I was certain that a shudder was passing through her. "So I've lived with this idea, you see? I thought the Catholics would be kinder to the dead, because Catholics themselves seem so much kinder."

I thought of Christine Barnhill's father, the liberties he'd probably take with an abundant corpse like Miss Askew's. He certainly wasn't above hacking her into halves and burying two coffins in order to increase income. Some Catholic undertaker probably would do the same thing.

"Once you're gone, Miss Askew, you're gone. It won't make any difference what they do to you."

She nodded under the reptilian eyes winking from the gas lights. "I know. I suppose I've just been foolish, brooding about such things. That sometimes happens after a person's been alone for so long."

"Maybe you ought to get married."

Her laugh came out sharp and deprecating. "Can you imagine anybody in his right mind wanting to marry me?"

"I'm in my right mind. I'd consider it an honor to marry a woman like you."

That seemed to strike something ugly in her, for her face twisted with panic and she struggled unsuccessfully to get up. "Don't say things like that," she finally pleaded. She was breathing hard. "You're young; you don't know what you're talking about. Can't you see how . . . how *grotesque* . . . I am?"

"You're beautiful," I said. "Even Miss Finkelstein thinks you're beautiful."

"You're young," she said bitterly, "and Miss Finkelstein was seeking a convert to Catholicism. You've both been blind to the facts."

"What about this fact?" I bent over and kissed the quiver of those cupid's bow lips, letting her feel John Henry growing proud against her thigh at the same time. At first, she seemed startled; then she whimpered down in her throat and stopped trying to pull away.

Her perfumed hand came up to the back of my head, pulling me harder to her. Her lips tasted like wet red fruit; lively as a cat's, her darting tongue was sweet and delicious. I saw stars and bright lights behind my closed eyes.

When our lips came unlocked with a pop, she said, "You shouldn't have done that."

"Why not?"

I could almost hear her brain scrambling about for excuses. "Because . . . I've never known a man," she finally said, obviously in the Biblical sense. "Because . . . I'm thirty-five years old, and I can't get up."

That seemed to be a very good sign; she had been reduced to talking nonsense.

"You can get up if you want to," I said. "I'll help you. The problem is that you keep your legs closed. You've got to open them to get leverage."

"Open my legs?" Her lips worked and puckered as though she might break out in tears. "Have you forgotten that I'm a lady?" she announced. Her voice sounded ominous. Being a lady was a very important thing in those days, even among certain black women.

We both started as sirens began wailing in the distance, growing louder, coming our way. "It's the police," I said. "Coming with a crane to pick you up, like you were a car wreck or something. Does that strike you as being ladylike?"

Soon, people would be coming from their houses, summoned by the commotion. And Miss Askew began to flail, making terrible noises in her throat.

"Help me!" she cried. "Hurry!"

I grabbed the fabric and ripped. She pulled her dress all the way up, hurriedly, as though being chased by the approaching sirens and people suddenly began pouring into the street, coming towards us. And those big fine things, clad in the sheerest silk—the spectacle that we had all jerked off to in our imaginations but had never seen—those silk-clad thighs gleamed triumphantly in the street lights as Miss Askew opened her legs.

It was as though the gates of a mighty city were being slowly parted by hordes of slaves to the sound of blaring trumpets. Or perhaps it was like the people of Moses watching the parting of the Red Sea, with the Egyptian hordes panting at their heels.

Again I thought of marches—*Aida*'s chief among them, remembering that the opera had been written especially to mark the opening of the Suez Canal in 1869—and of all the magnificent beauty of flowers opening their petals to the sun's warm penetration.

The gas lamps with their reptilian eyes seemed to leer down on us. Beyond them, the northern lights fanned out glimmering in sharp, gaudy colors. Miss Askew's thighs fell slack ... and exotic ships dotted with upright seamen slid through her emerald-colored canals while Egyptians on her banks sang fantastic chorales in rich voices. The ritual of Miss Askew opening her legs had ended. And the chimes at St. Philip Neri's rang the angelus, in praise of virgins, as I supported Miss Askew and she came majestically to her feet to a crashing of delirious cymbals inside my head.

The crowd, three police cars, and the crane arrived together. The men who had gone with Edwina Robinson came rattling back like dried reeds, emptied of all virility again. Harry Claiborne limped up exactly as he had been before Miss Askew's fall, while Nancy O'Reilly and Miss Edwina arrived wearing the smug dead expressions of roasted suckling pigs stuffed with apples and sperm. Up in her second floor window, the moaning woman eased her head and shoulders out again, resting on her elbows in the kind of sullen silence that is reserved for the presence of policemen.

Down with us, Miss Miriam Finkelstein finally arrived with Father McGarrity in tow. "She's up!" Miss Finkelstein cried, certainly in that same tone of mystification that had been used at the empty Easter tomb. "I was sure she was dying. Father, she took such a fall. I brought you to baptize her before she died."

"That was very thoughtful of you, I'm sure," Miss Askew said, in probably the driest voice she'd ever used.

"I'm sorry it took so long to get here," Father McGarrity said. "But I was administering last rites to a parishioner." A thin, wrinkled old priest, with white hair and magnetic black eyes, he had obviously felt Miss Askew's sarcasm. "Well, I don't suppose we'll be seeing you again at St. Philip Neri's," he said to her.

"I don't suppose so," Miss Askew said kindly. She lay a calming hand on Father McGarrity's arm, then turned away. She was an exquisite combination of beauty and grace as she walked to her house, making silken noises with her legs.

We all followed her at a small distance, certainly with the expectation that she might fall again. The gas lamps burned with unaccustomed brightness, as if they were also watching; and a chilly wind had risen. Behind us, the police cars flashed red and white lights, while the crane waited like some heated prehistoric monster with its pulley and hideous chains. The air was unaccountably perfumed, as though wreaths had been laid on our generation's imminent ending.

Miss Askew had reached her house now. Halfway up the stairs to the porch, she turned in the police lights and shaded her eyes until she found me. With her other hand, she held her torn dress together. "I am going to make some hot cocoa," she said. "Would you like to come in and finish our conversation?"

"I'd like to very much, ma'am."

Naturally everybody was watching me, all those grinning apes. So I acted nonchalant as I broke away from the crowd and went up the stairs with Miss Askew. I certainly did feel that I was our community's youngest, our biggest, and our best.

And as Miss Askew's door closed behind me, I suppose it was also the first time I became aware of how difficult it is for some people to do the forbidden.

Although for some people, of course, it must be very easy. There are always apes in trees somewhere, sniggering, coupling, listening to Kate Smith on the radio. While some of us hang even against our will in opened windows, singing our hurt sometimes, sometimes our joy.

DIONNE BRAND

I USED TO LIKE
THE DALLAS COWBOYS

I USED TO LIKE the Dallas Cowboys. Steel gray helmets, good luck gray, bad luck blue, skin tight, muscle definitioned thighs. I'd prepare for Sunday's game, beer and my pillows at the ready. Rushing to the kitchen between commercials, burning the chicken or the boiled potatoes, depending on whether there was money, or making split pea soup, scraping up the last grain of garlic and the onions growing stems in the dark corners of the cupboard below the sink. I'd neglect the dishes from the night before or the week before, depending on the week, set up a phone line with Tony or Jo as the case may be, put the bottles of beer in the freezer, if I had beer, and wait for the game, sit through the pre-game or the highlights, have a fifteen minute nap, time permitting. This was after I'd just risen from an eight hour sleep, most of which was devoted to regenerating the body after dancing and drinking till four in the morning. Whatever liquor wasn't danced out had to be slept out. Naturally sometimes even sleep would not produce the miracle of waking up without a vicious headache and feeling water-logged, but I had prepared for this by putting the television near to my arm.

Seems a while now, but back then, I used to really love the Dallas Cowboys. It's funny what things occur to you lying in a corridor at 3 A.M. in the morning in the middle of a war. Which is where I am now. The sky is lit bright from flares and there's a groaning F16 circling the sky like a corbeau. The flares give off the light of a red smoky dawn, except for their starkness which makes you feel naked. The air, seeping through the wood latticework, smells chemical. A few minutes ago, before the flares went up, the cat, who lives in the house whose corridor I'm huddled in, ran, screaming and scratching over my back. She had heard the incoming planes long before they hit the island again, on this second day . . . night of the war. Having no sixth sense like hers, the rest of us dove for the corridor only when the flares went up and we'd heard the crack of the F16's through the sound of speed. I wasn't asleep. Just waiting. Amazing, how your mind can just latch on to something, just to save you from thinking about how frightened you are. It reaches for the farthest thing away . . . That's how come I remember that I used to love the Dallas Cowboys.

The Cowboys shone, the Dallas sun glancing off their helmets. They weren't like other football teams. They were sleek where the others were rough, they were swift where the others were plodding, they were scientific where the others were ploughboys; they were precise where the others were clumsy mudwaders; they were slim, slender where the others were hulking, brutish. Even their linebackers had finesse. Not for them the crunch and bashing of the Steelers, the mud and squat of the Raiders; they were quick clean, decisive. Punters trembled before the upraised arm of Harvey Martin, linebackers dreaded his embrace. Too Tall Jones had too much oil, too much quickness for a defensive lineman, too long a right arm. It was ecstasy when Hollywood Henderson intercepted a pass or caught a running back for a loss. But most of all it was Drew Pearson, Tony Dorsett and Butch Johnson who gave you a look of perfection of the human, male, form.

Mind you there were a few from other teams, like Lynn Swann, who was with Pittsburgh. He was as graceful as the rest of his teammates were piggish. Sometimes, I think he flew. He was so lithe, I think, everyone on the field stopped to watch him, this bird of beauty among them, so tied to their squat bodies and the heavy ground. He should have been with the Cowboys really.

The Cowboys were fine. They had a move which befuddled their opponents while it raised something in me that . . . It was when they were waiting for the quarterback's call; hunched over, they would rise in unison for the quickest of moments and then settle in for the count again. The look of all those sinewy backs rising and falling was like a dance. A threatening dance. It reminded me of 'the breakdown' which we used to do every Thursday, Friday and Saturday night at the Coq D'Or.

Rufus Thomas started it with his song "Do the breakdown" and we just got better and better, perfecting the bend from the waist and the shudders to the left and right. Some of us added variations in the middle or with the hips and the motions of the crooked arm as the weeks went by, till the next new dance; but everything about Black dance was there, in the breakdown. So when the Dallas Cowboys did the breakdown, it really sent me. I was their fan, the moment I saw it.

Seems like I made a circle with my life. Then, I was in Toronto. Now, I'm back here on the island, not the one I came from in the beginning, but close by. Speaking of circles, there is . . . was a revolution here and I came to join. Correction, revolutions are actually not circles but upheavals, transformations, new beginnings for life. I'm graying by the minute in this corridor. I feel feverish.

That is a circle, ending where you began. The war outside is ending the revolution. We have nothing to listen to since the radio went off at 9 A.M. on the first day of the war, only the crack of the F16's over the house.

Rufus Thomas . . . tata ta tata tata pada ta pada pada boom . . . do the breakdown . . . That was in nineteen seventy or seventy-one. Seems a long time ago now, considering. That's when I first went to Toronto. I was sixteen. I went to school. I partied. I learned to like football. Not Canadian football, American football. Actually it was Sundays. Sundays. I had never liked Sundays. Back home everything stopped on a Sunday. The shop was closed; people didn't walk on the street, except in quiet penitence and their Sunday best; and worse, the radio no longer blared calypso and soul music but Oral Roberts' "the hour of decision."

Canadian football was too slow, the downs were too few and the ball seemed to be perpetually changing hands from one incompetent lot to the other, blundering up and down the field. American football, on the other hand, now . . . Well come to think of it, it was all the build-up, the pre-game assessment of the players, who was injured and who wasn't. You would swear that this was the most important event to take place in history—the tension, the coach's job on the line and the raw roar of winning. When my team lost, I cannot explain the deep loss, the complete letdown which would last until Monday morning. My sister and I would remark to each other every so often, in the middle of doing the washing or in the middle of a walk, "Cheups! Dallas could disappoint people, eh?" This would be followed by a pregnant silence and another "Cheups." The next Sunday, up until game time we'd be saying, "I can't watch that game, I just can't." But the call of the steel gray and the American star on the helmet was too much and Dallas! Dallas was good! You have to admit.

To be honest, if I really look back, it was the clandestine *True Confession* magazines from America which I read at thirteen that led to my love for the Dallas Cowboys. There was always a guy named Bif or Ted or Lance who was on the college football team and every girl wanted to wear his sweater. Never mind we didn't have sweaters or need them in the tropics, this only made them romantic items. We didn't have cars either in whose steamy back seats a girl became 'that kinda girl' or a wife.

So anyway because it was so boring in Canada on Sundays and because it was winter, morning, noon and night, I learned to like football.

And basketball. Mind, I always liked netball which was what they made girls play at Rima High School in San Fernando. And tennis, dying, dy..ing for Arthur Ashe to whip Jimmy Connors which he finally did at Wimbledon, which all north American sportscasters call wimpleton, which really gets me, like every broadcaster in north America says nukular instead of nuclear and they're supposed to be so advanced. Me and my sister couldn't bear to watch it, the tennis game that is, because we had already said too often,

"This Arthur Ashe can disappoint people, boy!"

Nevertheless we gave in. We were walking along Dufferin, that was when we used to live on Dupont, we were walking along Dufferin at Wallace and we suddenly made a run for Dupont after several long "cheups" and pauses and after hearing an Italian boy say something about the match to another Italian boy. We couldn't let Arthur go through that match alone. It was a battle of the races. Some people would be looking and cheering for Jimmy Connors. As we ran home it became more and more important that we watch the match to give Arthur moral support. Somehow, if we sat and watched the match, it would help Arthur to win. And if we didn't and he lost, it would have been our fault. So we sat in pain, watching and urging Arthur on, on the television. It was tense but Arthur played like a dream, like a thinker. Connors was gallerying, throwing tantrums like a white boy; but Arthur was cool. Connors would use his powerful forehand trying to drive Arthur to the base line, Arthur would send him back a soft drop shot that he couldn't make. Connors would send hard, trying to get Arthur to return hard, but Arthur would just come in soft. Arthur beat his ass ba . . . ad. I swear to God if we didn't sit and watch that match we would not have forgiven ourselves. This was like the second Joe Louis and Max Schmelling fight. Nineteen thirty-six all over again.

And boxing, I liked that too, and track. Never liked hockey, except when the Soviets came to play. And golf, would you believe. That's to tell you how far I'd go to escape the dreariness of Sundays in the winter. I'd even watch an old, lazy, white man's sport.

Last Sunday, here, was a little sad . . . and tense. Only, on Sunday, the war hadn't started yet. There was a visit to Mt. Morris from which you can see, as from most places on this island, the sea. Talk, a little hopeful but bewildered, that surrounded by water like this, one could never be prepared for war even if one could see it coming over the long view of the horizon.

The war was inside the house now. The light from the flares ignores the lushness of this island turning it into an endless desert.

I used to love the Dallas Cowboys like you wouldn't believe. How I come to love the Dallas Cowboys—well I've explained, but I left something out. See, I wasn't your cheerleader type; I wasn't no Dallas Cowgirl. I knew the game, knew all their moves and Dallas had some moves that no other football club would do. They would do an end around, which most other teams would think belonged in a high school or college game. So it would shock them that here was Dallas, America's team, doing a high school move.

I learned about American high school and college lore watching American football. In my own high school, where football was soccer, we didn't play it because I went to a girls' school. We played whatever we did play rough mind you, but it wasn't soccer. Football was played by Pres' College and (St) Benedict's. Boys' high schools. Benedict's always won but Pres' was the star boys. This was mainly because they were high yellow boys. Red skin, fair skin and from good families. Every high school girl was after them, god knows to do what with, because there was no place to do it that I could find. Benedict's was black boys, dark-skinned and tough, tall and lanky or short and thick like a wall. Convent girls and Rima girls vied for Pres' boys, Benedict's was a second choice. Benedict's boys were a little aloof though; they were the first ones to be turned on by the Black Power movement. They stopped wearing their uniform right, they were the first to grow afros and get suspended or expelled from school for it. They were the first to have a student strike and a protest march around the school. Then they became popular, or clandestine anyway. Pres' star boys looked pale against them and everybody now started to look for the darkest Pres' boy to walk with, because the boys in Pres' who weren't red skin began to join Black Power too. My friend Sylvia was the first to go afro in my school, and it was as if she had committed a crime, or as if she was a 'bad' girl or something.

That year, the Black Power year, I didn't get to go to see Pres' and Benedict's play in Guaracara Park. But I heard it turned into a Black Power demonstration. Well truthfully, I never got to go but once that I could remember, my family being so strict; and anyway, I was always at a loss to know what to do with a boy after, which was supposed to be the highlight of the evening and anyway, I never had a boyfriend really. The other thing was, I really couldn't get into jumping around in the stands as a girl, not looking at the game and yelling when everybody else yelled "Goal!" All of us who would leave without a boy would walk behind our next best friend who had one, looking at her boyfriend and snickering. The girls who had boyfriends on the teams that played were way above us.

But this was soccer, which we called football, so I didn't know American football.

I really didn't like soccer until television came in, in Trinidad, and not until years after that when we got a TV and we could watch Tottenham Hot Spurs at Trent and you could really see the game and the moves. And we watched the World Cup and found Brazil was who we could cheer for, because Brazil was Black; and then there was Eusebio of Portugal who was Black too. Now that's when the game got good. Pele and Eusebio made us cheer for both teams at the same time if they were playing each other because Black people had to shine anyhow they come. Never mind the Spurs, we wanted England to lose because they didn't have any Black players. That was an insult.

"What happen? They don't like Black people or what? They don't give Black people any chance at all?"

If the game was between two white teams, we'd root for the team with the darkest hair. So Italy and Mexico were our teams. If it was British teams, the most rough and tumble looking would be our favourites. So when TV came in, then is when I got into soccer.

Soccer didn't have any cheerleaders, but American football did. I was embarrassed when I saw them. They looked ridiculous and vulnerable at the same time. I suppose they were supposed to look vulnerable; but it looked like weak shit to me. Since I was a kid I had a disdain for that kind of girl or woman. I never liked not knowing exactly about a thing and I had always felt uncomfortable wearing a mini skirt or can can, when they were in fashion.

So I learned about American football. This standing around like a fool while men talked about football was not for me. Sometimes after Saturday night, and usually during the playoffs, someone, maybe Joe, would have a brunch and part of the programme was that we'd watch the game. That usually meant that the men would watch the game and the women would rap with each other (nothing wrong with that mind you), walk around, hassle or humour the men about watching the game or observe the new 'chick' belonging to whichever reigning cock on the walk. Well see, I never came with nobody except that one time that I was almost married. But that's another story, thank God. I'd get a place at the TV and not without feeling that I was ingratiating myself and that I wasn't quite welcome. Well, I'd make some comments about what call the referee made on such and such a play and nobody would take me on. Then I'd get a rise out of them if I said that their backs moved before the snap of the ball. Well, at first they humoured me. Mind you the worst of them left the room, objecting to watching football with a woman present. Then they realized that I know my game, you see. I'd bet them money too, just to prove how serious I was. I outmachoed the machoest. I yelled and pointed and called them suckers and then I'd laugh and tease them. Well, most of them were Trinidadian, so they rose to the bait. You could always catch a Trinidadian man in an argument defending the most unlikely prospect and the most ridiculous outcome.

Before you knew it, everytime I lost a game, to be sure that phone would ring and one of the guys would be taunting me saying, "You see how to play football? Dallas is dead, bet you ten bucks." I'd take the bet because the Dallas Cowboys were magicians. They could take sixty seconds left in a game and turn it into two touchdowns and a field goal. Robert Newhouse, before he got injured, could plough through a Steelers defense like an ant through a hibiscus hedge. See, I wasn't no cheerleader. I knew my game. Roger liked the Steelers cause they had Franco Harris but to me Franco was kinda clumsy. I know he ran so many yards and everything, but when he started to get old I figure he shoulda left, because he started to look bad to me. Other people wouldn't say that, but I didn't like the look of him. He looked too much like a white boy to me, which is why I hated quarterbacks. They were always white, except for James Harris who was with L.A. and then what's his name with the Bears. Roger Staubach I had to tolerate and anyway, he was clean. I mean he could throw a pass. He could go up the field in thirty seconds. Of course, one of *us*, Drew or Butch, had to be there to catch it. But Roger was clean. Never mind he was born-again and probably a member of the Klan, after all we're talking about Texas, where they still fly the Confederate flag and all.

Another thing about the Cowboys, all my football buddies used to say that they were the most fascist team. Well I agreed you know because football, or most any American sport, has that quality to it. I said that was exactly why I liked Dallas because in this gladiatorial game called football they were the most scientific, the most emotionless and therefore exactly what this game was about. I called my buddies a bunch of wimps. "How you could like football and then get squeamish? You got to figure out what it is you like, see!" Anybody can watch a game and say, "Oh I hate that. It's so violent." But they will live with it and in it. That person's just an intellectual. When I finally got to see the Dallas Cowboys in person, no set of intellectuals could have explained it and neither could anybody who didn't understand the game.

To cut a long story short, because I probably don't have time for a long story, even though I loved the Dallas Cowboys, I had to leave the country. So I had to wean myself off of football because where I was going there was no American football. There may be cricket but certainly no football. It wasn't easy. You get used to a way of life, even though you don't know it. And you take everything it has in it, even if you think you can sift out the good from the bad. You get cynical and hard-arsed about the bad, in truth. So you find a way to look at it. So cynical and hard-arsed that when you see good, it embarrasses you.

The jets breaking the sound barrier keep rushing over the house. I've never ever heard a noise like that. Oh, my God! It's a wonder I can remember anything. Remembering keeps the panic down. Remember your name, remember last week, . . . There's a feeling somewhere in my body that's so tender that I'm melting away, disintegrating with it. I'm actually going to die!

Someone in the corridor with me says, "It's the ones you don't hear . . ." Yesterday, we thought we heard MIG's overhead . . . Wishing . . . We know that no one will come to help us. No one can.

I was going to another kinda place, much quieter. A cricket match now and then, maybe . . . One Sunday, in March this year, I went to one. It was a quiet Sunday, the way Sundays are quiet in the Caribbean and I slept through half of the match. It was West Indies versus the Leeward Islands. Cricket is the only game that you can sleep through and it wouldn't matter. They say it started in the Caribbean as a slave master's game. Of course, they had all the time in the world. Matches can last up to five days. They break for tea and long lunches and they wear white, to show that it's not a dirty, common game. Even the spectators wear white.

You can tell that it was a slave masters' game if you notice where most cricket pitches are placed. You just look and you'll find them all laid out, green and close cropped grass, at some remote end of what use to be a plantation, or still might be for that matter. Remote enough so that the players would have some peace from the hurly-burly of slave life, but close enough in case of an emergency whipping or carnage. If you pass by a cricket pitch in the Caribbean, not the modern stadiums they built but the ones that have been there forever, there's a hush over them, a kind of green silence, an imperious quiet. You will notice that children never play on them. They play somewhere on the beach or in the bush. See, there's no place to hide on them, which is why slave owners liked them, I suppose. While they had their dalliances there, they could be sure to see a coming riot.

Which, oddly enough is why I left, here first, then there. I could no more help leaving Toronto than I could help going there in the first place or coming here eventually. I came to join the revolution; to stop going in circles, to add my puny little woman self to an upheaval. You get tired of being a slave; you get tired of being sold here and there; you assault the cricket pitch, even if it is broad daylight and the slave owner can see you coming; you scuttle pell-mell into death; you only have to be lucky once; get him behind the neck; and if it doesn't succeed, . . . well, you're one of millions and millions. Though lying in a corridor in the end, or for those lying dead, it doesn't feel that way, you're trembling, you lose sight.

So no Cowboys, no apartment buildings, no TV to talk about, not so much time to kill on a Sunday. Today, if it turns into day, it's not Sunday. What day is it? The red smoke dawn of the flares has given way to a daybreak as merciless as last night. Each day lengthens into a year. Another afternoon, God fled a blinding shine sky; wasps, helicopter gun ships stung the beach, seconds from the harbour. Four days ago the island was invaded by America. The Americans don't like cricket; but deep inside of those of us hiding from them in this little corridor and those in the hills and cemeteries, we know they've come to play ball. Dead eye ship, helicopter gun ships, bombers, M16's, troops. I've seen my share of TV war—hogan's heroes, the green berets and bridge on the river Kwai. Well none of that ever prepares you.

Because when they're not playing, the Cowboys can be deadly.

I've had four days to think about this. War is murder. When you're actually the one about to get killed, not just your physical self but what you wanted badly, well then it's close. I find myself having to attend to small things that I didn't notice before. First of all my hands and my body feel like they don't belong to me. I think that they're only extra baggage because there's nowhere to put them or to hide them. The truth is I begin to hate my own physical body, because I believe it has betrayed me by merely existing. It's like not having a shelf to put it on or a cupboard to lock it in; it's useless to me and it strikes me how inefficient it is. Because the ideal form in which to pass a war is as a spirit, a jumbie. My body is history, fossil, passé.

And my thoughts. I begin to think, why didn't I think of this? or that? I think, why isn't it yesterday? or last year? or year after next? Even a depressing day, any other day, a day when my menses pained me occurs to me like a hot desire. I try to evolve to a higher form. I want to think out of this place where I'm crouched with four other people; but my thoughts are totally useless and I know it, because I think that too.

And the noise of the war. That horrible, horrible noise like the earth cracked open by a huge metallic butchering instrument. That noise rankles, bursts in my ear and after a while it drones in my ear and that droning says that I'm not dead yet. I don't know when I'll get hit; the whole house could be blown away and this corridor which I chose, if I really think about it, and all the safety which I imbued it with. I would stand in the middle of the street and wave to the bombers in the sky to come and finish me off.

If I don't die today, the one thing that will probably dog me for the rest of my life is that I'm not dead. Why am I not dead now . . . now . . . now . . .

I began well. I tried to make it decent, to die clean and dignified; but I don't want to die and my greed to live is embarrassing. I feel like a glutton about how much my body wants to hang on and at the same time it does not want to be here, in this corridor, in this world where I'm about to die. And so, in the middle of the noise, through the gun fire, the bombs and the anti-aircraft guns, I'm falling asleep. Can you imagine! I'm falling asleep. Each time I hear the bombers approaching, I yawn and my body begins to fall asleep.

Like now. Someone else in the corridor is watching me trying to sleep in the middle of disaster. If we survive, she will remember that I tried to sleep. I will remember that she watched me, tears in her eyes, leaving her. We hum and flinch to each crackkk, each bomb . . . We're dancing the breakdown. But if I fall asleep, I know that I won't wake up, or I'll wake up mad.

For four days now, a war in the middle of October, on this small unlikely island. Four days. I crouch in a corridor; I drink bottles of rum and never get drunk. I stay awake, in case. I listen for the noise of the war because it is my signal, like the snap of the ball, that I'm not dead.

But the signal is not from my team. I'm playing the Dallas Cowboys.

The day I finally creep to the door, the day I look outside to see who is trying to kill me, to tell them that I surrender, I see the Dallas Cowboys coming down my hot tropical street, among the bougainvillea and the mimosa, crouching, pointing their M16 weapons, laden with grenade-launchers. The hibiscus and I dangle high and red in defeat; everything is silent and gone. Better dead. Their faces are painted and there's that smell, like fresh blood and human grease, on them. And I hate them.

OCTAVIA E. BUTLER

THE EVENING
AND THE MORNING
AND THE NIGHT

W HEN I WAS FIFTEEN and trying to show my independence by getting careless with my diet, my parents took me to a Duryea-Gode disease ward. They wanted me to see, they said, where I was headed if I wasn't careful. In fact, it was where I was headed no matter what. It was only a matter of when: now or later. My parents were putting in their vote for later.

I won't describe the ward. It's enough to say that when they brought me home, I cut my wrists. I did a thorough job of it, old Roman style in a bathtub of warm water. Almost made it. My father dislocated his shoulder breaking down the bathroom door. He and I never forgave each other for that day.

The disease got him almost three years later—just before I went off to college. It was sudden. It doesn't happen that way often. Most people notice themselves beginning to drift—or their relatives notice—and they make arrangements with their chosen institution. People who are noticed and who resist going in can be locked up for a week's observation. I don't doubt that that observation period breaks up a few families. Sending someone away for what turns out to be a false alarm. . . . Well, it isn't the sort of thing the victim is likely to forgive or forget. On the other hand, not sending someone away in time—missing the signs or having a person go off suddenly without signs—is inevitably dangerous for the victim. I've never heard of it going as badly, though, as it did in my family. People normally injure only themselves when their time comes—unless someone is stupid enough to try to handle them without the necessary drugs or restraints.

My father . . . killed my mother, then killed himself. I wasn't home when it happened. I had stayed at school later than usual rehearsing graduation exercises. By the time I got home, there were cops everywhere. There was an ambulance, and two attendants were wheeling someone out on a stretcher—someone covered. More than covered. Almost . . . bagged.

The cops wouldn't let me in. I didn't find out until later exactly what had happened. I wish I'd never found out. Dad had killed Mom then skinned her completely. At least, that's how I hope it happened. I mean I hope he killed her first. He broke some of her ribs, damaged her heart. Digging.

Then he began tearing at himself, through skin and bone, digging. He had managed to reach his own heart before he died. It was an especially bad example of the kind of thing that makes people afraid of us. It gets some of us into trouble for picking at a pimple or even for daydreaming. It has inspired restrictive laws, created problems with jobs, housing, schools. The Duryea-Gode Disease Foundation has spent millions telling the world that people like my father don't exist.

A long time later, when I had gotten myself together as best I could, I went to college—to the University of Southern California—on a Dilg scholarship. Dilg is the retreat you try to send your out-of-control DGD relatives to. It's run by controlled DGDs like me, like my parents while they lived. God knows how any controlled DGD stands it. Anyway, the place has a waiting list miles long. My parents put me on it after my suicide attempt, but chances were, I'd be dead by the time my name came up.

I can't say why I went to college—except that I had been going to school all my life and I didn't know what else to do. I didn't go with any particular hope. Hell, I knew what I was in for eventually. I was just marking time. Whatever I did was just marking time. If people were willing to pay me to go to school and mark time, why not do it?

The weird part was, I worked hard, got top grades. If you work hard enough at something that doesn't matter, you can forget for a while about the things that do.

Sometimes I thought about trying suicide again. How was it I'd had the courage when I was fifteen but didn't have it now? Two DGD parents—both religious, both as opposed to abortion as they were to suicide. So they had trusted God and the promises of modern medicine and had a child. But how could I look at what had happened to them and trust anything?

I majored in biology. Non-DGDs say something about our disease makes us good at the sciences—genetics, molecular biology, biochemistry. . . . That something was terror. Terror and a kind of driving hopelessness. Some of us went bad and became destructive before we had to—yes, we did produce more than our share of criminals. And some of us went good—spectacularly—and made scientific and medical history. These last kept the doors at least partly open for the rest of us. They made discoveries in genetics, found cures for a couple of rare diseases, made advances in the fight against other diseases that weren't so rare—including, ironically, some forms of cancer. But they'd found nothing to help themselves.

There had been nothing since the latest improvements in the diet, and those came just before I was born. They, like the original diet, gave more DGDs the courage to have children. They were supposed to do for DGDs what insulin had done for diabetics—give us a normal or nearly normal life span. Maybe they had worked for someone somewhere. They hadn't worked for anyone I knew.

Biology School was a pain in the usual ways. I didn't eat in public anymore, didn't like the way people stared at my biscuits—cleverly dubbed "dog biscuits" in every school I'd ever attended. You'd think university students would be more creative. I didn't like the way people edged away from me when they caught sight of my emblem. I'd begun wearing it on a chain around my neck and putting it down inside my blouse, but people managed to notice it anyway. People who don't eat in public, who drink nothing more interesting than water, who smoke nothing at all—people like that are suspicious. Or rather, they make others suspicious. Sooner or later, one of those others, finding my fingers and wrists bare, would take an interest in my chain. That would be that. I couldn't hide the emblem in my purse. If anything happened to me, medical people had to see it in time to avoid giving me the medications they might use on a normal person. It isn't just ordinary food we have to avoid, but about a quarter of a *Physician's Desk Reference* of widely used drugs. Every now and then there are news stories about people who stopped carrying their emblems—probably trying to pass as normal. Then they have an accident. By the time anyone realizes there is anything wrong, it's too late. So I wore my emblem. And one way or another, people got a look at it or got the word from someone who had. "She *is!*" Yeah.

At the beginning of my third year, four other DGDs and I decided to rent a house together. We'd all had enough of being lepers twenty-four hours a day. There was an English major. He wanted to be a writer and tell our story from the inside—which had only been done thirty or forty times before. There was a special-education major who hoped the handicapped would accept her more readily than the able-bodied, a premed who planned to go into research, and a chemistry major who didn't really know what she wanted to do.

Two men and three women. All we had in common was our disease, plus a weird combination of stubborn intensity about whatever we happened to be doing and hopeless cynicism about everything else. Healthy people say no one can concentrate like a DGD. Healthy people have all the time in the world for stupid generalizations and short attention spans.

We did our work, came up for air now and then, ate our biscuits, and attended classes. Our only problem was housecleaning. We worked out a schedule of who would clean what when, who would deal with the yard, whatever. We all agreed on it; then, except for me, everyone seemed to forget about it. I found myself going around reminding people to vacuum, clean the bathroom, mow the lawn. . . . I figured they'd all hate me in no time, but I wasn't going to be their maid, and I wasn't going to live in filth. Nobody complained. Nobody even seemed annoyed. They just came up out of their academic daze, cleaned, mopped, mowed, and went back to it. I got into the habit of running around in the evening reminding people. It didn't bother me if it didn't bother them.

"How'd you get to be housemother?" a visiting DGD asked.

I shrugged. "Who cares? The house works." It did. It worked so well that this new guy wanted to move in. He was a friend of one of the others, and another premed. Not bad looking.

"So do I get in or don't I?" he asked.

"As far as I'm concerned, you do," I said. I did what his friend should have done—introduced him around, then, after he left, talked to the others to make sure nobody had any real objections. He seemed to fit right in. He forgot to clean the toilet or mow the lawn, just like the others. His name was Alan Chi. I thought Chi was a Chinese name, and I wondered. But he told me his father was Nigerian and that in Ibo, the word meant a kind of guardian angel or personal god. He said his own personal god hadn't been looking out for him very well to let him be born to two DGD parents. Him too.

I don't think it was much more than that similarity that drew us together at first. Sure, I liked the way he looked, but I was used to liking someone's looks and having him run like hell when he found out what I was. It took me a while to get used to the fact that Alan wasn't going anywhere.

I told him about my visit to the DGD ward when I was fifteen—and my suicide attempt afterward. I had never told anyone else. I was surprised at how relieved it made me feel to tell him. And somehow his reaction didn't surprise me.

"Why didn't you try again?" he asked. We were alone in the living room.

"At first, because of my parents," I said. "My father in particular. I couldn't do that to him again."

"And after him?"

"Fear. Inertia."

He nodded. "When I do it, there'll be no half measures. No being rescued, no waking up in a hospital later."

"You mean to do it?"

"The day I realize I've started to drift. Thank God we get some warning."

"Not necessarily."

"Yes, we do. I've done a lot of reading. Even talked to a couple of doctors. Don't believe the rumors non-DGDs invent."

I looked away, stared into the scarred, empty fireplace. I told him exactly how my father had died—something else I'd never voluntarily told anyone.

He sighed. "Jesus!"

We looked at each other.

"What are you going to do?" he asked.

"I don't know."

He extended a dark, square hand, and I took it and moved closer to him. He was a dark, square man—my height, half again my weight, and none of it fat. He was so bitter sometimes, he scared me.

"My mother started to drift when I was three," he said. "My father only lasted a few months longer. I heard he died a couple of years after he went into the hospital. If the two of them had had any sense, they would have had me aborted the minute my mother realized she was pregnant. But she wanted a kid no matter what. And she was Catholic." He shook his head. "Hell, they should pass a law to sterilize the lot of us."

"They?" I said.

"No, but—"

"More like us to wind up chewing their fingers off in some DGD ward."

"I don't want kids, but I don't want someone else telling me I can't have any."

He stared at me until I began to feel stupid and defensive. I moved away from him.

"Do you want someone else telling you what to do with your body?" I asked.

"No need," he said. "I had that taken care of as soon as I was old enough."

This left me staring. I'd thought about sterilization. What DGD hasn't? But I didn't know anyone else our age who had actually gone through with it. That would be like killing part of yourself—even though it wasn't a part you intended to use. Killing part of yourself when so much of you was already dead.

"The damned disease could be wiped out in one generation," he said, "but people are still animals when it comes to breeding. Still following mindless urges, like dogs and cats."

My impulse was to get up and go away, leave him to wallow in his bitterness and depression alone. But I stayed. He seemed to want to live even less than I did. I wondered how he'd made it this far.

"Are you looking forward to doing research?" I probed. "Do you believe you'll be able to—"

"No."

I blinked. The word was as cold and dead a sound as I'd ever heard.

"I don't believe in anything," he said.

I took him to bed. He was the only other double DGD I had ever met, and if nobody did anything for him, he wouldn't last much longer. I couldn't just let him slip away. For a while, maybe we could be each other's reasons for staying alive.

He was a good student—for the same reason I was. And he seemed to shed some of his bitterness as time passed. Being around him helped me understand why, against all sanity, two DGDs would lock in on each other and start talking about marriage. Who else would have us?

We probably wouldn't last very long, anyway. These days, most DGDs make it to forty, at least. But then, most of them don't have two DGD parents. As bright as Alan was, he might not get into medical school because of his double inheritance. No one would tell him his bad genes were keeping him out, of course, but we both knew what his chances were. Better to train doctors who were likely to live long enough to put their training to use.

Alan's mother had been sent to Dilg. He hadn't seen her or been able to get any information about her from his grandparents while he was at home. By the time he left for college, he'd stopped asking questions. Maybe it was hearing about my parents that made him start again. I was with him when he called Dilg. Until that moment, he hadn't even known whether his mother was still alive. Surprisingly, she was.

"Dilg must be good," I said when he hung up. "People don't usually . . . I mean . . ."

"Yeah, I know," he said. "People don't usually live long once they're out of control. Dilg is different." We had gone to my room, where he turned a chair backward and sat down. "Dilg is what the others ought to be, if you can believe the literature."

"Dilg is a giant DGD ward," I said. "It's richer—probably better at sucking in the donations—and it's run by people who can expect to become patients eventually. Apart from that, what's different?"

"I've read about it," he said. "So should you. They've got some new treatment. They don't just shut people away to die the way the others do."

"What else is there to do with them?" *With us.*

"I don't know. It sounded like they have some kind of . . . sheltered workshop. They've got patients doing things."

"A new drug to control the self-destructiveness?"

"I don't think so. We would have heard about that."

"What else could it be?"

"I'm going up to find out. Will you come with me?"

"You're going up to see your mother."

He took a ragged breath. "Yeah. Will you come with me?"

I went to one of my windows and stared out at the weeds. We let them thrive in the backyard. In the front we mowed them, along with the few patches of grass.

"I told you my DGD-ward experience."

"You're not fifteen now. And Dilg isn't some zoo of a ward."

"It's got to be, no matter what they tell the public. And I'm not sure I can stand it."

He got up, came to stand next to me. "Will you try?"

I didn't say anything. I focused on our reflections in the window glass—the two of us together. It looked right, felt right. He put his arm around me, and I leaned back against him. Our being together had been as good for me as it seemed to have been for him. It had given me something to go on besides inertia and fear. I knew I would go with him. It felt like the right thing to do.

"I can't say how I'll act when we get there," I said.

"I can't say how I'll act, either," he admitted. "Especially . . . when I see her."

He made the appointment for the next Saturday afternoon. You make appointments to go to Dilg unless you're a government inspector of some kind. That is the custom, and Dilg gets away with it.

We left L.A. in the rain early Saturday morning. Rain followed us off and on up the coast as far as Santa Barbara. Dilg was hidden away in the hills not far from San Jose. We could have reached it faster by driving up I-5, but neither of us were in the mood for all that bleakness. As it was, we arrived at one P.M. to be met by two armed gate guards. One of these phoned the main building and verified our appointment. Then the other took the wheel from Alan.

"Sorry," he said. "But no one is permitted inside without an escort. We'll meet your guide at the garage."

None of this surprised me. Dilg is a place where not only the patients but much of the staff has DGD. A maximum security prison wouldn't have been as potentially dangerous. On the other hand, I'd never heard of anyone getting chewed up here. Hospitals and rest homes had accidents. Dilg didn't. It was beautiful—an old estate. One that didn't make sense in these days of high taxes. It had been owned by the Dilg family. Oil, chemicals, pharmaceuticals. Ironically, they had even owned part of the late, unlamented Hedeon Laboratories. They'd had a briefly profitable interest in Hedeonco: the magic bullet, the cure for a large percentage of the world's cancer and a number of serious viral diseases—and the cause of Duryea-Gode disease. If one of your parents was treated with Hedeonco and you were conceived after the treatments, you had DGD. If you had kids, you passed it on to them. Not everyone was equally affected. They didn't all commit suicide or murder, but they all mutilated themselves to some degree if they could. And they all drifted—went off into a world of their own and stopped responding to their surroundings.

Anyway, the only Dilg son of his generation had had his life saved by Hedeonco. Then he had watched four of his children die before Doctors Kenneth Duryea and Jan Gode came up with a decent understanding of the problem and a partial solution: the diet. They gave Richard Dilg a way of keeping his next two children alive. He gave the big, cumbersome estate over to the care of DGD patients.

So the main building was an elaborate old mansion. There were other, newer buildings, more like guesthouses than institutional buildings. And there were wooded hills all around. Nice country. Green. The ocean wasn't far away. There was an old garage and a small parking lot. Waiting in the lot was a tall old woman. Our guard pulled up near her, let us out, then parked the car in the half-empty garage.

"Hello," the woman said, extending her hand. "I'm Beatrice Alcantara." The hand was cool and dry and startlingly strong. I thought the woman was DGD, but her age threw me. She appeared to be about sixty, and I had never seen a DGD that old. I wasn't sure why I thought she was DGD. If she was, she must have been an experimental model—one of the first to survive.

"Is it Doctor or Ms.?" Alan asked.

"It's Beatrice," she said. "I am a doctor, but we don't use titles much here."

I glanced at Alan, was surprised to see him smiling at her. He tended to go a long time between smiles. I looked at Beatrice and couldn't see anything to smile about. As we introduced ourselves, I realized I didn't like her. I couldn't see any reason for that either, but my feelings were my feelings. I didn't like her.

"I assume neither of you have been here before," she said, smiling down at us. She was at least six feet tall, and straight.

We shook our heads. "Let's go in the front way, then. I want to prepare you for what we do here. I don't want you to believe you've come to a hospital."

I frowned at her, wondering what else there was to believe. Dilg was called a retreat, but what difference did names make?

The house close up looked like one of the old-style public buildings—massive, baroque front with a single, domed tower reaching three stories above the three-story house. Wings of the house stretched for some distance to the right and left of the tower, then cornered and stretched back twice as far. The front doors were huge—one set of wrought iron and one of heavy wood. Neither appeared to be locked. Beatrice pulled open the iron door, pushed the wooden one, and gestured us in.

Inside, the house was an art museum—huge, high-ceilinged, tile-floored. There were marble columns and niches in which sculpture stood or paintings hung. There was other sculpture displayed around the rooms. At one end of the rooms there was a broad staircase leading up to a gallery that went around the rooms. There more art was displayed. "All that was made here," Beatrice said. "Some of it is even sold from here. Most goes to galleries in the Bay Area or down around L.A. Our only problem is turning out too much of it."

"You mean the patients do this?" I asked.

The old woman nodded. "This and much more. Our people work instead of tearing at themselves or staring into space. One of them invented the p.v. locks that protect this place. Though I almost wish he hadn't. It's gotten us more government attention than we like."

"What kind of locks?" I asked.

"Sorry. Palmprint-voiceprint. The first and the best. We have the patent." She looked at Alan. "Would you like to see what your mother does?"

"Wait a minute," he said. "You're telling us out-of-control DGDs create art and invent things?"

"And that lock," I said. "I've never heard of anything like that. I didn't even see a lock."

"The lock is new," she said. "There have been a few news stories about it. It's not the kind of thing most people would buy for their homes. Too expensive. So it's of limited interest. People tend to look at what's doing at Dilg in the way they look at the efforts of idiots savants. Interesting, incomprehensible, but not really important. Those likely to be interested in the lock and able to afford it know about it." She took a deep breath, faced Alan again. "Oh, yes, DGDs create things. At least they do here."

"Out-of-control DGDs."

"Yes."

"I expected to find them weaving baskets or something—at best. I know what DGD wards are like."

"So do I," she said. "I know what they're like in hospitals, and I know what it's like here." She waved a hand toward an abstract painting that looked like a photo I had once seen of the Orion Nebula. Darkness broken by a great cloud of light and color. "Here we can help them channel their energies. They can create something beautiful, useful, even something worthless. But they create. They don't destroy."

"Why?" Alan demanded. "It can't be some drug. We would have heard."

"It's no drug."

"Then what is it? Why haven't other hospitals—?"

"Alan," she said. "Wait."

He stood frowning at her.

"Do you want to see your mother?"

"Of course I want to see her!"

"Good. Come with me. Things will sort themselves out."

She led us to a corridor past offices where people talked to one another, waved to Beatrice, worked with computers. . . . They could have been anywhere. I wondered how many of them were controlled DGDs. I also wondered what kind of game the old woman was playing with her secrets. We passed through rooms so beautiful and perfectly kept it was obvious they were rarely used. Then at a broad, heavy door, she stopped us.

"Look at anything you like as we go on," she said. "But don't touch anything or anyone. And remember that some of the people you'll see injured themselves before they came to us. They still bear the scars of those injuries. Some of those scars may be difficult to look at, but you'll be in no danger. Keep that in mind. No one here will harm you." She pushed the door open and gestured us in.

Scars didn't bother me much. Disability didn't bother me. It was the act of self-mutilation that scared me. It was someone attacking her own arm as though it were a wild animal. It was someone who had torn at himself and been restrained or drugged off and on for so long that he barely had a recognizable human feature left, but he was still trying with what he did have to dig into his own flesh. Those are a couple of the things I saw at the DGD ward when I was fifteen. Even then I could have stood it better if I hadn't felt I was looking into a kind of temporal mirror.

I wasn't aware of walking through that doorway. I wouldn't have thought I could do it. The old woman said something, though, and I found myself on the other side of the door with the door closing behind me. I turned to stare at her.

She put her hand on my arm. "It's all right," she said quietly. "That door looks like a wall to a great many people."

I backed away from her, out of her reach, repelled by her touch. Shaking hands had been enough, for God's sake.

Something in her seemed to come to attention as she watched me. It made her even straighter. Deliberately, but for no apparent reason, she stepped toward Alan, touched him the way people do sometimes when they brush past—a kind of tactile "Excuse me." In that wide, empty corridor, it was totally unnecessary. For some reason, she wanted to touch him and wanted me to see. What did she think she was doing? Flirting at her age? I glared at her, found myself suppressing an irrational urge to shove her away from him. The violence of the urge amazed me.

Beatrice smiled and turned away. "This way," she said. Alan put his arm around me and tried to lead me after her.

"Wait a minute," I said, not moving.

Beatrice glanced around.

"What just happened?" I asked. I was ready for her to lie—to say nothing happened, pretend not to know what I was talking about.

"Are you planning to study medicine?" she asked.

"What? What does that have to do—?"

"Study medicine. You may be able to do a great deal of good." She strode away, taking long steps so that we had to hurry to keep up. She led us through a room in which some people worked at computer terminals and others with pencils and paper. It would have been an ordinary scene except that some people had half their faces ruined or had only one hand or leg or had other obvious scars. But they were all in control now. They were working. They were intent but not intent on self-destruction. Not one was digging into or tearing away flesh. When we had passed through this room and into a small, ornate sitting room, Alan grasped Beatrice's arm.

"What is it?" he demanded. "What do you do for them?"

She patted his hand, setting my teeth on edge. "I will tell you," she said. "I want you to know. But I want you to see your mother first." To my surprise, he nodded, let it go at that.

"Sit a moment," she said to us.

We sat in comfortable, matching upholstered chairs, Alan looking reasonably relaxed. What was it about the old lady that relaxed him but put me on edge? Maybe she reminded him of his grandmother or something. She didn't remind me of anyone. And what was that nonsense about studying medicine?

"I wanted you to pass through at least one workroom before we talked about your mother—and about the two of you." She turned to face me. "You've had a bad experience at a hospital or a rest home?"

I looked away from her, not wanting to think about it. Hadn't the people in that mock office been enough of a reminder? Horror film office. Nightmare office.

"It's all right," she said. "You don't have to go into detail. Just outline it for me."

I obeyed slowly, against my will, all the while wondering why I was doing it.

She nodded, unsurprised. "Harsh, loving people, your parents. Are they alive?"

"No."

"Were they both DGD?"

"Yes, but . . . yes."

"Of course. Aside from the obvious ugliness of your hospital experience and its implications for the future, what impressed you about the people in the ward?"

I didn't know what to answer. What did she want? Why did she want anything from me? She should have been concerned with Alan and his mother.

"Did you see people unrestrained?"

"Yes," I whispered. "One woman. I don't know how it happened that she was free. She ran up to us and slammed into my father without moving him. He was a big man. She bounced off, fell, and . . . began tearing at herself. She bit her own arm and . . . swallowed the flesh she'd bitten away. She tore at the wound she'd made with the nails of her other hand. She . . . I screamed at her to stop." I hugged myself, remembering the young woman, bloody, cannibalizing herself as she lay at our feet, digging into her own flesh. Digging. "They try so hard, fight so hard to get out."

"Out of what?" Alan demanded.

I looked at him, hardly seeing him.

"Lynn," he said gently, "Out of what?"

I shook my head. "Their restraints, their disease, the ward, their bodies . . ."

He glanced at Beatrice, then spoke to me again. "Did the girl talk?"

"No. She screamed."

He turned away from me uncomfortably. "Is this important?" he asked Beatrice.

"Very," she said.

"Well . . . can we talk about it after I see my mother?"

"Then and now." She spoke to me. "Did the girl stop what she was doing when you told her to?"

"The nurses had her a moment later. It didn't matter."

"It mattered. Did she stop?"

"Yes."

"According to the literature, they rarely respond to anyone," Alan said.

"True." Beatrice gave him a sad smile. "Your mother will probably respond to you, though."

"Is she? . . ." He glanced back at the nightmare office. "Is she as controlled as those people?"

"Yes, though she hasn't always been. Your mother works with clay now. She loves shapes and textures and—"

"She's blind," Alan said, voicing the suspicion as though it were fact. Beatrice's words had sent my thoughts in the same direction. Beatrice hesitated. "Yes," she said finally. "And for . . . the usual reason. I had intended to prepare you slowly."

"I've done a lot of reading."

I hadn't done much reading, but I knew what the usual reason was. The woman had gouged, ripped, or otherwise destroyed her eyes. She would be badly scarred. I got up, went over to sit on the arm of Alan's chair. I rested my hand on his shoulder, and he reached up and held it there.

"Can we see her now?" he asked.

Beatrice got up. "This way," she said.

We passed through more workrooms. People painted; assembled machinery; sculpted in wood, stone; even composed and played music. Almost no one noticed us. The patients were true to their disease in that respect. They weren't ignoring us. They clearly didn't know we existed. Only the few controlled-DGD guards gave themselves away by waving or speaking to Beatrice. I watched a woman work quickly, knowledgeably, with a power saw. She obviously understood the perimeters of her body, was not so dissociated as to perceive herself as trapped in something she needed to dig her way out of. What had Dilg done for these people that other hospitals did not do? And how could Dilg withhold its treatment from the others?

"Over there we make our own diet foods," Beatrice said, pointing through a window toward one of the guesthouses. "We permit more variety and make fewer mistakes than the commercial preparers. No ordinary person can concentrate on work the way our people can."

I turned to face her. "What are you saying? That the bigots are right? That we have some special gift?"

"Yes," she said. "It's hardly a bad characteristic, is it?"

"It's what people say whenever one of us does well at something. It's their way of denying us credit for our work."

"Yes. But people occasionally come to the right conclusions for the wrong reasons." I shrugged, not interested in arguing with her about it.

"Alan?" she said. He looked at her.

"Your mother is in the next room."

He swallowed, nodded. We both followed her into the room.

Naomi Chi was a small woman, hair still dark, fingers long and thin, graceful as they shaped the clay. Her face was a ruin. Not only her eyes but most of her nose and one ear were gone. What was left was badly scarred. "Her parents were poor," Beatrice said. "I don't know how much they told you, Alan, but they went through all the money they had, trying to keep her at a decent place. Her mother felt so guilty, you know. She was the one who had cancer and took the drug. . . . Eventually, they had to put Naomi in one of those state-approved, custodial-care places. You know the kind. For a while, it was all the government would pay for. Places like that . . . well, sometimes if patients were really troublesome—especially the ones who kept breaking free—they'd put them in a bare room and let them finish themselves. The only things those places took good care of were the maggots, the cockroaches, and the rats."

I shuddered. "I've heard there are still places like that."

"There are," Beatrice said, "kept open by greed and indifference." She looked at Alan. "Your mother survived for three months in one of those places. I took her from it myself. Later I was instrumental in having that particular place closed."

"You took her?" I asked.

"Dilg didn't exist then, but I was working with a group of controlled DGDs in L.A. Naomi's parents heard about us and asked us to take her. A lot of people didn't trust us then. Only a few of us were medically trained. All of us were young, idealistic, and ignorant. We began in an old frame house with a leaky roof. Naomi's parents were grabbing at straws. So were we. And by pure luck, we grabbed a good one. We were able to prove ourselves to the Dilg family and take over these quarters."

"Prove what?" I asked.

She turned to look at Alan and his mother. Alan was staring at Naomi's ruined face, at the ropy, discolored scar tissue. Naomi was shaping the image of an old woman and two children. The gaunt, lined face of the old woman was remarkably vivid—detailed in a way that seemed impossible for a blind sculptress.

Naomi seemed unaware of us. Her total attention remained on her work. Alan forgot about what Beatrice had told us and reached out to touch the scarred face.

Beatrice let it happen. Naomi did not seem to notice. "If I get her attention for you," Beatrice said, "we'll be breaking her routine. We'll have to stay with her until she gets back into it without hurting herself. About half an hour."

"You can get her attention?" he asked.

"Yes."

"Can she? . . ." Alan swallowed. "I've never heard of anything like this. Can she talk?"

"Yes. She may not choose to, though. And if she does, she'll do it very slowly."

"Do it. Get her attention."

"She'll want to touch you."

"That all right. Do it."

Beatrice took Naomi's hands and held them still, away from the wet clay. For several seconds Naomi tugged at her captive hands, as though unable to understand why they did not move as she wished.

Beatrice stepped closer and spoke quietly. "Stop, Naomi." And Naomi was still, blind face turned toward Beatrice in an attitude of attentive waiting. Totally focused waiting.

"Company, Naomi."

After a few seconds, Naomi made a wordless sound.

Beatrice gestured Alan to her side, gave Naomi one of his hands. It didn't bother me this time when she touched him. I was too interested in what was happening. Naomi examined Alan's hand minutely, then followed the arm up to the shoulder, the neck, the face. Holding his face between her hands, she made a sound. It may have been a word, but I couldn't understand it. All I could think of was the danger of those hands. I thought of my father's hands.

"His name is Alan Chi, Naomi. He's your son." Several seconds passed.

"Son?" she said. This time the word was quite distinct, though her lips had split in many places and had healed badly. "Son?" she repeated anxiously. "Here?"

"He's all right, Naomi. He's come to visit."

"Mother?" he said.

She reexamined his face. He had been three when she started to drift. It didn't seem possible that she could find anything in his face that she would remember. I wondered whether she remembered she had a son.

"Alan?" she said. She found his tears and paused at them. She touched her own face where there should have been an eye, then she reached back toward his eyes. An instant before I would have grabbed her hand, Beatrice did it.

"No!" Beatrice said firmly.

The hand fell limply to Naomi's side. Her face turned toward Beatrice like an antique weather vane swinging around. Beatrice stroked her hair, and Naomi said something I almost understood. Beatrice looked at Alan, who was frowning and wiping away tears.

"Hug your son," Beatrice said softly.

Naomi turned, groping, and Alan seized her in a tight, long hug. Her arms went around him slowly. She spoke words blurred by her ruined mouth but just understandable.

"Parents?" she said. "Did my parents . . . care for you?" Alan looked at her, clearly not understanding.

"She wants to know whether her parents took care of you," I said.

He glanced at me doubtfully, then looked at Beatrice.

"Yes," Beatrice said. "She just wants to know that they cared for you."

"They did," he said. "They kept their promise to you, Mother."

Several seconds passed. Naomi made sounds that even Alan took to be weeping, and he tried to comfort her.

"Who else is here?" she said finally.

This time Alan looked at me. I repeated what she had said.

"Her name is Lynn Mortimer," he said. "I'm . . ." He paused awkwardly. "She and I are going to be married."

After a time, she moved back from him and said my name. My first impulse was to go to her. I wasn't afraid or repelled by her now, but for no reason I could explain, I looked at Beatrice.

"Go," she said. "But you and I will have to talk later."

I went to Naomi, took her hand.

"Bea?" she said.

"I'm Lynn," I said softly.

She drew a quick breath. "No," she said. "No, you're . . ."

"I'm Lynn. Do you want Bea? She's here."

She said nothing. She put her hand to my face, explored it slowly. I let her do it, confident that I could stop her if she turned violent. But first one hand, then both, went over me very gently.

"You'll marry my son?" she said finally.

"Yes."

"Good. You'll keep him safe."

As much as possible, we'll keep each other safe. "Yes," I said.

"Good. No one will close him away from himself. No one will tie him or cage him." Her hand wandered to her own face again, nails biting in slightly.

"No," I said softly, catching her hand. "I want you to be safe, too."

The mouth moved. I think it smiled. "Son?" she said.

He understood her, took her hand.

"Clay," she said. Lynn and Alan in clay. "Bea?"

"Of course," Beatrice said. "Do you have an impression?"

"No!" It was the fastest that Naomi had answered anything. Then, almost child-like, she whispered, "Yes."

Beatrice laughed. "Touch them again if you like, Naomi. They don't mind."

We didn't. Alan closed his eyes, trusting her gentleness in a way I could not. I had no trouble accepting her touch, even so near my eyes, but I did not delude myself about her. Her gentleness could turn in an instant. Naomi's fingers twitched near Alan's eyes, and I spoke up at once, out of fear for him.

"Just touch him, Naomi. Only touch."

She froze, made an interrogative sound.

"She's all right," Alan said.

"I know," I said, not believing it. He would be all right, though, as long as someone watched her very carefully, nipped any dangerous impulses in the bud.

"Son!" she said, happily possessive. When she let him go, she demanded clay, wouldn't touch her old-woman sculpture again. Beatrice got new clay for her, leaving us to soothe her and ease her impatience. Alan began to recognize signs of impending destructive behavior. Twice he caught her hands and said no. She struggled against him until I spoke to her. As Beatrice returned, it happened again, and Beatrice said, "No, Naomi." Obediently Naomi let her hands fall to her sides.

"What is it?" Alan demanded later when we had left Naomi safely, totally focused, on her new work—clay sculptures of us. "Does she only listen to women or something?"

Beatrice took us back to the sitting room, sat us both down, but did not sit down herself. She went to a window and stared out. "Naomi only obeys certain women," she said. "And she's sometimes slow to obey. She's worse than most—probably because of the damage she managed to do to herself before I got her." Beatrice faced us, stood biting her lip and frowning. "I haven't had to give this particular speech for a while," she said. "Most DGDs have the sense not to marry each other and produce children. I hope you two aren't planning to have any—in spite of our need." She took a deep breath. "It's a pheromone. A scent. And it's sex-linked. Men who inherit the disease from their fathers have no trace of the scent. They also tend to have an easier time with the disease. But they're useless to us as staff here. Men who inherit from their mothers have as much of the scent as men get. They can be useful here because the DGDs can at least be made to notice them. The same for women who inherit from their mothers but not their fathers. It's only when two irresponsible DGDs get together and produce girl children like me or Lynn that you get someone who can really do some good in a place like this." She looked at me. "We are very rare commodities, you and I. When you finish school you'll have a very well paid job waiting for you."

"Here?" I asked.

"For training, perhaps. Beyond that, I don't know. You'll probably help start a retreat in some other part of the country. Others are badly needed." She smiled humorlessly. "People like us don't get along well together. You must realize that I don't like you any more than you like me."

I swallowed, saw her through a kind of haze for a moment. Hated her mindlessly—just for a moment.

"Sit back," she said. "Relax your body. It helps."

I obeyed, not really wanting to obey her but unable to think of anything else to do. Unable to think at all.

"We seem," she said, "to be very territorial. Dilg is a haven for me when I'm the only one of my kind here. When I'm not, it's a prison."

"All it looks like to me is an unbelievable amount of work," Alan said.

She nodded. "Almost too much." She smiled to herself. "I was one of the first double DGDs to be born. When I was old enough to understand, I thought I didn't have much time. First I tried to kill myself. Failing that, I tried to cram all the living I could into the small amount of time I assumed I had. When I got into this project, I worked as hard as I could to get it into shape before I started to drift. By now I wouldn't know what to do with myself if I weren't working."

"Why haven't you . . . drifted?" I asked.

"I don't know. There aren't enough of our kind to know what's normal for us."

"Drifting is normal for every DGD sooner or later."

"Later, then."

"Why hasn't the scent been synthesized?" Alan asked. "Why are there still concentration-camp rest homes and hospital wards?"

"There have been people trying to synthesize it since I proved what I could do with it. No one has succeeded so far. All we've been able to do is keep our eyes open for people like Lynn." She looked at me. "Dilg scholarship, right?"

"Yeah. Offered out of the blue."

"My people do a good job keeping track. You would have been contacted just before you graduated or if you dropped out."

"Is it possible," Alan said, staring at me, "that she's already doing it? Already using the scent to . . . influence people?"

"You?" Beatrice asked.

"All of us. A group of DGDs. We all live together. We're all controlled, of course, but . . ." Beatrice smiled. "It's probably the quietest house full of kids that anyone's ever seen."

I looked at Alan, and he looked away, "I'm not doing anything to them," I said. "I remind them of work they've already promised to do. That's all."

"You put them at ease," Beatrice said. "You're there. You . . . well, you leave your scent around the house. You speak to them individually. Without knowing why, they no doubt find that very comforting. Don't you, Alan?"

"I don't know," he said. "I suppose I must have. From my first visit to the house, I knew I wanted to move in. And when I first saw Lynn, I . . ." He shook his head. "Funny I thought all that was my idea."

"Will you work with us, Alan?"

"Me? You want Lynn."

"I want you both. You have no idea how many people take one look at one workroom here and turn and run. You may be the kind of young people who ought to eventually take charge of a place like Dilg."

"Whether we want it or not, eh?" he said.

Frightened, I tried to take his hand, but he moved it away. "Alan, this works," I said. "It's only a stopgap. I know. Genetic engineering will probably give us the final answers but for God's sake, this is something we can do now!"

"It's something *you* can do. Play queen bee in a retreat full of workers. I've never had any ambition to be a drone."

"A physician isn't likely to be a drone," Beatrice said.

"Would you marry one of your patients?" he demanded. "That's what Lynn would be doing if she married me—whether I become a doctor or not."

She looked away from him, stared across the room. "My husband is here," she said softly. "He's been a patient here for almost a decade. What better place for him . . . when his time came?"

"Shit!" Alan muttered. He glanced at me. "Let's get out of here!" He got up and strode across the room to the door, pulled at it, then realized it was locked. He turned to face Beatrice, his body language demanding she let him out. She went to him, took him by the shoulder, and turned him to face the door. "Try it once more," she said quietly. "You can't break it. Try."

Surprisingly, some of the hostility seemed to go out of him. "This is one of those p.v. locks?" he said.

"Yes."

I set my teeth and looked away. Let her work. She knew how to use this thing she and I both had. And for the moment, she was on my side.

I heard him make some effort with the door. The door didn't even rattle. Beatrice took his hand from it, and with her own hand flat against what appeared to be a large brass knob, she pushed the door open.

"The man who created that lock is nobody in particular," she said. "He doesn't have an unusually high I.Q., didn't even finish college. But sometime in his life he read a science-fiction story in which palmprint locks were a given. He went that story one better by creating one that responded to voice or palm. It took him years, but we were able to give him those years. The people of Dilg are problem solvers, Alan. Think of the problems you could solve!"

He looked as though he were beginning to think, beginning to understand. "I don't see how biological research can be done that way," he said. "Not with everyone acting on his own, not even aware of other researchers and their work."

"It *is* being done," she said, "and not in isolation. Our retreat in Colorado specializes in it and has—just barely—enough trained, controlled DGDs to see that no one really works in isolation. Our patients can still read and write—those who haven't damaged themselves too badly. They can take each other's work into account if reports are made available to them. And they can read material that comes in from the outside. They're working, Alan. The disease hasn't stopped them, *won't* stop them." He stared at her, seemed to be caught by her intensity—or her scent. He spoke as though his words were a strain, as though they hurt his throat. "I won't be a puppet. I won't be controlled . . . by a goddamn smell!"

"Alan—"

"I won't be what my mother is. I'd rather be dead!"

"There's no reason for you to become what your mother is."

He drew back in obvious disbelief.

"Your mother is brain damaged—thanks to the three months she spent in that custodial-care toilet. She had no speech at all when I met her. She's improved more than you can imagine. None of that has to happen to you. Work with us, and we'll see that none of it happens to you."

He hesitated, seemed less sure of himself. Even that much flexibility in him was surprising. "I'll be under your control or Lynn's," he said.

She shook her head. "Not even your mother is under my control. She's aware of me. She's able to take direction from me. She trusts me the way any blind person would trust her guide."

"There's more to it than that."

"Not here. Not any of our retreats."

"I don't believe you."

"Then you don't understand how much individuality our people retain. They know they need help, but they have minds of their own. If you want to see the abuse of power you're worried about, go to a DGD ward."

"You're better than that, I admit. Hell is probably better than that. But . . ."

"But you don't trust us."

He shrugged.

"You do, you know." She smiled. "You don't want to, but you do. That's what worries you, and it leaves you with work to do. Look into what I've said. See for yourself. We offer DGDs a chance to live and do whatever they decide is important to them. What do you have, what can you realistically hope for that's better than that?"

Silence. "I don't know what to think," he said finally.

"Go home," she said. "Decide what to think. It's the most important decision you'll ever make."

He looked at me. I went to him, not sure how he'd react, not sure he'd want me no matter what he decided.

"What are you going to do?" he asked.

The question startled me. "You have a choice," I said. "I don't. If she's right . . . how could I not wind up running a retreat?"

"Do you want to?"

I swallowed. I hadn't really faced that question yet. Did I want to spend my life in something that was basically a refined DGD ward? "No!"

"But you will."

". . . Yes." I thought for a moment, hunted for the right words. "You'd do it."

"What?"

"If the pheromone were something only men had, you would do it."

That silence again. After a time he took my hand, and we followed Beatrice out to the car. Before I could get in with him and our guard-escort, she caught my arm. I jerked away reflexively. By the time I caught myself, I had swung around as though I meant to hit her. Hell, I did mean to hit her, but I stopped myself in time. "Sorry," I said with no attempt at sincerity.

She held out a card until I took it. "My private number," she said. "Before seven or after nine, usually. You and I will communicate best by phone."

I resisted the impulse to throw the card away. God, she brought out the child in me.

Inside the car, Alan said something to the guard. I couldn't hear what it was, but the sound of his voice reminded me of him arguing with her—her logic and her scent. She had all but won him for me, and I couldn't manage even token gratitude. I spoke to her, low-voiced.

"He never really had a chance, did he?"

She looked surprised. "That's up to you. You can keep him or drive him away. I assure you, you *can* drive him away."

"How?"

"By imagining that he doesn't have a chance." She smiled faintly. "Phone me from your territory. We have a great deal to say to each other, and I'd rather we didn't say it as enemies."

She had lived with meeting people like me for decades. She had good control. I, on the other hand, was at the end of my control. All I could do was scramble into the car and floor my own phantom accelerator as the guard drove us to the gate. I couldn't look back at her. Until we were well away from the house, until we'd left the guard at the gate and gone off the property, I couldn't make myself look back. For long, irrational minutes, I was convinced that somehow if I turned, I would see myself standing there, gray and old, growing small in the distance, vanishing.

CIVILIZATION

I WENT UP TO THE *Neurotic's House* because Fred got in my face. He went, put his hand on my shoulders, and then he said:

"I liked you, black man, I really liked you."

The world was rough on me, disenchantment reigned in my life. Example: Maestro Borino, who rented a room to me, drove me away and let some words loose in my ears in an uncomplaining way, but he let loose.

"That won't work, Paulie, people want to help, but you all . . ."

There it is, you all, blacks, colored people. The conductor betrayed himself, clearly, he betrayed himself. You all . . . or rather, you musicians, artists? NO! Maestro Borino couldn't stand me, clearly, in his shining living room. Someone reminded him of the clash, the disequilibrium in the environment . . . it's clear.

Then I stretched out my suitcase, and I took my few books from the shelf in the living room, with a sideswipe, as if picking up sparks for the beginning of an argument.

"People want to help, but you . . ."

I left then for a hotel, after examining the check for one hundred cruzeiros signed by Borino, for the lessons in harmony that I gave at his place. I almost spit on the check. Then I slept very badly. I got up three times in order to urinate. Feeling the greasy walls of the hotel, I felt that my life was changing. I really felt that my existence was rotting if I didn't take care of it, if I didn't like myself a little bit more. . . . My life was beginning to rot. My life was going to rot like a smashed fruit, rolled up under the bed by some child. On my side, in the bed, I

Translated by Carolyn Richardson Durham.

followed the flight of a beetle, zoom, so brief. My life is going to be a brief flight too, I thought, it would be good for me to die. I am an ugly guy, split by complexes. I am a screwed up black man, screwed up.

Miss Aída, the wife of maestro Borino, said that she needed to enjoy me more. Bolas. I liked her, but innocently, for God's sake. What beautiful eyes she has, what teeth, and what a half Mona Lisa smile. . . . I liked her in a pure way, and I never was a low life about it, for God's sake! She's old enough to be my mother.

Sometimes gloom assaulted me, and I became gloomier. I have these phases, I am a spontaneous guy in a crowd. I shout in the air and give compliments. Suddenly, I become gloomy, in the defective sense: I am brotherless, a solitary man among the people, in the streets that beget fights, I am an unfortunate boy.

Then, often Miss Aída used to arrive with a silver teacup (so much luxury, for what?) and she used to bring me a cup of tea, a compress. I almost used to cry with feeling, but she acted like she didn't notice and asked me to play "memories of an Ancient Castle." My wet eyes, my fine hands, my arms turned into angel wings might dare to touch Miss Aída. No low life trickery, no dirty thought. I couldn't like myself, but I liked Miss Aída. I liked her, yes, and I delighted myself in bed, avoiding imagining her. I am a confused guy. But I keep on thinking about the image of Miss Aída, without aspersions, without a flaw in my heart.

Then I played "Memories of an Ancient Castle" and my fingers, in grave sounds, brought together gloom, dragons, and moats. Miss Aída didn't move. My fingers resuscitated princesses with fevers, naked and cold walls of dungeons. But love, in the end, quivered on the keys and went triumphant, going up to the sharps, for a glorious finish.

"What a beautiful thing, Paulie."

"Miss Aída, I'm your musician. These memories are thine."

And I laughed about "are thine," words of a medieval knight courting a lady. But with me, no court. She could have been my mother, and I loved her, perhaps like my mother, who died very suddenly. Another thing, I was a virgin and Dona Aída knew it. She approached me, sometimes with her eyes, defeated and sad. Borino used to drink and spend the night out. I was crazy with fear, but it was my finish, since it couldn't be like that: Borino in the nightclubs and I in the house, under the same roof with Miss Aída. I asked God for Borino to behave, because it was not going to turn out right. I asked Borino to become the tranquil fellow that I met at the Morning Concerts, with his lightly silvered hair, indicating judgment, and the kind laugh with me and other boys, the big heart with a lot of understanding.

"Boy, you have a lot of talent, doggone it, and you are wasting yourself with these dumb little lessons. Come with me, boy."

I went. It was May. On the 13th of May I went to a lecture on "Negritude in Popular Songs" by Edward Embondeiro, an alias for Jose da Silva. Borino grumbled a lot during the conference, balanced his head and scratched his wrinkled forehead as if to unravel enigmas. "Negritude ... You are going to quit 'Negritudes' and other silly attitudes. You're going to stay with me. You are wasting yourself, boy, you are lost on that road. This way you are not going to become anything, do you hear? Not anything!"

"But I am black, and you tell me this about . . ."

"I didn't notice you were black. It is interesting, you are black."

Irony like a club, split my resistance in half. And he took me by the arm, rented me the empty room in his house and in the morning he asked, "How are you, did you like it?" And his wife Miss Aída brought breakfast for the two of us and sat down too. But this is like a dream, because everything happened and today, I am walking with other steps. Today, I breathe the air of insanity in the *Neurotic's House*.

But I cannot stop going back to Miss Aída, like a flower that hangs over my sleep and brushes my face at the time of a nightmare. I keep here an indescribable sadness. I am, by nature a debauched person, since debauchery became a powerful weapon for me and made me take giant steps to the *Neurotic's House*. I learned to laugh at the world and at myself. But there is a moment when I invent chastities in that house, where oral cripples disguised as little dirt balls covered with sugar are found. He passes himself off as an urchin, he thinks that he is a bonbon, and crack! he ate dirt and the street urchins laugh at him. He ate dirt! he ate dirt! he is a fool, fooled. I was that fool, I evolved ways of behaving myself. I. Chaste and hard, my eyes of steel gnawed on the scab of the dirtiness of the world. I, a boy of steel. I am the black one that wanted an example and was called fresh, with other amenities that mental pariahs use against a guy that holds himself back and doesn't get ahead.

But today, I am feeling the breath of insanity in my face, today my cover is of discouragement, anger. I am a cracked guy and I defend myself among many dirty tricks. I look for strange examples of disasters. I catalog them for Fred, the crazy man, who thinks me indispensable and pays me a high salary. I went up to the *Neurotic's House* because I am an intelligent, bright black man (in Fred's opinion) and also lacking shelter, after trying the beatitude. Fred read my little book of verses, "A Man Tries to Be an Angel," he laughed out loud, choked until he got red, and asked:

"You were like this? What a joke! Ah, ah, a joke, a joke!"

But I went up, I have money, thanks to that crazy rich man, and I don't pay attention to my shrewdness.

I left in the morning, bitten by fleas and with a nose stuffed up with snot.

You all, colored people . . .

That's it: He took me with him, I shook his hand, but inside I regretted having gone forward without evaluating the details. He didn't see that I didn't fit in that bedroom, in that living room, he didn't see that a black man takes a lot of space, if they leave him free and he is a guy who learned to fight, that is, educated, refined, covered with gold. That is the training, yes sir. A black man is a very smart guy. One discovers the hinge of success and works in the shadow shielded by a "Yes sir," "You are very kind to me," "Not so much madam," and reverences that are a pain in the behind, but push the train of success ahead.

I left then, in the morning, I sat down on a bench in the Plaza of the Republic where I conversed with José do Patrocínio (Patrocínio yes, sir, what a crust, he doesn't even know how to read, he drinks like a pig, he has a foul body odor, the shoeshine boys call him José do Patrocínio, oh José do Patrocínio!)

I opened my *Cruz e Souza*, that edition on cheap paper, by Zelio Valverde, I read two poems, they didn't move me. I found it strange: If *Cruz e Souza* doesn't move me it's because I'm good and ruined. I am beginning to become rotten and a rotten guy needs to earn money. If he doesn't stink, he ends up cracked and everybody says that he is down and out, and if he is a black man, he is a black man "Hey, you" and not a "You, Mr." Excuse me for talking like this, but I am bitter, really bitter. God knows that I may lose control of myself, behave like an idiot, but deep down I find myself to be a man, a man jogging along the road to the abyss, reticently striving, but a Man. Did you understand? A Man!

These thoughts of being an idiot flourish when I feel bribed by Borino's check. In the Plaza of the Republic, José do Patrocínio couldn't be bribed, since I ended up telling him about the derring-do of his illustrious namesake.

"Look here, a haughty black man bought a car. A long time ago, a tribune (I'll explain what a tribune is on another day) kissed the hand of the princess . . . You, perhaps, didn't find a check?"

I sat down on another bench, discouraged. I closed the book of *Cruz e Souza*, I looked at the young woman who was going by, beautiful (Oh white, bright forms, light forms) and perceived that I was "walled in." I perceived that "the miserable, the broken, are the flowers of the sewers." I perceived that I would rot in the morning and that something was going to happen to me. In that instant, something was going to warp the muzzle of life for the other side.

He was a guy of about fifty. Blond hair, blue eyes, thin lips, and a thin nose, a long head, revealing a very high intelligence. A good-looking man. I perceived without effort that he was a white man. He stopped in front of me, a cane in his hand, he raised his hat with a gracious inclination:

"You're reading."

"I'm reading."

He took a few steps forward, a malicious smile on his lips:

"You are not busy. You're reading. What is your job? If you pardon my indiscretion."

"A Professor of Piano and Harmony," I breathe a little in order to begin again.

He looked at me for a few seconds, and in his blue eyes I saw my black face, humid with Reno waters.

"You are a musician. You read. . . . Then what do you think of Bach?"

He made a face of very complex analysis. Bach ought to be the Sea and not Bach the river. He wrote the Old Testament of Music. Music owes as much to him as a religion owes its founder. The cantor of St. Thomas, keeps on, still, the greatest of composers.

My memory failed me, and my thoughts searched briefly: Kuert Fahlen, Schumann, and even Cladira Filho mixed in my despair, in such a way that I didn't know anything else about Bach.

I looked, then, at the morning that was on its way to afternoon, the buildings with their flat, concrete bellies, where the sun beat a yellow blur. I looked at the Plaza of the Republic. On the bench near the bandstand, José do Patrocínio snored.

"Bach is Bach, sir."

"I would like to talk to you, in another place. I enjoyed you, black man, I enjoyed myself" and he put his hairy hand on my knee.

"My card, Fred's card. Have you heard about the *Neurotic's House*? Well look for me, then look for me."

He extended his hand to me, leaning over. I smelled a sour scent of cologne, and his hair, stuck with a glue, seemed a shell of gold. And now a few meters from me, he repeated:

"I liked you, black man, I really liked you."

Today, I am in *Neurotic's House,* and Fred appreciates me. I arrive in the morning, and my function, beyond shuffling the cards and playing piano at lunch, is to converse with the people who come there. To converse officially and to quibble, also, officially. I must still learn quotes in several languages, read the encyclopedia, for at least two hours, and play in Klaverskribo, that method for a keyboard instrument, invented by the Dutchman, C. Pott.

In conclusion, Fred exhibits me as the apple of his eye, a young child brought up by a rich parent.

"I was born of a drunken, tubercular black woman without a husband, but he didn't put me in schools, nothing like that. He carried me with him, he gave me little white clothes, and, facing the fury of the family, uplifted me with the fineries of education, like a very beloved son of his, very loved."

My job, then, is to count the people who come to the *Neurotic's House:* my bitter road, my beginning as a little, black, *rahento* [ragged] boy, red socks, with a green patch in the behind (green-hope!) and kinky hair that was ignorant of a comb.

"I was born, ma'am, or better said, about to be born. My destiny cropped up full of holes, fenced in by zeros, a blind destiny, muddled and stupid. After Fred found me in the icy morning, I sold roses in front of a night club and sang 'God Save the King,' bungled but very loud.

"My mother learned 'God Save the King' in the home of an English madam, where she worked before getting sick—a tubercular drunkard and without a husband. My destiny cropped up full of holes, madam, but I repaired it with the help of Papa Fred."

When my listener laughs, I become satisfied with my truths, and she, in turn, is happy to allow herself to be carried along.

I went up to the *Neurotic's House,* because Fred got in my face, and he still does.

"I like you, black man. You proved that a black man can free himself of his burden. I like you, black man, I really like you."

And he adjusts the knot of my tie, smiling, very blond, very fine, and good looking, like a white man.

And his hand, on my shoulder, scratches the flesh to the bone, witnessing resistance . . .

"I like you, black man, I really like you."

A sour odor, of cologne, engulfs me, like clouds of Civilization.

AÍDA CARTAGENA PORTALATÍN

THEY CALLED HER AURORA
(THE LOVE OF DONNA SUMMER)

MAMA NAMED ME COLITA. Colita Garcia. But Miss Sarah enrolled me in school as Aurora. You can forget Colita! She shouted. So people called me Aurora, but inside I was Colita. I won't forgive the way you laugh when you call me Aurora, joking about whoever gave me that name "never saw the light of dawn." No! No way! I won't stay here with her. In her house. I don't care if she pays for my studies and goes around telling everybody how smart I am. I don't care. I'm tired of her and all the sisters at school—Sister Fantina, who's as tall and skinny as Twiggy. And Mother Superior—who's wise but as big and fat as I don't know what. And the hell with triangles, rectangles, and parallel lines! And the hell with getting punished and calling Miss Sarah and her jumping on me like a machine gun! No! No! No way!

I said no! I don't like Miss Sarah and I don't care about her nice home. I'm not going to grow old like some poor tree being beat down on by a hot August sun. No! I'm not going to live all sad and miserable like leaves in a rainstorm inside these walls surrounded by an evergreen lawn and bushes. Nor will I keep listening to that Aurora is such a smart little black girl or blacks really entertain me or blacks with their rhythm and their jazz or blacks make the whole world smile and go to the store and get me Donna Summer's latest record, and blacks should do something and it's great the way they entertain white people. No! No! No way! I like Donna Summer's music. It just goes on forever. I like how she makes her end-

---

Translated by James J. Davis and Terry L. Collier.

less high-pitched whines and how she lets go her sudden, full showers of sound. But Miss Sarah is not going to keep me cooped up forever in her house with all its music—jazz, boogoloo, ragtime, and everything. All that music just doesn't suit that old woman. She thought I wouldn't leave. I wish she could see me now rushing to the bus with this bag of clothes and books. Here, Sir, I'm getting off here in Haina.

I walk around a little, taking in the breeze from the sugarcane fields. I stop in at Candita Restaurant and have a cold Seven-up. Hungry. That's what I am. I go over to La Enana and have two rolls and a Pepsi. I hurry out. Donna Summer's music fills the little greasy spoon place and then spreads out all over outside. I can still hear that long musical moan. Her music and her voice spread all over the restaurant and the neighborhood. It's the same song that Miss Sarah gets all excited about. The hell with all that! Anyway, here I am, eight miles out of the capital. It's seven P.M. I go into the church and hide behind the altar of Saint Isidro Labrador. I want him to hide me. Don't let them find me. Saint Isidro, Saint Isidro, Saint Isidro. Homeless people in raggedy clothes are all over the street. La la la la laa, ya ya ya ya yaa.

Standing next to the wall in La Enana a girl bops back and forth to the music. Donna's voice gets louder as the lottery ticket vendor turns up the volume on the radio. Donna's music again fills the bar, the neighborhood, the whole town. I try to pull my hair in place. It's all stiff. Yes, I was born with it this way, and that's the way it's going to stay. The crazy thing is that they make fun of me and talk about how smart I am because I'm about to get my diploma. No. No Way! No! I'm sick of hearing about how all these millions of white people just love Donna Summer, the black girl with the sexy voice. At one time they just loved Louis Armstrong, then they just loved Makeba. All that rhythm all that jazz is just so happy-go-lucky. If I were Donna Summer, I'd go and take back all my records from all the stores, discos, cabarets, hotels, motels, and fine homes.

I run off to errands. I cook, I wash, I iron for this woman, and put up with all the crap from the grocer, the Italian woman's son who's always pulling my hair, saying little black girl . . . , where'd you come from, and all this and all that. And the gringo lady, saying Colita, why are you so late? I tell her that the Italian woman's son made me late or that I stopped to watch Giordano stab Manfredi all on account of some argument about whose funeral home was going to get the body of a man from the neighborhood, who had just died. I watch the policeman, who calmly says that the dead man is Giordano.

I'm going to have to get my mind together, like the classified ads you can find in any newspaper anywhere in the world. They drilled into me that this is the Free World. And here that woman from Ohio treats me like a slave. I don't understand Free World and Exploitation and Colita, you are really ignorant. I didn't know a thing about monopolies, like the Woolworth chain where I buy my bras, with its 300 manufacturing and sales centers. I didn't know anything about all the police running back and forth around here and more police over there. "Hey you! Watch it!" I shout to one of them who put his hand on one of my . . . (you know). I'm tired of all these police and ITTs and CIAs all over the world, and the violence and torture every day, like when they beat that homeless man up just on a simple suspicion. He looked like he was on drugs and he let them beat him up. This is not Dominican machismo. The police are becoming bullies like in the wild west movies. If this is the Free World, all this craziness and exploitation, I'm leaving. No! No way!

I go back to Miss Sarah's, with her constant Donna Summer music and her constant loud mouth yelling at me to stop talking nonsense. And the yelling gets louder when I read the newspapers about the injustices committed against blacks in South Africa. Don't keep silent about the lynchings in Soweto and Johannesburg. They mutilated Steve Biko in a jail cell in Pretoria. Miss Sarah grabs me by my hair screaming loud in my ears, stop talking nonsense, stop talking nonsense! She pulls me over to the record player and turns up the volume all the way. Now I can't even hear myself crying. Donna Summer, my dear Donna. Her voice and her music fill up the whole house . . . Miss Sarah's house.

CHERRY BOMB

I T WAS TWO SUMMERS before I would put my thin-penny bus token in the slot and ride the Fifth Street trolley all the way to the end of the line to junior high. Life was measured in summers then, and the expression "I am in this world, but not of it" appealed to me. I wasn't sure what it meant, but it had just the right ring for a lofty statement I should adopt. That Midwest summer broke records for straight over-one-hundred-degree days in July, and Mr. Calhoun still came around with that-old-thing of an ice truck. Our mother still bought a help-him-out block of ice to leave in the backyard for us to lick or sit on. It was the summer that the Bible's plague of locusts came. Evening sighed its own relief in a locust hum that swelled from the cattails next to the cemetery, from the bridal wreath shrubs and the pickle grass that my younger cousin, Bea, combed and braided on our side of the alley.

I kept a cherry bomb and a locked diary in the closet under the back steps where Bea, restrained by my suggestion that the Hairy Man hid there, wouldn't try to find them. It was an established, Daddy-said-so fact that at night the Hairy Man went anywhere he wanted to go but in the daytime he stayed inside the yellow house on Sherman Avenue near our school. During the school year if we were so late that the patrol boys had gone inside, we would see him in his fenced-in yard, wooly-headed and bearded, hollering things we dared not repeat until a nurse kind of woman in a bandanna came out and took him back inside the house with the windows painted light blue, which my mother said was a peaceful color for somebody shell-shocked.

If you parted the heavy coats between the raggedy mouton that once belonged to my father's mother, who, my father said, was his Heart when she died, and the putrid-colored jacket my father wore when he got shipped out to the dot in the Pacific Ocean where, he said, the women wore one piece of cloth and looked as fine as wine in the summertime, you would find yourself right in the middle of our cave-dark closet. Then, if you closed your eyes, held your hands up over your head, placed one foot in front of the other, walked until the tips of your fingers touched the smooth cool of slanted plaster all the way down to where you had to slue your feet and walk squat-legged, fell to your knees and felt around on the floor—then you would hit the strong-smelling cigar box. My box of private things.

From time to time my cousins Bea and Eddy stayed with us, and on the Fourth of July the year before, Eddy had lit a cherry bomb in a Libby's corn can and tried to lob it over the house into the alley. Before it reached the top of the porch it went off, and a piece of tin shot God-is-whipping-you straight for Eddy's eye. By the time school started that year, Eddy had a keloid like a piece of twine down the side of his face and a black patch he had to wear until he got his glass eye that stared in a fixed angle at the sky. Nick, Eddy's friend, began calling Eddy "Black-Eyed Pea."

After Eddy's accident, he gave me a cherry bomb. His last, I kept it in my cigar box as a sort of memento of good times. Even if I had wanted to explode it, my mother had threatened to do worse to us if we so much as looked at fireworks again. Except for Christmas presents, it was the first thing anybody ever gave me.

But my diary was my most private thing, except for the other kind of private thing, which Eddy's friend Nick was always telling me he was going to put his hand up my dress and feel someday when I stopped being babyish about it. I told that to my diary right along with telling the other Nick-smells-like-Dixie-Peach things I wrote every afternoon, sitting in my room with the bed that Bea and I shared pulled up against the door. I always wrote until it was time for my father to come home and take off his crusty brogans that sent little rocks of dried cement flying.

One evening after supper, I sat on the curb with Bea and Wanda calling out cars the way my father sometimes did with us from the glider on our front porch. The engine sounds, the sleekness of shapes, the intricacies of chrome in the grillwork were on his list of what he would get when his ship came in. Buick Dynaflow! Fifty-three Ford! Bea kept rock-chalk score on the curb until Nick rode up on his dump-parts bike. Situated precariously on the handlebars, he pedaled backwards, one of his easy postures. He rode his bike in every possible pose, including his favorite invention, the J.C., which had him sailing along, standing upright on the seat with his arms out in mock crucifixion.

"You wanna ride?"

Of course I wanted to, but Nick was stingy when it came to his bike, and I knew he was teasing.

"It's gettin dark, but I'll ride you up to the highway and back if you want to," he said. He sounded like he meant it.

"Okay, but no fooling around," I said, and at once I was on the seat behind him, close up to his Dixie Peach hair. Pumping up and over two long hills, we rode a mile in the twilight. Later with our knees drawn up, we sat to rest on the soft bluff overlooking the yellow-stippled asphalt road, calling out cars. Beyond the highway toward the river, I could see the horizon's last flames. The faint smell of bacon rode sweetly on the breeze from the packing house upshore.

"Star light, star bright, the first star I see tonight, I wish I may, I wish I might . . ."

At first Nick wouldn't look up. "I don't see no star," he said.

I pointed. "See right up there, it's the North Star."

"How you know?"

"My mother showed it to me."

Then he looked. "Bet that ain't it."

"Bet it is. When it gets all the way dark, it'll be on the handle of the Little Dipper."

"If it's on the handle by the time the nine o'clock whistle blows, you get to ride my bike tomorrow all day. If it ain't, I get a kiss."

"Uh-uh, Nick," I said. "Let's just bet a hot pickle."

"Okay, Mamma's-Baby, okay, Miss Can't-Get-No-Brassiere, Miss Bow-Legs," and he rubbed my leg.

"Quit!" I said, and brushed his hand away. He did it again and I knocked his hand away again.

"Bet nobody ever touched your pussy."

"Ain't nobody ever going to, either."

"See if I don't," and he pushed me backwards, stuck his salty tongue in my mouth. His groping fingers up the leg of my shorts scratched when he pulled at my underpants. Then, like an arrow, fast and straight, his finger shot pain inside me. I punched him hard and he—"Ow, girl!"—stopped. I jumped up—"I'm telling"—and ran. He grabbed my ankle. His "Don't tell," then his "You better not" filled the air around me. But my own steely "I ain't scared" walked me all the way home. Halfway there I heard the pad of bike tires behind me on the brick street, and Nick sailed by, standing on the seat, his arms out in a J.C.

"Girl, I sent Eddy out looking for you, where you been?" my mother asked.

"I was up by Janice's house," I told her.

That night the tinge of pink in my underpants said that I should put epsom salts in the bathtub and hope that nothing bad had happened down there. When my mother asked me what I was doing with epsom salts, I told her, "Chiggers."

But I spelled it all out to my diary in I-am-in-this-world language. Nick: his shiny black-walnut skin, the soft fragrance of Dixie Peach in his hair, the cutoff overalls he wore with only one shoulder strap fastened so that I had to hold on to his bare shoulders even though they were sweaty. And in but-not-of-this-world language I told my diary the wish I had for him to get some kind of home training, go to church, act right, and not want to feel in my panties, and the soft kiss I wanted him to learn. I also told my diary how Eddy was pretending to be able to see with his glass eye, but how I heard him crying at night because he wanted to go with Wanda Coles and she made a fool out of him by having him watch her hand move back and forth in front of his face.

The next morning, when I gave my father his lunch box and his ice-water thermos and held the screen door for him, I saw Nick leaning and looking to be noticed in the Y of his apricot tree across the alley that was the boundary between our backyards. It was washday, a good opportunity for me to ignore him.

"Four loads before the sun gets hot," my mother said, and we rolled the washer off the back porch and into the middle of the kitchen, with two rinse tubs set side by side on my father's workbench. I stripped the beds still full of Bea and Eddy and the tobacco smell of my father and soft scent of my mother's Pond's cream. Underneath the mattress in their bedroom I always saw the same envelope of old war bonds, the small book of old ration stamps. And this time I found a magazine, *True Romance,* and inside it a card with roses on the front and a my-love-grows message, unsigned. At first I thought it must be from my father to my mother or vice versa. But as I ran to the kitchen with my discovery, I suddenly thought of my *private* cigar box, and slowly I went back up the stairs to sort out the knot of bedclothes on the floor.

Nick waited until the last sheet was stretched and pinned and the long pole was jacked up to raise the clothesline higher before he said a word.

"Found a new pedal for my bike," he yelled. I went inside the screen door but turned to see him sliding down from his perch.

"You can ride all day," he said through the screen. "Aw, hi, Miss Wilson."

"What you doing running around this early?" my mother asked him. "I know your mamma left something for you to get done 'fore she gets home," she said. "I bet you haven't even washed your face yet."

"I already did everything," Nick lied. The naps on his head were still separate.

"Then you can get your friend Eddy out the bed, and y'all can go to the store for me. We need some more starch."

It tickled Nick that he had gained entrance to the goings-on of our house, and he raced up the back stairs calling out, "Hey, Eddy, let's go!" I was hanging up line number two when they jostled down the unpaved alleyway, picking up rocks and throwing them at birds. "Come on, girl," my mother called. "We got a mess of overalls in here."

On washdays, when my mother said "Catch as catch can," we revelled in the break of routine, eating whatever we could find raw in a bowl for breakfast—and whatever we could get between two slices of bread for lunch. That noon, in my mother's got-to-get-this-done expression, I tried to find the secret that must have brought her the card of roses. Suppose Nick gave me such a card. But I could not picture my mother looking at the man holding the woman on the front of *True Romance.* I made mustard-and-onion-sandwiches for me and Bea and wandered among the clotheslines, waiting for Nick to ride by so I could ignore him some more.

When the sun was at its highest point, Eddy and Nick came into the kitchen for a cool drink of water. Nick grinned at me through Eddy's entire speech to my mother about how hot it was, how the Missouri River had backed up enough from recent rains to fill the hole that wasn't even stagnant this summer, how the still water was so clear you could see the tadpoles, and how my father had said even *he* used to swim over there.

As Eddy went on, Nick said I could go swimming with them if I wanted to. I couldn't swim, and I knew that he knew it, which made his asking sweet.

"I saw the Dipper last night," he said. "You can ride my bike tomorrow since y'all have to wash today."

"I don't want to ride your bike," I said. "You don't know how to act. Besides, my father is building me one for myself, and it's going to be a girl's bike."

"You can't *make* a girl's bike," Nick said. "They don't throw away those kind of frames at the dump."

"Okay," my mother said to them. "Y'all can go. But Nick, you watch out for Eddy. He can't see as good as you can, so don't be cuttin the fool in the water. Y'all be back here 'fore supper, you hear?"

Nick winked at me. Rolling my eyes had become my best response. Undaunted, he pushed Eddy toward the screen door, and by the time it slammed, they were on Nick's bike, headed for the Missouri River hole.

My best friend, Cece, lived with her grandmother over the summer, too far away from our house. And so I hung around with Wanda most of the time, though I usually told her none of my secrets. Really, the only thing I had against Wanda was her long, straight hair in bangs and two braids that she made even longer with colored plastic clothespins clamped onto the ends.

"Can you come out?" she asked through the screen.

"Sprinkle the shirts and ball them up, and you can go," my mother said. I filled the ironing basket with sprinkled clothes and left with Wanda. Out under our crabapple tree we sat rubbing chunks of ice over our legs and arms in the still afternoon.

"I came to tell you something," Wanda said.

"What?"

"Guess," she said.

"I don't know."

"It has something to do with this," she said, and reached into the elastic band of her shorts. She struggled with the size of the thing until it cleared her pocket and she held it up. "See."

It was a small, thick diary, a tan color, with letters that read FIVE YEAR DIARY in gold on the cover, and when she felt around in her pocket, a small key—all just like mine. Then deftly she unlocked the lock.

"Read this," she said. I took the book from her and confirmed that each page held a lined section for each day of five years. It was enough to see that Wanda, who wasn't even my friend, had managed to secure for herself the same precious thing I had done Miss Gray's chores for. Because Miss Gray next door was grossly overweight and couldn't get her arms up, I had oiled and braided her thick, sticky hair. I had swept her house, rugs and all. Since she couldn't get around very well, I had run to the store to get her messy tobacco, and got the boneless ham too that she said she ought to cut back on—all in order to collect two dollars' worth of dimes in a sock for the journal that would record the most vital facts about five years of my life.

That was enough without Wanda insisting that I read it.

"I can't read your writing," I said.

She took the book from my hands. "It says, 'Today I became a woman. I didn't get the cramps like everyone said I would. Now I can wear heels and red-fox stockings, and know that I have put away all the childish things I used to do. I am truly happy.' You know what that means?" she asked me.

"Yeah, that's nice," was all I could muster.

"I think every girl should have a diary, because it happens to every girl and it's a day you should always remember. You ought to get one."

"Yeah," I said.

By the time my father got home, I had done my two-faced best to convince Wanda that she would look like Lena Horne if she just wore kit curlers to bed. All the while I delighted in the way her bangs fell like a stringy rag mop in her eyes that day.

By suppertime I was sick of Wanda and happy to go looking for Eddy and Nick at the river. My mother insisted Wanda should keep me company, and so off we went, hopscotching our way on the bricks until we came to the new concrete side-walk with cracks to avoid in the name of good luck. Down the soft slope above the highway we scooted, and when the whiz of cars broke, we flew across the high-way and ran down the muddy hollow to the plain of wild onion, garlic, aspara-gus, and no telling what kinds of snakes to the place where the stand of short trees leaned, and the noisy rush of cars gave way to the noisy rush of river to come.

There on the ground just through the trees, Eddy lay on his back with his arms careless at his sides. Something wavelike through me made the hairs stand up on my arms, and I took off running to him. I stood above him just long enough to see his blind eye staring before he jumped awake, opening his other eye. In that instant I realized that not since the cherry-bomb accident had I seen Eddy asleep, and therefore did not know that he slept with the eye open.

"What are you doing laying here like this? Where's Nick?"

"I got too tired and Nick didn't want to come out yet," Eddy said, and he got up, pulled on his undershirt, and picked up Nick's bike at his side.

Wanda and I went to the bank of the cloudy green pool and called for Nick to come out. We called again and again. "Nick! Nick! We're going to leave you here and take your bike!"

"Nick!" Eddy called from across the water. "Nick!" Eddy called again and it went through the hairs on my arms. Wanda and I couldn't hold back our "Nick! Come on!" We looked into the pool but saw nothing through the muddy green.

We ran around the pool to Eddy's side.

"You don't think he went on over to the river, do you?"

"Not without telling me," Eddy said.

"Then where is he? Where was he when you came out?"

"He was right there." Eddy pointed. "Right out there in the middle. He can swim better than anybody. Let's just wait, hear?"

"Uh-uh," Wanda said. "We ought to get somebody. Suppose something happened to him."

I hated Wanda more than anybody and anything. "Let's just wait," I echoed Eddy.

"I'm going," Wanda said. As she ran, she yelled, "I'm going to get y'all's daddy. My mamma's going to be mad. I ain't got no business by the river."

"Nick's gonna get it. Nick's gonna get it," Eddy kept repeating as we stood looking toward the river, hoping to see Nick's white-toothed, nappy-headed self come bopping through the short trees, looking for his bike to go off on while we walked home, probably meeting my father on the way, probably telling him never mind, and most likely rolling our eyes at Wanda, who always acts like she knows so much.

Nick's gonna get it. When I get my girl's bike I'm not letting him touch it unless he swears he will not show off like it's some piece of junk he doesn't have to treat right. Unless he says we can ride together up to the highway and he says he's sorry for not acting right. I am in this world, but not of it. I am in this world.

Eddy and I waited, watched the pool turn deeper green, and the sun slant light like fire through the trees.

First came my father, the sweat on his face and head shining, his arms wagging out at his sides as he sloshed through the tall grass toward us. Then mamma behind him in her flower-print wash dress, calling us like she couldn't see we were standing right there. Then, really bad, Nick's mother with her gray and crimson elevator operator's uniform still on from work, running in high-heel shoes, calling Nick. Then Bea with Wanda and Mrs. Coles holding Puddin's hand, walking fast, then standing still outside the realm of confusion. Then the questions and Nick's mother shaking Eddy and my mother snatching her away from us and my father jumping in with his overalls on and Nick's mother crying and my mother saying, "Hush, now, it's gonna be all right," and Eddy closing his good eye tight and me saying the Lord's Prayer for us all. Then my father spitting out water and hollering and going down again and up again and hollering, "Get them kids away from here, get 'em away!" and Wanda and her mother running toward the highway, and my mother making us go stand over by the trees and Nick's mother pulling away from Mamma like she was going to jump into the water herself.

When my father laid Nick's body on the grass, I could see that Nick's hands were curled like they could never be straightened. Mamma walked his mother over to him and they held those curled-up hands until the ambulance people came and covered up his face. Nick's mother and Mamma went with them. Wanda's mother took me and Eddy and my father and Bea home in their Dynaflow.

That night Mamma held her waist and cried a lot. Eddy put his bed up to his door so that nobody could go in. My father said that I could stay up as long as I wanted and he sat out on the porch with his cigarettes. I could hear the glider creak every now and then, and I knew he was dozing and waking in the dark. Bea was so quiet in our room, she was almost not there. I sat awake in our bed for what seemed like the longest time, as if I had been sentenced to wait for something that could never come. I didn't feel at all like I would cry. Blank was what I felt, blank and swollen tight.

Groping my way, I parted the coats between the mouton and my father's rough wool, stretched my arms, and walked my hands down the ceiling to the box. Although I could not yet bring myself to throw away a month of my recorded life, my diary would not be useful, I had nothing to write. I found the cherry bomb. In the kitchen, I took the box of matches from the shelf over the stove and crept out the screen door. The glider creaked, but I stole out of the yard across the alley, through Nick's yard, out to the sidewalk and on.

From the soft bluff, I could hear the rush of the river above the hum of locusts. A fingernail sliver of moon laid out the highway gray and bent. The Little Dipper tilted. I struck a match and lit the green stem. When it sizzled, I threw it high and far, exploding the whole summer.

AUSTIN C. CLARKE

GRIFF

Gᴿɪꜰꜰ ᴡᴀꜱ ᴀ ʙʟᴀᴄᴋ ᴍᴀɴ from Barbados who sometimes denied he was black. Among black Americans who visited Toronto, he was black: "Right on!" "Peace and love, Brother!" and "Power to the People!" would suddenly become his vocabulary. He had emigrated to Toronto from Britain, and as a result, thought of himself as a black Englishman. But he was blacker than most immigrants. In color, that is. It must have been this double indemnity of being British and black that caused him to despise his blackness. To his friends, and his so-called friends, he flaunted his British experience and the "civilized" bearing that came with it; and he liked being referred to as a West Indian who had lived in London, for he was convinced that he had an edge, in breeding, over those West Indians who had come straight to Canada from the canefields and the islands. He had attended Ascot many times and he had seen the Queen in her box. He hated to be regarded as just black. "Griff, but you're blasted black, man," Clynn said once at a party in his own home, "and the sooner you realize that fact, the more rass-hole wiser you would be!" Clynn usually wasn't so honest; but that night he was drunk. What bothered Griff along with his blackness was that most of his friends were "getting through": cars and houses and "swinging parties" every Friday night, and a yearly trip back home for Christmas and for Carnival. Griff didn't have a cent in the bank. "And you don't even have *one* blasted child, neither!" Clynn told him that same night. But Griff was the best-dressed man present. They all envied him for that. And nobody but his wife really knew how poor he was in pocket. Griff smiled at them from behind his dark-green dark glasses. His wife smiled too, covering her embarrassment for her husband. She never criticized him in public, by gesture or by attitude, and she said very little to him about his ways, in their incensed apartment. Nevertheless, she carried many burdens of fear and failure for her husband's apparent ambitionless attitudes. England had wiped some British manners on her, too. Deep down inside, Griff was saying to Clynn and the others, *godblindyougodblindyou!* "Griffy, dear, pour your wife a Scotch, darling. I've decided to enjoy myself." She was breathing as her yoga teacher had taught her to do. And Griffy said, *godblindyougodblindyou!* again, to Clynn; poured his wife her drink, poured himself a large Scotch on the rocks, and vowed, *I am going to drink all your Scotch tonight, boy!* This was his only consolation. Clynn's words had become wounds. Griff grew so centred around his own problems that he did not, for one moment, consider any emotion coming from his wife. "She's just a nice kid," he told Clynn once, behind her back. He had draped his wife in an aura of sanctity; and he would become angry to the point of violence and scare everybody, when he thought his friends' conversation had touched the cloud and virginity of the sanctity in which he had clothed her: like taking her out on Friday and Saturday nights to the Cancer Calypso Club, in the entrails of the city, where pimps and doctors and lonely immigrants hustled women and brushed reputations in a brotherhood of illegal liquor. And if the Club got too crowded, Griff would feign a headache, and somehow make his wife feel the throbbing pain of his migraine, and would take her home in a taxi, and would recover miraculously on his way back along Sherbourne Street, and with the tact of a good barrister, would make tracks back to the Cancer and dance the rest of the limp-shirt night with a woman picked from among the lonely West Indian stags: his jacket let loose to the sweat and the freedom, his body sweet with the music rejoicing in the happy absence of his wife in the sweet presence of this woman. But after these hiatuses of dance, free as the perspiration pouring down his face, his wife would be put to bed around midnight, high up in the elevator, high off the invisible hog of credit, high up on the Chargex Card; and Griff would be tense, for days. It was a tenseness which almost gripped his body in a paralysis, as it strangled the blood in his body when the payments of loans for furniture and for debts approached, and they always coincided with the approaching of his paycheck, already earmarked against its exact face value. In times of this kind of stress, like his anxiety at the race track, when the performance of a horse contradicted his knowledge of the *Racing Form* and left him broke, he would grumble, "Money is *naught* all." Losing his money would cause him to ride on streetcars, and he hated any kind of public transportation. He seemed to realize his blackness more intensely; white people looking at him hard—questioning his presence, it seemed. It might be nothing more than the way his color changed color, going through a kaleidoscope of tints and shades under the varying ceiling lights of the streetcar. Griff never saw it this way. To him, it was staring. And his British breeding told him that to look at a person you didn't know (except she was a woman) was *infra dig. Infra dig* was the term he chose when he told Clynn about these incidents of people staring at him on the streetcars. The term formed itself on his broad thin lips, but he could never get the courage to spit it at the white people staring at him. Losing his money: his wife would sometimes be placed in a position, where after not having had dinner, nor the money to buy food; the landlord locked the apartment door with a padlock one night while they were at a party; she would smile in that half-censuring smile, a smile that told you she had been forced against the truth of her circumstances, to believe with him, that money was "naught all." But left to herself, left to the ramblings of her mind and her aspirations and her fingers over the new broadloom in her girlfriend's home, where her hand clutched the tight sweating glass of Scotch on the rocks, her Scotch seeming to absorb her arriving unhappiness with the testimony of her friend's broadloom, or in Clynn's recreation room, which she called a "den"; in her new sponge of happiness, fabricated like the house in her dreams, she would put her smile around her husband's losses, and in the embrace they would both feel higher than anybody present, because, "Griffy, dear, you were the only one there with a Master of Arts."

"I have more brains than *any one* there. They only coming on strong. But I don't have to come on strong, uh mean, I don't *have* to come on strong, but . . ."

One day, at Greenwood Race Track, Griff put his hand into his pocket and pulled out five twenty-dollar bills, and put them on one race: he put three twenty-dollar bills on Number Six, *on the fucking nose—to win! Eh?* (he had been drinking earlier at the Pilot Tavern); and he also put two twenty-dollar bills on Number Six, *to show.* He had studied the *Racing Form* like a man studying torts: he would put it into his pocket, take it out again, read it in the bathroom as he trimmed his moustache; he studied it on the sweet-smelling toilet bowl, he studied it as he might have studied law in Britain; and when he spoke of his knowledge in the *Racing Form,* it was as if he had received his degree in the Laws of Averages, and not in English Literature and Language. And he "gave" a horse to a stranger that same day at Greenwood. "Buy Number Three, man. I read the *Form* for three days, taking notes. It *got* to be Number Three!" The man thanked him because he himself was no expert, and spent five dollars (more than he had ever betted before) on Number Three, *to win.* "I read the *Form* like a blasted book, man!" Griff told him. He slipped away to the wicket farthest away; and like a thief, he bought his own tickets: "Number Six! Sixty on the nose! forty to show!" and to himself he said, smiling, "Law o' averages, man, law of averages." Tearing up Number Six after the race, he said to the man who had looked for him to thank him, and who thanked him and shook his hand and smiled with him, "I don't have to come on strong, man, I *mastered* that *Form.*" He looked across the field to the board at the price paid on Number Three, and then he said to the man, "Lend me two dollars for the next race, man. I need a bet." The man gave him three two-dollar bills and told him, "*Any* time, pardner, any time! Keep the six dollars. Thank *you!*" Griff was broke. Money is *naught* all, he was telling the same man who, seeing him waiting by the streetcar stop, had picked him up. Griff settled himself back into the soft leather of the new Riviera, going west, and said again to the man, "Money is naught all! But I don't like to come on strong. Uh mean, you see how I mastered the *Form,* did you? . . ."

"You damn right, boy!" the man said, adjusting the tone of the tape-deck. "How you like my new car?"

The elevator was silent that evening on the way up to the twenty-fifth floor; and he could not even lose his temper with it: "This country is uncivilized even the elevators they make too much noise a man can't even think in them this place only has money but it doesn't have any culture and breeding so everybody is grabbing for money money money." The elevator that evening didn't make a comment. And neither did his wife: she had been waiting for him to come from work, straight, with the money untouched in his monthly paycheck. But Griff had studied the *Racing Form* thoroughly all week; and had worked out the laws and averages and notations in red felt-pen ink; had circled all the "longshots", and had moved through the "donkeys" (the slow horses) with waves of blue lines; had had three "sure ones" for that day; and had averaged his wins against heavy bets, against his monthly salary, it was such a "goddamn cinch!" He had developed a migraine headache immediately after lunch, slipped through the emergency exit at the side, holding his head in his hand, his head full of tips and cinches, and had caught the taxi which miraculously had been waiting there, with the meter ticking; had run through the entrance of the Race Track, up the stairs, straight for the wicket to bet on the Daily Double; had invested fifty dollars on a "long shot" (worked out scientifically from his red-marked, wavy-lined *Form*), and had placed "two goddamn dollars" on the favorite—just to be sure!—and went into the Club House. The favorite won. Griff lost fifty dollars by the first race. But he had won two dollars on his two-dollar bet. "I didn't want to come on strong," he told the man who was then a stranger to him. The man could not understand what he was talking about: and he asked for no explanation. "I didn't want to come on strong, but I worked out all the winners today, since ten o'clock last night. I *picked* them, man. I can pick them. But I was going for the "long shot." Hell, what is a little bread? Fifty dollars! Man, that isn't no bread, at all. If I put my hand in my pocket now, look . . . *this* is bread! . . . five *hundred* dollars. I can lose, man, I can afford to lose bread. Money don't mean anything to me, man, money is no *big* thing! . . . money is *naught* all." His wife remained sitting on the Scandinavian couch which had the habit of whispering to them once a month, "Fifty-nine thirty-five owing on me!" in payments. She looked up at Griff as he gruffed through the door. She smiled. Her face did not change its form, or its feeling, but she smiled. Griff grew stiff at the smile. She got up from the couch. She brushed the anxiety of time from her waiting mini skirt ("My wife must dress well, and look *sharp,* even in the house!"), she tidied the already tidy hairdo she had just got from *Azans,* and she went into the kitchen, which was now a wall separating Griff from her. Griff looked at the furniture, and wished he could sell it all in time for the races tomorrow afternoon; the new unpaid-for livingroom couch, desk, matching executive chair, the table and matching chairs where they ate, desk pens thrown in, into the bargain the salesman swore he was giving them, ten Friday nights ago down Yonge Street, scatter rugs, Scandinavian-type settee with its matching chairs, like Denmark, in the fall season, in style and design; he looked at the motto, CHRIST IS THE HEAD OF THIS HOME, which his wife had insisted upon taking as another "bargain"; and he thought of how relaxed he felt driving in the man's new Riviera. He took the new *Racing Form,* folded in half and already notated, from his breast pocket, and sat on the edge of the bed, in the wisteria-smelling bedroom. The wife had been working, he said to himself, as he noticed he was sitting on his clean folded pyjamas. But he left them there and perused the handicaps and histories of the horses. The bundle buggy for shopping was rolling over the polished wood of the livingroom floor. The hinges on the doors of the clothes cupboard in the hallway, were talking. A clothes hanger dropped on the skating rink of the floor. The cupboard door was closed. The bundle buggy rolled down from its prop against the cupboard and jangled onto the hardboard ice. Griff looked up and saw a smooth brown, black-maned horse standing before him. It was his wife. "Griffy, dear? I am ready." She had cleaned out her pocketbook of old papers, useless personal and business cards accumulated over drinks and at parties; and she had made a budget of her month's allowance, allowing a place in the tidied wallet section for her husband's arrival. The horse in Griff's mind changed into a donkey. "Clynn called. He's having a party tonight. Tennish. After the supermarket, I want to go round to the corner, to the cleaners' and stop-off at the liquor store for a bottle of wine. My sisters're coming over for dinner, and they're bringing their boyfriends. I want to have a roast. Should I also buy you a bottle of Black-and-White, Griffy, dear?": *they're at post! they're off! . . . as they come into the backstretch, moving for the wire . . . it's Phil Kingston by two lengths, Crimson Admiral, third, True Willie . . . Phil Kingston, Crimson Admiral, True Willie . . .* but Griff had already moved downstairs, in the direction of the cashiers' wicket! "Long-shot in your arse! Uh got it, this time, old man!" *True Willie is making a move. True Willie! . . . Phil Kingston now by one length, True Willie is coming on the outside! True Willie! It's True Willie!* "It's almost time for the supermarket to close, Griff dear, and I won't like to be running about like a race horse, sweating and perspiring I planned my housework and I tried to finish all my housework on time so I'll be fresh for when you come home I took my time, too, doing my housework so I won't get excited by the time my sisters come and I didn't bother to go to my yoga class" *it's True Willie by a neck! True Willie! What a run, ladies and gentlemen! what a run! True Willie's the winner, and it's now official!* "and I even made a promise to budget this month so we'll save some money for all these bills we have to pay we have to pay these bills and we never seem to be paying them off and the rent's due in two days, no, today! oh, I forgot to tell you that the bank manager called about your account, to say that" *it's True Willie, by a neck!* Griff smashed all the furniture in the apartment in his mind, and walked through the door. "Oh Griffy, dear! Stooly called to say he's getting a lift to the races tomorrow and if you're going he want you to . . ."

Griff was standing in the midst of a group of middle-aged West Indians, all of whom pretended through the amount of liquor they drank, and the "gashes they lashed," that they were still young black studs. "Man, when I entered that door, she

knew better than to open her fucking mouth to me! To *me? Me?*" The listening red
eyes understood his unspoken chastisement in his threatening voice.
"Godblindyou! she knew better than *that;* me? if she'd only opened her fucking
mouth, I would-have . . ." They raised their glasses, all of them, to make it a ritu-
alistic harmony among men. They would, each of them, have chastised their
women in precisely the same way that Griff was boasting about disciplining his.
But he never did. He could never even put his hand to his wife's mouth to stop
her from talking. And she was not the kind of woman you would want to beat:
she was much too delicate. The history of their marriage had coincided with her
history of a woman's illness which had been kept silent among them; and its physical manifestation, in the form of a large scar that crawled half-way around her
neck, darker in colour than the natural shade of her skin, had always, from the
day of recovery after the operation, been covered by a neckline on each of her
dresses. And this became her natural style and fashion in clothes. Sometimes, in
more daring moods, she would wear a silk scarf to hide the scar. "If my wife wasn't
so blasted sickly, I would put my hand in her arse, *many times!* many times I've
thought o' putting my hand in her arse, after a bad day at the races!" He had even
thought of doing something drastic about her smile and about his losses at the
track and at poker. It was not clearly shaped in his mind: and at times, with this
violent intent, he could not think of whom he would perform this drastic act on.
After a bad day at the track, the thought of the drastic act, like a cloud over his
thoughts, would beat him down and take its toll out of his slim body which itself
seemed to refuse to bend under the great psychological pressure of losing, all the
time. He had just lost one hundred dollars at Woodbine Race Track, when one
evening as he entered Clynn's livingroom, for the usual Friday night party of
Scotch and West Indian peas and rice and chicken, which Clynn's Polish wife
cooked and spoiled and learned to cook as she spoiled the food, he had just had
time to adjust his shoulders in the over-sized sports jacket, when he said, brag-
gingly, "I just dropped a hundred. At Woodbine."

"Dollars?" It was Clynn's voice, coming from the dark corner where he poured
drinks. Clynn was a man who wouldn't lend his sister, nor his mother—if she was
still alive—more than five dollars at one time.

"Money don't mean anything, man."

"A *hundred* dollars?" Clynn suddenly thought of the amount of Scotch Griff
had been drinking in his house.

"Money is *naught* all."

"You're a blasted . . . Boy, do you lose *just* for fun, or wha'?" Clynn sputtered.
"Why the arse you don't become a *groom,* if you like racehorses so much, then?
Or you's a . . . a pathological loser?"

"Uh mean, I don't like to come on strong, or anything, but, money is *naught* all . . ."

"Rass-hole put down my Scotch, then! You drinking my fucking Scotch!"

And it rested there. It rested there because Griff suddenly remembered he was among men who knew him: who knew his losses both in Britain and in Canada. It rested there also, because Clynn and the others knew that his manner and attitude towards money, and his wife's expressionless smile were perhaps lying expressions of a turbulent inner feeling of failure. "He prob'ly got rass-hole ulcers, too!" Clynn said, and then spluttered into a laugh. Griff thought about it, and wondered whether he had indeed caused his wife to be changed into a different woman altogether. But he couldn't know that. Her smile covered a granite of silent and apparent contentment. He wondered whether he hated her, to the bone, and whether she hated him. He felt a spasm through his body as he thought of her hating him, and not knowing about it. For so many years living together, both here and in Britain; and she was always smiling. Her constancy and her cool exterior, her smiles, all made him wonder now, with the Scotch in his hand, about her undying devotion to him, her faithfulness, pure as the sheets in their sweet-smelling bedroom; he wondered whether "I should throw my hand in her arse, *just* to see . . ." But Clynn had made up his own mind that she was, completely, destroyed inside: her guts, her spirit, her aspirations, her procreative mechanism, "hysterectomy all shot to pieces!" Clynn said, destroyed beyond repair, beneath the silent consolation and support which he saw her giving to her husband; at home among friends and relations, and in public among his sometimes silently criticizing friends. "I don't mean to come on strong, but . . ."

"You really want to know what's wrong with Griff?" Clynn's sister, Princess, asked one day. "He want a *stiff* lash in his backside! He don't know that he's gambling-'way his wife's life? He doesn't know that? Look, he don't have chick nor child. Wife working in a good job, for *decent* money, and they don't even live in a decent apartment that you could say, well, rent eating out his sal'ry. Don't own no record-player. *Nothing.* And all he doing is walking 'bout Toronto with his blasted head in the air! He ain' know this is Northamerica? Christ, he don't even speak to poor people. He ain' have no motto-car, like some. Well, you tell me then, what the hell is Griff doing with thirteen-thousand Canadian dollars a year? Supporting race-horse? No, man, you can't tell me that, 'cause not even the *most* wutless o' Westindians living in Toronto, could gamble-'way thirteen thousand dollars! Jesuschrist! that is twenty-six thousand back in Barbados! And he come up here to throw-'way thirteen-thousand Canadian dollars 'pon a race-horse? What the hell is a race horse? *Thirteen thousand?* 'Pon a race horse? But lissen to me! one o' these mornings, that wife o' his going get up and tell him that she with-child, that she *pregnunt* . . ." ("She can't get pregnunt, though, Princess, 'cause she already had one o' them operations!") "Anyhow, if his wife was a diff'rent person, she would 'ave walked-out on his arse *long ago!* Or else, break his two blasted hands! And she won't spend a *day* in jail!"

When Griff heard what Princess had said about him, he shrugged his shoulders and said, "I don't have to come on strong, but if I was a different man, I would really show these West Indian women something . . ." He ran his thin, long, black fingers over the length of his old-fashioned slim tie, he shrugged the grey sports jacket that was a size too large, at the shoulders, into shape and place, wet his lips twice, and said, "Gimme another Scotch, man." While Clynn fixed the Scotch, he ran his thumb and index finger of his left hand, down the razor edge of his dark brown trouser seams. He inhaled and tucked his shirt and tie neatly beneath the middle button of his sports jacket. He took the Scotch, which he liked to drink on the rocks, and he said, "I don't have to come on strong, but I am going to tell you something . . ."

The next Friday night was the first day of fete in the long weekend. There hadn't been a long weekend in Canada for a long time. Everybody was tired of just going to work, coming home, watching CBC television, bad movies on the TV, and then going to bed. "There ain' no action in this fucking town," Clynn was saying for days, before the weekend appeared like raindrops on a farmer's dry season head. And everybody agreed with him. It was so. Friday night was here, and the boys, their wives, their girlfriends, and their "outside women" were noisy and drunk and happy. Some of the men were showing off their new bell-bottom trousers and broad leather belts worn under their bulging bellies, to make them look younger. The women, their heads shining like wet West Indian tar roads, the smell from the cosmetics and grease that went into their kinky hair and on their faces, to make them look sleek and smooth, all these smells and these women mixed with the cheap and domestic perfumes they used, whenever Avon called; and some women, wives whose husbands "were getting through," were wearing good-looking dresses, in style and fashion; others were still back home in their style, poured against their wishes and the better judgment of their bulging bodies; backsides big, sometimes, too big, breasts bigger, waists fading into the turbulence of their middle age and their behinds, all poured against the shape of their noisy bodies, into evil-fitting, shiny material made on sleepy nights after work, on a borrowed sewing machine. But everybody was happy. They had all forgotten now, through the flavor of the calypso and the peas and the rice, the fried chicken, the curry-chicken, that they were still living in a white man's country; and it didn't seem to bother them now, nor touch them now. Tonight, none of them would tell you that they hated Canada; that they wanted to go back home; that they were going "to make a little money, first;" that they were only waiting till then; that they were going to go back before the "blasted Canadian tourisses buy-up the blasted Caribbean;" they wouldn't tell you tonight that they all suffered some form of racial discrimination in Canada, and that that was to be expected, since "there are certain things with this place that are not just right;" not tonight. Tonight, Friday night, was forgetting night. West Indian night. And they were at the Cancer Club to forget and to drink and to get drunk. To make plans for some strange woman's (or man's) body and bed, to spend "some time" with a real West Indian "thing," to eat her boiled mackerel and green bananas, which their wives and women had, in their ambitions to be "decent" and Canadian, forgotten how to cook, and had left out of their diets, especially when Canadian friends were coming to dinner, because that kind of food was "plain West Indian stupidness." Tonight, they would forget and drink, forget and dance, and dance to forget.

"Oh-Jesus-Christ, Griff!" Stooly shouted, as if he was singing a calypso. He greeted Griff this way each time he came to the Club, and each time it was as if Stooly hadn't seen Griff in months, although they might have been together at the Track the whole afternoon. It was just the way Stooly was. "Oh-Jesus-Christ, Griff!" he would shout, and then he would rush past Griff, ignoring him, and make straight for Griff's wife. He would wrap his arms round her slender body (once his left hand squeezed a nipple, and Griff saw, and said to himself, "Uh mean, I won't like to come on strong about it, but . . ."; and did nothing about it), pulling up her new mini dress above the length of decency, worn for the first time tonight, exposing the expensive lace which bordered the tip of her slip. The veins of her hidden age, visible only at the back of her legs, would be exposed to Griff, who would stand and stare and feel "funny," and feel, as another man inquired with his hands all over his wife's body, the blood and the passion and the love mix with the rum in his mouth. Sometimes, when in a passion of brandy, he would make love to his wife as if she was a different woman, as if she was no different from one of the lost women found after midnight on the crowded familiar floor of the Cancer. "Haiii! How?" the wife would say, all the time her body was being crushed. She would say, "Haiii! How?" every time it happened; and it happened every time; and every time it happened, Griff would stand and stare, and do nothing about it, because his memory of British breeding told him so; but he would feel mad and helpless afterwards, all night; and he would always want to kill Stooly, or kill his wife for doing it; but he always felt she was so fragile. He would want to kill Stooly more than he would want to kill his wife. But Stooly came from the same island as his wife. Griff would tell Clynn the next day, on the telephone, that he should have done something about it; but he "didn't want to come on strong." Apparently, he was not strong enough to rescue his wife from the rape of Stooly's arms, as he rubbed his body against hers, like a dog scratching its fleas against a tree.

Once, a complete stranger saw it happen. Griff had just ordered three drinks: one for his wife, one for himself, and one for Stooly, his friend. Griff looked at the man, and in an expansive mood (he had made the "long shot" in the last race at Woodbine that afternoon), he asked the stranger, "What're you drinking?"

"Rum, sah!"

"I am going to buy you a goddamn drink, just because I like you, man."

The stranger did not change the mask on his face, but stood there, looking at Griff's dark-green lenses. Then he said, "You isn' no blasted man at all, man!" He then looked behind: Stooly was still embracing Griff's wife. It looked as if he was feeling her up. The man took the drink from Griff, and said, "You no man, sah!"

Griff laughed; but no noise came out of his mouth. "Man, that's all right. They went to school together in Trinidad."

"In *my* books, you still ain' no fucking man, boy!" The stranger turned away from Griff; and when he got to the door of the dancefloor, he said, "Thanks for the drink, *boy.*"

The wife was standing beside Griff now, smiling as if she was a queen parading through admiring lines of subjects. She looked, as she smiled, like she was under the floodlights of some premiere performance she had prepared herself for, a long time. She smiled, although no one in particular expected a smile from her. Her smiling went hand in hand with her new outfit. It had to be worn with a smile. It looked good, as usual, on her; and it probably understood that it could only continue to look good and express her personality if she continued smiling. At intervals, during the night, when you looked at her, it seemed as if she had taken the smile from her handbag, and had then powdered it onto her face. She could have taken it off any time, but she chose to wear it the whole night. "Griffy, dear?" she said, although she wasn't asking him anything, or telling him anything, or even looking in his direction. "Haiii! How?" she said to a man who brushed against her hips as he passed. The man looked suddenly frightened, because he wanted his advance to remain stealthy and masculine. When he passed back from the bar, with five glasses of cheap rum-and-cokes in his hands, he walked far from her. Griff was now leaning on the bar, facing the part-time barman, and talking about the results of the last race that day; his wife, her back to the bar, was looking at the men and the women, and smiling; when someone passed, who noticed her, and lingered in the recognition, she would say, "Haiii! How?" A large, black, badly dressed Jamaican (he was talking his way through the crowd) passed. He stared at her. She smiled. He put out his calloused construction hand, and with a little effort, he said, "May I have this dance, gal?" Griff was still talking. But in his mind he wondered whether his wife would dance with the Jamaican. He became ashamed with himself for thinking about it. He went back to talking, and got into an argument with the part-time barman, Masher, over a certain horse that was running in the feature race the next day at Greenwood. Masher, ever watchful over the women, especially other men's, couldn't help notice that the calloused-hand Jamaican was holding on to Griff's wife's hand. With his shark-eyes he tried to get Griff's attention off horses and on to his wife. But Griff was too preoccupied. His wife placed her drink on the counter beside him, her left hand still in the paws of the Jamaican construction worker's, whom nobody had seen before, and she said, "Griffy, dear?" The man's hand on her manicured fingers had just come into his consciousness. But he tried to be cool. It was the blackness of the Jamaican. And his size. Masher knew he was upset. The Jamaican reminded Griff of the "Congo-man" in one of Sparrow's calypsos. Masher started to laugh in his spitting kee-kee laugh. And when Griff saw that everybody was laughing, and had seen the Congo-jamaican walk off with his wife, he too decided to laugh. "It's all right, man," he said, more than twice, to no one in particular, although he could have been consoling the Jamaicancongo man, or Masher, or the people nearby, or himself.

"I sorry, suh," the Jamaican had said. He smiled to show Griff that he was not a rough fellow. "I am sorry, suh, I didn't know you was with the missis. I thought the missis was by-sheself, tonight, again, suh."

"It's no *big* thing, man," Griff said, turning back to talk to Masher, who by now had lost all interest in horses. Masher had had his eyes on Griff's wife, too. But Griff was worried by something new now: the man had said, "*by sheself, tonight, again, suh:*" and that could mean only one thing: that his wife went places, like this very Club, when he wasn't with her; and he never thought of this, and he never even imagined her doing a thing like this; and he wasn't sure that it was not merely the bad grammar of the Jamaican, and not the accusation in that bad grammar, "*but language is a funny thing, a man could kill a person with language, and the accusation can't be comprehended outside of the structure of the language*" . . . "*Wonder how you would parse this sentence, Clynn . . . a Jamaican fella told me last night, 'by-sheself, tonight, again, suh'; now, do you put any emphasis on the position of the adverb, more than the conditional phrase?*" Griff was already dozing off into the next day's dreams of action, thinking already of what he would tell Clynn about the incident: . . . "*which is the most important word in that fellow's sentence structure? 'By-sheself,' 'again,' or 'tonight'?*" "Never mind the fellow looks like a canecutter, he's still a brother," Griff said to Masher, but he could have been talking into the future, the next day, to Clynn; or even to himself. "I don't want to come on strong, but he's a brother." The CBC television news that night dealt with the Black Power nationalism in the States. The Jamaican man and Griff's wife were now on the dance floor. Griff stole a glimpse at them, to make sure the man was not holding his wife in the same friendly way Stooly, who was a friend, held her. He thought he could find the meaning of '*by-sheself*,' '*again*,' and '*tonight*' in the way the man held his wife. Had the Jamaican done so, Griff would have had to think even more seriously about the three words. But the Jamaican was about two hundred and fifty pounds of muscle and mackerel and green bananas. "Some other fellow would have come on strong, *just* because a rough-looking chap like him, held on . . ."

"Man, Griff, you's a rass-hole idiot man!" Masher said. He crept under the bar counter, came out, faced Griff, broke into his sneering laugh, and said, "You's a rass-hole!" Griff laughed too, in his voiceless laugh. "You ain' hear that man say, *'by-sheself,' 'tonight' 'again'*? If I had a woman like that, I would kill her arse, be-Christ, just for *looking* at a man like that Jamaikian-man!" Masher laughed some more, and walked away, singing the calypso the amateur band was trying to play: "*Oh Mister Walker, Uh come to see your daughter . . .*" Griff wet his lips. His bottom lip disappeared inside his mouth, under his top lip; then he did the same thing with his top lip. He adjusted his dark glasses, and ran his right hand, with a cigarette in it, over his slim tie. His right hand was trembling. He shrugged his sports jacket into place and shape on his shoulders . . . "*Oh, Mister Walker, uh come to see ya daughterrrrrr . . .*" He stood by himself in the crowd of West Indians at the door, and he seemed to be alone on a sun-setting beach back home. Only the waves of the calypsonian, and the rumbling of the congo drum, and the whispering, the loud whispering in the breakers of the people standing nearby, were with him. He was like the sea. He was like a man in the sea. He was a man at sea . . . "*tell she is the man from Sangre Grande . . .*" The dance floor was suddenly crowded: jam-packed. Hands were going up in the air, and some under dresses, in exuberance after the music; the words in the calypso were tickling some appetites; he thought of his wife's appetite and of the Jamaican's, who could no longer be seen in the gloom of the thick number of black people; and tomorrow was races, and he had again mastered the *Form*. And Griff suddenly became terrified about his wife's safety and purity, and the three words came back to him: *'by-sheself,' 'tonight,' 'again.'* Out of the crowd, he could see Masher's big red eyes and his teeth, skinned in mocking laugh. Masher was singing the words of the calypso: "*Tell she I come for she . . .*" The music and the waves on the beach, when the sun went behind the happy afternoon, came up like a gigantic sea, swelling and roaring as it came to where he was standing in the wet white sand; and the people beside him, whispering like birds going home to branches and roof tops, some whispering, some humming like the sea, fishing for fish and supper and for happiness, no longer in sight against the blackening dusk . . . "*she know me well, I gi' she a'ready! . . .*" Stooly walked in front of him, like the lightning that jigsawed over the rushing waves; and behind Stooly was a woman, noisy and Trinidadian, "this par-tee can't done till morning come!" like an empty tin can tied to a motor car bumper. All of a sudden, the fishermen were walking back to shore, climbing out of their boats, laden with catches, their legs wet up to their knees; and they walked up to the brink of the sand. In their hands were fish. Stooly still held the hand of a woman who laughed and talked loud, "fete for so!" She was like a barracuda. Masher, raucous and happy, and harmless, and a woman he didn't know, were walking like Siamese twins. One of his hands could not be seen. Out of the sea, now resting from the turbulent congo drumming of the waves in the calypso, came the Jamaicancongoman, and his wife.

"Thank you very much, suh," he said, handing Griff his wife's hand. With the other hand, she was pulling her mini skirt into place. "She is a first class dancer, suh."

"Don't have to come on *strong,* man."

"If I may, some other time, I would like to . . . ," the man said, smiling and wiping perspiration from his face with a red handkerchief. His voice was pleasant and it had an English accent hidden somewhere in it. But all the words Griff heard, were "*I know she well, I gi' she a'ready*". . . . and there were races tomorrow. His wife was smiling, smiling like the everlasting sea at calm.

"Haiii!" she said, and smiled some more. The Jamaicanman moved back into the sea for some more dancing and fish. The beach was still crowded; and in Griff's mind it was crowded, but there was no one but he standing among the broken forgotten pieces of fish: heads and tails, and empty glasses and cigarette butts, and some scales broken off in a bargain, or by chance, and the ripped-up tickets of wrong bets. Masher appeared and said in his ear, "If she was my wife, be-Christ, I tell you . . ." and he left the rest for the imagination. Griff's wife's voice continued, "Griffy, dear?" Masher came back from the bar with a coke for the woman he was with. When he got close to Griff, he said in his ear, ". . . even if she was only just a screw like that one I have there . . ."

"Griffy, dear, let's go home, I am feeling . . ."

". . . and if you was *something,*" Masher was now screaming down the stairs after them. Griff was thinking of the three little words which had brought such a great lump of weakness within the pit of his stomach.

"Masher seems very happy tonight, eh, Griffy, dear? I never quite saw Masher so happy."

". . . you, *boy!* you, *boy! . . .*"

"Masher, Haiii! How?"

"If it was mine," Masher shouted, trying to hide the meaning of his message, "if it was mine, and I had put only a two-dollar bet 'pon that horse, that horse that we was talking about, and . . . and that horse *behave'* so, well, I would have to *lash* that horse, till . . . *unnerstan?*"

"Griffy, dear? Doesn't Masher really love horses, eh?"

They were around the first corner, going down the last flight of stairs, holding the rails on the right hand side. Griff realized that the stairs were smelling of stale urine, although he could not tell why. His wife put her arm round his waist. It was the first for the day. "I had a *great* time, a real ball, a *lovely* time!" Griff said nothing. He was tired, but he was also tense inside; still he didn't have the strength or the courage, whichever it was he needed, to tell her how he felt, how she had humiliated him, in that peculiar West Indian way of looking at small matters, in front of all those people, he could not tell her how he felt each time he watched Stooly put his arms round her slender body; and how he felt when the strange Jamaican man, with his cluttered use of grammar broken beyond meaning and comprehending, had destroyed something, like a dream, which he had had about her for all these fifteen years of marriage. He just couldn't talk to her. He wet his lips and ran his fingers over the slim tie. All she did (for he wanted to know that he was married to a woman who could, through all the years of living together, read his mind, so he won't have to talk), was smile. The goddamn smile, he cursed. The sports jacket shoulders were shrugged into place and shape. "Griffy, dear? Didn't you enjoy yourself?" Her voice was like a flower, tender and caressing. The calypso band, upstairs, had just started up again. And the quiet waltz-like tune seemed to have been chosen to make him look foolish, behind his back. He could hear the scrambling of men and crabs trying to find dancing partners. He could imagine himself in the rush of fishermen after catches. He was thinking of getting his wife home quickly and coming back, to face Stooly and the Jamaican man; and he wished that if he did come back, that they would both be gone, so he won't have to come on strong; but he was thinking more of getting rid of his wife and coming back to dance and discuss the *Racing Form;* and tomorrow was races, again. He imagined the large rough Jamaican man searching for women again. He saw Stooly grabbing some woman's hand, some woman whom he had never seen before. But it was *his* Club. He saw Masher, his eyes bulging and his mouth wide open, red and white, in joy. And Griff found himself not knowing what to do with his hands. He took his hands out of his jacket pockets; and his wife, examining her mini dress in the reflection of the glass in the street door they were approaching, and where they always waited for the taxicab to stop for them, removed her arm from his waist. Griff placed his hand on her shoulder, near the scar, and she shuddered a little, and then he placed both hands on her shoulders; and she straightened up, with her smile on her face waiting for the kiss (he always kissed her like that), which would be fun, which was the only logical thing to do with his hands in that position round her neck, which would be fun and a little naughty for their ages like the old times in Britain; and his wife, expecting this reminder of happier nights in unhappy London, relaxed, unexcited, remembering both her doctor and her yoga teacher, and in the excitement of her usually unexcitable nature, relaxed a little, and was about to adjust her body to his, and lean her scarred neck just a little bit backward to make it easy for him, to get the blessing of his silent lips (she remembered then that the Jamaican held her as if he was her husband), when she realized that Griff's hands had walked up from her shoulders, and were now caressing the hidden bracelet of the scar on her neck, hidden tonight by a paisley scarf. He thought of Stooly, as she thought of the Jamaican, as he thought of Masher, as he squeezed, and of the races—tomorrow the first race goes at 1:45 P.M. And the more he squeezed the less he thought of other things, and the less those other things bothered him, and the less he thought of the bracelet of flesh under his fingers, the bracelet which had become visible, as his hands rumpled the neckline. He was not quite sure what he was doing, what he wanted to do: for he was a man who always insisted that he didn't like to come on strong, and to be standing up here in a grubby hallway killing his wife, would be coming on strong: he was not sure whether he was wrapping his hands round her neck in a passionate embrace imitating the Jamaican, or whether he was merely kissing her. But she was still smiling, the usual smile. He even expected her to say, "Haiii! How?" But she didn't. She couldn't. He didn't know where his kiss began and ended; and he didn't know where his hands stopped squeezing her neck. He looked back up the stairs, and he wanted so desperately to go back up into the Club and show them, or talk to them, although he did not, at the moment, know exactly why, and what he would have done had he gone back into the Club. His wife's smile was still on her body. Her paisley scarf was falling down her bosom like a rich spatter of baby food, pumpkin and tomato sauce; and she was like a child, propped against a corner, in anticipation of its first step, toddling into movement. But there was no movement. The smile was there, and that was all. He was on the beach again, and he was looking down at a fish, into the eye of reflected lead, a fish left by a fisherman on the beach. He thought he saw the scales moving up and down, like small bellows, but there was no movement. He had killed her. But he did not kill her smile. He wanted to kill her smile more than he wanted to kill his wife.

Griff wet his lips, and walked back up the stairs. His wife was standing against the wall by the door, and she looked as if she was dead, and at the same time she looked as if she was living. It must have been the smile. Griff thought he heard her whisper, "Griffy, dear?" As he reached the door, Stooly, with his arm round a strange woman's body, took away his arm, and rushed to Griff, and screamed as if he was bellowing out a calypso line, "Oh-Jesus-Christ-Griff!"

Masher heard the name called, and came laughing and shouting, "Jesus-Christ, boy! You get rid o' the wife real quick, man! As man, as *man*." Griff was wetting his lips again; he shrugged his sports jacket into place, and his mind wandered . . . "show me the kiss-me-arse *Racing Form,* man. We going to the races tomorrow . . ."

COLUMBA

WHEN I WAS TWELVE my parents left me in the hands of a hypochondriacal aunt and her Cuban lover, a ham radio operator. Her lover, that is, until she claimed their bed as her own. She was properly a family friend, who met my grandmother when they danced the Black Bottom at the Glass Bucket. Jamaica in the twenties was wild.

This woman, whose name was Charlotte, was large and pink and given to wearing pink satin nighties—flimsy relics, pale from age. Almost all was pink in that room, so it seemed; so it seems now, at this distance. The lace trim around the necks of the nighties was not pink; it was yellowed and frazzled, practically absent. Thin wisps of thread which had once formed flowers, birds, a spider's web. Years of washing in hard water with brown soap had made the nighties loose, droop, so that Charlotte's huge breasts slid outside, suddenly, sideways, pink falling on pink like ladylike camouflage, but for her livid nipples. No one could love those breasts, I think.

Her hair stuck flat against her head, bobbed and straightened, girlish bangs as if painted on her forehead. Once she had resembled Louise Brooks. No longer. New moons arced each black eye.

Charlotte was also given to drinking vast amounts of water from the crystal carafes standing on her low bedside table, next to her *Information Please Almanac*—she had a fetish for detail but no taste for reading—linen hankies scented with bay rum, and a bowl of soursweet tamarind balls. As she drank, so did she piss, ringing changes on the walls of chamber pots lined under the bed, all through the day and night. Her room, her pink expanse, smelled of urine and bay rum and the wet sugar which bound the tamarind balls. Ancestral scents.

I was to call her Aunt Charlotte and to mind her, for she was officially *in loco parentis.*

The Cuban, Juan Antonio Corona y Mestee, slept on a safari cot next to his ham radio, rum bottle, stacks of *Punch, Country Life,* and something called *Gent.* His room was a screened-in porch at the side of the verandah. Sitting there with him in the evening, listening to the calls of the radio, I could almost imagine myself away from that place, in the bush awaiting capture, or rescue, until the sharp PING! of Charlotte's water cut across even my imaginings and the scratch of faraway voices.

One night a young man vaulted the rail of a cruise ship off Tobago and we picked up the distress call. A sustained SPLASH! followed Charlotte's PING! and the young man slipped under the waves.

I have never been able to forget him, and capture him in a snap of that room, as though he floated through it, me. I wonder still, why that particular instant? That warm evening, the Southern Cross in clear view? The choice of a seachange?

His mother told the captain they had been playing bridge with another couple when her son excused himself. We heard all this on the radio, as the captain reported in full. Henry Fonda sprang to my movie-saturated mind, in *The Lady Eve,* with Barbara Stanwyck. But that was blackjack, not bridge, and a screwball comedy besides.

Perhaps the young man had tired of the coupling. Perhaps he needed a secret sharer.

The Cuban was a tall handsome man with blue-black hair and a costume of unvarying khaki. He seemed content to stay with Charlotte, use the whores in Raetown from time to time, listen to his radio, sip his rum, leaf through his magazines. Sitting on the side of the safari cot in his khaki, engaged in his pastimes, he seemed like a displaced white hunter (except he wasn't white, a fact no amount of relaxers or wide-brimmed hats could mask) or a mercenary recuperating from battle fatigue, awaiting further orders.

Perhaps he did not stir for practical reasons. This was 1960; he could not return to Cuba in all his hyphenated splendor, and had no marketable skills for the British Crown Colony in which he found himself. I got along with him, knowing we were both there on sufferance, unrelated dependents. Me, because Charlotte owed my grandmother something, he, for whatever reason he or she might have.

One of Juan Antonio's duties was to drop me at school. Each morning he pressed a half-crown into my hand, always telling me to treat my friends. I appreciated his largesse, knowing the money came from his allowance. It was a generous act and he asked no repayment but one small thing: I was to tell anyone who asked that he was my father. As I remember, no one ever did. Later, he suggested that I say "Goodbye, Papá"—with the accent on the last syllable—when I left the car each morning. I hesitated, curious. He said, "Never mind," and the subject was not brought up again.

I broke the chain of generosity and kept his money for myself, not willing to share it with girls who took every chance to ridicule my American accent and call me 'salt.'

I used the money to escape them, escape school. Sitting in the movies, watching them over and over until it was time to catch the bus back.

Charlotte was a woman of property. Her small house was a cliché of colonialism, graced with calendars advertising the coronation of ER II, the marriage of Princess Margaret Rose, the visit of Alice, princess Royal. Bamboo and wicker furniture was sparsely scattered across dark mahogany floors—settee there, end table here—giving the place the air of a hotel lobby, the sort of hotel carved from the shell of a great house, before Hilton and Sheraton made landfall. Tortoise-shell lampshades. Ashtrays made from coconut husks. Starched linen runners sporting the embroideries of craftswomen.

The house sat on top of a hill in Kingston, surrounded by an unkempt estate— so unkempt as to be arrogant, for this was the wealthiest part of the city, and the largest single tract of land. So large that a dead quiet enveloped the place in the evening, and we were cut off, sound and light absorbed by the space and the dark and the trees, abandoned and wild, entangled by vines and choked by underbrush, escaped, each reaching to survive.

At the foot of the hill was a cement gully which bordered the property—an empty moat but for the detritus of trespassers. Stray dogs roamed amid Red Stripe beer bottles, crushed cigarette packets, bully-beef tins.

Trespassers, real and imagined, were Charlotte's passion. In the evening, after dinner, bed-jacket draped across her shoulders against the soft trade winds, which she said were laden with typhoid, she roused herself to the verandah and took aim. She fired and fired and fired. Then she excused herself. "That will hold them for another night." She was at once terrified of invasion and confident she could stay it. Her gunplay was ritual against it.

There was, of course, someone responsible for cleaning the house, feeding the animals, filling the carafes and emptying the chamber pots, cooking the meals and doing the laundry. These tasks fell to Columba, a fourteen-year-old from St Ann, where Charlotte had bartered him from his mother; a case of condensed milk, two dozen tins of sardines, five pounds of flour, several bottles of cooking oil, permission to squat on Charlotte's cane-piece—fair exchange. His mother set up housekeeping with his brothers and sisters, and Columba was transported in the back of Charlotte's black Austin to Kingston. A more magnanimous, at least practical, landowner would have had a staff of two, even three, but Charlotte swore against being taken advantage of, as she termed it, so all was done by Columba, learning to expand his skills under her teaching, instructions shouted from the bed.

He had been named not for our discoverer, but for the saint buried on Iona, discoverer of the monster in the loch. A Father Pierre, come to St Ann from

French Guiana, had taught Columba's mother, Winsome, to write her name, read a ballot, and know God. He said he had been assistant to the confessor on Devil's Island, and when the place was finally shut down in 1951 he was cast adrift, floating around the islands seeking a berth.

His word was good enough for the people gathered in his seaside chapel of open sides and thatched roof, used during the week to shelter a woman smashing limestone for the road, sorting trilobite from rock. On Sunday morning people sang, faces misted by spray, air heavy with the scent of sea grapes, the fat purple bunches bowing, swinging, brushing the glass sand, bruised. Bruises releasing more scent, entering the throats of a congregation fighting the smash of the sea. On Sunday morning Father Pierre talked to them of God, dredging his memory for every tale he had been told.

This was good enough for these people. They probably couldn't tell a confessor from a convict—which is what Father Pierre was—working off his crime against nature by boiling the life out of yam and taro and salted beef for the wardens, his keepers.

Even after the *Gleaner* had broadcast the real story, the congregation stood fast: he was white; he knew God—they reasoned. Poor devils.

Father Pierre held Columba's hand at the boy's baptism. He was ten years old then and had been called 'Junior' all his life. Why honor an un-named sire? Father Pierre spoke to Winsome. "Children," the priest intoned, "the children become their names." He spoke in an English as broken as hers.

What Father Pierre failed to reckon with was the unfamiliar nature of the boy's new name; Columba was 'Collie' to some, "Like one damn dawg," his mother said. "Chuh, man. Hignorant smaddy cyaan accept not'ing new." Collie soon turned Lassie and he was shamed.

To Charlotte he became 'Colin,' because she insisted on Anglicization. It was for his own good, she added for emphasis, and so he would recognize her kindness. His name-as-is was foolish and feminine and had been given him by a *pedophile*, for heaven's sake.

Charlotte's shouts reached Columba in the kitchen. He was attempting to put together a gooseberry fool for the mistress's elevenses. The word *pedophile* smacked the stucco of the corridor between them, each syllable distinct, perversion bouncing furiously off the walls. I had heard—who hadn't?—but the word was beyond me. I was taking Latin, not Greek.

I softly asked Juan Antonio and he, in equally hushed tones, said, "Mariposa . . . butterfly."

Charlotte wasn't through. "Fancy naming a boy after a bird. A black boy after a white bird. And still people attend that man . . . Well, they will get what they deserve," she promised. "You are lucky I saved you from that." She spoke with such conviction."

I was forbidden to speak with Columba except on matters of household business, encouraged by Charlotte to complain when the pleat of my school tunic was not sharp enough. I felt only awkward that a boy two years older than myself was responsible for my laundry, for feeding me, for making my bed. I was, after all, an American now, only here temporarily. I did not keep the commandment.

I sought him out in secret. When Juan Antonio went downtown and while Charlotte dozed, the coast was clear. We sat behind the house under an ancient guava, concealed by a screen of bougainvillea. There we talked. Compared lives. Exchanged histories. We kept each other company, and our need for company made our conversations almost natural. The alternative was a dreadful loneliness; silence, but for the noises of the two adults. Strangers.

His questions about America were endless. What was New York like? Had I been to Hollywood? He wanted to know every detail about Duke Ellington, Marilyn Monroe, Stagger Lee, Jackie Wilson, Ava Gardner, Billy the Kid, Dinah Washington, Tony Curtis, Spartacus, John Wayne. Everyone, every name he knew from the cinema, where he slipped on his evening off; every voice, ballad, beat, he heard over Rediffusion, tuned low in the kitchen.

Did I know any of these people? Could you see them on the street? Then, startling me: what was life like for a black man in America? An ordinary black man, not a star?

I had no idea—not really. I had been raised in a community in New Jersey until this interruption, surrounded by people who had made their own world and 'did not business' with that sort of thing. Bourgeois separatists. I told Columba I did not know and we went back to the stars and legends.

A Tuesday during rainy season: Charlotte, swathed in a plaid lap-robe lifted from the *Queen Mary*, is being driven by Juan Antonio to an ice factory she owns in Old Harbour. There is a problem with the overseer; Charlotte is summoned. You would think she was being transported a thousand miles up the Amazon into headhunter territory, so elaborate are the preparations.

She and Juan Antonio drop me at school. There is no halfcrown this morning. I get sixpence and wave them off. I wait for the Austin to turn the corner at St Cecilia's Way, then I cut to Lady Musgrave Road to catch the bus back.

When I return, I change and meet Columba out back. He has promised to show me something. The rain drips from the deep green of the escaped bush which surrounds us. We set out on a path invisible but to him, our bare feet sliding on slick fallen leaves. A stand of mahoe is in front of us. We pass through the trees and come into a clearing.

In the clearing is a surprise: a wreck of a car, thirties Rover. Gut-sprung, tired and forlorn, it slumps in the high grass. Lizards scramble through the vines which wrap around rusted chrome and across black hood and boot. We walk closer. I look into the wreck.

The leather seats are split and a white fluff erupts here and there. A blue gyroscope set into the dash slowly rotates. A pennant of the Kingston Yacht Club dangles miserably from the rearview.

This is not all. The car is alive. Throughout, roaming the seats, perched on the running board, spackling the crystal face of the clock, are doves. White. Speckled. Rock. Mourning. Wreck turned dovecote is filled with their sweet coos.

"Where did you find them?"

Columba is pleased, proud too, I think. "Nuh find dem nestin' all over de place? I mek dem a home, give dem name. "Dat one dere nuh Stagger Lee?" He points to a mottled pigeon hanging from a visor. "Him is rascal fe true."

Ava Gardner's feet click across the roof where Spartacus is hot in her pursuit.

Columba and I sit among the birds for hours.

I thank him for showing them to me, promising on my honor not to tell.

That evening I am seated across from Charlotte and next to Juan Antonio in the dining room. The ceiling fan stirs the air, which is heavy with the day's moisture.

Columba has prepared terrapin and is serving us one by one. His head is bowed so our eyes cannot meet, as they never do in such domestic moments. We—he and I—split our lives in this house as best we can. No one watching this scene would imagine our meeting that afternoon, the wild birds, talk of flight.

The turtle is sweet. A turtling man traded it for ice that morning in Old Harbour. The curved shell sits on a counter in the kitchen. Golden. Delicate. Representing our island. Representing the world.

I did not tell them about the doves.

They found out easily, stupidly.

Charlotte's car had developed a knock in the engine. She noticed it on the journey to the ice factory, and questioned me about it each evening after that. Had I heard it on the way to school that morning? How could she visit her other properties without proper transport? Something must be done.

Juan Antonio suggested he take the Austin to the Texaco station at Matilda's Corner. Charlotte would have none of it. She asked little from Juan Antonio, the least he could do was maintain her automobile. What did she suggest? he asked. How could he get parts to repair the Austin; should he fashion them from bamboo?

She announced her solution: Juan Antonio was to take a machete and chop his way through to the Rover. The car had served her well, she said, surely it could be of use now. He resisted, reminding her that the Rover was thirty years old, probably rusted beyond recognition, and not of any conceivable use. It did not matter.

The next morning Juan Antonio set off to chop his way through the bush, dripping along the path, monkey wrench in his left hand, machete in his right. Columba was in the kitchen, head down, wrapped in the heat of burning coals as he fired irons to draw across khaki and satin.

The car, of course, was useless as a donor, but Juan Antonio's mission was not a total loss. He was relieved to tell Charlotte about the doves. Why, there must be a hundred. All kinds.

Charlotte was beside herself. Her property was the soul of bounty. Her trees bore heavily. Her chickens laid through hurricanes. Edible creatures abounded!

Neither recognized that these birds were not for killing. They did not recognize the pennant of the Kingston Yacht Club as the colors of this precious colony within a colony.

Columba was given his orders. Wring the necks of the birds. Pluck them and dress them and wrap them tightly for freezing. Leave out three for that evening's supper.

He did as he was told.

Recklessly I walked into the bush. No notice was taken.

I found him sitting in the front seat of the dovecote. A wooden box was beside him, half-filled with dead birds. The live ones did not scatter, did not flee. They sat and paced and cooed, as Columba performed his dreadful task.

"Sorry, man, you hear?" he said softly as he wrung the neck of the next one. He was weeping heavily. Heaving his shoulders with the effort of execution and grief.

I sat beside him in silence, my arm around his waist. This was not done.

THE VISIT

T HE WOMAN SAT LEANING slightly forward. Left elbow on leg, left hand holding up her chin, clamping shut her lips. Not hiding their look of sullen disinterest. From the doorway, her daughter watched her. Took in the droop of the shoulders, the emptiness in the heavy-lidded black eyes.

"You watching that program?"

Miriam shrugged, not moving her hand, not moving her eyes from the television. Catherine sighed, leaned in the doorway and turned her eyes towards the television. Jensen's Dream! The woman was trying to prevent Jensen from getting the deal on the plantation. Catherine hoped that he would find out in time to stop her. She glanced over at her mother. Lord! Look at her! Just look at her! She had to choose the most uncomfortable chair in the room, quite in the corner over there! and look at her face! Anybody come in here and see her looking like that must think I making her see trouble! Just look at her! Catherine sucked her teeth and turned away from the doorway, moving back to the kitchen.

Martin looked up from his job of washing dishes at the kitchen sink. He chuckled. Stepped back and blocked his sister's path with his elbow. "Behave yourself, non!" he said in a low voice. "Leave the lady alone!"

Catherine matched his tone. "Go and watch her! Go and see how she sit down poor-me-one as if somebody thief she best clean-neck fowl!"

Martin laughed quietly, the sound staying down in his throat. He picked up a glass and placed his hands back in the water. "Behave yourself," he repeated, "leave her alone!"

His answer was a prolonged sucking of the teeth as his sister moved towards the refrigerator.

Jensen was confronting his secret adversary. He was beginning to suspect that something not quite right was going on.

Miriam had heard the whispering. Guessed that it had something to do with her. She removed her hand from under her chin, frowned, looked cross-eyed at the door, shifted herself sideways in the chair, crossed her legs and leaned her head cautiously back. Her right ear just touched the cushion.

An advertisement. Some kind of sauce. Miriam didn't hear what sauce it was. A far-off memory came back to her. An advertisement on radio years ago. "Don't just say Worcester! Say Bee and Digby's!"

Miriam cleared her throat and hunched her shoulders. Couldn't they do something to make it a little warmer? Put on the fire or something? Miriam yawned. She would have liked to go and lie down. Cover up. She smiled. *Kooblay* up! But for sure Catherine would want to know if she was ill or something. Quietly, so as not to be heard, Miriam sucked her teeth and turned in the chair. Her body was curved, head down, her back turned now towards the television.

April in England. Catherine and Martin had said when they wrote that it was a good time to come. Not very hot, but good weather. Springtime! Good weather! Well I wouldn't like to see bad one! Last week, when they had gone to visit Cousin Bertrand in Huddersfield, it had snowed! Miriam shivered. Martin who wasn't a bad child, really . . . Not like his sister. Is as if she think England is hers and she doing me a favor to have me here! Favor? I want to go home, yes! I want to go home where me is woman in me own house!

Martin said that Huddersfield and that whole area around there was like that. Always cold. Always cold. When there was snow in Huddersfield, he said, it didn't mean that there was snow in London, too. In fact afterwards they knew that it hadn't snowed in London that day. But snow or no snow, it well cold! It well, well cold!

I tell you, eh, it hurting me heart. Catherine! Look at Catherine, non! I remember how I nurse that child! Puny, puny, she did nearly dead, yes! They didn't even think she would survive! And now acting with me like if she think she is queen!

When she had sat there in Peggy's Whim, high up on the hill above Hermitage, writing Martin and Catherine here in England, she never would have thought that England was like this. No. 30 Rose Mansions, Bedford Street, London NW . . . NW . . . either 3 or 5, she could never remember. Those England addresses were so long! Rose Mansions! Rose Mansions! She had expected . . . she had expected . . . well, not a *mansion*, but something different to this. This high, high building, all the markings on the wall downstairs, and you had to travel up in a dark, dark elevator! Like a hole! And even those steps! Miriam lifted her head, turned, looked around her. I mean, when you reach inside here, it not bad. It nice, she conceded. They have the place well put away! Well put away!

Furtively, she looked around the room. The little carpet well nice, the bookcase in the corner well neat, the pictures on the wall, well . . . not my choice, these kind of mix-up colors that you don't even know what you looking at, but is all right. Miriam's eyes moved to the records stacked in the corner, the music set on the side by the television. Everything well put away! Is to be expected. Both of them know from time how to take care of a place. They didn't grow up anyhow, if even self we was poor. Her eyes traveled around the room. She looked down at the corners. The place clean. The place well clean. Catherine could work. I know that. And Martin never had nobody servanting for him. He accustom cooking and looking after himself. He spend enough time looking after the house and seeing after Catherine while I go to work! So they all right. They could see after theyself from time!

But . . . Miriam looked around the room again, sucked her teeth softly, leaned her head back against the cushion. So this England is place to live too, then? Only coop up, coop up inside a house all the time? Miriam sucked her teeth again, too loudly this time.

"You all right, Mammie?" Catherine asked from the doorway, unbuttoning her jeans at the waist to ease the pressure.

"Yes," Miriam answered in an almost questioning tone, a resigned sort of tone that infuriated Catherine. "Yes, I all right, yes."

"Well Mammie, how you doing *kabusé, kabusé* so? As if you seeing trouble?" Miriam sniffed, held on to the arms of the chair and drew herself to a more upright position. "Why you sit down there in the chair looking poor-me-one, poor-me-one so? Lively up yourself, non!"

"Madam Catherine, if you don't want me to sit down in you chair, just tell me, yes. I not beggin nobody for a cup of water, non! I have me house, yes. I didn't ask allyou to come up here. So I could pack me things and go whenever allyou ready! All I will ask you is to drop me on the airport please. And even self you don't want to do that, I sure I could find me way. I not beggin nobody for a drop of water, non! I could go back home in me house this evening self, self!"

Martin pushed past his sister, walked towards his mother, laughing. "So who is allyou now?" he asked. "Who you cursing in smart there?" He sat on the arm of the chair, hugged her, leaned his head against hers.

"You smell of onion, boy! Don't try to mamaguy me at all! Move away from me!"

"Come on, Mums. Don't take things so hard." He put his other arm around her. Catherine grumbled something and moved back into the kitchen.

"I want to go home, yes," said Miriam. "Youall just drop me on the airport let me find me way, please. I don't want to come in people place come and give them trouble!"

"Mum, why you acting as if you with strangers? How you mean in *people* place come and give them trouble? Who is this *people?*"

"I don't have time bandy words with you and you sister, non! I . . ."

"My sister? You daughter, yes! Come on, Mums!"

He shook her gently. "Is just a short holiday. Relax and enjoy yourself. You're so tense up! Is only because Catherine wants to see you happy. You just sit there looking so sad, hardly eating . . . How you think we feel?"

"I not trying to make youall unhappy, so let me go where I happy. I don't like this place. It cold, cold; you can't move; if it little bit bright, which is hardly, and I want to take a walk outside, I have to say where I going, as if me is some little child; I have to ring doorbell to annoy people for them to let me in again . . . How people could live like that? In a house, in a house all day long?"

"Mums, that's the way it is here. And it's more difficult because we have to be running around, getting Carl to school and to the baby-sitter; we couldn't take our holidays same time, so I have to be rushing off to work sometimes; it's different! But it's just a short holiday! Enjoy yourself! We want to see you feeling happy! And look, you even have a chance to meet your grandson for the first time!"

"That self is another thing. Perhaps you should have send that child home for me since after the mother dead. The two of you letting him do exactly what he want. The child talking to you just as he want, saying what he feel? No. Is not so. Is so England children is, then? No wonder it have so much bad thing happening all over the place!"

Martin removed his arms. Linked his fingers, unlinked them and leaned towards the small table to pick up the remote control for the television.

"You not watching that, non?"

"What?" His mother's eyes followed the direction of his glance. "No. No. I not watching no television!"

Martin pressed a button on the control. The image faded. "Carl's all right, Mum. He's doing pretty well at school and . . . I encourage him to express his ideas." He leaned forward again, put down the control, sat looking at the photograph of his son on the side table. Carl was holding a ball, looking straight into the camera, his tongue out. That had been taken last summer, up on Hampstead Heath. Carl was wearing a T-shirt and shorts. Martin's long face was serious, thoughtful, as he watched his son's laughing face. He turned his eyes towards his mother's face. "Carl's a fine child, Mums."

"Papa, take care of allyou children as allyou want, you hear. Is your responsibility. I just want to go where I living!"

"You only have two more weeks, Mum."

"If you could organize it for me to leave before, I will be very grateful."

Martin hunched his shoulders. Cracked his fingers. "Okay," he said. "Okay, Mum. Whatever you want." He sat there a while longer, then stood up and moved back towards the kitchen.

I know he feeling bad, but I just don't like this place! Not me and England at all! After a while, Miriam pushed herself up from the chair and walked slowly out to the kitchen.

"We're almost finished," Martin said.

"Nothing I could do?" Miriam asked.

Catherine turned from taking something off a shelf. Picked up the jug of juice. "Just put this juice on the table for me, Mammie. And if you want, while I setting the table, you could take out those clothes in the washing machine and hang them up in the bathroom."

"All right."

It had started from the time she reached the airport here, really. Before that, Miriam had been excited about the visit. It was only when she reached Heathrow that she started feeling perhaps she should have stayed at home.

Walking up in that line and waiting to go to one of those customs officers. Was customs, non? Customs, or immigration, or something. One of them. Just standing in that line she had remembered school, all those donkey years ago. Standing in line for the ruler from Teacher Alfred. And that man was a beater! She remembered a day when she didn't know all of her poem. She could even remember the book! Royal Readers, Book . . . book . . . She couldn't remember which number Royal Readers, but it was Royal Readers, anyway. And the lesson was

> *Lives of great men*
> *All remind us*
> *We can make our lives sublime*
> *And departing leave behind us*
> *Footprints on the sands of time*
>
> *Footprints that . . .*

And that's the part that she had forgotten. Standing in line at Heathrow airport, Miriam realized that she *still* couldn't remember it.

Standing taking clothes out of the washing machine, she didn't remember it still. Miriam laughed at herself, out loud. Said, "Well yes, wi!" Catherine and Martin exchanged glances.

The man at the airport desk had asked a lot of questions. And Miriam had started to feel guilty. She didn't know why, because she didn't have anything to hide. But she had felt really guilty. It was as if he thought she was lying about something.

"You say your daughter and son invited you here on this holiday?"

Miriam had cleared her throat, put her hand to her mouth, said, "Sorry!" Inclined her head slightly. "Yes, sir."

"And this here; this is the address you're going to?"

"Yes, sir!"

"What does your daughter do?"

"She's a teacher, sir."

"Your daughter is a teacher in this country?"

He had looked up at her then, lifting his eyebrows questioningly.

So what the hell? You think I can't have a teacher daughter here? "Yes, sir."

He kept her waiting while he looked through her passport again. There was nothing to see. She had only traveled to Trinidad on it before. Many times. To sell things in the market there. And to Barbados once. He seemed to examine each stamp. Then he picked up her ticket. Examined that, too.

"Will your daughter be here at the airport to meet you?"

"Yes, sir."

"You'll be here for three weeks?"

Well look at the flicking ticket, non! "Yes, sir."

Finally, he had looked up at her and his eyes seemed to say, "Well, I guess I'll let you go through, even though I'm sure you're lying." His lips didn't say anything more. He stamped her passport.

By the time Miriam had got through customs and walked out to find Catherine, Martin and Carl, Martin's six-year-old son, waiting for her, she was near to tears. Something that hadn't happened for a long time. Her shoulders were hunched and she was feeling as small as Cousin Milton's little Maria back home, Maria who usually stayed with her in Peggy's Whim.

She had felt strange with her children and grandson from the beginning. She found that she just couldn't laugh and talk with them as usual. Especially when Carl said, "*You're* my nan?" And she started off wondering why he had said it like that.

And then she found that Carl wasn't like a child at all. He asked big people questions, talked all the time, and Catherine and Martin just wouldn't shut him up. That must be England style. They didn't grow like that at all.

And Miriam's voice began to sound strange in her own ears, especially when Carl talked to her in that funny accent of his. It made him sound even more like big people.

Two more weeks away! The second of May. Miriam wondered if Martin would try to get the date changed. She wouldn't say it again, but she hoped that he would remember.

It rained on April the twenty-seventh. They traveled by the underground train. Took a taxi to the station, hurried out in the rain, and went with the two suitcases down the escalator to take the Northern line to King's Cross. Then they changed to the Piccadilly line, which went all the way out to Heathrow airport.

At the BWIA airline counter, Miriam began to brighten up. She smiled often. Even seemed to be holding herself back from exploding with laughter. She touched Carl on the head and said "Young Mister Carl, eh!"

"You must come again, Nan," Carl said.

"All right, son." Miriam laughed, glanced at Catherine.

"You know you're only saying that," said Catherine, leaning across and straightening her mother's collar. "You didn't like it at all."

"Well," Miriam shrugged, still smiling, "all place have their people."

"Yes, Madam Diplomat," said Martin.

Miriam laughed again, leaning back in the way that they remembered. Martin and Catherine looked at each other and shook their heads. Catherine's smile was disbelieving. "So Mammie you just start to enjoy yourself, then?" she marveled.

"Child, leave me alone, non. Is home I going, yes." Miriam touched her daughter's face. "Don't mind. Don't mind that!"

"Well I never!" said Catherine.

They sat in the airport cafeteria and drank orange juice. "This orange juice could have do with a little touch of something stronger in it!" laughed Miriam.

"But," she added with a laugh as they both looked up at her, "is all right; is all right; I will make do."

Catherine folded her lips and said nothing. Martin laughed. "The lady start to enjoy sheself when she going, yes! Yes. Mammie! Ye-e-s! You not joking!"

Miriam leaned back and smiled at her grandson.

"You're nice, Nan," said Carl, looking at her critically. "When will you be back?"

"Son, I don't know, non. Is you to come to visit me now!"

"Yes!" said Carl enthusiastically. "Yes, Nan." Carl looked from his father to his aunt.

"Don't look at me," said Catherine. "That is you and your father's business."

"Dad?"

"Yes. We'll have to plan it. We're overdue for a visit."

"Well that is all you'll hear now until the date is set." Catherine drained her orange juice, leaned across and handed a tissue to Carl. "Wipe your mouth, Carl."

The three were quiet as they watched Miriam walk through to emigration. She turned and waved, her round face smiling broadly, the light brown hat that she liked to wear perched almost jauntily on her head, her body looking smaller than when she had first arrived, but her face shining with health and happiness. Martin looked down at his sister. Back at his mother. "Is now I could see how much you two look alike," he said. "Short same way. Same round face. And then both of you stubborn same way."

Catherine chuckled. "She not joking in truth, you know."

"Your mother looking well young, you know, girl."

They waved again. Miriam disappeared around the corner. Carl shouted, "See you in Grenada, nan!"

They stood for a while looking at the wall around which Miriam had disappeared. "Never me again," said Catherine, as they turned away. "Never me again."

"Never me again," said Miriam to Cousin Milton the next morning. They were sitting under the tamarind tree on the hill just near to her house. "You see that little devil?" she asked in a lower voice, looking down the hill towards a boy of about six who was moving backwards, staring at them, finger in his mouth. "Is me tambran he coming after, you know. See he see us here, he backing back now. But is me tambran he was coming after."

Cousin Milton glanced at the retreating youngster, turned his attention back to Miriam. "But girl, how you mean you don't like England, dey? So England is place not to like, then?"

"I don't care what you say!"

"All round you, you seeing England pounds putting up house; all who stay in England for thirty years and more coming back put up house to dead in luxury, you self saying you don't like England? How you mean? Girl, don't talk this thing hard make people laugh at you at all! Keep that to yourself!"

Miriam laughed. "You all right yes, Cousin Milton. Anyway, that is one episode that over! Dead and bury. Not me and England, non. Never me again! Give me me place where I could sit down outside and see people, do what I want. Not me at all. All place have their people! Never me again!"

Milton sighed. Opened his mouth and seemed about to say something. Lapsed into thoughtful silence.

"Never!" pronounced Miriam.

NIGHT THOUGHTS

She was reading of larks singing and country girls dancing in summery English meadows. The scent of cut hay brushed past their muslin dresses and one of the girls paused to pick a spray of pink roses and lay it along her flushed cheek. In the dairy a woman churned cool, white milk into butter, another brought an apronful of apples, glowing a boisterous red, into the farm kitchen. The men left the harvest in the late summer evening and walked to the farm house to drink long glasses of cider.

All the wars that lay behind them in history had been transformed into heroic legends. The clash of battles transmuted into crests, woven into tapestries which hung far away in grand manors and turreted castles. Best of all, the age of the miserable realist novel had not yet begun. Ah, the softness and fragrance of those long gone English summers weaving their spell in books propped open by this child in a cold, Canadian winter evening, or that boy, retreating from the harsh Bombay glare to a cool corner of the verandah, and that girl on a Caribbean island, slowing her reading to savor more fully the turn of the churn which pulls up smooth, yellow butter from the milk.

And so it was that somewhere else became more real, more vivid than the jasmine blooming just outside her own window and happiness seemed to be an English summer day always beyond her grasp. For the Indian boy, who years later became a doctor and wore fine woollen suits and settled his family in Sudbury or Dorking, on that shaded verandah he had experienced a sweet happiness which he could never recapture in the neat English gardens and rows of grey houses with chimney pots thrusting into the starless nights.

For the girl on the Caribbean island, the steps into womanhood went by so quickly and always she was plagued by a sense of, this is not how it's supposed to

125

be. She did not know either just how it was supposed to be but she stopped reading gentle books and entered the modern world of realism, of books that were like films that were like newspapers that were like paintings, so much of it hard edges and sharp, brutish colors. The realism moved to her own streets as the bars and grilles went up over the faces of the houses shutting out each other, shutting in the hard won material possessions, shutting out the stars, the full moon which shines now more clearly from the pages of a book picked up by a man, settled comfortably in his house in Sudbury or Dorking as the cold March winds whip through the streets. He swims in the warm Caribbean sea, at night he meets the woman and walks close beside her under a clear, starry sky and he knows that he can be truly happy with such a woman, in such a place.

The Caribbean woman sat in her room and stretched her arms. Tomorrow, another day in the office, but tonight she saw that the orchids on her verandah had bloomed. She brought them indoors and placed them on a round table covered with a fine, linen tablecloth which someone's aunt had embroidered. She never did like orchids, they reminded her of her father's funeral. A large bouquet of them, incredibly intricate patterns with strange colors, browns, mauves, yellows and here and there an outrageous bright pink against the dark box, slipping now into dark earth. The lowering into the earth was an illusion. The coffin with its crown of orchids slid noiselessly into a secret place to be consumed by the crematorium fire. A man lived then was silent, covered with strange blooms as he moved into another world.

In Dorking or Sudbury, the Indian doctor hung his fine woollen suit carefully in his bedroom closet and sank wearily into bed. He had bathed with his usual meticulous attention to detail, still the smell of the hospital hung over him. He thought about his patients, working class English women who disliked him. He would have to tell this one that she must have a hysterectomy, that one that she had cancer of the cervix. Rows of perished reproductive organs waited for him each day in the ward as cheerful nurses swished curtains around and took temperatures with no regard for the collapse of tubes and wasted ovaries which lay hidden, secret inside the women until he would reveal them. Charted and enemaed they lay ready for his probing knife. They were all so pale. He hated that first incision when the blood welled up dark against the skin. He couldn't rid himself of the idea that each woman he touched grew older at that exact moment. His colleagues rated him a fine surgeon, he was saving lives. He curled his arm around his pillow and moved his face away from the window where the streetlight cast a sickly yellow glow against the net curtains. He couldn't sleep. He pictured the children at home who would be happy to have Ma back from the hospital making tea, putting fish fingers and chips on plates and drawing the curtains against the dark. Waiting for Dad to come home from the factory, they would watch telly dimly aware of her clearing the plates, scarping globs of ketchup into the sink. He saw her putting the children to bed and climbing into her own bed, beside Dad, her scar covered with a Marks and Spencers nightie.

He couldn't sleep. His youth had hurried along hospital corridors and shut itself away in libraries. Grey streaked his thick black hair and his body felt soft, flabby. His English Indian children slept in their room where cool colors climbed the wallpaper, interrupted here and there with posters of rock stars who looked savagely down at the sleeping children. His mother was coming to live with them soon. She was too old to live alone in Bombay. Would he get to know her now, he wondered. In his childhood she was always busy, supervising maids or organizing her work for the many charities she supported. In the evenings she emerged on the verandah briefly, soft and scented, ready to greet his father. He hadn't known them at all.

It seemed to him now that he had always hurried past the people who he might have known. His patients only knew him by the generic name, Doctor, and he only knew them by their diagnoses. He shifted his position and gazed at his wife sleeping curled away from him right at the edge of the bed. Did she feel the need to protect her own ovaries and tubes from him? He must be crazy to be thinking like this. He stared at the flowers on the wallpaper. They reminded him of something, yes, yes the garden in Bombay, clumps of pink flowers by the wall. Now what was their name? He couldn't remember, or perhaps he had never known. What the hell did it matter. He didn't know the name. Perhaps his mother would know. His mother was coming and she was a stranger to him.

As the Caribbean woman turned the pages of her book, he had an image of her. A woman, somewhere far away, in a room with a table covered with a linen cloth. The image was somehow consoling. He loosened his grip on the pillow and fell asleep.

After her father's funeral, she thought about happiness, what makes it, where does it spring from, why does it seem to be another place thing, like the people always setting off from her island, off to somewhere else where that happiness thing can be found. It was not something she could discuss, the word had become so unfashionable, a calendar word found now only in the racks of cards for Happy Birthday, Happy New Year. Once she fell in love and she thought that that was happiness, standing on the street watching him walk up towards her and everything was wonderfully sharp and clear and she had never seen that street before even though she went there every day, never seen the women sitting on the pavement with their baskets overflowing with fruits and vegetables, the plenty of it, the round fat richness of it. But he was a very intelligent man, he lived in America where people knew such things and he said that there was no such thing as love. It was a bourgeois fantasy and women who clung to such fantasies would be forever unhappy.

She resolutely put away the other place happiness and looked carefully at the world around her. The beauty, the poverty, the betrayals, they bloomed into strange cactus shapes. She couldn't find space to put them all and took to arranging them on paper in piles on her desk. Friends went to other countries, children grew up. Days took on an ordered quiet as age crept in through the window. Until she picked up the book. It had a faintly familiar feel to it. Ah yes, larks singing, girls in muslin dresses. The lure of the smooth, beautiful prose pictures flowed around her evening chair, the lamp tipped slightly to shed light on the small print. But gradually pictures of her own life were swimming up to interrupt her concentration.

Flashes of her childhood, young motherhood, perfection of the small ones, this one running, that one sleeping against her, small moist mouth slightly open leaving a fragrant trail of baby breath against her skin. This passionately held cause, the ousted lover, they paraded insistently through the pages. Suddenly it seemed to her that it was all real, beautiful, and the other place happiness finally did not exist.

In her home, the Caribbean woman shut the book with a small, impatient gesture, shutting out the woman churning butter, the girls in their muslin dresses, the farmers drinking cider. She could hear tree frogs singing outside in the mango tree, she could see the moon full above the mountains and a faint breeze brought the scent of jasmine in through the window. She opened the door, called in the dog and locked up the house for the night. The purple orchid trembled slightly from her bustling in the room. The door opening to admit the dog, the light switched off, the radio silenced. She went upstairs to bed. The orchid glowed in the room below.

AVENUES

WHEN I UNDERSTOOD THE FUTURE and I sired a young child in it, the little boy that I had been was born again, slingshotting my fellow man, keeping an
eye on the carambola fruit[1] of the lady next door, giving and taking dreams and
sexual curiosity, and landing my private airplane on a naked tree branch again.
Heaven was low and I asked questions of the angels. My answers were always
delayed. When the angels brought them to me with Our Lord's authorization,
they no longer mattered to me, since I had a bunch of new questions. The cheru-
bim, who were quite solicitous, returned to Paradise carrying my doubts. One day
I confused them with swallows and I hit one of them, right in the head. He said
some harsh words about the Apocalypse to me. I shook in my boots and promised
to reform myself by reading the Bible more. When he turned his back, I opened
up my little pornographic magazine.

The years went by slowly. When I came to my senses, there were enormous bags
of adolescent doubts to carry. The little angels began to demand taxes, in renun-
ciations. I paid honestly, however, I didn't understand spiritual oaths. Adults, who
surrounded me with their puffy eyes and their labored breathing, couldn't help
me with the interminable calculations.

I kept on thinking about the carambola fruits, at the same time worried about
the terrible stories passed off by the celestial agents, when a black rooster on a
corner said to me, "Come here!"

Translated by Carolyn Richardson Durham.

1. The carambola is a red fruit that is native to the tropics. In this case it is a symbol of sexual desire,
similar to the apple in the Garden of Eden.

Frightened, I went. After all he was a guy tossing in pain on the curb. I asked as I approached, "What happened?"

With his legs tied up with black and red tape, his neck broken, the bird hardly responded.

"Carry me over there," pointing to the crossroads of the two large avenues of my life, with a difficult movement with one broken wing.

I waited for more words. Nothing. His silence had a very profound effect. I covered my stammering with a yellow and green smile.[2]

I looked all around. Nobody was going by. It was twelve o'clock noon on the dot. The shout of a victim of my emotional traffic was not permitted to be heard in that rush hour. But everything was deserted. I didn't feel so ill at ease. The solitude is a breeze that comes along, shedding light.

I looked more closely at the chicken coop in an attempt to choose the manner of picking him up without making his deplorable state worse. I perceived two round, very bright tears that slowly ran down to his beak and then rolled down and fell on the ground, hopping, bound for the requested place, where they evaporated. I thought about my little marbles, clear as crystal. This memory filled me with tenderness. It was easier to take the necessary care to carry the sick one by the neck. He kept the warmth of life strong. I walked lightly up to the indicated spot. I placed him gently in the center where the avenues crossed each other.[3]

There, on the asphalt, he agonized, he agonized, he agonized . . . Until candles emerged around us, covering the entire extension of the two roads.

Among the candles, the cadavers of angels were rotting, and daisies were sprouting on them. The rooster sang long and strong and was getting up. In his pains, he had acquired red, blue, and yellow resplendences. After singing for the third time, he opened his wings wide, moving them with exuberance, in a calm and harmonious flight, to the sound of a music box.

I was brought to this place of peace, safely on his legs, free of angels and Our Lords. It is my own heaven that I didn't know about for so long.

---

2. "A yellow and green smile" refers to the colors of the Brazilian flag.

3. The custom of placing a black rooster at a crossroads is part of the African-Brazilian religious tradition. This sacrificial offering to the Orisha is made in order to seek positive energy and to assist one in making decisions.

SAMUEL R. DELANY

TAPESTRY

They noticed that virginity was needed,
To trap the unicorn in every case,
But not that, of those virgins who succeeded,
A high percentage had an ugly face.
—Auden, *The Quest*

IMAGINE ONE LOOSE thread pulled violently—huntsmen, virgins, hounds, hedge sparrows, hawks, and that leering Varlet will all snarl, distort, mangle, and tear apart. The bone of the tapestry is coarse linen, lined and backed with something resembling canvas. And all the faces and hands of all the hundred figures throughout the seven tapestries are woven in a distorted way. Look. Examine the hand of that man with his sleeve fallen halfway down his forearm. What is it? Thread, silk, nothing living, only pale grey and white stitching.

The panel there is incomplete. Note the torn edges. How much smaller it is! But it was once as big as the others. Extrapolate the threads, pull them together, and watch the Virgin woven into her virginity again. The Unicorn is white, the only animal displayed with his sex recognizable, whereas hounds, foxes, and the tight-crotched and doubleted hunters all seem to be placed in conveniently decent positions—or castrated. Extend the torn cloth, continue the intertwining of flower and vine that makes the background. Who has captured whom? Has the pale, imprisoned girl seduced this god-horse, or has—by all the laws of logic— the horse seduced her? The rest of the tapestry is gone. We do not know. Europa and the white bull—the godhead metamorphosed into a virile animal, whose virility is thread and silk and brocade. The witch who left us instructions on how to catch Unicorns failed to mention whether the Virgin was good for more than one throw.

There is blood in every tapestry but the first.

A wild boar is goring a hound. The Unicorn is pierced through the side in his corral, and the Virgin . . . is no longer a Virgin. The leering Varlet from the castle is slain in a hunting accident.

Notice that there is no water in any of the tapestries except through the artificial means of a fountain. No rivulet, no seascape in the distance, no dew or rain in any scene. And the fountain is not on a panel which shows blood, signifying that this is not a Christian allegory. Or is, at any rate, only supposed to look like one to the uninitiate. Blood as a Christian symbol must always be accompanied by water: Christ's pierced side, and the rains that followed; the wine transubstantiated into blood at the Last Supper is only given its power through the water with which Christ washed the feet of the disciples. No, the women who designed these tapestries wove into them something other than religious mysteries, but, to avoid heresy, gave it a seeming religious cast by the Unicorn with the pierced side: the Christ crucified. Without the sea, the order of rivers, the royalty of waves, there is no true religious dignity. The Jordan, the Ganges, the Euphrates, or the Styx, the river through the Vale of Tempe, or the Boreal streams around Ultima Thule: and there is a lake at Nemi.

There is no hint of the sea here, and so something else is intended. Look at the fragmentary tapestry again. What was woven into the missing part? Take time and wind it in gold, red, and turquoise filaments. Wind those into woods' flowers, make elders and beech trees, oaks and yews with purplish bark. This fragment purportedly showed the Virgin luring the Unicorn to the trap. How? Take time, take twenty minutes, and weave it into a tapestry. Oh, she must have stood at least that long in the forest, waiting, uncomfortably, her corset too tight and the brocade of her paneled skirt caught with bits of leaves. She bites at a hangnail on her thumb, starts as a jay or a lapwing utters its condensed shriek. The forest floor beneath the embroidered flowers is damp and moistens her thin soles. She has sweated in the heavy dress, even though the air is cool, and she fears her underarms will smell through her perfume. Half-heartedly she looks for mint to chew but cannot find it in the profusion of weeds and undergrowth.

A sound. She whirls her head and stops it, jaw-jarring hard, transfixing the darkness beyond the trees; and her hair shakes in its coiffure beneath the veil of her conical cap. The leaves shiver in front of her, and the fear she feels twists in her stomach, a squirming knot of little animals she'd never known nested there. Her train ruffles, and the breeze ruffling it moves leaves from a stretch of dirty white: the shoulder of the beast. He'd been sleeping all afternoon in a damp bower where the leaves had mostly fallen off the trees, and he had rubbed the grass down to a frizzle with his thrashing-around nights. The Unicorn has not bathed in four months, and issues an unpleasant, horsey smell. Rising, he pokes his head into the thicket, the horn cleaving blossoms and quivering. The Virgin sees immediately that its spirals are not really regular at all. Obviously he has not taken care of it because it is tarnished and chipped. His eyes are large, brown, and the whites, which show just at the back and front of the almond-shaped aperture of his eye sockets are bloodshot. Mucus has strung down from them, as on a lap dog who has not had its eyes washed with boric acid. The black labia of his nostrils expand.

The Virgin is disgusted.

So is the Unicorn: although he finds the smell of her sweating flesh attractive, the medicinal pungency of alcohol and ambergris, the rancid hair oil, sweetened with dead flowers, revolt him. But he is still sleepy, and comes nearer. His hooves are muddy, she notes. Men who don't wash their feet, at least before getting into bed, have always annoyed her—as a concept; she *is* a virgin and only knows about such things through reading. His horn should be polished. She takes a step nearer and stops when he snorts; snot flies in globules and strings. Then he winks a nostril at her and whinnies. The Virgin is fascinated by his vulgarity. Her stomach feels a little weak—but she is fascinated. Staring at the mess on his nose, she is about to abandon the whole silly thing and make her way back to the castle, when suddenly the animal bends his head and wipes it off on the grass, leaving the blades darker, shiny, broken. Well, it's off his face. As he raises his head, the Virgin takes one more step.

The Unicorn is encouraged and leaps forward.

The Virgin shrieks, tries to run backward, trips over the end of her train, and sprawls, spread-eagled, the wind knocked out of her; her cap has come off; she can feel her hairdo gone loose; and the silly Unicorn is leering down at her with the oddest grin she can possibly picture on the teeth of a horse. Gingerly she tries to roll over but the beast is standing on her dress. She glances through his forelegs and sees that his stomach is almost hairless, pinkskinned like the belly of a rat, incredibly dirty. The whole area of his sex is matted and muddy and gives the impression of something profoundly useless. The only way it could have possibly gotten in that condition, she thinks, is from masturbating on a muddy log.

He neighs at her, and her face is splattered with drops of saliva. Goddamn it, she thinks. Violently she rolls aside—the dress rips beneath his muddy hoof. Then she screams, because the Unicorn has bent down and flicked her back to her back with his horn, ripping her bodice and opening a cut from an inch over her nipple to above her collar bone, tearing a shoulder ligament. It hurts like hell. "You cut that out," she cries. Tears whirl into her eyes, making them burn. There's blood on her fingers.

Again she pulls; the dress rips more, but the Unicorn jumps back, perhaps afraid of the blood. The Virgin manages to get to her feet, holding her skirt up with one hand and her bodice closed with the other. The Unicorn backs away, walks in a circle (his rectum is matted with dung halfway down his thighs, and his tail is burred with nettles and wood-lice), paws the ground. Again he faces her, coming toward her with watered thighs and the silver of his hooves visible in flakes through dried mud. The green boughs dip and whisper oppressively, and the sun suddenly scatters gold coins over his back that slip off, one by one, as he walks forward. She walks backward, terrified and bleeding.

Her back comes up against bark.

With rubies in his eyes he brings his head toward her, and the flies crawling in his ear simmer like green glass in the stained marble trumpet. His nose, wet velvet, pushes her neck, and he moves his shoulder and foreleg against her, and her hand is on the rough pelt, shivering in the decision whether to push him away, or to press him closer as her father has instructed. He whispers to her in a voice like sand ground into crumpled leaves. Among hoarse gasps and neighings, she hears: "You fool! You fool! I'm only a myth in Unicorn's clothing, but I'll rip you to bloody pieces! . . ." Pressure hardens into a bent knee on her belly. Protests get all snarled up with what is in her throat. She breaks away, trips, regains her footing, flees. . . .

Something turns forest to cathedral in her head. As she stumbles, the labyrinth of trees becomes halls, galleries, carved stone, a haphazard cloister of apsways and narthex posts in which is suddenly raised the image of a crucifixion of someone not her. Vines petrify before her into classical friezes. And his feet on the sod sound like metal balls flung at granite. Like mad hags and tree wraiths, leaves whip her on, whip her shoulder where the dress is torn; twigs like spread fingers slap her forehead and catch her hair as she ducks beneath a low limb, which is for her the buttress flying by the choir columns of oak. He is close to her, a rhythm of hooves syncopated with limb snappings, skittering rocks, and the battering of leaves on her forelegs. She will run, and the pain builds burning in her chest, and she will canter, while terror solidifies into rotten logs in the path, flailing black branches, and the raking cries of seven rooks, circling; and she will. . . .

RENÉ DEPESTRE

ROSENA ON THE MOUNTAIN

How beautiful are the feet of the messenger on the mountain
when he brings good tidings.

—Isaiah

1

That year I wanted to become a saint. My vocation was welling up like water in a cistern. Leaving school one afternoon in November, I went through the gates of Saint Martial's School and Seminary, which was run by the Fathers of the Holy Spirit. I asked to see Father James Mulligan. They told me to wait in the parlor because the priest had not yet finished his classes that day. The Irish missionary had acquired the reputation of a man of great wisdom and learning. He was teaching philosophy at the high school on the Street of Miracles.

He welcomed me cordially and invited me to follow him into his chambers. The room had the good smell of lavender and fresh linen. The walls were covered with bookshelves. Stacks of books also towered on his night table and even on his prie-dieu [kneeling bench]. On the priest's desk fresh roses from that morning adorned an orderly mess of notebooks and folders. The sunlit branches of a tree brought the lyrical songs of birds to the window. This was not exactly the way I had pictured the cell of a saint, but the studious comfort and cleanliness of the room impressed me.

Translated by Carrol F. Coates.

The minute I sat down, I began to tell him the reasons for my visit. I explained why I was making my request to a religious order rather than to the secular clergy. I felt destined to rise at two o'clock each morning of my life and to utter only three words a week. My ideal would have been the Trappists, but there was no Trappist monastery in our country. If the world is a vale of tears, Haiti is the best watered corner on the globe. Since I was born Haitian, sainthood seemed to me to be the only way to attract Christ's attention to a planet without tenderness or consolation.

For more than an hour, I developed these ideas with a vehemence that left my jaws aching. Father Mulligan found it admirable to respond to an inner call resounding so forcefully. He shared my opinion that the worst of misfortunes in the Americas was to be born in Haiti. He could understand why I envisioned the extreme alternative of suffering and renouncement. He added that the seditious fires burning within had not tarnished the child's candor in my features. In his eyes, my face stood out boldly from the banality of the young men in that year's philosophy class. He was happy that he could not sense in me any vendor of imported merchandise, senator or minister of state. I was a young man in a state of revolt, called to the great adventure of the priesthood. God had planted me in this ungrateful and sterile terrain for his own purposes. As he spoke, the wrinkles at the corners of his Irish eyes took on an expression of joy.

"My son, accept the mystery and the violence of this call. Do not rush the flow of the sap. Sainthood is a tree biding its time in the Lord's eternal plan. Beware impatience! It is an arrow in Satan's bow."

Then he questioned me about my parents and my background in Port-au-Prince.

I was the eldest of a family with seven children. Years ago, following my father's premature death, we had been left penniless. My mother tried ten other jobs and then became a seamstress. She worked at her Singer sewing machine day and night to keep a roof over our heads, feed us, clothe us, and send us to school.

In the poor section of Tête-Boeuf, our house had two rooms but no electricity or running water. Our toilet was a ditch over which there was a kind of little shack covered with haphazard planks. It was located in the courtyard with absolutely no privacy. When the ditch was full, we called the *bayakou*. These men worked up to their waists shoveling fecal matter out of the ditch. Those nights, nobody in Tête-Boeuf could close an eye. Everyone in the area waited for dawn and the departure of the truck that would take away the odiferous load. We imagined the workers with vulture wings or jackal maws. When we discovered that they were really human beings, we hurled stones, empty bottles, and epithets at them.

I ought to have become a tailor's or cobbler's apprentice long before, but my mother would not hear of this. She wanted me to get a high school diploma and go to medical school. Her fondest dream was to see me in a doctor's white smock, working in the posh sections of Port-au-Prince. In order to see it come true, she said that she would be capable of prostituting herself with the merchants along the waterfront when her sewing machine was ready for the junkyard. She repeated this with a kind of icy rage in her voice, even when there was company. It did not lower her in people's estimation since, in our area, hunger eventually drove most women to sell their bodies.

I confided to Father Mulligan that during the slow season, when my mother could find nothing to sew, she strung the family budget together by telling fortunes for masons, tinsmiths, servants, boilermakers, prostitutes, thieves, and other neighbors in Tête-Boeuf. They would come to consult her all day long. She would read the future in out-of-work hands. Sometimes she would pretend to be mounted by Vodun spirits. Her face would become long, with hardened features, and she would give advice and encouragement in a falsetto tone to the customers who listened to her in this trance-like state. As soon as they left, she broke into raucous laughter in front of us, without disguising the tears that betrayed her extreme dignity.

Each year she sent her little ones off in the *taptap* toward Croix-des-Bouquets. At a fork in the road, the bus would stop and we would cover some ten kilometers on foot to Dorelia Dantor's farm. During the two or three days that we spent with this well-known mambo, each of us received a magic bath prepared with orange leaves, holy water, jasmine flowers, barley water, rum, and powdered almonds. Dorelia would also bathe us in a mixture with garlic, chives, thyme, cassava flour, rum, salty coffee, and *bwakaka* [a Haitian tree]. She had us swallow herb teas and concoctions of various aromatic plants or she would give us a large glass of castor oil that had been boiled with soap shavings. In order to make our blood too bitter for sorcerers, she fed us cockroaches fried in castor oil, spiced with garlic and nutmeg. These treatments would scare bad luck, the evil eye, and supernatural maladies out of our bodies like rabbits. On occasion, two men would grab one of us by our legs and swing us head down for a minute over a ritual fire. At that moment, the drums beat along with the chants of the *ounsi* [postulants] and the participants invoked Gede-Nibo, General Grand-Bois, Captain Maloulou, and Boumba-Lord-of-Cemeteries. These spirits were all as familiar to us as the ants and rats at home in Tête-Boeuf. The ceremony in their honor would last all night. Dressed in red, ears and nostrils stuffed with cotton, and wearing a three-horned hat of tin or a Chinese hat, Dorelia would officiate. One evening, she threw all her clothes to the devil and offered her nude body to the erect flames. Once the mystical union had been consummated, there was not a single trace of a burn on her smooth flesh.

This last account led Father Mulligan to question me about my sexual experience. Had I already committed the sin of the flesh? I told him everything I knew. I came from a background where people were generally not ashamed of their private parts nor of their ability to enjoy them to the fullest. We talked about them and used them freely. Boys and girls were proud of their penis or vagina when they discovered these organs as a source of pleasure that brought them a sense of well-being and health. Everybody quickly discovered the meaning of menstruation, rounded buttocks, breasts, and the swaying of girls' backs and hips. The same was true of the penis, testicles, erection, ejaculation, and sperm for the boys. Far from provoking guilt, this discovery brought a joyful self-confidence to both sexes. The initiation to physical relationships came about in the most natural manner through chance encounters and animated sessions of petting in the shadows of porches.

The naked truth is that, strange as it may seem, I had never yet known a woman, not in the full sense of the expression. I knew everything that you can know about the act of love. I had spied on couples making love. This spectacle had seemed quite healthy and had a beauty about it that took my breath away every time. I had tried fornicating, alone or in a group, without fear or disgust but with a kind of spontaneous delight. Like most of my friends, I had massaged my penis with cocoa butter in the hope of increasing its diameter and length. Once or twice, when I was in the country, I had tried fucking with a goat or a heifer but without much enthusiasm. In spite of these precocious experiences, I had never yet had the experience of disappearing ecstatically into a girl's vagina. If the act of love was a sin, I claimed no virtue for not having committed it. If chastity was a virtue, I was practicing it by instinct.

According to the priest, the fact that I had been wallowing in paganism for years without spoiling my innocence was proof that my calling had been sprouting in fertile terrain. When God is going to confide a great mission to one of his children, He often works deliberately to try that individual's soul and flesh in the miasma of sin. The history of the Church teems with men forced to traverse swamp after swamp without soiling their purity. This was undoubtedly what had happened to me. From now on, however, it would be necessary to break with the pagan eccentricities of Vodun and to found my destiny on chastity.

Then we talked about the practical aspects of my vocation. I was in an advanced class at Pétion Lycée, with two more years of classical studies to finish before beginning theological studies. Was I gifted in Latin? Father Mulligan grabbed one of Seneca's works and asked me to translate a passage chosen at random. The text was laced with difficult translation problems that I could not resolve, although I was one of the best students in my class. I was extremely upset, but the priest closed the book and told me not to worry. It was no secret that the pupils in Pétion did not shine particularly in Latin and Greek. The professors of that impious establishment undoubtedly had better things to do with their time. He was prepared to help me catch up and volunteered to give me Latin lessons three times a week. In fact, he had a better proposal to make: every year he spent the hot season in a retreat that the Fathers of the Holy Spirit maintained in the mountains. I could simply go with him next summer. My Latin would improve decisively and I could participate in his priestly exercises.

When I was out in the street once more, I could tell that my inner well was overflowing. *Vocatus! Vocatus!* With the Latin word, my calling resounded with fresh emotion in the Haitian night, flooding my banks, spreading its poinciana-laden branches within me.

2

One day, after lunch, all three of us were seated on the porch of a little house hidden in the lush forest, a hundred meters from Lamark Chapel. We had left Port-au-Prince a month earlier. Father Mulligan was smoking his after-dinner cigar in silence. I was helping Rosena to husk the rice in a winnowing basket.

The priest had asked the mother of one of his pupils to find a housekeeper for his vacation. The woman had sent Rosena Rozel. She was a young woman of about nineteen, half-clove, half cinnamon as far as her complexion and perfume went. She had finished her secondary schooling and, in some less stifling kingdom, her talents, beauty, and queenly bearing would have brought her a better station in life. It would have been necessary to articulate each syllable with the tongue in order to state that she was RE-SPLEN-DENT. And, once that was said, a philosophy teacher in a religious school or a future priest needed a whole string of Hail Mary's to bring his circulation back to normal.

"I was expecting someone to clean house," said Father Mulligan. "They've sent a lioness, a biological scandal! May misfortune befall those who create scandals."

The scandal was there. It was breathing the same air that we did, under the same roof day and night. It was preparing our meals, washing and ironing our linens, making our beds, serving us meals and, most of the time during the week, Rosena the scandal was the only one of the faithful kneeling in the chapel as I assisted the priest in the pre-dawn Mass. At that very moment, the tiger-eyed scandal was winnowing the evening rice, shaking her shoulders and breasts above our souls cooled only by the shade of the Lord's mystical almond trees.

"Tomorrow is market day," said the priest.

"Yes, Thursday already," said Rosena. "Who is going with me this time, Father, you or Alain?"

"Alain has his Latin homework. I'll go with you just like the last time," the priest decided imperatively.

"What if we take the mule?" suggested Rosena.

"A good idea, Rosie. We could buy a stalk of aromatic bananas."

"And maybe a kid," suggested Rosena.

"Ah, a barbecue!"

"With yams, onions, roucou sauce, cayenne pepper!" exclaimed Rosena.

The market was about an hour's trip from the foothills where the chapel was perched. I had gone with Rosena the first Thursday after our arrival. We set out right after the Mass. We followed the peasant women who were converging from all sides of the mountain to the main path toward the market. Some were on foot, others were riding bareback on donkeys with hooves covered by dew. Along the way, buntings, woodpigeons, and even couples of guinea fowls flew up with a whirring of wings and rustling of leaves. The mountains were slowly emerging from the shadow and unveiling here and there shacks from which the aroma and steam of the first coffee rose agreeably. We were progressing in silence at a steady pace. Rosena forged ahead undaunted, pulling me in her wake and paying no attention to the brambles that kept scratching her long, bare legs. Her strides communicated pure lyricism to her buttocks. Thanks to the host that I had swallowed a few minutes earlier, I associated those curves with some innocent design of God.

At the market, I admired her talent for instinctively selecting the best watermelon, the ripest avocados, the freshly laid eggs, the eggplants, tomatoes, and cucumbers that promised the most beautiful salads. I could also see that the vendor was not yet born who could induce Rosena to pay an inflated price for a hen or a quarter-stalk of fig bananas. We returned loaded like donkeys and were forced to rest and regain our breath as we proceeded up steep slopes in a luminescence as tawny as Rosena Rozel.

"Is it true that you want to become a priest?" she asked during one of our stops.

"Yes, I feel the vocation."

"What's it like when somebody feels the VO-CA-TION?"

"It's like a burst of light inside. You have a taste for humble, tender things," I answered.

"How's that?"

"You keep the spirit of childhood that most men quickly lose for the rest of their life when they become an adult. You follow God's gentle commandments night and day. You scorn the fleeting sensations of the flesh."

"My word, you already sound like a priest in the pulpit! So God forbids you to taste a woman?"

"Yes. Chastity is a commitment that you make for life," I replied.

"And why do our *lwa* make love freely when they are gods too? Dambala Wédo is married, you know. He's not a black male for nothing. Agwé Taroyo's exploits on the sea are no more notorious than his oar strokes in the flesh of Ezili Freda!"

"Our *lwa* are only concerned with terrestrial affairs. Their faith is practical. They are ambitious spirits—hard-drinking, crafty, lewd fellows. They like to eat, drink, dance, and fornicate. They forget their own souls in their revelry!"

"Has Father Mulligan stuffed your head with that nonsense? Huh? That's his affair if he wants to keep his prick in the Holy Spirit's cooler all his life! I think that our *lwa* are right to limber up their limbs when they feel like it," chided Rosena.

"Those are pagan words, Rosena!"

"Pagan! It feels so good to be pagan from head to foot! There's no evil in that. Look, you can feel the heat of paganism working on my flesh," she said as she placed my hand flat on her belly. "The soul! You can't talk about anything but that wisp of hot air! I'm not ashamed of being a woman with an oven under my dress!"

She pulled her blouse open. "Look, why should I be ashamed of these perky breasts? And my thighs!" She pulled her skirt up to her belt. "Do you think that they bring bad tidings to the hills?"

All of a sudden, everything had begun to spin: huge trees, breasts, sky, the joyful explosion of the mountain, paths, thighs, and solemn buttocks in the morning light. An impulse to slap Rosena on the mouth boiled inside as that rapacious rascal I had once tamed began rising inside my pants. I was nailed to the spot, fists clenched, head bowed, and tears rolled down my blushing cheeks.

"I'm sorry, Alain," she said. "I didn't mean to hurt you. It's stronger than I am when it hits. When I was born, somebody must have rubbed hot peppers on the soles of my feet and the hot points of my body. Forgive me."

She came closer and dried my cheeks. Little pearls of sweat were shining on her forehead and arms. She was almost pressed against me. I could smell the aroma of cinnamon and feel her hot breath. I saw my damnation taking on the color and sparkle of her eyes. She was a satanic force of seduction, and her breasts were pulsating against my throat.

"Let's make peace, little brother," she pouted tenderly. "I promise never to talk that way again. Tell me, my sweet pastor, will you make peace with Rosena?"

"Yes," I said without looking at her.

Now, she was shaking the basket and putting the husked rice onto a metal platter. That innocent chore, like everything that she did, was charged with electricity. She must have exercised her charms on him in the same way. The Thursday before, the priest had gone with her to the market. Since then, I had noticed a change in their relations. A kind of familiarity had appeared between them. He called her Rosie now. He allowed himself to make little jesting remarks on her coquetry. He paid more attention to his clothes. He no longer wore his cassock and did not roll up the cuffs of his trousers, not even when he went to cut wood. He trimmed his beard and mustache. Every afternoon, he changed shirts and sprinkled himself with lavender water after his bath. The fine wrinkles at the corner of his eyes were always smiling. He had gotten rid of his suspenders and was wearing a tobacco-brown belt and metal buckle embossed with the initials J. M. When Rosena leaned over to pour his soup, I kept waiting for the priest's eyes to light directly on her breasts. But I suppressed all these suspicions as unworthy of my piety. They kept coming back to mind even stronger. The previous night, I was awake and praying anxiously when I saw the priest get out of bed. A thin partition separated us from Rosena and we could notice every time she turned over, moved her legs, or talked in her sleep. The priest looked at me for an instant. Seeing that I was motionless, he stepped onto a chair with all the stealth of a wildcat on the prowl and began staring over the top of the partition. After a long moment of reflection, he went back to bed and lit a cigarette. I understood why he was set on accompanying Rosena to the market once more.

After the incident with Rosena, I had hurried to confess everything to the priest the same day. He praised the arms with which my purity had held off the demonic assault on my flesh. He reproached my lack of skill, however. In the future,

I should prove myself a more ingenious pastor. The soul of this kind of pagan is a skein that must be artfully unraveled. Confronted with the young woman's impious passion, I should have pretended to be seriously caught up in it in order to guide her wisely to the lap of God.

"Grace is not contagious, my dear boy," he said to me. "It's a matter of patience."

God had let this diabolic dew fall on my path in order to test the quality of the grass growing in my life. I must pray lest the droplets falling from the most satanic part of the sky appear one fine morning to be a benediction! I promised to follow his advice. And then, while I was awake that night, this holy man, who perhaps had a direct line to the Mother of Christ, had gotten up with feline stealth and trembling beard to drink in Rosena's defenseless nakedness. You could bet that this Thursday would be a decisive day. The priest and Rosena would fall onto the short grass of the mountain together, one on top of the other, intertwined in a panic of the senses. Satan would winnow them like a sizzling basket of rice under the Haitian summer sun . . .

3

Several hours later, I accompanied Rosena down the steep road that led through a growth of fern to the river. She led the way. The rhythm of our descent made her thighs vibrate, which had a violent effect on my own blood pressure. I was carrying the buckets that we had to fill.

Usually, she made the trip for water alone. She would come back sparkling each afternoon, with a clean dress and without her apron. The priest would be reading his breviary on the porch while I knelt in the chapel, gazing devotedly toward the lamp on the altar. I heard some steps behind me: It was Rosena coming toward me with clacking sandals and outrageously swinging her paganism in front of the holy sacrament.

"I'm sorry to disturb you. Come help me carry the buckets."

"Father Mulligan won't be happy if I go to the river with you. He'll scold me."

"You and your red-haired god make my tits ache!"

"Rosena, are you forgetting where you are?"

"That's true," she said making the sign of the Cross. "Are you afraid of being devoured?"

"It's not that, but Father Mulligan strictly ordered me not to be alone with you."

"Since when?"

"Since the day when you showed me your . . ."

"Imagine that! You'll go to hell because you saw my . . ."

"Rosena, not here, please!"

"Excuse me."

She crossed herself again, kneeling this time.

"Come on, be nice. Come give Rosena a hand."

"OK, I'll come. Wait for me a minute at the hollowed road. I'll be with you in a minute."

"Thank you, Saint Alain of Tête-Boeuf!" (She laughed aloud in the chapel.)

Toward the river, the road dropped vertiginously as the shadows of fern closed in around us. The path took a brusque turn to the clearing at the steep bank, scattered with flat, multicolored, polished stones. The rushing stream made a hairpin turn and formed a large basin upstream. At certain places, you could lose your footing. As soon as we arrived, I bent over the water and began to fill the two buckets. Standing beside me, Rosena observed me with a suggestive glance, something like two glowing coals of searing sensuality. When I had filled both buckets, I took the handles and was ready to start back up.

"Don't you want to take a dip?" she asked.

"No, I already washed right here at four o'clock."

"Doesn't the water tempt you again?"

"No, Rosena."

"Will you wait for me then? Turn around. It won't take me long."

I set the buckets down and turned my back to Rosena. I could hear her undressing behind me. A moment later, she was splashing noisily in the river.

"The water's great!"

I did not answer. I felt ridiculous and did not even feel like praying. My favorite "Ave Maria" was stuck in my throat now, and I had a slight sensation of nausea. My blood was coursing through my eyes, cheeks, hands, and, especially, my testicles. I turned around abruptly. Rosena was standing in the least shallow part of the river, up to her calves in the water. She smiled.

"Well, little Jesus-of-Prague! Make up your mind."

I kept quiet, without taking my eyes off her. I had never looked at anything with such amazement. My eyes were literally washing her and she made no effort to hide. I felt terribly awkward with my trembling hands and my swollen trousers. Trying to regain my composure, I bent over and picked up a little rock, pretending that I was going to throw it at her. She dove and came up several meters further away, laughing and shaking her head in defiance.

"Why don't you throw it? I'm not afraid of you."

I held on to my pebble. My vision was blurred with shame and desire. Rosena took several steps in my direction and began to splash me with water.

"I baptize you in the name of my mouth, my breasts, and my holy spirit," she yelled in a burst of laughter as she showered me again.

I backed up to the grass. She took several more steps. Her breasts loomed above the current. She kept coming toward the bank, still splashing water. Suddenly, at her middle, an eagle appeared with its wings deployed for battle and it was swooping down on me with the furious cries of its kind. In all my clothes, I dashed toward the flaming black triangle. I pushed Rosena over into the river. We fell onto a sandbar. We rolled in the shallow water, with our bodies, hands, and lips mingled, reaching desperately for each other like drowning people. She got up, escaped from my grasp with a jerk of her hips, and began running upstream.

I ran after her, tripping in my wet shoes. I joined her beneath a canopy of silken fern where she had stretched out with her arms under her head. I threw my clothes to the four winds. I could feel her heaving buttocks between my thighs. I arched my body against hers. Rosena turned over in ecstasy and offered me her tongue, her teeth, her eyes, her ears, her dimples, her belly, and her sovereign breasts. Her long legs arched in a sunny cross over my back as her waist ineluctably became unknotted. Her mound suddenly became the foliage of sensation. It was a beautiful, muscled, bulging vulva, generous in savor and fire. I was grafted onto Rosena and her blood flowed with mine, far from the coast, blending life and death, marvelously reconciled in the dual rhythm of our breathing. We plummeted breathlessly, measuring our overheated boundaries, kneading each other, and swelling into a full, knowing, glorious fruition as we launched into a final, piercing ecstasy.

4

Father Mulligan saw a transfigured couple arriving on the plateau that evening. What we had just done must have shone so intensely on our faces that he shaded his eyes. He understood at first glance that it was not the same Rosena or the same Alain who had returned from the river.

"What happened to you?" asked Father Mulligan.

"Nothing, Father," I answered as Rosena disappeared into the kitchen.

"What do you mean 'nothing'? You're all wet."

"I slipped into the water as I was helping Rosena to fill the buckets."

"And the ecstasy I see on both your faces? Did the river do that to you?"

"Where did I fall?" I asked with a sinking feeling.

"You're asking me? You are betraying your vocation without shame! Rosena, come here! What happened at the river?"

"Nothing serious, Father. Alain slipped while he was helping me."

"Is that why you both have that look?"

"What look is that?" she said innocently.

"This is too much! Should I draw you a picture? You must take me for a raving idiot. You are both dripping with sin and lies. You've just been fornicating! You're a miserable pair of fornicators!"

"It's true, Father," I answered. "Pardon us."

He turned toward Rosena looking for an expression of contrition. But she kept still. Her eyes flashed anger and her breasts were more insolent than ever.

"Rosena, do you persist in lying?"

"We did nothing wrong. We made love, Father. It was good, good, good!" She closed her eyes.

"Shut up! You have sullied this boy and that's all that you can say!"

"There's nothing dirty about love," we said.

"You treat vile fornication as love? Aren't you ashamed to profane a word so close to our Lord? You wallowed like pigs in the slime at the edge of the river!"

"That's enough!" yelled Rosena, beside herself. "I've had it with your hypocritical raving. It's nothing but jealousy bothering you. Don't lie, Father. Do you think I haven't been aware of your strutting around like a rooster? 'Rosie, this! Rosie, that!' Your eyes haven't stopped caressing my 'good angel.' You would have loved to be in Alain's shoes. He clipped the grass under your spurs, that's all!"

The priest was dumbstruck. Words seemed to well up into his mouth like new teeth. He glanced at Rosena and then at me, with a crazed look and dangling arms. His beard looked like the fur of a scalded cat and he seemed like a small boy holding back his tears.

"Leave me alone, please," he finally told us.

Rosena went to the kitchen. I went out into the evening, headed for the chapel.

5

The next day, after the Mass, which I served without taking Communion, the priest with an apparently relaxed manner asked me to go to market in his place with Rosena. We left toward dawn, in good spirits. We walked clear to the market in silence, each of us pretending simply to watch the people we met and to note the little stirrings on the mountain. She made her purchases with determination. Before 9:00 A.M., we were ready to return. I went first and pushed the brambles out of Rosena's way. In spite of our loads and the steep road, we were making good time and breathing deeply in the shimmering daylight. We had already covered half the road, totally absorbed in watching where we stepped. Rosena broke the silence.

"Alain, let's rest for a minute."

"Sure, Rosena dear."

I was surprised by what I said. I put down the provisions I was carrying and turned around. Drops of sweat were rolling down Rosena's cheeks. I pulled out my handkerchief and gently wiped her face. She rested against my shoulder a minute and then changed her mind and sat down on the grass in the shade.

"We were really trotting along."

"Like flying . . ."

"Because of what we did, right?"

". . ."

"You're not answering."

"Yes, love."

She raised her eyes with astonishment. Her lips and her nostrils quivered. Her bosom was heaving beneath her dress. The serious look on her face changed bit by bit to a kind of grateful affection.

"I love you, Alain."

A delicious aroma of Rosena-cinnamon filled my arms. We placed our bundles behind a bush and stretched out on the grass. I slipped my hand under her dress. With crab fingers and closed eyes, I caressed her from the soles of her feet to her breasts, which awakened to form distinct silhouettes. I went straight to her center. The triangle conveyed ecstasy and intimate knowledge of consummate form. This was a mill to make the blood flow, the prodigy that began life before fire and rain, before sand and wind, and particularly before any mythology had denatured the female womb into the great misshapen monsters of the species. Beneath the mountain sunlight, Rosena opened up once more. My diamond-prick sculpted the radiance of her harmonies, her curves, her golden number.

6

The evening of the same day, I found myself alone with Father Mulligan. We were reading in silence. He had Maritain's essays on *The Spirit in Its Carnal State* and I was reading the story of a little prince who had escaped from an asteroid with the help of a flock of wild birds. Rosena had already gone to bed. Since our return from the market, I had been looking for a chance to set matters right with my confessor. In his look, there was no animosity, just a virile, self-aware kindness that even seemed to be affectionately understanding toward us.

"'Scandal' won the first round," he said.

"And I have to look out, right, Father?"

"We both have to look out. We were both in the ring, weren't we?" he replied.

"What surprises me is that I don't feel as if I've sinned. I feel as pure as before. It's as if I just sampled the tip of ecstasy. Rosena made me experience the other four-fifths of an incredible state of grace."

"It's not right, my son, to compare grace to an iceberg. If that were the case, I would have seen two frozen statues coming back from the river. Confess that this wasn't true," he said, laughing.

"Maybe a divine 'iceberg,' submerged in our blood contains the very warmth of God."

"You are completely caught up in your fascination with evil. It's blasphemous to associate grace with a mere adventure of the flesh."

"And yet, Father, I prayed for a long time yesterday evening. The more I asked God's forgiveness, the more it seemed to me that he was blessing me for having dipped my soul like a piece of toast in the honey of the mountain. Why should evil be more fascinating than good? Why should I have experienced Rosena like a life-giving explosion?"

"Now you are touching on one of the great mysteries of creation. Light comes from Satan, also. According to the designs of the Creator, it would be too simple if the demon always appeared with the familiar look of a minion of darkness. . . ."

"So, in your eyes, Rosena is evil incarnate?"

"I've already told you that God sometimes submits his chosen ones to the illusions of the flesh in order to test their mettle. It is all to the better if this trial has not exhausted your store of purity. But it would be a serious sin to confound Satan's brilliance with the limpid incandescence of grace!"

"I don't feel the least remorse. The little bit I felt last night was swept away this morning. God placed the pristine form of woman's sweet flesh in my hands. These hands are entranced for the rest of my days!"

"My son, you need help!"

"Help me, Father," I replied.

"Let's go pray together."

He got up, took the hurricane lamp and started along the path leading to the chapel. I followed him through the night. He placed the lamp at the foot of the altar and knelt. His deep voice rose with gravity and sonority as he intoned the "Pater noster" and the "Ave Maria."

I responded, "Holy Mary, Mother of God, pray for us, poor sinners, now and at the hour of our death. . . . Our Father, who art in Heaven, . . . I salute you, Mary."

As I uttered these sacred words, tears came into my eyes. A different memory and a new piety brought the name of Rosena and our experience at the river to mind, forcibly replacing the image of the Mother of God.

"I salute you, Rosena, full of grace, now and at the hour of our death. . . ." Suddenly my voice cracked with sobs.

"Don't be ashamed of your tears, my son," said Father Mulligan. "They are flowing down the cheeks of the marvelous woman who is listening to us."

He got up and I followed him. My heart was ready to burst. My legs would barely carry me. The transparent, fresh night of the mountain must be Rosena. The lactescent, starry sky is Rosena, is it not? And my pillow and sleep that night: Rosena!

7

Had anybody watched us during the following weeks, they would have thought that the peace of the Lord was reigning beneath the shady foliage around Lamark Chapel. At dawn, I continued to assist Father Mulligan at Mass. Rosena kept kneeling behind us each morning. When I changed the place of the Missal on the altar, I glanced at her and her smile told me that we were following the same religion. When I rang the bell for the consecration and Rosena piously bowed her head, I knew that the bread and wine, mysteriously changed into the body and blood of Christ by the priest, had a special savor for us like the beautiful work of our flesh. Father Mulligan observed the Mass in accordance with the most orthodox Roman rites as he unknowingly celebrated the secret rites by which Rosena and I experienced our delirious identity in love. The gods of our childhood were slyly alert behind our Christian ritual.

Once she had served breakfast, after Mass, Rosena disappeared for several hours to take care of her kitchen and housekeeping chores. Father Mulligan gave me Latin lessons in the cool shade of a tree below the porch. He was also initiating me to philosophy. He often spoke to me about a current of Catholic thought that particularly interested him at that time—neo-thomism. He was acquainted with its principal proponent, Jacques Maritain, then teaching at Columbia University and at Princeton. The priest wanted to invite Maritain to give some lectures in Haiti.

Once a week, he received his mail from the capital. He gave me commentaries on the war, which was in full swing. That summer, the big news was the English resistance to the German offensive in Libya and the admirable strengthening of the Red Army, in the Caucasus and on the Don. The communiqués also mentioned the attacks by the Japanese forces in New Guinea and the bloody stages of the campaign of Guadalcanal. Father Mulligan's passion, however, was for Free France. He never tired of talking about what had happened at the beginning of the summer in the Libyan countryside. For almost two weeks, General Charles de Gaulle's troops had heroically resisted German Stukas and General Rommel's heavy artillery.

"Beginning with Bir Hakeim, France has come back into the war in the finest tradition of its past," he explained.

He repeated the text that the head of Free France had addressed to the heroes of Bir Hakeim: "General Koenig, you and your troops should know that France watches you and that you are her pride."

"You would think that this was one of Napoleon's edicts," exclaimed Father Mulligan.

At the time, I knew nothing about the political divisions of the modern world. The familiar names of the war, Guadalcanal, Tobruk, the Dneper, Timoshenko, El Alamein, the Crimea, and Montgomery, mixed with the names of Latin authors such as Cicero, Titus Livy, and Pliny the Younger. They all took their place beside the name of the woman who was offering me an entirely different bread of life. . . .

At lunch, we ate together. Without fail, the priest and I would congratulate Rosena on her culinary ability—not the least of her talents. After lunch, we helped her with the dishes, shelling peas, peeling potatoes, cleaning the lamps, cutting wood, and other household tasks. Father Mulligan always carried his medical kit with him and he had the gravity and assurance of a doctor when he attended cases of fever, yaws, kwashiorkor, and other maladies endemic to the Haitian countryside. Rosena and I served then as his attentive nurses. We discovered the avitaminosis that affects both children and adults. We heard explanations given by the priest on rickets, scurvy, beriberi, and pellagra. When we returned to the house, we walked in silence while the beauty of the trees in which the birds chased each other singing and the joyful summer of the mountain made us bleed inwardly from the misery that left us powerless. The same disarming sadness made Father Mulligan more somber. At those times, Rosena and I felt a bit abashed at our secret celebrations.

In fact, when the priest thought that I was piously kneeling in the chapel at prayer time, I had often run top speed to join Rosena in the shade of a bush or at the river bank. We made love in dazzling harmony. As soon as we had reached climax, I ran back to kneel in the chapel.

One morning, we had taken each other standing in the kitchen. We were so ecstatic that it seemed our legs had vaporized and our bodies floated over the pots and the incandescent coals. Often toward dawn, after making sure that the priest was asleep, I slipped into Rosena's room. The silence in which we gently excited our circulation was so full, so good, so dizzy that it seemed like the very embodiment of the vagina in which my existence centered.

Once, when we had spent three days without touching each other, we made love on a pew in the chapel, feverishly blending our orgasms with the very breath of God. As for the priest, he began treating Rosena with a highly paternal respect. "Now he knows the kindling that I am burning. He is cautious, but basically the Irish rooster in him isn't asleep," said Rosena.

One afternoon, toward four o'clock, a peasant arrived as breathless as the horse he was riding. He had come to take Father Mulligan to a dying man several leagues from Lamark. He said that the man had lived a good, Christian life and, since he had heard of the priest, did not want to die without the final sacraments. The peasant added that if he drove his mule hard, the priest could get back before sunrise. As he was leaving, Father Mulligan took me aside and pointed out the danger I was in, remaining alone in the house with Rosena Rozel after such a torrid August day. He advised me to spend all night praying in the chapel.

"Look out, my son. The earth will be devastated this evening by the wars of the flesh. It will be an agonizing vigil!"

I promised to keep my lamp lit.

Our honeymoon began in the river. In the fantastically starlit night, we went back to the house without dressing. We had a feast of oranges, melons, bananas and other fruit brought from the market the day before. By the light of the hurricane lamps, we pushed the three beds together in order to enlarge the arena for our nuptial games. Hours later, intoxicated and fatigued from mutual delight, we fell into the sleep of children, the insane, and lovers.

We did not hear the priest come in. When I opened my eyes, I did not know how long he had been there watching us sleeping with interlocked arms and legs. The lamps were still lit. The priest's eyes were bulging out of his head and his prickly beard was darting red flames. The veins in his neck were beating, and his Adam's apple stood out like a curious erection. I grabbed a sheet and covered Rosena, who was still asleep. I got up to put on my pajamas. Father Mulligan threw himself on me. With a rough prod, he pushed me against the wall. He punched me right in the face. Then he hit me on the nose. I stifled a cry of pain.

"Stop, or I'm going to start punching, too," I said.

He poked me in the mouth. My nose and lips were bleeding. I was reeling from more blows, but kept taking them like a fool, forgetting that I was an athlete. Finally, our struggle aroused Rosena. Seeing my disarray, she fled to the kitchen and ran back in immediately with a machete in one hand. Father Mulligan turned. Without letting go of her weapon, she threw off the cumbersome sheet. She was splendidly naked with the knife in her fist. She was staring at a precise part of the priest's anatomy. The man saw in her eyes that Rosena was determined to cut *them* off, once and for all.

"Drop your trousers," ordered Rosena Rozel.

Like an automaton, the mesmerized priest unbuckled his belt with incredible humility. The trousers fell at his feet, baring his sturdy legs, all covered with red hair.

"Your shorts, too," said Rosena with the same commanding tone.

He obeyed, revealing a tumescent organ that appeared pugnacious and warlike, ready to face any danger. Rosena took a step and struck with all her strength. I rushed at her, pushed her frantically into the other room, and disarmed her. Then I flew back to the missionary's aid. He was bent in two, pulling cotton out of a first-aid kit and trying to stop the bleeding from the ugly wound.

"I don't need your help," he growled. "Take her away! Get out of here, couple from hell!"

We dressed and threw our affairs into one packet. With tears in our eyes, we set out into the fresh, sparkling dawn.

In mid-September, I tried discreetly to get some news about Father James Mulligan from a nurse I knew in the municipal hospital. I found out that he had fallen victim to a serious accident in Lamark, where, according to his custom, he had gone for the summer. A vicious horse had given him such a violent kick on the tender parts that he was now in convalescence. At last report, he was accepting his condition philosophically.

UNDER THE ROSE

THE ELDEST

I was the battering ram; my looks attest to it. Every freedom was wrung by action: I endured the wails of a frightened mother when I came home disheveled after dark; the rage of an ineffectual father stiffened my shoulders and narrowed my eyes. I tried it all. If I could not be doted upon, I could be worried about; I would get out into the world. Can't you imagine? Can you blame me? Three years later came my first sister, and then the baby, the darling.

At first we loved her too, and sometimes called her Cookie, she was so round and perfectly baked. She was a hoarder. Weaned from the breast too late, she would tuck a spoonful of pablum in the pouch of her cheek like a hamster. For how long had we thought those cheeks were naturally puffed, the round face of a cherub! But one afternoon she stumbled over a ripple in the hall rug and with a thud her chin hit the parquet; a clump of masticated banana spurted from between her lips and lay before us, mother and two older sisters, like the indecent gelatinous workings of a snail scraped from its shell. Alerted, every evening Mother would check Babs' mouth for signs of hoarded food, and each evening found packed between gum and cheek the soggy remains of bread, or green beans blackened from saliva. In time those baby teeth, soft pearls, began to decay; despairing, Mother brushed them after every meal with a mixture of salt and baking soda. Oh, the screams when that bracing paste met raw gums! And yet this did not cure her. One by one the teeth dropped out until there was no retaining wall for the hoarded food, and she was forced to swallow. By the time her adult teeth came in, strong, straight, and white, she had forgotten the old habit.

What could prompt a toddler to store up nourishment like a chipmunk sniffing winter? What could she know already of life, how it whittles? Or was she no more than an animal following instincts, proclamations of Enlightenment, delayed gratification and propriety notwithstanding? Hasn't she been this way always—continually stocking the cave with nuts against the impending frost?

This last daughter was the first one to Get Out. This was my disgrace. Even if she left against her will, even if the Turn of Events spelled Tragedy to our House . . . *I* was the one destined to break out of the nest, *I* was my parents' heartache. All my life I had been practicing to disappoint them, and then nothing—no scandal, no hairy groom nor inappropriate lover—could outshine Beauty's contract. What neat upstaging! What sabotage!

After much thought, I decided on a course of action nobody would have expected of one so flamboyant, so carefree: I decided to stay put. Never to marry but to wither into old maidhood. I simply refused to participate in the ancient games: I abandoned my jewels and silks, I put away the hankies scented with dried violets and the talcs laced with thin curls of tangerine peel. Each morning I scrubbed my body with a hunk of brown soap such as the farmers use; I eschewed the wooden tub and stood in the courtyard before the pump, betraying not so much as a gasp as ice water shot up from the bowels of the earth to rinse me squeaky-clean.

It was easier than I had imagined; it was hardly denial at all. How little the soul needs, finally! If there are no plums it will feed on the pits, or on the dream of pits or, finally, on itself. And it eats so slowly; it grows faster than it can be consumed.

THE MIDDLE ONE

No one watched me. No one Paid Attention. The first time I understood this, observed the never-changing scene at the dinner table and saw how clearly I didn't count, I felt as if the carpet under me had opened with a terrifying wave of pity, whispering *Let go* but I took off, let loose, cast my flaking soul on the waters—what a freedom to be the ampersand.

THE MOTHER

Yes, I spoiled her. She was the youngest: she ruined my body, she kicked away the scaffolding and stood by, cooing as the last of pre-war grandeur, my flaking gold, came crumbling down. I spoiled her because she was all there was left; I wanted her to have it, Beauty, all the things that were free for the asking. Because I had grown away from all that; my Youthful Adventure was over. I suppose I hated her just a little, I can see that; but mostly I was giving her an education.

When she grew old enough to read, I told her stories; I made her the heroine. This was a mistake, because she grew up believing all endings would be if not happy, then at least neatly turned. She grew up confident that life could be conducted with grace.

I had married my husband because he was malleable. That I loved him is beside the point—Love, too, is a matter of education. I balanced my desire for the things of the world with the house he built; I compared the clamorous sighs of other suitors with his good smile above the merchant's waistcoat; I thought of the trips he would make while I baked pies in the kitchen, gazing out into the clearing, I imagined the gilt mirrors he would bring back, accepted in trade but utterly useless to the few tired wives in the region; I thought a *mirror in every room* and when he proposed I did not hesitate.

I have not regretted that decision, although my buoyant, fecund life has become a magnificent mulch. Just consider my daughters, each a product of my horticulture and each so remarkably different. Martha bloomed faster than I could complete the trellis; unsupported, she ran wild and burst early. Her bold brain grew too heavy for its spine; I could see the strain in her face as she struggled to defy us—and of course the first disappointment chilled her. *Nipped in the bud,* she did not wither so much as freeze, rigidly accepting the stasis of the present, refusing the uncertainties of anticipation. She simply stopped, arrested all growth, and in time began imperceptibly to shrink, darkening around the edges like an arrangement of dried wildflowers.

Then Megan, who never understood the battle for sunlight. Content to be marginal, she valued above all her capacity to be innocuous and made a virtue out of small, efficient movements. Even her name was a compression: not as robust as Martha, more arid than Mother. I did not realize the pattern I had fallen into, the progression of M-words humming through our house, until Megan was three. Then came Beauty.

Barbara, Babs, Baby—a wild attempt to start again, to break the chain. After all, my real name, before Wife and Mother, had been Beatrice; but none of the names I gave her would stick. My husband called her Beauty, her sisters dubbed her Cookie—and the sisters were right; she *was* a cookie, the kind you nibbled with a glass of milk; a sweetness that fired the blood, only to produce a drop in energy minutes afterward: To gorge oneself on this delicacy meant to come out much weaker than before.

BEAUTY

As for my looks—I was lucky. Looks are a matter of fashion, and my complexion, my figure, happen to be in accordance with the age. A mere generation ago in the great cities beyond the lake, women were delicious when they bore a pale countenance on a precarious stalk, heads like peeled eggs. They plucked their eyebrows, even shaved back their hairline to accommodate the illusion of a regal brow. The stark white facial powder contained a lead base, so that the more they applied, the more their skin was eaten away. And the two spots of rouge imitating china dolls in a toymaker's window—these, too, carried their weight in lead. Beneath the bald-eyed countenance of Elizabethan beauties, the virginal flesh rotted like pears.

Roses? I'm rather afraid of them, though nobody has guessed; men will believe anything. Even when I told him to stop he piled them at my feet, in my lap; their fiery heads sprawled across white tablecloths or tucked under my pillow like a bloodstain, a tubercular dribble in the night. They weren't really for me. After all, he was the one who had squandered an entire garden plot on them, a brute in search of Romance way before I came along. I see him stumbling through the rows with his pruning shears, trimming back growth, or gently lifting the flushed lip of a petal with a sweaty paw to get at the aphids in their cunning green industry, humming "I'm in the Mood for Love." When he discovered my father, he found another sentimental fool; the two hearts gushed in recognition. I was merely the expedient: legal tender.

It was never the rose; that's the biggest irony. I prefer silks. Thousands of tiny worms spinning week upon week in order to produce one handkerchief's worth of glimmering breath: That's the kind of dedication I appreciate.

It was never the rose but the idea of a rose, the sort of thing expected from fair young maidens. I made my request in January, in the dead of winter, so my wish was more than charming or frivolous—it was impossible. I had mocked my father. He did not fail me.

My sisters asked for the easy pleasures but I was the youngest; I stood flat-chested and scrawny under a flannel nightshirt and watched them frowning into their mirrors; I knew how little the stuffs of the world satisfy. As a child I had caught my mother crying over the stove and when I asked her why she was crying she would make up yet another gooey story starring the Invincible Princess Rose, stories guaranteed to put me to sleep within five minutes. How could I tell her I was more interested in the pungent taste of millet soup?

Those weeks I lay in terror of his approach; his stench was insupportable. The merest brush of his cheek against mine left angry red welts. Nothing in my life had prepared me for this abandonment. His touch was discreet, but his eyes! Liquid with sex, they held me in their glistening fever until I lost all appetite, even for my favorite *pâté de foié gras;* one wet glance and I began to regurgitate effortlessly, all that gluttonous liver loosening. The sight of a golden plate made my jaws ache.

So I ran back to mama who wept openly this time, pressing her soggy cheek to mine. My sisters looked on, silent. That I had not yet been defiled was of no consequence; it was only a matter of time. As a sister I no longer existed. I had preempted them, but someday they might have to follow, and so they watched for clues. When, in the mirror, I first saw him stagger, I packed my bags. I had driven him mad, and like the thief fatally proud of the perfect execution of a crime, I felt compelled to return to the scene.

By the time I arrived, I found him aswoon between rows of new hybrids. Flies were already collecting in the frothy corners of his lips. I was moved by pity but also the desire to avoid Ugliness; although to die for love is not in bad taste, to be the lethal perpetrator of longing is always unsavory.

How gloriously my tormentor had staged my return! By bending over the dim rosebeds I could see that he had just shaven; he was languishing but nowhere near the demise promised so ravishingly.

Yes, that was it: he merely looked ravished; laid out for my delectation, awaiting my kiss. He allowed me to lead him through the crowds of scents to the villa, past corridor upon corridor of doors shut and bolted against the wind that was rising, an evening wind that swept through the hallways and guttered the candles.

Crazed by my extended absence, he had made of my sleeping chamber a garden as well, filling the very pillowcases with petals, installing a fountain on the balcony so that all night the liquid veil sizzled. In this madhouse of desire he had slept, ordering meals brought up by the eunuchs, the most exquisite delicacies, each and every one flavored with the essence of attar: rose gelée on white toast, rose wine and rose-petal bouillon, golden curry studded with rose hips.

All this he whispered into my shoulder, the quenched wicks smoking; the air smelled heavy and burned, like incense. Where was the Moment of Transformation? When would the beast melt, harden into a prince? Did I really yearn for a prince? Which is more likely to have a soul, an animal or a rose? And when I was opened—*deflowered*—what glutted mass would spew out, and how could I ever hope to stopper that scent?

And yet my chest kept rising and falling. I wrenched the casements wide till moonlight poured over my hands, the silken parquet, the glacial bedsheets forming a fervid cocoon. Now, I thought, moving into his furred arms. Now, at last, I am anonymous.

SUZANNE DRACIUS-PINALIE

SWEAT, SUGAR, AND BLOOD

I DON'T KNOW IF Emma loves Emile. But that's not the point.

The mulatto girl is sixteen. As milky white as a corrosol, as tender as a heart of palm, in just two days a wedding will officially make her my great-aunt Emma B.

The day after tomorrow Emma is going to marry the eminent Mr. Emile B., Esq., a lawyer from Fort-de-France. Everything is ready: from the lilies, the organdy, the damask, the tulle, the vertiginous chiffon down to the royal orchids brought from Balata, still trembling and damp from the tropical forest, everything is immaculately white. All you hear around her is talk of trousseaus, hairdos, veils, fittings, her train, her posture, and then her attire again.

Emma getting married is like being engulfed in a whirlwind of white.

The third day after the wedding, Mr. Emile B. gave her a quick peck on the lips and then advised her in leaving that under no circumstances should she venture off in the direction of the distillery. Besides his law office located on the rue Perrinon in Fort-de-France, in the center of town, Mr. Emile B. has inherited an ancient little distillery that has managed to subsist up on the Didier plateau. Because the property is vast, he has restored the old plantation house, made of old stones and wood from Guiana. This is where Emma is now living with a new husband—new to her alone, for there's quite a bunch of cabins in Morne Coco now who can claim that they're B.'s little bastards. But Emma never meets any of these illegitimate kids. She never goes to Morne Coco on the other side of the road. That's not a place for her, according to the plump cook, Mama Sonson. Every

---

Translated by Doris Y. Kadish.

God-given day, Mr. Emile drives to his office, leaving her alone at Haut Didier with the women of the house: Mama Sonson and the little Da Sirisia. Emma didn't think she needed any other help.

Every morning it's the same peck, the same "have a good morning," and the same advice: "Don't go walking in the direction of the distillery."

"What does he think?" wonders Emma, protesting to herself. "Is he worried that I'm going to get drunk on rum? Who does he think I am? I'm not a baby anymore! Besides the decanters are all within my reach on the pedestal table in the living room; they're not even locked up. If I felt like getting drunk, I'd just have to reach for them."

Maybe Emile is afraid of the powerful erotic charge that emanates from those big, supple bodies with their long, bulging muscles and their skin pearled with sweat? Emma barely caught a glimpse of the workers from the distillery when they came—their hair all marcelled and slicked down with vaseline, all dressed up wearing ties and smelling of eau de Cologne "Etoile"—to present their congratulations to the newlyweds. But they disappeared as fast as they came.

Thus went the first weeks of her marriage.

On the morning of the eighth day, while Emile was busy washing and dressing—a daily activity that always seemed to last as long as a day without bread—Emma made sure, by peering into the bathroom, that her husband was busy passing his straight-edged razor over his greenish mulatto beard, carefully tailoring the contour of a goatee that Emma caught herself at that moment finding a tiny bit ridiculous. Only half awake, the young bride flew as in a dream to the end of the veranda, at the other end of the house from the bathroom, to the spot where she knew she'd be hidden by the foliage of the poinsettias and the crimson curtain of the Barbados hibiscus. From there she knew she could look all she wanted at a couple of the turns in the road leading to the distillery. True she'd never be able to take in the whole road in a single glance: tufts of giant bamboos hid most of it. But there was a spot, a part in the vegetation's woolly crop of hair, where a spot of light shone through revealing a part of the road. That's all Emma needed.

The veils of early morning had lifted in silence. The blackbirds in the filao trees had begun their racket: Between chirping and squawking, they had enough to keep them busy until nightfall. Noisy but serene, the early morning dampness gave new, throbbing life to trees alive with the rocking of sissis, to roosters rushing to cockadoodledoo just to beat out the cackling hens and prove their supremacy, to acrobatic anolis spread out on the frond of a dwarf date palm hoping to catch their first prey, and to Emma, who had leaped from her bed, barefoot on the damp tiles, drawing the lace of her nightgown over her breast with her hand.

"How cool it is at dawn!" Emma says to herself shivering—with cold? with fear? with a sense of having no business being there?

Suddenly, clearly, penetrating the air there arises the masculine voice of some fellow that unfortunately Emma can't see.

She closes her eyes and listens carefully:

"I pé ké ni siklon, man di'w! Pa fè lafèt épi mwen! Asé bétizé, ou ka plen tèt mwen épi tout sé kouyonnad-la!"

(Ain't gonna be no hurricane, ya hear me? Don't want to hear nothin' about it! Stop that nonsense. I've had it up to here with your crap.)

A second voice loses patience, rings out stubbornly.

"Fé sa ou lé! Mwen, man za paré. Zalimet, luil, pétrol, bouji, man za fè tout provizyon mwen, Kité Misyé Siklon vini!"

(Do what you want! I'm ready. I've got me enough matches, oil, kerosene, candles. Come and get us, Mr. Hurricane.)

"Gadéy! I pa ka menm kouté. Yen ki chonjé i ka chonjé toubonnman."

(Look at him! He's not even listening. All he does is daydream, daydream . . .)

That voice is new; it's trying to cover the other one and will succeed, without any difficulty. It's a third man who's speaking. Emma can't recognize either the tone or the language of the first two. This one speaks a heavy creole that sounds rough and choppy. So, he's from the North! she thinks, without wondering why.

"Sa ou ni an ka-kabèch ou, nèg? Asé dépotjolé ko-ko'w! ou ka sanm an t-toupi mabyal."

(Hey, what's got into your sk-skull, man? Stop wo-worrying so much! You look like a crazy spinning t-top, a higher voice snickers.)

Which one of them just spoke? She can't figure it out. She's sure it's not the first man. Now that she's heard it she'd recognize his voice out of a thousand. She becomes flushed. She represses a shudder. This time is it a fever? Oh, she can't wait for them to get to the clearing soon so that she can see them!

But when they get there she can't hear them anymore. Their voices are already fading, the words wafting off in the air. She can't make out what they're saying anymore. All she hears now is a burst of the same, incoherent, hammered-out syllables—té-té-ké-ké-pé-ka-pou-pouki—the steady barking of the one who stammers and articulates louder than the others, probably to compensate, she thinks.

"The air is healthy in Haut-Didier, but at this time of year you still have to be careful about spiders, moths, and cockroaches that are leaving deposits and laying all kinds of eggs in the hems of your clothes," the little Da explains to Emma.

Startled, Emma quickly leaves her secret observation point.

And Mama Sonson adds, "You keep your clothes in the closet forever and ever, ain't no way you're still going to find them there! . . . Hey Sirisia, girl, stop jumping around, you're not going to be able to do your ironing, girl, my lord! You'll work yourself up into a fever! . . . If you think you're going to use that hot iron wearing sopping wet clothes and you all covered with cold sweat you've got another thing coming."

Mr. Emile must have finished his endless morning routine by now for, tall and straight, with triumphal beard, he comes to perform the daily ritual: Have a good morning, here's a good kiss, take my good advice.

There, it's over, he's left at the wheel of his Panhard.

Up there in the big house, Emma is bored.

A hot smell of caramel and sugar cane alcohol rising from the distillery tickles her nostrils. They're making rum, and the young woman enjoys the mystery that comes from inhaling the disturbing emanation, stronger than the odor of punch, more intoxicating than a planter's punch or that tropical cocktail they serve at the Annual Grand Officers' Ball.

As she waits for Madame to get pregnant, the little Da busies herself fancifully tending to the trousseau of the future first-born child. There's no end to what you can do with a trousseau. Sirisia never stops washing, rewashing, ironing, and then washing again the diapers, bibs, little shirts, little sheets with English embroidery, the minuscule mosquito net. There's no point in keeping in mothballs anything that will touch the newborn in any way! "Poor little thing, his skin would come off and he'd suffocate from the smell," Mama Sonson asserts knowingly. It's a matter of honor of the Da to keep a jealous guard over Mr. B.'s future progeny, even if he hasn't been conceived yet, even if there's more going on in Emma's mind now than in her womb. Whether Madame likes it or not, a child will be born and he'll be male, there's no two ways about it, "no squirming out of it," Mama Sonson would chime in if there were any questions on the matter. Besides, a boy's first name has already been designated; if the misfortune of its being a girl arises, they'll just put an 'e' at the end. If Mr. B. had picked "Arsène" instead of "Henri," it would have been even easier, there'd be nothing to change at all. That's Mama Sonson's opinion; even though "Arsène" means virile, she sees nothing wrong with imposing it on a girl, who'll be feminine enough, you can be sure! Anyway Mama Sonson doesn't know Greek. That's really the least of her concerns. On the other hand, there's a serious problem for the baptism, because the person who's been picked in advance refuses to be a godfather for the first time in his life for a member of the feminine race: "It's bad luck." He's only agreed for a boy. For a girl it's another matter: He hadn't even thought of that possibility when he proudly said yes. It's an honor to be the godfather of a little male, but for some little female pissecrette . . .

Sure Emma enjoys listening to the moralistic lamentations of Mama Sonson, who tells the beads on the rosary of past, present, and future miseries while she scales fish.

But then there's the mystery of those men!

Mr. B. announced in leaving that he won't be back for lunch today. As is often the case, he has a business luncheon that will keep him in Fort-de-France. Sometimes he even lowers himself to buy lunch at the market, eating off of big wooden trestle tables, getting a blaff or a fish stew seasoned with red pepper served by imposing câpresses.

Mr. B. has never mentioned bringing Emma there some day.

She assumes that it's not done.

"Little rummy, so you're sipping your punch without even waiting for me?"
Aunt Herminie just arrived.

Of course, Godmother's having lunch here today, obviously! Every time Mr. B.
needs to have lunch downtown, he assigns "Cousin Herminie"—Godmother for
Emma, for she's not only her aunt but was her godmother for her baptism. She's
a B. from Saint Pierre, not from Fort-de-France, and that's a big difference. The
B. family from Saint-Pierre has a certain paternalistic condescension toward the
B. family from Fort-de-France; a square bears their name in the center of Saint-
Pierre in honor of one of their family members who was a notable personage of
that city—Emma can't remember why—but the B. family of Fort-de-France has
more money.

The historically prominent but nevertheless impoverished mulatto lady gargles
with pride as she affirms that the B. family is a great family, but Emma responds
by bursting out laughing: "You shouldn't confuse 'great family' with 'large family'!"

Great or not, the B. family has never intrigued Emma.

Lunch drags on. Godmother talks to herself without realizing it: Emma's not
with her anymore. Emma's lost in thought. Emma's thoughts wander off from the
house.

If there's one thing she can't stand it's not being able to know things, to know
only one side of life.

She can't see or know anything, at least not by herself. Because she's "the mulatto's wife," "the boss' wife," a mulatto herself, she doesn't have the right to go see
what's going on below, what they're doing over there, inside, within the distillery.
All she can do is steal a few bits of conversation when they arrive in the morning
or when they leave in the evening, when their workday is over. If she hears them
it's because they're still invisible and, finally when she sees them, she can't hear
them anymore because they're too far away. Then they go into the distillery. There
she can't see anything, she can only imagine what happens afterwards, after the
last twist in the road where she has her last view of the group of tall men walking, who despite the distance always seem tall: She's never stepped foot inside that
beastly distillery! For her the interior of the distillery is an unknown world. She
wants to go inside, see what they do there, know how they go about it, find out
about these men that she sees from afar every day, that she observes on the sly
and, yes, find out how they manage to perform the metamorphosis of the juice
from sugar cane into rum. Emma has drunk rum, with a lot of syrup and lime.

She's tasted sugar cane. But what about the forbidden alchemy . . .

Oh! She learned many things at the Colonial Boarding School on rue Ernest-
Renan, attended in Fort-de-France by all the daughters of the "best families,"
snobbish, straight-laced but nonetheless tolerant and committed to humanist
values. But she stopped learning things all of a sudden! Emma yearns to know
more. She wasn't a bad student, she digested whole chapters of the history of
France and Navarre: She's very familiar with school programs in the natural and

physical sciences and even in world geography; she knows quite well who broke the Soissons vase and there's nothing she doesn't know about auricles and other ventricles. Yet she knows nothing about the fabrication of rum that's taking place over there, a few feet away from her.

Nothing seems more mysterious to her today than what's right there, so near to her, in that distillery that holds within its walls the tall men that she only sees passing by, with their handsome blue-black bodies. Here she is now: married, a woman, a wife, the lady of the house, potentially a mother. Yet nothing is more foreign to her than that world that is so close by, than that side of humanity to which she has no access.

A barrier has been built between Emma and that world, between Emma and their creole language.

A barrier has been built between their world and hers, between their language and hers, between their skin and hers, between their sex and hers.

Taking advantage of Godmother's nap, Emma has slipped away like a swift mongoose to the edges of the Other World. She's gotten away secretly, furtively, without Mama Sonson suspecting anything, and even without Sirisia knowing, she who normally knows everything.

It's the hour of the break, for them too, it would seem. That's to be expected: With Godmother you have to eat early out of respect for her age.

At the doorway stands a man, naked to the waist. After the work he's done he puts his shirt back on so as not to catch his death. The stretched-out fabric of his jersey sticks to his sweat-covered skin. Emma recognizes him right away: he's the one with the voice, the first voice, the clearest, the one that cuts through the air the best at sunrise each day. She'd swear to it.

What he needs is a good shower. But a cold or even cool shower on a body all covered with sweat is just what you need to get sick. At least that's what grown-ups always preach, so forget the shower, there's no way around it. If Mama Sonson was there, that's what she'd say, Lord, she would! Just as long as he knows it.

The man with the sweat-drenched jersey stretches his long limbs and then goes off slowly to crouch down in the shade, off a way.

Others join him outside, sit down with him under the biggest mango tree. From their lunchpail they extract a big piece of breadfruit, some fried balao, some acra, a piece of codfish: It's Friday. They concentrate on eating, saying not a word. Wet Jersey pours everyone big glasses filled with a clear liquid, probably rum, or maybe just water?

Emma doesn't dare go over to talk to them. She doesn't even dare come close to them. Is it their silence that intimidates her? She only knows them when they speak, when she spies on them each morning. It's first and foremost through language that their complicity has arisen, it's through the shared secret of all those words that she steals from them, day after day—those creole words . . . Is it their silence that stops her, or is it the insurmountable barrier between her and their universe? It may be insurmountable but surely one can get round it. . . .

Emma goes around the group of men, at some distance, so as not to be seen.

She almost gets down on all fours to reach the back of the building, which she succeeds in entering by crawling through the opening of a low window.

Her blood spurts on the sugar cane, splattering the cane trash.

The escapade at the distillery has cost Emma three fingers. That's the price. And at that, only because she screamed and because the men ran back, amazed by the sound of the machine inexplicably set in motion. They thought quickly and stopped the crusher in time while one of them, the strongest, Wet Jersey, grabbed onto Emma's body with the full force of his muscles, straining to the breaking point.

The man managed to hold back the voracious movement of the machine.

"If he hadn't it would have crushed her hand, her whole hand, and then her arm, and then her whole body, who knows! . . . Ah, Jesus, Mary and Joseph, and all the saints, why did Madame need to go play with those machines!" laments Mama Sonson.

One of their cousins, a good doctor who answered the emergency call, has given the necessary treatment to Emma's mutilated hand, and Mr. Emile B., called away from his office, makes no comment. Hasn't she been punished enough for her disobedience? He has never been so silent. She has never been so pale, but with a glow in her eyes that will never go out. Yes, it is a light of jubilation that illuminates Emma's eyes. . . .

Having lost the use of the fingers that she used the most, Emma B. lived her life as a lady from Fort-de-France awkwardly, wearing a glove on one hand, the left one: first a white glove, then a navy one, and finally a pearl grey one. Fools would say, "Fortunately it wasn't her right hand!"

For some people the whole thing was mysterious; for others it had a sort of troubling charm; still others interpreted it as a sign of uniqueness or a kind of provocation, although they would have been hard pressed to say what kind. Very few knew what it was all about; very few knew the secret of Emma's rebellion.

When Emma died, at the age of one hundred and two, Oreste, her seventeenth child, approached her deathbed—or should I say her wedding bed?—and slipped on the pearl-white glove, the first one that she had worn until the day of her silver wedding anniversary. Washed, rewashed, and ironed, it wasn't even yellowed with age.

Forget "Crick, crack."

This is not a story.

It really happened to my great aunt, Emma B.

Thanks to that mixed frenzy of sweat, sugar, and blood, Emma had at least one strong sensation in her lifetime.

GLOSSARY

Acra: Fritters made with codfish or vegetables.

Anolis: Little green lizards.

Balao: A type of tropical seafish, also known in English as halfbeak.

Blaff: A plate of fish seasoned by cooking on Indian wood.

Câpre, Câpresse: Dark-skinned child of black and mulatto parents.

Chabin, Chabine: Person of mixed-blood who appears to bear the characteristics of only the lighter skinned parent; sometimes referred to in English as being "yellow."

Cockadoodledoo (translation of "coquiyoquer," a word invented by the author): to crow.

Corrosol: A tree of medium height resembling a European pear tree bearing a juicy, refreshing fruit considered to have a calming effect.

Crick, crack: Caribbean expression, like "Once upon a time," used to begin the recounting of a story.

Da: Black nursemaid for creole families.

Filao: Casuarinas; graceful trees from Madagascar that resemble weeping willows.

Marcelled (translator's choice for translation of "calamistré"): A style of carefully waved hair attributed originally to the nineteenth-century French hairdresser Marcel.

Pissecrette: Creole word for a little fish which, while evoking smallness, also evokes the image of a "little pisser" (information provided by the author).

Sissis: Little birds comparable to sparrows.

Vaseline: A special hair product used in Martinique made from vaseline and a mixture of other cosmetic products (explanation supplied by the author).

HENRY DUMAS

ARK OF BONES

Headeye, he was followin me. I knowed he was followin me. But I just kept goin, like I wasn't payin him no mind. Headeye, he never fish much, but I guess he knowed the river good as anybody. But he ain't know where the fishin was good. Thas why I knowed he was followin me. So I figured I better fake him out. I ain't want nobody with a mojo bone followin me. Thas why I was goin along downriver stead of up, where I knowed fishin was good. Headeye, he hard to fool. Like I said, he knowed the river good. One time I rode across to New Providence with him and his old man. His old man was drunk. Headeye, he took the raft on across. Me and him. His old man stayed in New Providence, but me and Headeye come back. Thas when I knowed how good of a river-rat he was.

Headeye, he o.k., cept when he get some kinda notion in that big head of his. Then he act crazy. Tryin to show off his age. He older'n me, but he little for his age. Some people say readin too many books will stunt your growth. Well, on Headeye, everything is stunted cept his eyes and his head. When he get some crazy notion runnin through his head, then you can't get rid of him till you know what's on his mind. I knowed somethin was eatin on him, just like I knowed it was *him* followin *me*.

I kept close to the path less he think I was tryin to lose him. About a mile from my house I stopped and peed in the bushes, and then I got a chance to see how Headeye was movin along.

Headeye, he droop when he walk. They called him Headeye cause his eyes looked bigger'n his head when you looked at him sideways. Headeye bout the ugliest guy I ever run upon. But he was good-natured. Some people called him Eagle-Eye. He bout the smartest nigger in that raggedy school, too. But most time we called him Headeye. He was always findin things and bringin 'em to school, or to the cotton patch. One time he found a mojo bone and all the kids cept me went round

164

talkin bout him puttin a curse on his old man. I ain't say nothin. It wont none of my business. But Headeye, he ain't got no devil in him. I found that out.

So, I'm kickin off the clay from my toes, but mostly I'm thinkin about how to find out what's on his mind. He's got this notion in his head about me hoggin the luck. So I'm fakin him out, lettin him droop behind me.

Pretty soon I break off the path and head for the river. I could tell I was far enough. The river was gettin ready to bend.

I come up on a snake twistin toward the water. I was gettin ready to bust that snake's head when a fox run across my path. Before I could turn my head back, a flock of birds hit the air pretty near scarin me half to death. When I got on down to the bank, I see somebody's cow lopin on the levee way down the river. Then to really upshell me, here come Headeye droopin long like he had ten tons of cotton on his back.

"Headeye, what you followin me for?" I was mad.

"Ain't nobody thinkin bout you," he said, still comin.

"What you followin long behind me for?"

"Ain't nobody followin you."

"The hell you ain't."

"I ain't followin you."

"Somebody's followin me, and I like to know who he is."

"Maybe somebody's followin me."

"What you mean?"

"Just what you think."

Headeye, he was gettin smart on me. I give him one of my looks, meanin that he'd better watch his smartness round me, cause I'd have him down eatin dirt in a minute. But he act like he got a crazy notion.

"You come this far ahead me, you must be got a call from the spirit."

"What spirit?" I come to wonder if Headeye ain't got to workin his mojo too much.

"Come on."

"Wait." I grabbed his sleeve.

He took out a little sack and started pullin out something.

"You fishin or not?" I ask him.

"Yeah, but not for the same thing. You see this bone?" Headeye, he took out that mojo. I stepped back. I wasn't scared of no ole bone, but everybody'd been talkin bout Headeye and him gettin sanctified. But he never went to church. Only his mama went. His old man only went when he sober, and that be about once or twice a year.

So I look at that bone. "What kinda voodoo you work with that mojo?"

"This is a keybone to the culud man. Ain't but one in the whole world."

"And *you* got it?" I act like I ain't believe him. But I was testin him. I never rush upon a thing I don't know.

"We got it."

"We got?"

"It belongs to the people of God."

I ain't feel like the people of God, but I just let him talk.

"Remember when Ezekiel was in the valley of dry bones?"

I reckoned I did.

". . . And the hand of the Lord was upon me, and carried me out in the spirit to the valley of dry bones.

"And he said unto me, 'Son of man, can these bones live?' and I said unto him, 'Lord, thou knowest.'

"And he said unto me, 'Go and bind them together. Prophesy that I shall come and put flesh upon them from generations and from generations.'

"And the Lord said unto me, 'Son of man, these bones are the whole house of thy brothers, scattered to the islands. Behold, I shall bind up the bones and you shall prophesy the name.'"

Headeye, he stopped. I ain't say nothin. I never seen him so full of the spirit before. I held my tongue. I ain't know what to make of his notion.

He walked on pass me and loped on down to the river bank. This here old place was called Deadman's Landin because they found a dead man there one time. His body was so rotted and ate up by fish and craw dads that they couldn't tell whether he was white or black. Just a dead man.

Headeye went over to them long planks and logs leanin off in the water and begin to push them around like he was making somethin.

"You was followin me." I was mad again.

Headeye acted like he was iggin me. He put his hands up to his eyes and looked far out over the water. I could barely make out the other side of the river. It was real wide right along there and take coupla hours by boat to cross it. Most I ever did was fish and swim. Headeye, he act like he iggin me. I began to bait my hook and go down the bank to where he was. I was mad enough to pop him side the head, but I shoulda been glad. I just wanted him to own up to the truth. I walked along the bank. That damn river was risin. It was lappin up over the planks of the landin and climbin up the bank.

Then the funniest thing happened. Headeye, he stopped movin and shovin on those planks and looks up at me. His pole is laying back under a willow tree like he wan't goin to fish none. A lot of birds were still flyin over and I saw a bunch of wild hogs rovin along the levee. All of a sudden Headeye, he say:

"I ain't mean no harm what I said about you workin with the devil. I take it back."

It almost knocked me over. Me and Headeye was arguin a while back bout how many niggers there is in the Bible. Headeye, he know all about it, but I ain't give on to what I know. I looked sideways at him. I figured he was tryin to make up for followin me. But there was somethin funny goin on so I held my peace. I said 'huh-huh,' and I jus kept on lookin at him.

Then he points out over the water and up in the sky wavin his hand all round like he was twirlin a lasso.

"You see them signs?"

I couldn't help but say 'yeah.'

"The Ark is comin."

"What Ark?"

"You'll see."

"Noah's Ark?"

"Just wait. You'll see."

And he went back to fixin up that landin. I come to see what he was doin pretty soon. And I had a notion to go down and pitch in. But I knowed Headeye. Sometimes he gets a notion in his big head and he act crazy behind it. Like the time in church when he told Rev. Jenkins that he heard people moanin out on the river. I remember that. Cause papa went with the men. Headeye, his old man was with them out in that boat. They thought it was somebody took sick and couldn't row ashore. But Headeye, he kept tellin them it was a lot of people, like a multitude.

Anyway, they ain't find nothin and Headeye, his daddy hauled off and smacked him side the head. I felt sorry for him and didn't laugh as much as the other kids did, though sometimes Headeye's notions get me mad too.

Then I come to see that maybe he wasn't followin me. The way he was actin I knowed he wasn't scared to be there at Deadman's Landin. I threw my line out and made like I was fishin, but I wasn't, cause I was steady watchin Headeye.

By and by the clouds started to get thick as clabber milk. A wind come up. And even though the little waves slappin the sides of the bank made the water jump around and dance, I could still tell that the river was risin. I looked at Headeye. He was wanderin off along the bank, wadin out in the shallows and leanin over like he was lookin for somethin.

I comest to think about what he said, that valley of bones. I comest to get some kinda crazy notion myself. There was a lot of signs, but they weren't nothin too special. If you're sharp-eyed you always seein somethin along the Mississippi.

I messed around and caught a couple of fish. Headeye, he was wadin out deeper in the Sippi, bout hip-deep now, standin still like he was listenin for somethin I left my pole under a big rock to hold it down and went over to where he was.

"This ain't the place," I say to him.

Headeye, he ain't say nothin. I could hear the water come to talk a little. Only river people know how to talk to the river when it's mad. I watched the light on the waves way upstream where the ole Sippi bend, and I could tell that she was movin faster. Risin. The shakin was fast and the wind had picked up. It was whippin up the canebrake and twirlin the willows and the swamp oak that drink themselves full along the bank.

I said it again, thinkin maybe Headeye would ask me where was the real place. But he ain't even listen.

"You come out here to fish or fool?" I asked him. But he waved his hand back at me to be quiet. I knew then that Headeye had some crazy notion in his big head and that was it. He'd be talkin about it for the next two weeks.

"Hey!" I hollered at him. "Eyehead, can't you see the river's on the rise? Let's shag outa here."

He ain't pay me no mind. I picked up a coupla sticks and chunked them out near the place where he was standin just to make sure he ain't fall asleep right out there in the water. I ain't never knowed Headeye to fall asleep at a place, but bein as he is so damn crazy, I couldn't take the chance.

Just about that time I hear a funny noise. Headeye, he hear it too, cause he motioned to me to be still. He waded back to the bank and ran down to the broken down planks at Deadman's Landin. I followed him. A couple drops of rain smacked me in the face, and the wind, she was whippin up a sermon.

I heard a kind of moanin, like a lot of people. I figured it must be in the wind. Headeye, he is jumpin around like a perch with a hook in the gill. Then he find himself. He come to just stand alongside the planks. He is in the water about knee deep. The sound is steady not gettin any louder now, and not gettin any lower. The wind, she steady whippin up a sermon. By this time, it done got kinda dark, and me, well, I done got kinda scared.

Headeye, he's all right though. Pretty soon he call me.

"Fish-hound?"

"Yeah?"

"You better come on down here."

"What for? Man, can't you see it gettin ready to rise?"

He ain't say nothin. I can't see too much now cause the clouds done swole up so big and mighty that everything's gettin dark.

Then I sees it. I'm gettin ready to chunk another stick out at him, when I see this big thing movin in the far off, movin slow, down river, naw, it was up river. Naw, it was just movin and standin still at the same time. The damnest thing I ever seed. It just about a damn boat, the biggest boat in the whole world. I looked up and what I took for clouds was sails. The wind was whippin up a sermon on them.

It was way out in the river, almost not touchin the water, just rockin there, rockin and waitin.

Headeye, I don't see him.

Then I look and I see a rowboat comin. Headeye, he done waded out about shoulder deep and he is wavin to me. I ain't know what to do. I guess he bout know that I was gettin ready to run, because he holler out. "Come on Fish! Hurry! I wait for you."

I figured maybe we was dead or somethin and was gonna get the Glory Boat over the river and make it on into heaven. But I ain't say it out aloud. I was so scared I didn't know what I was doin. First thing I know I was side by side with Headeye, and a funny-lookin rowboat was drawin alongside of us. Two men, about as black as anybody black wants to be, was steady strokin with paddles. The rain had reached us and I could hear that moanin like a church full of people pourin out their hearts to Jesus in heaven.

All the time I was tryin not to let on how scared I was. Headeye, he ain't payin no mind to nothin cept that boat. Pretty soon it comest to rain hard. The two big black jokers rowin the boat ain't say nothin to us, and everytime I look at Headeye, he poppin his eyes out tryin to get a look at somethin far off. I couldn't see that far, so I had to look at what was close up. The muscles in those jokers' arms was movin back an forth every time they swung them oars around. It was a funny ride in that rowboat, because it didn't seem like we was in the water much. I took a chance and stuck my hand over to see, and when I did that they stopped rowin the boat and when I looked up we was drawin longside this here ark, and I tell you it was the biggest ark in the world.

I asked Headeye if it was Noah's Ark, and he tell me he didn't know either. Then I was scared.

They was tyin that rowboat to the side where some heavy ropes hung over. A long row of steps were cut in the side near where we got out, and the moanin sound was real loud now, and if it wasn't for the wind and rain beatin and whippin us up the steps, I'd swear the sound was comin from someplace inside the ark.

When Headeye got to the top of the steps I was still makin my way up. The two jokers were gone. On each step was a number, and I couldn't help lookin at them numbers. I don't know what number was on the first step, but by the time I took notice I was on 1608, and they went on like that right on up to a number that made me pay attention: 1944. That was when I was born. When I got up to Headeye, he was standin on a number, 1977, and so I ain't pay the number any more mind.

If that ark was Noah's, then he left all the animals on shore because I ain't see none. I kept lookin around. All I could see was doors and cabins. While we was standin there takin in things, half scared to death, an old man come walkin toward us. He's dressed in skins and his hair is grey and very woolly. I figured he ain't never had a haircut all his life. But I didn't say nothin. He walks over to Headeye and that poor boy's eyes bout to pop out.

Well, I'm standin there and this old man is talkin to Headeye. With the wind blowin and the moanin, I couldn't make out what they was sayin. I got the feelin he didn't want me to hear either, because he was leanin in on Headeye. If that old fellow was Noah, then he wasn't like the Noah I'd seen in my Sunday School picture cards. Naw, sir. This old guy was wearin skins and sandals and he was black as Headeye and me, and he had thick features like us, too. On them pictures Noah was always white with a long beard hangin off his belly.

I looked around to see some more people, maybe Shem, Ham and Japheh, or wives and the rest who was suppose to be on the ark, but I ain't see nobody. Nothin but all them doors and cabins. The ark is steady rockin like it is floating on air. Pretty soon Headeye come over to me. The old man was goin through one of the cabin doors. Before he closed the door he turns around and points at me and Headeye. Headeye, he don't see this, but I did. Talkin about scared. I almost ran and jumped off that boat. If it had been a regular boat, like somethin I could stomp my feet on, then I guess I just woulda done it. But I held still.

"Fish-hound, you ready?" Headeye say to me.

"Yeah, I'm ready to get ashore." I meant it, too.

"Come on. You got this far. You scared?"

"Yeah, I'm scared. What kinda boat is this?"

"The Ark. I told you once."

I could tell now that the roarin was not all the wind and voices. Some of it was engines. I could hear that chug-chug like a paddle wheel whippin up the stern.

"When we gettin off here? You think I'm crazy like you?" I asked him. I was mad. "You know what that old man did behind your back?"

"Fish-hound, this is a soulboat."

I figured by now I best play long with Headeye. He got a notion goin and there ain't nothin mess his head up more than a notion. I stopped tryin to fake him out. I figured then maybe we both was crazy. I ain't feel crazy, but I damn sure couldn't make heads or tails of the situation. So I let it ride. When you hook a fish, the best thing to do is just let him get a good hold, let him swallow it. Specially a catfish. You don't go jerkin him up as soon as you get a nibble. With a catfish you let him go. I figured I'd better let things go. Pretty soon, I figured I'd catch up with somethin. And I did.

Well, me and Headeye were kinda arguin, not loud, since you had to keep your voice down on a place like that ark out of respect. It was like that. Headeye, he tells me that when the cabin doors open we were suppose to go down the stairs. He said anybody on this boat could consider hisself *called*.

"Called to do what?" I asked him. I had to ask him, cause the only kinda callin I knew about was when somebody *hollered* at you or when the Lord *called* somebody to preach. I figured it out. Maybe the Lord had called him, but I knew dog well He wasn't *callin* me. I hardly ever went to church and when I did go it was only to play with the gals. I knowed I wasn't fit to whip up no flock of people with holiness. So when I asked him, called for what, I ain't have in my mind nothin I could be called for.

"You'll see," he said, and the next thing I know we was goin down steps into the belly of that ark. The moanin jumped up into my ears loud and I could smell somethin funny, like the burnin of sweet wood. The churning of a paddle wheel filled up my ears and when Headeye stopped at the foot of the steps, I stopped too. What I saw I'll never forget as long as I live.

Bones. I saw bones. They were stacked all the way to the top of the ship. I looked around. The under side of the whole ark was nothin but a great bone-house. I looked and saw crews of black men handlin in them bones. There was crew of two or three under every cabin around that ark. Why, there must have been a million cabins. They were doin it very carefully, like they were holdin onto babies or somethin precious. Standin like a captain was the old man we had seen top deck. He was holdin a long piece of leather up to a fire that was burnin near the edge of an opening which showed outward to the water. He was readin that piece of leather.

On the other side of the fire, just at the edge of the ark, a crew of men was windin up a rope. They were chantin every time they pulled. I couldn't understand what they was sayin. It was a foreign talk, and I never learned any kind of foreign talk. In front of us was a fence so as to keep anybody comin down the steps from bargin right in. We just stood there. The old man knew we was there, but he was busy readin. Then he rolls up this long scroll and starts to walk in a crooked path through the bones laid out on the floor. It was like he was walkin frontwards, backwards, sidewards and every which a way. He was bein careful not to step on them bones. Headeye, he looked like he knew what was goin on, but when I see all this I just about popped my eyes out.

Just about the time I figure I done put things together, somethin happens. I bout come to figure them bones were the bones of dead animals and all the men wearin skin clothes, well, they was the skins of them animals, but just about time I think I got it figured out, one of the men haulin that rope up from the water starts to holler. They all stop and let him moan on and on.

I could make out a bit of what he was sayin, but like I said, I never was good at foreign talk.

> *Aba aba, al ham dilaba*
> *aba aba, mtu brotha*
> *aba aba, al ham dilaba*
> *aba aba, bretha brotha*
> *aba aba, djuka brotha*
> *aba, aba, al ham dilaba*

Then he stopped. The others begin to chant in the back of him, real low, and the old man, he stop where he was, unroll that scroll and read it, and then he holler out: "Nineteen hundred and twenty-three!" Then he close up the scroll and continue his coming towards me and Headeye. On his way he had to stop and do the same thing about four times. All along the side of the ark them great black men were haulin up bones from that river. It was the craziest thing I ever saw. I knowed then it wasn't no animal bones. I took a look at them and they was all laid out in different ways, all making some kind of body and there was big bones and little bones, parts of bones, chips, tid-bits, skulls, fingers and everything. I shut my mouth then. I knowed I was onto somethin. I had fished out somethin.

I comest to think about a sermon I heard about Ezekiel in the valley of dry bones. The old man was lookin at me now. He look like he was sizin me up.

Then he reach out and open the fence. Headeye, he walks through and the old man closes it. I keeps still. You best to let things run their course in a situation like this.

"Son, you are in the house of generations. Every African who lives in America has a part of his soul in this ark. God has called you, and I shall anoint you."

He raised the scroll over Headeye's head and began to squeeze like he was tryin to draw the wetness out. He closed his eyes and talked very low.

"Do you have your shield?"

Headeye, he then brings out this funny cloth I see him with, and puts it over his head and it flops all the way over his shoulder like a hood.

"Repeat after me," he said. I figured that old man must be some kind of minister because he was ordaining Headeye right there before my eyes. Everythin he say, Headeye, he sayin behind him.

> *Aba, I consecrate my bones.*
> *Take my soul up and plant it again.*
> *Your will shall be my hand.*
> *When I strike you strike.*
> *My eyes shall see only thee.*
> *I shall set my brother free.*
> *Aba, this bone is thy seal.*

I'm steady watchin. The priest is holdin a scroll over his head and I see some oil fallin from it. It's black oil and it soaks into Headeye's shield and the shield turns dark green. Headeye ain't movin. Then the priest pulls it off.

"Do you have your witness?"

Headeye, he is tremblin. "Yes, my brother, Fish-hound."

The priest points at me then like he did before.

"With the eyes of your brother Fish-hound, so be it?" He was askin me. I nodded my head. Then he turns and walks away just like he come.

Headeye, he goes over to one of the fires, walkin through the bones like he been doin it all his life, and he holds the shield in till it catch fire. It don't burn with a flame, but with a smoke. He puts it down on a place which looks like an altar or somethin, and he sits in front of the smoke cross-legged, and I can hear him moanin. When the shield it all burnt up, Headeye takes out that little piece of mojo bone and rakes the ashes inside. Then he zig-walks over to me, opens up that fence and goes up the steps. I have to follow, and he ain't say nothin to me. He ain't have to then.

It was several days later that I see him again. We got back that night late, and everybody wanted to know where we was. People from town said the white folks had lynched a nigger and threw him in the river. I wasn't doin no talkin till I see Headeye. Thas why he picked me for his witness. I keep my word.

Then that evenin, whilst I'm in the house with my ragged sisters and brothers and my old papa, here come Headeye. He had a funny look in his eye. I knowed some notion was whippin his head. He must've been runnin. He was out of breath.

"Fish-hound, broh, you know what?"

"Yeah," I said. Headeye, he know he could count on me to do my part, so I ain't mind showin him that I like to keep my feet on the ground. You can't never tell what you get yourself into by messin with mojo bones.

"I'm leavin." Headeye, he come up and stand on the porch. We got a no-count rabbit dog, named Heyboy, and when Headeye come up on the porch Heyboy, he jump up and come sniffin at him.

"Git," I say to Heyboy, and he jump away like somebody kick him. We hadn't seen that dog in about a week. No tellin what kind of devilment he been into.

Headeye, he ain't say nothin. The dog, he stand up on the edge of the porch with his two front feet lookin at Headeye like he was goin to get piece bread chunked out at him. I watch all this and I see who been takin care that no-count dog.

"A dog ain't worth a mouth of bad wine if he can't hunt," I tell Headeye, but he is steppin off the porch.

"Broh, I come to tell you I'm leavin."

"We all be leavin if the Sippi keep risin," I say.

"Naw," he say.

Then we walk off. I come down off that porch.

"Man, you need another witness?" I had to say somethin.

Headeye, he droop when he walk. He turned around, but he ain't droopin.

"I'm goin, but someday I be back. You is my witness."

We shook hands and Headeye, he was gone, moving fast with that no-count dog runnin long side him.

He stopped once and waved. I got a notion when he did that. But I been keepin it to myself.

People been askin me where'd he go. But I only tell em a little somethin I learned in church. And I tell em bout Ezekiel in the valley of dry bones.

Sometimes they say, "Boy, you gone crazy?" and then sometimes they'd say, "Boy, you gonna be a preacher yet," or then they'd look at me and nod their heads as if they knew what I was talkin bout.

I never told em about the Ark and them bones. It would make no sense. They think me crazy then for sure. Probably say I was gettin to be as crazy as Headeye, and then they'd turn around and ask me again:

"Boy, where you say Headeye went?"

QUINCE DUNCAN

A LETTER

I don't feel no ways tired.
I come too far from where I started from.
Nobody told me the road would be easy.
I don't believe He brought me this far
To leave me.

—Gospel Song arranged by James Cleveland

IT'S BOILING.

Water buried in the veins of the earth, the porous, humid earth, igniting wind and fire. Contrasts. It is a heterogenous world huddled on the edge of town, containing a hidden unity that explodes in the polychromy of its vegetation.

Various metallic sounds drown out the plaintive voice of the land, which is stifled by great need, anguish and intense heat. Shouts rise up stronger than the sound of iron rusted by usage and time. It is the monotonous plea of a town that is seething.

"Get ya hot bread, hot bread, good hot bread, coconut candy . . . meat patties, coconut candy, meat patties, patties, patties . . ."

In that unchained melody, you can intimately feel the rhythm of a race that refuses to fall. It's in their eyes, in their voices. Siquirres is in turmoil; it's falling to pieces.

Translated by Dellita Martin-Ogunsola.

"Yucca, yucca, yucca, *bofe*... fish ... *bofe* ... fish ... meat patties ... patties ... patties ..."

When the train stops, passengers scurry. Siquirres oozes through the town's pores; breasts dehydrate, children's throats dry out in the searing heat. Looking out the door of the mail car, the conductor bows. Someone smiles in response. A barefoot child goes stumbling by, hurriedly pursuing an invisible goal. He slips, falls, gets up rubbing his hands, and continues indifferent to everyone, losing himself in anonymity.

"Don't the gentleman wants to buy ... some homemade coconut candy? Taste 'em; these fried ones the best."

"Three patties. Are they fresh?"

"What you expect?"

"What can I say?"

"That they real good, and then you ain't seen nothin' yet."

Out of boxcars come food for a whole nation, liquor that dulls the senses, and ice that quenches the intense heat consuming it.

An old woman waits with hope-filled eyes. Her face, mellowed by age, is a plethora of wrinkles, her hair, disheveled. She has on an apron which hangs from her waist, symbolizing the creative spirit that dwells within. Her toes peep out at the world through torn shoes and tattered stockings.

Cruel, almost inhuman, a voice tears into her: "No, Miss Spence, there're no letters for you today."

The wind picks up the voice, playing with it. The wind nails the savage fist of its laughter. Too heavy for the air to sustain, the mockery is dashed against the rocks. The echo catches the story and smears it in the old lady's ears, eyes, nostrils and mouth: "No, Miss Spence, there aren't any letters for you today; there'll never be any." But with all that, she kept the faith.

Slowly the train resumes its journey, drowning out with its characteristic noise the hum of that daily litany. The wind unfolds, scatters, regroups, stirring up whirlpools, robbing the town of its supplication only to convert it into dust.

Arms wave goodbye. So much sweat, so much weight does not allow for more. Some boys hang from the moving train, recklessly casting their fate to the wind. A little farther on they hop off and run a stretch before stopping and returning.

Siquirres is boiling, sweating, falling apart.

"Miss Spence" (Was it the Angel of Resurrection or the air?).

"Miss Spence, Lippo's callin' you. He says he did find a letter of yours."

The old woman tried in vain to recapture the wind's laughter, but it was silent.

For how many endless days had she made that same trip during the last two years. Great was her unwavering faith in God; abundant were her prayers. In the rain sometimes, at others withstanding the scorching heat of the plain, water and sun equally inclement. Sometimes when it was neither raining nor sunny, she had to put up with the inconvenience of dragging her 57-year-old body from Brooklin downtown without any respect from the unbearable heat, and to sit down on wooden benches made for chastising the bones instead of resting them. And then, fatigued from misery, anguish and heat, to get from Lippo, to whom she was invisible, the same disinterested, automatic response: "No, Miss Spence, there're no letters for you. No, ma'm, there's nothin', m'am."

Today the world was expanding its horizon—her son had written! Didn't she recognize his handwriting on the envelope? God moves in mysterious ways His wonders to perform!

She advanced with great difficulty.

It was not easy to cross railroad tracks with innumerable wooden slats, sharp stones, and potholes. Her feet were barely covered with what had once been a good pair of shoes. Her sight was failing, for the years were betraying her.

Like a muletrain at dusk, it was necessary for her to proceed slowly with the heavy burden of cocoa on her back, like life in Siquirres—slow, but never steady.

Siquirres was disintegrating little by little.

She finally got to the small shack that was the family dwelling. Seven heads peeped through the window: seven different faces, like baby chickens flinging themselves headlong to get under their mother's wings.

Seven brothers and sisters. Only one was missing—the oldest, who lived with his mother. Clustered around her, the others had made her old age more oppressive. But there was nothing she could do. They were bone of her bone and flesh of her flesh, her son's bloodline.

The grandmother propelled herself forward by quickening her steps. A ray of hope whose sparks had already spread to the children illumined her. She broke the seal and stood there looking at the letter, inside of which lay a beautiful bill of currency. A light breeze absorbed a little of the heat from the atmosphere and departed, carrying with it praises and honor that quickly sought God's ears.

That Sunday the children ate fish for the first time in two years. The Sunday after Easter she had made white rice and fish and, like they did every year, the children arrived one by one accompanied by their respective mothers. From that time on she could never allow herself such a luxury. With good reason the children sucked their fingers, licked their plates, smacked their tongues and finally sucked their teeth.

Also that Sunday bought eighteen tickets of Number 40 from the illegal lottery and ten from the Panamanian lottery; and because the Devil made her do it, she also bought ten from the national pot. But she had experienced bad luck up to that very moment: Number 38 came out. "I was close," she thought; "perhaps I'll hit the jackpot later."

She enjoyed seeing the children eat. Po' lil' things. Dropped jus' like that. At the beginning she doubted that they were her grandchildren, but as they grew the Spence family traits stood out more clearly. And that was enough to endear them to her. They were her own bloodline.

Was it they fault for having fast mammas? On the other hand, how could you blame her son when such womens should have known better? And what a lack of spunk on the part of these mothers not to love they own chil'ren.

How she had struggled with her own three. She had lived for them. Over the washtub, over the basin, over the stove: she had lived for them. By giving up her own possibilities for progress and happiness—through honest and dishonest propositions—she had remained faithful to her children, devoting herself entirely to them. And today with equal devotion, she bore the responsibility for her grandchildren, and because of that selfsame love she incurred the disdain of her neighbors, for whom she was the biggest fool in the whole Atlantic Province.

"Miss Spence," the mothers announced one after another. "I'm gon' leave the lil' one here. He a grandchild of yourn and his daddy gone. Y'all mistaken if you think I'm gon' take care him."

"But . . ."

"You the grandmother; get it straight with yo' son. Miss Spence, I'm leavin' your lil' grandbaby here. You see 'bout him."

Jus' like that. With they kinky li'l heads and hope-filled eyes, they was left with her one by one. Her neighbor lady thought she was a mad woman. Even the priest told her she wasn't obliged to take on such a load. But what could she do? What would the priest have done with his own grandchil'ren if he had any?

They were bone of her bone, her son's flesh and blood.

Neither was it something for which she repented. The children compensated her with a lot of joy.

Two years of silence passed like that, with her taking in other people's washing, selling little boxes of jelly, plaintain torts and yucca pudding. That way she earned her daily bread, at least the bread part. But then so great a burden undermined her strength little by little until it made her sick. She kept the faith though. "He know I got the lil' angels. He won't let me down. The reason he don't write me is 'cause he don't have nothin' to send. That's the only reason he don't write me." And as if he had heard her, the letter said exactly that. In addition, it revealed some other things that were more disturbing, those which a mother's heart had already intuited. Nevertheless, things were now going better for him. He had begun to earn a good living, which was very important. Besides, he had enrolled in night school, and that was even more important.

"An' here I am thinkin' it was already too late for him. My boy!"

That's what she would say to those who were quick to point out her son's faults: "My boy. Y'all gon' see what he capable of."

Someone was whispering a kind of gray poem in the density of the wind. Eight children, seven of whom had no-good mothers. He fled one dawn saying, "Mama, I can't stand it no mo'; I'm goin' to the big city." Then, two years of silence, and finally, a one-page letter. And the ultimate—enclosing in the same a 100-dollar bill. Yes, they was signifyin' 'bout her boy.

But he could also do other things. That had already been demonstrated. Yes, he aspired to do great things, quite the opposite of Bromly and Agnes, who were turning tricks in Limon. Feeling jubilant, she kissed the letter. She left a spot of coconut oil stamped on the fly, smelling like fish and onions.

Outside, the water in the earth's veins was still boiling.

THE MIRACLE

Aт тнат momeNт, I was strolling on the levee, enjoying the freshness of the evening breeze. It had been a day of feverish activity in the port. There were still huge stacks of rice and coffee sacks that the tired stevedores were continuing to move toward the dock. I was just about to sit down when a stranger approached.

"May I have a cigarette?" he asked me in a foreign accent.

I tried to look at the stranger's face, half hidden by the thick foliage of the almond trees, but before I could answer him, he tried to put me at ease:

"Don't be afraid. I'm not who you think I am."

"I'm not thinking about anything," I said to him in a strained voice.

"You think I am an assailant," he contradicted me firmly. "Will you give me the cigarette I asked for?"

"I don't have any," I said lying to him, hoping he would go away.

"If you give me one, you'll have three left in your pack."

"How do you know that?" I asked, showing my annoyance. "Did you see it?"

"I didn't have to see it."

Grudgingly, I offered him the cigarette.

"Do you realize that there are exactly three left in your pack?" he said smugly.

"Yes," I agreed, forcing myself to smile slightly.

"You are surprised and you are tired. You have worked hard."

"It's been an exhausting day," I admitted reluctantly.

"Come on, let's sit down. May I have a match?" he asked.

Translated by Ann Venture Young.

He lit his cigarette and savored it. We sat down. I kept asking myself, "Who is this man? He looks like a childhood friend with whom I experienced the misfortune of the horse in the river," I said to myself. He answered me:

"I am not the friend you are thinking about. You and I have never met. I am Juan Caminos, at your service."

He extended his hand which I shook. Then he added:

"I didn't have anything to do with the horse that drowned while crossing the river."

I was dumbfounded.

"How . . . ?" I was about to finish my question, but he interrupted me while blowing dense puffs of smoke:

"Don't be alarmed. I read everybody's mind."

Being slightly annoyed, I tried to get away from him by saying:

"Forgive me, but my wife is waiting for me across the street in the supermarket. I know you'll understand that I must . . ."

"I beg your pardon," he said smiling, "you are a bachelor and no one is waiting for you there, not even your girlfriend."

"What girlfriend?"

"Marcia."

"Sir," I said to him while getting up, seized by a mixture of anger and annoyance, but he grabbed my arm and restrained me, all the while gazing at me. Then he asked:

"Are you finally going to see the Black and White Sisters' strip-tease act?"

"I hadn't planned to go," I answered, sitting down again.

"And what about those tickets in your wallet?"

"You are mistaken. I don't have any."

"See if you don't."

"Ah," I thought, "he is a nervy rascal. He's been watching me. He's trying to frighten me so that he can attack me. He thinks I'm going to show him my wallet. Then he'll rob me. He's probably a slick international thief."

I felt more afraid, despite the fact that several persons were strolling through the area and there was a policeman making his regular rounds.

Indifferent to my discomfort, he continued:

"You're not the only one that life has played cruel tricks on. Sometimes we feel sorry for ourselves because we don't attain a goal in life. The truth of the matter is that even when man accomplishes a goal, he's still not satisfied. There is always something more that he wants."

"I don't know what you're getting at."

"A little while ago you were feeling sorry for yourself because you failed to obtain your law degree. When a luxury car passed by, you felt disadvantaged, because the owner was one of your classmates who is now a distinguished jurist."

"I stared at him from head to toe, feeling an even greater displeasure. But he just smiled, and I said to him:

"Lawyer? Yes. The car? OK . . . But who are you?"

"I've already told you. Shall we go to see the Black and White twins? You won't be sorry."

"The truth is," I confessed, "that I plan to invite my buddy to go with me . . ."

"OK then, give Fortunato a call . . ."

"Fortunato?" I interrupted. "I have three good buddies. How do you know that he's the one I plan to invite?"

"Even I can't explain how I know, but that's the way it is."

Believing that I had reached the height of astonishment, I said to him:

"Come with me to the phone booth."

We walked in silence. I knew that he was reading my mind, so I began to feel it was quite unnecessary for me to speak. When I came out of the booth, he said to me:

"Since your friend can't go, the two of us can attend."

"OK. Let's go."

"I hope Pablito doesn't get any worse."

"What Pablito?" I asked him, trying to verify his power, since he had stayed a good distance from the phone booth while I was talking to Fortunato, and I had not mentioned the boy's name.

"Fortunato's youngest son. Let's get going. You'll like the show. It's a little corny, but there's no place else to go. Furthermore I want to give you a demonstration of real mental telepathy."

When we got to the nightclub it was crowded. The master of ceremonies announced the performance of the Black and White Sisters. At that very moment, a middleaged man in a wheelchair burst into the aisle which separated the two rows of seats. He managed his wheelchair with dexterity and situated himself on the front row.

"Do you know the invalid?" he asked me.

"No. And you?"

"Neither do I, but it makes no difference to me. I'm reading his mind like I'm reading yours and I know what Marcia is thinking about also. The girl in the rose-colored dress, the one who is seated next to the invalid, is thinking about you in spite of being annoyed at the unexpected company. Both girls are remembering the incident that happened this morning . . ."

"What incident?" I asked him believing that he was trying to intimidate me.

"The one that took place in the Dumarest Department Store, when Marcia was going to pull her by her hair, but you restrained her . . ."

I stood there dumbfounded.

"Don't go on, please. You know too much." I looked at him.

The orchestra began to play and a few couples went out on the dance floor. I invited Juan to a booth where, from behind the beaded curtain, we could observe the show without being seen.

"Forget that business about the check," he said. "You are worrying for nothing."

"What check?" I inquired, to test his knowledge again.

The truth is that at that moment I was thinking about the consequences of my error that afternoon in the office.

"The check that was cancelled afterwards. Your boss knows that your mistake was not on purpose. And he hasn't lost his confidence in you."

"I hope that's true," I replied, no longer astounded by the accuracy with which he was reading my thoughts.

"I told you that I wanted to demonstrate my powers. One day you will write about me."

"Write?" I asked, with tongue in cheek, because up to that time I had never written anything in my life other than business documents.

I went along with him. He suggested that I find a friend and get a good supply of paper for the experiment. I left and came back with Antonio. I introduced them and placed the paper on the table.

"The proof is easy," he told us. "Both of you will write without my saying a word to you."

"And how is that possible?" a surprised Antonio asked.

"Be patient. You'll soon understand everything." Then he addressed me: "I will read the mind of any person in this audience whom you choose and the two of you will write what I dictate to you mentally. Understood?"

"Understood," we both answered together.

"Choose a subject," he told me.

I asked Antonio to help me. We looked at the audience.

"The man in the wheelchair?" I suggested to my friend.

"Good," he agreed.

We sat down pointing out the invalid to him.

"Him?" he asked us in disbelief.

We confirmed our choice. Then he instructed us:

"Sit down and make yourselves comfortable. Take a pen and a good supply of paper. I will communicate to you mentally what you are supposed to write. Please, a cigarette," he asked me.

"That'll leave me two," I answered.

"I don't want one of the three. Give me one from the pack that you bought on the corner, before you came back with Antonio."

"How did he find out?" Antonio asked in amazement.

The stranger answered him with a smile.

I handed him the pack. He lit up one, and put the rest in his shirt pocket.

"Thanks a lot for getting them for me," he said, smiling.

"You're welcome," I replied, to Antonio's surprise.

"Don't worry so much, Antonio," he said. "Your friend on the high seas is thinking about you and wants me to tell you that he will be in port this morning at three-thirty but you are not to meet him where you did last time. This time you're to go to the carob tree by the bay . . ."

"Do you know that spot? Do you know Pedro Pablo?" he asked while getting to his feet. "Tell me the truth because what you're dealing with now is very serious. And we'll have to keep an eye out for the watchmen."

"You just have to follow his instructions. That's why I told you not to worry. It won't take us more than two hours here. That'll give you plenty of time."

"We're ready," I reminded him. "Get yourself ready, Antonio."

The third bell sounded. The orchestra became silent. And the Black and White Sisters came out on the stage.

"Let's begin," Juan Caminos told us. "Let's begin writing down that crippled fellow's thoughts."

"A literal transcription," I advised Antonio. "And afterwards we'll compare notes . . ."

"And you'll see that they're the same," he interjected. "Ready."

We wrote:

". . . it looks like them they are exactly eighteen years three months and eight days old Dr. Cortés told me that there has never been another case like it in the world and he was the one who took care of Lupe when I read at home that they had made their stage debut in Guayaquil I decided to wait until they came to Quito before seeing them at least here nobody knows me and I can dispell my doubts I wonder what their real names are because this thing of Black and White Sisters is just their stage name what beautiful girls how slim what poise they show in their dancing and how lovely their songs and what figures and what busts with that sensual mouth the black one reminds me of Sophia Loren with their exuberant bosoms they've charmed the audience listen to the applause I think they are the ones how eagerly Lupe and I awaited the birth of our first child I wanted a boy and she wanted a little girl and when I saw them what a shock how could white parents have a black girl what a sense of shame what a scandal at first I thought it was a joke but Dr. Cortés confirmed it telling me simply that they are my daughters and he didn't even congratulate me how could he congratulate me on the birth of a phenomenon did Lupe deceive me or not I never found out she took the secret with her to her grave."

Under the table, Antonio touched me on the foot. When I looked at him, his hand was trembling and his face was pale.

"Is that what the man in the wheelchair is thinking?" I asked.

"That's it exactly. What I'm dictating to you is an exact transcription."

Antonio and I compared notes. We laughed like fools when we discovered that they were exactly the same.

"Shall we go on?" he asked us.

"By all means."

Again he told us to begin writing, and we copied:

". . . I hated that black girl from the first I didn't kiss Lupe when I left the hospital I went home and spent the early morning hours drinking and thinking about that unusual birth how my co-workers at the office and my friends at the club were going to laugh at me would murmur about horns the way they always did when there was the slightest doubt I didn't go to work that day racking my brain suffering at noon I remember it as clearly as if it were today bitter memories from the past always seem to be relived in the present at noon I cried like a baby the disgrace the dishonor me with a black daughter I would never be able to accept it I didn't go visit Lupe that day and at night some friends came to congratulate me I felt the ridicule underneath their well-wishes making me suffer I almost threw them out of the house how their congratulations hurt me I could hardly sleep that second night and in the morning when I was on my way to visit Lupe the height of insult this time undisguised two enormous horns painted black hanging over the front door blowing in the wind I got enough courage to go visit my wife she found me changed and she told me so and without mentioning the black horns to her I told her that I did not feel any affection for the little black girl I still referred to her as the girl it was the last time because from then on I called her monster or phenomenon but how she dances even better than the white girl I wonder who gave them their stage name where did they get it and the truth is that it suits them very well the Black and White Sisters is it they we'll see in the next set I'll get a little closer to see them better I know how to identify them I remember their special features if I only knew their age but maybe they don't even know it themselves what a shame that they have finished their first number I'm not interested in watching these other jokers dance I hate all dancers except those two I truly admire them and I don't envy them I'll go out for a few minutes to catch a breath of fresh air I'm lucky that no one recognizes me or knows my secret or what I'm thinking."

"Want a smoke?" Juan Caminos asked us, handing us the pack.

The invalid made his way toward the door, handling his chair with extraordinary dexterity. We smoked and watched the spirited dancers.

"Can you read his mind even without seeing him?" Antonio inquired.

"It's just as easy as when I'm looking at him. Shall we try it?"

"OK," I replied.

"Start copying," he said, and we continued writing.

". . . and sometimes I think they're the ones and at other times I'm not sure I behaved very badly I really killed Lupe with my reproaches I shouldn't have acted that way life has its mysteries and perhaps this is one of those that we are not meant to understand perhaps not even the scientists waiter bring me a shot of whiskey on the double."

"Whiskey?" I asked of Caminos.

"I'm sorry," he explained, "that's what he's ordering from the waiter. I should have told you."

"All right," I said, "let's have something to drink."

"Thanks, but I don't drink. But you go right ahead."

I called the waiter and he promptly brought us a bottle and some glasses. He asked us if we wanted to go on writing or if we preferred to talk for a while. We decided to chat and he told us some stories from his many experiences. When the twins began their second set, he dictated to us mentally:

". . . Now, yes, I'm sure they're the ones the black girl has two dimples and the white girl has only one on her right cheek there is no doubt the white one is my daughter but how much she resembles the black girl in almost every way the black

girl is not my daughter she can't be I don't have any black blood in me and neither did Lupe have any of that damned blood in her veins poor Guadalupe how
she suffered when I arranged the disappearance of the black child from our house
I had to do it because her presence there was like a living testimony to the scandalous act and the black horns in the garden on the fences on the roof one day I
got a package that was supposed to contain a gift but when I opened it I found a
pair of those damned black horns I gave her to a friend to take her to another city
I paid him well when she was gone I felt relieved for the first few months afterwards I was overcome by repentance Lupe cried as if her heart would break did
she suspect that I was the one responsible when Lupe cried my heart ached and
it even seemed that Glenda cried she was hurt by the absence of the black girl
oh when I remember this I feel a tightness in my heart and I get weak all over
one day I grabbed Lupe by the throat oh how well they dance and how beautifully they sing and how they applaud them I grabbed her by the throat and I demanded a confession I almost strangled her but the only reply I got was negative
that she had never been unfaithful to me that her honor and mine were unblem-
ished that she swore before God and on her mother's ashes that there had never
been another man I threw her to the ground and mad with rage I accused her of
infidelity while kicking her brutally she was reduced to a formless mass of flesh
her clothes bloodied but she never shed a tear nor made a single sound I left the
house puffing and blowing like an angry lion when I returned Glenda was not in
her cradle I didn't attach much importance to it but when I didn't see her the next
day I found out what had happened Lupe told me that she was not in the house
because I had frightened her with my behavior I confronted her again with my
suspicions and I said many unkind things to her and she swore again that she was
innocent where did that bat come from then I asked her that black stain on the
family honor if not from fornication can you explain this insult I couldn't take
any more sometimes we are just not responsible for what we do I took out my gun
but how strange these songs are they're singing now how strange to sing about
and portray a father who desired his daughter when he saw her one morning taking off her brassiere how delightfully risqué their performance without baring their
breasts I took out my gun I aimed it at her and she fell to the floor but I didn't kill
her the bullet got stuck she died the victim of a broken heart yes damn it my behavior killed her some said that the shame of giving birth to a black baby killed her
when she fell dead I became as stiff as a board afterwards I had to use this damned
wheelchair in the beginning what difficulty what anguish what anger what envy
to see everyone else moving about normally later I resigned myself to the condition and accepted it as God's punishment I never heard any more about Glenda
or about the black child it was as if the earth had swallowed them up how agile
these girls are they move as if they have no bones they are like dancing serpents
how pretty without realizing it I applauded them."

The twins finished their second number, and the audience applauded them so
frantically that they came back for three curtain calls. The invalid went outside
again.

"Incredible!" Antonio exclaimed, wiping the perspiration from his brow. "I never would have believed that I could write like this—except from spoken dictation."

Juan Caminos just smiled. Some couples came out on the dance floor. We compared what we had written and, more astounded than ever, we found that it was identical. The stranger was somehow different now. He was no longer the same jovial person who had approached me on the docks. I told him my impression and he confirmed it:

"You're quite right." He urged us to have a drink and he filled our glasses. He continued to talk: "I feel Death's shadow, as cold as the grave, the same way I felt it that time in Bombay."

"Are you going to tell them that he's their father?" he asked him.

"Perhaps, but the situation would become very serious."

"They have a right to know. Tell them," I urged him.

"Is that really what you want?" he asked me, more with his eyes (as I felt them meet mine) than with his voice.

"Yes," I answered him, without giving any thought to the consequences.

"Since it is what you want, I'll do it," he said in a grave tone.

The cripple returned at the beginning of the third number. Juan, visibly changed, instructed us to continue writing and we wrote:

". . . listen to the audience applaud people today are just interested in sex my generation is not like that how can women who call themselves ladies enjoy such voluptuous contortions it's a pity they have to earn a living doing striptease I do not want to see my daughter naked in this place or anywhere else I don't care about the black girl it really is Glenda my heart is telling me and the dimples it is they my God there is no longer the slightest doubt."

"Give me a cigarette!" Juan demanded, his voice trembling.

"You have them in your shirt pocket," I reminded him. He lighted one up hurriedly. His face was flushed.

"Whiskey, give me a drink!" he requested.

"Didn't you say that you don't drink?" I chided him.

"Pour me a drink fast," he retorted and I served him just as the Black and White Sisters had stripped down to transparent garments, the white girl in black and the black girl in white. "They've tuned in!" he shouted. "They've recognized him. The thoughts of all three of them are interwoven."

He observed the scene; the girls moved like butterflies in flight, their sheer dresses serving as wings. Suddenly:

"More whiskey!" he demanded.

"Don't drink any more," I told him, seizing the bottle.

As if possessed he threw his glass crashing to the floor. All three of us were nervous. The twins sang a very sad ballad. The lyrics told of a cruel man, who out of jealousy killed his wife and evicted his two young daughters on a winter's night and how when they were grown they became accomplished prostitutes. When they had finished their song, they spoke to each other in a whisper and to the beat of a slow, sensual song, beneath multicolored lights, they slowly began to undress. We were all dazzled by the girls' extraordinary beauty, when he shouted:

"Write it down, quick . . ."

He took a couple of swallows from the bottle; we wrote:

". . . my daughters I am just like the evil man you just sang about in your song how embarrassing don't undress before my eyes listen to me Glenda he is the murderer yes Norma I feel in my heart that he's the wretch who killed her it's his fault that we are doing striptease we are so unhappy we can't even dream of having a home of our own because who would marry a woman who displays her body in public let's kill him no because he's our father he was not our father let's just forget all about him he's paying for his sins in his wheelchair let's repay him with contempt I am going to embrace them oh my God it's a miracle I can walk and a strong light illumines my brain (excuse me miss excuse me sir don't be concerned please I can walk damn it leave me alone I know what I'm doing) because of you my daughters I can walk again how wonderful it is to walk again like everybody else a hug never vile murderer cruel husband cruel father forgive me (let me go they are my daughters and I'm going to take them away so that they will never have to undress again in public only in front of their husbands) a hug my daughters don't undress yourselves no for the love of God (no I'm not crazy) Oh God."

We ceased writing. Our hands were trembling. We observed the scenario with intrigue. It became a labyrinth of confusion. The twins, naked, remained motionless like resplendent petrified statues, illuminated by the blinking multicolored lights, engulfed by uproarious applause. The father lay at their side. Someone threw a cigarette butt at him and he began to burn. The firemen rushed in with their extinguishers. The audience began to disperse.

"It's not my fault!" Juan Caminos exclaimed, trembling from head to toe, with his eyes rolling in his head. He left the booth and we never saw him again. Antonio and I went to my room where we compared our notes until the wee hours of the morning when my friend left to keep his appointment by the carob tree on the bay. Since then I have walked on many levees and frequented many nightclubs, hoping, in vain, to see Juan Caminos again.

Now that I am writing about this episode in my life, I know that he was right when he said, to my surprise, that one day I would write about him.

RANDALL RANDALL

RANDALL HALPERN RANDALL

189 Wayland Avenue   Apt. 51   Providence, Rhode Island

8:10 A.M., Sunday, November 23, 1980

Miss Holly Diehl
Apt. 41
189 Wayland Avenue
Providence, RI

Dear Holly:

 I am distressed that it has come to this. I had hoped that there would be no reason for me to compose this letter, but it seems the matter at hand will not straighten itself out, considering this morning's condition in the driveway rear of this building.
 Please permit me to state MY SIDE of the matter in question!!!
 My dear wife, a good woman who knits constantly and who makes baby booties for people she doesn't even know, has enjoyed over 20 years of extremely peaceful and harmonious relations with the tenants in this building, and I certainly have tried my best to preserve such a condition in spite of some recent goings-on such as door slamming by tenants on the fourth and sixth floors, etc.
 We have attempted to quietly and without disturbing anyone else on any floor take care of the rubbish and/or garbage from our apartment . . . to the large green dumpster, as detailed in our lease and yours . . . daily (not just weekends as you seem to have deduced, per

Claudia!). However, I usually do it . . . and a major reason is that Claudia suffered a fracture to her knee cap (patella) some time back when she fell on some ice outside the convenience store and had to wear a brace for weeks. And of course I have thrombophlebitis, as did our former president Mr. Nixon, two years ago, throughout my left leg and must watch myself when descending the 87 *steps down to the first floor and out the rear door of this building!!!*

I contacted Mr. Harry Bottoms following your "to whom it may concern" note (which I still have in my possession) and asked him WHO was probably the nicest and most quiet and agreeable tenant in the building—aside from him and Lucy. He said without pause that it is YOU!!! That is WHY I could not understand HOW any such fine person *would block the rear door to prevent passage to the big green dumpster.* . . . Aside from *the probability that the fire department could NEVER get in, in case of a fire in the building!!! I remember vividly when those yellow lines were painted, and I NEVER saw any car in that area right up close blocking the door until your car was there!!!*

You KNOW that once I stopped into your fine apartment and was received most cordially and enjoyed speaking with you about your plants and collection of small dinner bells, etc. I could NOT somehow believe that it was YOUR car (never thought it was for one minute) that was blocking us from the dumpster.

I was planning to seek you out for a discussion of the matter, but the condition, and it was a condition and not a situation as my wife insists, was so serious this morning that I had to state MY side of the case to Mr. Pluckett!!! I HOPE that this will be the end of it—and that my poor wife won't have to cart our waste out and around, so publicly, around three (3) sides of the building to reach the dumpster!!! Mr. Bottoms was just up here again—Claudia spoke with him at length only to discover that you and others have accused me of over-reacting. *Please do not speak about me further and I shall do the same for you.*

Sincerely,
  R.H.R.

P.S.—I don't care what you or anyone else thinks, I am NOT a "trouble-maker" and want a peaceful home just as you no doubt do. I DO try to be alert, however, because there have been several burglaries in the 27 years Claudia has been here and the 16 years that I have been here. And of course the Osco drugstore was broken into again last week.

Randall folded the letter and sealed it in an envelope. He waved it in the air in front of his wife's face as if to say, "This should take care of it."

"It's not such a big deal, Randall," Claudia said.

"What if I were breaking the rule," Randall asked. "What if it was me? You think it would just be let go? No, it wouldn't." He sat down at the kitchen table and scratched at a chip in the formica. "No, it wouldn't and I'll tell you why. It's because she's a young woman and Pluckett's a dirty old man."

Claudia slapped a skillet onto a burner of the gas stove. She laughed.

"Shut up."

"I bet old Pluckett is down there right now having a little party with Miss Diehl." She melted butter in the pan while she opened the refrigerator.

"I only want one egg this morning," Randall said.

"Bacon or sausage?"

"Sausage."

"We're out of sausage," Claudia said.

"Then why did you ask me?"

She put the bacon on the counter next to the carton of eggs. "I wanted to give you a choice."

"But I didn't have a choice."

"You chose, didn't you? You just made the wrong choice." She cracked an egg into the hot skillet. It sizzled.

"Well, I don't want bacon," Randall said.

"Then I won't make you any."

He looked at her in her lavender robe and cream-colored slippers. She was dressed in street clothes, but still she wore that robe over them and those slippers. He hated the way the heels of her feet looked, hard and calloused, white, porous.

"Do you want toast?"

"Is there any bread?"

"Yes."

"Then, yes, I want toast."

Claudia flipped one of the eggs. "I broke your yolk," she told him. She lit a cigarette and put the lighter back down on the sill above the sink.

"I want to put plastic runners down over the carpet in the front room," Claudia said.

"Plastic runners."

"To protect the carpet from wear."

Randall laughed. "Wear? Oh, yeah, from all the visitors we get."

Claudia fell silent as she slid the eggs onto the plates. She pulled the bread from the toaster and put breakfast in front of Randall. She sat with him at the table.

Randall buttered his toast. "This neighborhood is going to hell."

Claudia tore her toast and dipped a corner of it into the yolk of her egg.

"Gangs and drugs," Randall said. "Punks." He watched Claudia eat for a while. "What's wrong with you?"

"Nothing's wrong with me."

"Something's wrong," he said.

"I'll tell you what's wrong. I don't have anybody to talk to. That's what's wrong."

"Here we go again," Randall sighed. "I'm talking to you right now."

Claudia continued to eat.

Randall put his fork down. "Listen, I'm going out to get my medicine. Is there any money in the house?"

Claudia looked up at him. "In my purse."

"What?"

"There's some money in my purse," she repeated.

Randall went into the front room and grabbed Claudia's pocketbook from the buffet. He brought it back to the doorway of the kitchen and found the money in it. "Do you need anything while I'm out?"

"No."

"I'm not going out again, so tell me now if you need anything."

"I don't need anything."

"Okay, but I asked. You can't tell me I didn't ask."

Randall walked out, pulling the door closed behind him. He went down one flight of stairs and stood at number 41. He slipped the note under the door of Holly Diehl's apartment. At that moment the door opened and there was Holly Diehl, a small woman with short blonde hair and she was looking at Randall.

"Just delivering a note to you," Randall said.

Holly Diehl bent and picked it up, looked at the envelope.

Randall realized that he had not put her name on it.

"How do you know it's for me?" she asked.

"It's for you," he said and he turned away and started walking toward the stairs.

"Is this from you?" Holly Diehl asked.

But Randall was gone. He walked down the stairs and out onto Wayland Avenue. The cold wind blew open his jacket and he pulled it closed, zipped it as he walked. He looked in through the window of the Oriental rug store where none of the salesmen spoke English, at least pretended not to speak English. Randall had gone in when the shop first opened, but when he figured out how much they were trying to tell him a rug sold for he got mad. He turned his gaze away when one of the mustached salesmen waved to him.

A blast of heat pushed through Randall when he entered the Osco drugstore and made him too hot. He unzipped his jacket and let out a breath.

"Morning, Mr. Randall," the young clerk, Susie, said. She was setting up a display of blank video tapes.

"Hi, Susie," Randall said. He liked her, liked to look at the way her make-up curved up at the corners of her eyes. He had always thought that Claudia would look good like that, but had never said anything, knew she would take it the wrong way. Claudia could try something, he thought, more make-up or wear her hair differently. She didn't even try. All she ever did was complain about her knee. Susie always smiled at him, so he knew he was still an attractive man.

At the back of the store, the druggist, a fat man named Willy, was in his booth. Randall hated looking up at the man. He didn't like Willy, was sure that the man was cheating him somehow, maybe putting less medicine in each capsule.

"How's the pressure?" Willy asked.

"Under control," Randall said. "How's yours?"

"Oh, I don't have a problem. I watch my diet and walk to work."

Randall nodded as Willy turned away to collect his medicine. "Sure you do, you fat bastard," he said under his breath.

"Excuse me?" Willy said.

"Nothing."

"Oh, I thought you said something." Willy reached through the window and handed down the vial of pills in a small white bag. "There you go."

"Thanks."

"You ought to get some exercise," Willy said. "Gotta stay in shape just to run from the thugs in this neighborhood nowadays."

"You can't outrun them bastards," Randall chuckled.

"Don't need to. Not now."

Randall nodded and walked away down the aisle of foot care items. He remembered once when he had athlete's foot and how good that spray had felt. It was funny he had thought then, and thought now, that his feet didn't usually feel good, bad, or otherwise. It was something when that spray had felt good. He met Susie at the check-out.

"Is that it?" Susie asked.

"That's it." Randall looked at her eyes. "I like your eyes," he said. "The way you paint them." He had never mentioned them to her before. "How's school?"

"Stopped going."

"Oh. Are you still going out with that guy? That cook guy." Randall remembered his white clothes from when he would pick up Susie from the drugstore.

"No. He thought he was hot stuff because he was going to Johnson and Wales."

"Oh."

"I'm trying to get a job as a cosmetician," Susie said.

"You'll be good at it. You always look really pretty." He paused, watching her nails on the register keys. "I hope you don't mind me saying that."

"No, I don't. Thank you, Mr. Randall. That will be twelve-forty-seven."

He handed her a ten and a five. "This stuff just keeps going up."

"Everything does," Susie said. She counted his change out to him. "Want your receipt?"

"I guess."

"Bye now."

Randall waved and walked away, the blast of heat at the doorway bothering him once more as he exited.

Randall paused at the entrance to his building, looked up its side to his window. He decided to walk around back and check on the situation with the driveway and dumpster. He rounded the corner and saw the car before he was there. He couldn't believe it. After all his complaining and his last letter, here was Holly Diehl's car, big as life, in the very same spot, blocking the dumpster. He saw exhaust coming out of the tailpipe and realized that the car was running. Holly Diehl must have just run inside for something. He walked to the driver's side and peered through the window at the purse on the seat. Dumb girl, Randall thought.

Mr. McRae came out of the back door with a bag of garbage and had to squeeze by the blue Honda.

"Can you believe this?" Randall said.

McRae looked at the car. "Pretty tight."

"I've begged her not to park here. It's a fire zone, you know."

McRae nodded and tossed his bag into the container. "I guess, it's not a good idea, all right." He was back at the door now. "Nice car, though." He was gone.

Randall looked at the car, then at the closed door. He thought about taking Holly Diehl's purse, to teach her a lesson, then it occurred to him that he should just take her car. He could get into her car and park it around the block. She'd get the point then.

There was no one on the street at that moment and Randall opened the car door. His heart was racing. He looked around again, then fell in behind the wheel, keeping his eye on the door of the building. He stepped on the clutch, put the car into reverse and released the brake. He backed out slowly, still watching for Holly Diehl. He drove forward away from Wayland Avenue and toward the stop sign at the corner, but he didn't stop, he rolled through it, turning right and noticing behind him a Providence city police car. The cop turned on his blue light.

Randall was sitting in Holly Diehl's car, her open pocketbook beside him. He had taken the car without her permission. He had stolen it. His foot pressed more firmly on the accelerator. The policeman honked his horn. Randall looked at him in the mirror, saw the cop see him looking. He floored it. The car lurched forward and Randall sped away toward the university. The cop turned with him and switched on his siren. Randall felt a pressure in his chest. He careened through a series of alleys and side streets and lost the police car when it slid into a white Plymouth. He saw the cop talking on his radio as he rolled out of sight.

Randall was terrified. He was a criminal on the run. Holly Diehl had no doubt called the police by now to report her car stolen. It occurred to Randall that the policeman could have gotten hurt in his crash. What if that had happened? He would be to blame. He saw the man on the radio, but what if he was calling for an ambulance? What if he had sustained internal injuries or had a bad heart? He could be dying. Randall Halpern Randall could be a murderer. He looked at the little white bag on the seat beside him. He needed one of the pills now. He tried to breathe calmly and deeply, tried to slow his body down. What he needed to do was stop the car and get out, run, hide and sneak back to his apartment. No one knew that he was the car thief. McRae had seen him by the car though. He needed to get to a phone and call Claudia, tell her to tell anyone who asked for him that he was in the bathroom or something like that. He began to slow to a stop when another siren blast pushed his foot to the floor. The tires of the blue Honda squealed as he narrowly missed hitting a woman with a sheep dog. A light snow began to fall. The cop was right behind him, talking on his radio as he drove. Randall found himself on busy Thayer Street, college students everywhere, cars everywhere, people pointing.

There were two police cars behind him now, lights flashing, sirens blowing. Randall imagined he heard his name over a loud speaker. He made a sharp right and headed down the bus-only tunnel toward downtown. The police were caught off guard by this maneuver and slammed into each other at the mouth of the tunnel.

To Randall's surprise there were no police at the bottom of the tunnel. He screeched to a halt and got out of the car, ran along Main Street for a half block, then up through someone's yard, through a couple of yards and up the hill until he was on the campus. In fact, he was suddenly back on Thayer Street, just a block from the accident involving the two police cars. People were standing around, watching, telling each other what they had seen. But no one was looking at Randall even though he was panting and his clothes were grass and dirt stained from his scurry up the hill. He walked away from the commotion, looking up at the snow, which was falling harder now. The white flakes made him think of his white bag and he remembered that he had left his medicine sitting on the seat of Holly Diehl's car.

He found a phone booth on a corner in front of a gas station. He closed the door, fumbled through the change in his pocket, dropped in a quarter and called Claudia.

"Where are you?" Claudia asked.

"Shut up and listen," he barked.

"Don't you tell me to shut up," she said. "Where are you?"

"Has anyone asked for me?"

"Randall? What's going on?"

"Has anyone asked for me?" he repeated.

"No, no one has asked for you. Why?" He could hear her sitting down on the recliner. "Where are you?"

"If anyone calls or comes by just tell them I'm in the bathroom."

"Why?"

"Just do it!"

"Don't yell at me," Claudia said.

"I'm sorry. Do it, please?" Randall hung up the phone, knowing that she wouldn't do it. An ambulance rolled by him, lights flashing. The cop was hurt. He knew it. He couldn't count on Claudia. He was suddenly very cold. The snow was beginning to stick to the grass and bushes.

Randall pushed through the wind to the gas station office. He pieced together forty cents and dropped the coins into the vending machine. He collected his bag of cheese curls from the tray and pulled it open, began to eat as he watched the weather. The man behind the desk, a big greasy man, was staring at Randall. Randall left, shoving the remains of his snack into the pocket of his jacket.

Randall counted his money. He had nearly seven dollars, not enough for anything, certainly not enough for a life on the lam. If only that cop hadn't died in that collision. He was sure the matter could be straightened out if not for that. The cold air was beginning to make his lungs ache when he entered a branch of his bank that he had never visited. There was no line and he went directly to a teller, a youngish woman with big glasses and a gold crown that showed in the back of her mouth when she said,

"May I help you?"

"I'd like to withdraw some money," Randall said. He felt his pocket and realized he didn't have his checkbook. "But I'm afraid I don't have my checkbook."

"What's your account number then?" the woman asked.

"I don't know."

She looked at him over the rim of her glasses.

"My name is Randall, Randall Randall," he said.

"Randall Randall," she repeated. "Would you mind waiting here for a second."

"I just want my money," Randall said.

"I'll be right back." The woman fell away from her stool and walked briskly across the floor to another woman and together they regarded Randall.

Randall looked around. The bank was empty of customers. The guard was by the door looking at him. He looked up and saw the video camera looking at him. Randall began to whistle. He turned, continuing to whistle as he moved toward the door.

"Sir," the young teller called to him, but Randall was gone. He ran down the street and around the corner, stopping finally, hands on knees, panting.

Randall went back to Thayer Street and boarded a bus. There were a couple of kids in the back and a blind man up front next to the driver. They rolled toward the tunnel, and Randall saw the faces of the policemen. Their cars were connected to purple tow trucks with Buzz painted on the doors. The bus passed by and went through the tunnel. Randall looked at his watch and thought about that armed forces ad that said soldiers did more before eight than most people did all day. It was nine-thirty.

Randall wandered into a McDonalds to get warm. He bought a cup of coffee and sat in the middle of the restaurant, away from the windows. His mind was racing but could find nowhere to go. He wouldn't be able to sit here forever. Too long, and the workers would get suspicious. Besides the little, yellow, plastic chairs hurt his butt.

A man in a tattered coat had been sitting in a booth when Randall arrived. He wasn't eating or drinking, just sitting. A kid in a McDonalds hat came and asked him to leave.

"It's cold out there," the man said.

"I'm sorry, sir, but you're going to have to leave."

"It's cold out there."

The kid looked back into the kitchen and caught the eye of another man. He said something to someone Randall couldn't see and came out to the scene.

"He won't go," the kid said.

"Sir, we're trying to run a business here," the new man said. He was tall, lanky and not too old himself. He wore a brass tag that said MANAGER.

"And I'm trying to stay the fuck alive."

"Listen," the manager was getting tough. "You gotta get out of here right now."

"Or what?" The man in the tattered clothes looked the manager up and down. "Or what? You candy-ass, made-up little prick-faced, boy scout."

The manager got mad. "Listen, asshole, the police are coming, already been called."

"The police are coming," the man repeated. "Is that because you can't *handle* the situation?" The man pulled himself up and out of the booth.

The manager and the kid fell back a step.

"Boo," the man said.

The manager got mad and started for the man in tattered clothes, but the kid stopped him.

"You'd better stop him," the man said, headed for the door. "Don't make me have to hurt the sorry-ass."

The manager stopped pushing and said, "Get out of here, you boozed-up, pathetic, homeless motherfucker."

The man in the tattered clothes stopped, held the door open, and looked back at the manager. His eyes were steady. "I ain't pathetic."

Randall watched the man walk past the window and out to the street. He got up himself and threw away his empty cup. He had to use the toilet, but he wanted to be gone when the police arrived.

Randall Randall was scared. He couldn't go home and he had no one to whom he could turn. He thought about the people who liked him. Susie liked him. He liked her. Maybe she would help him. He wondered what she could do, being just a cashier at the Osco. She could go to his apartment and get the checkbook. He would call Claudia and tell her that Susie was coming by for it, but then Claudia would see Susie and get jealous, jealous of her youth, jealous of her make-up, and then she would get mad and not give it to her. For that matter, why couldn't Claudia just bring the checkbook to him herself or even go to the bank and bring him the cash. Because she wouldn't, that was why. She had always insinuated that he was only interested in her money and this would just prove it. And what would he say when she asked him when he was coming home? It was her fault that he was in this mess. He had no problem with the dumpster, he was just worried about her knee, all her complaining.

Randall went back to his neighborhood and from a couple of blocks away he could see that things weren't quite right. There were a couple of cops standing on the sidewalk across the street from his building.

He found another pay phone, this one in the back of an arcade. This phone had a dial and it felt funny on his finger, had to work to remember his number. It was difficult for him to hear over the bells and buzzers of the nearest pinball machine, but he knew that Claudia sounded funny when she answered.

"Oh, hello, Randall," Claudia said. "Where are you, dear? You're late. I've been so worried."

Randall hung up. He looked over to find the leather-jacketed, late teens pin-baller staring at him. "What are you looking at?" Randall asked.

"Nothing," the kid said, staring right at him. "I'm looking at nothing."

Randall got mad for a second, then became afraid. He left the arcade and decided the public library was a good place to hide and keep warm.

The very tall woman with the tower of books in her arms disappeared down the stairs, leaving Randall alone on the floor, he believed. He sat on a step stool in the middle of an aisle, a book full of pictures of India on his lap. He'd never wanted to go to India, and these pictures of sand and elephants and cobra snakes and people with spotted foreheads weren't causing him to want to go there now, but still he wished he were there.

He looked through many, many books about Asia, suffering through the occasional visitor to his section of the stacks. Out the window he could see the sky starting to darken, the snow still falling. The library would close soon and he figured it was best to get out without being asked, so he left.

It was nearly five and the Osco would be closing. He wanted to catch Susie as she was leaving work and ask her to help, though he wasn't sure what he would be asking her to do. Perhaps she would allow him to sleep at her place. It was much colder now and the snow was piling up.

Randall was glad it was dark, feeling he could now move about more freely. His jacket was not nearly warm enough. If he had a credit card he could just take off, go to the bus station or the airport, but he didn't have one. A life on the lam didn't sound so bad, city to city, new people.

Susie was bundled up in her long, down parka, coming out of the front door of the drugstore. The coat was a dark pink and seemed to match her eye make-up. Randall was standing at the corner of the building, at the entrance to the alley, in the shadows.

"Susie," he whispered to her, startling her. "Susie, it's me, Randall Randall."

She looked at him, clutching her bag. "Mr. Randall?" Susie did not come closer. "The police came in today asking questions about you."

"I need your help, Susie."

Susie looked up and down the street, took a step away. "Listen, I've got to go."

"I didn't do anything, Susie."

The young woman walked away, looking over her shoulder at Randall. The snow swirled around her.

Randall went back into the alley and fell to sitting on the ground, leaning against the brick wall, between a green dumpster, like the one behind his building, and some empty cardboard cartons. He heard the back door of the Osco come open and he pushed and pulled himself to his feet, his legs stiff. He saw Willy, the druggist locking up.

"Willy," Randall said.

"Who's there?"

"It's me."

Willy put the package he was holding into his other hand and reached into his pocket.

Randall moved closer. The flash hurt his eyes. He felt a dull push at his middle and he was confused. He was sitting on the ground, looking down at his lap. His ears were ringing. He moved his eyes back up to see Willy. The fat man showed fear. Randall saw something drop from the fat man's hand. Randall rocked in the cold air, then lay back, looked up at the snow.

GUY-MARK FOSTER

THIS MAN AND ME

Some day I shall rise and leave my friends
And seek you again through the world's far ends,
You whom I found so fair
(touch of your hands and smell of your hair!),
My only god in the days that were.
— Rupert Brooke (1887–1915)

I HAVE BEEN IN LOVE only once. I was twenty-one years old and lived in the city I think of sometimes as my pretend birthplace, though I was not born there. That city was small and clean and architecturally pleasing to the eye. I can close my lids and picture the slender cherry blossom trees, tall and pink-colored, lining the wide avenues; the Tidal Basin, and the two great rivers calmly opposite one another—the Potomac and the Anacostia—where my father sometimes went to fish. There was, I recall, an abundance of sunny days, people smiling, and the nostalgia of quickly changing seasons. I remember nothing but happiness in that city; though to be sure there were sad times, too. But these I can't recall as clearly.

In that city, because neither this man nor myself had money, we often took long, rambling walks. Our shoulders now and again bumped one another, and the hair on my bare arms stood up and tingled. Some days we would stop at a sidewalk cafe and ask for a table in the uninhabited rear, near the toilets, and split the cost of a large, wet fruit salad. He fed me from his fork and I was promptly awed by his attentiveness, and, too, by the strange, new flutterings taking place in my body.

When he and I were together there was, when I walked, always a hardly perceptible, springy layer of cloud between the soles of my shoes and the hard, weather-

199

beaten pavement. At night he would lay me on his single mattress and hover in the air above me. Often I would forget to breathe. I would leave my body and from a distance watch him trace the outline of my face with the sweaty tips of his fingers. He shoved a digit up inside a still nostril and withdrew an index hung with mucilage. He bit into my flesh until my body would jerk.

Downstairs, hardly out of earshot, his aged mother sat drinking can after can of Piels beer. She wore what appeared to be the same hairnet over her greying head every time I saw her. And her toothless jaw caved in under the despairing burden of what horrified me to imagine could be a person's memories. His weight lay pressed upon me, and I thought, as in Whitman: *This is not only one man!* His tongue lathered my lashes so that I could not see but with my body; it was as if I was surrounded. I could hear the television in the background: "Rowan and Martin's Laugh-In," or "Maude." It was this soundtrack of canned, vertiginous hilarity which punctuated my moans of pleasure, of gratitude, and simple lust. The fitted sheet on his bed was like his mother's hairnet, always the same one whenever I visited: a shade of dullest white with thick swirls of brown waves in the pattern. Smeared upon this threadbare fabric was the proof of our bond: there, mixed in with the undulations and food stains was his gummy semen mingled with my own, and the dark, oily excrement or fart fucked out to exhaustion from both our saliva-slickened bodies.

In the middle of the night he would awake to find me gazing at his uncircumcised penis, amazed at the now calm sheathe of flesh which had been, only hours before, violently chafing against the inflamed walls of my rectum. Sometimes, when he had to urinate, I asked if I could hold this warrior for him, pull back the shield of foreskin and guide the stream into the bowl. For some reason he always declined, amusement in his brown eyes. I thought, self-praisingly: *My love is so large and uncontainable that it will, sometimes, simply burst out with the most aboriginal of requests.*

Months later, because of the nature of his work, he told me of his plans to relocate to this other city. I did not know yet what kind of a city it was, of its reputation as a murderer and a cheat, as an unconscionable liar. And so I asked him to take me away with him—away from the cherry blossom trees and the wide, forking rivers; and because I was young and persuasive enough in my argument and I humored him, and because he loved me, too, I think, he did this.

The apartment we moved to was directly opposite a small park. But the trees had not grown of their own accord—I could tell this; but rather they were planted with questionable intentions by what seemed to me a vain and desperate city. I could never look at those trees without feeling a slight discomfort in my chest. At the beginning these trees were pruned regularly by a man in a dull-green, belted jumper. Under the pretense of an esthetically perfected landscape, bandages were wrapped around certain limbs to direct the growth of the branches. I thought, indignantly: *This would never have happened to the venerable cherry blossoms in my city.* In every way these trees were being prevented from flowering into the full extensions of their true selves. This horrified me, and yet I averted my eyes and behaved as if such oppression could not concern me.

It was at this point that I began to hold my love more and more loosely in my grip. Other men caught my attention. I would stare after them, smile, and once caught I would snatch my eyes away in embarrassment. I did not understand this behavior and when I was alone with the man I lived with I would lavish more and more attention upon him, to make up for having strayed earlier with my mind. But whichever direction I faced there stood before me always this implacable guilt. I turned and I turned and I turned my head until a kind of terror shook me.

"I'm lost," I thought.

Avoiding those trees, I began to leave the apartment when he was away and I would walk along dark streets looking strange men in the eye. If ever anyone displayed the slightest curiosity I would panic and accelerate to a brisk pace. I only wanted these men, for an instant, to witness my impossible interest in them. I played my eyes over their bodies until I sensed their arousal, and then, like a shot, I would bolt. I never wanted them to respond: for then I would be committed to them instead of to the man I had come to this city devoted to, and I could not risk such a betrayal.

During those days we seldom had friends over. But when they came this man I lived with would become suddenly more vivacious and brighter than he was when with me alone. I did not take offense to this. I enjoyed the many variant angles to his persona. With him I was always surprised and always, simultaneously, on the surest footing. In honor of the arrival of these people in our apartment he would drape colorful African cloth over his chest and sit cross-legged on our murex purple carpet and tell funny stories, gesticulating with his blunt, flat-tipped, expressive hands. White candles in tall cylindrical jars would be lit throughout the room and soft music would play on the turntable: Peabo Bryson or Brenda Russell, singers he liked. He was in the theater and so were many of these friends. I was outside all that. I had been inside but, in the end, he and these people I thought were more committed, not to mention adept, at this type of work than I ever hoped to be; and, anyhow, I felt the need to uncrowd them all by stepping down and out of, what seemed to me, their already too immense and over-populated circle.

After a while I began to unbuckle my trousers on some of those walks I made at night and stroke my penis to erection. Sometimes, if it was cool, I carried a jacket to drape over me in case of an unsympathetic passerby, or a woman. I lived in an exalted fear of being seen by one of our many friends, and of them reporting back to my lover my nocturnal habits. In my worst hours I craved for this. In time I grew very brave, and often some man would stop to chat with me. He and I would stare at one another, each waiting for the other to grab him where he was most elongated; and both of us, too, incorrigibly lusty, full of a secret, exhilarating, nasty, dual fright.

The city was at its ugliest then; it was even common to see grown men taking a piss in full view out on the sidewalk. Besides, the buildings were all covered with soot and in various states of disrepair. Access to the sky was severely restricted by the ludicrous height of these block-shaped edifices. Each morning a new rash of killings covered the headlines. When I returned to our apartment, if he had come in I would tell the truth: that I had been out taking a walk. Or else, shamelessly, I would lie. During the night I somehow would lose sight of these wanderings and by the morning the memory was all but obliterated. At rest all those hours, next to his dark, regenerative body, somehow this absolved my soul: for he never judged me, or otherwise gave indication that I was not to be trusted. I felt it was therefore incumbent on me not to disappoint him. As in the beginning, by sunrise it was as if I had died and been reborn all in the long, purifying interval of night giving way to the diurnal. I became my old innocent, sweet-natured self: a bit irascible but harmless. I rolled over to him and we made love, or we simply kissed one another upon our fat, ancestral lips, and the trial began all over.

One evening I met a friend of his, a certain actor from the south who was not very attractive. He was tall and absurd with his body—the perfect hick. He spoke with the customary twang in his voice, and always leaned forward to clutch a person on the shoulder when talking. I remembered he had one of those highfalutin society names, as from a Henry James novel: Charles or Frederick.

It began simply enough. I loathed him. He had no sense of moderation and saturated himself in musk-scented oils. He reeked of it. Instead of making him more desirable, this repelled me. And it did. But then I felt badly for him. He so wanted to be a part of the 'in' crowd, stylish and in the 'know,' like the man I lived with, and all the others in his profession—those who paraded themselves in bright plumage and behaved as if a camera were recording their every gesture. He reminded me of myself: the outsider who longs desperately to be inside but who simply does not fit; who isn't popular or even talented, or especially well-liked, but who is merely tolerated as the embarrassing love-object of one in their ranks; who has simply lucked in on a certain crowd, as I assumed I had with this man and his friends. But after a while I could not stay away from him, nor he me. We phoned each other and confessed in quick, movie-script voices:

"Don't you want me?"

"He'll find out."

"But you want me, right?"

"No."

"*Liar.*"

At his apartment we circled each other. He had already bathed himself in his favorite scent and it was all I could do to keep from retching. To my horror, he wore a short-sleeved, plaid shirt a size too small, and loose-fitting generic blue-jeans with loopy stitching on the back pockets.

"No," I thought, when he held me. He did not remind me of myself, but rather of boys I had gone to school with, boys I had admired yet had not been friendly with since they had claimed a much stronger kinship with girls; or, as he told me, in his case, with large-hipped women. Nevertheless, that first time he exuded caution for only an instant. Soon he had bruised my neck with his uneven teeth and I had torn a button off his shirt. In no time both our jeans lay undone at our ankles and we ground or bodies together, liberally, as if to reach the core of something we both believed lay concealed in the deepest recess of the other. He did not have as finely muscled a body as the man I lived with. His was of a larger mass, but it was soft and there was a surprising opacity to his copper complexion; it did not give, but took. In our lovemaking there was no confidence: it was all crying out and mad panic, as though we were sure the world would end because of our il-licit groping. And yet I knew it was too late to turn back.

Some nights I lay next to the man I lived with and did not know him. I was twenty-three or twenty-four years old and had grown very skittish. I began to hide my various new faces from everyone who entered our lives. When friends visited I discouraged them from staying long by storming out of the room, or by showing them the door when I decided enough time had lapsed. Leaving, they merely smiled at one another or said, "Oh, Mark's just being Mark. Isn't he cute?" I had lost my identity and I resented these people for telling me who I was, and when they'd gone I would become an emotional gymnast before that man; it was as though I'd gone mad. He was calm and loving, and sometimes he would say my name aloud to cool me off, or sit astride my body and ride my erect penis to exhaustion; other times he would take up his sketch pad and draw mythical figures of tall dark men with scales along their backs and a bit of schizophrenia in the eyes.

We never returned to that other city, the one we had left. He often went alone to visit his aged, alcoholic mother and I would wait for him after my nights of walking the streets. I had adapted too well to this new city. I misplaced all mem-ory of the parades my mother had taken my brothers and I to see every year along Constitution Avenue, for the cherry blossoms. I forgot the picnics on the grounds of the Smithsonian. When I was with some other man, and not the one I lived with, I would be caught off-guard sometimes by a recollection. A vivid sadness would wash over me and I would drift back in time to when he and I would ride the Metro from the housing project where he lived with his mother into the cen-ter of that historic city. He would sit next to me and just as the doors closed he would shut his eyes. I sat in silence beside him, awed by his trick of blotting out the world through meditation, as I had been awed once by his fork between my lips. This mastery of myself was what I wanted, but I could not be confident that I would come back from such depths; therefore, I leaned upon the proven sol-idness of his frame for support and guidance instead of searching for it from within. I thought: *I dare not risk such a journey for fear of losing myself inside my vast, chaotic self.*

When I was twenty-five or twenty-six he came home from being weeks away and confessed his love for some other man over me. This was in the summer, and while he had been away I had undergone yet another rebirth and was more deter-mined than ever to hold my love more firmly in my grasp. I had not seen that musk oil–wearing actor for some while, nor any other man. I had been cleansed this time not by his presence but by his very absence. It left a hole in me the size of that city which had initially nurtured our love, and I had stared bravely into it while he was gone. The depth of it stunned me; I did not want to ever be without him. I could not, I thought, survive it.

We tried to wait it out. When he left in the evenings to rendezvous with this other man I would fire up sticks of incense to burn the stench of jealousy away. I played his favorite records over and over like a mantra, especially "If Only For One Night"—a song he had serenaded me with in our courtship. I would extinguish all the lamps and, with a single white candle, sit in that heavy darkness and try to glean from Brenda Russell's mellifluous voice and, too, from the guilt I felt, what could be salvaged from my shattered world.

Eventually, it was no good. One night this occurred to me and I lay up in our loft bed, sobbing. The windows were opened and all our neighbors could hear the despair flying out of my body like birds being freed from an aviary. We had often lay there ourselves listening to the desperate fucking, and the curses in English, but in Spanish too, which was the language of that part of the city. For seven hours the deluge was unceasing. The man I loved lay listening in the next room. I did not know to what extent he was aware of my infidelities, but I was sure that this was the very reason that had pushed him, finally, to form this sudden alliance. The planet had abruptly come spinning off its axis and was now shockingly out of control: I had not truly imagined that this could happen, no matter how often or rarely I strayed. If anyone, I thought, reminded me of those adolescent boys from my youth—in whose arms I imagined lay my eventual salvation—it had been him all along; and yet for years I had felt that I was suffocating with him, and that simultaneously I was living the greatest pleasure a man could fabricate out of the stuff of his dreams.

Later that summer I moved out of the second floor walk-up he and I had shared in that city, into a one-bedroom affair across the bridge. I did this decisively, and yet in spite of my packed boxes I could not quite believe in my actions, or in the actions of those friends who assisted me with my belongings. It was not my body, I told myself, that this was happening to, but some other poor man's worn-out, adulterous body. I was very much like those trees across from our building, I thought, who had suffered, in years past, a similar asphyxiation of spirit. Like them, I felt paralyzed at having my expansive potential for love smothered so early in life, without having a say in the matter. I shut my eyes to what seemed a ruling beyond my self-government and, instead, I fashioned an alternate reality to compete with the obviously untenable one that faced me. For months afterwards, and then for years, I convinced myself that as far as those trees were concerned, the filthy pieces of sackcloth would eventually rot and drop from around their bark-covered bodies, and with a vengeance an unprecedented blooming would occur. In my patience I willed for a similar reconstitution of justice to happen for this man and me. I clung with fingers and nails to the hope that if I were patient and good—something I had not been before, but had wanted to be and failed—then he would forgive my indiscretions and, because he had once loved me, come back to me.

After all, he was my god.

ERNEST J. GAINES

THREE MEN

Two of them was sitting in the office when I came in there. One was sitting in a chair behind the desk, the other one was sitting on the end of the desk. They looked at me, but when they saw I was just a nigger they went back to talking like I wasn't even there. They talked like that two or three more minutes before the one behind the desk looked at me again. That was T. J. I didn't know who the other one was.

"Yeah, what you want?" T. J. said.

They sat inside a little railed-in office. I went closer to the gate. It was one of them little gates that swung in and out.

"I come to turn myself in," I said.

"Turn yourself in for what?"

"I had a fight with somebody. I think I hurt him."

T. J. and the other policeman looked at me like I was crazy. I guess they had never heard of a nigger doing that before.

"You Procter Lewis?" T. J. said.

"Yes, sir."

"Come in here."

I pushed the little gate open and went in. I made sure it didn't swing back too hard and make noise. I stopped a little way from the desk. T. J. and the other policeman was watching me all the time.

"Give me some papers," T. J. said. He was looking up at me like he was still trying to figure out if I was crazy. If I wasn't crazy, then I was a smart aleck.

I got my wallet out my pocket. I could feel T. J. and the other policeman looking at me all the time. I wasn't supposed to get any papers out, myself, I was supposed to give him the wallet and let him take what he wanted. I held the wallet out to him and he jerked it out of my hand. Then he started going through everything I had in there, the money and all. After he looked at everything, he handed them to the other policeman. The other one looked at them, too; then he laid them on the desk. T. J. picked up the phone and started talking to somebody. All the time he was talking to the other person, he was looking up at me. He had a hard time making the other person believe I had turned myself in. When he hung up the phone, he told the policeman on the desk to get my records. He called the other policeman "Paul." Paul slid away from the desk and went to the file cabinet against the wall. T. J. still looked at me. His eyes was the color of ashes. I looked down at the floor, but I could still feel him looking at me. Paul came back with the records and handed them to him. I looked up again and saw them looking over the records together. Paul was standing behind T. J., looking over his shoulder.

"So you think you hurt him, huh?" T. J. asked, looking up at me again.

I didn't say anything to him. He was a mean, evil sonofabitch. He was big and red and he didn't waste time kicking your ass if you gived him the wrong answers. You had to weigh every word he said to you. Sometimes you answered, other times you kept your mouth shut. This time I passed my tongue over my lips and kept quiet.

It was about four o'clock in the morning, but it must've been seventy-five in there. T. J. and the other policeman had on short-sleeve khaki shirts. I had on a white shirt, but it was all dirty and torn. My sleeves was rolled up to the elbows, and both of my elbows was skinned and bruised.

"Didn't I bring you in here one time, myself?" Paul said.

"Yes, sir, once, I think," I said. I had been there two or three times, but I wasn't go'n say it if he didn't. I had been in couple other jails two or three times, too, but I wasn't go'n say anything about them either. If they hadn't put it on my record that was they hard luck.

"A fist fight," Paul said. "Pretty good with your fists, ain't you?"

"I protect myself," I said.

It was quiet in there for a second or two. I knowed why; I hadn't answered the right way.

"You protect yourself, what?" T. J. said.

"I protect myself, *sir*," I said.

They still looked at me. But I could tell Paul wasn't anything like T. J. He wasn't mean at all, he just had to play mean because T. J. was there. Couple Sundays ago I had played baseball with a boy who looked just like Paul. But he had brown eyes; Paul had blue eyes.

"You'll be sorry you didn't use your fists this time," T. J. said. "Take everything out your pockets."

I did what he said.

"Where's your knife?" he asked.

"I never car' a knife," I said.

"You never car' a knife, what, boy?" T. J. said.

"I never car' a knife, *sir*," I said.

He looked at me hard again. He didn't think I was crazy for turning myself in, he thought I was a smart aleck. I could tell from his big, fat, red face he wanted to hit me with his fist.

He nodded to Paul and Paul came toward me. I moved back some.

"I'm not going to hurt you," Paul said.

I stopped, but I could still feel myself shaking. Paul started patting me down. He found a pack of cigarettes in my shirt pocket. I could see in his face he didn't want take them out, but he took them out, anyhow.

"Thought I told you empty your pockets?" T. J. said.

"I didn't know—"

"Paul, if you can't make that boy shut up, I can," T. J. said.

"He'll be quiet," Paul said, looking at me. He was telling me with his eyes to be quiet or I was go'n get myself in a lot of trouble.

"You got one more time to butt in," T. J. said. "One more time now."

I was getting a swimming in the head, and I looked down at the floor. I hoped they would hurry up and lock me up so I could have a little peace.

"Why'd you turn yourself in?" T. J. asked.

I kept my head down. I didn't answer him.

"Paul, can't you make that boy talk?" T. J. said. "Or do I have to get up and do it?"

"He'll talk," Paul said.

"I figured y'all was go'n catch me sooner or later—sir."

"That's not the reason you turned yourself in," T. J. said.

I kept my head down.

"Look up when I talk to you," T. J. said.

I raised my head. I felt weak and shaky. My clothes was wet and sticking to my body, but my mouth felt dry as dust. My eyes wanted to look down again, but I forced myself to look at T. J.'s big red face.

"You figured if you turned yourself in, Roger Medlow was go'n get you out, now, didn't you?"

I didn't say anything—but that's exactly what I was figuring on.

"Sure," he said. He looked at me a long time. He knowed how I was feeling; he knowed I was weak and almost ready to fall. That's why he was making me stand there like that. "What you think we ought to do with niggers like you?" he said. "Come on now—what you think we ought to do with you?"

I didn't answer him.

"Well?" he said.

"I don't know," I said. "Sir."

"I'll tell you," he said. "See, if I was gov'nor, I'd run every damned one of you off in that river out there. Man, woman and child. You know that?"

I was quiet, looking at him. But I made sure I didn't show in my face what I was thinking. I could've been killed for what I was thinking then.

"Well, what you think of that?" he said.

"That's up to the gov'nor, sir," I said.

"Yeah," he said. "That's right. That's right. I think I'll write him a little telegram and tell him 'bout my idea. Can save this state a hell of a lot trouble."

Now he just sat there looking at me again. He wanted to hit me in the mouth with his fist. Not just hit me, he wanted to beat me. But he had to have a good excuse. And what excuse could he have when I had already turned myself in.

"Put him in there with Munford," he said to Paul.

We went out. We had to walk down a hall to the cell block. The niggers' cell block was on the second floor. We had to go up some concrete steps to get there. Paul turned on the lights and a woman hollered at him to turn them off. "What's this supposed to be—Christmas?" she said. "A person can't sleep in this joint." The women was locked up on one end of the block and the men was at the other end. If you had a mirror or a piece of shiny tin, you could stick it out the cell and fix it so you could see the other end of the block.

The guard opened the cell door and let me in, then he locked it back. I looked at him through the bars.

"When will y'all ever learn?" he said, shaking his head.

He said it like he meant it, like he was sorry for me. He kept reminding me of that boy I had played baseball with. They called that other boy Lloyd, and he used to show up just about every Sunday to play baseball with us. He used to play the outfield so he could do a lot of running. He used to buy Cokes for everybody after the game. He was the only white boy out there.

"Here's a pack of cigarettes and some matches," Paul said. "Might not be your brand, but I doubt if you'll mind it too much in there."

I took the cigarettes from him.

"You can say 'Thanks,'" he said.

"Thanks," I said.

"And you can say 'sir' sometimes," he said.

"Sir," I said.

He looked at me like he felt sorry for me, like he felt sorry for everybody. He didn't look like a policeman at all.

"Let me give you a word of warning," he said. "Don't push T. J. Don't push him, now."

"I won't."

"It doesn't take much to get him started—don't push him."

I nodded.

"Y'all go'n turn out them goddamn lights?" the woman hollered from the other end of the block.

"Take it easy," Paul said to me and left.

After the lights went out, I stood at the cell door till my eyes got used to the dark. Then I climbed up on my bunk. Two other people was in the cell. Somebody on the bunk under mine, somebody on the lower bunk 'cross from me. The upper bunk 'cross from me was empty.

"Cigarette?" the person below me said.

He said it very low, but I could tell he was talking to me and not to the man 'cross from us. I shook a cigarette out the pack and dropped it on the bunk. I could hear the man scratching the match to light the cigarette. He cupped his hands close to his face, because I didn't see too much light. I could tell from the way he let that smoke out he had wanted a cigarette very bad.

"What you in for?" he said, real quiet.

"A fight," I said.

"First time?"

"No, I been in before."

He didn't say any more and I didn't, either. I didn't feel like talking, anyhow. I looked up at the window on my left, and I could see a few stars. I felt lonely and I felt like crying. But I couldn't cry. Once you started that in here you was done for. Everybody and his brother would run over you.

The man on the other bunk got up to take a leak. The toilet was up by the head of my bunk. After the man had zipped up his pants, he just stood there looking at me. I tightened my fist to swing at him if he tried any funny stuff.

"Well, hello there," he said.

"Get your ass back over there, Hattie," the man below me said. He spoke in that quiet voice again. "Hattie is a woman," he said to me. "Don't see how come they didn't put him with the rest of them whores."

"Don't let it worry your mind," Hattie said.

"Caught him playing with this man dick," the man below me said. "At this old flea-bitten show back of town there. Up front—front row—there he is playing with this man dick. Bitch."

"Is that any worse than choking somebody half to death?" Hattie said.

The man below me was quiet. Hattie went back to his bunk.

"Oh, these old crampy, stuffy, old ill-smelling beds," he said, slapping the mattress level with the palm of his hand. "How do they expect you to sleep." He laid down. "What are you in for, honey?" he asked me. "You look awful young."

"Fighting," I said.

"You poor, poor thing," Hattie said. "If I can help you in any way, don't hesitate to ask."

"Shit," the man below me said. I heard him turning over so he could go to sleep.

"The world has given up on the likes of you," Hattie said. "You jungle beast."

"Bitch, why don't you just shut up," the man said.

"Why don't both of y'all shut up," somebody said from another cell.

It was quiet after that.

I looked up at the window and I could see the stars going out in the sky. My eyes felt tired and my head started spinning, and I wasn't here any more, I was at the Seven Spots. And she was there in red, and she had two big dimples in her jaws. Then she got up and danced with him, and every time she turned my way she looked over his shoulder at me and smiled. And when she turned her back to me, she rolled her big ass real slow and easy—just for me, just for me. Grinning Boy was sitting at the table with me, saying: "Poison, poison—nothing but poison. Look at that; just look at that." I was looking, but I wasn't thinking about what he was saying. When she went back to that table to sit down, I went there and asked her to dance. That nigger sitting there just looked at me, rolling his big white eyes like I was supposed to break out of the joint. I didn't pay him no mind, I was looking at that woman. And I was looking down at them two big pretty brown things poking that dress way out. They looked so soft and warm and waiting. I wanted to touch them right there in front of that ugly nigger. She shook her head, because he was sitting there, but little bit later when she went back in the kitchen, I went back there, too. Grinning Boy tried to stop me, saying, "Poison, poison, poison," but I didn't pay him no mind. When I came back in the kitchen, she was standing at the counter ordering a chicken sandwich. The lady back of the counter had to fry the chicken, so she had to wait a while. When she saw me, she started smiling. Them two big dimples came in her jaws. I smiled back at her.

"She go'n take a while," I said. "Let's step out in the cool till she get done."

She looked over her shoulder and didn't see the nigger peeping, and we went outside. There was people talking out there, but I didn't care, I had to touch her.

"What's your name?" I said.

"Clara."

"Let's go somewhere, Clara."

"I can't. I'm with somebody," she said.

"That nigger?" I said. "You call him somebody?"

She just looked at me with that little smile on her face—them two big dimples in her jaws. I looked little farther down, and I could see how them two warm, brown things was waiting for somebody to tear that dress open so they could get free.

"You must be the prettiest woman in the world," I said.

"You like me?"

"Lord, yes."

"I want you to like me," she said.

"Then what's keeping us from going?" I said. "Hell away with that nigger."

"My name is Clara Johnson," she said. "It's in the book. Call me tomorrow after four."

She turned to go back inside, but just then that big sweaty nigger bust out the door. He passed by her like she wasn't even there.

"No, Bayou," she said. "No."

But he wasn't listening to a thing. Before I knowed it, he had cracked me on the chin and I was down on my back. He raised his foot to kick me in the stomach, and I rolled and rolled till I was out of the way. Then I jumped back up.

"I don't want fight you, Bayou," I said. "I don't want fight you, now."

"You fight or you fly, nigger," somebody else said. "If you run, we go'n catch you."

Bayou didn't say nothing. He just came in swinging. I backed away from him.

"I wasn't doing nothing but talking to her," I said.

He rushed in and knocked me on a bunch of people. They picked me clear off the ground and throwed me back on him. He hit me again, this time a glancing blow on the shoulder. I moved back from him, holding the shoulder with the other hand.

"I don't want fight you," I told him. "I was just talking to her."

But trying to talk to Bayou was like trying to talk to a mule. He came in swinging wild and high, and I went under his arm and rammed my fist in his stomach. But it felt like ramming your fist into a hundred-pound sack of flour. He stopped about a half a second, then he was right back on me again. I hit him in the face this time, and I saw the blood splash out of his mouth. I was still backing away from him, hoping he would quit, but the nigger kept coming on me. He had to, because all his friends and that woman was there. But he didn't know how to fight, and every time he moved in I hit him in the face. Then I saw him going for his knife.

"Watch it, now, Bayou," I said. "I don't have a knife. Let's keep this fair."

But he didn't hear a thing I was saying; he was listening to the others who was sicking him on. He kept moving in on me. He had both of his arms 'way out— that blade in his right hand. From the way he was holding it, he didn't have nothing but killing on his mind.

I kept moving back, moving back. Then my foot touched a bottle and I stooped down and picked it up. I broke it against the corner of the building, but I never took my eyes off Bayou. He started circling me with the knife, and I moved round him with the bottle. He made a slash at me, and I jumped back. He was all opened and I could've gotten him then, but I was still hoping for him to change his mind.

"Let's stop it, Bayou," I kept saying to him. "Let's stop it, now."

But he kept on circling me with the knife, and I kept on going round him with the bottle. I didn't look at his face any more, I kept my eyes on that knife. It was a Texas jack with a pearl handle, and that blade must've been five inches long.

"Stop it, Bayou," I said. "Stop it, stop it."

He slashed at me, and I jumped back. He slashed at me again, and I jumped back again. Then he acted like a fool and ran on me, and all I did was stick the bottle out. I felt it go in his clothes and in his stomach and I felt the hot, sticky blood on my hand and I saw his face all twisted and sweaty. I felt his hands brush against mine when he throwed both of his hands up to his stomach. I started running. I was running toward the car, and Grinning Boy was running there, too. He got there before me and jumped in on the driving side, but I pushed him out the way and got under that ste'r'n' wheel. I could hear that gang coming after me, and I shot that Ford out of there a hundred miles an hour. Some of them ran up the road to cut me off, but when they saw I wasn't stopping they jumped out of the way. Now, it was nobody but me, that Ford and that gravel road. Grinning Boy was sitting over there crying, but I wasn't paying him no mind. I wanted to get much road between me and Seven Spots as I could.

After I had gone a good piece, I slammed on the brakes and told Grinning Boy to get out. He wouldn't get out. I opened the door and pushed on him, but he held the ste'r'n' wheel. He was crying and holding the wheel with both hands. I hit him and pushed on him and hit him and pushed on him, but he wouldn't turn it loose. If they was go'n kill me, I didn't want them to kill him, too, but he couldn't see that. I shot away from there with the door still opened, and after we had gone a little piece, Grinning Boy reached out and got it and slammed it again.

I came out on the pave road and drove three or four miles 'long the river. Then I turned down a dirt road and parked the car under a big pecan tree. It was one of these old plantation quarter and the place was quiet as a graveyard. It was pretty bright, though, because the moon and the stars was out. The dust in that long, old road was white as snow. I lit a cigarette and tried to think. Grinning Boy was sitting over there crying. He was crying real quiet with his head hanging down on his chest. Every now and then I could hear him sniffing.

"I'm turning myself in," I said.

I had been thinking and thinking and I couldn't think of nothing else to do. I knowed Bayou was dead or hurt pretty bad, and I knowed either that gang or the law was go'n get me, anyhow. I backed the car out on the pave road and drove to Bayonne. I told Grinning Boy to let my uncle know I was in trouble. My uncle would go to Roger Medlow—and I was hoping Roger Medlow would get me off like he had done once before. He owned the plantation where I lived.

"Hey," somebody was calling and shaking me. "Hey, there, now; wake up."

I opened my eyes and looked at this old man standing by the head of my bunk. I'm sure if I had woke up anywhere else and found him that close to me I would've jumped back screaming. He must've been sixty; he had reddish-brown eyes, and a stubby gray beard. 'Cross his right jaw, from his cheekbone to his mouth, was a big shiny scar where somebody had gotten him with a razor. He was wearing a derby hat, and he had it cocked a little to the back of his head.

"They coming," he said.

"Who?"

"Breakfast."

"I'm not hungry."

"You better eat. Never can tell when you go'n eat again in this joint."

His breath didn't smell too good either, and he was standing so close to me, I could smell his breath every time he breathed in and out. I figured he was the one they called Munford. Just before they brought me down here last night, I heard T. J. tell Paul to put me in there with Munford. Since he had called the other one Hattie, I figured he was Munford.

"Been having yourself a nice little nightmare," he said. "Twisting and turning there like you wanted to fall off. You can have this bunk of mine tonight if you want."

I looked at the freak laying on the other bunk. He looked back at me with a sad little smile on his face.

"I'll stay here," I said.

The freak stopped smiling, but he still looked sad—like a sad woman. He knowed why I didn't want get down there. I didn't want no part of him.

Out on the cell block, the nigger trustee was singing. He went from one cell to the other one singing, "Come and get it, it's hot. What a lovely, lovely day, isn't it? Yes, indeed," he answered himself. "Yes, indeed . . . Come and get it, my children, come and get it. Unc' Toby won't feel right if y'all don't eat his lovely food."

He stopped before the cell with his little shiny pushcart. A white guard was with him. The guard opened the cell door and Unc' Toby gived each one of us a cup of coffee and two baloney sandwiches. Then the guard shut the cell again and him and Unc' Toby went on up the block. Unc' Toby was singing again.

"Toby used to have a little stand," Munford said to me. "He think he still got it. He kinda loose up here," he said, tapping his head with the hand that held the sandwiches.

"They ought to send him to Jackson if he's crazy."

"They like keeping him here," Munford said. "Part of the scheme of things."

"You want this?" I asked.

"No, eat it," he said.

I got back on my bunk. I ate one of the sandwiches and drank some of the coffee. The coffee was nothing but brown water. It didn't have any kind of taste—not even bitter taste. I drank about half and poured the rest in the toilet.

The freak, Hattie, sat on his bunk, nibbling at his food. He wrapped one slice of bread round the slice of baloney and ate that, then he did the same thing with the other sandwich. The two extra slices of bread, he dipped down in his coffee and ate it like that. All the time he was eating, he was looking at me like a sad woman looks at you.

Munford stood between the two rows of bunks, eating and drinking his coffee. He pressed both of the sandwiches together and ate them like they was just one. Nobody said anything all the time we was eating. Even when I poured out the coffee, nobody said anything. The freak just looked at me like a sad woman. But Munford didn't look at me at all—he was looking up at the window all the time. When he got through eating, he wiped his mouth and throwed his cup on his bunk.

"Another one of them smokes," he said to me.

The way he said it, it sounded like he would've took it if I didn't give it to him. I got out the pack of cigarettes and gived him one. He lit it and took a big draw. I was laying back against the wall, looking up at the window; but I could tell that Munford was looking at me.

"Killed somebody, huh?" Munford said, in his quiet, calm voice.

"I cut him pretty bad," I said, still looking up at the window.

"He's dead," Munford said.

I wouldn't take my eyes off the window. My throat got tight, and my heart started beating so loud, I'm sure both Munford and that freak could hear it.

"That's bad," Munford said.

"And so young," Hattie said. I didn't have to look at the freak to know he was crying. "And so much of his life still before him—my Lord."

"You got people?" Munford asked.

"Uncle," I said.

"You notified him?"

"I think he knows."

"You got a lawyer?"

"No."

"No money?"

"No."

"That's bad," he said.

"Maybe his uncle can do something," Hattie said. "Poor thing." Then I heard him blowing his nose.

I looked at the bars in the window. I wanted them to leave me alone so I could think.

"So young, too," Hattie said. "My Lord, my Lord."

"Oh shut up," Munford said. "I don't know why they didn't lock you up with the rest of them whores."

"Is it too much to have some feeling of sympathy?" Hattie said, and blowed his nose again.

"Morris David is a good lawyer," Munford said. "Get him if you can. Best for colored round here."

I nodded, but I didn't look at Munford. I felt bad and I wanted them to leave me alone.

"Was he a local boy?" Munford asked.

"I don't know," I said.

"Where was it?"

I didn't answer him.

"Best to talk 'bout it," Munford said. "Keeping it in just make it worse."

"Seven Spots," I said.

"That's a rough joint," Munford said.

"They're all rough joints," Hattie said. "That's all you have—rough joints. No decent places for someone like him."

"Who's your uncle?" Munford asked.

"Martin Baptiste. Medlow plantation."

"Martin Baptiste?" Munford said.

I could tell from the way he said it, he knowed my uncle. I looked at him now. He was looking back at me with his left eye half shut. I could tell from his face he didn't like my uncle.

"You same as out already," he said.

He didn't like my uncle at all, and now he was studying me to see how much I was like him.

"Medlow can get you out of here just by snapping his fingers," he said. "Big men like that run little towns like these."

"I killed somebody," I said.

"You killed another old nigger," Munford said. "A nigger ain't nobody."

He drawed on the cigarette, and I looked at the big scar on the side of his face. He took the cigarette from his mouth and patted the scar with the tip of one of his fingers.

"Bunch of them jumped on me one night," he said. "One caught me with a straight razor. Had the flesh hanging so much, I coulda ripped it off with my hands if I wanted to. Ah, but before I went down you shoulda seen what I did the bunch of 'em." He stopped and thought a while. He even laughed a little to himself. "I been in this joint so much, everybody from the judge on down know me. 'How's it going, Munford?' 'Well, you back with us again, huh, Munt?' 'Look, y'all, old Munt's back with us again, just like he said he'd be.' They all know me. All know me. I'll get out little later on. What time is it getting to be—'leven? I'll give 'em till twelve and tell 'em I want get out. They'll let me out. Got in Saturday night. They always keep me from Saturday till Monday. If it rain, they keep me till Tuesday—don't want me get out and catch cold, you know. Next Saturday, I'm right back. Can't stay out of here to save my soul."

"Places like these are built for people like you," Hattie said. "Not for decent people."

"Been going in and out of these jails here, I don't know how long," Munford said. "Forty, fifty years. Started out just like you—kilt a boy just like you did last night. Kilt him and got off—got off scot-free. My pappy worked for a white man who got me off. At first I didn't know why he had done it—I didn't think; all I knowed was I was free, and free is how I wanted to be. Then I got in trouble again, and again they got me off. I kept on getting in trouble, and they kept on getting me off. Didn't wake up till I got to be nearly old as I'm is now. Then I realized they kept getting me off because they needed a Munford Bazille. They need me to prove they human—just like they need that thing over there. They need us. Because without us, they don't know what they is—they don't know what they is out there. With us around, they can see us and they know what they ain't. They ain't us. Do you see? Do you see how they think?"

I didn't know what he was talking about. It was hot in the cell and he had started sweating. His face was wet, except for that big scar. It was just laying there smooth and shiny.

"But I got news for them. They us. I never tell them that, but inside I know it. They us, just like we is ourselves. Cut any of them open and you see if you don't find Munford Bazille or Hattie Brown there. You know what I mean?"

"I guess so."

"No, you don't know what I mean," he said. "What I mean is not one of them out there is a man. Not one. They think they men. They think they men 'cause they got me and him in here who ain't men. But I got news for them—cut them open; go 'head and cut one open—you see if you don't find Munford Bazille or Hattie Brown. Not a man one of them. 'Cause face don't make a man—black or white. Face don't make him and fucking don't make him and fighting don't make him—neither killing. None of this prove you a man. 'Cause animals can fuck, can kill, can fight—you know that?"

I looked at him, but I didn't answer him. I didn't feel like answering.

"Well?" He said.

"Yeah."

"Then answer me when I ask you a question. I don't like talking to myself."

He stopped and looked at me a while.

"You know what I'm getting at?"

"No," I said.

"To hell if you don't," he said. "Don't let Medlow get you out of here so you can kill again."

"You got out," I said.

"Yeah," he said, "and I'm still coming back here and I'm still getting out. Next Saturday I'm go'n hit another nigger in the head, and Saturday night they go'n bring me here, and Monday they go'n let me out again. And Saturday after that I'm go'n hit me another nigger in the head—'cause I'll hit a nigger in the head quick as I'll look at one."

"You're just an animal out the black jungle," Hattie said. "Because you have to hit somebody in the head every Saturday night don't mean he has to do the same."

"He'll do it," Munford said, looking at me, not at Hattie. "He'll do it 'cause he know Medlow'll get him out. Won't you?"

I didn't answer him. Munford nodded his head.

"Yeah, he'll do it. They'll see to that."

He looked at me like he was mad at me, then he looked up at the bars in the window. He frowned and rubbed his hand over his chin, and I could hear the gritty sound his beard made. He studied the bars a long time, like he was thinking about something 'way off; then I saw how his face changed: his eyes twinkled and he grinned to himself. He turned to look at Hattie laying on the bunk.

"Look here," he said. "I got a few coppers and a few minutes—what you say me and you giving it a little whirl?"

"My God, man," Hattie said. He said it the way a young girl would've said it if you had asked her to pull down her drawers. He even opened his eyes wide the same way a young girl would've done it. "Do you think I could possibly ever sink so low?" he said.

"Well, that's what you do on the outside," Munford said.

"What I do on the outside is absolutely no concern of yours, let me assure you," the freak said. "And furthermore, I have friends that I associate with."

"And them 'sociating friends you got there—what they got Munford don't have?" Munford said.

"For one thing, manners," Hattie said. "Of all the nerve."

Munford grinned at him and looked at me.

"You know what make 'em like that?" he asked.

"No."

He nodded his head. "Then I'll tell you. It start in the cradle when they send that preacher there to christen you. At the same time he's doing that mumbo-jumbo stuff, he's low'ing his mouth to your little nipper to suck out your manhood. I know, he tried it on me. Here, I'm laying in his arms in my little white blanket and he suppose to be christening me. My mammy there, my pappy there; uncle, aunt, grandmammy, grandpappy; my nan-nane, my pa-ran—all of them standing there with they head bowed. This preacher going, 'Mumbo-jumbo, mumbo-jumbo,' but all the time he's low'ing his mouth toward my little private. Nobody else don't see him, but I catch him, and I haul 'way back and hit him right smack in the eye. I ain't no more than three months old but I give him a good one. 'Get your goddamn mouth away from my little pecker, you noteef, rotten, egg-sucking sonofabitch. Get away from here, you sister-jumper, God-calling, pulpit-spitting, mother-huncher. Get away from here, you chicken-eating, catfish-eating, gin-drinking sonofabitch. Get away, goddamn it, get away . . . '"

I thought Munford was just being funny, but he was serious as he could ever get. He had worked himself up so much, he had to stop and catch his breath.

"That's what I told him," he said. "That's what I told him. . . . But they don't stop there, they stay after you. If they miss you in the cradle, they catch you some other time. And when they catch you, they draw it out of you or they make you a beast—make you use it in a brutish way. You use it on a woman without caring for her, you use it on children, you use it on other men, you use it on yourself. Then when you get so disgusted with everything round you, you kill. And if your back is strong, like your back is strong, they get you out so you can kill again." He stopped and looked at me and nodded his head. "Yeah, that's what they do with you—exactly. . . . But not everybody end up like that. Some of them make it. Not many—but some of them do make it."

"Going to the pen?" I said.

"Yeah—the pen is one way," he said. "But you don't go to the pen for the nigger you killed. Not for him—he ain't worth it. They told you that from the cradle—a nigger ain't worth a good gray mule. Don't mention a white mule: fifty niggers ain't worth a good white mule. So you don't go to the pen for killing the nigger, you go for yourself. You go to sweat out all the crud you got in your system. You go, saying, 'Go fuck yourself, Roger Medlow, I want to be a man, and by God I will be a man. For once in my life I will be a man.'"

"And a month after you been in the pen, Medlow tell them to kill you for being a smart aleck. How much of a man you is then?"

"At least you been a man a month—where if you let him get you out you won't be a man a second. He won't 'low it."

"I'll take that chance," I said.

He looked at me a long time now. His reddish-brown eyes was sad and mean. He felt sorry for me, and at the same time he wanted to hit me with his fist.

"You don't look like that whitemouth uncle of yours," he said. "And you look much brighter than I did at your age. But I guess every man must live his own life. I just wish I had mine to live all over again."

He looked up at the window like he had given up on me. After a while, he looked back at Hattie on the bunk.

"You not thinking 'bout what I asked you?" he said.

Hattie looked up at him just like a woman looks at a man she can't stand.

"Munford, if you dropped dead this second, I doubt if I would shed a tear."

"Put all that together, I take it you mean no," Munford said.

Hattie rolled his eyes at Munford the way a woman rolls her eyes at a man she can't stand.

"Well, I better get out of here," Munford said. He passed his hand over his chin. It sounded like passing your hand over sandpaper. "Go home and take me a shave and might go out and do little fishing," he said. "Too hot to pick cotton."

He looked at me again.

"I guess I'll be back next week or the week after—but I suppose you'll be gone to Medlow by then."

"If he come for me—yes."

"He'll come for you," Munford said. "How old you is—twenty?"

"Nineteen."

"Yeah, he'll come and take you back. And next year you'll kill another old nigger. 'Cause they grow niggers just to be killed, and they grow people like you to kill 'em. That's all part of the—the culture. And every man got to play his part in the culture, or the culture don't go on. But I'll tell you this; if you was kin to anybody else except that Martin Baptiste, I'd stay in here long enough to make you go to Angola. 'Cause I'd break your back 'fore I let you walk out of this cell with Medlow. But with Martin Baptiste blood in you, you'll never be worth a goddamn no matter what I did. With that, I bid you adieu."

He tipped his derby to me, then he went to the door and called for the guard. The guard came and let him out. The people on the block told him good-bye and said they would see him when they got out. Munford waved at them and followed the guard toward the door.

"That Munford," Hattie said. "Thank God we're not all like that." He looked up at me. "I hope you didn't listen to half of that nonsense."

I didn't answer the freak—I didn't want have nothing to do with him. I looked up at the window. The sky was darkish blue and I could tell it was hot out there. I had always hated the hot sun, but I wished I was out there now. I wouldn't even mind picking cotton, much as I hated picking cotton.

I got out my other sandwich: nothing but two slices of light bread and a thin slice of baloney sausage. If I wasn't hungry, I wouldn't 'a' ate it at all. I tried to think about what everybody was doing at home. But hard as I tried, all I could think about was here. Maybe it was best if I didn't think about outside. That could run you crazy. I had heard about people going crazy in jail. I tried to remember how it was when I was in jail before. It wasn't like this if I could remember. Before, it was just a brawl—a fight. I had never stayed in more than a couple weeks. I had been in about a half dozen times, but never more than a week or two. This time it was different, though. Munford said Roger Medlow was go'n get me out, but suppose Munford was wrong. Suppose I had to go up? Suppose I had to go to the pen?

Hattie started singing. He was singing a spiritual and he was singing it in a high-pitched voice like a woman. I wanted to tell him to shut up, but I didn't want have nothing to do with that freak. I could feel him looking at me; a second later he had quit singing.

"That Munford," he said. "I hope you didn't believe everything he said about me."

I was quiet. I didn't want to talk to Hattie. He saw it and kept his mouth shut.

If Medlow was go'n get me out of here, why hadn't he done so? If all he had to do was snap his fingers, what was keeping him from snapping them? Maybe he wasn't go'n do anything for me. I wasn't one of them Uncle Tom-ing niggers like my uncle, and maybe he was go'n let me go up this time.

I couldn't make it in the pen. Locked up—caged. Walking round all day with shackles on my legs. No woman, no pussy—I'd die in there. I'd die in a year. Not five years—one year. If Roger Medlow came, I was leaving. That's how old people is: they always want you to do something they never did when they was young. If he had his life to live all over—how come he didn't do it then? Don't tell me do it when he didn't do it. If that's part of the culture, then I'm part of the culture, because I sure ain't for the pen.

That black sonofabitch—that coward. I hope he didn't have religion. I hope his ass burn in hell till eternity.

Look how life can change on you—just look. Yesterday this time I was poontanging like a dog. Today—that black sonofabitch—behind these bars maybe for the rest of my life. And look at me, look at me. Strong. A man. A damn good man. A hard dick—a pile of muscles. But look at me—locked in here like a caged animal.

Maybe that's what Munford was talking about. You spend much time in here like he done spent, you can't be nothing but a' animal.

I wish somebody could do something for me. I can make a phone call, can't I? But call who? That ass-hole uncle of mine? I'm sure Grinning Boy already told him where I'm at. I wonder if Grinning Boy got in touch with Marie. I suppose this finish it. Hell, why should she stick her neck out for me. I was treating her like a dog, anyhow. I'm sorry, baby; I'm sorry. No, I'm not sorry; I'd do the same thing tomorrow if I was out of here. Maybe I'm a' animal already. I don't care who she is, I'd do it with her and don't give a damn. Hell, let me stop whining; I ain't no goddamn animal. I'm a man, and I got to act and think like a man.

I got to think, I got to think. My daddy is somewhere up North—but where? I got more people scattered around, but no use going to them. I'm the black sheep of this family—and they don't care if I live or die. They'd be glad if I died so they'd be rid of me for good.

That black sonofabitch—I swear to God. Big as he was, he had to go for a knife. I hope he rot in hell. I hope he burn—goddamn it—till eternity come and go.

Let me see, let me see, who can I call? I don't know a soul with a dime. Them white people out there got it, but what do they care 'bout me, a nigger. Now, if I was a' Uncle Tom-ing nigger—oh, yes, they'd come then. They'd come running. But like I'm is, I'm fucked. Done for.

Five years, five years—that's what they give you. Five years for killing a nigger like that. Five years out of my life. Five years for a rotten, no good sonofabitch who didn't have no business being born in the first place. Five years . . .

Maybe I ought to call Medlow myself. . . . But suppose he come, then what? Me and Medlow never got along. I couldn't never bow and say, "Yes sir," and scratch my head. But I'd have to do it now. He'd have me by the nuts and he'd know it; and I'd have to kiss his ass if he told me to.

Oh Lord, have mercy. . . . They get you, don't they. They let you run and run, then they get you. They stick a no-good, trashy nigger up there, and they get you. And they twist your nuts and twist them till you don't care no more.

I got to stop this, I got to stop it. My head'll go to hurting after while and I won't be able to think anything out.

"Oh, you're so beautiful when you're meditating," Hattie said. "And what were you meditating about?"

I didn't answer him—I didn't want have nothing to do with that freak.

"How long you're going to be in here, is that it?" he said. "Sometimes they let you sit for days and days. In your case they might let you sit here a week before they say anything to you. What do they care—they're inhuman."

I got a cigarette out of the pack and lit it.

"I smoke, too," Hattie said.

I didn't answer that freak. He came over and got the pack out of my shirt pocket. His fingers went down in my pocket just like a woman's fingers go in your pocket.

"May I?" he said.

I didn't say nothing to him. He lit his cigarette and laid the pack on my chest just like a woman'd do it.

"Really, I'm not all that awful," he said. "Munford has poisoned your mind with all sorts of notions. Let go—relax. You need friends at a time like this."

I stuffed the pack of cigarettes in my pocket and looked up at the window.

"These are very good," the freak said. "Very, very good. Well, maybe you'll feel like talking a little later on. It's always good to let go. I'm understanding; I'll be here."

He went back to his bunk and laid down.

Toward three o'clock, they let the women out of the cells to walk around. Some of the women came down the block and talked to the men through the bars. Some of them even laughed and joked. Three-thirty, the guard locked them up and let the men out. From the way the guard looked at me, I knowed I wasn't going any-where. I didn't want to go anywhere, either, because I didn't want people asking me a pile of questions. Hattie went out to stretch, but few minutes later he came and laid back down. He was grumbling about some man on the block trying to get fresh with him.

"Some of them think you'll stoop to anything," he said.

I looked out of the window at the sky. I couldn't see too much, but I liked what I could see. I liked the sun, too. I hadn't ever liked the sun before, but I liked it now. I felt my throat getting tight, and I turned my head.

Toward four o'clock, Unc' Toby came on the block with dinner. For dinner, we had stew, mashed potatoes, lettuce and tomatoes. The stew was too soupy; the mashed potatoes was too soupy; the lettuce and tomatoes was too soggy. Dessert was three or four dried-up prunes with black water poured over them. After Unc' Toby served us, the guard locked up the cell. By the time we finished eating, they was back there again to pick up the trays.

I laid on my bunk, looking up at the window. How long I had been there? No more than about twelve hours. Twelve hours—but it felt like three days, already.

They knowed how to get a man down. Because they had me now. No matter which way I went—plantation or pen—they had me. That's why Medlow wasn't in any hurry to get me out. You don't have to be in any hurry when you already know you got a man by the nuts.

Look at the way they did Jack. Jack was a man, a good man. Look what they did him. Let a fifteen-cents Cajun bond him out of jail—a no-teeth, dirty, overall-wearing Cajun get him out. Then they broke him. Broke him down to nothing—to a grinning, bowing fool. . . . We loved Jack. Jack could do anything. Work, play ball, run women—anything. They knowed we loved him, that's why they did him that. Broke him—broke him the way you break a wild horse. . . . Now everybody laughs at him. Gamble with him and cheat him. He know you cheating him, but he don't care—just don't care any more . . .

Where is my father? Why my mama had to die? Why they brought me here and left me to struggle like this? I used to love my mama so much. Her skin was light brown; her hair was silky. I used to watch her powdering her face in the glass. I used to always cry when she went out—and be glad when she came back because she always brought me candy. But you gone for good now, Mama; and I got nothing in this world but me.

A man in the other cell started singing. I listened to him and looked up at the window. The sky had changed some more. It was lighter blue now—gray-blue almost.

The sun went down, a star came out. For a while it was the only star; then some more came to join it. I watched all of them. Then I watched just a few, then just one. I shut my eyes and opened them and tried to find the star again. I couldn't find it. I wasn't too sure which one it was. I could've pretended and choosed either one, but I didn't want lie to myself. I don't believe in lying to nobody else, either. I believe in being straight with a man. And I want a man to be straight with me. I wouldn't 'a' picked up that bottle for nothing if that nigger hadn't pulled his knife. Not for nothing. Because I don't believe in that kind of stuff. I believe in straight stuff. But a man got to protect himself . . . But with stars I wasn't go'n cheat. If I didn't know where the one was I was looking at at first, I wasn't go'n say I did. I picked out another one, one that wasn't too much in a cluster. I measured it off from the bars in the window, then I shut my eyes. When I opened them, I found the star right away. And I didn't have to cheat, either.

The lights went out on the block. I got up and took a leak and got back on my bunk. I got in the same place I was before and looked for the star. I found it right away. It was easier to find now because the lights was out. I got tired looking at it after a while and looked at another one. The other one was much more smaller and much more in a cluster. But I got tired of it after a while, too.

I thought about Munford. He said if they didn't get you in the cradle, they got you later. If they didn't suck all the manhood out of you in the cradle, they made you use it on people you didn't love. I never messed with a woman I didn't love. I always loved all these women I ever messed with. . . . No, I didn't love them. Because I didn't love her last night—I just wanted to fuck her. And I don't think I ever loved Marie, either. Marie just had the best pussy in the world. She had the best—still got the best. And that's why I went to her, the only reason I went. Because God knows she don't have any kind a face to make you come at her . . .

Maybe I ain't never loved nobody. Maybe I ain't never loved nobody since my mama died. Because I loved her, I know I loved her. But the rest—no, I never loved the rest. They don't let you love them. Some kind of way they keep you from loving them . . .

I have to stop thinking. That's how you go crazy—thinking. But what else can you do in a place like this—what? I wish I knowed somebody. I wish I knowed a good person. I would be good if I knowed a good person. I swear to God I would be good.

All of a sudden the lights came on, and I heard them bringing in somebody who was crying. They was coming toward the cell where I was; the person was crying all the way. Then the cell door opened and they throwed him in there and they locked the door again. I didn't look up—I wouldn't raise my head for nothing. I could tell nobody else was looking up, either. Then the footsteps faded away and the lights went out again.

I raised my head and looked at the person they had throwed in there. He was nothing but a little boy—fourteen or fifteen. He had on a white shirt and a pair of dark pants. Hattie helped him up off the floor and laid him on the bunk under me. Then he sat on the bunk 'side the boy. The boy was still crying.

"Shhh now, shhh now," Hattie was saying. It was just like a woman saying it. It made me sick a' the stomach. "Shhh now, shhh now," he kept on saying.

I swung to the floor and looked at the boy. Hattie was sitting on the bunk, passing his hand over the boy's face.

"What happened?" I asked him.

He was crying too much to answer me.

"They beat you?" I asked him.

He couldn't answer.

"A cigarette?" I said.

"No—No—sir," he said.

I lit one, anyhow, and stuck it in his mouth. He tried to smoke it and started coughing. I took it out.

"Shhh now," Hattie said, patting his face. "Just look at his clothes. The bunch of animals. Not one of them is a man. A bunch of pigs—dogs—philistines."

"You hurt?" I asked the boy.

"Sure, he's hurt," Hattie said. "Just look at his clothes, how they beat him. The bunch of dogs."

I went to the door to call the guard. But I stopped; I told myself to keep out of this. He ain't the first one they ever beat and he won't be the last one, and getting in it will just bring you a dose of the same medicine. I turned around and looked at the boy. Hattie was holding the boy in his arms and whispering to him. I hated what Hattie was doing much as I hated what the law had done.

"Leave him alone," I said to Hattie.

"The child needs somebody," he said. "You're going to look after him?"

"What happened?" I asked the boy.

"They beat me," he said.

"They didn't beat you for nothing, boy."

He was quiet now. Hattie was patting the side of his face and his hair.

"What they beat you for?" I asked him.

"I took something."

"What you took?"

"I took some cakes. I was hungry."

"You got no business stealing," I said.

"Some people got no business killing, but it don't keep them from killing," Hattie said.

He started rocking the boy in his arms the way a woman rocks a child.

"Why don't you leave him alone?" I said.

He wouldn't answer me. He kept on.

"You hear me, whore?"

"I might be a whore, but I'm not a merciless killer," he said.

I started to crack him side the head, but I changed my mind. I had already raised my fist to hit him, but I changed my mind. I started walking. I was smoking the cigarette and walking. I walked, I walked, I walked. Then I stood at the head of the bunk and look up at the window at the stars. Where was the one I was looking at a while back? I smoked on the cigarette and looked for it—but where was it? I threw the cigarette in the toilet and lit another one. I smoked and walked some more. The rest of the place was quiet. Nobody had said a word since the guards throwed that little boy in the cell. Like a bunch of roaches, like a bunch of mices, they had crawled in they holes and pulled the cover over they head.

All of a sudden I wanted to scream. I wanted to scream to the top of my voice. I wanted to get them bars in my hands and I wanted to shake, I wanted to shake that door down. I wanted to let all these people out. But would they follow me—would they? Y'all go'n follow me? I screamed inside. Y'all go'n follow me?

I ran to my bunk and bit down in the cover. I bit harder, harder, harder. I could taste the dry sweat, the dry piss, the dry vomit. I bit harder, harder, harder . . .

I got on the bunk. I looked out at the stars. A million little white, cool stars was out there. I felt my throat hurting. I felt the water running down my face. But I gripped my mouth tight so I wouldn't make a sound. I didn't make a sound, but I cried. I cried and cried and cried.

I knowed I was going to the pen now. I knowed I was going, I knowed I was going. Even if Medlow came to get me, I wasn't leaving with him. I was go'n do like Munford said. I was going there and I was go'n sweat it and I was go'n take it. I didn't want have to pull cover over my head every time a white man did something to a black boy—I wanted to stand. Because they never let you stand if they got you out. They didn't let Jack stand—and I had never heard of them letting anybody else stand, either.

I felt good. I laid there feeling good. I felt so good I wanted to sing. I sat up on the bunk and lit a cigarette. I had never smoked a cigarette like I smoked that one. I drawed deep, deep, till my chest got big. It felt good. It felt good deep down in me. I jumped to the floor feeling good.

"You want a cigarette?" I asked the boy.

I spoke to him like I had been talking to him just a few minutes ago, but it was over an hour. He was laying in Hattie's arms quiet like he was half asleep.

"No, sir," he said.

I had already shook the cigarette out of the pack.

"Here," I said.

"No, sir," he said.

"Get up from there and go to your own bunk," I said to Hattie.

"And who do you think you are to be giving orders?"

I grabbed two handsful of his shirt and jerked him up and slammed him 'cross the cell. He hit against that bunk and started crying—just laying there, holding his side and crying like a woman. After a while he picked himself up and got on that bunk.

"Philistine," he said. "Dog—brute."

When I saw he wasn't go'n act a fool and try to hit me, I turned my back on him.

"Here," I said to the boy.

"I don't smoke—please, sir."

"You big enough to steal?" I said. "You'll smoke it or you'll eat it." I lit it and pushed it in his mouth. "Smoke it."

He smoked and puffed it out. I sat down on the bunk 'side him. The freak was sitting on the bunk 'cross from us, holding his side and crying.

"Hold that smoke in," I said to the boy.

He held it in and started coughing. When he stopped coughing I told him to draw again. He drawed and held it, then he let it out. I knowed he wasn't doing it right, but this was his first time, and I let him slide.

"If Medlow come to get me, I'm not going," I said to the boy. "That means T. J. and his boys coming, too. They go'n beat me because they think I'm a smart aleck trying to show them up. Now you listen to me, and listen good. Every time they come for me I want you to start praying. I want you to pray till they bring me back in this cell. And I don't want you praying like a woman, I want you to pray like a man. You don't even have to get on your knees; you can lay on your bunk and pray. Pray quiet and to yourself. You hear me?"

He didn't know what I was talking about, but he said, "Yes, sir," anyhow.

"I don't believe in God," I said. "But I want you to believe. I want you to believe He can hear you. That's the only way I'll be able to take those beatings—with you praying. You understand what I'm saying?"

"Yes, sir."

"You sure, now?"

"Yes, sir."

I drawed on the cigarette and looked at him. Deep in me I felt some kind of love for this little boy.

"You got a daddy?" I asked him.

"Yes, sir."

"A mama?"

"Yes, sir."

"Then how come you stealing?"

"'Cause I was hungry."

"Don't they look after you?"

"No, sir."

"You been in here before?"

"Yes, sir."

"You like it in here?"

"No, sir. I was hungry."

"Let's wash your back," I said.

We got up and went to the facebowl. I helped him off with his shirt. His back was cut from where they had beat him.

"You know Munford Bazille?" I asked him.

"Yes, sir. He don't live too far from us. He kin to you?"

"No, he's not kin to me. You like him?"

"No, sir, I don't like him. He stay in fights all the time, and they always got him in jail."

"That's how you go'n end up."

"No, sir, not me. 'Cause I ain't coming back here no more."

"I better not ever catch you in here again," I said. "Hold onto that bunk—this might hurt."

"What you go'n do?"

"Wash them bruises."

"Don't mash too hard."

"Shut up," I told him, "and hold on."

I wet my handkerchief and dabbed at the bruises. Every time I touched his back, he flinched. But I didn't let that stop me. I washed his back good and clean. When I got through, I told him to go back to his bunk and lay down. Then I rinched out his shirt and spread it out on the foot of my bunk. I took off my own shirt and rinched it out because it was filthy.

I lit a cigarette and looked up at the window. I had talked big, but what was I going to do when Medlow came? Was I going to change my mind and go with him? And if I didn't go with Medlow, I surely had to go with T. J. and his boys. Was I going to be able to take the beatings night after night? I had seen what T. J. could do to your back. I had seen it on this kid and I had seen it on other people. Was I going to be able to take it?

I don't know, I thought to myself. I'll just have to wait and see.

ACCIDENTS

By the time we manage to push and shove our way up to the front, the cops decide to get ugly and brandish their nightsticks, looking, for all the spit and polish of their uniforms, like drunk, dangerous modern-day pirates. But we want to *see*, like everybody else, even though we're not smiling the way everybody else is—that transfixed, gruesome smile you'd expect to see on the face of a real vampire just after he licked his lips—the serial killer's smile. Melvin's with me, although since he's taller and wider across the shoulders than I am, he has less trouble than I do fighting his way up there through the crowd. So, just what I thought would happen, happens: He gets so excited that he lets go of my arm. Normally, when that happens in a situation like this, I panic and race after him, all cold and sweaty, like back in the time I hate to remember. But that time isn't tonight or coming anywhere near, and right now I'm feeling pretty safe, even with this crazy slobbering crowd, because I can see his back and those two long shoulder blades sticking out like ridges beneath his plaid shirt. He can see, but the way these people are shoving—just trying to hold myself up, I step on a young girl's foot. I can tell from her features that she's probably Dominican, probably no more than fourteen.

She says—"Why don't you watch out!" As she screams this at me, adding a furious *qué pendejo maricón,* her face, otherwise pretty in a dark Caribbean way (like mine, some people tell me; definitely like Melvin's), contorts into ugly twisted rage. It's a little much, and before I can even begin to stammer out an apology she's already slipped away into the crowd, yelling—it sounds like her voice amidst all these other screamers—for someone named Noellia.

"They're bringing her out!" Melvin shouts, and as I wave up to him (a little more frantically now, I'll admit), he of course turns his head and misses me. He's

227

not even looking for me; I can see him focusing in different directions like all these other people, with that same look on his face.

Get back here, would you . . . but I've got to say this out loud so that—

"Mel! Yo, get back here, would you? Mel!"

—he can hear me. All around you can feel this type of rising hysteria: It's time to leave. But there's that voice I haven't heard in so long, a nasty taunting voice right inside my ear canal that always comes back to me when something bad's about to happen: *If you leave now he'll never find you.* . . . With a few good pushes it's just fifteen seconds before I'm behind him, then beside him, missing by only a few inches banging my knees on one of the blue police car fenders.

"They're bringing her out," he says, all out of breath. "She's young, too. Looks pretty bad."

I'm amazed all at once by how many colors there are, and their ferocity in this evening's light: the cold red angry swirls of the ambulance light, the helpless pink and white hands of the paramedics, the snarling vicious-red faces of the police and the dark blue sweat patches under their arms, the dull refrigerator white of the ambulance, and the awful brownish-red blobs and blots on the white sheets covering the thing they're putting into the ambulance—whatever it is now, it can't be alive anymore, so lumpy and still. And that car—ruined and smoking with a fragmented windshield . . . the driver's seat so crushed in that you knew anything removed from there would have to have been something maybe once pretty, now hideous—*mangled* is the word; once a human, now—what? A pile of something or ash? I can tell you right now that I've never been a soldier; neither has Mel, nor has anyone of our age or generation we know. But here we are, looking. We see. It's all colored like what we imagine to be war. Here, in this place. There'll be screams somewhere tonight—all of it upended over three or four dark pools, a glutinous mess seeping over the asphalt, shallow dark-purple lakes that make sticking-sucking noises on the bottoms of the paramedics' clean white shoes.

Just for a second I look down toward my hands to make sure they're still the same color. I can't find them. At the same time somebody else's hand brushes my side, only to pull away as if burned in the same instant. What feels like a large crotch presses an intrusive, creepy tumescence against my right buttock. Now the police are furious and move closer to us, nightsticks swinging like parade girls' batons, but less gracefully, more insistent.

"Mel."

He turns after a minute to look at me; his eyes saying, not with the light of drunken good-natured foolishness, that he's about to be sick.

"Come on. Let's go." He doesn't need to get sick here. I'd probably laugh to see everybody scream and push back to give us space, but it wouldn't really be funny.

"What?" Grunting, swallowing the mess rising in his throat.

"I *said*, let's go. Come on, now." I've got a hold on his arm, pulling him back through the crowd, but now it's as if they're glad we're leaving, making space for us as we walk, although we can barely feel our feet touch the ground—at least I can't. And there's our parking space with our little blue Hyundai, still there (and why *shouldn't* it be?); I throw a glance his way as he opens the door on his side.

"Are you sure you want to drive?" Now, this is brave of me and probably even at this point a crazy thing to offer, but I have to say it. It's Mel.

"Yeah. I'm better." He looks over at me. "Get in." And that familiar smile lets me know he means it, just as clearly as I can see the glow in his face—that faint glow of sadness and weird pleasure at the uncommon fact that I am leading him away from danger, for once.

His voice was different on the way back:

"Pretty gruesome, huh?" This as he lit up a cigarette, checking the rear-view mirror in almost the same moment. The ashtray's there—I found it after a minute (and it did take me nearly a minute, you'd think that by now my hands would know *ashtray, lower left center*) and pulled it out for him. We were almost at the bridge.

"Well, wasn't it?" he insisted.

"The—yes, *yes*. What do you want me to say? I didn't know her." And I don't think I would have wanted to, either, I thought. Hell, no.

"Lucky."

"Who?"

"Some people. I don't know."

This didn't make any sense to me: A sign that he was going off into some unreachable thoughts of his own on the subject. Then he took a deep drag on the cigarette, turning to blow a long stream of smoke sideways, twisting his mouth as he did it, a mannerism of his I've always hated. It's always reminded me of a woman to whom I'd been introduced some years ago, at lunch with some friends in an Upper West Side Columbus Avenue cafe—a place called Café Recherché, or something just as pretend-French-silly; the kind of place that got you wondering just what the French must think when they visited here: Was this some sort of unqualified, hysterical Francophilia that had dreamt its way into one hundred silly, overdone restaurants?—I remembered that woman, not so much because of the way she'd dressed, actually very becomingly in pink and lavender, but because of the way she'd blown cigarette smoke sideways out of the window adjacent to our table, while rambling on about the benefits of natural foods and the company she'd soon be starting in SoHo, which would sell only *the* best balsamic vinegar and goat's-milk cheeses and pure, fresh yogurt with absolutely no preservatives or canned fruit added. "I'm calling it *Pains aux Naturels*," she'd trilled, very much like one of those mechanical songbirds you see sometimes on the tops of expensive music boxes. "Names are important. I *love* this one. A good name adds that certain *some*thing, a little panache." She'd invited a few of us to work for her as stock- and salespeople, but I was still in school then and couldn't spare the time. I still am and I still can't—now mostly because of the trouble of that time that put me out of school for a while. It all came down at once until the quiet time that helped. But at the table I'd been thinking that a better name for her company would have been *Des Crudités.* Of course I hadn't had the guts to say this. And then dessert had come.

"It's like some people," Mel was saying, speeding up to pass a small jeep dawdling in the right lane—"some people, that kind of thing doesn't bother at all. It's like they live on it, like something out of—gimme an example of a sick, scary movie."

"A *sick,* scary movie? Dag, now, Melvin, I don't know." (Talk about liars! I could think of a bunch of them.)

"But anyway it did bother me. So I *know* it bothered *you.*"

I turned the radio on. They were playing a song with slow, mournful lyrics, one we'd both heard before and liked. Somehow this song seemed right for the moment—nice and quiet and soft, like what you'd hear pouring out of a roadside stand in the country somewhere, a hazy summer night's song for a place without any people around—until the D.J. spoiled it by breaking in and announcing a new contest that was coming up if we kept it right there, on the power. I changed to something jazzy and cool and wild, music for the autumn season and these autumn moons.

"What do you mean, it bothered me? Why?"

He looked over at me, frowned, looked to his left and squeezed in behind a fat yellow taxi, cutting off an expensive-looking car behind us. The driver sped up and passed us on the right after making an obscene gesture at me; then wove in and out of the cars ahead, his brake light flashing on, flashing off: a quick, clipped warning. Some of the lights were off on the bridge; Mel drove a little slower. A subway train was rumbling past on his side, grumbling over the tracks; you could see a big patch of graffiti: ROSA LOVES BILLY 4-EVER. Big white letters on the steel sides, moving over the tracks.

He was still frowning. "You *know* what I mean." He paused and gave me that look that made his eyes relax. He almost smiled. "Gimme another cigarette."

I didn't have to look at him. But I did for a moment. The span lights overhead were forming bars, then small triangles, then crosses across his cheekbones and high, strong, dark forehead. In that light he was earth-colored; you could see in him the richest loam tones that matched his eyes and complemented the African colors in both our skins. What a beauty, I thought. His beauty excited me. You know when you're lucky. I could say I had it like that. I thought about how strange it still seemed to me sometimes, yet almost royal, a gift—one man loving another, doing things for him and to him that no one else would—or had better, I used to tease him. Loving another man wasn't strange; people can't hate the idea enough to change it, for us or anybody. The whole thing itself was the quirk. And is. And having such things done to and for yourself—that simple reciprocal thing or shadowed look; the funny feeling of knowing all the secret, intimate things our parents probably knew but had never wished to discuss, and which withholding had inevitably led to those bitter arguments that would almost always end in the icy, intractable silences of untranslatable years. It seemed so just then as pressing one of his cigarettes into the round fiery-hot lighter, I inhaled gently on it before passing it to him; that's when I knew his fingers would brush across mine the way they always did, our way. I looked down at his long, slim fingers, where they rested on the gear shift, and thought about all the rest of him that I liked. They were brown and delicate, bony at the knuckles for such a tall man (six-one). My glance was like a flirt, one he knew well, and shy. As well I knew his smell (bay rum and books), and which joints in his body would always creak at some times and snap at others to support him, and the faint whistle-and-grunt of his snore, and the dark-brown glow of his skin when the moon managed to slip itself over our roof and through our bedroom window . . . things that were nice to know about somebody. I'd only ever wanted to know them about him.

I do have a thing about car accidents, what he was hinting at before, wanting to know if tonight bothered me. I don't talk about it much. My mother died a couple of years ago, just before I started freshman year. She had been missing for two days, on the way back from my grandmother's, in New Jersey, when we heard, first from the police, then on the radio news five hours later, that she'd driven her gray Sentra right off the road and into the Johnsons' lake. The lake had adjoined the Johnsons' property, and they still hadn't returned from Algeria, where Mrs. Johnson had been writing a book on the effects of intermarriage in some populations. I've since forgotten which ones. All I really remember from that time is my mother, because soon after that was when everything to do with cars had started to happen. My mother had been in that lake for two days. She'd just sat there at the bottom, seatbelted and progressively becoming a mass of wrinkles. When the divers did get to her, she, the thing she'd become, *it,* had become heavy with washed-over mud. The water had soaked into her wool plaid coat. And the eels. They'd had to tell us about the eels.

That was a bad time for some of us. Sometimes I can still see it, when Melvin's not with me and everything's far away and the city darkens and all you hear are the screeches of cars, and gunshots, and screams; everybody dying everywhere, the way they do now. I can hear the songs they sang to keep each other company then, back in that place where I spent time. I sang them too, through how many hours I can't remember. I can hear them in every breath of the wind our apartment gets, and the voices and the sighs, old as the oldest spirits I still sometimes see; and the fire of that time they tried to shock out of me. I just remember, past those white-lit rooms and the strangers and the huge black spiders of that room I lived in, for a few years, it seemed. It was quiet with voices and water. Sometimes, now, I can just close my eyes and leave all this, leave Melvin and all of it, and see those leaves in that water and feel myself down there in the leaves, in the leaves. That peace.

The really bad part of it's over now. It's been over for a while. I look pretty much the way I used to, hair, weight, and all, and I don't have this thing anymore about going off piers or locking myself in with some good exhaust. It's not as if you could do it that many times, but you get better at it. And now it's like she's close sometimes, when I'm talking, and Mel's not in on it. He'd never understand how it feels when it's about to happen—the time when everybody finally shuts up.

After all that, you just want to get away from it for a while. You feel like there's nothing really good left in you anymore. It had all seemed a good place to get away from, that place of lakes with eels in them, and winding roads and skid marks, and stupid, slow-witted cops, and neighbors who had been away when they should have been there at home, ready to help and guide you on which way to walk if you couldn't see, even if your eyes had been open. My mother's eyes, when they'd found her, had been open and staring and just vacant, the rusty color of the leaves on the lake's surface. The brown of her skin had paled. My father's eyes have always been deep brown and since that time they have remained open and staring—staring at nothing except the black doorknob of that room they put him in, that silent room that speaks to him with the same blue electricity that the events of my time there still speak to me.

Melvin's eyes were closed.

"Melvin—Mel, wake up!"—and it was true, as he told me later, that I'd actually screamed at him—but that was the time when you felt like you weren't in a car at all; instead, you were on your way someplace else, high above everyone in the world, although you could still see them before it was all over. And also, that for one horrible minute I'd seen how Melvin would look when he was dead.

All at once he was jamming the car into first gear, then realized his mistake and pulled it back. It took me a short while, as we groaned and jerked and then swerved right up on the steel grid wall on my side, to realize that I was sitting bolt upright in the seat with the car door handle gripped in my right hand and my left knee in my left hand. That was the feeling you got when you were about to jump out, I remembered. From a car, from a car. This one.

Then we were off the bridge. A voice on the radio was singing a slow song now; the lyrics were incomprehensible and the singer sounded as though she were in tears.

"Christ." It was Melvin.

"What?"

"I'm sorry."

"___"

"D'you hear me? I'm telling you—"

"It's OK" (It *wasn't.*)

"—I'm sorry. Are you all—"

"*Yes.*"

"You know I never do that. It must be later than I thought."

I remained silent: someone had once told me that it wasn't good for a man to talk too much, and anyway there was nothing to say except:

"Are *you* OK?"—and when he nodded I shut up again. But you can imagine it. It's everything you remember: Those minutes when you smell the electric shock in the air, just like when they say *Hold still please, this won't hurt;* the shock in the shudderings of the car itself, as if for one moment we had been balanced like two eggs on the sloping bridge spans and could see every cold orange light over that water of no end—then the deep blackness of the river below, knowing that we (with just a breath or a sigh) could have fallen into that blackness, unaware of any pain or trauma or sensation of falling; just that awful blackness and the power it would have to swallow us down into itself far away from any lights, lights, which just then for us would have had the beauty of men on camels in the desert, bearing water and loaves of thick, crusty brown bread, rescue wreathed in smiles. I still hadn't released my grip on the car door handle or my knee as we drove the rest of the way home with the radio off, as we listened to all those ancient faraway sounds, like voices, echoing. Old voices, echoing.

It's our neighborhood: In this part of Brooklyn, one of those still-quaint, tree-lined brownstone-ish areas unctuously described by real-estate agents (who probably live on Park Avenue; ours did) as "charming," "up-and-coming," "the new *perfect* place to raise a family." A place a lot of white people have been known to call "delightfully ethnic." Many families do live here, most them poor, middle-aged Puerto Ricans. There are many beautiful, clear-eyed children, almost all of whom attend the Catholic elementary school a few blocks west of the park. I moved in here with Mel soon after we met just over a year ago, after I'd gotten good and cleaned up and away from everybody. Now that I'm back in school it's a long trip every day by subway. I don't really mind. I'd never think of asking him to drive me in, since he has to commute out to Nassau County every day, to the South Shore Hospital he works in. Once I surprised him out there and we had lunch on the grass; it was pretty nice even for a hospital. Most of the time that I see him he's tired. That's what gets me scared, when he drives back late from out there. What almost happened tonight could almost happen out there. Or happen. It would happen, the way things are now. The thing is, you have to be ready for it when it happens. It would be *what was left of him under that white sheet with red and brown spots all over it when he was brought back with all those people smiling and wanting to see; people we had never known. And if you looked into my eyes you would see how they would stay open for years, especially at night because there would be those demons, those demons behind the door and the things that still live there. Because what—*

(*—what everybody always tells you, what they always rush to tell you, is never true, about how those things aren't there and can't get you. They do get you. Even if you're dreaming that they got you, you never really wake up. Not ever. Never and can't*).

"*Hey.*" Mel's voice. "Are you coming to bed or what?" He was giving me this very annoyed look.

"What's up with you?" he said. We'd gotten all the way up the stairs and into the apartment and through to the bedroom, and I was just standing there in front of the mirror with my shirt off, holding it in my right hand. He was smiling, weary, and just at the edge of fatigued impatience, showing the smooth shoulders and pretty dark nipples that, from their place beneath his T-shirt, pressing perfect points up beneath the cotton, didn't tempt me tonight.

"Come *on.*"

I finished undressing and got into bed. I was trembling. His arms and shoulders felt warm and safe. I moved closer to him.

He turned out the light, butted my arm with his face, put a hand in its favored place on my ass, and grunted good night.

"Mel?"

"*Oh . . .* yeah?"

". . . nothing—" I couldn't sleep. It was close to a full moon. There weren't any noises. Only the sound of his breathing.

Four nights later, five nights, six. . . . I still couldn't sleep. Mel was working the four to twelve shift at the hospital and then had called to say that he'd had a fight with some loudmouthed, do-it-*this*-way type nurse and had told them all to go fuck themselves good, and that with luck and clear traffic he'd be home a little before midnight, but first he'd be stopping off to eat at an expressway restaurant in Massapequa with one of the guys from X-ray—Johnny Mercado, did I remember him? *No.* The rest of it was fine with me. At least for a little while yet there wouldn't be anyone else around.

—That's what I was thinking after I hung up. I just didn't feel like speaking to anybody. In fact, I didn't feel like doing much of anything. There were a few papers I could have worked on, and some books I should have read a week ago already and discussed in the classes I missed yesterday and the day before, but instead I'd turned off the light early in the evening and had just sat there in the comfortable dark, thinking. It seemed like there was a lot to think about all of a sudden . . . like the ocean at Quogue last summer . . . that place where we'd spent a week with some friends of Mel's: a husband and wife neurology team at the hospital out there. They hadn't been all that bad for older people, in their forties, and they hadn't tried to make us feel stupid, either, the way some doctors do to people, all condescending in white. That had been their summer-weekend house, right on the beach, and we'd spent every evening but one, the rainy one, sitting and talking and drinking fancy drinks on the redwood porch facing the beach. You could feel the ocean everywhere—eating its way along the edge of the beach and licking at the legs of the neighbor's little boy who had played at the water's edge every day. Sometimes he would waddle on chubby kid legs over to us to show us something he'd found—a pretty shell or a rock—and I'd always wanted to grab him to tell him to stay away from the water, because couldn't he see it was dangerous? The ocean *had* been everywhere: in the air, in the house, on our skin, even inside us; you couldn't get away from it. Every now and then a town police jeep had bumped past on the beach, leaving huge tire marks and flashing its red light like an awful, swollen, bloody red eye. Even the sun had been red. The sun had been red and the ocean had been everywhere and you couldn't get away from them.

Except in the dark. When I'm in the dark and I can't see, I can tell everything's going to be all right. It's something you know. Even if any monsters or flashing lights or greedy oceans or black rivers are here, I won't see them and they won't get to me because I can't see them.

I can't see them!

That was me, in a loud, clear voice. Before the door moved with—

"Who are you talking to? I said 'Hi,' for the second time," Mel's voice came from behind the kitchen door. He made it even sooner than he'd said he would (*but just leave me the fuck alone, would you? Always breaking in like a goddamn—*)

"Hi. What's this miracle?—what time is it?"

"I don't know . . . late. We didn't bother to stop. You know that place is *not* the real deal for any kind of dinner after eight o'clock."

"Um-hmm." It sounded clumsy. Had he come home early to see what I was up to? Why the *fuck*—

"So what're you sitting in the dark for?"

"'Cause I feel like it. It was quiet."

"Yeah? Since when?" He was fumbling in the refrigerator for something; pushing aside things wrapped in tin foil, rolling around what sounded like cucumbers.

"What're you looking for?"

"A beer."

"I think we're out. See if there's any Coke."

"I don't *want* a Coke. What d'you mean, we're out? How could we be out?"

"*I* want a Coke. Oh, wait." A few days ago he'd bought two six-packs of some new Japanese beer that had sounded good and I'd promised to put them away. I'd forgotten. "Mel."

"What? You're right, we are out. Jesus Christ."

"No, there're two six-packs on the floor. By the garbage can. I forgot to put them in. On the floor, the Sapporuchi something."

"Warm beer? Unh-*unh,* baby. That ain't gettin it. So." He came into the living room where I could almost see him, tall and familiar in the dark. "Since when're you into sitting in the dark? You going all loco on me, hombre?"

"*Don't* turn it on." With, quickly: "It's an ugly lamp. It makes the room look pink."

"It's . . ."

"It's nice like this, when you can't see anything. Check out the street lights, honey!"

"Who can see . . . it's dark as *hell.*" He was tired, affectionate, just worn out, really. Not only had it been a long day for him, ending with that stupid nurse, but then he'd had to come home and find warm beer when it should have been fresh-cold from Japan, and me sitting in the dark, not even playing the stereo the way I used to do, sometimes for hours, until he'd come home. It was all so different so fast. And now it was like I wasn't even alone with him. I could feel it.

"Just leave it off. Did you bring my Coke?"

"Come and get it." I got up and went to him. It was all dark as I crossed the room and took the Coke as he gave me his hand and pulled me in a little. That was when I saw her. The leaves were covering her.

No sleep. Tonight there are a few noises, noises of cars and cats and the late street-sweepers. The living room faces the street, across the hall from our bed-room, and usually the few street noises there are don't reach us in there; tonight I'm listening for them carefully, watchfully. The sounds never seem to be enough; there are never enough of them. It gets so quiet you can hear your own heart, thumping like some soft clumsy thing inside you. I hear it: It's beating louder and louder, ocean-sounds. Well, the ocean's here. I see it, all white and gray and angry. This has to be Quogue or some other place, a nameless, faceless beach with only the ocean and me staring at each other. It's whispering, and the whispers sound like one big, ugly hiss.

What do you want?—quietly, so Mel won't hear.

It's not answering me. Just staring and whispering.

When this happens, you have to *make* it answer.

What do you want? Louder now. I don't think Mel can hear me here. I'm on the beach and he's asleep. Sleeping like the dead.

You, it says, shifting and rolling itself.

Why? Rolling itself over and over, back and out to the edge of the sky and back again, until it says: *Because.*

Because what? Mel's so far away—all these shadows here and him so far away with no answer from the ocean and these noises hurting in my head. Like, *Hold still please, this won't hurt.* The scumbags lie, you remember it.

I nod. I'm nodding. I'm walking into the ocean and from some point far off in the distance I hear a voice calling me, *Stop,* calling my name, *Stop!* Mel or some-body.—I'm walking in with my eyes open as the ocean keeps staring *and oh dear God I will not stop walking in deeper and deeper, deeper and deeper. Marry me.*

The radio was on. Brash as a buzzsaw and loud—what time was it, what time?—and then that voice, announcing . . . a DC-10 crashed in Boston last night, killing all two hundred and seventy-three aboard. This was a dream, it had to be.

There was Mel, sitting on the edge of the bed, smoking and watching me. He looked more tired than ever.

"Morning."

"Umh."—"What time?"

"Seven-eighteen."

"Hup." It hurt to clear my throat.

"Listen."

"——"

"Are you—are you—"

He wanted to finish with *all right?* I knew it. I hated him. I looked at him and didn't say anything. He should have been dressed already and on his way out. He was still in the T-shirt and undershorts he'd slept in, sitting there calmly looking at me; only he wasn't calm. I hated him. (Since when?) I hated him.

"I'm fine." I could hear my voice, so far away, as he looked down at his hands, then back up at me. "*You* look tired. You look like hell." He wouldn't stop *looking* at me. "You don't smell that great, either," I added.

"Thanks."

"Did *you* sleep well? You didn't!" I couldn't take it when he looked like that. I felt like burning him with something, or tearing him to screaming, bloody shreds. Bastard, sitting there staring at me. A born bastard. And now my head was hurting again.

"No. But take a look at yourself."

"Why?"

"Just do." (A surprise?) I jumped out of bed and went to the mirror.

So, I looked as though I hadn't slept for days. I haven't. The only difference was that now there were black rings under my eyes, small black lines. But I still felt as though I could get into a high-speed car in two seconds and race off for miles, never touching the earth.

He was still looking at me—his head off to one side, legs crossed, drumming his fingers on his bare thigh as he blew smoke out of the side of his mouth. That habit I hated all over again, as he put the cigarette out in the ashtray on top of the blanket and came over to put his hot, horrible hands on my head. Next it would be his mouth, and then he might even have tried to hold me down, looking at me the whole time, saying *What's wrong?*—when there was nothing wrong at all. I just had to get away from him. It was him, today, now.

(*To where?*)

—the leaves, the lake, the lights flashing dream-red, dream-white, so pretty . . . I'd been there before, in those places, sometime. It had been so very quiet with no one.

I was already in the bathroom, trying to find something to hold on to—the toothbrush, the toothpaste tube, soft, plastic, cold—right there.

"What's wrong?"—if I'd had a gun right then I would have shot him. *Gotten rid of him.* There were noises of him opening a drawer, the drawer that always stuck and made splinters, as he searched for a shirt to wear. Those little noises made my head hurt more.

"Nothing. I'll be late," I said. The newscaster was still snapping out details of the crash and quoting the statements of airline officials. There were so many victims: *a tragic event,* one official said. But this was peace for some of us. Just to stand here, and listen.

Another night and still no sleep. Now, at last, it was nice. Finally, just some time when you could stay awake for hours, staring at the walls, watching them move and shift in the dark. With the moon's passing it was darker tonight. There were no noises anywhere. I couldn't even hear breathing, or snoring. It was like I didn't have to pretend anymore that maybe he was dead after all and wouldn't ever wake up, just like I'd never go to sleep. The day after tomorrow and the day after that and on and on for years, he'll be lying there next to me as I keep sitting up listening to the ocean sucking out and back and the jets that crash and burn people to ash. And that small, sneaky sound of books that have to turn their own pages because I—*I*—can't read them.

Yes; today I pretended that I was getting ready to go to classes and then came right back after Mel was gone. *¡Qué estupido!* the Spanish neighborhood ladies would say, anyone could fool him. I was here to pull down the shades. I sat in the dark to listen. Because you never know when there'll be an accident that you'll hear that you'll want to see, and you'll know that it's an accident with all those sirens and firetrucks and people screaming as they see the runway come up closer from way down there with those huge, beautiful engines as they burn up and you know that you will soon burn with them. I sat in the dark all day to listen; I heard the voices of cats. Also the floor creakings and the shadows. I could hear them breathing as I sat there thinking. They were here for hours until the woman came. And she's back now.

It *is* her. That bloody woman from the accident that was when? A month or three weeks ago. Standing by the door next to the mirror over the cabinet, looking at me. (How can she see me?) Seeping . . . that neck is so shredded. I see the blood glinting on the walls behind her. I see that white sheet on her.

Mel, *I'm whispering*, you better get up. She's here. I can see her. Why don't you look?

The bastard's asleep. I have to wake him up, for *this*. Get up, Mel! Still asleep. *That woman is standing over there.*

(*And you should know why, says a voice that is Melvin's voice but it is different. He's rising to sit. And I can see you better now than I've ever seen you before, Mel. I can see the demon that I always knew was in you, the same demon I have been feeling these last weeks, this last year, however long the whole world has been hurting my head like this. Your face is gone except for those red eyes and red teeth, red like the sun on the beach and the blood. Now you know because everyone knows as she bleeds and starts to cry that she is doing this, that you are doing this and that we will have to leave this room now, get out of here to live, because no one is crazy here, we are not crazy in any way or shape.*)

A few seconds later you hear someone screaming, screaming like a monster or the way she screamed as the car smashing into the lamp post cut off her legs and pulled out her hair and ripped her neck from end to veined end; no, the way she screamed as the muddy water swept down her throat and made bubbles in her blood until it was all darkness and the leaves in protest swirled up like bat wings around her and covered her for the living to haul up because by then she was anyway sewage dead with the weight of sewage; no, the way, he screamed when smiling white cops told him she was gone and his screams echoed through the screams and laughter and tears until the final silence of that room they put him in: Screaming like the dead who will never rise to inherit the earth or whatever kingdom is promised any number of king-

doms from one day to the next; screaming like him now with his mouth open and dry as something under his chin tries to push his mouth shut; earwitnesses will say It must be someone out on the street dying under the cold city skeleton lights in the alleyways where cats maul and screw . . . somebody on the runway, stifling under all the foam they sprayed there, screaming for the ambulance. Trying now to remove those many arms about you; feeling the killing grip will strap you into that place and drown you. What is that thing under your chin. A hand. A smell once familiar. The hand of the lake choking you choking all . . . the last thing now in the world of fire; that other's burning face, Melvin's face screaming Let me help you: words spoken through red teeth until all dims to the black water color. And now

—no noises. The girl gone. How many creatures swim through the water. And how he swims. He and he. And the silent screams and the sirens of that time; the red revolving lights like bright hungry fish. And the fire. Watching him.

I can't tell you what day it is. Maybe the next day but I can't be sure anymore when all I hear are lies, whispers, and lies. And now *the days pass by so quickly, yellow, green, red, until the nights come, the black nights: There must be three or four of them at a time sometimes, they last so long. They just go on and on, like space, empty like space, and the moon's not full anymore so you can't see anything. You can't see the stars or the walls of the walls of your room or even the earth, although you know it's out there. Blue. You know it's out there and you look for it but you can't see it. It's dangerous because if you can't see it you'll crash and wind up on the radio after the song hour. The sad songs they play at night, the songs of dreams.*

They're playing a song on the radio now. The words to it are coming through clearly in this dream. We're in the Hyundai, heading for the bridge, some bridge I don't remember, to get to this hospital, a white hospital . . . Mel's driving. He looks so tired, and now he looks different, like a shadow. He doesn't look real. He's a dream-person. He looks like the shadows the sun makes on bridges. I'm dreaming this, I have to be dreaming this. And the dream-pictures, like photo snaps all muddled, blurry-faced, come rushing up, stay for a second, then race off. To the bridge.

And he's driving too fast. *This trip wasn't my idea.* He planned everything as always. He thinks there's something wrong with me and wants me to go to the E.R. of this hospital so they can poke me around until I come out sounding stupid. He's not saying anything. I know him. After all this time I can read his mind. He thinks they'll be able to fix me because there's something wrong with me even though I feel fine. I just don't want to go to sleep anymore. In fact I'm never going to sleep again.

"Mel, you're driving too fast." *I hate the way he drives and sits on the bed and stands up blowing smoke out of the side of his mouth—like that. He's doing it. I'm just glad he's a shadow. He shouldn't be real. People should blow smoke sideways when they're dreaming not when they're driving and sitting down and standing up. That woman used to do it.*

"Mel, you're driving too fast." We're at the bridge now. What if he drives too fast and we drive off the earth? They'll tell it on the radio. People I care about will go out and have an accident. There are always so many trucks. The trucks that bring supplies, the trucks that block everyone's vision, the trucks of dreams.

This truck is in front of us and somebody on the radio is screaming. *Watch out, we're going to go off the earth*

"Mel, watch out!—it's too *fast!*" And now I

—reach over and hit him and see the bright red on my hand. I must have hit him in his teeth. *They're so red. Always red, more and more like his eyes. This is the steering wheel. We can't, we can't go off the earth.*

In front of us, the noise of a crash: A plane must have crashed on the bridge, killing everybody aboard. There's a crash behind us and we are flying forward, hard, flying. I was belted in so I would never leave the bottom of the lake, but Mel's not belted so he can escape, flying, big black brown pretty jet right through the glass. I see him, there he goes. *Too much noise.* . . . Cracked glass, red, the smell of fire . . . he's gone. He escaped and left me under this red sky. I would never ever have left him, never . . . the radio's screaming about accidents; there are accidents everywhere.

But I'm out of the car, running. I know I should be *waking up* but I'm here running on the bridge, feeling the thin, dreamy-delicious air parting itself, carrying me up. Mel must be somewhere close by. What happened— . . . *but you have to be OK, Mel, somewhere I can't see you.* I'm running . . . my eyes are open but I can't see and I'm still running. The sun is melting over everything like hot angry orange taffy, and even the bridge is running and melting under the sky that just keeps hanging there, a world of red burning dreams, burning gold . . . the neighbors who could help me see and take me home are in Africa, writing a book. I have to cross the water to get to them. Maybe even the ocean. It's there, under the bridge.

I keep hearing the horns of cars, angry honks. Only they aren't cars, they're trumpeting elephants. I'm out in the open, running with the elephants, and the plane that crashed is burning nearby under a red sky and a red sun as the ocean roars in anger, in terror, far away. *Africa.* I'm close. I can't find Mel anywhere. He must have melted into the bridge.

I have to cross the water. *It's the dream.* And there's the water: I can see it, black, old, deep, swirling to Africa, telling me *not to be afraid, to walk on its back, to follow it to*

Red lights . . .

Dreams. Voices calling. Calling—

The sounds of elephants . . .

The bridge is burning.

Dear God—

And now listen. Just listen. This is the long dream beginning. *The long dream.* You can't see anything but fire all around here. *Hot.* And now all you can hear for miles—for miles and miles—are screams.

LORNA   GOODISON

BY LOVE POSSESSED

SOMETIMES, SHE USED TO WAKE UP and just look at him lying asleep beside her; she would prop herself up on one elbow and study his face. He slept like a child, knees drawn up to his stomach, both hands tucked between his thighs. His mouth was always slightly open when he slept, and his mouth water always left a damp patch on the pillowcase; no matter how many days after, it seems the patch would always be damp and every time she washed it, she would run her finger over the stain and her mind would pick up the signal and move back to the image of him lying asleep. When the radio next door began to play the first of the morning church services, she would know that it was time to begin to get ready to go to work. From Monday to Saturday, every day, her days began like this. She would go to the kitchen to prepare his breakfast, then she would leave it covered up on top of the stove over a bowl of hot water. Then she would go to the bathroom, bathe in the cold early morning water and then get dressed. Just before she left, she always placed some money on the top of the bureau for his rum and cigarettes, then she would say to his sleeping form, "Frenchie, ah gone, take care till I come back." Dottie sometimes wondered how she was so lucky to be actually living with Frenchie. He was easily the best looking man in Jones Town, maybe in the whole of Jamaica and she, ten years older than him, tall and skinny and "dry up." She had never had luck with men and she had resigned herself to being an old maid a long time ago. She was childless, "a mule" as really unkind people would say. She worked hard and saved her money, and she kept a good house. Her two rooms in the big yard were spotless. She had a big trunk bed, that was always made up with pretty chenille spreads, a lovely mahogany bureau, a big wardrobe with good quality glass (mirrors) and in the front room, in pride of place, her China Cabinet. Nobody in the yard, maybe in Jones Town, maybe in the whole of Jamaica, had a

China Cabinet so full of beautiful things. Dottie had carefully collected them over the years and she never used them. Once a year when she was fixing up her house at Christmas, she would carefully take them out, the ware plates, cups and saucers, tureens, glasses, lemonade sets, serving dishes and teapots, and she would carefully wash them. This took her nearly a whole morning. She washed them in a pan of soapy warm water, rinsed them in cold water, then dried them with a clean towel. Then she would rearrange them artistically in the Cabinet. On that night, she would sometimes treat herself to a little drink of Porto Pruno wine, sitting by herself in her little living room and would gaze on her China Cabinet enjoying the richness within, the pretty colors and the lights bouncing off the glasses. Her sister always said that she worshipped her possessions; maybe she did, but what else did she have? Till she met Frenchie.

There was one other thing that Dottie really liked, she liked the movies and that is how she met Frenchie. She was in the line outside the Ambassador theater one Saturday night, waiting to get into a hot triple bill when she struck up a conversation with him. He was standing in the line behind her and she remembered feeling so pleased that a man as good looking as this was talking to her. They moved up in the line till they got to the cashier, and she being ahead of him, took out ten shillings to pay for herself. It was the easiest most natural thing in the world for her to offer to pay for him when he suddenly raised an alarm that his pocket had been picked. If she had been seeing straight, she would have noticed that some people were laughing when he raised the alarm. But she didn't see anything but the handsome brown skin man with "good hair," straight nose and a mouth like a woman's. It was the best triple bill Dottie ever watched. He had walked her home. All the way home they talked about the movie . . . His favorite actor was Ricardo Montalban, she liked Dolores Del Rio, for that is how she would like to have looked, sultry and Spanish, for then she and Frenchie would make a striking couple, just like two movie stars. As it was she looked something like Popeye's girlfriend Olive Oyl and he was probably better looking than Ricardo Montalban.

Frenchie did not work. He explained that he used to have a job at the wharf but he got laid-off when his back was damaged unloading some cargo. She sympathized with him and some nights she would rub the smooth expanse of his back with wintergreen oil. He said he liked how her hands felt strong. Frenchie moved in with Dottie about two weeks after they met. At first, she was a little shy about having a man living in her room, then she began to be very proud of it. At least she was just like any other woman in the yard. As a matter of fact, she was luckier than all of them, for Frenchie was so good looking. "She mind him. Dottie buy down to the very drawers that Frenchie wear," said her sister, "not even a kerchief the man buy for himself." The people in the yard would laugh at her behind her back, they wondered if Frenchie kept women with her. Winston her nephew said, "Chu, Rum a Frenchie woman, man, you ever see that man hug up a rum bottle?"

Now that was true. Frenchie loved rum and rum loved him, for he never seemed to get drunk. As a matter of fact, every day he spent a good eight hours like a man going to work, in Mr. Percy's bar at the corner. After Dottie had gone to work at the St. Andrew House where she did domestic work for some brown people, Frenchie would wake up. He would bathe, eat the breakfast that Dottie had left for him and get dressed, just like any man going to work. He always wore white short sleeved shirts which Dottie washed whiter than "Pelican shit"; he favored khaki pants, so she ironed both shirt and pants very carefully.

He would get dressed very, very carefully; put some green brilliantine in his hair and brush it till it had the texture of a zinc fence, or as one of the men in the yard said, "Everytime I see you hair Frenchie, I feel sea-sick." Frenchie would laugh showing his gold crown on his front teeth, run his hand over his hair and say, "Waves that behaves, bwoy, waves that behaves." When his toilette was over, he would walk leisurely up the road to the bar. The one thing which made you realize that he could not have been going to work like any other decent man was his shoes: he always wore backless brown slippers. Frenchie would sit in the bar and make pronouncements on matters ranging from the private life of the Royal Family (Princess Margaret was a favorite topic), to West Indian Cricket (he always had inside knowledge on these matters), general world affairs and most of all the movies.

Everybody was in awe of Frenchie, he was just so tough, handsome and in control of life. His day at the bar usually ended at around 5:00 P.M., just like any other working man. Then he would walk home and join the Domino game which went on constantly in the yard. Usually Dottie would find him at the Domino table, when she burst in through the gate, always in a hurry, anxious to come home and fix his dinner. She always said the same thing when she came through the gate, "Papa, ah come" and he looking cool and aloof, eyes narrowed through the cigarette smoke, would say "O, yu come." Dottie always experienced a thrill when he said that, it was a signal of ownership, the slight menace in his voice was exciting, you knew it gave the right to say, "Frenchie vex when I come home late . . ."

She would hurry to fix his dinner and set it on the table before him. She hardly ever ate with him, but sat at the table watching him eat. "Everyday Frenchie eat a Sunday dinner," Winston would say. It was true, Dottie cooked only the best for Frenchie, he ate rice and peas at least three times per week unlike everybody else who only ate it on Sunday . . . Dottie would leave the peas soaking overnight and half boil them in the morning, so that they could finish cooking quickly, when she hurried home in the evenings. He also had beef steak at least twice a week and "quality fish" and chicken, the rest of the week.

Dottie lived to please Frenchie. She was a character in a film, "By Love Possessed." Then one day in Mr. Myers' bar, the movies turned into real life . . . Frenchie was sitting with his usual group of drunkalready friends talking about a movie he had seen, when a stranger stepped into the saloon, actually he was an ordinary man. He had a mean and menacing countenance, because he was out of work and things were bad at home, he walked into the bar and ordered a white rum and sat on a barstool scowling, screwing up his face everytime he took a sip of the pure 100% proof cane spirit, and suddenly Frenchie's incessant talking began to bother the stranger. The more Frenchie talked, the more it bothered him. He looked at Frenchie's pretty boy face and his soft looking hands and he hated him.

Then Frenchie reached a high point of the story he was telling. He was painting a vivid picture of the hero, wronged by a man who doubted his integrity and Frenchie was really into it . . . he became the wronged hero before everyone's eyes, his voice trembled, his eyes widened in disbelief as the audience gazed spellbound at him . . . "Then the star boy say," said Frenchie, him say, "What kind of man do you think I am?" The stranger at the bar never missed a beat . . . he replied, "A batty Man." And the bar erupted. The laughter could be heard streets away, the barmaid laughed till they had to throw water on her to stop her from becoming hysterical, all the people who had ever wanted to laugh at Frenchie, laughed at him, all the people who envied him, his sweet boy life, laughed at him, everybody was laughing at him. The uproar didn't die down for almost half an hour and people who heard came running in off the streets to find out what had happened. One man took it upon himself to tell all the newcomers the story, over and over again. Frenchie was sitting stunned, he tried to regain face by muttering that the man was a blasted fool . . . but nobody listened.

Finally, the self-appointed raconteur went over to him and said, "Cho Frenchie, you can't take a joke?" The he lowered his voice, taking advantage of the fallen hero and said, "All the same yu know everybody must wonder bout you, how a good looking man like you, live with a mawgre dry up ooman like Dottie, she fava man, she so flat and crawny . . ." Upon hearing this, Frenchie got angrier and funnily enough, he wasn't angry at the man, he was angry at Dottie. It was true, she didn't deserve him, she was mawgre and crawny and dry up and really was not a woman that a handsome sexy man like him should be with . . . No wonder the blasted ugly bwoy coulda facety with him, he understood what the hero meant in the movies when he said he saw red . . . Frenchie felt like he was drowning in a sea of blood . . . he wanted to kill Dottie! He got up and walked out of the bar to go home. When Dottie hurried in through the door that evening, saying breathlessly, "Papa ah come," she was met with the following sight. Frenchie was standing at the door of her front room with her best soup tureen in one hand and four of her best gold rimmed tumblers stacked inside each other in the other hand, and as soon as he saw her he flung them into the street. He went back inside and emerged with more of the precious things from her China Cabinet and he flung them into the street where they broke with a rich full sound on the asphalt. After a while, he developed a steady rhythm, he began to take what looked like the same amount of steps each time he went into the house, then he'd emerge with some crockery or glass, walk to the edge of the verandah taking the same amount of steps and with an underarm bowling action, fling the things into the street. Dottie screamed, she ran up the steps and clutched at him, he gave her a box which sent her flying down the steps. Everybody screamed, the men kept saying that he had gone rass mad . . . nobody tried to restrain him for he had murder in his eyes . . . and he never stopped till he had broken all of Dottie's things and then he walked out of the yard.

"Frenchie bad no rass bwoy . . . You see when him just fling the things, chuh."
Frenchie's name became a great legend in the neighborhood, nobody had ever
seen anybody "mash it up" like that, so nobody had ever seen anybody in such a
glorious temper, "mash up the place to blow wow" . . . Nobody remembered him
for "What kind of man do you think I am?" Even poor broken Dottie remembered
him for his glorious temper . . . She would have forgiven him for breaking her precious things, she would have liked to have told the story of how bad her man was
and the day he broke everything in her China Closet and boxed her down the steps
. . . But he didn't give her a chance. She kept going to the Sunday night triple bills
at the Ambassador, but she never saw him again and after that, she took a live-in
job and gave up her rooms in the Yard.

SHE WAKES

... SHE WAKES. She is not Enid Thomas. Let's make that clear. She is Patricia Williams. Patricia Whittaker-Williams. Author of her own story. This gift. This daughter. Wife of this worried face. This anxious questioning. Eventually she is lying back on heaped pillows listening to his breathing, the dream seeping into the room. She has never met, never even heard of an Enid Thomas. I'm telling you Daughter reality is beyond my poor comprehension. As if she didn't have problems enough. What with a husband intent on moving to her island. And a Canada intent on giving him good reason. If she smoked this would be a good time for a cigarette. Bars of moonlight across the coffin cross, his father's, handed to his mother before the mattress and the shovelfuls of earth and stone. Since her death passed on to him. Mysterious in grey blue light. He has begun to snore lightly. She is hot, throat sore, dry. The secret dream-life as strenuous as other rebellions.

> The bed is a ghostly galleon floating the moonlit sea
> Enid Thomas comes sailing   sailing   sailing
> Enid Thomas comes sailing up to the old Bounty

She slips as quietly as her bulk allows out of the bed, and from the room. Sitting, standing, pacing, she outstares the story. Daughter this is yours, and Enid Thomas's who ever she may be.

She finds her image *Butterfly on a Pin* then begins with the dream:

> In such dream-quickened dark everything looms   streetlights
> corner bank   drugstore   even small houses in small

246

gardens gather their skirts   lean
in their intent night-windows a scythe-moon
glitters   and this is where a poem begins   innocent
insistent   *she finds herself at the corner*   dream
sense of stifled horror   to know
once and for all what it is that eludes
and teaches   in such a space the night is wet   dank
streetlights are blue/orange/red in pavement   a wind
a plastic bag that lifts and skids and blows
gleams *ghostly as flimsy as i in the schoolyard*
twirling   twirling to music that not even the dream
reveals   what is a dream *without revelation*
i watch as from a great distance above how *she*
comes face to face with her self   that other that
in the dream *is glimmering*   trailing   not always
there   not all there   sudden as dreams are sudden
the city glows in her forehead
her eyes are islands   dark Caribbean seas
a yellow light on her face   deft peculiar grace
my mouth open straining to fit in to   reach what
is there   on that street corner in Calgary below
the bluffs and dry poplars   *to fit into*
infiltrated by the bitter orange glow of midnight streets
to reach what there is teasing beyond the edges and
heaven's bruised light spilt i am crying   *i am Enid*
Thomas   my voice rising i think it is my voice   *i am*
Enid Thomas   voice as if my hands were tied behind
my back as if someone were denying me
a name *i am Enid Thomas*

When she wakes for the second time, grey light fills the room like an unwanted visitor. Her head is stuffed, bulging with the night's images. Walking about the room she touches everything, claims the bright spines of detective fiction, the Inca head, the Warri beads. She runs her hands over the television screen, the Brecht, the Spaniards. Reads the titles of all the Africans. Then stands shivering before the open window trying to pierce the storm-driven torment of snow to the bluffs and sentinel towers. As if to reassure herself. As if some vital truth of herself, some proof susceptible to the hand, the eye, lingered on the surface of things. So could bear witness.

When she first come to tell me this story, she say, "Great Aunt, what happen here? What it is that really happen?" Is a question Patricia always asking, as if she suspicious, she want the whole world to have meaning. She is a child that never believe in accident, in chance. She tell me she read somewhere "God don't play dice." Well, if it ain't dice He playing, is card He pulling. But she can't believe that yet. It going to come. She got some more living to do.

Well to go back to the beginning. The whole trouble start with this dream she have. Simple as that. Patricia have a dream. Everybody have nightmares, but hers have to be dramatic! They have to have atmosphere! Is a worse thing: they have to have meaning! So she set like a comet on somebody path. She got to interfere with Enid Thomas. While she standing there at that window, pretending that everything she see is hers . . . she seeing changing it, you understand . . . laser eyes . . . that poor woman. Jocelyn, who don't even know her, who is getting out of bed, pushing those heavy blankets back, pulling her pink brushed nylon nightgown up over her head, and struggling a little, seeing as she forget the buttons at the neck, and liking how it soft, and how she smell she own sweetish warm scent, and wondering if is so Lloyd does smell it when he sleep over, and how she got to get that Ashley out of bed, and the porridge on the stove; that woman who don't believe in this cornflakes thing, and the child only picking up, picking up from that damn TV, but porridge does stick to the ribs, and she going to put an egg in it, no child of hers going to school hungry, and blast! the child have a dentist appointment this morning, she hope Marilyn, since she owe her one, going to cover when she take Ashley . . . that place so far, is the LRT she going to have to take and then a bus, it go take two hours, if she go early and use the lunch hour perhaps sourface Garth ain't going to mind, but is a kind dentist, she talk real soft and she Black, and not stuck up because she professional, but is so darn far; that woman who don't have no time for water trouble now, so is what wrong with the tap . . . is only hot water coming, she ain't got time for this fiddling fiddling this morning, she really got to get in early . . . ah is now the water coming good; that woman who stand under the shower who throw she head back who let water fall on she face like rain on the banks of the Lopinot river, the water pockmarked the cocoa trees darkening and glistening in the rain, and the sound of it like thunder . . . you see what I mean, this Jocelyn who thinking like a normal person about what is real: what happen already, what she know going to happen because it happen already, whose life ain't no fantasy, that woman going to have to deal all unexpected with Patricia who think she and God in this together. Together they creating everything she see, everything she touch. I tell you life ain't no equal contest. Just think how no Carib, no Iroquois, could ever imagine that somebody could leave their own place, come thousands of miles to this place and think to take he land from him, think he have a right to take he land, not only he land, he world, he very self. And calling he 'Indian'. In the same way this poor woman who once call she self Enid Thomas can't even imagine what go happen to she, can't even prepare she self for this thing what coming.

This morning she puts on the loose floating African gown she affects, then drifts into the kitchen. From the door of the broom closet she takes the huge barbeque apron and fastens it on. This is an egg morning. There is the unexpected school holiday, the snow on the balcony banked up against her glass wall, the soft muffling sound of sky slanting into heavy white drifts, wind-howl rising every now and again to penetrate the triple windows. As if it were a whisper, a secret breathed in her ear, she begins to hear words, phrases, the poem she dreamt last night. She connects the blanks, begins to design the whole, to lay the poem out in her head.

While the water for her poached egg boils, she cuts the crusts off whole wheat slices. That done, she drops creamy Danish butter into the small china jar, breaks an egg into the butter, hesitates over thyme, a drop of tabasco, a sprinkle of cheese; or salt, white pepper, a dusting of paprika. She decides on a plain egg, but at the last moment fishes the jar out of the boiling water, unscrews the stainless cover and adds a twist of black pepper to the orange-yellow yolk. One part of her quietly enjoys the breakfast ritual, the silence, the other part of her works furiously at the poem she intends to write.

I can see Patricia now sitting there prim as prim, looking like she mother and planning something. The next thing you know she pick up the phone. She tell me it have twenty-three E. Thomas in the phone book, one E.J. Thomas, one Edwin Thomas, one Ethelridge Thomas, one Edgar, one Eulah. She figure it have to be one of the E. Thomases, but Ethelridge sound like a West Indian name so she try there first. Well, is an English man answer, she ask for Enid anyhow, but she knew was a waste of time. In she mind, Enid single. I have to tell you she ain't think twice about any of this. She have a writing plan, nothing else matter. I know how this shaping up it sound bad for my girl. You have to remember what they teach she there. Is a big country is Canada, is advanced; people there think theory matter more than human being. She learn a writer have a right to write anything, do anything for the writing. Never matter who life it bruise, who life rough up. Is freedom of speech all the way. If words does kill, she ain't grow enough to know that. Bull in a china shop. I tell you now, is so people delicate. Is easy to mangle them, and words does mangle better than iron. It ain't have no cripple like a soul-cripple, and no one so dangerous. But she ain't think so far yet. Patricia like a child. She want every life she see, every life she dream. She ain't want to live it, no, just to lay it out on paper, like a butterfly on a pin.

"Hello."
"May I speak to Enid Thomas, please?"
"It don't have no Enid Thomas here."
"Is this Eulah Thomas?"
"Yes, whom am I speaking to, please?"
"I represent the Heritage school. It runs on Saturdays at the Multicultural Centre from 9:30 to 3:30 P.M. Its purpose is to put African and Caribbean children in touch with their heritage and themselves."

"Well, we don't have any kids in this house. But it sound like a good idea."

"Please tell your friends; we rely on word of mouth."

She writes down the dialogue for nuance and flavor. Then continues the long trek through the E. Thomases.

"Hello."

"May I speak to Enid Thomas, please?"

"I'm sorry, you must have the wrong number."

"Oh, I'm sorry."

"Goodbye."

The brisk Northern formula speeds things up, but there are no more West Indians, no possible Enid Thomas.

The slender dark-skinned woman with the high cheekbones and great dark eyes is not present in any voice she has heard. Yet she knows she is there somewhere. And a great story with her. It has taken one and a half hours to phone. If she is to get anything done today she must hurry. She calls the various West Indian associations, she calls a few spokepersons, she calls the food bank, the battered women's shelters (who incidentally would give out no information). She calls the Remand Centre, the hospitals, Unemployment Insurance. In all these places she is trying to get in touch with 'her cousin' who came to Calgary and vanished. Sometimes she is surprised and cheered by the helpfulness. But she cannot find Enid Thomas. She has a cup of tea and decides to phone Immigration. Somebody must have a record of a West Indian woman, a recent immigrant to this country. Outside the snow has stopped. Blue, blue sky, white and cold. "Bone-chilling" the radio says. She is so keyed up, so excited by the search, that her hands are trembling as she dials the Department. Somehow the very elusiveness of her dream-woman makes the search more important, the possible story looms fantastic in her mind. It never for one moment occurs to her that Enid Thomas may not exist. That she may be simply the figment of her dream, a name she once heard and last night put to a use of her own. Normally brimming with the psychological imperative, she does not recognize it now.

The Immigration Department is cautious; she is put on hold, then a man comes to the phone. Brennan wants to know where last she saw Miss Thomas. When she tells him Trinidad, he begins to suggest places she might check. They are chatting, getting on quite famously, reviewing various possibilities when she suggests the Multicultural Centre. He tells her they've moved to larger quarters, gives her the new address. She thanks him and is about to ring off when he says, "You will of course let us know if you find her." When she hesitates, he tells her withholding information is a criminal offense. She has not given them her real name. Ethelready Thomas, she had said. Now outraged by the menacing tone, she simply puts down the receiver. "Her own status may be in jeopardy." She notes the weasel words as she writes it down. It is clear she will be able to find a use for it.

If it had stop there, if only. Ain't those the saddest words. And every story have them, even if they ain't said aloud. But no, she had to put on the coat. In spite of all that snow and cold and wind, all what it had for weather, she cover she face with ski mask. Patricia don't ski, but she have ski mask to mind poor Jocelyn business. She put on big high boots and go down to the Multicultural Centre. She say she think perhaps somebody there could tell her something. All this because of a dream. Life is something, yes! Somebody dream and you life mash-up! Patricia tell me it was only eight blocks from her, and she couldn't call a taxi, so she walk. This is the same girl, everybody have to leave whatever they doing to come with the car and carry she wherever she want to go. That was when she in Trinidad, and she wasn't walking no place. Now she leave she warm house to walk eight blocks in ice. The same distance as from here to the river. I remember how I used to see Jocelyn coming there to the ledge, every Thursday with that boy from town . . . Burri. Everybody know he was no good. Woman get under he skin and he jumpy. First one flower, then another, then another. When he get in that accident, the only person surprise was he. Jocelyn mother send she to she aunt in Calgary. Was for a visit; to have the child in secrecy. When she never come back, the poor mother tell everybody she going university. I don't know who believe that! By the time Jocelyn leave here, the child rounding she arms and thing, she hair thick and shining. A pretty-pretty girl . . . They say if you don't trouble trouble, trouble won't trouble you . . . is a long penance that girl pay and paying still and for what? She young, she innocent, she trust where she love.

Sheets of steel blow off the Bow River. Patricia is thrust forward by each gust, and in the end the wind carries her along the icy pavement at a half trot. Today ice frosts the mouth holes of ski masks, forms icicles on beards and moustaches. Normally noisy with the bustle of Adult Vocational Students on the way to class, the streets are lonely. Only the cars sweep by in the blue cold, and the heavy trucks grind past. Many of these who are out, red-faced and smiling, carry a jaunty air. Below the din of the asthmatic traffic, they exchange quick amused glances with her. There is an air of secret triumph, of camaraderie, as if this were an adventure. She smiles absentmindedly at everyone who glances at her, and while part of her mind notes every stance and gesture, she is busy plotting the discovery of Enid Thomas. She expects the Centre will have employment records, volunteer lists, mailing lists. If she can only get a lead, she is certain she will find Thomas. In any case, someone there may have heard of her. It's such a relief to escape the cold that she finds her way through the maze of corridors and security doors, where her back door entry has led her, with ease. Finally, she comes to a hall enlivened with the bright, clear art of children. She passes through a half-opened door to a small reception room furnished with green plastic chairs, mustard walls, with posters of functions both past and future. On the receptionist's desk there is a brave croton. The person at the desk is about fifty, well groomed. With great poise and assurance, Patricia introduces herself as a writer who has lived in the city for many years.

"I have been asked by my aunt, quite old actually, to get in touch with a cousin, Enid Thomas." The lie trips off her tongue, dances in the air. "We know she's in the city, but no one has heard from her for years. Such a pity when families drift apart, don't you think?"

The receptionist agrees. "Family is really important to ethnic people. We have gathering with children every Sunday. First the Mass, then the big dinner."

"Do you really? Where are you from? Are you Latvian?"

The woman is surprised.

"How you know?"

"A friend whose father is Latvian. They farm outside of Beiseker. When I lived in the islands, we did the gatherings. I miss it now. I wonder if I could see your mailing lists? Perhaps my cousin is on them?"

"Today, everything is on computer."

"Is the manager of the Centre in?"

"Oh yes! She got in early."

Half an hour later Patricia sits at a long table in the bare conference room beyond. Through the open door she can hear and see what is obviously the multicultural daycare centre. No doubt because of the storm, there is an unusually wide age range of child painters happily attacking large sheets of brown paper tacked up on the walls of the corridor. She has already gone carefully through the mailing lists. No Enid, no E. Thomas. She has begun to work her way through a varied list of volunteers, paid workers, and possible volunteers.

"We update this list every three years. So any one who has done anything here, even attending a meeting, is on this. We haven't done the deletions yet."

Patricia is half-way through the list, and still certain that she will find Thomas, when she becomes aware that a woman is standing in the doorway of the daycare centre arguing with a furious small girl. The girl is about eight, and is making her feelings clear about staying in a daycare for toddlers. Something about the child's eyes, the diamond slant of her face, trigger a memory. Eight years old and still Pat to all and sundry, she is standing on the verandah of the house at Lopinot, staring horrified at a girl she doesn't know. A girl her own age, who, eyes glazed with admiration, is holding out a gift, two firm, plump mangoes, a spray of hibiscus. A girl, whose face marked with the same awe, the same suppressed excitement she has seen on the faces of the white girls chosen to present flowers to the Governor's wife, she never forgets. She is told the girl's name is Jocelyn, Jocelyn Romero. And Jocelyn's shy smile comes and goes, but she stands there her hands rooted to her sides, making no effort to take the fruit from her. Finally, her mother pushes her forward, she takes the fruit, says a low "thank you." Jocelyn runs back to her mother smiling hugely. Mrs. Romero smiles at her parents on the verandah, and with her daughter continues on their way to the village. But she stands staring after them, tears pouring down her cheeks. She has begun to sob uncontrollably.

That was the first time she meet Jocelyn, far as I know, was the only time they ever talk, if you can call it talk. Jocelyn give her the fruit, and she stand there bawling like somebody do her an injury. Embarrass everybody that child. Is not one cry she cry you know. After the mother take her inside, and she can't stop the child crying. I go in after them. I tell the mother leave her with me. I get a glass of cold water, a wash rag, and a towel. I pick her up off the pillows, and make her stand up. I wash she face and make her drink the glass well slow. And I ain't talk at all. Then I hold she hands by she side, and I make her breathe with me. Slow-slow breathing. Then we wash the face again. I say to her. "Tell me the truth, what take you so?" She look like a misery, but she ain't say nothing. I hold both she soft little hands in my cocoa hands, an I say "So tell me, just tell me how it come." She say Jocelyn just like she. "What you mean? You is a girl, Jocelyn is a girl. All-you-two the same age. How you mean that?" She say it ain't have no difference. She could be Jocelyn, Jocelyn could be she. She look in Jocelyn eye and feel she self Jocelyn. What if she wake up one morning and find she self Jocelyn? She ain't want to be poor. What it have to say to child like that? Everybody know it have rich and poor in the world. She eight years old and she see is accident. Come to think of it, must be that what make her decide God don't play dice! Is a idea she don't want to risk. Anyway, I hold she hard-hard in my arms, rocking she. She say she ain't no "royal personage." Is so she used to talk. Plenty-plenty words. Read too much. I know right then that child go see trouble. The world is a hard place for them what see further than the eye. And for who have to live with them.

And is that same seeing that lead her to Jocelyn. For is Jocelyn self was there standing in the doorway with Ashley. Jocelyn who once, just once, call she self Enid Thomas.

Is when Burri leave she pregnant by the river and go he way. The mother know one time was disgrace. A child with no name for she one daughter. And she proud. She sit down and write the sister in Canada. Just as they getting everything together, the registry office burn down in Arouca.

Well! The government announce how anybody could replace their papers with two sign pictures and two important signatures, in any registry office in the area. They see they chance, Jocelyn and she mother. They seize it.

Is so it start, this Enid Thomas thing, so easy-easy. First they take pictures with she hair crimp and comb up in a big Afro. Then they fool the headmaster to sign is Enid Thomas. You can't expect the man to remember everybody what pass through a district school. Children coming from everywhere. Next, they went quite Port-of-Spain to a real fashionable hairdresser to get it straighten and so. With that they take pictures and get the priest to sign is Jocelyn Romero. Is so she get the two identification, and the two passport to go to Canada. Once she pass in the country, was a easy thing to burn up Enid Thomas. She just go back to being she. The mother say she go to school nights. She bear a real pretty-pretty girlchild, that one, and intelligent for so. With nobody to help she. Is so when you too proud. They ain't even apply for immigration. Just sneak in the people country. Live like a thief. Always frighten-frighten. Prouder than pocket! It don't pay. Then one day Jocelyn look up and see my great-niece.

The two of them just start moving towards each other. They hold out their hands and they move across the room. Like is a magnet. Like they can't stop. They on track and they can't stop. People say thing like that is God's will. If I was God, lightning and thunder! That is slander, yes! Think about it. Something lead to blood and guts in the street, and you saying is God's will. What kind of God is that? Such a God! Too much like people for people to be safe. If He was wanting her to dead, you ain't think He could let her dead in bed. Private like! With some dignity! God! My foot! You ain't think is time priest come up with a reason what better than that?

They are laughing, their hands still clasped together, all of home in their palms, when she feels Jocelyn stiffen, sees her face go rigid. Ashley too is still, her eyes wide. She looks over her shoulders, sees two men hurrying down the long hallway towards them. Perhaps it's their slight swagger. She knows immediately. Immigration! Immigration! Immig . . . Jocelyn grabs Ashley, races down that long hall.

"STOP! STOP! IMMIGRATION! ENID THOMAS! ENID THOMAS! STOP! IMMIGRATION!"

Shouldering Patricia aside, sweeping her against the wall, they run past. Startled, horrified beyond belief, she stands for a moment, and sees Jocelyn, her dark green coat flying out behind her, half dragging Ashley as she tugs at the heavy doors. The child struggles with her red back-pack as she runs.

At the door, Ashley looks back, her small face intent, terrified. Patricia begins to run now, through halls that seem to narrow inexplicably, are dark, towards the brilliant patch of light at the door. She pushes the door open and finds that she is on Sixth Avenue, where cars and trucks come pounding through to the overpass, sweep over the Langevin to Memorial. As she reaches the curb, Patricia sees Jocelyn's scarf on the street, and looks wildly around. Then in the gap left between two trucks, she sees Jocelyn herself on the median. Such a look on her face! Together, their mouths widen into a scream. When the trucks move on she sees the Immigration officers on the opposite sidewalk, their lips shaped in an O, their eyes wide and staring. At first she does not see Ashley. And always afterwards Patricia is to believe she called "Jocelyn come back! This way! Come back!" but she can never be sure what if anything she says before the tableau is complete.

On the far side of the far lane, a brown car has caught the child. She cannot see her head, her face; only the one arm lifted, a red rag of coat, a foot like a doll's in a white stocking. There is blood and mud. Snow clots and burns. Cars, trucks, buses are grinding to abrupt halt. The shrieks of tires, bang, jangle, crash of metal is repeated again and again as cars crash into the backs of cars. It seems to her that Jocelyn falls in slow motion to her knees in the snow; that the wind picks up, sends loose-leaf sheets whirling into the air; that the sky begins to fall in thick white drifts; that the distance between her curb and Jocelyn is all the years between that girl on the verandah, and that woman who dreamt . . .

She stands   stretches   closes the notebook. It is four and a half hours later. She slips back into bed falls into a healing dreamless sleep.

WILSON HARRIS

KANAIMA

Tumatumari is a tiny dying village on a hill on the bank of the Potaro River, overlooking roaring rapids. The bursting stream foams and bunches itself into a series of smooth cascading shells enveloping backs of stone. Standing on the top of the hill one feels the gully and river sliding treacherously and beautifully as though everything was slipping into its own curious violent inner concentration and energy, and one turns away and faces the tiny encampment and village with a sensation of loss—as of something alive and vibrant and wholehearted, whose swift lure and summons one evades once again to return to the shell of this standing death.

A beaten trail that keeps its distance from the dangerous brink of the gorge winds its spirit over the hill, through the village, like the patient skin of a snake, lying on the ground with entrails hanging high as husks of vine, dangling and rotting in the ancient forest.

The village seems to hold its own against the proliferation of the jungle with great difficulty, dying slowly in a valiant effort to live, eternally addressed by the deep voice of the falls, conscious too of a high far witness across the slanting sky— a blue line of mountains upholding a fiction of cloud.

A tiny procession—about a dozen persons in all, mostly women and children— was making its way across the trail. The man who led them, a rather stocky Indian, had stopped. His face bore the mooning fateful look of the Macusi Indians, travelling far from home. They lived mostly in the high Rupununi savannahs stretching to Brazil, a long way off, and the village encampment at Tumatumari was composed of African and Negro pork-knockers, most of whom were absent at this time, digging the interior creeks for diamonds. They had left a couple of old watchmen behind them at Tumatumari but otherwise the village (which they used as a base camp) was empty. The leader of the newcomers reconnoitered the situation, looking around him with brooding eyes, rolling a black globule and charm on his tongue, and exhibiting this every now and then against his teeth under his curling lips with the inward defiance of an experienced hunter who watches always for the curse of men and animals.

The six o'clock parrots flew screeching overhead. The Indians looked at the sun and corrected their mental timepiece. It could not have been later than four. The sky was still glowing bright on the mountain's shoulder. In the bush the hour was growing dark, but here on the snake's trail which coiled around the huts and the shuttered houses the air still swam with the yellow butter of the sun.

One of the old decrepit watchmen left by the Negro pork-knockers was approaching the Macusis. He shambled along, eyeing the strangers in an inhospitable, barren way. "Is no use," he said when he reached them, shaking his head at them with an ominous spirit, "Kanaima been here already." The Indians remained silent and sullen, but in reality they were deeply shaken by the news. They started chattering all of a sudden like the discordant premature parrots that had passed a few moments before overhead. The sound of their matching voices rose and died as swiftly as it had begun. Their stocky leader with the black fluid betel on his tongue addressed the old watchman, summoning all the resources of the pork-knocker's language he was learning to use. "When Kanaima"—he spoke the dreadful name softly, hoping that its conversion into broken English utterance deprived it of calling all harm, and looking around as if the ground and the trees had black ears—"when Kanaima come here?" he asked. "And which way he pass and gone?" His eyes, like charms betokening all guarded fear, watched the watchman before him. They glanced at the sky as if to eclipse the sentence of time and looked to the rim of the conjuring mountains where the approach of sunset burned indifferently, as though it stood on the after-threshold of dawn, rather than against the closing window of night.

"He gone so—that way." The old Negro pointed to the golden mountains of heaven. "He say to tell you"—his voice croaked a little—"he expect you here today and he coming tonight to get you. He know every step of the way you come since you run away from home and is no use you hiding any more now. I believe"—he dropped his voice almost to a whisper—"I believe if you can pass him and shake him off your trail in the forest tonight—you got your only chance."

The Indians had listened attentively and their chattering rose again, full of staccato wounded cries above the muffled voice of the waterfall, dying into helpless silence and submersion at last. "We got take rest," the leader of the party declared heavily and slowly, pronouncing each word with difficulty. He pointed to everyone's condition, indicating that they stood on the very edge of collapse. They had come a long way—days and weeks—across steep ridges and through treacherous valleys. They must stop now even if it was only for four or five hours of recuperative sleep. The burden of flight would be too great if they left immediately and entered the trail in the night.

"Is no use," the old man said. Nevertheless he turned and shambled towards a shattered hut which stood against the wall of the jungle. It was all he was prepared to offer them. The truth was he wanted them to go away from his village. His name was Jordan. Twenty years of pork-knocking—living on next to nothing, expending nearly every drop of heart's blood in the fever and lust of the diamond bush—had reduced him to a scarecrow of ill-omen always seeing doom, and Kanaima, the avenging Amerindian god, who could wear any shape he wished, man or beast, had come to signify—almost without Jordan being aware of it—the speculative fantasy of his own life; the sight of strange Indians invariably disturbed him and reminded him of the uselessness of time like a photograph of ghosts animated to stir memories of injustice and misfortune. He always pictured them as bringing trouble or flying from trouble. They were a conquered race, were they not? Everybody knew that. It was best to hold them at arm's length though it seemed nothing could prevent their scattered factions from trespassing on ground where he alone wanted to be.

The light of afternoon began to lose its last vivid shooting color, the blazing gold became silver, and the resplendent silver was painted over by the haze of dusk. In the east the sky had turned to a deep purple shell, while an intensity of steel appeared in the west, against which—on the topmost ridge of the ghostly mountains—the trees were black smudges of valiant charcoal emphasizing the spectral earth and the reflection of fury. A few unwinking stars stood at almost vanishing point in the changing spirit of heaven.

The Indians witnessed the drama of sunset, as if it were the last they would see, through the long rifts in the roof of the house, and out beyond the open places in the desolate walls. The stupor of their long day enveloped them, the ancient worship of the sun, the mirage of space and the curse of the generations.

Kanaima had been on their heels now for weeks and months. Their home and village, comprising about sixty persons, had been stricken. First, there had been an unexpected drought. Then the game had run away in the forest and across the savannahs. After that, people had started dropping down dead. Kanaima planted his signature clear at last in the fire he lit no one knew when and where; it came suddenly running along the already withered spaces of the savannahs, leaving great black charred circles upon the bitten grass everywhere, and snaking into the village compound where it lifted its writhing self like a spiritual warning in the headman's presence before climbing up the air into space.

They knew then it was no use quarreling with fate. Day after day they had traveled, looking for somewhere to set up a new encampment, their numbers dwindling all the time, and every situation they came to, it was always to find that Kanaima had passed through before them. If it was not nature's indifference—lack of water or poor soil—they stumbled upon barren human looks and evil counsel, the huts they saw were always tumbling down, and the signs upon the walls they visited were as arid and terrible as flame, as their own home had looked when they had left to search for a new place. It was as if the world they saw and knew was dying everywhere, and no one could dream what would take its place.

The time had surely come to stop wherever they were and let whatever had to happen, happen.

It was a hot, stifling night that fell pitch-black upon them. Jordan and the other aged watchman the pork-knockers had left at Tumatumari had nevertheless lit a fire in the village, over which they roasted a bush cow they had shot that morning. It was rare good fortune at a time when the country was yielding little game. The flame blazed steadily, painting a screen on the trees and the shadows of the two men seemed to race hither and thither out of a crowded darkness and back into multitudes still standing on the edge of the forested night. It seemed all of a sudden that another man was there in the open, a sombre reticent spectator. His shadow might have been an illusion of a glaring moment on the earth, or a curious blending of two living shapes into the settlement of a third moving presence.

He was taller than the two blind watchmen over whom he stood. He studied them from behind a fence of flaming stakes, a volcanic hallucinated gateway that might have belonged to some ancient overshadowed primeval garden. It was as if, though he stood near, he was always too far for anyone to see his flowing garb. It appeared as if his feet were buried in a voluminous cloak whose material swept into a black hole in the ground, yet when he moved it was with perfect freedom and without a sign of stumbling entanglement. He occasionally glided over the enfolding majestic snake of his garment that obeyed his footsteps.

All at once sparks flew and his shadow seemed to part the two men in a rain of comets, dispatching one with a great leg of beef to the hut where the Indians were, while with another imperious gesture his muffled hand turned the roasting cow into a comfortable position for the one who remained by the fire to slice a share of the breast for dinner. It was the tenderest part of the meat and the stranger devoured a ghostly portion. A distant breeze stirred the whole forest and the fire lifted a tongue up to heaven as though a nest of crucial stars remaining just above a mass of dark trees had finally blown down on earth's leaves.

All around the fire and under the stars the night had grown blacker than ever. The crowding phantoms of the bush had vanished, turning faceless and impotent and one with Kanaima's cloak of trailing darkness; the strong meat of life over which the lord of death stood had satisfied them and driven them down into the blackest hole at his feet. The aged watchmen too had their fill and seemed unable to rise from their squatting heels, dreaming of a pile of diamonds under the waterfall. The Macusi headman came to the door of the hut and stood looking towards every hidden snake and trail in the jungle. His companions were sound asleep after their unexpected meal. They had picked the bone clean and then tossed it into the uncanny depths of the lost pit outside their window. Even if they had wanted to resume their journey, the headman felt, it was impossible to do so now. The sound of the Tumatumari Falls rose into the air like sympathetic magic and universal pouring rain. But not a drop descended anywhere out of a sky which was on fire, burning with powder and dust choked with silver and gold, a great pork-knocker's blackboard and riddle, infinitely rich with the diamonds of space and infinitely poor with the wandering skeletons of eternity.

The headman let his chin drop slowly upon his breast, half-asleep in awe and with nameless fatigue and misery. It was no use complaining, he said to himself. Tumatumari was the same as every other village through which they had come, uniform as the river's fall and the drought standing all over the forgotten land from which they had fled, insignificant as every buried grave over which they had crossed. All the trails were vanishing into a running hole in the ground and there was nothing more to do than wait for another joint of roasting meat to fall upon them from the stars that smoked over their head.

There was a movement in the hut behind him, the shaking of a hammock, and a woman appeared in the door beside him. He recognized her in the dim light. She was his wife. She said something to him and began descending the steps, rolling a little like a balloon and half-crouching like an animal feeling for sand before it defecates.

The headman suddenly raised an alarm. He realized she had taken the wrong direction, her eyes half-bandaged by sleep. She had misjudged the trail and had blundered towards the waterfall. His voice was hardly out of his throat when her answering shriek pierced him. She had come to the yawning blind gully, had tried to scramble for the foothold she was losing, and had only succeeded in slipping deeper and deeper. The headman continued to shout, running forward at the same time. He perceived the cloud of unknowing darkness where the chasm commenced and far below he felt he saw the white spit of foam illuminated by starshine, blue and treacherous as a devil. The voices of his companions had followed him and were flying around him like a chorus of shrieks, and it seemed their cry also came from below. The two village-watchmen had also been aroused and they were heaving at the low fire, squandering a host of sparks, until they had acquired flaming branches in their hands. They began to approach the gully. The flaring billowing light forked into the momentous presence of their infused companion, the shadow of the god who had attended the feast. He had been crouching at the fire beside them as though he presided over each jealous spark, his being shaped by the curious flux of their own bodies which wove his shape on the ground. Now his waving cloak swirled towards the great pit and it seemed that no one realized he was there until the headman of the Macusis saw him coming at last, a vast figure and extension of the dense frightful trees shaking everywhere and shepherding the watchmen along.

"Kanaima," he screamed. The whole company were startled almost out of their wits, and Jordan—who had met the Indians that afternoon when they arrived in the village—gasped, "I tell you so." He repeated like a rigmarole, "I tell you so."

Then indeed, as if they were proving what they had known all along, they perceived him, his head raised far in the burning sky and his swirling trunk and body sliding over the illuminated cloud above the waterfall. Yet in spite of themselves they were all drawn towards the precipice and the roaring invisible rainfall in the night. The flaring torches in their hands picked out the snaking garment which streamed upon the hideous glitter of the angry river, whose jaws gaped with an evil intent. They were lost in wonder at what they saw. The woman who had fallen hung against the side of the cliff, half-sitting upon a jutting nose of rock, her hands clasping a dark trailing vine that wreathed itself upwards along a ragged descending face in the wall. The torches lit up her blind countenance and her pinpoint terrified eyes were enabled to see grinning massive teeth in the face on the wall. Tremblingly holding the vine—as if it were a lock of beloved hair—she began to climb upon the staircased-teeth, brushing lips of stone that seemed to support her, and yet not knowing whether at any moment she would be devoured by falling into the roaring jaws of death.

The watchers waited and beheld the groping muse of all their humanity: Kanaima alone knew whether she would reach the cliff top.

PRESENCE

I'M OUT NEAR THE POOL holding a handful of ratchet sockets, watching Spike change the plugs and filters on the used LTD he has bought from a welder this morning, when Danny, this guy we don't know too well, comes sauntering out of his apartment carrying a six-pack of bottled beer. We've seen Danny in the pool back when it was warmer, and we know that he laughs a lot and drives an eighteenwheeler. He usually parks it over by the fence and it takes up a lot of space, but it's not there today. I've bummed a smoke from him once or twice and he's bummed one from me.

He is already drinking one of the beers, and he offers one to Spike and me. He sets the six-pack on the pavement by the right front tire and sort of rotates his shoulders, like his back hurts. But he's smiling as always, his blond eyebrows kind of naturally arched with amusement.

"I'm going to Myrtle Beach at four in the morning," he says.

"Business or pleasure?" I ask.

"Work. Coming right back tomorrow night. But I hate to think there won't be some fun."

I touch Spike's arm with a cold bottle and he tells me to set it down until he's finished. So I put the ratchet sockets in my pocket and start drinking the beer myself.

"Where's your truck?" I ask Danny.

"I ain't driving," he says. "They took my license away some more yesterday. My damn sister. She's thirty-eight years old with two teenage boys and still living at home. My folks went to Oklahoma for a visit so I called the house for three hours yesterday to check on her, and the line was busy the whole time. So I put in an emergency call, and the operator said my sister was hanging up but she never did.

It's because of her that I left home. We've gotten her jobs, I don't know how many, and she's quit or got fired from each one. I set her up with a buddy of mine who's a multimillionaire, got her moved in with him, and she even messed that up.

"So I went over there and she wouldn't open the doors. She could see it was me, and I could see her walking around checking the windows, all the while with the phone to her ear. I said, 'This is my daddy's house. This ain't your house. You can't lock me out.' Two days before that I went over there and she was remodeling the kitchen, soon as they had left. There she was painting the wallpaper, making the kitchen like she wanted it to be. I didn't want to call out to Oklahoma, 'cause my daddy's got a bad heart—he's had one heart attack already. Everybody knows my sister is trying to kill him. He's been supporting her and her boys forever and she won't do nothing to help. I went around to the bathroom—this was yesterday again—where the phone won't reach and climbed in the window. She yelled at me, asking what I thought I was doing, and I said I was taking out the phone.

"I went down to the basement where the main line is and she came up behind me and hit me on the head and neck with a metal pipe. I popped her on the forehead like this. Pop, you know, and that got her off me, knocking her back some. I didn't hit her hard like you hit a man, but she said she was gonna call the police. I'm thinking, This is my daddy's house. So I said, 'Call the police. That's right. Just call the police.'

"They pulled up out front in two cars and I went out there and invited them in. I wasn't scared, but you know what presence they have with all that heavy leather and metal and wood hanging on them. I don't know why she called them, and I told them that. 'This is just a family thing,' I said. 'I don't know why she called you. This ain't even her house.'

"'What is your name, sir?' one of them said.

"'My name is the same as my daddy's,' I said. 'This is my daddy's house.'

"'Do you mind stepping into another room while we talk to the lady?' he said.

"So I did. Then she told them I was drunk and didn't have a license. My license was revoked last year and I was doing all right with only a month to go. I know she told them that, 'cause I read her lips through the French doors; I know she did. Hell, I was standing there with a beer in my hand, the same beer I climbed through the window with and the same I had when I met the cops outside. I wasn't no way drunk. The police motioned for me to come back in and said to me, 'Do you have somewhere you can go sleep tonight?' I mean they saw I was drinking. I wasn't going nowhere, you know what I'm saying? They'd get me for DWI as soon as I cranked up.

"I told them I didn't have no place to go. She told them I did; I told them I didn't. So they left. I waited about fifteen or twenty minutes while my sister was locked in the bedroom and as soon as I got to the top of the hill there they were, the same police. She's gonna pay for that. She likes to dye her hair, so I'm gonna get some of that Neet hair remover and put it in her hair dye. Or maybe I'll get some peroxide and turn her hair as white as the witch's hair ought to be, but that might get in her eyes and mess her up, so I'll get some Neet. So long as she knows it's me that did it.

"The one police who'd been doing all the talking took me downtown and on the way I cried like a baby. I didn't want to go to jail. That's why I'm standing here right now. I'm standing here, right? By the time we got to the station I had told that policeman my whole life's story 'cause I'm trying to make him cry, too. But I'll fix her good. I hate to think that I won't. Myrtle Beach is a long way and I'm glad not to drive, you know? So I'll have my pleasure, that's for sure."

Danny takes a swig of his beer and looks at me like it's time for me to speak, but I don't know what to say. Spike is still under the hood, and I'm wondering about that sister, like what is her name and how to warn her about Danny. Then I decide to let it drop. I hold out my Newports and Danny takes one. The whole thing is none of my business.

Danny walks around the car sliding his hand over the surface, which is candy-apple red with flecks of gold. Spike pulls up from under the hood and gets himself a beer out of the carton.

"Thanks," he says to Danny.

"Start it," Danny says, nodding to the car. "Let's go get some more. Let's see how this beauty sounds. I got most of the day."

KELVIN CHRISTOPHER JAMES

CIRCLE OF SHADE

WITH THE FIRST CROWING of the old rooster that slept high in the thorny lime tree in his backyard, Striker! opened his eyes. Through the bare window space of his mud-and-wattle *ajoupa,* the fullmoon beamed its pale yellow gaze on him. He glared at it, sucking down his lips ugly, and abruptly rolled off the coconut-fibre mattress that slept him naked from the hard earth floor. As he stood up, he hawked and spat a mouthful through the window, high at the foredawn sky. A soft breeze came seeking past his face and left the single space of the room, still bearing all its comfort. "Don't need no moon eye fix on me," Striker! mumbled and, needing to piss, started through the door space for the snakepit.

Last new moon, as he set out on business deep in the night, the brightness at the doorway had stopped him for notice. Although the moon was blade skinny, starlight was so strong, shadows were forming their own colours. Taking it in, all of a sudden Striker! had noticed a glitter shifting just past the clearing of the yard; a sheen sliding along around the bole of the old red zaboca tree; a gleaming darkness that slipped through the underbrush with barely a rustle.

Striker!, smooth and silent over the yard's clean-swept dirt, had quicked over to see the snake gradually disappearing into a hole under the buttress roots of the old tree: a big macawoeul, fat around as Striker!'s lithe waist, and two, three times long as him. Judging from its sluggishness and the bulge of its belly, it had just fed, and was returning to its nest to digest the meal.

The two weeks since that morning, that's where Striker! pissed: right down the snakepit every morning, noon, and night. In the long run, when the snake came out hungry again, it would've grown to accept his scent and to take it as a natural part of its nest, allowing Striker! to tame it easily. In his business, a big old snake was always useful.

He targeted a strong stream and, thinking of business, pictured the land-grabbing woman he had woken up to deal with this morning: one of a settle of families who—despite his undermining efforts—had remained squatting in Striker!'s forests. This one a woman in her prime with two boy children, she had shiny, dark-chocolate skin, short-tempered eyes, a ready, rude mouth, and a long, bold stride. He conjured up her slim-thick legs, her pouting rump swaying defiant. He saw himself with her—on her—holding her wrists to the ground, pegging her, spreading those hostile thighs, licking the angry sweat off her breasts, absorbing all her struggle until there was just submission in her eyes. Then he'd tongue the salt of surrender from her belly, tasting her, teasing her, taunting her will.

Caught in his dream, flushed and panting, Striker! squeezed and tugged the thick shaft of his swelling cock. But when he imagined her hot chocolate face again, the disgusted grimace he pictured there abruptly curdled his passion. And his skin crinkled to the chill in the air, as instead he recalled the one real time he had gone by her board-and-concrete house to try courting.

It was a cool, sunshiny afternoon end of rainy season. Bursting cedar flowers were filling the breezes with winged seeds and woodscent. Broad-leaf tania had flourished like tall grass all under the forest, and the hordes of wild pigs rooting tubers were easy to kill—they so dotish on the plenty. From the best hung in his *'joupa,* he had taken along a boucaneered haunch for the woman's kitchen. He had crossed the narrow gravelled cart road to their wicket gate, leaned over, and put the meat just inside their low bamboo fence. Then he called the house and waited.

He could hear them, feel them, scrutinizing him through their front jalousies. But only the dog came around: hostile, growling suspicion at his meat, sniffing at it with not even a try at a nibble, and glaring red eyes at him. Then Striker! sighted her younger son sidling along in the shadow of the house. Screwed-up-faced, he carried a piss-pot of whatever. Quick and scrawny, the ten-year-old had scuttled up and made his awkward toss, nearly splashing himself, most of the mess plopping on the meat, while Striker! easily jumped well out of range.

Half holding to hope, half holding back temper, Striker! had eyed his stunk-up meat and said to the boy, "Sonnyboy, tell yuh mother, I jus' want friendship. Is all. The boucan was a kitchen present." He couldn't stop his voice rising. "Is too much pride to foul good food so. All you shouldn't do ting so."

"I doh' carry message for no ol', ugly bushman!" the boy retorted, and scampered back to a side door.

Then she set the dog at him; it rushing threats and snarls but well keeping its place behind the bamboo fence. Striker! had given up. Not because of the stupid dog—he could always silence dogs—it was rejection had beaten him down, had dampened his anger like water dousing fired coal.

With half a year though, that same rejection had brewed him a bitter, smouldering resentment at her. While six times the night's pale eye went from golden goad to glittering blade, Striker! watched her house and brooded on why she threw shit at him; on why she felt too high-blood proud and pretty for him. She would've made a fine female friend, but now he'd have to rid himself of her and her boy soldiers altogether. For as she chose to be, he had no need for such a formidable woman. And finally, he had hit on the manner of his revenge: his early job today.

Striker! went back in the *ajoupa* and pulled his hunting pants up over his nakedness and tied its leather belt tight. The coarse dirt-brown canvas fitted like a loose skin, supporting the weight of his balls, protecting his skinny legs right down to his ankles, shielding him. Wearing the hard cloth, he felt boarhog to the densest bush.

Next, from his special corner, and using his left hand, he concentrated on gathering materials he needed into a snakeskin draw-pouch. Same left-handed, Striker! put the pouch into a left-side pocket. Lastly, he hitched the knife sheath to his belt and slid his big blade into it. Then he left the 'joupa for his home of forest.

In the foredawn darkness under the canopy, Striker! strode along swiftly and silent, his great callused feet familiar and confident of step. He was in his own place, where he was born free. Every crick and cranny, every pale green peeping bud, every rotten root and balding knoll, every grassy flat in the woods this side the mountain was his yard, his safeplace. He had come up here, nurtured to natural growing rhythms. Same was his father: born of girl stolen by a bushman grandfather run'way from the yoke fresh off the hellboat. They'd all grown up in these safe forests, all bred in remembered ways, all raised by free men honouring ancient gods of the ancestors and remaining ever untamed.

And now concrete house and engines were invading this sacred place; and among them was his high-assed, hot chocolate woman who felt she could spit on him.

Thinking bitterness, and with special needs in mind, Striker! headed for another squatter's claim a half mile past the sidetrack to the woman's place. This family—man, woman, four big boys, and a ripe young girl—had greedily boundaried off whole four acres. They worked the plot like oxen, making a garden of short crops like tomatoes, bodie beans, table greens, and such. Once a week, a noisy, smoking jitney groaned up the gravel road to pick up produce they sold in town. Every Saturday evening, the band of them returned grinning over the money they'd reaped out of Striker!'s birthright. Second on his list, he intended a harsh justice for them. For now, though, he only needed a sacrifice.

At night a guard dog prowled their yard, but time ago Striker! had made friends with it. Now he softly called the brute to him, and petted it some before giving it a bit of meat from his pocket. The dog gulped down the tidbit and came slobbering for more. Striker! cuffed it away roughly, stood up from his crouch, and started for the backyard trees where the fowls slept.

Easily, quietly, Striker! climbed up the tree towards the white cockerel. When it was in reach, with practiced moves he stifled the bird's head with one hand and twisted sharply, gathering its shuddering body close under his arm to smother the efforts of its flapping wings.

Quickly to the ground, Striker! at once ripped the young cock's head off, tossed it away, and drank deeply of the pulsing blood. It splashed warmly on his face and whiskers, his chest, where he absently rubbed it in, matting his hair into sticky clumps. When he had to pause, gulping to breathe, he felt the power from the libation rush through him and fill his head almost to a swoon. Striker! closed his eyes and thought prayers of homage to his ancient forest gods. With the grin of a hungry dog, he invoked ferocious Kutua Kalivudun, and frightful Culisha, and Tagwadome Fafume, the malicious forest wraith. From the cockerel's ragged neck, he relished the fresh, gushing blood for them, gorging their terrible appetites, and in exchange, he begged that the might of their fierce magic'd be on his side.

But already the blood was clotting sluggish on his palate. So he pulled the neck-skin and feathers down and, using his teeth, tore open the bird's chest. The thick, fresh-warm aroma of the entrails filled his nose and his head, and made his mouth water. He swallowed ready, viscous spit and probed a careful finger around in the opened body until he located the gallbladder. He cut that out with the left little fingernail, and that done, gave in to gouging out the pink, bubbly lungs and stuffing his mouth with the sweet raw meat.

In response to the gorging, his bulging bowels suddenly rolled loosely, demanding immediate relief. He squatted down there under the fowls' roosting tree and shat, chuckling at the confusion he imagined the later-found turds would cause the landgrabbers. For, with their trust in their fence, and their watchdog, and their skittish, noisy fowl, they'd never stop thinking wild creatures. Wondering what monster of a hunting animal had made such a lump of shit. And that'd be only their lighter frightener. For what if they did think about the dread bushman?

Done, he wiped his asshole with the feathery pelt and, on the way back to his forest's tracks, tossed the cockerel's carcass to the slavering watchdog, smiling again at the trouble it'd pay for its choice early-morning snack.

Just as he had planned, Striker! got to the woman's place as day was cleaning. Opposite in the gloom of the forest, he squatted and waited for her house to come to life. After a while, as usual, the older boy emerged from the kitchen door, and went up the backyard to the latrine. In due time, the little wiry one followed suit. Patiently, Striker! waited until wisps of blue smoke told him the morning wood-fire was lit, and the boys would begin their daily routine—the big one making breakfast, the other sweeping the yard. Then Striker! got up, ready to be contrary.

He jogged lightly across the gravelled road, approached their low bamboo fence with a burst of speed, and leapt cleanly over it—only to land challenged as their growling watchdog appeared from nowhere, and with a furious snarl launched itself at him. Quickly bracing himself, and swinging powerfully from his shoulder, Striker! punched the flying dog in the nose. With a brief howl, it fell heavily against the fence, and lay shuddering.

Striker! looked up from the brained dog to find the smaller boy, straw broom in hand, lip hanging slackly, staring in horror. Striker! bared his teeth and grunted at him. The boy shot off towards the back of the house screaming, "Mammy!

Mammy! The bushman, the bushman! The dreadman coming. And he just kill Princess!"

Striker! grinned. "Damn right," he muttered, starting for the back of the house, "the dreadman is coming! And he coming set powerful to move out all a' you!" In his left pocket, his hand began dipping into the pouch to gather some special stuff he'd brought.

A window banged open side of the house, and the woman was screaming at him, "Mister man, what you doing in my yard?"

Striker! looked at her without answering. This close, she was even prettier; even though she was roused for war, and still rising. Her eyes were wide in her face—hard black marbles staring from white heat. Forming through her flush, sweat beaded rapidly and rolled over her cheeks and temples.

She screamed again, "Ah talking to you, mister man. What you doing in my yard? What right you have? Why you here stinking down my morning, frightening my children, and making my place ugly? Why the hell you deviling my yard?"

This was what particularly irritated Striker! about the whole set of them—this claim of the land they kept repeating. Where did she—they—get this right from? He said angrily, "Y'all think put up fence is all to do, and you inherit land, eh? Own it just so, eh?"

"I do what everybody else do, and for that matter, I do much less than most. So don't pick on me! You better leave me alone and go nasty someplace else."

"Is not me that have anywhere to go, madam," said Striker! slowly, "and is not only y'own hot mouth and y'own high pride that goin' t'have you goin'."

"Going? Who saying I going? Look here! Don't you threaten me, mister. Don't you mistake me. I ent no putty woman for you or anybody to shape up as they feel like. You don't frighten me at all. I's mih father one chile. Dead and gone, he jumbie still mih Tauvudun, and for man like you I have all strength. So you measure close the steps you take with me, mister. . . ."

The bigger boy interrupted, "Mum. Is true dat he kill Princess!"

The woman's marble stare blinked swiftly, and cleared to a dangerous cast. "What's that you saying, chile?" she asked.

The boy replied, "Princess dead. She neck break or something. She laying down by the gate, bleeding from the mouth, but she dead, or soon so."

The woman turned to Striker!, eyes glittering. She screamed at him terribly, "God blast your tricks! You evil fool. I warn you not to try to walk on me." She slammed the window shut and disappeared.

Satisfied, Striker! grunted: She seemed convinced he was serious. She'd soon realize her only way out now was his way. And to make the point, he started for the back where her yardfowl roosted in an old cocoa tree. This morning when they flew down hungry, they'd be gobbling up handfuls of poisoned corn he planned to toss from a pocket. The next matter'd be his knife to the yard animals. And, all or nothing, then it'd be the soldier boys.

Under the cocoa tree, Striker! looked up at feathered bellies and claws of chickens, guinea fowl, turkeys, ducks, pigeons; at all the snoozing yardfowl fluffed and huddled up against the early morning chill, yet unready to meet day, allowing Striker! time to summon support of his dread gods. The gods he needed to harden his mind to frenzy he could terrorize from, and to harden his hands into talons of stone to hurt and maim.

He stretched out belly down, humbling himself to his demons, grubbing his nose into the dirt and rotting leaves and fowlshit, fresh and stale. The soil's warm, stinky-sweet aroma rose up from the little gully his rooting chin and nose formed. He sucked the earthy breath noisily into his belly, holding the indraught long, bloating up himself, clearing way to his soul for the spirits he sought.

And he could feel them coming in. Low in his throat, he moaned into the ground—the vibrations travelling down his chest and guts to his groin, rousing and thickening his nature. And as his gods' grip took hold, Striker!'s eyes rolled up white and vacant. Then, serpent-supple, he slowly stood up straight and tall, entranced, unmerciful, a weapon cast.

From the corner of his vision, swift movement: The quick younger son, beginning a wail, was coming at him. From a calabash, the boy flung a cloud of powder that hit Striker! square in the face. That made him gasp for air, further smothering himself as the dry, stinging stuff crammed his lungs and forced his chokes and wheezing.

Overhead, alarmed by his hoarse, unstifling coughs, the startled fowl began clucking and squawking: a cackling and fluttering that faded gradually, and most strangely eased his breathing to a hollow-shell sound more and more muffled and distant, lazy, heavy-moving, as if his raging storm of discomfort were suddenly being squelched in a lake of molasses.

Striker! closed his bulging eyes to the confusing world changing about him—only to confront a multitude of weird shapes and commingling colours shifting through the black window of his mind. Without pattern, they stood or rolled and fused or weaved and thinned or danced and made him think of how the round green grassy once frolicked with the black ice smiles of sunny . . . shine . . . shine . . .

He shivered helplessly in the brilliance. The sky's bright grin was falling down, scattering about him in great cold chunks. From all around, the woman's voice came booming and scratching into him, words like needles piercing every hair root, screaming: "Hear now, bully man, I warn you fair to leave me be, and pass me by. But morning come or no, you choose to bind yourself to midnight. Well, dreadman, now I command you just so. Stay fast with your choice!"

A stifling darkness overcame his mind. Her sayings—massive, clammy—covered him like rain clouds, exploded heavy in his head like thunderbolts. Then, subject to their demanding sentence, his will dense, weighed down, Striker! at once commenced pacing round and round the shade under the cocoa tree.

Dully stepping. Steadfast stepping. Stepping a careful circle. Staying in the shade. Stepping where he dared not desert. Panicked yardfowl fluttered from their roost, colliding with Striker! in descent. Still he trod true at his circle. Wings and claws flapped and scratched his chest and shoulders. He only continued slapping his broad feet in their constant rut. One guinea hen's foot caught in his braids, clamouring with beating wings until it tore away a lock of hair and was free. Yet Striker! remained unriven from his wheeling way. Off and on, loads of steaming fowlshit splattered down on him. No matter. Striker! kept steadily stepping. Stolid, stupid, step after step . . .

The world went around with a hollow rushing, like dry leaves pushed along on a big *whooosshh* of wind. Yoked to the slapping-feet rhythm of his trek, his mind caught wispy dreams about his squatter-woman driver. He saw her standing arms akimbo in a sunny field, dressed in men's trousers and banded for war with white cloths about her head and belly. She straddled the ground, fiercely guarding it as if it'd dropped from her womb, as if she'd bloody the black dirt defending it, be ruthless for it. . . .

He saw her strolling in a garden with her shaman—a cottonheaded man, short to her knees, who pranced about her like a playful child, now this side, now that. The ancient carried a square leather box under his arm, and every now and again he'd peek into it and grin huge, toothless glee at the joke he saw inside.

Striker!'s soul squirmed with yearning to know the contents of the box: what powers, potions, secrets? And by enormous striving, he finally got a glimpse: In the box was a cage that held a tiny garden, and under a low tree with swollen leaves dripping milk, a dark, hairy man was chained up like a slave. Big white drops bathed his brow, but he could not drink; his lips were pinned together with great curved spines.

Yet the desperate man, his head strained back and tears of pain a stream into his ears, was slowly forcing his mouth open against the cruel spines, gradually ripping apart his purpled, punctured lips, so he could suck his own blood and slake his horrid thirst. Then Striker! realized the poor, tortured slave was he. . . .

Long and deliberate as an old tree grows, vague time passed. Weary, despairing of the endlessness, compelled to trudge the shade of the roosting tree yet again, he went snivelling around . . .

Beyond his stepping feet, the world was haze: a shimmering glare where things—animals? *vudun*? people?—moved about at odd angles and brightnesses. A nibble of fear, once cowering in his belly, had long grown into a consuming *corbeau* scavenging his mind peck after peck. . . .

Over and over, one main concern beat on him: She had him altogether now! He couldn't get away. This idea pelted down on him like rain. Only *it* was plain. He could not escape, although he was hardly there to them. . . .

The land-grabbing woman, her children, her fowls, her animals in the yard, all went about their business in the daze, treating him like a tree stump. They moved around him as though he were another lump of dirt in their yard. He felt empty of presence to them, the way his open *ajoupa* in its forest clearing was without him. . . .

Off and on, an enormous melancholy would rise up and choke him, and, without relief, Striker! would weep. . . .

Later still, blind in his swoon, unknowing whether he was whispering, or thinking, or heard, or not, Striker! cried out, "Oh, please, miss lady, let me go!" Through the mess of snot and tears, he begged, "Please, lady, lemme go."

More time later, Striker!'s world began slowly righting, and making sense in simple ways. Pain was close on him like sweat. All over—tired back and neck and straining shoulders—scrapes and scratches stung wickedly. But the distress made sense. . . .

He breathed the sweet, very cool air over his rasped throat, starting and flinching as it scraped down to his hot lungs. Still, it soothed. . . .

His eyes were sore, his jaws hurt. With every step, he now smelled the stale shit slicking in his pants. He tried to talk, only managing a hoarse groan. But it wasn't so bad. . . .

Eventually, looking about blearily, Striker! focused on the spry boy scrutinizing him and, cringing fearfully, began a violent trembling.

"Mammy, the bushman waking up!" the boy boomed, each word erupting pain volcanoes in Striker!'s fragile mind. He could only cradle sweaty hands around his tormented head and trudge along drooling like a feebled bull.

The woman came out, dressed in men's trousers, her hair bound up, her head banded in white. She approached and commanded, "Stand steady, you!"

Striker! stood. His eyes fell to his foul, crusty toes.

"So! You still want to war with me, mister man?" she asked.

Every part of every word hammered echoing hurt into Striker!'s head. Afraid to speak answer and make more noise, he tried to shake his head in silent surrender, but at that, the world shimmered unsteady again. He felt himself close to being down and crawling before her, and grasped at the air for balance. And, dreading a fall to that final lowness, he just stood swaying, cowed, and quiet.

The woman said, "So, you is a cockroach now? You can't even mumble? And you want me let you walk and go, eh? And you want to go 'way and come back no more? And you want to leave me and mine in peace? Eh, bushman? Is that all what you want now? Eh? Nothing else?"

Striker!, drudged by the hot, jumping pains in his head and the punishing whip in her tone, couldn't answer. Instead, he began weeping again. After a bit, clearing his throat, he managed to whisper, "Just lemme go, miss lady. Please. No more."

"Listen to him, sons," the woman said, "look at him good. This is what man could be. No more! he says. Pleading now, he is. Remember him so! And you, mister man, don't you ever cross my pathways no more, y'hear!"

Then, from a bowl in her hand, she sprinkled some liquid on his face. "Now, take all the bad yuh bring, and leave my yard in peace!" she commanded, and turned her back on him.

Then, and only then, Striker! felt free to go.

Anxiously, careful to close the wicket gate behind him, Striker! realized the crimson sun setting meant she had trapped and stolen his spirit for a full day.

What a power she must have! he thought, shuddering as he slunk across the gravelled road and padded back into the forest. Just inside the sheltering fronds, Striker! turned and gazed befuddledly at her place one last time. Then, wearily, woozily, he homed towards his mud-and-wattle den, to huddle and to heal.

CHARLES JOHNSON

ALĒTHIA

GOD WILLING, I'm going to tell you a love story. A skeptical old man, whose great forehead and gray forked beard most favor (when I flatter myself) those of that towering sociologist W. E. B. Du Bois, I am hardly a man to conjure a fabulation so odd in its transfiguration of things, so strange, so terrifying (thus it now seems to me) that it belongs on the pale lips of the poetic genius who wrote *Essentials* and that hallucinatory prosepoem called *Cane*. But even though I'm an old man (I know my faults: failing memory, an infernal Faustian leer), I can still tell a first-rate tale of romance.

The girl always came late to my evening seminar—Kant this semester—sashaying seductively, pulled into the room by rental-library books held close to her chest, clomping in black leather boots around the long table to sit, her brown knees pressed together, left of my lectern. When she first "appeared" to me, I believe I was stalking Kant, thumbs hooked in my vest, by way of a playful verse attributed to Bishop Berkeley:

> *There was a young man who felt God*
> *Must find it exceedingly odd*
>> *When he finds that this tree*
>> *Continues to be*
> *When there's no one about in the Quad.*

> *"Dear sir, your astonishment's odd;*
> *I am always about in the Quad.*
>> *And, therefore, this tree*
>> *Will continue to be*
> *As observed by yours, faithfully, God."*

274

Lecturing, I seldom noticed her, only a dark blur, a whiff of sandalwood, but this winter, after thirty years of teaching, years as outwardly calm as those of a monk or contemplative, devoted to books, my study of Kant led to a nearly forgotten philosopher named Max Scheler, who said—and this shook me deeply— "Contemplation of essence, the fundamental approach to Being peculiar to metaphysical knowledge, demands an attitude of loving devotion," so yes, I did see Wendy Barnes, but with the flash of clear vision, the focus, the gasp of recognition that slaps you, suddenly, when a tree drawing in a child's book (the dome of leaves, I mean) recomposes itself as a face. My mouth wobbled. If I had been standing, I would have staggered. I forgot my lecture; I sent my Kant scholars home.

Legging it back to my office in Padelford Hall, a building as old—so I put it to myself—as a medieval fortress, I could not pull my thoughts together. *Shame,* I thought. *O shameful* to have hot flashes for a student. My room of papers (halffinished books that had collapsed on me in midmanuscript, or changed as I was chasing them), closed 'round me comfortably when I slumped behind my desk, flipping through my gradebook. The girl Wendy, an Equal Opportunity Program student, was failing—no fault of mine—but it saddened me all the same, and now I suppose I must tell you why.

Time being short, I must explain briefly, hoping not to bore you, that a Negro professor is, although reappointed and tenured, a kind of two-reel comedy. Like his students, like Wendy, he looks back to the bleak world of black Chicago (in my case), where his spirit, if you will, fought to free itself—as Hegel's anxious Spirit struggles against matter—from a life that led predictably to either (a) drugs, (b) a Post Office job, (c) Marion Prison, (d) Sunset Cemetery (all black), or (e) the ooga-booga of Christianity. And what of college? There, like a thief come to table, he hungrily grabs crumbs of thought from their genuine context, reading Hume for his reasoning on the self, blinking that author's racial slurs, "feeling his twoness," as Du Bois so beautifully put it in a brilliant stroke of classic Dualism, "an American, a Negro; two souls, two thoughts, two warring ideals in one dark body." Regardless, he puts his shoulder to the wheel, pushing doggedly on as I did: a dreamy, first-generation student in a paint-by-numbers curriculum, fed by books for Negro uplift—the modern equivalent, you might say, of Plutarch's *Lives of the Noble Grecians* (which I swore by). Not exactly biography, these odd books from the Negro press, and with titles like *Lives That Lift*—written by blacks to inspire blacks—but myths about men who tried, in their own small way, to create lives that could be, if disciplined, the basis of universal law. He embraces—and this is the killing part—the lofty balderdash of his balding, crabbed-faced teachers about sober Truth and Science when they, shaken by Wittgenstein, had in fact lost faith and were madly humping their teaching assistants.

So, I mean to say, that Scheler, the night before in my study, pulled me up short. Lately, I live alone in three untidy, low-ceilinged rooms I rent in Evanston near

Northwestern University. I get up at three each morning, read Hebrew, Greek, or Sanskrit at my roll-top desk, but no tabloids or lurid newspapers. Nights, I soak in a hot bath of Epsom salts, never forget my thought exercises—perceptual tricks pulled from Husserl's *Ideen*—and eat my dinners (no meat or eggs) in a nearby diner, slowly because I have an ulcer, bad digestion, and a bathroom cabinet spilling open with pills for migraines, stomach cramps, and potions (Dr. Hobson's Vegetable Prescription, McClean's Tar Wine Compound) for rest. At fifty, I sleep poorly. So it has been for years. Barricaded in by books, bleary with insomnia, I read Scheler's *Philosophical Perspectives*, my medicines beside me on my desk, and it came to me, sadly—I felt sad, at least, as if I'd misunderstood something any salesgirl knew instinctively—that living for knowledge, ignoring love, as I had, was wrong, because love—transcendental love—*was* knowledge. True enough, "love" is on the lips of every sentimental schoolgirl (or boy), and cheapened by maudlin songwriters. A thoughtful man doubts, and rightly so, these vulgar reports.

But Scheler wrote—if I've got this right—that Mind, revealed by Kant to be only a relation in the worldweb, was a special kind of window, a gap in Being, an opening that, if directed toward another, allowed him (or her) to appear—like Plato's form of "The Good"—as both moral and beautiful. The implications, I daresay, were staggering, for Nature, contrary to common sense, needed man to clarify its meaning. (Of course, there was a paradox in this: To say "Man clarifies Nature" is to say, oddly, that "Nature clarifies Nature," because man is a part of Nature, which suggests, stranger still, that man—if self-forgetful—is not an actor or agent at all.) Scheler's happy term *alēthia*, "to call forth from concealedness," advanced the theory that each man, each moment, each blink of the eye, was responsible for obliterating the petty "Old Adam" and conjuring only those visions from perceptual chaos that *let be* goodness, truth, beauty. So what? So this:

How a better scholar would interpret this, I do not know; but to a plodding, tired man like myself, *alēthia* meant the celebration of exactly that ugly, lovely black life (so it was to me) I'd fled so long ago in my childhood, as if seeing beauty in every tissue and every vein of a world lacking discipline and obedience to law were the real goal of metaphysics; as if, for all my hankering after Truth in the Academy, Truth had been hidden all along, waiting for my "look" in the cold-water flats between Cottage Grove Avenue and the Rock Island right-of-way.

I was under the spell of this extravagant idea when Wendy Barnes came barreling into my office, sore as hell, banging the door against my wall, and blew noisily up to my desk. "You know what my adviser, the punk, just pulled on me?" She was chewing gum with her mouth open, punishing the wad as if it might be her adviser.

"There now," I said, professorial. I pushed back my swivel chair. "Tell me about it."

She slammed shut the door with her hip, then threw herself into a chair. Here then was Wendy in a loose white blouse and open-top brassiere, with a floss of black hair, a wide, thick mouth, and a loud, vibrating voice. I judged her to be twenty-five. She had large, uncanny eyes that sometimes looked brown or sepia, sometimes black with no iris like blobs of oil, sometimes hard and gray like metal. And what of her character? She might have been one of three sassy, well-medicated blues singers backing up James Brown down at the Regal. I thought her vulgar. "I've got to get a B to stay in school." She dipped into her purse for a pack of Kools—"Or they kick me out, see?"—then lit a cigarette. Her hands shook, bobbling the flame of her match; then she lifted her head, slanting her eyes at me. "I'll do *any*thing to get that grade."

"Anything?" I asked. "Perhaps an incomplete for—"

"You still don't get it, do you?" She blinked away cigarette smoke curling up her wrist. "Like, I been here goin' on six years now, and if nothing else, I know how this place works. Like, I ain't got nothin' against you, but I ain't *about* to go back to no factory, or day-work. If I don't ace this course—are you listenin'?—I'm gonna have to tell your chairman Dick Dunn and Dean David McCracken that you been houndin' me for trim."

"Me?" I looked up. "Trim?"

"Look"—from my desk she lifted a fountain pen—"I'll give you an ostensive definition." Uncapping it, she slowly slid the pen back into the cap. "See?"

Lord, I thought. *O Lord.*

"Like, it's nothin' personal, though." She was at pains to keep this catastrophe on a friendly basis. Aboveboard. "But if *I* flunk," she said, "you're finished." Then, like a trap door, Wendy's face sprang open in a beautiful smile. She touched my hand. "I *can* be nice, too, you know, once you get to know me."

I didn't believe her. She'd have to be crazy to say this. It was, for a timid Negro professor who never thought of using his position for leverage, an all-hands-to-the-pump panic. My heart started banging away; I could not snap the room into clarity. She was armed with endless tricks and strategies, this black girl, but Wendy was nobody's fool—she used Niggerese playfully, like a toy, to bait, to draw me out. She was a witch, yes. A thug. But she had me, rightly or wrongly, at bay. I drew deeply for air. I asked, fighting to steady my voice, "You'd do this?"

"Yeah," she said. Her nose twitched. "Mrs. Barnes's baby daughter is strictly business tonight." And then: "Say what you're thinkin'."

My voice shattered. "I haven't *done* anything! Nothing! Not to you. Or anyone! Or—"

"So don't be stupid." She was standing now, crushing out her cigarette. Her blouse pulled tightly against her bosom. "My mama only got as far as second grade, but she always said, 'If you gonna be accused of somethin', you might as well *do* it.'" She smiled. Deep in my stomach I felt sick. What I felt, in fact, was trapped. Rage as I might, I felt, strangely, that this disaster was somehow all my own doing. Now she opened the office door. "Can we go someplace and talk? Do you hang out?"

Although I do not "hang out" (I checked my fly to make sure), she pulled me in tow downstairs to her sports car, clicked on her tape deck, then accelerated along the Lake Michigan shoreline, her speedometer right on seventy, damned near blowing off both doors, then tooled down Wacker Drive. She drove on, head back, both wrists crossed on the wheel. My square black hat crushed against the roof, hands gripped between my knees, I listened, helplessly, to Michael Jackson on station WVON, then saw the silver hood nose into Chicago's squalid Fifth Police District. What was this woman thinking? Were we stopping here? In this sewer? Wendy parked beneath the last building on a side street. Lincolns, Fleetwoods, El Dorados were everywhere. Onto the sidewalk braying music spilled from an old building—hundreds of years old—that looked from below like a cinder block. I sucked in wind. "You *live* here?"

She gave a quick hiss of laughter. "Are you afraid?" Her eyes, small as nails, angled up to mine.

"Yeah, I know you, Professor. We're really 'gods fallen into ruin,' right? Ain't that what you said in class? Didn't you read that when you were a lonely, fat little boy? And you wasted all those years, learned twelve foreign languages, two of them dead ones, you dimwit, wanting Great Sacrifices and trials of faith, believing you could contribute to uplifting the Race—what else would a fat boy dream of?— only to learn, too late, that nobody wants your goddamn sacrifices. For all the degrees and books, you're still a dork?" Waving her cigarette, she talked on like this, as if I had been perfectly blind my whole life. "Civil rights is high comedy. The old values are dead. Our money is plastic. Our art is murder. Our philosophy is a cackle, obscene and touching, from the tower. The universe explodes silently nowhere, and you're disturbed, you fossil, by decadent, erotic dreams, lonely, hollowed out, nothing left now but the Book—that boring ream of windy bullshit— you can't finish." Her hair crackled suddenly with electricity. "Or maybe one last spiritless fuck, you passéiste, with a student before you buy the farm. Yeah," she said, opening her door, "I *know* you, Professor."

I was too stunned to speak. If I'd known she was this smart, I'd have given her an A the first week of the term. Wendy pulled me, tripping, holding my head ducked a little, down cement steps into a hallway of broken glass and garbage, then into a long apartment so hazed with the raw, ugly scent of marijuana hashish congolene and the damp smell of old cellars that I could taste as well as smell these violent odors as they coalesced, take hold of them in my hands like tissue. For a moment I was dizzy. Someone was sprawled dead drunk in the doorway. Sound shook the air. The floorboards trembled. Yet what most confounded me were the flashy men in white mink jackets who favored women, the women who looked, in this pale, fulgurating light, like men. Meaning was in masquerade. I felt my head going tighter. Let me linger too long and I would never regain the university. Remembering what she'd said, I felt tired, fat, and old. Damned if I seduced her. Damned if I didn't. Ten, maybe fifteen dancers, like dark chips of paint peeled from the shadows, swept me from my briefcase and Wendy. Someone pressed a pellet into my palm. That scared me plenty. But what moved invisibly in this hazy room, this hollow box of light, this noise-curdled air, was more startling than the seen. Music. It played hob with my blood pressure. It was wild, sensual, clanging and languid by turns, loud and liquid, an intangible force, or—what shall I say?—spirit angling through the air, freed by cackling instruments that lifted me, a fat boy and student still, like a scrap of paper, then dropped me, head over heels, into a dark corner by a man or boy—I could not tell which—snorting white powder off a dollar bill. He had a dragon tattooed on his left arm, long braids like a Rastafarian, and a face only a mother could love. Lapping up the last of the powder, he gave me an underglance. "What you lookin' at, chief?" "Nothing," I said. "You gettin' high?" "No," I said. "You drinkin'?" "No." "You *queer?*" "No!" "Then what the fuck you doin' here?"

What had brought me here? Even I was no longer sure what brought me. I became aware that my palm was empty. *Lord.* My hand had brought the pellet to my lips without telling my brain. *O Lord.* Hours passed. Twice I tried to raise my arm, but could not budge. Neither could I look away. Silently, I watched. Helplessly, I accepted things to smoke, sniff, and swallow—blotter acid Budweiser raw ether Ripple. The room turned and leaned. Slowly, a new prehension took hold of me, echoing like a voice in my ear. That man, the one in the Abo Po, lightly treading the measure, was me. And this one dressed like Walt (or Joe) Frazier was me. If I existed at all, it was in this kaleidoscopic party, this pinwheel of color, the I just a function, a flickerflash creation of this black chaos, the chaos no more, or less, than the *I.* There was an awful beauty in this. Seer and seen were intertwined—if you took the long view—in perpetuity. As it was, and apparently shall ever be, being sang being sang being in a cycle that was endless. I gazed, dizzily, back at the girl. She danced now fast, now slow. I followed her minutely as she moved. And then, perhaps I suffered hypnosis, or yet another hallucination, but my eyelids lowered, relaxing her afterimage into an explosion of energy, a light show in the blink, the pause before the world went black, and I suddenly saw Wendy—not as the girl who shotgunned me with blackmail back at Padelford Hall, who made me jump like a trained seal; who stood outside me as another subject in a contest of wills—but, yes, as pure light, brilliance, fluid like the music, blending in a perfectly balanced world with the players Muslims petty thieves black Jews lumpenproles Daley-machine politicians West Indians loungers Africans the drug peddlers who, when it came to the crunch, were, it was plain, pure light, too, the Whole in drag, and in that evanescent, drugged instant, I did indeed desperately love her.

Hours later, when I came out of this drug coma, the building was full of daylight, quiet, the loud party long past. Things, no longer hazed, had a stylized purity of line. Was there more to come? Was I done? I wondered if I had dreamed the connectedness of Being the night before, or if now, awake, I dreamed distinctions. I didn't know where I was for an instant. My bones felt loose, unlocked in my body. Through misty eyes I saw Wendy in an upholstered chair nearby, her arms around one brown knee, one bare foot on my briefcase, looking at me sadly, then away. I was twisted in covers on the mattress of a low bed, under a bare electric bulb, wearing only long flannel underwear limp from my sweat. Her bedroom was rayed by sunlight, cool as a basement. She sighed, a long stage sigh: "You poor fool." Her voice was flat and tired. "You're still thinking like a fat boy." She pulled off her blouse, her skirt, her other boot, and threw her cigarette still burning into a corner. As she lay down, her cold feet flat against me, I lifted my arm to let her move closer, and at last let my mind sleep.

EDWARD P. JONES

THE FIRST DAY

On an otherwise unremarkable September morning, long before I learned to be ashamed of my mother, she takes my hand and we set off down New Jersey Avenue to begin my very first day of school. I am wearing a checkeredlike blue-and-green cotton dress, and scattered about these colors are bits of yellow and white and brown. My mother has uncharacteristically spent nearly an hour on my hair that morning, plaiting and replaiting so that now my scalp tingles. Whenever I turn my head quickly, my nose fills with the faint smell of Dixie Peach hair grease. The smell is somehow a soothing one now and I will reach for it time and time again before the morning ends. All the plaits, each with a blue barrette near the tip and each twisted into an uncommon sturdiness, will last until I go to bed that night, something that has never happened before. My stomach is full of milk and oatmeal sweetened with brown sugar. Like everything else I have on, my pale green slip and underwear are new, the underwear having come three to a plastic package with a little girl on the front who appears to be dancing. Behind my ears, my mother, to stop my whining, has dabbed the stingiest bit of her gardenia perfume, the last present my father gave her before he disappeared into memory. Because I cannot smell it, I have only her word that the perfume is there. I am also wearing yellow socks trimmed with thin lines of black and white around the tops. My shoes are my greatest joy, black patent-leather miracles, and when one is nicked at the toe later that morning in class, my heart will break.

I am carrying a pencil, a pencil sharpener, and a small ten-cent tablet with a black-and-white speckled cover. My mother does not believe that a girl in kindergarten needs such things, so I am taking them only because of my insistent whining and because they are presents from our neighbors, Mary Keith and Blondelle Harris. Miss Mary and Miss Blondelle are watching my two younger sisters until

281

my mother returns. The women are as precious to me as my mother and sisters. Out playing one day, I have overheard an older child, speaking to another child, call Miss Mary and Miss Blondelle a word that is brand new to me. This is my mother: When I say the word in fun to one of my sisters, my mother slaps me across the mouth and the word is lost for years and years.

All the way down New Jersey Avenue, the sidewalks are teeming with children. In my neighborhood, I have many friends, but I see none of them as my mother and I walk. We cross New York Avenue, we cross Pierce Street, and we cross L and K, and still I see no one who knows my name. At I Street, between New Jersey Avenue and Third Street, we enter Seaton Elementary School, a timeworn, sad-faced building across the street from my mother's church, Mt. Carmel Baptist.

Just inside the front door, women out of the advertisements in *Ebony* are greeting other parents and children. The woman who greets us has pearls thick as jumbo marbles that come down almost to her navel, and she acts as if she had known me all my life, touching my shoulder, cupping her hand under my chin. She is enveloped in a perfume that I only know is not gardenia. When, in answer to her question, my mother tells her that we live at 1227 New Jersey Avenue, the woman first seems to be picturing in her head where we live. Then she shakes her head and says that we are at the wrong school, that we should be at Walker-Jones.

My mother shakes her head vigorously. "I want her to go here," my mother says. "If I'da wanted her someplace else, I'da took her there." The woman continues to act as if she has known me all my life, but she tells my mother that we live beyond the area that Seaton serves. My mother is not convinced and for several more minutes she questions the woman about why I cannot attend Seaton. For as many Sundays as I can remember, perhaps even Sundays when I was in her womb, my mother has pointed across I Street to Seaton as we come and go to Mt. Carmel. "You gonna go there and learn about the whole word." But one of the guardians of that place is saying no, and no again. I am learning this about my mother: The higher up on the scale of respectability a person is—and teachers are rather high up in her eyes—the less she is liable to let them push her around. But finally, I see in her eyes the closing gate, and she takes my hand and we leave the building. On the steps, she stops as people move past us on either side.

"Mama, I can't go to school?"

She says nothing at first, then takes my hand again and we are down the steps quickly and nearing New Jersey Avenue before I can blink. This is my mother: She says, "One monkey don't stop no show."

Walker-Jones is a larger, newer school and I immediately like it because of that. But it is not across the street from my mother's church, her rock, one of her connections to God, and I sense her doubts as she absently rubs her thumb over the back of her hand. We find our way to the crowded auditorium where gray metal chairs are set up in the middle of the room. Along the wall to the left are tables and other chairs. Every chair seems occupied by a child or adult. Somewhere in the room a child is crying, a cry that rises above the buzz-talk of so many people. Strewn about the floor are dozens and dozens of pieces of white paper, and people are walking over them without any thought of picking them up. And seeing this lack of concern, I am all of a sudden afraid.

"Is this where they register for school?" my mother asks a woman at one of the tables.

The woman looks up slowly as if she has heard this question once too often. She nods. She is tiny, almost as small as the girl standing beside her. The woman's hair is set in a mass of curlers and all of those curlers are made of paper money, here a dollar bill, there a five-dollar bill. The girl's hair is arrayed in curls, but some of them are beginning to droop and this makes me happy. On the table beside the woman's pocketbook is a large notebook, worthy of someone in high school, and looking at me looking at the notebook, the girl places her hand possessively on it. In her other hand she holds several pencils with thick crowns of additional erasers.

"These the forms you gotta use?" my mother asks the woman, picking up a few pieces of the paper from the table. "Is this what you have to fill out?"

The woman tells her yes, but that she need fill out only one.

"I see," my mother says, looking about the room. Then: "Would you help me with this form? That is, if you don't mind."

The woman asks my mother what she means.

"This form. Would you mind helpin me fill it out?"

The woman still seems not to understand.

"I can't read it. I don't know how to read or write, and I'm askin you to help me." My mother looks at me, then looks away. I know almost all of her looks, but this one is brand new to me. "Would you help me, then?"

The woman says Why sure, and suddenly she appears happier, so much more satisfied with everything. She finishes the form for her daughter and my mother and I step aside to wait for her. We find two chairs nearby and sit. My mother is now diseased, according to the girl's eyes, and until the moment her mother takes her and the form to the front of the auditorium, the girl never stops looking at my mother. I stare back at her. "Don't stare," my mother says to me. "You know better than that."

Another woman out of the *Ebony* ads takes the woman's child away. Now, the woman says upon returning, let's see what we can do for you two.

My mother answers the questions the woman reads off the form. They start with my last name, and then on to the first and middle names. This is school, I think. This is going to school. My mother slowly enunciates each word of my name. This is my mother: As the questions go on, she takes from her pocketbook document after document, as if they will support my right to attend school, as if she has been saving them up for just this moment. Indeed, she takes out more papers than I have ever seen her do in other places: my birth certificate, my baptismal record, a doctor's letter concerning my bout with chicken pox, rent receipts, records of immunization, a letter about our public assistance payments, even her marriage license—every single paper that has anything even remotely to do with my five-year-old life. Few of the papers are needed here, but it does not matter and my mother continues to pull out the documents with the purposefulness of a magician pulling out a long string of scarves. She has learned that money is the beginning and end of everything in this world, and when the woman finishes, my mother offers her fifty cents, and the woman accepts it without hesitation. My mother and I are just about the last parent and child in the room.

My mother presents the form to a woman sitting in front of the stage, and the woman looks at it and writes something on a white card, which she gives to my mother. Before long, the woman who has taken the girl with the drooping curls appears from behind us, speaks to the sitting woman, and introduces herself to my mother and me. She's to be my teacher, she tells my mother. My mother stares.

We go into the hall, where my mother kneels down to me. Her lips are quivering. "I'll be back to pick you up at twelve o'clock. I don't want you to go nowhere. You just wait right here. And listen to every word she say." I touch her lips and press them together. It is an old, old game between us. She puts my hand down at my side, which is not part of the game. She stands and looks a second at the teacher, then she turns and walks away. I see where she has darned one of her socks the night before. Her shoes make loud sounds in the hall. She passes through the doors and I can still hear the loud sounds of her shoes. And even when the teacher turns me toward the classrooms and I hear what must be the singing and talking of all the children in the world. I can still hear my mother's footsteps above it all.

THE FISHERMAN'S HOUSE

CATHERINE, SCULPTOR, STANDING in the glare of the Ibiza sun, is working on *The Negress.* Catherine, wife of Ernest, considers herself a neo-realist. Neo-realists, she explains in her Southern accent, the deep accent of an educated Southerner, blend reality and fantasy. I am a satirist and literary prankster whose favorite narrators are fictitious narrators with their own idiosyncracies. I am on the terrace of the fisherman's house, la casa del pescador ("la casa del pecador," Catherine calls it; but "pescador" means fisherman, while "pecador," everyone knows, means sinner). I'm in the peacock's chair reading the impressionist Chekov and Feodor Sologub's *The Petty Demon* and more Sologub, "In Bondage," in the bright glare of the same Ibiza sun.

"I'm not a mosquito," the boy says in the story. "I'm a prince." I'm not a mosquito, I should tell you, and I'm not a princess either, though sometimes, like Catherine, I play the witch. I'm not a mosquito, I'm a common woman. Isn't it better to be a common woman and free? ("Common African American woman," Catherine whispers. I insist that my readers know that already.)

"A common drunkard," mumbles Catherine, the cosmopolitan. Brandy, that old corrupter. I'm a common African American woman reading Sologub's "In Bondage." Isn't it better to be a common African American woman and free?

Catherine sees me drunk again and whistles through her teeth, as she drapes braids on her new sculpture, *The Negress.* If there are African American princesses, then it is this Catherine, whistling through her teeth, the deep accent of an educated Afro-Southerner. But isn't it better to be a common African American woman and free? The wind whistles through my necklace made of crocodiles teeth. I'm not a mosquito. I'm not a princess. I'm not a common drunkard.

Catherine, sipping hot tea in the Ibiza sun in her sundress. The long-beaked avocet. ("What's an avocet?" asks Catherine.) Semantic ambiguities.

🐚   🐚   🐚

There are caves on Ibiza and cartographers shops like in the ancient world. Shrimp boats and pindoba trees, or is that Brazil? Aquatic birds. The fool Amanda's drunk again. Draping braids on my sculpture, I whistle through my teeth. Princess, she calls me and herself a common woman? Which one of us could better play the witch in the storybook? (From here one can see the Cathedral-fortress, on an island as white-washed as any Greek. I dream of the Moorish conquest.)

—How can you be drunk and read Bunin? I can't understand Bunin when I'm sober. No, not Bunin, Zamyatin. In Spain, anyhow, girlfriend, you should be reading Cervantes or Goytosolo. How can you be drunk and read Bunin? Go to Moscow and read Bunin.

—This ain't Bunin, it's Sologub.

Amanda in her palazzo pants and hobo bag. Doppelgangers. Madam Zucchini or the Notorious Eleanor.

—You must think you're a European, girlfriend. You're a jiggaboo just like the best of us.

It's a private joke. Let me explain. Once during one of my art exhibitions in a museum in Detroit, we overheard someone say, She must think she a European. She ain't a European, she a jiggaboo just like us. Amanda playfully covered my ears, then she wanted to introduce me as the artist, to make sure they knew I was the artist, to embarrass me, you know. Then she was certain that I'd flee the museum. But when she got upon them she didn't introduce me, but tried to explain my art: "Maybe that's because she study art in Germany." (She said "she study.") And they says, "Yeah, she think she a European. She just a jiggaboo like the best of us, I mean, the rest of us." Her and her wise-gal phrases. How can they think I'm European with jazz playing in this museum? Don't we all like jazz? (Jazz is the logic that advances the narrative.)

🐚   🐚   🐚

Neither one of dem is natives of dis island. Me I'm from de Sea Islands off de coast of Georgia and Catherine she from Atlanta. Catherine she call me Aunt Jane but de other peoples dey calls me Gullah Jane. Me I ain't never been out of Georgia till Catherine she bring me to dis other island, dis Ibiza, which is off de coast of Spain. Catherine, she Catherine Shuger, de famous African American sculptress. Naw, she don't like for me to use de word sculptress. She call herself sculptor. She say dat de womens don't need to have no second-class name, dat de womens should have de same name as de mens. Dat a woman poet ain't no poetess she a poet, same as de poet mens. I ask her what about de sorceress, but she don't answer dat. But when I calls us Negresses, she say Aunt Jane don't say dat word, dat a slavery-time word. It ain't slavery time Aunt Jane, it de modern world and you cosmopolitan now, Aunt Jane.

Catherine, she done rented a fisherman's house on dis island where she work on her scuptures. Amanda, she sometimes be looking over my shoulder when I'm writing in dis notebook. And she be saying, Aunt Jane, dere ain't no action in your story. And Catherine she be saying, Dat's because us ain't peoples of actions, we's peoples of thought.

Amanda she calls us exiles and me I ask exiles from what? Is de natives of Ibiza, is dey exiles? Amanda she say dat you can put anything in a book, de true and de ain't true. Catherine she say dat it be more interesting if I writes about de Sea Islands and not Ibiza. Ernest, who de husband of Catherine, he don't give no advice on dis story, like he de only one of de three of dem dat thinks I got my own mind.

Do you like my new sculpture? ask Catherine.

Yeah.

Tell me de truth.

Dat de truth. De pure truth.

She don't call me no liar cause I'm Aunt Jane, but dat de look. I likes de sculpture, I repeats, but I heard dat Amanda say dat de radical critics dey don't like de new sculpture cause it ain't African American enough for dem and de fact dat she dwells on de island of Ibiza dey don't like dat neither. I like de sculpture, I says again. I don't know what dey means by de radical critics.

Catherine is one of dem little womens, de kind dat can charm anybody. Amanda she one of dem big womens, and when de big womens got de sly eyes dat make dem look twice as sly.

I have run out of writing paper and Aunt Jane says that I may scribble in her notebook. Ibiza has the same healthy climate. The sun is very hot. I've developed the habit of getting up early and working on my sculpture. Ernest? He's working on his popular science articles and Amanda's drinking rum. Aunt Jane looks like she just stepped off a plantation, but perhaps that's why I've brought her here, the incongruity of Ibiza. Negress? I tell her this is the modern world. Her and her blue kerchief. Negress? When Amanda was a child, she was very poor, but now she gambles all her money.

What nonsense! I'm not a gambler. It's not true. Es Verdad, estaba pobre como niña. But that gambling business, that's nonsense. First you fantasize about me being a drunkard and now it's gambling. Readers, Catherine Shuger, though she behaves like a Southern princess is not nobility. She's merely middle-class.

She's a real fantasist, this girl. And when she's not gambling she's drunk. When she comes back from the mainland I always test her to see how drunk she is.

—Draw a straight line.

—I can't. You're the artist.

—Draw a straight line.

—I don't want to.

—You'd better draw a straight line girl.

She's a rascal, a rogue.

—Draw a straight line.

—I can't even draw a straight line when I'm sober.

Negress? What's the word for that? A throwback. Retrogressive sculpture. Anyhow the bitch is working on a new sculpture. Draw a straight line, my ass. You're the artist. I can't even draw a straight line when I'm sober. You're the artist.

—What do you have to say for yourself, Ernest?

—I've told Ernest not to talk to you when you're drunk, girl.

—He can listen to me then.

Ernest, writer of popular science articles (I've read his article about the horse-shoe crab and the one about the African baobab) is playing Chinese Checkers.

As for Catherine, she's a fan of holy legends. She thinks she's a savior. The bitch. Draw a straight line. I can't even draw a straight line when I'm sober. So we listen to flamenco guitar. Flamenco guitar, she says, is the closest to love. I drink. And I grab the flamenco guitar, the closest thing to love.

Catherine she a short-statured woman with green eyes. Dat give her a curious look, a brown-skinned woman with green eyes. She's bought us all masks for carnival and she's got de mask on the breakfast table and she's entertaining herself putting on first one of de masks and den de other one. Amanda's scribbling one of her short stories called "Mr. Poteet" and Ernest he playing a game of Chinese Checkers.

Catherine put on de bird mask and I'm reading de tale of "Mr. Poteet":

MR. POTEET

That Mr. Poteet, she say.

Who Mr. Poteet.

That Mr. Poteet. Me and he call usself going together.

I'm helping my great Aunt serve punch in the reception room. They having this reunion for forty-year graduates of the college. She say forty-year ago she and Mr. Poteet call themself going together and she keep saying he name, Mr. Poteet.

That's when this usedta be a all African American college, that's why you see you all African Americans, she say.

I know.

I'm surprise she say African American, but my great Aunt always keep up with the name change, while I hear other people her generation they still be saying colored.

Somebody come up to the table and us pour them little cup of punch. One of them be looking at Aunt Jane like she know her.

Ain't you. . . .

Honey, I'm. . . . And then Aunt Jane explain to her she ain't no fellow student but the girl used to work in the kitchen or the laundry room. But she ain't no student there.

Woman thank Aunt Jane for the punch, and then she go introduce herself or re-introduce herself to one of the reunion people. And then I see her over there talking to that Mr. Poteet.

Mr. Poteet, she say again. Us usedta go together. Back when this was a all-African American college. Founded by the Poteets.

Mr. Poteet, he the founder of this college?

Naw, not that Mr. Poteet, the slaveholder Poteet. All the African American Poteets they name Poteet on account of slaveholder Poteet.

How can African Americans attend a college founded by a slaveholder? I ask.

He founded it after de war. Weren't no other colleges where de Negro could go to except for dis one. And you talking bout not going to de colleges founded by no slave-holder, dey was all founded by de slaveholder.

That ain't true, Aunt Jane. Lotta them was founded by abolitionist and them Northern Philanthropist.

But dey all made dere money de same way. Lotta dem shipbuilders in de North dey be talking anti-slavery dis and anti-slavery dat while a lot of dey ships was off de coast of Africa and use in de Middle Passage and dey might as well been de trader deyself. Dat is de true story. All de New World countries dey was built on dat slavery. De wealth of de New World dat is slavery wealth. . . . But what you says is de truth. Dat's why Mr. Poteet left dis school he-self, found out dat it were a slave trader dat founded it. And him one of de smartest of de smartest and talking bout him being another Washington Carver and all dat, and den he working in de library and come across dese slave-trading documents and den about de Poteet dat founded de college, and den him come tell me he leaving de college cause he can't go to no slave trader college. . . . But us call us-self going together in dem days.

I wait for her to tell me they love-story, but she don't. Or how maybe he ask her to leave the college with him, but she don't tell that tale.

Mr. Poteet, except he don't use de name Poteet, dey say he live in Africa now and call himself one of dem Africa name.

How come he to come back to the reunion, he ain't graduate? I ask.

I don't know. I never could understand dat Mr. Poteet. I ask him if he going North. He say de North built as much on slavery as de South. It's him told me bout de ship-builders and stuff. He say he going to Africa.

He ask you to come with him?

Yes, he did. Cept in dem days I didn't feel like no African. I didn't feel de African dat he did. Here come Mr. Poteet.

Mr. Poteet come up to de punch table and I pours his little cup of punch. I'm standing there waiting for they reunion. But she just pour him his little cup of punch, but she don't say Mr. Poteet and Mr. Poteet—if he really Mr. Poteet—he don't say Jane.

I think she going to say something bout Mr. Poteet not recognize her, but she don't. She just serve the other reunion peoples they punch. As for me I'm pretty sure he ain't no Mr. Poteet anyhow, or whatever he African name, cause never could understand dat Mr. Poteet or not, I don't think he be coming to no reunion at no slave-trader college. Not somebody dat feel dey African.

Ginseng tea and syncopated jazz. There are two kinds of obscurity in art. That which can be deciphered and that which can't. Catherine tells Amanda of the ladder of Plato, from the material to the spiritual. (Amanda thinks she means platonic love.) And what does Amanda believe. She believes they can exist in the same plane. Not a duality, but a modality, a mode.

Ginseng tea and syncopated jazz.

Catherine works on *The Negress,* a sculpture of beauty and fantasy. She disobeys the rules. It's certain that Amanda, a writer, believes in clarity in art while Catherine an avante-garde sculptor, believes in obscurity. Like this new sculpture, *The Negress,* of Catherine's, for example.

(Aunt Jane wonders whether she's the same Aunt Jane in the story of Mr. Poteet.)

But the purpose of this story is to study aspects of love, not art.

(Art like love's a form of intuition; subjective elements predominate.)

I am a sculptor. My sculptures, like *The Negress,* are vague, imprecise, ideal. I am an iconoclast. My style is at times pseudoautobiographical. *The Negress* is not Aunt Jane. *The Negress* is merely a metaphorical figure, perhaps even satire.

(I am one of those women who try, when possible, to evade the subject of love. I prefer the subject of freedom.)

My Aunt Jane is not the same Aunt Jane in the story of Mr. Poteet. . . .

Ernest looks up from his Chinese Checkers.

—She's drunk again, says Catherine. Draw a straight line.

—I can't even draw a straight line when I'm sober.

—Let her sleep it off. Sleep's the best medicine for intoxication.

—And what's the best medicine for love?

In the Roman garden, Amanda is kissing Ernest. Is she drunk or sober? Is the kiss spontaneous or calculated? It is an asymmetrical kiss like my sculpture. Perhaps hers is calculated spontaneity. Or spontaneous calculation.

It is not the purpose of short stories to resolve conflicts. As for Amanda, she only reconciles love with love. As for Aunt Jane, she enjoys proletarianizing and deboogifying boogified tales such as this one. (Plus, someone said the kiss ain't African. But then what of Africans in the new world? But Ibiza's the old world. And note the Moorish architecture even in the fisherman's house.) This is a small study in the psychology of love, but I do not know whether it is Gullah Jane or Catherine or Amanda or Catherine's husband Ernest who is telling the story.

While Catherine sculpts, Ernest plays Chinese Checkers. While Catherine sculpts, Aunt Jane writes in her notebook rumors of a kiss.

I am drinking aguardiente.

JOHN R. KEENE

TRANSITS

SEVEN WREATHS, green, caparisoned forelocks, garland the upper tier of windows of the Trust Company branch: We are lurching out of Harvard Square. My pen skates towards stability as this bus speeds around its circuit, which also skitters a cappuccino cup about the blue rink of my lap. Beside me, a sketcher. His freckles and beard scattered specks and spun strands of ginger, he wears his darker, oily curls like a delicate, handwoven calotte. His pencil's rapid route draws my gaze until the bus shifts so that he shifts, obscuring his designs. Sneakers nesting atop the wheels of a capsized skateboard, before dislodging to let the woman pass. The bus rests for a second, his hand revs up. Ah, I see, he is capturing in pencil this December scene that enfolds us, when those girls, three, stumble, trip, topple onto me. I wait, but they proffer no excuses to right their momentary losses of poise, just sneers in triplicate as they cluster at the rear of the car. What else to do but roll my eyes at their crude masks of contempt while the sketcher simply sketches on.

The station is humming with commuters. A roguery swells outwards from each car's half-open shutter like the bulb of an inflating balloon. We creep closer, cropping, as through a telescope: hair—ash-gray, cobalt, lime-white, bituminous—cumbers like boulders with peaks upon crowns or climbs the sheer, cleft crags of brows or carves a river's passage across the acrylic valleys of shoulders. Necks hunch or huddle in scarves, wool, satin, silk, synthetic. Hands are sliding in and out of gloves, up and down every manner of pole. On straps, a second's nap. Collarbones shimmy beneath their serge tents of coats, hips tug against their rings of elastic. Feet, in boots, in duckshoes, in galoshes, skip across the linoleum to each car's violent rocking. Closer, until the sounds conjure forms before us: the squeals of infants, their mother's clucks and sighs. Like magpies we hop about then settle in abandoned perches while others forced to stand now strut, cardinaling and crowing. Nestled, we begin picking through our growing store of sights, when suddenly, the train slingshots its head into the station, to the vibraphonic thrumming of Vietnamese.

His usual haunts, visited today on a much later jaunt than usual. First, the straits of the upstairs consignment shop, where he did not browse but paid like a greenhorn for a vest he had set aside. Next the milliner's—and how he had longed to match this word—*millinery*—to something he could smell, touch, feel! A gambler: Only this and a bowler flattered the flourbag of his head, despite the salesgirl's sugary persuasions. Thereupon some strollclip browsing, until a halt before the shoeshop's glass, yet a quick check revealed that his claim slip had absconded and his shoes still sat unsewn, so he struck out on the pavement anew. Over there, the overheated used-book store, where the early-Baldwin cupboard lay bare, which forced him, like any desperate fictionwriting apprentice, to purloin a tattered Dos Passos. Farther on, more delights behind panes, but for his pocket mint of pennies. Further still, beneath the café now crowded with shadows, the market whose produce "sells itself." His loaf, he left! Freighted now with baglets, bags, and sacks of books, he could savor the evening's arrival, and the serene, unhurried ride towards home.

Pauses, as we part with Ashmont. Small puddles intermittently dot the car floor, a lacustrine landscape viewed as would a bird. These faces, with their innumerable, inviting referents, like guidebooks read and studied but incompletely understood. At last, a few words alight, the interplay of languages, my atlas. This one crosses her legs, fillips her purse, feigning an air of incuriosity, but the nervous flicker on the screen of her pupils alerts me that she is observing. This one, her seatmate, his head a black floret of jhericurl, scribbles maniacally on the box between his legs, though this action, like the periodic growls and barks, merits nary a slight turn of our heads. This other one purses his lips in disgust, that one proceeds to her book's denouement, these two declaim with such passion of tongue that the transcript of their conversation scrolls before us. Then, in strolls another, irises, lips afire, who sits, lolls, slackbacked upon my bench. The disinterested one stares, he spins away. I tune my eyes to record. She stares some more, he returns a glare—I am jotting as furiously as I can. Finally he challenges her to a bout of pouts at which neither combatant triumphs, though in the end I award him the win since such eyes on such guys always sway this arbiter!

The thigh, plump and nyloned, assured in its repose, like a newly fitted length of tubing. It rolls, reclines, on its black bed of seat beside me, making sure it has fixed my gaze. Now it freezes, as if captured in an instant print: It awaits the first hint of my reaction. I turn, it does not move. I turn again, yet it fails to budge. I turn once more, then it jumps just an inch to mystify my attentions. Well, of course, I jump an inch too! We both exhale from the severe exertions of this game, then resume our statuary hauteur. O thigh, is it fatigue or fashion that stills you so, or maybe a cheimonic ennui? Are you planning craftily, anticipating warily some imminent, extended exercise? An amble, perhaps, a prolonged peregrination, a run to a far-off station and yet another impatient train? O tantalizing *cuisse,* my tacit accomplice, what adventures, what diversions, are you dreaming of now?

Scenes of triple-deckers and factories, schools and apartment buildings concealed behind the screens of the winterstripped oaks and lighted by an insomniac sun. Features, details flee us, solid colors blend, bleed, run. Our train, in transit. A trio of garrulous schoolgirls switch tracks to enter town with the Quincy crowd when a voice announces, "Andrew next." Faces shift with the subtlety, the dreary gray of the track of tile beneath our feet, turn slowly without acknowledging the rows of others like them, similarly indifferent orbs. A mother and daughter in testifying garb, beside a gauntess in saltcaked brogues. One rider, his hand fanned open in Saigonese elegance, gestures to blurs beyond the plexiglass. A stark shower of sunlight briefly whitens the car's west side, rinsing out our eyes with squints. "Next stop, Andrew." The gaunt woman rises, raises her arms, invoking some unseen god, before shrieking at, then spitting on, a thoroughly engrossed magazine reader. He starts, suspires, his torso quaking with exasperation, while the disbelieving circle of our faces discomposes as we implore the doors to open.

The tranquilizing murmur of the overhead fluorescence, its electric, antinomian hum. Observe, on the facing platform, faces of friends, our forebears, the future! There, a man, his head a cap of hoar, cants lazily about his paces. Aroma of lather, scent of leather, one's head grows airy as if ethered. Against the train's waxing tide, the light-music subsides. How our locomotive sends this vault into convulsions, how we shudder as it sidles up! Some awaken, others break from the second circle of their figure-eights, still others cease their maundering to wander back among us. Quickly a flock assembles, for each car's beck lasts but so long. Briefcases, purses, brownbags, satchels suspend from each hurrying frame, the carefully queued shuffle towards the few free lots, doors bang closed to bar the few stragglers. They recede in shouts, in waves as we scud into the tunnel's darkness. Ensconced, we so efficiently assume our usual routines that the train, now relieved of its brief, supervisory tenure, lumbers almost jealously along.

A hubbub, some young brothers, from the station's other end, eclipsed by the advancing roar. The invisible cape of wind aback the swiftly inrushing train knocks us backwards in a splitsecond swoon. "All aboard," all board, aboard. A fellow rider shakes to what eavesdropping limns as the outline of a probing bass—hiphop? rock? r&b? salsa?—yet its inner shades of harmony elude me. His amber nails traverse the black ridge of buttons that rise up the side of his Walkman, but our interest scatters to other corners. Silence. Stares, with that "what on earth are you writing?" glare. We glide across the bridge atop the mirror of the river, we gawk at the shimmer-ice. Through the window, the white frame of snow and dark filigree of Boston buildings, the background of this tableau an indulgent platinum sky. At Charles. A jug of water cradled between marmoreal fingers that taper into frets of the palest mica. A jerk, before the fingers slide beneath the culverts of corduroy pockets, which leaves us with only a faint memory of the knuckles. "Park Street, Park Street Station." In the tunnel's darkness the outside rumbles past, then other board or deboard to commence or complete their journeys.

A threnody, for those sites of the past that served as ports, way stations, crossroads! A song for those future venues where the paths of travelers cross, convene: here, their contemporary countenance, the airport terminal! Welter of sounds, of voices, acme of disharmony, such hullabaloo, more hooplah than one can truly bear! Tongues warbling, whistling, wheedling; lips shooing, smacking, shushing; an ear-deadening hurdy-gurdy, but not a word yet uttered! Now monologues, dialogues, pantalogues, rantalongs, admonitions, susurations, disquisitions, expositions, prattle, persiflage, impassioned pettifoggery, but never that achieved caesura that each new percussive aria augurs! And to this inimitable din please add the planes' tympan-numbing boom! Besides, the recheecheechereeching of a dot-matrix printer, the ring-ping-puh-ding of the check-in registers, the ding-ding-aring of so many courtesy carts, why not claim it for art! The jingle on the TV sets, the jangling of rings of keys, a dense, defiant jungle of sound: Not enough? Well, more hovers above: papers harripping, speakers waaawwaaaaing, crepe soles seeawkaweeking, and then the underlying gasconade of the airport's nighttime lifeline, its lights, from all sides, in all areas, inaudible, but for the terminal's undying drone.

Thaws, as though a thousand unseen faucets had turned on. Serenades of slush and sloshing, saraband of this stretch of road, still sullen, half-sulking in its parget coat. You ford the river of cinders to navigate its middle like Spring's first intrepid herald, past the crumbling, knee-high pyramids of snow, of snowfleas, in the throes of their final ecstatic dance. I halt, inhaling the new season's aroma, as you tense, the distant rumble of a train visible in your glance. There, under the wintered hawthorn, that tabby, adept avoider of any weather's vicissitudes, darts from beneath an Oldsmobile, pauses, bares her claws, poses, primps in the afternoon pallor. I drop to my haunches to engage her, you grimace. She paws at purls in a puddle formed from the curb's outflow. I waddle, carefully, towards her. "Kitty, sss, come here, Kitty." She creeps to just beyond my reach then freezes, before your "The train is coming, come on!" hauls us away. Kitty sits, supposing that we always scurry off so, without taking our proper leaves, to other more important appointments.

Whorls of swallows, sparrows pursue one with ease. Look, squirrels are running their parcourse of wet benches, garbage cans, low fences, trees! Gulls blaze a white path through this barren arbor, where I am mounting the Commons' main hill. Before me, the Obelisk, insolent in its snowless solitude, peers out upon the greening expanse. A pack of pigeons titter then flap off, regarding this: "Notice: No Loitering." Like the monument, the stone memorializing the nurses of the Armed Services has shed its snowcape, though some of the ground lies still encraped where the men are jabbering in Spanish. Whose guitar strums that redolent tune? Dogs caper in the sunlight further on, beneath the brick red blazon of Beacon Hill. Here you slidewalk, as one often does on ice, following the drabbled trail that empties into Arlington. Lovers pass, gloves entwined or rubbing thighs, berets, ski-hats bowed in thought, sunglasses hide the bright blooms of eyes, torsos tremble in their drapes of down or wool in this Aprilled air, calves sigh, until a caravan of cars rives our vision. Along the wrought-iron fence, stalks have begun to poke up from the snow like rattoons, reeds, though this is the Public Garden. Wendell Phillips orates in cast iron before the colonnade of abjuring elms, the stern tribunal of Four Seasons' facade. Gulls return, in swoops, bearing their song of the sea. And here Thomas Cass, here Kościuzko, here William Ellery Channing! At last, before the draggle of automobiles, solemn elms, this is where today's journey ends! Alas, past the gauntlet of coffee sippers, gazetteers, unaware of this afternoon's drama.

Through a breach in the ice you trundle to the subway's mumbles below, to the grief of the exit of the old year, now underneath a vast mid-January shroud. Another sale, and yet another, beside still other closeouts: How many storefronts have darkened with foreclosures? They are pointing, asking, Can we park here, will we be ticketed? until he shakes his head in ignorance, nods, strides on. Leers. Several "Yo brother, can you spare me a dollar?" to which you mime a fingering of your pockets' dry wells, hardly a satisfying or sufficient gesture, though it garners only grimaces and a yawn. Sunlight crests on car rooves, swirls about the crowns of trees, coronets, as if to say, Hey, I understand. A klaxon. Diners' eyes stray up from the boxes of their dinners, step carefully out onto the barren boulevard. Boylston, Boston. While every other window sings a hymn to Palladio, a few, tourists perhaps, study maps, fold-out guides, beguiled that they will now be able to figure out the grid of streets. A thought gradually begins to follow you, like a shadow, stares from behind each plate of glass: You are hungry. Shifting your backpack on the shelf of your back, you dine on the beauty of the few passersby, by distinguishing the figures beneath the shearlings, peacoats, parkas, this eye-play always affording a private delight. In the offing, another's plodding, he slips, so that all tread more carefully. Now you notice the sky so dark and quiet where the bay lies, how it blues towards the horizon as if to garner your attention, how soon your hunger abates and you hurry on, how *you* remember that *you* at least have a meal waiting at home.

Angle of the sun as it skims the water's surface, kestrel's or sturgeon's coign. Overhead a jet, one lone steel cross, to temper the sky's white insolence. Laughter soars in the space around me, sniffles, barks, March's soughing. Beneath this bridge at midday, a Saturday: In a month how many powerboats will ply these sparkling narrows, which sailor will be the first to raise her mast? Joggers blur, momentary blazes of color, mere flashpoints in the ripening breeze. Where the cars whiz fastest, the asphalt has shed its cloak, alleys no longer impeded by snow. Runners gun by, their faces drawn as the dead, thus you avail yourself of the monotony of the guardrails. On the street three cyclists on a long lean perilous track, the trek continues, other pedestrians putt by, past, bags bow one courier, legs slow another, but she deftly darts among the drying passes. Walls, sidewalks flame with the promise of spring, windows, porches brim with the new season's lights, though at night a touch of winter will sweep through. Behind a van someone empties a bottle, a bladder. Some halt; I stride by, my own guide, nonplussed.

As the afternoon deepens, the kalorama presses inwards like an immense bas-relief, extends endlessly on all sides like a self-perpetuating mural, these effects no mere tricks of optics. But wait, witness what it truly does as you wend your way through: It binds you to its surface like a fresco.

Inhabit a character, the writer. Describe what it was like when our stares first interleaved, how few pleasures ever approximate such moments. Write that we had no need of caressing, kissing, just the bliss that we tap by permitting desire to drain its saps, to flow, as it will, into that space between us. Passion that the others missed, concealed as we had both hoped beneath our outward peace, until you sat down beside me. Sliding the shaft of my arm into the seam of your shoulder, I relaxed, though you feigned not to notice. "Pardon me," I almost voiced as my leg grew a vine about yours; "excuse me," I voicelessly cooed as your fingers drummed a march upon my knee. For a second I forgot that to live one needs to breathe, the bus's lunge proving no reminder. Your uninterest ignited, flared in intensity, erupted in a groan as the next stop, mine, was nearing through the smear of window behind us. I wondered whether I should stay here with you, dismiss my plans, ride on, as I had never done, to this route's unimagined end? Should I? Ought I? Why? Why not? Well, but . . . a burst of air, your hand mounting my thigh, my—stop. You pulled away, I rose. There we were, but it was not, and would not be; I pressed towards the front, you glared, I smiled, you averted your gaze as I whispered goodbye, but my delight burned as I crossed the street, undoused by your shame-draped guise.

He enters, into our cycle of chatter. Some rise in unison, exeunt. Three suitcases of coarse linen sprawl out under the knoll of a knee. For a while a leg lavishes its force, its affections on them, till their owner snatches each up and storms off. Four places away, he crouches beneath a canopy of dreadlocks, looks out upon the whirring solemnity of the tunnel. Index and thumb consult the compass of face, whose eyes' needle charts a map of my expressions. Torso, arms, legs, feet ensheathed in black, so much black that rills like candlewax from the less-black Naugahyde seats, as if he did not desire for all to see him *except* as shadow. I want to say, "I'm writing about you anyways," but we turn suddenly to the glass behind him, to the semistuck door, and no wonder: The blaring box of dancehall trails its owner out, beneath the inspector's supercilious stare. Beyond the curtain of poles, doors, this other brother in uniform flips through a newspaper amused, something soundless to us piping through his headphones. Our caboose's unsteady slither strains his concentration, so that he fixes on the newsprint to focus his thoughts. The windows, like the glass in a projectionist's booth, transpose two images before me: The first, we who idle in this car like holograms, just light and all that your sight filters through, translucent as newts, the second the city that clamors, courses in concreteness beyond. Now, the necklace of lamps adorning Dorchester Avenue, the yellow gloat of Field's Corner Station, before that double tableau to which our eyes return, that replays like a dream in real time.

(CHICAGO CODA)

On the narrow, rickety platform, where we shiver awaiting the trains. In the distance, headlights—how many?—two, like the first glimmers of an idea or crisis. A roundelay, from competing recorders: Remind me, *which* city is this? The chilly air scours our uncovered necks, hands, the virgin felt square of our foreheads. The heated booth quickly fills. Someone jostled out into the slap of the air scurries back, her scarf now a helmet about her head. Hands cup, clap, as if they were loco-focos, trying to strike a palm-sized flame. We quiver, seesaw from the ball of each foot to the other, dance around to deny the frost. One locomotive, but the wrong one, then another. Ours? Not yet. You grow antsy, prance across the planks to the silent, wintry score, the economy of your movements better testimony than anything heard. Then you whisper, "John, it's so cold I want to cry!" and I'd reply, but *my* jawbone has frozen. Finally our express slinks in, embarrassed, empties, is off. Onwards, all, to Evanston!

WILLIAM MELVIN KELLEY

MY NEXT-TO-LAST HIT

CALVIN COOLIDGE JOHNSON WRITES:

My next-to-last hit got very personal in several ways. And everybody in the Business knows he can't let the hit get personal. One messes up, makes mistakes. I find I do better work when I don't care but just do it dispassionately.

I doubt I could have gotten very far in the Business if I had conducted myself in a passionate manner. Generally Reupeons didn't trust Africamericans. Many of them didn't like to have us around at all. Some maintain that *laos neggaos* lack courage and loyalty, that we talk too much. I broke many barriers in those years, but I'll confess I think I progressed in the Business because I knew the Daon from childhood days, even before I worked in his father's bakery on White Plains Avenue in the Bronx, New York. The Daon and I grew up on the same block. We played stoopball and stickball and mooshball and hardball and all the other balls together. At eleven or so we even measured boners, but I'll never tell you who had the bigger one or who shot off quicker. Just kid stuff.

Then in 1945, at age fifteen, I'd gone to work for Papa Capeurtao before and after school, learning the baker's trade. In the daytime, I continued at Evander Childs, graduating in June 1948 first in my class, mostly Italian kids then and a few Reupeons and a handful of brown-colored kids including me. Every so often, I'd do a job for Roff, the future Daon, but already a rising young thug, mostly collecting numbers receipts from the brothers in Harlem allied with him, occasionally beating up guys, once sticking an icepick through some man's palm, though I didn't do my first legitimate hit till after I returned to the city from Harvard in 1953 when no other opportunities opened up. And of all my hits, this next-to-last one turned weird and personal from the second Roff Capeurtao (the Daon) came into the bakery, which I had run for him since the death of his father and after that section of the Bronx went from Reupeoamerican to Africamerican.

"Come in back, Cooley." The Daon hadn't even waited for his bodyguards, Laon and Saom, solid like two brass bookends, to check the premises. He rolled by me, an armored vehicle in the best worsted, through the swinging doors, into the oven room. "Wants to bug with my holes . . ." The doors deadened his utterance.

I nodded at Laon, his chief protector. "Which ones?"

"The holes went on strike."

"On strike?" I put down a tray of cookies I'd just brought to the front of the shop. "Next you'll say they formed a union." I'd started to despise unions when I found out how easily we corrupted them.

"Laughing at me?" Laon scowled, his gun hand twitching. He resented my childhood relationship with the Daon. "Huh?"

"I better get in back."

"Yaoh."

I went in the oven room.

". . . wants to bug with my holes heads!" The Daon had removed his overcoat and jacket, stood in naked bulletproof vest and trousers. "Tell me about this Hamilton Dapper."

I had to think a moment. Hamilton Dapper. TV Host. Political pundit. Syndicated columnist. Media Analyst. Professional feminist. Television spokesperson for at least one financial institution. A prepschool old boy and Ivyleaguer. Scion of a wealthy cracker (i.e., WASP) family. Friend of presidents. World traveler. Sometime war correspondent, but only if the war played well to the dinner audience. Theater critic. Book reviewer. Roff the Daon could hardly have missed him as a fellow citizen of his time and place, but except for political fund-raisers they lived in two different orbits. And even at political fund-raisers, Daon Roff Capeurtao and Mediamond Hamilton Dapper sat in two different sections, the Daon in the shadows, Dapper in the spotlight.

"He has a couple of TV shows."

"I want you to dush him." He gave the order like a man switching a channel with a handheld remote control unit. "Give you ten thousand."

My heart made my chest quake. Already I didn't like the feel of this assignment. But I couldn't just say No. "How much in front, Daon?"

"What's wrong, Cooley? Think I'll screw you?"

At moments like these in the Business, a man could speak honestly but always respectfully. "You might."

"Smart *neggao,* son of a saint!" His face cracked into a smile. "How's your Mom doing?"

I couldn't tell if he'd just threatened my mother, so I gave a neutral reply. "She's in good health, Roff. *Baola Saleudao.*"

"May she live many more years," he replied in Reupenese, giving me a quick, strange look, all the hardness dropping away in an instant. "Does she still sit on the porch and read? I ever tell you about one day, Pop beat me good with the belt for spilling a basket of bread. Fists too. I ran out the house and down the block. Saw your mom on the porch reading. So I ran up on the porch. Begged her to save me from Pop. Your little mom! So here comes Pop. A belt in one hand and a broom handle in the other. 'Roff, get down here!' I shit my short pants. Musta been maybe eleven. But she stood up to him. 'You don't supposed to beat'im that way, Mr. Cap.' He said, 'Yes, Mrs. Johnson.' Walked me back home." The Daon stopped. He'd told the story often, every time he wanted me to dush somebody for him.

I dared a question. "He ever beat you again?"

"You kidding?" He snorted. "When we got home, he broke my fuggin jaw."

I remembered then the real topic under discussion. "With respect, Roffi, Hamilton Dapper leads a very public life." I had other reservations too.

"What d'you want? Public place or private?"

The Daon really wanted Hamilton Dapper done. Usually the assignment came in a package. Time and place and manner. The Daon had gone deep into Specialization. A rare Capeurtao had attended Harvard Business School and the Daon listened to him. "Private."

"Easy. We got a hole in his office." He sensed my hesitation, my weakness. "What else?"

"But Roffi, what does he have to do with our Business?" I'd stepped over a line. Troops did not question the motives of the Daon. You did not want to question his motive because then you would know it, too. It would become your motive, or it wouldn't. Either way, knowing the Daon's motive made you less efficient. You messed up.

The Daon reached out and tapped my forehead with his forefinger. "He bugs with my holes' heads with his horsehump. You know you start a revolt with the women!"

"Laon told me the holes went on strike." I still couldn't conjure up his motive. "Dapper's into one of them?"

"That Dapper had three holes on his show one morning. Now they call themselves High Rise Hookers, want double their fee, and free cocaine. So dush him for me, Cooley." He clutched my right earlobe with his left hand. "Hear this, Cooley, I make you judge. And if you decide, execute! Dush! If not, I can get somebody else."

The Daon told me an address. I'd report there at two the next afternoon, bringing my own weapon. The Business would get me into Hamilton Dapper. I might do him in his bed. Or in his garage. Or taking a piss in the executive washroom. I might end up as his caddy and finish him on the back nine. One man I sold a poisoned pork sausage to at a street fair, an out-on-loan assignment. Most of the time, they'd slip me into a target as a deliveryboy. Several times, I've delivered

Death in a brown paper bag, especially when the Business wanted to muscle into Entertainment.

At two the next afternoon, I reported for duty. The man there gave me a pair of overalls, on the back of which he'd stenciled SMITH CARPETING CO. I perceived the plan immediately, the maintenance man gambit. I'd used the class structure and racism often to gain access to prohibited places. A few years ago, an Africamerican dressed in clean coveralls and carrying a toolkit could get into any downtown Manhattan building, day or night. Nowadays, it takes more ingenuity to penetrate places.

After I dressed, I checked my weapon, a revolver with a silencer. I fired off a shot to make sure it worked. I hadn't spent much for the revolver, having bought a half-dozen on a recent trip to the South. I'd paid a lot for the silencer which I always took away with me. Actually, I rather dislike the sound of firearms; a silent weapon would provide a breakthrough for our profession. In another age, I'd have used knives exclusively. The revolver I usually left at the scene of the crime, where it could tell the police nothing. Sometimes it might even lead investigators to rule the death a suicide.

Inhaling some cocaine, I tried to make myself into a guided missile, a mind thing I do like an actor's sense memory. I imagine myself as a missile, already fired and homing in on my target. Nothing can call me back. I see myself whirling burrowing smashing through skin fat muscle bone, emerging on the other side in a shower of blood; escaping with the life of my target.

This time I had some difficulty getting myself into a mood to wipe out Hamilton Dapper. The assignment had gotten too personal, ironically because the Daon wanted him squashed not for something really personal, a brother killed or a territory seized, but for causing his high-priced prostitutes to think. I'd never before heard of his ordering an assassination over an idea. I consider that kind of killing closer to politics. What people thought did not usually concern him, only what they did. People made laws against drugselling and taking, against gambling, prostitution, and murder, then broke all the laws. The Daon respected only the law of human behavior. What did a man want and how badly did he want it? Would he kill for it? I heard him ask such questions on several occasions of men with whom he had contradictions. But first he would ask, How much does he want? Then he'd want to know how much pain the man could endure. He had only four weapons. Money. Fear. Pain. Death. With due respect for his criminal mind, I knew that Death did not work well on Ideas. Especially if the Idea had value, and even if it didn't.

I pride myself on my logic but found myself engaged in an illogical enterprise. Finally I resolved to wait and see. The Daon had made me judge after all. I didn't have to tell him what I really thought. I could just say that I hadn't found Hamilton Dapper alone.

I left for Dapper Enterprises at three-thirty and walked crosstown. I wondered if anybody passing could imagine that I might take someone's life within the hour. Sometimes death comes that close and we don't even know it.

At Dapper Enterprises, in a townhouse he owned in the East Sixties, the hole had made an appointment for Mr. Skippy Smith from Smith Carpeting to restaple the carpet in Mr. Dapper's office. During the night, vandals had broken in and slightly wrecked the place, pulling up the carpet as if looking for hidden riches. The receptionist told me this while I waited to get in. "Mr. Dapper's willing to endure the upset for one day, no more. Reasonable overtime won't bother us, if you finish tonight."

"Yes, ma'am," I said politely. I had a few years on her, but I knew my role. "Definitely will finish tonight."

I sat for fifteen minutes, as the receptionist (I wondered if she was the hole) took phone calls and ran little errands. She had a cute way of bouncing her first few steps getting up from her desk, a folded note clamped between thumb and index finger. I liked watching her life dance.

The fifth time she left her desk, I stood and walked into the bowels of the set-up. I carried my toolkit past cubicles and corners where young people, mostly female, talked on phones or hunched over reading matter or stared off into space. The females staring off into space seemed to have the more attractive work places, provocative and evocative clippings and photos tacked to their walls, flowers on their desks. The thick smug carpets made my steps silent. I didn't know which office held Hamilton Dapper, but I knew enough about office hierarchy to guess correctly. I followed the power vibration right to his door, finding it slightly open. I put on workgloves and knocked softly, then entered.

Hamilton Dapper looked at me over his halflens reading glasses. "You came to fix the rug." He sounded disappointed. "Will it be unpleasantly noisy?"

"I work silently, Mr. Dapper." I reset the door, slightly open, where he'd had it. The vandals (I imagined younger clones of Laon and Saom gleefully going about destruction) had torn a sixteen-by-four foot section of carpet from the floor in front of Hamilton Dapper's desk and piled it in a corner near the wall-to-ceiling bookshelves. I began to untangle it and spread it onto the naked wood floor.

He sat at an electric typewriter, staring at the humming machine. He typed, then stopped, then typed and didn't seem pleased with what he'd written. He made more noise at his work than I did at mine.

"Now I'm gonna try the gun, Mr. Dapper." I opened my toolkit and took out the giant stapler. "If it makes too much noise, I'll come back tomorrow."

"O God, no! Do it now and be done."

I started stapling in the corner furthest away from him and where some passing female couldn't see me. The rug muffled the thump of steel spike into wood floor. "This okay, Mr. Dapper?"

He typed to the end of his sentence. "You said what?" He typed another sentence. "O, yes."

I returned to my stapling, getting into the work. I didn't enjoy it as much as baking, but if I had to make a living at it, I wouldn't mind. I got some satisfaction from seeing the carpet going down smooth and blue. I'd almost finished when I became aware that I didn't hear his typewriter clattering. I looked up.

Hamilton Dapper sat back, smoking a cigarette, studying me. "Do I know you from some place?"

I looked him dead in the eye. "That depends on the place, Mr. Dapper." I shot the last staple into the floor.

"Stop that a minute. Let me get a good look at you." He indicated a black wooden armchair facing his desk, the official patented Harvard chair. Every suite of rooms at Harvard contained one for each man. When he left, one had the right to buy it. Everybody has a hustle.

I sat facing him.

"It seems I met you a long time ago." He studied me some more. "I see the face I know in the face I see." I saw he liked the sentence he'd made. "Did you ever work in Cambridge?"

"England?" I toyed with him a bit, way ahead of him now. I'd always thought he'd gone to Yale. He seemed like a Yalie, not quite as smart as he thinks. More style than substance.

He shook his head. "Massachusetts. Near Boston. You couldn't have gone to Harvard."

"Why not?" I enjoyed the flicker of shock in his eyes. "Class of fifty-three."

"No shitting! Well, I'll sure be a horse's ass."

After all, we got down. I got interested in him. And I thought he got interested in me. His office transformed itself into a room in Adams House at Harvard, back in the early fifties when the Africamerican knew his place, and the Euramerican too.

Me at Harvard. Talking to some high class WASP about Life, meaning Money and Power. We hardly ever talked about Sex. Back then they didn't even allow females into a man's room after seven p.m. on weekdays. A Harvardman had to get his snatch before dinner. But no man talked about it. So the B.S. ran to Money and Power. Come to think of it, we didn't talk too much about Money either. Pop had worn out his heart and left some insurance. Tuition 'round a thousand. I had a scholarship. And I worked on the Dorm Crew, cleaning toilets with a brush. I could charge necessities like records and clothes at the Coop. Every so often, the Capeurtaos sent me a couple hundred. So Money didn't bother me.

Power. We talked about Power. Assuming we would have it (even naive brown me); attending Harvard to learn how to wield it. The Fine Art of Ruling Others. Assuming that admission to Harvard signified permission to have and wield Power. They gave you a diploma when you got in! Even if you didn't get a degree, you didn't go away empty-handed. You'd already reached the upperclass. Obviously the gods had smiled. And if the gods smiled on a man, Cooley—my pop would say—not only would a man get rich, he would get smart. It followed then, if a man had money for more than one generation, that smartness would stack up like interest, becoming wisdom.

Pop had prepared me to meet American nobility at Harvard. Somewhere back in Georgia before he ran away from childhood, Pop must have met a cracker who blew his mind, combining the stature of George Washington (who grew hemp and loved walnuts) with the brilliance of Thomas Jefferson (who grew ideas and loved sweet Sally Hemings), an android of Gary Cooper with the streetsmarts of Humphrey Bogart.

Evenings in the early forties, Pop and I'd sit at the yellow kitchen table, opening and munching walnuts. He told me about one WASP he met in Chicago who gave him a job just because Pop had courage enough to ask for it. Pop had never done accounting work before but had confidence in his math, and said so, and the man had gone for it. Got the job. Did well. Till the Big (1917) War opened, and drafted Pop went to France to tend the Cavalry's horses. Never saw combat. Saw France sweeping up horse shit. Years later, he still couldn't talk about it. I had to find out about it from Mom.

Poor, uptight Pop, he expected great things of the WASP. If dealt with patiently and tactfully, he'd do righteously. Once he accepted our humanity, he'd do well by us. He'd pay us our back wages. He'd brag to the world about our accomplishments. How he couldn't have built America without us. How the partnership between the Englishman (doing the planning) and the African (doing the plotting) resulted in a pie big enough to feed the wretched and poor runaways of Europe.

We've been in America longer than anybody but the English, Pop stressed, early as I can remember. "And before most of them." Pop disregarded the original People, displaying racism in regard to them.

Pop raised me to trust the WASP, who mostly came straight. Either he hated you or he loved you, but never fibbed about it. If he called you nigger behind your back, he called you nigger to your face, especially if you worked for him. Now I found myself in earnest conversation with one of the exalted WASPs of my time. If he had known, Pop's chest would have swollen with pride.

I began to genuinely enjoy my conversation with Hamilton Dapper, and the pleasant memories it stirred up. Then a strange thing happened. We had conversed for fifteen minutes on the general state of the world, when I decided to get more specific, and asked him about the state of the nation, as seen from his lofty perch, and its chances of survival.

His blue eyes looked into my brown two, then his voice said, just simple and quiet: "I don't know, Skippy."

"You don't know. The great American idea tottering on the edge of the historical dustbin and you tell me you don't know if we'll make it or not?"

He looked at me across his typewriter, his eyes sorrowful and sheepish. "You needn't bother to heap recrimination on me. Your people certainly haven't fulfilled their potentialities as citizens. You rarely vote."

"You folks rarely vote your ownselves."

"Everybody's bored," he said.

"Everybody's bored," I agreed. "Even black folks are bored. If you don't have the latest attachment for your TV, forget it. Vote today? That means they'll keep breaking into my TV tonight. But in a class and race society, which you admit we have here, it's the responsibility of your class and race not to get bored. If you're born with all the breaks, you have a responsibility to your subjects."

Hamilton Dapper shrugged, sighed, took a puff on his cigarette. "It's a bloody mess. What would you do about it?"

"If I knew, I'd be the President's valet, whispering advice while I helped him squeeze into his tux. But I do notice you folks always do the same thing. Complicate and mystify. Throw money at problems. Form a committee. Why not be brave enough to simplify? Especially your class. The ruling class. Set a new tone. Enough yachts already. Give us a good example of diligence and frugality. You can't imagine how demoralizing it gets for a poor man to watch you folks going through your wasteful changes. You give your subjects no choice but to believe you're either incompetent or corrupt." Never scold a WASP, Pop had taught: He doesn't take scolding well. He thinks it means you don't like him. "Nothing personal, you understand."

"I understand." Hamilton Dapper peeped at his wristwatch. "But you misunderstand one essential point, Skippy. My class isn't raised to rule. We don't consider you our subjects. We're merely raised to be polite and to say bright things at cocktail parties. We have no class or race consciousness." He stood and extended his hand, blue eyes bright. "I guess we'd better get on with our work now."

I removed my right glove, but grabbed his right wrist with my gloved left hand and gripped it tight, at the same time reaching into my coveralls for my weapon. When he saw the pistol, he tried to squirm away, giving me his right temple for a target. Before he could utter a syllable, I put a bullet into his brain, silent as a puff of wind. Dush! The staple gun had made more racket. Dead, he slumped back into his chair, his head thudding forward onto his typewriter. Blood leaked onto his halfdone page.

I put my glove back on and wiped the pistol clean of fingerprints and removed the silencer. Then I pressed the pistol into his right hand, his smoking hand. I found the cigarette he'd just lit and mashed it out, then gathered up my toolkit and stepped out of his office. A few females glanced up, but seeing me and not Hamilton Dapper, returned to their reading and phonecalls. I closed the door behind me.

"The man says not to disturb him a few hours," I told the receptionist. "The staple gun made too much noise, so he got behind in his work. But I finished the job, so you can drop the check in the mail."

"Fine." She smiled, but through me. "Look for it 'round the first of the month."

Next day the tabloids crowed the news. Even the *Times* mentioned it, though it made short shrift of Hamilton Dapper on its Obit page. TV HOST TAKES OWN LIFE. Typewritten Note Expresses Pessimism. Recent Divorce Seen as Contributing to Despondency. Bugged with her brain too. Roff the Daon had amazing perceptions about people. Talented as hell, but never a very stable character. He had everything, money, power and position, but none of it made him happy, continued Mr. Lipshutt, longtime associate and agent of the deceased. Some men are just naturally morose. Maybe it goes with the talent. Reached at the home of her mother, the former Mrs. Dapper broke down on receiving the devastating news she had not heard before. It can't be true, it just can't, she shrieked. It must be some macabre trick. Ham always did have a sick sense of humor. You wait. He'll turn up in a few days, the bastard!

Wonder if she gets any dough now. But the Herald has obtained a copy of his bloodstained last testament to the world. His head fell, thud! Drip. Drop. It reads in part:

"These recent revelations recall to remembrance my oft-used wheelbarrow image. Only now it turns out the wheelbarrow we approach—Hell, it costs seven times its real value. And may not even last until we get to Hell. Everyday we receive more evidence that our society hurdles headlong toward self-destruction. We all know it. We complain. But we don't change our ways."

It all made interesting reading on my flight to Colombia, where I went the next day for some rest and recreation. In the following days I did little but read accounts of it in English-language periodicals coming in from the United States. I'd inhale fine cocaine, then sit by the pool ogling the young bodies and reading about the Dapper Suicide. By the time it faded to the back pages and into the Beyond, I knew the time had come to return to the Bronx and my baking.

THE ORIGIN OF WHALES

T HE WOMAN SAT. She sat on a porch under the roof of an old white house, with a massive oak before her, apple trees and plum trees and peach trees to the right and left, a grape arbor at the edge of the backyard, and an abandoned chicken coop at the other end near an empty smokehouse. She sat in a wicker-bottomed rocking chair like some grim guardian, peering into the late-September air as if searching for the place where the air gives way.

A car approached from the distance, creating a mean and dusty cloud that rose up and vanished. The car stopped in front of the house. The woman who drove the car stepped out and a boy jumped out from the other side: the boy clad in ripped and sporty clothes, his shoes unlaced; the woman nicely coiffured, smartly dressed.

"How you doing today, Aunt Essie?"

"Fine, child, just fine." The old woman's voice trembled like ripples across a pond. "Can't complain. Things sho could be whole lot worser. How you doing, gal? You and Thad ready to go?"

"Yes, ma'am. Soon as I get Little Thad straightened away with you, we'll be ready to go." Her voice was small but sharp, like a bird's. She absently watched the boy over by the ditch at the edge of the yard poking at something with a branch.

"Well, I knows y'all is looking forward to it."

"Yes, ma'am, we are. And I want to thank you for looking after Thad for us."

"Tain't no trouble atall. Where his things at?"

"In the car. He'll get them." The woman turned on the porch, her high heels clicking on the wood, and called to the boy, telling him to get his suitcase and tote bag out of the car, Mama's got to go, and did he have his books to study?, and to be good.

Through all this the boy continued to kick at clods of dirt around the ditch, his hands in his pockets, his head down.

"Thad, did you hear me?"

"Yeah," said the boy, without looking up.

"Come on, Thad. I've got to get on the road."

"You do it then." He did not look at her.

Closing her eyes as if in pain, she started toward the car.

"Wait." Essie stopped rocking. "Boy," her voice rolled forth. "You get your little black butt to that car and get your mess out. This very minute. Do you hear me?"

The boy stood still and stared at the older woman. After a while he did as she'd told him, without saying a word.

The mother sighed. "Seems I just can't do anything with him these days. I really do appreciate your keeping him, Aunt Essie. I hope he doesn't give you too much trouble."

Essie commenced to rock. "Now don't you worry about a thing, child. You all enjoy the convention and we'll be fine."

"Thank you, Aunt Essie." The woman gave a little girl's prim smile. "Oh, and Aunt Essie, how is Cousin Ruth? I heard she wasn't doing too well."

The old woman fixed her with a peculiar narrowing of the eyes. "Well, I don't know, girl. I just don't know. Saw her yestidy. Reverend Greene took me. Didn't look good. Had another stroke, you know." She shrugged. "But the Lord do know best, don't he?" Her voice trailed off into the blue. "You know." Essie's face lightened. "You know, me and her was born on the same day."

"Yes, Thad told me."

"Did?"

The woman smoothed the pleats in her dress with the palms of her hands. She glanced at her watch. "Oops! I better head on out."

The boy climbed the steps carrying his bags and looking stern. His mother smiled sweetly. "Now you be a good boy and do what your Aunt Essie says. Okay?"

He groaned.

She tried to kiss him, but he stepped back. "Aw, come on, Ma."

"Give your mama a good-bye kiss, boy, or I'll put this here walking stick upside your head. Go on now. Do it."

He gave the old woman a who-the-hell-do-you-think-you-are? glare but kissed his mother, grudgingly.

The mother thanked Essie again and walked to her car.

The old woman watched the car slide down the dirt road. She turned to the boy, who peered at her. She rolled her eyes. Presently the boy made his way over to the opposite side of the porch, walking its edge like a tightrope.

Essie turned her gaze toward the sky again. She told him where to put his bags and where he would be sleeping. She asked him if he was hungry. He said no. She told him they would eat in about half an hour.

"I'm going to look around."

"What?"

"I said I'm going out to take a look-see around in the yard. Okay?"

"You are?"

"Yeah."

"Is that a fact?" Essie bent over her cane, the gray wig on her head a little askew. She cocked her head to the side the way a listening fawn would.

The boy crossed his arms and tapped his feet. She began to tap her cane in counterpoint. They went on, ta-tap-tap, ta-tap-tap, like a couple of retired vaudevillian hoofers, their eyes locked in determination.

Finally the boy said, "*May* I go scout around?"

"'Scout around'?"

"Ah, come on. Give me a break."

"Beg your pardon?" Her expression did not change nor did she stop tapping her stick.

He dropped his hands to his side. "Miss Aunt Essie, ma'am, may I *please* go out in the yard to play, Miss Aunt Essie, ma'am, thank you, may I, please, ma'am?" He bugged his eyes and stretched his mouth sorrowfully.

"Well, I reckon if you got the sense to ask somebody, you can go." The boy dashed down the steps, only touching one with his foot. "You stay out of them ditches!" she yelled after him. "And don't go no further than the yard."

Essie slowly made her way inside and down the hall, past the heavily framed sepia photographs of stern-looking men and women and past vases of dried flowers on doily-covered tabletops to the kitchen. She lifted a pot and filled it with water. Measured out cornmeal. Dipped out lard. Washed and drained a silvery-steel pan full of green-hued collard and mustard leaves. Stuffed them in a pot. Measured out a cup of rice. Put more water on to boil. Her hands moved about the cups and spoons and jars with an exaggerated deliberateness.

"Pssst! Pssst! Aunt Essie. Aunt Essie."

She peered out the window over the sink. "What you want now, boy?"

"Want to play hide-and-go-seek?"

Her expression did not change. She wiped her hand with a cloth. "Okay. Be right out." She checked the pots and the water and walked out the back door, pausing to look at a clock.

At the foot of the back door steps he met her.

"All right. Who's gone be It?"

"You."

"Uh-uh. You always hide. I'm gone hide this time, feller."

The boy heaved an impatient sigh, shifted his weight, and rolled his eyes. "Okay. Okay. I'll be It. Ready?"

The woman started to walk way. "Well? Turn around now. And start counting, why don't you? And don't count too fast neither. To a hundred."

"A hundred!"

"Yeah, a hundred. And don't peep neither. Turn round, I say."

"Good enough?" The boy had his back to her, his hands over his face. "One-hundred, ninety-nine, ninety-eight . . ."

Essie crept away as best she could, tip-tip-tippy-toed. She walked over to the old chicken coop, the door off its hinges. She peeked in, paused, and shook her head *no*. She turned to the grape arbor.

". . . seventy-six, seventy-five, seventy-four . . ."

She crouched slightly behind the big mother-stalk at its center, which was twice as wide as she.

". . . twenty-four, twenty-three, twenty-two . . ."

She hunched there grinning, her back to the stalk, leaning on her cane. She glanced into the net of green-dark leaves above her head, saw a cluster of grapes, and plucked one off.

". . . nine, eight, seven . . ."

With a grimace and a pucker she spat out the unripe grape, then quietly spat out more of the hull.

"Ready or not, here I come!"

She tilted her head to the right and listened. She tiptoed to a post at the edge of the arbor and peeked out. Little Thad was tiptoeing, just as she had, toward the front of the house. When he had vanished from sight, Essie snuck out from the arbor toward the steps. She began to smile, for she had almost arrived at home base. Something grabbed her elbows—

"Got you!" Thad had come up from behind her.

Essie jumped with a start. "Whooooweeee! You scared the devil out of me, you little—" Playfully, laughing, she swung her cane at him. He ducked like a gazelle.

"Your turn. Your turn." His face betrayed glee.

Essie advanced to the steps.

"Turn your back and close your eyes now."

"I know, boy. I know. I was playing this before your daddy was a itch in his daddy's breeches. Now go on and let me count. One hundred, ninety-nine, ninety-eight, ninety-seven . . ." Essie stopped counting out loud.

"Aunt Essie. Keep counting. Come on now, play fair."

"I am playing fair." She grinned. ". . . eighty-eight, eighty-seven, eighty-six, eighty-five . . ."

She looked through her hands through the screen door into the house, straight to the front door and out, across the fields in the front, out and out.

". . . thirty-five, thirty-four, thirty-three . . ."

Above her head she noted a spiderweb, and in it a spider making a living mummy out of freshly caught prey. A wooden thud sounded in the distance not far behind her. A smirk spread across her face.

". . . four, three, two, one. Ready or not, I'm gone get you." She turned and with a mockingly purposeful walk made her way toward the chicken coop. At its door she paused and inspected the ground around it.

"Now, Thad. I know you're in there and ain't but one way out. So come on, I got you."

No sound came from the henhouse.

"Come on, boy."

She bent over and peered in.

Suddenly Thad jumped up, yelling: "You got to get me fore I get to base." He tried to make a run for it, but Essie quickly stuck out her cane, tripping him to the ground.

Tears welled up in the corners of her eyes and slipped down her cheeks, and she could hardly catch her breath for laughing.

"Teach you. Teach you to mess with ole Essie. Teach you."

The boy sat stunned in disbelief and soon began to laugh along with her. They giggled and snickered outside the henhouse, pointing and poking at one another.

Essie suddenly stood up straight and gasped.

"Aunt Essie? What? What is it?"

"My collards, boy. I bet they's burnt." With that she made her way as quickly as she could to the house.

In the kitchen, over the pot, she sighed with relief when she found a smidgen of water left. Her breathing came short and she awkwardly sat in the chair. "Getting old. Getting old. Can't keep doing this foolishness. Gone kill me sho," she murmured as she tried to catch her breath and calm her breast. After a spell she rose, with more effort than before, and finished preparing the meal.

"Boy, come on in here and wash your face and hands and get ready for some supper. Hear?"

"Okay. What's for grub, Granny?"

"Watch your lip, son. Your grandma's dead. I'm your Aunt Essie. Remember that." She kept her eyes on the iron skillet as she tended the frying cornbread with a spatula.

The boy came back from the bathroom and sat at the table. The woman served his plate.

"Now you eat."

"What's this?"

"What you mean, 'What's this?'" She looked as perplexed as if someone had asked her why the sun burned in the sky. "It's collards, with some mustard greens mixed in. A little bit a fatback, rice, and cornbread. What you been eating all your life. What you think it is?"

"Collards!" The boy squinched his face up into an awful frown. "I can't eat no collards or no fatback neither." He stared at the plate as though it held a pile of dung.

"Boy, you eat that somethingtoeat. I ain't slaved all this time in this here kitchen to put up with your mouthing bout what you is and ain't gone eat. Eat." She looked at him hard, and he lifted his fork and ate. He mumbled something to himself.

"Your maw ate this here food when she was coming up. Your paw ate this here food when he was coming up. I ate it. My maw and paw ate it, and if it were good enough for them I reckons it'll suit you." She served her plate and slowly sank into her chair across the table from the boy, who picked at his food as though stirring leaves.

"Boy, stop picking in that food and start eating. Y'all chilren don't know what good eating is. Get you some nice smothered collard greens, some fatback, a nice piece of cornbread. Uh-uh. Now, boy, that's eating. Y'all young folks don't know. You just don't know." She stuffed some more collards into her mouth. The boy's eyes were fixed on his plate.

"You say you don't love no collards. You ever hear talk of my brother Hugh?"

"No, ma'am."

"Well, I don't know why. You should. He was my brother. Now, Hugh—he loved him some collard greens. You hear me? Sho did. I remember one time. Round August. Maw had cooked a great big ole pot of collards. Now ole Hugh—he couldn't a been more than your age—well, he knew them collards was about done. We was all out in the fields. So Hugh, he slips back to the house, you know, cause Maw left the pot on. And he ate that whole pot of collards."

"A whole pot! How? He couldn't have. He—"

"If I'm lying, I'm flying. Ate the whole blessed pot. Well, we come home for supper and there ain't no collards. Paw's furious. Say he's sho that Hugh done and ate them collards. 'No, no, paw,' Hugh say. 'Twon't me. I seen a bear, paw. I bet hit was a bear.'

"Now Paw wont no stupid man. He knew Hugh ate them collards. But he was a slick one, Paw was. So he just scratched his head a mite and say: 'Now, boy, if twas a bear they ought to be tracks, now oughten they?'

"Well, Hugh agreed, cause there wont nothing else to do but say he ate them collards, and he sho didn't want Paw to lay into him. So Paw and Hugh went out and I figured they was going to the woodpile so Paw could whup Hugh good. But guess what?"

"What?" Thad spoke from behind wide eyes and through a mouth full of greens.

"See, there had been a rainstorm the night before and the ground was soft. Hugh and Paw come back and say he be damned if there wont some tracks out yonder. Now I could see that ole Hugh didn't know what to think, cause he knowed he was lying. But Paw didn't give him a whupping, since he seen them tracks sho enough.

"But that night Hugh couldn't get to sleep. He twisted. He turned. He paced the floor."

"What was wrong with him?"

"He had the runs."

"The runs?"

"Diarrhea. The squirts. You know what I'm talking bout, boy."

"Oh. Well, why didn't he just go to the bathroom?"

"Cause,"—Essie threw her head back and chuckled—"son, in them days we didn't have no bathrooms in the house. No, Lord, we had a outhouse."

"Why didn't he go there?"

"Cause! He was scared the bear was gone get him."

"What happened?"

Essie took a swig from her lemonade. "Well, ole Hugh lasted till about eleven-thirty—in them days we went to bed at about nine or ten o'clock—and he just had to get out of there to make a stink real bad. So he went out the door. Bout two minutes later we heard yelling and screaming and in come Hugh, yelling: 'Paw, Paw, get your gun, get your gun, I seen a bear,' and he had messed all over himself. Paw whupped him good too."

"What about the bear?"

"Tsk." Essie rolled her eyes and picked up her fork. "Wont no bear, fool." Her eyes lit with the chewing of the greens and she nodded and rocked as she ate to show how good the food tasted to her. She winked at the boy. After a time of silence she began to hum. A low, rich tune. A hymn.

After supper Thad helped Essie clear the table, put away food, and wash dishes.

"Help me with my homework?" Thad rubbed a dishtowel across a plate until it squeaked.

"Don't I always?"

On the cleared kitchen table, atop the green-and-white oilcloth. Thad piled up his books: modern mathematics, spelling, social studies, science. Essie went to her black purse in the hall for her eyeglasses, which had round lenses and silver frames.

Thad and Essie sat at the table. By and by the brilliant horizon could be seen through the window; the sun was just setting; blues mingled with reds mingled with yellows as if the air were ablaze.

"Science first. We're doing biology now. Evolution. This says that all animals began as lower animals and adapted into what they are now. Do you believe that, Aunt Essie?"

"Not particularly." She frowned over her spectacles at the color-bright picture of dinosaurs and shaggy elephants in the book.

"Whales even were supposed to walk on the earth with legs and stuff once upon a time. Cause they're mammals like us and not fishes like goldfishes and sharks. Do you believe that?"

"No, I—"

The phone rang.

She jumped as if someone had come into her house uninvited.

"Boy, get that for me." She struggled to get to her feet, reaching for her walking stick. The boy ran to the phone in the front hall.

"Hello," he said. "Yes. Yes, ma'am . . . This is Thad . . . Thad Williams . . . Yes, ma'am . . . Aunt Essie is . . . Yes, ma'am . . . No, ma'am, I'm Thad Williams, the dentist's son . . . Yes, ma'am, Leota's boy . . . No, ma'am, my mama's Denise . . ."

"Who that, boy?" Essie looked almost angry with worry. The boy, confused, handed the phone to her. She took it while still asking him who it was.

"Hello!" She yelled into the receiver as though she had to push her voice through the wire. "Whasay? . . . Uh-huh, yeah . . . This *is* Essie. Hattie, that you? . . . Oh, girl, how you doing? . . . Uh-huh. Uh-huh. Yeah. What?

Lordchildyouknowitaintso . . ." She became silent for a time, nodding occasionally. The boy went back to the kitchen table, flipping through his book.

"Which hospital is she in?"

The boy looked out the window into the newly harvested soybean field, into the ever-darkening sky.

"Who there with her?"

Through the window in the door before which she stood, Essie watched a squirrel scamper up the oak tree in the front yard. It had an acorn in its mouth and its movements were quick and sharp.

"Well, I wisht I could go see bout her, but I'm keeping this boy of Thad's . . . Uh-huh . . . And, well, I might bring him with me in the morning. Uh-huh. Well, the Lord's time ain't man's time. Yes, Lord."

Essie hung up the phone.

"Who in the hospital?"

"Don't vex me, boy."

Essie took off her eyeglasses and gently placed them by the phone. Haltingly, visibly tired, she walked out the front door to the porch and her rocking chair. The sky gathering velvet. Evening tangible. The squirrel darted up and about tree limbs like some devilish dervish. Essie sat in the chair and began to hum. After a few bars she stopped; but her rocking continued.

Thad stood in the doorway, behind the screen door, watching Essie. She rocked. Finally he opened the door, carefully so as to keep it from creaking, and sat down on the floor next to the metronome figure rocking back and forth. He reached up for her hand, but as his neared hers he stopped. He stared at her hand on the arm of the chair: pecan-colored, large-veined, the nails clipped short, wrinkles like stitching. He balled his fist up tight, looked at it, drew it to his chest.

"Gone help me with my homework?"

"Directly."

JAMAICA KINCAID

SONG OF ROLAND

Hᴉꜱ ᴍᴏᴜᴛʜ ᴡᴀꜱ ʟɪᴋᴇ ᴀɴ ɪꜱʟᴀɴᴅ in the sea that was his face; I am sure he had ears and nose and eyes and all the rest, but I could see only his mouth, which I knew could do all the things that a mouth usually does, such as eat food, purse in approval or disapproval, smile, twist in thought; inside were his teeth and behind them was his tongue. Why did I see him that way, how did I come to see him that way? It was a mystery to me that he had been alive all along and that I had not known of his existence and I was perfectly fine—I went to sleep at night and I could wake up in the morning and greet the day with indifference if it suited me, I could comb my hair and scratch myself and I was still perfectly fine—and he was alive, sometimes living in a house next to mine, sometimes living in a house far away, and his existence was ordinary and perfect and parallel to mine, but I did not know of it, even though sometimes he was close enough to me for me to notice that he smelt of cargo he had been unloading; he was a stevedore.

His mouth really did look like an island, lying in a twig-brown sea, stretching out from east to west, widest near the center, with tiny, sharp creases, its color a shade lighter than that of the twig-brown sea in which it lay, the place where the two lips met disappearing into the pinkest of pinks, and even though I must have held his mouth in mine a thousand times, it was always new to me. He must have smiled at me, though I don't really know, but I don't like to think that I would love someone who hadn't first smiled at me. It had been raining, a heavy downpour, and I took shelter under the gallery of a dry-goods store along with some other people. The rain was an inconvenience, for it was not necessary; there had already been too much of it, and it was no longer only outside, overflowing in the gutters, but inside also, roofs were leaking and then falling in. I was standing under the gallery and had sunk deep within myself, enjoying completely the despair I felt at

317

being myself. I was wearing a dress; I had combed my hair that morning; I had washed myself that morning. I was looking at nothing in particular when I saw his mouth. He was speaking to someone else, but he was looking at me. The someone else he was speaking to was a woman. His mouth then was not like an island at rest in a sea but like a small patch of ground viewed from high above and set in motion by a force not readily seen.

When he saw me looking at him, he opened his mouth wider, and that must have been the smile. I saw then that he had a large gap between his two front teeth, which probably meant that he could not be trusted, but I did not care. My dress was damp, my shoes were wet, my hair was wet, my skin was cold, all around me were people standing in small amounts of water and mud, shivering, but I started to perspire from an effort I wasn't aware I was making; I started to perspire because I felt hot, and I started to perspire because I felt happy. I wore my hair then in two plaits and the ends of them rested just below my collarbone; all the moisture in my hair collected and ran down my two plaits, as if they were two gutters, and the water seeped through my dress just below the collarbone and continued to run down my chest, only stopping at the place where the tips of my breasts met the fabric, revealing, plain as a new print, my nipples. He was looking at me and talking to someone else, and his mouth grew wide and narrow, small and large, and I wanted him to notice me, but there was so much noise: all the people standing in the gallery, sheltering themselves from the strong rain, had something they wanted to say, something not about the weather (that was by now beyond comment) but about their lives, their disappointments most likely, for joy is so short-lived there isn't enough time to dwell on its occurrence. The noise, which started as a hum, grew to a loud din, and the loud din had an unpleasant taste of metal and vinegar, but I knew his mouth could take it away if only I could get to it; so I called out my own name, and I knew he heard me immediately, but he wouldn't stop speaking to the woman he was talking to, so I had to call out my name again and again until he stopped, and by that time my name was like a chain around him, as the sight of his mouth was like a chain around me. And when our eyes met, we laughed, because we were happy, but it was frightening, for that gaze asked everything: who would betray whom, who would be captive, who would be captor, who would give and who would take, what would I do. And when our eyes met and we laughed at the same time, I said, "I love you, I love you," and he said, "I know." He did not say it out of vanity, he did not say it out of conceit, he only said it because it was true.

His name was Roland. He was not a hero, he did not even have a country; he was from an island, a small island that was between a sea and an ocean, and a small island is not a country. And he did not have a history; he was a small event in somebody else's history, but he was a man. I could see him better than he could see himself, and that was because he was who he was and I was myself but also because I was taller than he was. He was unpolished, but he carried himself as if he were precious. His hands were large and thick, and for no reason that I could see he would spread them out in front of him and they looked as if they were the missing parts from a powerful piece of machinery; his legs were straight from hip to knee and then from the knee they bent at an angle as if he had been at sea too long or had never learnt to walk properly to begin with. The hair on his legs was tightly curled as if the hairs were pieces of thread rolled between the thumb and the forefinger in preparation for sewing, and so was the hair on his arms, the hair in his underarms, and the hair on his chest; the hair in those places was black and grew sparsely; the hair on his head and the hair between his legs was black and tightly curled also, but it grew in such abundance that it was impossible for me to move my hands through it. Sitting, standing, walking, or lying down, he carried himself as if he were something precious, but not out of vanity, for it was true, he was something precious; yet when he was lying on top of me he looked down at me as if I were the only woman in the world, the only woman he had ever looked at in that way—but that was not true, a man only does that when it is not true. When he first lay on top of me I was so ashamed of how much pleasure I felt that I bit my bottom lip hard—but I did not bleed, not from biting my lip, not then. His skin was smooth and warm in places I had not kissed him; in the places I had kissed him his skin was cold and coarse, and the pores were open and raised.

Did the world become a beautiful place? The rainy season eventually went away, the sunny season came, and it was too hot; the riverbed grew dry, the mouth of the river became shallow, the heat eventually became as wearying as the rain, and I would have wished it away if I had not become occupied with this other sensation, a sensation I had no single word for. I could feel myself full of happiness, but it was a kind of happiness I had never experienced before, and my happiness would spill out of me and run all the way down a long, long road and then the road would come to an end and I would feel empty and sad, for what could come after this? How would it end?

Not everything has an end, even though the beginning changes. The first time we were in a bed together we were lying on a thin board that was covered with old cloth, and this small detail, evidence of our poverty—people in our position, a stevedore and a doctor's servant, could not afford a proper mattress—was a major contribution to my satisfaction, for it allowed me to brace myself and match him breath for breath. But how can it be that a man who can carry large sacks filled with sugar or bales of cotton on his back from dawn to dusk exhausts himself within five minutes inside a woman. I did not then and I do not now know the answer to that. He kissed me. He fell asleep. I bathed my face then between his legs; he smelt of curry and onions, for those were the things he had been unloading all day; other times when I bathed my face between his legs—for I did it often, I liked doing it—he would smell of sugar, or flour, or the large, cheap bolts of cotton from which he would steal a few yards to give me to make a dress.

What is the everyday? What is the ordinary? One day, as I was walking toward the government dispensary to collect some supplies—one of my duties as a servant to a man who was in love with me beyond anything he could help and so had long since stopped trying, a man I ignored except when I wanted him to please me—I met Roland's wife, face to face, for the first time. She stood in front of me like a sentry—stern, dignified, guarding the noble idea, if not noble ideal, that was her husband. She did not block the sun, it was shining on my right; on my left was a large black cloud; it was raining way in the distance; there was no rainbow on the horizon. We stood on the narrow strip of concrete that was the sidewalk. One section of a wooden fence that was supposed to shield a yard from passersby on the street bulged out and was broken, and a few tugs from any careless party would end its usefulness; in that yard a primrose bush bloomed unnaturally, its leaves too large, its flowers showy, and weeds were everywhere, they had prospered in all the wet. We were not alone. A man walked past us with a cutlass in his knapsack and a mistreated dog two steps behind him; a woman walked by with a large basket of food on her head; some children were walking home from school, and they were not walking together; a man was leaning out a window, spitting, he used snuff. I was wearing a pair of modestly high heels, red, not a color to wear to work in the middle of the day, but that was just the way I had been feeling, red with a passion, like that hibiscus that was growing under the window of the man who kept spitting from the snuff. And Roland's wife called me a whore, a slut, a pig, a snake, a viper, a rat, a low-life, a parasite, and an evil woman. I could see that her mouth formed a familiar hug around these words—poor thing, she had been used to saying them. I was not surprised. I could not have loved Roland the way I did if he had not loved other women. And I was not surprised; I had noticed immediately the space between his teeth. I was not surprised that she knew about me; a man cannot keep a secret, a man always wants all the women he knows to know each other.

I believe I said this: "I love Roland; when he is with me I want him to love me; when he is not with me I think of him loving me. I do not love you. I love Roland." This is what I wanted to say, and this is what I believe I said. She slapped me across the face; her hand was wide and thick like an oar; she, too, was used to doing hard work. Her hand met the side of my face: my jawbone, the skin below my eye and under my chin, a small portion of my nose, the lobe of my ear. I was then a young woman in my early twenties, my skin was supple, smooth, the pores invisible to the naked eye. It was completely without bitterness that I thought as I looked at her face, a face I had so little interest in that it would tire me to describe it, Why is the state of marriage so desirable that all women are afraid to be caught outside it? And why does this woman, who has never seen me before, to whom I have never made any promise, to whom I owe nothing, hate me so much? She expected me to return her blow but, instead, I said, again completely without bitterness, "I consider it beneath me to fight over a man."

I was wearing a dress of light-blue Irish linen. I could not afford to buy such material, because it came from a real country, not a false country like mine; a shipment of this material in blue, in pink, in lime green, and in beige had come from Ireland, I suppose, and Roland had given me yards of each shade from the bolts. I was wearing my blue Irish-linen dress that day, and it was demure enough—a pleated skirt that ended quite beneath my knees, a belt at my waist, sleeves that buttoned at my wrists, a high neckline that covered my collarbone—but underneath my dress I wore absolutely nothing, no undergarments of any kind, only my stockings, given to me by Roland and taken from yet another shipment of dry goods, each one held up by two pieces of elastic that I had sewn together to make a garter. My declaration of what I considered beneath me must have enraged Roland's wife, for she grabbed my blue dress at the collar and gave it a huge tug; it rent in two from my neck to my waist. My breasts lay softly on my chest, like two small pieces of unrisen dough, unmoved by the anger of this woman; not so by the touch of her husband's mouth, for he would remove my dress, by first patiently undoing all the buttons and then pulling down the bodice, and then he would take one breast in his mouth, and it would grow to a size much bigger than his mouth could hold, and he would let it go and turn to the other one; the saliva evaporating from the skin on that breast was an altogether different sensation from the sensation of my other breast in his mouth, and I would divide myself in two, for I could not decide which sensation I wanted to take dominance over the other. For an hour he would kiss me in this way and then exhaust himself on top of me in five minutes. I loved him so. In the dark I couldn't see him clearly, only an outline, a solid shadow; when I saw him in the daytime he was fully dressed. His wife, as she rent my dress, a dress made of material she knew very well, for she had a dress made of the same material, told me his history: it was not a long one, it was not a sad one, no one had died in it, no land had been laid waste, no birthright had been stolen; she had a list, and it was full of names, but they were not the names of countries.

What was the color of her wedding day? When she first saw him was she overwhelmed with desire? The impulse to possess is alive in every heart, and some people choose vast plains, some people choose high mountains, some people choose wide seas, and some people choose husbands; I chose to possess myself. I resembled a tree, a tall tree with long, strong branches; I looked delicate, but any man I held in my arms knew that I was strong; my hair was long and thick and deeply waved naturally, and I wore it braided and pinned up, because when I wore it loosely around my shoulders it caused excitement in other people—some of them men, some of them women, some of them it pleased, some of them it did not. The way I walked depended on who I thought would see me and what effect I wanted my walk to have on them. My face was beautiful, I found it so.

And yet I was standing before a woman who found herself unable to keep her life's booty in its protective sack, a woman whose voice no longer came from her throat but from deep within her stomach, a woman whose hatred was misplaced. I looked down at our feet, hers and mine, and I expected to see my short life flash before me; instead, I saw that her feet were without shoes. She did have a pair of shoes, though, which I had seen: they were white, they were plain, a round toe and flat laces, they took shoe polish well, she wore them only on Sundays and to church. I had many pairs of shoes, in colors meant to attract attention and dazzle the eye; they were uncomfortable, I wore them every day, I never went to church at all.

My strong arms reached around to caress Roland, who was lying on my back naked; I was naked also. I knew his wife's name, but I did not say it; he knew his wife's name, too, but he did not say it. I did not know the long list of names that were not countries that his wife had committed to memory. He himself did not know the long list of names; he had not committed this list to memory. This was not from deceit, and it was not from carelessness. He was someone so used to a large fortune that he took it for granted; he did not have a bankbook, he did not have a ledger, he had a fortune—but still he had not lost interest in acquiring more. Feeling my womb contract, I crossed the room, still naked; small drops of blood spilt from inside me, evidence of my refusal to accept his silent offering. And Roland looked at me, his face expressing confusion. Why did I not bear his children? He could feel the times that I was fertile, and yet each month blood flowed away from me, and each month I expressed confidence at its imminent arrival and departure, and always I was overjoyed at the accuracy of my prediction. When I saw him like that, on his face a look that was a mixture—confusion, dumbfoundedness, defeat—I felt much sorrow for him, for his life was reduced to a list of names that were not countries, and to the number of times he brought the monthly flow of blood to a halt; his life was reduced to women, some of them beautiful, wearing dresses made from yards of cloth he had surreptitiously removed from the bowels of the ships where he worked as a stevedore.

At that time I loved him beyond words; I loved him when he was standing in front of me and I loved him when he was out of my sight. I was still a young woman. No small impressions, the size of a child's forefinger, had yet appeared on the soft parts of my body; my legs were long and hard, as if they had been made to take me a long distance; my arms were long and strong, as if prepared for carrying heavy loads; I was not beautiful, but if I could have been in love with myself I would have been. I was in love with Roland. He was a man. But who was he really? He did not sail the seas, he did not cross the oceans, he only worked in the bottom of vessels that had done so; no mountains were named for him, no valleys, no nothing. But still he was a man, and he wanted something beyond ordinary satisfaction—beyond one wife, one love, and one room with walls made of mud and roof of cane leaves, beyond the small plot of land where the same trees bear the same fruit year following year—for it would all end only in death, for though no history yet written had embraced him, though he could not identify the small uprisings within himself, though he would deny the small uprisings within himself, a strange calm would sometimes come over him, a cold stillness, and since he could find no words for it, he was momentarily blinded with shame.

One night Roland and I were sitting on the steps of the jetty, our backs facing the small world we were from, the world of sharp, dangerous curves in the road, of steep mountains of recent volcanic formations covered in a green so humble no one had ever longed for them, of three hundred and sixty-five small streams that would never meet up to form a majestic roar, of clouds that were nothing but large vessels holding endless days of water, of people who had never been regarded as people at all; we looked into the night, its blackness did not come as a surprise, a moon full of dead white light travelled across the surface of a glittering black sky; I was wearing a dress made from another piece of cloth he had given me, another piece of cloth taken from the bowels of a ship without permission, and there was a false pocket in the skirt, a pocket that did not have a bottom, and Roland placed his hand inside the pocket, reaching all the way down to touch inside of me; I looked at his face, his mouth I could see and it stretched across his face like an island and like an island, too, it held secrets and was dangerous and could swallow things whole that were much larger than itself; I looked out toward the horizon, which I could not see but knew was there all the same, and this was also true of the end of my love for Roland.

YANICK LAHENS

THE BLUE ROOM

I KNOW I MUST HAVE BEEN a little girl of six or seven. I cannot say precisely how this event happened; it is a memory somehow more than a memory, a fleeting gleam among all my memories, as if from a distant shore, shimmering briefly on the water's surface.

I recall the house distinctly—it is located at the end of the hibiscus-lined alley, with its big dark sitting room and three bedrooms lined up along the right side. My father's parents' bedroom opens on a small porch, where every morning a gentle light coaxes objects out of the shadows. My parents occupy the middle room. Only its blue color gives it any particular character. And my younger sister and I share that last room at the end of the hall. On the left side, two small rooms are separated by a thin wall, one my father's office, the other my mother's sewing room. In the large room in the back of the house, we all gather for our meals.

Before this event, the sitting room is for me the mysterious heart of the house. I enter it, always, with barely controlled emotions. And, ever in fear that my voice will be mysteriously snatched by the alarming silence of this place, I shrink from uttering the faintest sound, withholding even my breath.

This big room guards its solemnity behind doors and curtains that are always closed. A half-light reveals a thin veil of dust, like a pollen dropped by an unknown hand during the night. Sometimes the sun passes a timid arm through the shutters and lightly brushes objects with its fingers. Like a sacred fire, the light marks the threshold of this magic territory where creatures of secrecy and ghosts of darkness rise.

Translated by Kathleen M. Balutansky.

324

This sitting room strangely fascinates my young soul. Some mysterious emanation seems to animate its objects and its furniture. It is possessed, filled with familiar spirits, perhaps ferocious werewolves. I avoid it, pursuing my numerous imaginary adventures elsewhere in the house. I am convinced that spirits sit around on the imposing dark mahogany armchairs, conversing quietly. And if I disturb them, I risk—or so I used to think—being severely reprimanded, just as when my characteristic curiosity drives me to interrupt adults in conversation. Often, without the grown-ups even noticing, I stand among them, listening to their talk. Their conversations—on illnesses, on the old days, on politics, or on death—are both enchanting and troubling at the same time.

The sitting room curtains and doors open only for marriages, for first communions, for christenings, and for funerals—to receive uncles, cousins, aunts, and friends. But for coups d'états, of course, for insurrections, at times of curfews, my grandparents and my parents have the curtains drawn and close the doors as they gather around the low rectangular sitting room table. This arrangement allows them to exchange their opinions on the political actors of the moment without fear of being heard by neighbors or anyone not enjoying the absolute trust of the house. And on these same occasions, when they sit on the porch, they exchange innocuous remarks in loud and intelligible voices.

Many years later I would understand that my parents' seemingly contradictory patterns of behavior were in fact manifestations of the same feeling: a terror that either hid behind the transparency of words or concealed itself in silence. They protected themselves by hiding their fear behind a mask of innocence.

In our carefree days, my younger sister and I enjoy with rare pleasure these family reunions in the sitting room. For us the element of surprise always overcomes our anxiety. We invent games to match these circumstances and try to fit our voices and our gestures to those of the adults, whose unusual proximity is a complicity and a reassurance at the same time. This privilege and joy are all the more acute for our inability to predict these events. Yet, we feel instinctively that only momentous and grave events can so suddenly change our daily routine. But we are children and these events seem to belong to the world of adults—only later would we learn that they were political events and that they had also changed the course of our lives.

It was one day in August 1963 that those elusive events unfolded that have possessed my memory ever since.

Some days earlier, the door to my parents' blue room had been locked because of work being done on the roof, or so they said. While this work goes on, my parents occupy the room that I normally share with my younger sister, while she and I join our grandparents in their room. These seemingly harmless changes will shatter forever the harmony in which I have always lived.

From this day on, the heart of our home would beat elsewhere, and its secret would gravitate around those few blue square meters. The sitting room, which for so long has enjoyed absolute prestige in my eyes, becomes banal with disconcerting suddenness. . . . After this day I will spend hour after hour engrossed in the depths of this memory.

As I become accustomed to this new order of things, a secret sting alerts me to my parents' and grandparents' change of attitude. Like an attentive animal, I keep my eyes, ears, and nostrils on alert, checking the scene at all hours of the day, surrendering with a certain delight to my natural curiosity. I spy upon the slightest gestures of those around me with sustained attention so that nothing escapes me and, because my curiosity is well known, with discretion so as to avoid suspicion.

The scanning of this horizon exhilarates me for days. It will change the course of my life. And it is precisely on one of these days that I spy my grandfather furtively making his way along the hall that leads to the bedrooms. I carefully shut the door to my room, leaving only enough space to watch with my right eye. The strange way I see grandfather walking along the hall first catches my attention, then upsets me and leaves me with a strong sense of alienation in the midst of this setting I know so well. Once grandfather reaches the blue room, he looks to the right, then to the left, then again to the right to be sure that no one has followed him. His three knocks on the door are sharp and distinct. As if by magic, the door opens. Before I can see who or what moved the knob from the inside, grandfather slips into my parents' blue room and the door pulls shut, containing in its secret. My heartbeat quickens, I hold my breath, completely stunned, transfixed by the silence that follows this scene and prolongs its effect. A few minutes later, I venture out a few steps. I recall wanting to listen with my cheek against the wood of the door, but I also remember being suddenly afraid and changing my mind.

Since that day, I hear the three sharp and distinct knocks. It's a sound that will always follow me in my sleep. But that night I sleep with my head full of doors that open mysteriously, of blue prisons and paradises. The next day and the following days, I note my grandfather's repetition of the same little game that becomes for me a magic ritual. While by night an entire procession of colors and images crosses my dreams, by day my life is a feverish anticipation. This anticipation and this fever give the hours an exceptional flavor. I know nothing, and this ignorance feeds my childish fear. I do forget it in rare moments, but mostly I can't help thinking about it very intensely. The three knocks haunt me, entice me, and terrify me at the same time. And one day of this same August of 1963, I meet the secret head on.

My parents have gone to work early in the morning and will not return until the end of the business day. This solves the problem of their whereabouts, but leaves unsettled the problem of those who remain in the house. I quickly check the kitchen to make sure the cook is minding her own business. To overcome my grandparents' watchfulness, I allow them to catch me two or three times lost in the reading of a picture book. As he usually does, my grandfather is sipping a cup of coffee and disappears behind a cloud of smoke. My grandmother keeps her eye on her work as she repeats, "You smoke too much, you drink too much coffee." To which he seldom answers. By the time of his death, grandfather must have smoked an entire tobacco field and drunk a whole coffee plantation.

My little game lasts until my grandparents surrender to the summer heat, probably intensified by the weight of their years, and fall asleep on the deck chairs on the porch in the early afternoon. I silently put away my book and undertake my journey down the hall leading to the blue door, at the mystery's edge. Even the tales I have heard with amazement at dusk have no more fabulous characters than the one I personify at this moment. I duplicate gestures that I have observed grandfather repeat for days. I knock three times on the door. When it opens, I find myself in the presence of what I, at first, take for a shaggy monster sitting on the edge of my parent's bed. A beard rings his face and a gun rests on his right thigh. Our eyes meet for a brief moment of recognition. My terror is indescribable but multiplies when I see this hideous creature become paralyzed by a feeling that strangely resembles my own mixture of surprise and fear, but which I construe as a threat. A moment of white silence, and then I recover just in time to ask myself how such a monster can be affected by a six-year-old child. But that is a fleeting thought. And more concerned about being devoured by this monster than about vain speculations, I run away from the room, screaming all the way through the house and out to the porch. There is a monster in the blue room! At the same time, I am utterly aware that I've committed an enormous blunder. But under the circumstances, I choose a sound spanking from real people over being devoured by this dreadful creature.

Curiously, I am spared the anticipated spanking. My grandparents are speechless. Startled awake by my racket, they first try to calm me by repeating that I'm imagining things. Grandfather manages to bring me back inside the house and offers me a few pennies to buy some candy. But such an offer only a half-hour before a meal violates their own rule—a rule that cost me many a memorable spanking. This unsettles me even more. And this is not the end of my surprise. In fact my amazement only increases when I gradually hear in their voices the muffled sound of insurrection and coups d'états. The long wait for my parents' return does nothing to diminish my anxiety but only increases it because mischief committed in their absence is liable to draw additional punishment.

The exceptional nature of this event is further confirmed by my parents' own unexpected behavior. When my grandparents tell them about what they attribute to my overflowing imagination, my parents lavish attention upon me. By the end of the afternoon, I am treated to a ride to my favorite cousins at Babiole, and to the pleasure of a vanilla ice cream right in the middle of the week and right in the heart of the city.

The next day the roof is miraculously repaired, and the very next day after that, the blue room is once again open to all. It opens its doors to the world but snatches away its secret and takes away a part of my childhood, which returns only as a faint glimmer that shimmers on the water's surface sometimes, from a distant shore.

MARRIAGE BONES

H E SLEEPS IN THE BED beside hers, floating on the air mattress that keeps his skin from troubling into sores.

She has tucked him in according to the rhyme and ritual he once used with their daughters, wondering, as she anchored the blanket at the foot of the bed, how the shrunken man before her could be the same one who loved to dance.

He cries out, and she isn't sure if it is pain, or the language of release sleep brings. A mourning for what this day, just closing, has claimed. She reaches out across the gulf between their beds to touch his back and moves her fingers along the slackened skin to feel the outline of each rib, thinking how bones ought to endure.

At her touch he stirs and settles further into night.

She closes her book and turns off the light. "Bones," she says to herself, trying to think of armature, of structure itself, as open to ruin. She has never, no matter how hard she has tried, been able to picture the start of the disease that is taking him, there in the marrow, and she lies awake, her fingers on his back, and tries to imagine the sinister conquest going on beneath her hand.

With the sound of his breathing as background she has known for forty years, she thinks back over the day.

&   &   &

That morning he had turned to her as she was putting down his breakfast tray, and asked, "Ina . . . where are we today?" and she had quietly, patiently, said that they were "home." "Home," he had repeated as he fought to raise himself from lying to sitting.

Ina helped him up with her steady hands, feeling the strain in her own tired back, and kissed him. "Home, Pelman. You're home with me."

Explaining the transition from the hospital to their house that had happened several times, she got him started on his breakfast and then helped him wash and dress and got him settled in the den. He sat and stared at the shelf of framed photographs beside his chair, arching his numb fingers together into steeples.

He tried, as he did each day, to place himself within the display of captured moments that told the story of his life. Staring at the pictures on the shelf, he saw his daughters, Cam and Brenda, and reached out to touch the raised flowers along the edge of the silver frame. Brenda. He knew those toddler legs that propelled her to the ocean's edge, and the upraised arms scattering water in exclamation at the joy of breaking waves. And there was Cam, her infant features just taking shape, in one of his fedora hats. A flash of memory came to him of her tiny feet on top of his as they danced around the room. He looked at their pictures and he recognized them. Brenda and Cam.

Pelman looked on and saw his own childhood, and Ina's, too, in the brownish photos that were fuzzy and cracked, noticing how their faces were painted in to make them look less brown. He remembered the stiff woolen clothes, which almost made him itch to look at them, and the high shoes with small leather buttons that required a hook. As he peered at the weeping willow backdrop and his own boyhood face, the smell of that day surfaced, of the photographer's cigar smoke, of dust and closed-in heat. He looked at the picture of Ina in curls and a big stiff bow, and he saw the Ina he knew in the determined set of the girl's mouth, in the way she clutched her folding fan.

There were pictures of graduations and grandchildren, and the family portrait with everyone spiffed up and smiling big. He knew that red dress of Ina's, red with little white curved moon shapes, that he had given as a birthday gift.

He found a tether to some thing in each picture, and then he realized, lacing his fingers together tighter and tighter, that he didn't know how long ago any of the moments he was looking at had passed, nor how they fit together to make where he had been.

Telling himself that it would make a whole if he tried, Pelman focused on the posed portrait of his wedding day. He saw how lovely Ina was, her open face and thick dark hair crowned with flowers. And that was him in a black suit, standing next to her, next to Ina, his arm around her waist. *We are gathered here . . .* the words came back to him, but where was "here?" He didn't know. *Here . . . we are gathered here . . .* Reaching out to pick up the picture, he knocked it to the floor.

Hearing something fall, Ina rushed in, hands wet from soaking soiled sheets, and was relieved to find that he was safe. There was nothing to be mopped up or swept up or pieced together. But his apology, and the angry fear she detected in it, inspired her to bend and smooth the hair back from his clay-brown face, and glancing from Pelman to the picture as she put it on the shelf, she stopped and thought, "They're still his eyes."

Often, lately, Ina finds herself searching for recognizable things. Her glance strays sometimes to the figurines that have always stood on the hall table, and she stops before the gold clock they received as a wedding gift, bending to look in at the works and weighted pendulum, safe behind the curved glass front. She picks up the coffee canister and inhales its familiar smell or turns her wedding band round and round and round.

Sometimes she opens the kitchen cabinets and touches the smooth blue mixing bowl that was known by the hands of women she has loved, pausing to recall the chip that reveals the rough tan clay beneath the glaze as she reaches over the rim and down the side to feel her way to the curved bottom that is veiny with dark lines. Remembering her Nana and her mother, who held the marine blue bowl in the bend of an arm while stirring, she can hear the spoon against the crockery and the rhythm of their quiet voices, talking as they worked.

She looked at Pelman as she returned the wedding portrait to the shelf, and having found the known thing, she whispered to herself, "His eyes . . . his eyes are still the same."

And as she set it down and straightened it, she remembered, too, their wedding day: the music and the faces and the heavy, stone smell of the church. The ivory fabric of her dress with its hooks and stays, and the thick scent of lilies that left their mark of orange pollen dust. His arms around her while they danced and their first naked touch. Pelman's soft, umber eyes and the vows they made, which he said were like the skeleton of their life together: their "marriage bones."

Ina looked at the picture and a rush of recollections surfaced from that day. The day that marked *from this day forward. In sickness and in health.*

In the middle of his favorite afternoon program he asked her "Do we have any chocolate, Ina . . . any . . . chocolate in there?" and she reminded him, for the third time that day, that he couldn't eat chocolate, that it made him sick. She tried to say it patiently and handed him the remote control so that he could change the T.V. channels as he wished. And then she sat for a bit, while he flew from program to program in a blur of images and sounds, and she rested from a morning of finding misplaced things and righting what had gone awry. She would stop, she thought, for a minute, and then she would shower and dress while he was occupied with lunch.

Soon she was up and back to waging her war against stains and odors, thinking how little grace there was in the decline of things. On her knees scrubbing, Ina thought that even if she did manage to erase the tale of things spilled and leaked and broken, their traces were imprinted in her head forever, along with the smell of vacant sameness that she identified with hospital food. The smell that met you when you entered the ward, the smell underneath the covered dinner tray, she could remember into the present at any time.

And then Pelman was calling her and she got up and rinsed her hands and went to him, hearing in his voice a fury that had been part of their lives. The anger at reductions, the raging for a wider definition of himself. She heard him calling for help and she was there, answering his need.

To have and to hold.

He kicked when she brought dry clothes, and there it was, rising up, the fire she knew as his, fierce man of infantile strength, kicking with withered calves where the blood once coursed. He kicked and shook his fist and looked away to save them both from shame as she reached beneath his knees to lift him for the diaper. She talked steadily while she fixed him, in the reassuring, cheerful voice she had used with their girls, and when she met the eyes that had that morning linked her to their past, he asked her in his look if she didn't know, if she didn't know that he was proud.

As she eased his foot into a pant leg he shoved her hands away and declared, silently, jaw clenched, that he didn't need her help. She left the room and waited, just outside the door, returning ten minutes later to find him in the same spot, his trousers halfway on. But when she bent her aching back again to offer help, he kicked and shouted and shook his fist, refusing her healing cleaning feeding hands.

He pushed away her hands, the hands for which he often reached when he woke, blank and then smiling, whispering that it was her, her, he had been dreaming of.

In sickness and in health.

After he had his nap and was propped in his chair for the talk shows, Ina saw him wincing and she asked him, her touch upon his arm, if he was hurting. He turned away and frowned, as if speaking it would give it life. But she went and got his pills, thinking how he had spoken only once of insurance and house notes and what they had saved up. They had never talked of death, and now he took the pill she offered in silence as she watched his jaw flex against the pain.

"Are Cam and Brenda coming," he asked Ina. "Are they coming tonight?" She reminded him that Brenda had the kids and Cam would be there that weekend. He smiled and said, "Ina . . . maybe she'll bring fudge," and they laughed, together, then, at the family joke told for years and years. Ina sat with him and they relived the time when Cam, barely five-years-old, had discovered that Ina had never had chocolate growing up. She had cried over Ina's poverty, and spent her next allowance on the biggest piece of chocolate fudge she could afford for her mother. "She's adopted it as a cause," Pelman said. "As if she's trying to help you make up for lost time," and every Christmas and birthday she sent fudge.

They laughed and Ina said to Pelman, pulling him close with old times, "Remember when Brenda fixed that dinner, serving noodles that hadn't been cooked?" Yes, yes they both remembered. And he said, "Remember the first time we took them to the beach?" Ina turned off the T.V. and they sat in the den, as the afternoon settled into evening, and assembled pieces of the past they shared, remembering the time his Uncle Russell had backed his car all the way over that bridge, and the crazy stories he told. As they talked, Pelman thought how they had traveled a long way together, he and Ina, and how it had been hard and it had been sweet. They sat together in the last blue light of the day and his eyes said, "Look, Ina. Look where we've been."

From this . . . from this day forward.

Soon he was asking when they would eat and she was answering, again and again, that it would be soon. Focused on remaining joys, he watched T.V. and he ate, asking all day for sweets. If she wasn't careful, he would make his way to the pantry and she would find him eating jam straight from the jar. After dinner she gave him three helpings of ice cream, and still, he held out his bowl.

While Pelman watched the news, Ina got ready for bed, rubbing cold cream into her face at the bathroom sink and looking forward to propping up in bed with a book and having the chocolate she had saved for a special treat. After Pelman was asleep she would have her quiet time, the part of the day she claimed for herself.

And then, from the bathroom, she heard him fall.

He had gone on his own, stumbling to the kitchen without his walker, in search of something sweet. She heard him fall, taking down cups and saucers as he went, and when she came to the kitchen doorway, she saw him sitting on the floor, clutching the little paper bag of chocolate she had saved as he crammed the candy into his mouth.

Ina stood watching him, open-mouthed, and then yelled and left him on the floor with the chocolate on his hands and his clothes, and slammed the door. Sitting on the back porch, she tried to bring down her anger as her pulse pounded and her eyes filled with tears.

She reminded herself, out loud, that he didn't know, he didn't know, that he was merely seeking the small good thing that was fixed, beyond reasoning, in his mind. And she felt small that she had hidden the candy in the cabinet, all the way to the back, and let her anger get out of control. It was such a little thing, she said, sobbing, and it was Pelman who was dying, after all.

When she returned from the porch, she saw in those umber eyes, before he masked it with anger, that he didn't understand, that he was scared. And then he clutched the candy bag, empty now, and shook his fist. Shook his fist and banged it, scattering pieces of broken china across the tiled floor. Taking what was promised so long ago, that where their lives had brought them could not have been conceived.

In sickness and in health . . . To have and to hold . . .

Taking what was promised, each to the other, and taking what was hers.
She let him spend his rage and then helped him up and into the bedroom,

where she cleaned his hands and sponged him off and got him into dry pajamas, knowing that the time when they would pay for his chocolate binge was still to come. She tucked him in and when he met her eyes that time, they said, "Look, Ina. Look where we are."

She lies beside his sleeping body now, and tries to think of the "her" before the "them." Closing her eyes, she struggles to picture only herself, thinking that surely she has her own story, surely she does. What with cooking since she was eight and helping her mother with housekeeping and catering jobs, minding and dressing and plaiting hair, and watching the grandkids in that gap between school and Brenda's coming home, she tries to see herself. She's been cleaning and feeding and listening all her life, and Pelman often said she "didn't work."

She looks over to his dresser at his desk set and plaque from work, thinking how proud he had been to be "the first Negro clerk" at that job. The day he had retired and come home with a box of papers and things from his desk, he had looked so lost. He had put the box down on the floor and gone directly to bed, and it had sat there until she unpacked and displayed a few of the things, and put the rest away.

Pelman had loved his job and he had loved to dance, she thinks, looking at him raised upon the mattress filled with air. How long, she wonders, since they had danced? He had been fluid and graceful, whether he was Lindy Hopping or doing a waltz. She can't remember when they last danced.

The sound of his breathing as background, Ina whispers, "When did we dance?" unable to imagine her own tired body feeling light and free enough to move that way. She has noticed that she can't get her breath after bending and lifting him, but she knows, too, that she can't give in to being as exhausted as she is.

She's tired and afraid, and although she doesn't know it, she calls out, too, sometimes, in the accepting night. She calls for strength and help. She calls his name.

'Til death . . .

Can this be the man, she thinks, reaching over to listen with her hand to his breathing in and out, who inspired and enraged, delighted and disappointed her? Whom she has had and held through all the gifts and trespasses that are carried in the streams of time and love?

'Til death do us part.

Ina rests her fingers on the bones of Pelman's ribcage, which remind her of arching cathedral beams, built to house the tender, sacred heart.

Her hand travels down, over the last curving rib, and she turns to face the dark.

SHOEMAKER ARNOLD

SHOEMAKER ARNOLD STOOD at the doorway of his little shoemaker shop, hands on hips, his body stiffened in that proprietorial and undefeated stubbornness, announcing, not without some satisfaction, that if in his life he had not been triumphant, neither had the world defeated him. It would be hard, though, to imagine how he could be defeated, since he exuded such a hard tough unrelenting cantankerousness, gave off such a sense of readiness for confrontation, that if Trouble had to pick someone to clash with, Shoemaker Arnold would not be the one. To him, the world was his shoemaker shop. There he was master and anyone entering would have to surrender not only to his opinion on shoes and leather and shoemaker apprentices, but to his views on politics, women, religion, flying objects, or any of the myriad subjects he decided to discourse upon, so that over the years he had arrived at a position where none of the villagers bothered to dispute him, and to any who dared maintain a view contrary to the one he was affirming, he was quick to point out, "This place is mine. Here, I do as I please. I say what I want. Who don't like it, the door is open."

His wife had herself taken that advice many years earlier, and had moved not only out of his house but out of the village, taking with her their three children, leaving him with his opinions, an increasing taste for alcohol, and the tedium of having to prepare his own meals. It is possible that he would have liked to take one of the village girls to live with him, but he was too proud to accept that he had even that need, and he would look at the girls go by outside his shop, hiding, behind his dissatisfied scowl a fine, appraising, if not lecherous, eye; but if one of them happened to look in, he would snarl at her, "What you want here?" So that between him and the village girls there existed this teasing challenging relationship of antagonism and desire, the girls themselves walking with greater flourish and style when they went past his shoemaker shop, swinging their backsides and cutting their eyes, and he, scowling, dissatisfied.

With the young men of the village his relationship was no better. As far as he was concerned none of them wanted to work and he had no intention of letting them use his shoemaker shop as a place to loiter. Over the years he had taken on numerous apprentices, keeping them for a month or two and sometimes for just a single day, then getting rid of them; and it was not until Norbert came to work with him that he had had what could be considered regular help.

Norbert, however, was no boy. He was a drifter, a rum drinker, and exactly that sort of person that one did not expect Arnold to tolerate for more than five minutes. Norbert teased the girls, was chummy with the loiterers, gambled, drank too much, and, anytime the spirit moved him, would up and take off and not return for as much as a month. Arnold always accepted him back. Of course he quarrelled, he complained, but the villagers who heard him were firm in their reply: "Man, you like it. You like Norbert going and coming when he please, doing what he want. You like it."

More than his leavings, Norbert would steal Arnold's money, sell a pair of shoes, lose a side of shoes, charge people and pocket the money, not charge some people at all, and do every other form of wickedness to be imagined in the circumstances. It must have been that because Norbert was so indisputably in the wrong that it moved Arnold to exhibit one of his rare qualities, compassion. It was as if Arnold needed Norbert as the means through which to declare not only to the world, but to declare to himself, that he had such a quality; to prove to himself that he was not the cantankerous person people made him out to be. So, on those occasions when he welcomed back the everlasting prodigal, Arnold, forgiving and compassionate, would be imbued with the idea of his own goodness, and he would feel that in the world, truly, there was not a more generous soul than he.

Today was one such day. Two weeks before Christmas, Norbert had left to go for a piece of ice over by the rumshop a few yards away. He had returned the day before. "Yes," thought Arnold, "look at me, I not vex." Arnold was glad for the help, for he had work that people had already paid advances on and would be coming in to collect before New Year's day. That was one thing he appreciated about Norbert. Norbert was faithful, but Norbert had to get serious about the right things. He was faithful to too many frivolous things. He was faithful to the girl who dropped in and wanted a dress, to a friend who wanted a nip. A friend would pass in a truck and say, "Norbert, we going San Fernando." Norbert would put down the shoes he was repairing, jump on the truck without a change of underwear even, and go. It wasn't rum. It was some craziness, something inside him that just took hold of him. Sometimes, a week later he would return, grimy, stale, thin, as if he had just hitch-hiked around the world in a coal bin, slip into the shop, sit down and go back to work as if nothing out of the way had happened. And he could work when he was working. Norbert could work. Any shop in Port of Spain would be glad to have him. Faithful worker. Look at that! This week when most tradesmen had already closed up for Christmas there was Norbert working like a machine to get people's shoes ready. Appreciation. It shows appreciation. People don't have appreciation again, but Norbert had appreciation. Is how you treat people, he thought. You have to understand them. Look how cool he here working in my shoemaker shop this big Old Year's day when all over the island people feteing.

At the door he was watching two girls going down the street, nice, young, with the spirit of rain and breezes about them. Then his eyes picked up a donkey cart approaching slowly from the direction of the Main Road which led to Sangre Grande, and he stood there in front his shoemaker shop, his lips pulled back and looked at the cart come up and go past. Old Man Moses, the charcoal burner, sat dozing in the front, his chin on his chest, and the reins in his lap. To the back sat a small boy with a cap on and a ragged shirt, his eyes alert, his feet hanging over the sides of the cart, one hand resting on a small brown and white dog sitting next to him.

Place dead, he thought, seeing the girls returning; and, looking up at the sky, he saw the dark clouds and that it was going to rain and he looked at the car. "Moses going up in the bush. Rain going to soak his tail," he said. And as if suddenly irritated by that thought, he said, "You mean Moses aint have no family he could spend New Year's by," his tone drumming up his outrage. "Why his family can't take him in and let him eat and drink and be merry for the New Year instead of going up in the bush for rain to soak his tail? That is how we living in this world," he said, seating himself on the workbench and reaching for the shoe to be repaired. "That is how we living. Like beast."

"Maybe he want to go up in the bush," Norbert said. "Maybe he going to attend his coal pit, to watch it that the coals don't burn up and turn powder."

"Like blasted beast," Arnold said. "Beast," as if he had not heard Norbert.

But afterwards, after he had begun to work, had gotten into the rhythm of sewing and cutting and pounding leather, and had begun the soft firm waxing of the twine, the sense of the approaching New Year hit him and he thought of the girls and the rain, and he thought of his own life and his loneliness and his drinking and of the world and of people, people without families, on pavements and in orphanages and those on park benches below trees. "The world have to check up on itself," he said. "The world have to check up. . . . And you, Norbert, you have to check up on yourself," he said broaching for the first time the matter of Norbert's leaving two weeks before Christmas and returning only yesterday. "I not against you. You know I not against you. I talk because I know what life is. I talk because I know about time. Time is all we have, boy. Time. . . . A Time to live and a time to die. You hear what I say. Norbert?"

"What you say?"

"I say, it have a time to live and a time to die. . . . You think we living?"

Norbert leaned his head back a little, and for a few moments he seemed to be gazing into space, thinking, concentrating.

"We dying," he said, "we dying no arse."

"You damn right. Rum killing us. Rum. Not bombs or Cancer or something sensible. Rum. You feel rum should kill you?"

Norbert drew the twine out of the stitch and smiled.

"But in this place, rum must kill you. What else here could kill a man? What else to do but drink and waste and die. That is why I talk. People don't understand me when I talk; but that is why I talk."

Norbert threaded the twine through the stitch with his smile and in one hand he held the shoe and with the other he drew out the twine: "We dying no arse!" as if he had hit on some truth to be treasured now. "We dying . . . no arse."

"That is why I talk. I want us . . . you to check up, to put a little oil in your lamp, to put a little water in your wine."

Norbert laughed. He was thinking with glee, even as he said it, "We dying no arse, all o'we, everybody. Ha ha ha ha" and he took up his hammer and started to pound in the leather over the stitch "Ha ha ha ha ha!"

Arnold had finished the shoe he was repairing and he saw now the pile of shoes in the shoemaker shop. "One day I going to sell out all the shoes that people leave here. They hurry hurry for you to repair them. You use leather, twine, nails, time. You use time, and a year later, the shoes still here watching you. Going to sell out every blasted one of them this New Year."

"All o'we, every one of us," Norbert chimed.

"That is why this shoemaker shop always like a junk heap."

"Let us send for a nip of rum, nuh," Norbert said, and as Arnold looked at him. "I will buy. This is Old Year's, man."

"Rum?" Arnold paused. "How old you is, boy?"

"Twenty-nine."

"Twenty-nine! You making joke. You mean I twenty-one years older than you? We dying in truth. Norbert, we dying. Boy, life really mash you up." And he threw down the shoe he was going to repair.

"We have three more shoes that people coming for this evening," Norbert said, cautioning. "Corbie shoes, Synto shoes and Willie Paul sandals."

Arnold leaned and picked up the shoe again. "Life aint treat you good at all. I is twenty-one years older than you? Norbert, you have to check up," he said. "Listen, man, you getting me frighten. When I see young fellars like you in this condition I does get frighten. . . . Listen. Norbert, tell me something! I looking mash up like you? Eh? Tell me the truth. I looking mash up like you?"

Norbert said, "We dying no arse, all o'we everybody."

"No. Serious. Tell me, I looking mash up like you?"

"Look, somebody by the door," Norbert said.

"What you want?" Arnold snapped. It was one of the village girls, a plump one with a bit of her hair plastered down over her forehead making her look like a fat pony.

"You don't have to shout at me, you know. I come for Synto shoes."

"Well, I don't want no loitering by the door. Come inside and siddown and wait. I now finishing it." He saw her turn to look outside and she said something to somebody. "Somebody there with you?"

"She don't want to come in."

"Let her come in too. I don't want no loitering by the door. This is a business place." He called out, "Come in. What you hanging back for?"

The girl who came in was the one that reminded him of rain and moss and leaves. He tried to look away from her, but he couldn't. And she too was looking at him.

"You 'fraid me?" And he didn't know how his voice sounded, though at that moment he thought he wanted it to sound tough.

"A little," she said.

"Siddown," he said, and Norbert's eyes nearly popped open. What was he seeing? Arnold was getting up and taking the chair from the corner, dusting it too. "Sit down. The shoes will finish just now."

She watched him work on the shoe and the whole shoemaker shop was big like all space and filled with breathlessness and rain and moss and green leaves.

"You is Synto daughter?"

"Niece," she said.

And when he was finished repairing the shoes, he looked around for a paper bag in which to put them, because he saw that she had not come with any bag herself. "When you coming for shoes you must bring something to wrap it in. You can't go about with shoes in your hand just so."

"Yes," she said. "Yes." Quickly as if wanting to please him.

He found some old newspaper he was saving to read when he had time and he folded the shoes in it and wrapped it with twine and he gave it to her and she took it and she said "thank you" with that funny little face and that voice that made something inside him ache and she left, leaving the breathlessness in the shoemaker shop and the scent of moss and aloes and leaves and it was like if all his work was finished. And when he caught his breath he pushed his hand in his pocket and brought out money and said to Norbert, "Go and buy a nip." And they drank the nip, the two of them, and he asked Norbert, "Where you went when you went for the ice?" And he wasn't really listening for no answer, for he had just then understood how Norbert could, how a man could, leave and go off. He had just understood how he could leave everything and go just so.

"You had a good time?" Though those weren't the right words. A good time! People didn't leave for a good time. It was for something more. It was out of something deeper, a call, something that was awakened in the blood, the mind. "You know what I mean?"

"Yes," Norbert said, kinda sadly, soft, and frightened for Arnold but not wanting to show it.

Arnold said, "I dying too." And then he stood up and said sort of sudden, "This place need some pictures. And we must keep paper bags like in a real 'establishment,' " and with that same smile he said, "Look at that, eh. That girl say she 'fraid me a little. Yes, I suppose that is correct. A little. Not that she 'fraid me. She 'fraid me a little."

When they closed the shop that evening they both went up Tapana Trace by Britto. Britto was waiting for them.

"Ah," he said, "Man reach. Since before Christmas I drinking and I can't get drunk. It aint have man to drink rum with again. But I see man now."

They went inside and Britto cleared the table and put three bottles of rum on it, one before each one of them, a mug of water and a glass each, and they began to drink.

Half an hour later the *parang* band came in and they sang an *aguanaldo* and a *joropo* and they drank and Norbert started to sing with them the nice festive Spanish music that made Arnold wish he could cry. And then it was night and the *parang* band was still there and Britto wife family came in and a couple of Britto friends and the women started dancing with the little children and then Josephine, Britto neighbor, held on to Arnold and pulled him onto the floor to dance, and he tried to dance a little and then he sat down and they took down the gas lamp and pumped it and Britto's wife brought out the portion of *lappe* that she had been cooking on a wood fire in the yard and they ate and drank and with the music and the children and the women, everything, the whole thing was real sweet. It was real sweet. And Norbert, more drunk than sober, sitting in a corner chatting down Clemencia sister picked up another bottle of rum, broke the seal and about to put it to his lips, caught Arnold's eye and hesitated, then he put it to his lips again. He said, "Let me dead." And Arnold sat and thought about this girl, the one that filled the world with breathlessness and the scent of aloes and leaves and moss and he felt if she was sitting there beside him he would be glad to dead too.

CLARENCE MAJOR

CITY FLESH
AND COUNTRY MANNERS

My mother says she feels too much self pity. After all these years. . . . What is going on inside her?

The town people seem friendly in a small way. What is going on inside them? Why are they so quiet in summer days and where are their children? The lawns are pretty like my mother's. Fathers play baseball with their boys. Everything in me resents it—the father I never walked with. Baseball was a game played under blue night lights. First base blues, second base blues, third base . . . home runs and strikes!

My mother never learned to drive a car. My father drove balls into left field. The night was burning in my guts! I was too young to write well, my headache was in my head—not in the pavement. I trembled. Not the street. All this dishonesty is too much to look back on. Rain on one side of the street, dry on the other. This town was hell. Bird shit sliding down the glass of taverns where I first learned to drink.

I picked up a hotel phone. Is Wolf up there? I was Casey. Jimmy was tigerboy. Forty-seventh and Cottage was the jazz world. Miles played there. The elevators were padded. Wolf was deadly. Wolf's room: one small cot against the wall, a desk, a chair. A huge blonde woman on the bed. And there was Wolf's piano! He loved it and played it. The Spanish girl from down the hall came and sang alongside it as tigerboy and I propped ourselves against the wall with an air of jaded authority. We were too young, too pretty! The blonde bitched about the lack of money. The Spanish girl in black and gold tights rehearsed with Wolf who was watched by his woman—the blonde. We looked too. I sat on an ashtray, burning my seat.

340

Then Wolf played and since tigerboy was a genius at the keyboard—and didn't approve (and I wasn't impressed either!) we exchanged glances, said nothing. Wolf had a facial scar. He scratched it. When he spoke he was mad, he said: the weird stranger comes cloaked in his own flesh. A passionate pig—he dares us where we stand, this pose! He seems solid in the rain, even charming—while soaked, sad, and sucked by the whim of the moon. The stranger comes, as with you two—soaked in tough skin! Like Rimbaud. He comes with more than lust. His anger is there, too. He throbs with the urge to poke fun. He turns and is imperishable in his turn, as he vanishes in the mist. So romantic, this guy! I thought; tigerboy said, the blonde winked.

Spanish took me in the hallway, said: he's a criminal, the Marquis de Sade, he sells dope; he, she said, is backward—crazed; some sort of Flaw of his generation. But he's optimistic—watch his chin! He can't sleep. His own face multiplies in dreams. He sees himself coming along an incline, he stumbles. Thinks he's beautiful. He carries plagues with him. He looms into a monster. Be careful around him! My eyes burn, she said, watching the personality combinations he produces!

Tigerboy—years later—told me he was in the dark outhouse. Chickens clucking below, eating the stuff; a summer day, a country boy. He clutched a hen with both hands and impaled it on his organ. Being Catholic he never overcame the guilt of the hot anal cavity, the chicken fear pulling his shaft. Poor boy, the scream and his grandmother chasing him with her broom! Which reminded me of the girl next door discovering my sex. And with glazed eyes teaching me how to unbuckle her leg braces; how to put my "tale" in her "hole." We were cannibals with cunning logic. We ripped the heart out of caste mixing. A black tree trunk drenched in yellow fuzz, from root to branch. I also rode a wild west horse in a vampire movie! Pleasure was a thing of the future! A large mouth—teeth, tongue, jaws, pulled at me, causing my head to buzz twenty years later.

My mother, the town people, Miles, Cottage, the Casey I was, my memory of Wolf and tigerboy, all changed; I walked upside-down against the sky. But my eyes were right-side up! Snow and ice, cold winds from the lake whipped me toward home. Odor of exhaust fumes and no place to be myself! Frozen to the bone, shaking—while my red eyes searched for the next hour. Who could help me, then? Not the president! Not the guru!

The dishonesty is necessary? My first grown-up lover was a woman whose lips drove me into a new world of cursed mystery! At twenty-three truth does not count! I said to her, You are silent behind your rasping voice. Church bells ring in it; jewhorns and cool centuries rest behind your bright, light erotic facade. I like the way you don't have to run for cover. Even when they had you twisted in agony at the foot of the cross, your son dying up there, nails in his feet, in his hands. You are your own woman—yet you're not, as the screaming—with no known origin—goes on down the years! Your red garment was ripped on twigs of male glory; the silence behind your cry is a response, I guess, to the lost witch in the early craft. The terror is not yours alone. *Smile, you're on!*

You are always on and it's never the solution: it is this now, itself, the precise way another woman, a friend, not a lover, tried to resolve the dilemma: by making a connection between herself and this—she was a white girl standing on a street handling out leaflets to a cause. She was a girl standing in a black section passing out ideas she did not fully understand but she meant well. She was standing on centuries of white ideas, passing out, finally from failure. She went to work as a restaurant girl. Suddenly she turned completely around, the biggest smile in her face: teeth—and behind her: mirror, flowers, coffee cups.

I moved to a city where I could feel intense among rug dye factories and bull fighters who kill paper bulls in bohemian apartments. This city was full of virgins trying to discover a way to live without men—men were so bad. If a woman then wanted to have a child she could impregnate herself with a chemical from her own body. That's how detached a lot of people had become. There's no metaphor for such a place. Anyone could be shot or made king. Ingrown interests and cold print were common. I found a way, though, to expand laughter. My father was now dead.

I said nothing that I had not tried out first. These were not the iron years for money, where I punched a clock and welded metal together.

That was earlier, sometimes in a crane at the controls looking down on men who hated me, thinking what would happen if I—accidentally—dropped ten tons of steel on them. They would not get to punch their time cards anymore—no more overtime. All the hours would end. That was back in the town of dirty el trains. They stop. The sun shines, at times, into those moving boxes. There was always something to drain my energy, stifle my imagination. I smoked cigarettes like a tough guy and tried to look like Jack London at the furnace door. I made my surveying mark of beauty. Saw myself ripped to pieces on the rails as the train shot up out of the ground at Roosevelt Road.

But all that has ended and with it my attempt to speak profoundly to people. Jesus, I used to say things like: it is the wish of the general public to conclude that you—black man—enjoy your so-called inferiority though I, from the start, could have told them that you did not, technologically, take no shit off nobody. I went on like that raving about the immortal leadership spirit of the underground railway, about the black women with glittering ornaments. They wore gold, flat plates in their lower lips hundreds of years before slavery. And *that* was beauty. I cried out about poverty and death in Mexico! I felt my own face. It was a billboard facing a Mexican marketplace; beggars whimpering; people calling—Help me! Tears and dogs! Bony children in doorways; shitting in the sand, crazy with hunger. The ocean there leaves for the sky—leaving its mood in the people. A group of tourists snapped pictures of the misery, the basket-making! That was a brief stay but I knew then that I had never known real poverty; that my story about the black woman who'd give a vicious dog a place to sleep was rather touching but not profound.

Better to be quiet, as on a Sunday morning as in a green telephone booth, unclear like an old woman searching the coin return slot dressed in 1923 high heels—the laced up kind. I claim this view for all time. She goes into the booth almost too quickly as though something were urgent, pretends to look for a thing in her pocket. Black coat and thin white face at the top of it.

I know the slot is always empty; as she searches it, the phone to her ear, pretending to talk. In the ten years it was possible to run into that sort of pain.

I worked sheers with guys who threw ten gauge—sixty by a hundred and twenty sheets around like paper napkins. That's how mean the world was then. They were racists, too. They walked through pigeon shit. All for two twenty an hour and union dues knocking the hell out of the need to take off.

I moved to a city where I could see steam coming out of the mouths of people still breathing. I smelled whisky on breaths. Women understood me. I did not understand them, their trembling faces, their starts. The damage in the rooms was fierce! We all slept like rough savages. Some of these ladies floated up into another world—so intense were the pressures around them. They left babies in cribs, got lost in love groans, said to hell with guest rooms, fell in love on the kitchen floor. Possessed with keys to their own dark places, they turned mad! They broke down before drunk husbands, clutching yellow rent stubs and smearing their blood on Sears and Roebuck furniture. They stayed hidden in corners even when new boyfriends came.

There wasn't a new flute in the world that could bring a smug chant to their ears. Guys—as nightriders—not on horseback, but in Buicks, were arriving at eighty miles an hour. Even I, the ex-Casey, came like this. I cared no more for the shut-in maid either nor did I wish to serenade her below the window; nor climb the vines of the castle wall. My concern was for the tough boogie-woogie girl with sweat under her arms. The pill did not rhyme with castle!

The night still burned me out; the Spanish woman warned me well; the large mouth of pleasure still loomed in the logic of the future; my honesty became the way through necessary mystery. My lets and lips trembled when I promised a woman I wanted to marry that she and I would sun on beaches with gold for sand. No church bells rang behind her gentle words.

I waited wet in winter sunlight. She never came. What will I do alone? Against that question rests the quiet one of privacy, I slept in the sweat of her armpit. In our furious need she went right on swooning under me on the portable sofa as I was grave and deep in my mission in her, trying to make her swell with child. You know how triangles revitalize everything? I played with the idea with my tongue. At such moments I was wind or fire—or nothing definite. Sex or guilt, white or gray, her metabolism, her fat, my generation, her age, speech or singing, none of these made any sacred sense. Her smile could not be captured in a restaurant mirror. She was Woman—on her cool back with one blue stockinged leg up, toes wiggling; no wedding ring on her ring finger. Yet I planned to stay in her city: deep in the narrow streets, expecting nothing but blood, failure and wings in an emergency. I was planning to stay.

I said: I consist of all that you are though I take issue with the ache in my own body. I might have gone flying over dye factories—but no, rather than leaning against my own death at fifteen thousand feet above the earth in a chartered radar equipped plane with deep sorrow, moving geography, trying not to do something irrational I sweated my way along the floor of an orgy of heavy laughter, dry tongues; voiceless friction, dry areas; yellow eyes, red skin, sharp fingernails; breasts uneven and staccato teeth that left prints; I climbed into frowns, broke my way through polka dot shame and awkward rhythm. Pried opened and entered salient spirits; slept well while growling, yodeling and chewing sounds surrounded me like a circle of Indians about to kill George Armstrong Custer.

Up in the aircraft I might have watched the propeller wave at the wavers below. Innocent fun. People stuck to the ground are hard to figure out. With the others I could have wondered at my own unhappiness—flying so low to the angle of the sun showing us the plane moving in shadow down there across the pink earth. Tits for mountains.

I might have been too furious to read the cold print of the magazines. But I would have been moving out. And I might have looked to the dark side of myself—not for perception or insight but for a simple symbol—a tree, a sunrise, an ocean, a confession, quiet and in myself, to go along with one of these—a self-confession of modesty before the overwhelming immodest presence of Everything.

Well, my short dictionary of philosophy was simple: I still did not understand how a period stopped. Metaphors could not explain bohemia, time clocks, the death of my father, the coldness of steel, and for lack of an answer I got together a gang of shadows and captured the black angels, let them down into the slow waters of my own bad eyesight. When I slept deeper I saw them riding seaweeds and seahorses. They lynched my mother at daybreak; short devils danced around their activity, singing death and rebirth songs.

I now find pieces of my mother's flesh and hair in my bowl of soup. I tore open the chest of history, and hundreds of years of blood and misery poured out. I became the king with deep holes for eyes. I prayed for goodness but kept doing all the wrong things. I wore a shaggy beard. Gave up the thought of love—it was a hopeless situation. Wore robes of silk, carried a tall staff. Lectured my subjects on the town I left, Mexico, the lack of clarity in slots and customs. Made them swoon to my descriptions of snake men dancing around the victims of justice in the cellar.

They had no idea the city was this fearful. Is human flesh cooked here? You better believe it! The king is the first to taste it—though he has no taste for it. It is his sensitivity that compels him.

Those were bleak times. I pulled through and went on tour with a mike on a string around my neck—I earned a living that way. To pay the rent people speak. I spoke to Puerto Rican, Italian, Negro mothers sunning their infants of copper faces—of ironstone. Actually, I came close to singing hymns: iron words on Sundays. Yet not even with the best will or intentions could I break and grind their interests to the smoothness of understanding.

My tongue got caught on the inside of my own lower and upper borders. Yet I continued to speak, even to the empty benches. I gauged myself. I moved to another part of the city where violence was less intense. The key to my dark apartment always stuck in the door.

I tried to go on vacation and discovered I could not leave myself. Mouth to mouth attempts with trial mates did not help. Lunch with stars did not either. The flag up its pole, morning warm as the space between breasts was little comfort. Steam coming out of people now only meant they were overheated.

To be in the middle of somebody—except myself—seemed less reassuring. Fat, hair and skin, noses—ears: all seemed so difficult to touch. The hard frown of concentration on trying to be good again came like the downward pressure of an airplane beginning to descend. Yet I watched people around me pull apart and understand nothing as they turned. Eyes and seeing, hearing and ears: explained nothing. No boogie-woogie girl could see me through. Nor could I regress.

Faith would not let me join the others with cocked ears; swearing before food. It does not matter that one brought barley, another cream. Walter or John. With horns on his plate, one prayed to the devil. Someone crunched an apple.

It was no help at all that a speaker spoke of starving children in Africa, India, South America. Everybody had fun? Maybe—we rode to the island, some went on boats up the river and it seemed like happiness. Roving the hills, hiding and seeking each other.

When the food ran out I helped them connect our net to the net in the sand and we caught fish. But my heart wasn't in it. We drove our words into stone—yet they refused to stay. So we joined hands and closed our eyes.

PAULE MARSHALL

SOME GET WASTED

A SHOUT HURLED AFTER HIM down the rise: "Run, baby. Run, fool!" and Hezzy knew, the terror snapping the tendons which strung together his muscles, that he had been caught in a sneak, was separated from his People, alone, running with his heart jarring inside his narrow chest, his stomach a stone weight and his life riding on each rise and plunge of his legs. While far behind, advancing like pieces of the night broken off, were the Crowns. He couldn't dare turn to look, couldn't place their voices because of the wind in his ears, but he knew they were Crowns. They had to be.

"Run, baby, run. You running real pretty, but we's with you all the way. . . ."

And he was running pretty. So that he began to feel an ease and lightness. His feet skimmed the path while his arms cut away the air around him. But then he had learned how to run from the master. Him and the Little People was always hanging around the block watching Turner and the Big People practice their running. Turner was always saying, "Dig, you studs, one thing, don't never let another club catch you in a sneak. Especially you Little People. Don't never get too far away from the rest of the guys. In this club when we go down everybody goes together. When we split, everybody splits together. But if you should get caught in a sneak, haul ass out of there. Run, baby. Your legs is your life then, you can believe that."

Yeah, Turner would dig the way he was running. He would go round the block tomorrow, all cool like nothing had happened and say—ignoring Turner but talking loud enough so's he hear—"Man, dig what happened to me last night after the action in the park. Them dirty Crowns caught me in a sneak, man. Come chasing me all over the fuggen place. But I put down some speed on them babies and burned their eyes."

346

Even now, their jeers seemed fainter, further away: "Run, baby . . . like we said, you running pretty. . . ." The night was pulling them back, making them part of it again. Man, he could outrun those punks any time, any place. His heart gave a little joyous leap and he sprinted cleanly ahead, the pebbles scattering underfoot.

The day, this night, his flight had begun a week ago. The Little People had gotten the word that something was up and had gone over to the Crib where the Noble Knights, their Big People, hung out. The Crib was the square of bare earth in front of the decaying brownstone where Turner lived.

"The jive is on," Turner said as soon as they were assembled.

And before the words were barely out, Sizzle who lived only to fight, said, "Like I been telling you, man, it's about time. Them Crowns been messing all over us. Pulling sneaks in our turf. Stomping and wasting our Little People like they did Duke. Slapping around our broads when they come outta school . . . Man, I hate them studs. I hate them dirty Crown Buggers."

"Man, cool your role," Turner said. Then: "Like I said, the jive is on. And strong this time. We ain't just goin' down in their turf and stomp the first Crown we see and split, like we always do. This is gonna be organized. We already got word to the Crowns and they're ready. Now dig. Next Monday, Memorial Day, we look. Over in Prospect Park, on the Hill. Time the parade ends and it starts getting dark, time the Crowns show, we lock. Now pick up on the play. . . ."

Hezzy, crowded with his guys on the bottom step of the stoop listened, his stomach dropping as it did on the cyclone in Coney Island. Going down with the Big People at last! Down with the hearts! And on Memorial Day when every club in the city would be gangbusting. The Italian cats in South Brooklyn, them Spanish studs in East Harlem. And on the Hill—Massacre Hill they called it— where many a stud had either built his rep or gotten wasted.

He had heard how three years ago on Easter Sunday when the Noble Knights clashed with the Crusaders on the Hill, Turner had gotten the bullet crease on his forehead and had started his bad rep. Heard how the cat had gone to church packing his zip that morning and gone down to lock with the Crusaders that afternoon.

Hezzy looked up over the other heads at the bullet crease. It was like the cat's skin was so tough the bullet had only been able to graze it. It was like nothing or nobody could waste the cat. You could tell from his eyes. The iris fixed dead-center in the whites and full of dark swirls of colors like a marble and cold, baby. When Turner looked sideways he never shifted his eyes, but turned his head, slow, like time had to wait on him. Man, how them simple chicks goofed behind that look. The stud didn't even have to talk to 'em. Just looked and they was ready to give him some. . . .

"Dig, we ain't wearing no club jackets neither," Turner was saying. "Cause they ain't no need to let The Man know who we is. And another thing, it's gonna be dark out there, so watch whose head you busting." The unmoving eyes fixed the Crosstown Noble Knights. "You studs down?"

"We down, man."

"You all down?" His chin flicked toward the Little People at the bottom of the stoop.

"Yeah, we down," Hezzy answered.

"We don't want none of you Little People coming up weak," Turner said.

"Man, I ain't saying we ain't got some punks in the Division, but we leaves them studs home when we bopping."

All around the eyes glanced his way, but he kept his gaze on Turner.

"What's your name again, man?" Turner said and there was a tightness in his voice.

"Hezzy, man," and he touched the turned down brim of the soiled sailor hat he always wore where his name was emblazoned in black.

"You suppose to be president of the Little People since Duke got wasted?"

"Ain't no suppose, man. I am the president."

"All right, my man, but cool your role, you dig?"

He was all flushed inside. His head felt like it was twisted behind drinking some wine—and when the meeting was over and he and his little guys were back on their corner, they pooled their coins for a pint of Thunderbird and drank in celebration of how bad and cool he had been in front of the Big People.

Late that night he wandered alone and high through his turf. And all around him the familiar overflow of life streamed out of the sagging houses, the rank hallways, the corner bars, bearing him along like a dark tide. The voices loud against the night sky became his voice. The violence brooding over the crap games and racing with the cars became the vertigo inside his head. It was his world, his way— and that other world beyond suddenly no longer mattered. Rearing back he snatched off his hat, baring his small tough black child's face. "Hezzy," he shouted, his rage and arrogance a wine-tinged spume. "Yeah, that's right, Hezzy. Read about me in the *News* next week, ya dumb squares."

The night before Memorial Day he wet his bed, and in the morning awoke in the warm wet rankness of himself, shaking from a dream he couldn't remember, his eyes encrusted with cold. Quickly pulling on his hat, he shoved his half-brothers from around him.

"Boy, what time you got in here last night?"

He jammed a leg into his trousers.

"You hear me? What time? Always running the streets . . . But you watch, you gonna get yourself all messed up one of these days . . . Just don't act right no more. I mean, you used to would stay round the house sometime and help me out . . . used to would listen sometime . . . and go to school. . . ."

It was the same old slop, in the same old voice that was as slack as her body and as lifeless as her eyes. He always fled it, had to, since something in him always threatened to give in to it. Even more so this morning. For her voice recalled something in his dream. It seemed to reach out in place of her arms to hold him there, to take him, as she had sometimes done when he was small, into her bed. Jumping up, he slammed the door on that voice, cutting it off and almost threw himself down the five flights of stairs. As he hit the street the sun smacked him hard across the face and he saw his Little People waiting for him on the corner.

The parade was half over when Hezzy and his guys following Turner and the Big People some distance ahead reached Bedford Avenue. Old soldiers, remnants of the wars, shuffled along like sleep-walkers, their eyes tearing from the dust and glare. Boy Scouts, white mostly, with clear eyes and smooth fresh faces, marched under the rippling flags to the blare of "America, America, God shed his grace on thee . . ." and the majorettes kicked high their white legs, the flesh under the thighs quivering in the sunlight. Their batons flashed silver. And the crowd surged against the barricades with a roar.

"Man, dig the squares," Hezzy said, the smoke flaring from under the sailor hat.

"They sure out here, ain't they," the boy beside him said.

"Man! You know, I feel sorry for squares, I tell you the truth. They just don't know what's happening. I mean, all they got is this little old jive parade while tonight here we are gonna be locking with the Crowns up on the Hill. . . ."

Later, in Prospect Park he watched scornfully from behind his oversized sunglasses as the parade disbanded: the old soldiers wheezing and fanning under the trees, the Boy Scouts lowering the heavy flag, the majorettes lolling on the grass, laughing, their blond hair spread out as if to dry. "Yeah," he said, "I feel real sorry for squares."

As always whenever they came to Prospect Park they visited the small amusement area and Hezzy seeing that they had gotten separated from Turner and the Big People suddenly let out a whoop and clambered aboard the merry-go-round, his four guys behind him. Startling the other children there with their bloodcurdling cries, they furiously goaded their motionless painted mounts, cursing whenever they grabbed for the ring and missed.

"Man," he said laughing as they leaped off together into the trampled grass and dust. "You all is nothing but punks riding some old jive merry-go-round."

"Seems like I seen you on there too, baby."

"How you mean, man? I was just showing you cats how to do the thing."

Later they sneaked through the zoo, and forcing their way close to the railing with their cocked elbows, teased the animals and sounded each other's mother:

"Yoa mother, man."

"Yours, Jim."

Leaning dangerously over the rail, they gently coaxed the seals out of the water. "Come on up, baby, and do your number for the Knights. The Noble Knights of Gates Avenue, baby."

They stood almost respectfully in front of the lion cage. "Lemme tell ya, Jim, that's about a bad stud you see in there," Hezzy said. "You try locking with that cat and get yourself all messed up. . . ."

And all the while they ate, downing frankfurters and Pepsis, and when their money was gone, they jostled the Boy Scouts around the stands and stole candy. Full finally, they climbed to a ridge near Massacre Hill and there, beneath a cool fretwork of trees and sun they drank from a pint bottle of wine, folding their small mouths around the mouth of the bottle and taking a long loud suck and then passing it on with a sigh.

The wine coupled with the sun unleashed a wildness in them after a time and they fell upon each other, tussling and rolling all in a heap, savagely kneeing each other and sending the grass and the bits of loosened sod flying up around them. And then just as abruptly they fell apart and lay sprawled and panting under the dome of leaves.

"Man, you seen the new Buick?" one of them said after a long silence. "I sure would like to cop me one of them."

"Cop with what, man? You'll never make enough bread for that."

"Who's talking about buying it, Jim. Ain't no fun behind that, I means to steal me one."

"For what? You can't even drive."

"Don't need to. I just want that number sitting outside my house looking all pretty. . . ."

Hezzy, silent until then, said, shaking his head in sad and gentle reproof. "That's what I mean about you studs. Always talking about stealing cars and robbing stores like that's something. Man, that slop ain't nothing. Any jive stud out here can steal him a car or rob a store. That don't take no heart. You can't build you no real rep behind that weak slop. You got to be out here busting heads and wasting cats, Jim. That's the only way you build you a rep and move up in a club. . . ."

"Well, we out here, ain't we?" one of them said irritably. "Most of the guys in the division didn't even show this morning."

"Them punks!" he cried and sat up. At the thought of them out on the corner drinking and jiving the chicks, having a good time, safe, the wine curdled in his stomach. For a dangerous second he wanted to be with them. "Let's make it," he shouted, leaping up, and feeling for the section of lead pipe under his jacket. "Let's find Turner and the rest of the guys." And as they plunged down the rise, he looked up and squinting in the sunlight, cried, "Who needs all this sun and slop anyways. Why don't it get dark?"

As if acceding to his wish, the sun veered toward Massacre Hill and paused there for a moment as if gathering its strength for the long descent. Slowly the dusk banked low to the east began to climb—and all over the park the marchers departed. The merry-go-round stood empty. The refreshment stands were boarded up. And the elephants, sensing the night coming on, began trumpeting in the zoo.

They found their Big People in a small wood on the other side of Massacre Hill, the guys practicing the latest dance steps, drinking from a gallon bottle of wine, playfully sparring, cursing—just as if they were in the Crib, although there was an edginess to all they did, a wariness.

Turner, with Sizzle and Big Moose—the baleful Moose who had done in a Crown when he was Hezzy's age, thirteen, and gotten busted, rehabilitated, paroled and was back bopping with the cats—was squatting under a tree, his impassive gaze on the path leading to the Hill.

Hezzy saw the bulge at his pocket. The cat was packing his burn! And suddenly he felt as safe as the guys back on the corner drinking and jiving with the chicks. Everything was cool.

The dusk had begun slowly sifting down through the trees when Sizzle sprang up—and it was seeing a tightly coiled wire spring loose. "Them sneaky Crown bastards," he cried, almost inarticulate with rage. "They ain't gonna show. Just like the last time. Remember?" he shouted down at Turner. "Remember how the pricks sent us word they was coming down and then didn't show. Punked out. Every last one of the bastards. Remember?"

Turner nodded, his eyes still fixed on the path.

And Big Moose said petulantly, "I never did go for bopping in Prospect Park no ways. Give me the streets, baby, so if I got to haul ass I'm running on asphalt. Out here is too spooky with all these jive trees. I won't even know where I'm running— and knowing me I'm subject to run right into The Man and find myself doing one to five for gangbusting again."

"Man," Turner said laughing, but with his eye still on the path. "There ain't no need to let everybody know you punking out."

"I ain't punking out," Moose said. "It's just too dark out here. How I'm going to know for sure it's a Crown's head I'm busting and not one of our own guys?"

And Hezzy said, his voice as steady, as chiding as Turner's. "You'll know, man. Just smell the punk's breath before you smash him. Them cheap Crowns drink that thirty cents a pint slop."

"Who asked you?" Big Moose swung on him.

"Cool, man," Turner caught Moose's arm and turned to Hezzy. He stared at him with eyes filled with the dusk. "Moose, man," he said after a time, his gaze still on Hezzy, "Looks like I might have to put you out of the club and move up my man Hezzy here, especially if the stud fights as bad as he talks. I might even have to move over, Jim . . ."

Hezzy returned the dark and steady gaze, the chilling smile—and again he felt high, soaring.

The Crowns came at the very edge of the day. A dozen or more small dark forms loping toward them down the path which led to the hill. They spotted the Noble Knights and the wind brought their cry: "The Crowns, punks. It's the Crowns."

There was a moment's recoil among the Noble Knights and then Turner was on his feet, the others behind him and their answering shout seemed to jar the trees around them. "The Noble Knights, muh-fuggers! The Noble Knights are down!"—and with Turner in the lead and Sizzle, Big Moose and Hezzy just behind, they charged up the rise from the other side, up into the descending night and as they gained the low crest and met the oncoming Crowns, the darkness reached down and covered them entirely.

The battle was brief as always, lasting no more than two or three minutes, and disorderly. They thrashed and grappled in the dark, cursing, uncertain whom they were hitting. The cries burst like flares: "The Crowns!" "The Noble Knights, baby!" The dull red spurt of a gun lit the darkness and then they were fighting blind again.

In those minutes which seemed like hours a rubber hose smacked up against Hezzy's head, knocking off his hat and blinding him with pain for a second. He did not mind the pain, but the loss of his hat, the wind stinging his exposed head, terrified and then enraged him. He struck out savagely and something solid gave way beneath the lead pipe in his hand—and as it did something within him burst free: a sap which fed his muscles and sent his arm slashing into the surging darkness. Each time someone rushed him shouting, "The Crowns, punk!" he yelled, "The Noble Knights, baby!" and struck, exulting.

The pipe flew from his hand and he drew his shiv, the blade snatching a dull yellow gleam from somewhere and as he held it at the ready, shouting for a Crown he heard the first whistle then the next, shrill, piercing the heart of the night. For an instant which seemed endless, there was silence on the hill. And it was as if the sound of the whistle had cut off the air in their throats. Their bodies froze in the violent attitudes of the fight—and it was as if they were playing "statues." Knights and Crowns were one suddenly, a stunned, silent, violently cohered mass. Comrades. For the whisper passed among them without regard to friend or foe: "The Man, baby! The Man." Then the darkness exploded into fragments that took on human form and they scattered headlong down the hill.

The ground below was a magnet which drew Hezzy to it and he plunged helpless toward it, bruised and terrified and suddenly alone as the others behind him raced down another path. And then no longer alone as the shout sounded behind him, "There goes one of the punks, I betcha. Let's waste the muh-fugger."

He had been caught in a sneak.

"Run, baby . . . Like we said, you running pretty . . . But we're still with ya. . . ."

And he was, as they said, still running pretty. He was certain of his escape now. The black wall ahead would soon give way, he knew, to a street and neon signs and people and houses with hallways to hide him until he could get back to his turf. Yet a single regret filtered down through the warm night and robbed the flight of its joy. He longed for his hat. Tears of outrage started up. If only he had wasted one of the bastards to make up for his loss. Or shived one of them good. He ran crying for the hat, until overwhelmed by his loss, he wheeled around and for a moment stood cursing them. Then, turning, he ran ahead.

But in that moment they were on him. It was as if they had known all along that he would pause and had held back, saving themselves till that error. Now they came on swiftly, intent, suddenly silent. The distance between them narrowed. The sound of their approach welled out of the night; and out of the silence came a single taunt: "What's the matter, baby, you ain't running so pretty no more?"

His fear suddenly was a cramp which spread swiftly to all his muscles. His arms tightened. His shoulders. The paralysis reached his legs so that his stride was broken and his feet caught in the ruts of the path. Fear was a phlegm in his throat choking off his air and a film over his eyes which made the black wall of trees ahead of him waver and recede. He stumbled and as he almost went down, their cry crashed in his ears: *The Noble Knights, punk! The Knights are down!*

He turned as if jerked around and over the loud rale of his breathing he listened, unbelieving, to the echo of the words. They called again, "The Knights, muh-fugger!" nearer this time, and the voices clearly those of Turner, Sizzle and Big Moose. And Hezzy's relief was a weakness in his legs and a warmth flooding his chest. The smile that everyone always said was so like his mother's broke amid his tears and he started toward them, hailing them with the shiv he still held, laughing as he wept, shouting, "Hey, you bop-crazy studs, it's . . ."

The gun's report drowned his name. The bullet sent a bright forked light through him and pain discovered the secret places of his body. Yet he still staggered toward them, smiling, but stiffly now, holding out the knife like a gift as they sped by without looking. Even when they were gone and he was dead, a spoor of blood slowly trailed them. As if, despite what they had done, they were still his People. As if, no matter what, he would always follow them. Overhead the black dome of the sky cleared and a few stars glinted. Cold tears in the warm May night.

JOHN McCLUSKEY JR.

SPECIMEN

FEBRUARY 16, 1854

Dear Queenie,

I write this from this teensie room in Richmond, about the same as a hog pen. At first they had me down at a stable, straw thick as the baby crib. Tomorrow I go out and parade in front of strangers still wet behind the ears.

A free colored man is a blacksmith here and he heard about me sleeping in a barn and now this shed. He told me I could sleep with him and his family. He say he got a clean spare room. He didn't act scared or nothing when he saw my spots. I'll ask Dr. Calderwood about it tonight, how long we'll be staying.

They say it snowing on up the road around Washington.

Your loving husband,
Stewart

February 20, 1854

Dear Stewart,

You go in front of strangers is bad enough. I still go into town with Miss Leona and she make me carry a whole bushel of things in my arms—calico, gingham, and such as that. I be strong as a bull-calf before too long. I see Ariel and Solomon in town and we try to talk some but Miss Leona won't let me go on much. It's so now I can carry a basket on my head and one under my arms. One lady offer to buy me when she see me do that. I reckon she think I can tote two, three more. Look at me like she look at a horse.

354

It warm here, Stewart, warm for February. What it like in Richmond? Is it two day's ride like you said? How long you be there, dearest Stewart?

Your loving wife,
  Queenie

February 21, 1854

Dear Queenie,

When they come up this time they scared to touch my arm. So Doc, he say go ahead and touch my arm. It just the vitigo,* he say. Won't nothing happen to you. It ain't 'tagious. I ask him later what 'tagious mean and he laugh and say it mean my spots won't stick on the boys hands when they touch me. So one of them step right up and look real quick at my arm and neck. "Silas, you sure your daddy wasn't one of them pinto horses that got loose over by Monticello?" Before I can tell him my name ain't Silas he giggling like a little girl. Everybody laugh, but Doc remind them they gone be doctors, too, before long and better learn all they can about everything. You can't be teasing about no disease you never seen before, he say. But he didn't really mean it because he cover his mouth like he want to laugh, too. When I speak up strong and say my name ain't Silas, who hear?

Your loving husband,
  Stewart

February 27, 1854

Dearest Stewart,

Asberry lost his front tooth today. The other front one is loose, too, so I think it gone fall out soon, too. I remember I lost my tooth at six, seven, too. Maybe everybody do. We all miss you here. Edna broke out in hives the other day and Luther think she just did that all by herself in her head. Like the time he said she stopped into the poison ivy patch to keep from going to the fields last August. Whoever heard of such? Sometimes I wish they lived clean on the other side of the quarters.

Love, Queenie

---

*Vitiligo is an acquired, often disfiguring, pigmentary anomaly of the skin manifested by depigmented white patches surrounded by a normal or hyperpigmented border.... The patches are of various sizes and may have various configurations. ... The pigmentation may be generalized or universal. (Source: *Andrews' Diseases of the Skin,* 8th edition)

March 1, 1854

Dear Queenie,

We in Petersburg now and they had me up again this morning. Just before me they had a cow up, a skinny thing that can't give milk. Been like that for four years, her owner claim. Doc and another man use a lot of fancy-sounding names, then have the boys come up and touch it on the teat. They act kind of scared of it, like our Saba was the first time she got close to a cow. Then I come up and stand under the bright lights, bright as the sun. Must be thirty candles up close. Doc do all the talking this time and they come up like they always do. Then all of them writing something down.

It cold here. I get bumps because I have to take my shirt off. You say it warm there? I be glad when we get back home. We go to another place tomorrow. Some place warmer, Doc tell me. How the babies?

Love, Stewart

March 2, 1854

Dearest Queenie,

They say I could be famous with these spots. But where do the money go? I get my little bit each time. Doc tell me I ought to buy a good horse with the money I make going around with him. I just shake my head to keep him going. I talk to him a little bit about us and how we like growing a few beans and collards. How you and me enjoy our little garden patch so much. He seem to hear a little bit, then he go on talking about what just jumped in his head, like me and the birds and the rivers ain't even around for this morning. We aiming to Lynchburg, be there in another day.

Stewart, your loving husband

March 4, 1854

Dear Queenie,

Hands this time, just your ordinary hands. Here in Lynchburg they want to claim now that my hands big as a bear's paw. Who among them seen a bear's paw? None of those boys ever pulled home a full-grown bear. They probably re-member something they daddies maybe talked about. Truth is, they will know my hands, every scar, every callous, before they see a bear they done killed with they own hands. That go for Doc, too, far's I'm concerned.

Then they asked Doc how come I can't grin. He tell them it's the hands they should be studying about. If I grin, it will be teeth next. I know my hands ain't no bigger than that white trash Bradshaw's. That man's got hands big as shovels. Doc asked me again what I want to do with the money. He still think I want to buy one of Bradshaw's broken down Appaloosas. What he know? I'm buying something that live longer than horses, that live longer than me and you.

We be home, soon, I think.

Very truly yours, Stewart

March 9, 1854

Dear Stewart,

The babies doing good. It stormed here some bad last night. It started just about dusk-dark, coming out of the west roaring. Little limbs start to flying first, then the rain hit real real hard and it stay like that all night long, throwing the covers off the window. The baby start to crying, so I had to sit up with her through the night. I rock her and rock her and every so often I have to get up and peek out. There was lightning so big it made night go to noon. The thunder shook the walls like a big man hitting them with all his might. We had three big puddles on the floor. Most of the time me and the baby sleeping and waking up and I go to humming. The others just slept right along.

Two big poplar trees fell up by the big house. And somebody scream loud in the next cabin, probably Edna or her big Dinah, one. I guessed it must have been the two that stand at the curve in the road and this morning I see I was right. The men was chopping it up this morning so the wagons could get through. Then real sudden-like last night the wind die down, 'way long about midnight, but the rain still coming. Then it stop, too, and you can only hear it dripping off the leaves. The dogs start barking like they chasing off some ghostses. Then it quiet and all you can hear is the children sleeping.

Husband, when you coming home?

Your loving wife, Queenie

March 15, 1854

Dearest Wife,

I can't move my arm. That's the way it was Monday. Here it is Wednesday morning and I can't barely walk neither. I move slow, slow to write you this with the only thing moving, my fingers. I can't feel nothing in my arms and legs—is there a floor? Can I hop up and sit in the top of that sugar maple yonder? No, I ain't even gone try to move. He better tell me something or I stay a statue, a tree, something that can't walk but something stay put in Appomatox County. What he gone say then?

Love, Stewart

March 16, 1854

Dear Queenie,

He decided to say nothing. He want to hold my money until I tell him I'm gone buy a horse or something. I can be stubborn, too. But I got to thinking. Tomorrow night I could leave. I could come down from the stable loft quiet as a cat. I could leave. You could hear me one night, my call coming the same as a owl's or a cardinal out real late. And you could be ready to go. Every night you could be ready to go and pack the children's clothes every night and unpack during the day so nobody would suspect. We could leave. I could be the tree in the night, singing. Trust me. I could be the river whispering in the darkness. Step into my coldness and we could leave.

He could see me one last time, this statue, this pinto everybody touch like they scared. I will whistle softly one night and I want you to dream with me of Phildelphia or Canada. This I mean. Burn this letter or bury it, one. Meanwhile cross my knife and fork across my plate when you set the table from now on.

Love, Stewart

March 17, 1854

Dearest Stewart,

Ellis come by last night and whisper that Johnnie Ruth's wild boy Cicero done run off from the Dawkins plantation. He didn't tell nobody nothing, not even Johnnie Ruth. Ellis say he left his mama a sign—turned up his drinking cup and carved a picture of a bird next to it. Some tried to say it was the worms in his belly so bad that make him do that way. Hound dogs been on him for two days now, you can hear them day and night back forth across the ridges. They gone catch him. Everybody know they gone catch him. You know them dogs. Old Raven would be rich as Doc if he hired them out as much as white folks want. You know and I know they never missed but those two times. If Rufus hadn't drownded and floated up against that log, he would have never found him. They ain't never found Jake. Sandy claim he turned into a hawk and in New York right now.

You know your mind better than me, but I know a little about your heart. And rage is in your heart now. Can you wait just a little bit more? I pray Doc ain't lost all his senses now. He a hard man, but there some good in him. He will see us through.

Your loving wife, Queenie

March 18, 1854

Dearest Stewart,

Yes, yes, he'll see us through. I saw you and him and me in my dream last night. We was walking in a field of high grass, just you and me at first, grass tall as corn in early August. The ground was soft and muddy and we would slip every once in awhile, but hold each other up. We in the middle of this field and I see two hawks floating just over our heads. We smell smoke, both of us, 'bout the same time. I scream fire, I fix my mouth to say it again but it somebody else voice. . . . I start running one way and you pull me in the other. You say it the only way to run. We outrun the fire and it hot on our back. Then we walk into a room where it cool and dark. There Dr. Calderwood sitting and he wave his hand at two cups of tea and he grinning. "Sit down and rest a spell," he say. "No fire can reach you here." You look at me and I sit down. But you stand and sip your sassafras tea and everything quiet. That's what I dreamed last night, love. Don't it signify help?

Queenie

March 25, 1854

Dear Queenie,

I can't know what those dreams signify. That's woman-talk anyway. I only go on what I see with both eyes open and it's like I say. I go before strangers every-day. I take off my shirt and wait while Doc talk about the spots on my chest and neck. I show my hands. After he talk they come close to point to my neck and ask questions. How come you know it ain't lepersy, somebody always asking Doc. They ask the same questions all the time and Doc explain what he explain. Then he tell them that only five colored in the whole state of Virginia got it—two free and two other slaves beside me.

I ask him about the money again and he blow up real big and give me a dollar. Say he saving the rest until we get here. He know our secret now, except I tell him I want to buy my freedom first. I don't believe he saving. How I know he ain't spend-ing it on those big cigars he blow on after supper? He say he through talking.

Tomorrow we go up to the school in Charlottesville. Write me there. Where Johnnie Ruth boy now?

Your loving husband, Stewart

March 30, 1854

Dearest Stewart,

You know no spots didn't make no nevermind to me. I didn't marry your skin. Don't let no child-doctors worry you. They don't know your heart. They don't see you handling the horses or chopping the wood or singing the loudest and best at the meetings. All they see is what Doc say they should see. I miss you. Come home.

Love, Queenie

March 30, 1854

Dear Queenie,

Yesterday a boy say I should go to London or Phildelphia where they got parks with animals and they could put me 'side wild animals in cages. Dr. Calderwood tell him to shut, tell him he can't run medicine running his mouth like he do. I like Doc for saying that but taking up for me don't mean I forget. One of us be free by the time the corn ripe. Where Johnnie Ruth boy at?

Stewart

April 5, 1854

Dear Stewart,

Flowers showing up already. Crocuses been up. It seem like it stay warm right along, waiting for you to come on home. People be asking about you all the time. The baby been low with the croup lately. I'm chewing a juniper root and drinking tea and staying out of the night air. Johnnie Ruth boy still out there somewhere. They gave up on the dogs. That no-'count Raven lost a lot of money betting them dogs bring Cicero back. 'Course he been making it plenty warm for everybody in the fields. Do Doc know about Cicero leaving? He'll say something, watch. He can't keep a secret, watch.

I been studying hands since you said it in one of your letters. Look at the babies, everybody in the fields, and even Miss Leona's hands. She got green rivers running over hers, look like. Little lines going everywhere. What could the young doctors learn from looking at hers, I wonder? You do what best for all of us, I know you will. Be particular.

Love, Queenie

April 5, 1854

Dearest Queenie,

Charlottesville won't take us too long. We just here for three days. I hope you drinking tea and staying out of the night air. Folks all through the quarters get the spring fever every year. I just ate a big meal with a colored family here what like to take in travelers. I give them one of Dr. Calderwood's dollars for their hospitality. I guess I'm so full now I don't need to eat for awhile, but I'm running when this letter is through. Cross my knife and fork on the plate, then turn my cup down. I'm moving by myself. If you hear a tree or bird talking to you, just listen and smile. Teach their songs to the babies.

Love, Stewart

THE MORE I LIKE FLIES

Aʟʟ ʀɪɢʜᴛ, ᴍᴀɴ, so I'm bussing down tables—we gotta do our own here, and we gotta sweep, mop, wash dishes and do just about everything else too—and trying to keep flies off my arms and the sweat out my eyes and the seam of these polyester monkey suit pants from working into the crack of my ass. I ain't even gonna tell you how disgusted I am with all this wreckage these ape-neck cadets have left behind. And we gotta throw all this crap away, too. Three and a half gallons of milk, four, maybe five pounds of scrambled eggs, a whole pig's worth of bacon, enough French toast to feed France, and then, like, from nowhere ol' Kelly goes, "What's so great about bein' goddamn white?" Hello! I say to myself. There he goes. Good ol' Kelly. But I keep my mouth shut, naturally. No sense going into it. This is Kelly.

But still, I'm thinking, How about this, ya dope: Try walking down the street at night, minding your own beeswax, and a white couple comes at you from the opposite way? and it's hot outside, so you're ambling, just ambling, and it's not all that late, just blue black with a few stars, like you like it, and you're thinking about, say, nothing really, OK? and you don't even mind the water sprinklers spitting on your right side. And the crickets sound nice, don't they? Then when Ken and Barbie get within a half block of you they cut across the street like you're a hissing viper hell hound man, bristling with Uzis and hypodermic needles. You can barely keep yourself from hollering, *Oh, come ooonnn. I gotta Korean girlfriend and my best buddy's white, and you people got to simply lay off watching so many goddamn drug lord movies.* Weenies. What's so great about being white is you get to act like everybody else in the world is a scary monster.

Like I say, all this I keep to myself cause once this old melonhead's got his mind made up to say something, you can't stop him. He's like a four-foot stack of plates tipped at a forty-five degree angle. Get em that far gone and you can kiss a big hunk of your paycheck goodbye. That's Kelly. Soon's he opens his mouth he's already at forty-five degrees. Too late. Man says what he's gotta say. "You think we'll get our pay today?" I ask him, even though I know it won't make a damn bit of difference what I say. I look at him and see him working them bones in his temples, working em. You'd think he was chewing cornhusks. But didn't have a damn thing in his mouth but his own words. He says, "You colored guys make it sound like don't nobody else in the world feel pain."

"Hey look, Kelly, I ain't said jack to you, man. Go talk to Mendez; he's the one pissed you off."

"Move," he says, then sweeps in front of me, then behind.

I say to him, "You know, we'd get done quicker if we sweep at the same time and clear at the same time, and wipe at the—"

"Mendez don't listen." He swipes his hand through the air, stands straight and leans on his broom. "At least you listen. And Mendez gets loud, too. I can't talk to him, cause no matter what you say he gets loud. I can't talk to loud people."

"Do you wanna get the mop, or me?"

"A guy like that'll never learn shit. You look at him. He's supposed to be our shop steward, setting an example for younger lads like yourself, and what's he doing?"

"Same as usual, walking around with a pitcher fulla drumsticks and talking smack while he's supposed to be working."

"Fat son of a bitch."

"Yeah, well, I'll mop and you can clean the silverware and plates." I walk into the kitchen and just about drop from the heat. Jesus, how can these cooks take this nonsense? I walk past the ovens and see they're empty. They haven't even started lunch yet, I notice, and start wondering where Mendez got the chicken legs. I look for George, which is easy, cause he's the only one here who wears a cloth chef's hat. Everybody else wears paper. I find him at the chopping block, skinning garlic. This is pretty much where you can expect to find George, and that's what he'll be doing when you find him. Skinning garlic. He's got a year before he retires, so I guess no one'll say squiddly to him about goofing off.

"Georgie Pordgie."

"Say babe, what's to it?"

I don't care much for the ways guys around here call each other "babe." I know they don't mean nothing funny by it, but the only person I call babe is Hwasook, my girlfriend. But lately I've been kind of joking with Ray by calling him babe. He'll walk into our apartment and I'll say, "Hey, babe," and he'll say, "Hey, babe," and we'll both get a grin out of that. We did it once when Hwasook was over, and you could tell it made her uncomfortable. Even after we explained it was a joke she still didn't get it.

"Say, George, where'd Mendez get the birdlegs?"

"Cooler."

"He's grubbing a whole pitcher full of cold chicken legs?"

"Microwaves em in Salazar's office."

"You mean Salazar don't care?"

George said he didn't care, so I said, "See you George," and went back to the soap room to get the mop and bucket. I was a little twicked off about finding out that a guy like me'll get written up by Salazar for snatching a hand full of shrimp while Mendez gets away with a pitcher or a plate full of whatever the hell he wants all day long. We're not supposed to eat any leftovers, but most guys do. Better not get caught, though, cause they will nail you, even though it takes an act of Congress to actually fire a civil servant. But Mendez does whatever he wants. Maybe it's because most everybody likes him. Maybe because he's shop steward. But it isn't because, like Kelly says, that Mendez is a "colored Mexican," and in cahoots with Salazar. Mendez'll tell anybody who wants to listen that he's Panamanian. But to me the guy's all Brooklyn. I figure a guy like Kelly, though thinks anyone with a Latino name is a Mexican. As far as I can see, Mendez and Salazar despise each other, it's just that Salazar's terrified of Mendez. Mendez knows it and loves to rub Salazar's face in it. I mean all you gotta do is compare one to the other and you can see why. Salazar can't be taller than five foot four, and if he weighs much over one-twenty on any given day it's cause he's carrying his grocery money in quarters. And he's got about as much personality as he's got body weight and height. Big ol' meaty Mendez could have the dude fried up crispy, carry him around in a pitcher, and munch him in maybe four quick bites. Mendez is all personality, big, quickstepping, fast-talking lug is everywhere at once, in sight and sound. Cahoots my butt. Mendez owns the place, and you gotta admire him sort of. But still this chicken-in-O'-pitcher crap twicks me off and I tell Kelly about it when I get back to our section. All Kelly says is, "Proves my point." And before I can stop myself I ask him what he means, so he says, "When you finish mopping, we'll take a break." *Hello! Anybody home?* Forget about it. Kelly twicks me off too.

So I sit down for break after I'm done and Kelly comes from the kitchen with the usual yogurt, the usual orange, and the usual sausages. He bathes the sausages with Frank's Louisiana Hot Sauce, and as per usual asks me why I'm not eating, and as usual I tell him I don't eat breakfast. Then I say, "You know, if we don't get our checks today, I'm gonna tell Salazar to pay my rent."

"It's just like I'm saying, Scott, what's so goddamn great about bein' white?"

Plates, I tell you. Plates, stacked four feet high, heading straight down like a gunshot victim and there's nothing I can do.

"I mean look," he says, "You don't get your check. I don't get my check. How's my color make it any better for me?"

"Couldn't tell you, all I know is that Civil Service pay is supposed to be guaranteed on time."

"And do I get a tax break cause I'm white?"

"Nine extra days is just too damn long to wait, if you ask me. Hey, how come it's taking so long anyway?"

"Scotty. You know why I retired early from the Corps?"

I give up, so I say, "You got shot. You told me."

"Know why I got shot? He pushes his paper hat back off his brow, then dumps salt and more hot sauce on his sausages. I tell him no I don't know why he got shot. "You know who shot me?"

"You weren't shot in Viet Nam?"

Kelly stabs a sausage with his fork, pops it into his mouth, and chews it so hard I can hear his teeth knock together. I wave a fly off my ear. After a minute Kelly says, "There was this kid in my company, well, not really a kid like some of the boots in my company. This lad had seven years in. Did a couple tours in Viet Nam, too, but was only a private first class."

"So why'd he shoot you?"

"Did I say he shot me?"

"Well get to the—"

"No, I didn't, so let me—"

"All right! All right!"

"You never listen."

"Kelly, just ten minutes ago you said . . . OK, Kelly, you're right. I don't listen."

"They called him Barney for some damn reason, but at the inquest and the court martial they called him by his real name, but I don't remember it. Never forget what he looked like, though. This fella had one a them bull necks, built like a little oak stump. They guy was Indian, but I don't know the tribe or nothing. But that's what made him wild. Mean, lazy, and smart, too, I'm telling you.

"You know, I'd walk into the squad bay sometimes, for some reason or another, and I'm telling you, it'd be like ten, eleven hundred in the morning and there'd this kid be, in his boots, trousers, and undershirt, just snoozing like a papoose. Course I'd wake him up and he'd tell me some kind of bullpuckie like he'd just given blood, or was suffering heat stroke, or didn't nobody bother to wake him up at reveille, or like that, and I'd go, 'Well where's your med-pass?' or 'Whycome you're in uniform?' or something and he'd get pissed off, get his ass up, put on the rest of his uniform, and get his Indian ass to work." Kelly sniffs and holds his coffee cup under his nose, just staring off into space. I look at his nose hairs, and his bushy knuckles, and his arms, which are fuzzy as a dog's leg, and I say to myself, Well, looks like some white people got it better in winter, but I sure wouldn't wanna be you in all this heat. Kelly sniffs again and sips his coffee. "Goddamn right I did," he says, as if I've just said, Gosh, Kelly, really.

"But nobody else would," Kelly says. "Company commander didn't say shit, hell, his own platoon sergeant didn't say shit. I did. Good ol' Gunny Sergeant William P. Kelly did. I never understood this, Scott, I never did. Some guys seemed to respect him cause of all the chest cartoons he'd picked up in combat. Man, you shoulda seen that boy in dress uniform. Had a chest fulla combat ribbons, enlistment stripes on his sleeve, too, of course, but just one goddamn stripe. One."

Kelly's pointing a finger in my face like I can't count. "That told me everything I needed to know. It was like he was saying to everyone, 'Lookit me, I done my time, so lea-me alone and lemme collect my paycheck.' Nobody but me seemed to care. Kid wasn't even in my platoon. I was motor pool; he was comm, but you think any one a them shitbirds in the comm platoon'd say something to 'im.

"Well, one day I caught him in the rack and it was something like thirteen hundred hours in the afternoon or what have you, and so I nudge him with my foot and he sits up like a dead body'll do if it lays around a few days. Well, he says, "What time is it, gunny?'

"'It's time somebody wrote you up,' I say, 'if you don't have an excuse for being in that rack, PFC.' And get this: He jumps out his rack, throws his blouse and cover on, telling me he's got an excuse, but that he's gotta go get it. Well that little son of a bitch walked out and never did come back. I wasted twenty minutes waiting for his dumb ass to come back, but he never did. Well, I was mad enough to piss fire, but I let it go. Wasn't in the mood that day, I guess."

Kelly pops that last sausage into his mouth and has some more coffee. Those little skull bones are working like he's got at least a dictionary or two worth of words in his mouth. He stares down at his plate and chews. I sit back and wait. This obviously ain't his point, though, with ol' Kelly, you just never know. The plates ain't hit the floor yet. I swipe at a fly and it vanishes somewhere past Kelly's ear. "So what's this got to do with why white folks got it so bad?" I say.

"You know, breakfast is the most important meal of the day, Scott. You oughta take advantage. Only thirty cents a meal, lad." I just hiss and shake my head. Then my heart just about pops when I'm jolted by someone's meathook slapping down solid on my shoulder.

"What you boys think this is?" When I turn I'm staring right into little Salazar's mustache, even though I'm sitting and he's standing. ". . . a retirement home?" he says.

"Break ain't over yet," says Kelly. Salazar ignores him and looks at me. "I need someone to hit you section one more time with the mop, Mr. Winters. Sergeant Klutsky spilled some coffee between table five and table six."

"Someone. You mean me."

"Everybody else is eating."

"Hey," says Kelly, "we getting paid or not?"

"Paychecks are in my safe," says Salazar, then he scoots away on those size six patent leather shoes of his. Damn things squeak and glimmer like a couple a mechanical toys. Kelly's looking at em too, them shoes. Looks at em like he hates em.

"Why's he always come to me for crap like that?" I ask Kelly, and he says he does it cause I let him. I guess that's true, but I'm new here and can't afford to act like I own the place, like I'm Mendez. I've got a month and a half of probation left. But even if I was a full civil service employee I don't think I'd play the jigaboo some of em expect me to. That's the kind of thing you just can't explain to an old bone-brain like Kelly. It might not be so, but you always feel white people are watching you, waiting for you to screw up, pissed off a little if you don't. And they can't really make up their minds about us. I mean, they call you lazy, but every so often I overhear white dudes in the locker room say, "Yeah, babe, busted my ass today, worked like a nigger, I'm telling ya." But, I can't make up my mind either, cause what I can't figure is whether I look more like a "jigaboo" if I don't try to slide by with hardly any work, or if I kow tow to de boss man. Can't win as long as someone else calls your game, I guess. And, like, would it be OK working during break time if a white guy had asked me to? Skip it, I tell myself. All I wanna do is keep my job for now.

I get up, stretch. "Well," I say, "by the time I get back from the soap room, break'll be over anyhow."

"Fuck Salazar."

"Not my type."

"Sit down."

"Well, what damn difference is it gonna make two minutes from now? The point is *I'll* be the one who has to do it anyway. You ain't gonna do it. Mendez, Piper, Ski, Morales, those guys ain't gonna do it. So . . ." And I just stand there with my knuckles on my belt, trying to look tough, but my trouser seams are wedged up my butt; and in my paper hat, short sleeve white shirt, and red monkey jacket, and knowing that I'm on my way to the soap room so I can clean up a mess that no one else will, I don't feel so tough. Kelly gets the message anyway. He sits there, staring at me with his flat blue eyes jiggling side to side like they always do, when he's twicked. It always makes me sort of nervous. I can't understand how a guy's eyes could do that. Must be some kind of palsy. Then he squints and says, "You noticed how hot it is? It ain't even lunch time yet and it's just plain damn hot in here."

We're setting up the lunch dishes. In less than an hour we'll be shoveling chow at the jr. flyboys and girls. That's what I really hate about this job. That, and cleaning up after them, which pretty much means I hate the whole job. I'm not saying I've got anything against these cadets, not personally. They're smart and polite and everything, but I hate the way the upper classmen harass the doolies. I hate it when the kids have to stand up at attention right in the middle of a meal and have to spout the chain of command or the parts the M–16 rifle. I hate when a bunch of em are made to stand up and shout football cheers or wing cheers or flight cheers or squadron cheers. I hate when you're just getting the ravioli or whatnot to your hundredth flyboy when the first ten are asking for more milk and juice and after you give em the milk and the juice, ten people here want more green beans and twenty there want more corn and bread, and there's cheers and chants, and heat and steam and flies and Air Force blue and pink heads everydamnwhere you look, and you're pulling your hot cart all overthedamnplace and it's big, the size of a V.W. bus, when you're tired, but then the flybabes split all neat and orderly like, leaving you all this cleaning up to do. All the waste. All the waste. It really gets to me: feed a Boyscout Jamboree with the leftover burgers. Fatten every poor baby on the south side of Colorado Springs with the leftover milk. Ship the green beans, the rice, the macaroni to the shelters all over town and you ain't gotta feel guilty for at least half a week. Abscond with the spuds—fried, baked, au gratin, hashed and browned, boiled, ranched—and open up your own damned potato restaurant at zero percent food cost. I mentioned all this to Kelly once and he told me, "Volume buying. Don't cost em nothing. And don't give me that trash about starving people and that, cause the gover'ment pays for it and pays your rent, food, clothes, and gas, too, and they can do what they please with us *and* the food."

But I can't think about all that now, cause I got to hustle buns and get the stuff laid out. Yesterday. Cause lunch is just about ready and I know Kelly ain't gonna be much help today since he's steady yakking my ear off about this Barney guy. "Well," he says, "I had duty that very night, anyway, which means I had reveille the next morning and you could bet your sweet ass that little shitbird was getting outta that rack at oh-five-thirty sharp. I knew how to get jarheads up, I tell ya. I'd rap my nightstick on their bedposts, wink the lights, kick over shit cans, and if that didn't work, I'd grab an ankle and pull the guy out. And see, with this Barney kid, I'd not only wake him, but I'd make sure he stayed up by giving him a lawful order to help me get other Marines up."

I said to Kelly, "Say, you want me to get the pitchers laid out or you want to?"

Kelly wipes his brow with the inside of his wrist and says, "But when I grabbed his ankle the boy went three kinds of ballistic. Scott, I tell you that not only did this boy take a swing at me, but he pushed over five or six wall lockers and racks. Goddamn things went over like dominoes . . . You better polish them spoons; they look like hell—and then, see, and then he starts screaming, 'motherfucker! motherfucker! I got something for your ass!' And next thing you know he starts punching out windows."

"With his fist?"

"Hell, yeah, with his fist. He punches out four before I even know what the hell he's doing. Rattled me pretty bad. That's one of the reasons I retired from the Corps when I did. Crazy hopheads like that, well, you never knew what they were gonna do.

"Well, so this big colored fella, name of Lance Corporal Whitaker, just pushes by me and says, 'Dust,' which I thought was some kind of colored cuss word for white man, but found out later he meant what they call angel dust, PCP, know what that is?"

He missed my sarcasm when I said, "No, Kelly. Tell me."

"It's a goddamn drug is what it is. A goddamn drug. So this Lance Corporal Whitaker just walks over to Barney when he's on his seventh or eighth window, cutting himself and shedding his blood like he's got an extra couple quarts in his wall locker and don't care, see, and this Whitaker guy just touches Barney on the shoulder and says something like, 'Morning, Barn,' and Barney just stops. Stops dead. I mean he don't move, and neither does anybody else. Everybody's just staring at this kid's bloody hands and arms, and all the blood here and there. But then this Whitaker fella, just as calm as you please, grabs a towel off Barney's rack, wraps it up and walks Barney to the infirmary. Hey, Scott, we got some bent forks here. Scrounge some good ones, will ya, lad?"

The dining hall is wall to wall blue, and Kelly shuts up for awhile. But I know he's at sixty degrees cause those bones are struggling under his skin like a bag fulla kittens. Things are going smooth and my mind's not even on my work. I'm thinking about taking a long shower, getting into some non-polyester clothes and calling up Hwasook to make plans for the weekend. Since we're getting paid today the weekend's looking good. We'll go to Deckers, maybe, and she'll take her suntan lotion, a nice bikini, and a book and I'll take my fishing stuff and wine and crackers, cheese, fruit, and so forth. Maybe I'll bring a good sci-fi pulp, myself. If the sun cooperates, we'll be fine. As long as we don't run into a bunch of gawking rednecks. Hwasook doesn't understand, but that's why I don't care much for going to the mountains, big, blue-green, and beautiful as they are, cause of all the RV, truck, and motorcycle necks who stare at her like she's some kinda slut and stare at me like they know she wouldn't be as close as a parsec to me if not for my twelve-inch unit and my briefcase fulla heroin.

Hwasook argues that a neck's neck is just as red in town as it is in those hills, and she's got a point, but I have my doubts. Something funny happens to some people when they start huffing pine wood air, drinking beer in the hot sun, eating ash-flavored food. They start feeling like pioneers, muleskinners, cowboys, desperadoes. To them Hwasook and me start looking like runaway slaves or bloodthirsty savages. They start up with the yee-haaaaws and revving their engines, yelling hey nigger out their windows as they drive by. She doesn't get it, though, and neither does Kelly. I'm getting pretty twicked off thinking of all this stuff and can't wait till things slow down and he can get to his point, which I plan to shoot down with all this stuff I've been thinking about.

Finally, things do slow down, but before I can talk to ol' Kelly, I spot Mendez coming our way with a hamburger in his fat mitts. "Hey, Mendez," I say.

"Hey, babe."

"Is it true we're getting paid today?"

Mendez shrugs, "Ask Salazar."

"Fuck Salazar," says Kelly.

"Too skinny," I say, and at the same time Mendez says, "Nobody's talking to you, Kelly."

Kelly's eyes start to jiggle. "You can kiss my ass, Mendez."

"Wouldn't kiss that wrinkly thing with your *own* lips, old man." The he turns back to me. "Look here, bruh, Salazar needs someone to help Peggy clean up a mess on the east section."

"He don't have to—"

"It's okay, Kelly, I got it." And I do get it, leaving Mendez and Kelly to argue with each other over the rattle and clatter of 90 waiters in monkey suits cleaning up after 4,500 cadets, throwing away probably a quarter ton of food, telling jokes, lies, stories. I hear Mendez say "racist" at least a half dozen times. I hear Kelly use the phrase "silver platter." I roll my eyes and keep walking.

My only problem with working next to Peggy is that I'm pretty sure she's got a crush on me. I'm not being conceited, or anything, cause I'm no stud and Peggy's no fox. She's tall, skinny, forty-five-ish, with platinum hair, veiny hands, and sky-blue, ice-blue eyes. She always calls me gorgeous, which I find hard to respond to in a likewise way. She ain't ugly, but I don't like giving her ideas. Right now I'm trying to be polite to her but keep by eyes on the grape juice I'm swabbing up. The flies are having a party. There's a zillion more in her section than there are in Kelly's and mine. "Who's your partner today, Peg," I ask.

She locks her unbelievably blue eyes on me and smiles at me the same say Mendez smiles at ribs. "Freddy Washington, but I'll trade him for you, gorgeous." I ignore that and ask her where Freddy is. "Salazar's got him in the office, chewing him out for coming in at four-fifty this morning. I'm sure Salazar's having a tougher time than Freddy in there."

I chuckle and say something like Yeah, or, I'll bet, but I notice my hands are trembling and I feel almost sick to my stomach. I'll admit that Peggy usually makes me nervous, but there's something more right now, something I can't get the finger on till two things happen. One: a fly lands on my hand, and I flick it away so hard I drop my mop. Then two: Peggy bends to pick it up for me, as I bend over she looks me right square down deep in the eyes. Then I remember. "So where is Freddy?" I say.

Peggy smiles, no doubt thinking she's got me in one of those magic moments where a guy finally notices how beautiful a woman is. "Someone's been working too hard," she says.

I say, "I mean, what time did Freddy come in, you say?" I notice her neck is all mottled up red, and I say to myself, Oh Lord, and I look up at her face and she winks and says, "About five, gorgeous." I wish I could tell her it's not her half moon beauty, but it does have to do with her, and these flies, and Kelly, and her color and mine, and especially her eyes, the most beautiful thing about her. And now that I really look at her it's got to do with her thin, chapped lips, her hawk nose, her long neck. She reminds me of this girl I thought was my friend for about a semester back in high school. Her name was Dianna Dillman, and she was my lab partner in tenth grade biology. I never had, like, a crush on Dianna or anything, but I liked her a lot. She was extremely funny and used to write little notes to me while Mr. Buller was yammering about pond scum, or mitosis, or some such crap. I figure because of Dianna I got C's instead of B's in that class, but for almost a whole semester it was worth it. If her little notes didn't crack me up, she'd go for what Buller used to call the 'lowbrow' stuff like pretending to get high from breathing the Bunsen burner gas, or just filling her cheeks with air and staring at me for five minutes. Guess you just had to be there. But one day all that stuff just stopped. Dianna acted like I was absent. Bad day, I told myself. So pretty much near the end of bio class, Mr. Buller asked me to stay after. I nudged Dianna with my elbow and whispered to her, "Wonder what this is all about. Nobel Prize, you think?" Dianna didn't say jack. She stared straight ahead and blushed red as her own lipstick.

Turns out the day before, Dianna's had her wallet lifted from her purse, and since she noticed it missing after bio class, and since I sat right smack next to her at our little black table, she figured I'd snagged it. I didn't take her wallet, and I was glad Buller believed me, but he told me that Dianna didn't wanna be my lab partner anymore. I didn't see her the rest of that day, so I never got the chance to argue my case. And the next day I found a note that she'd slipped into the vents of my locker. I knew it was her, cause it was in the same microscopic handwriting of all those funny little notes she'd slip me in class. It went, and I quote, "Only two things in this world that I despise / One of them's niggers / The other one's flies / Only one thing to say about each of these guys / The more I see niggers / The more I like flies." That was it. Not even a "Love, Dianna."

So this is one more thing to tell Kelly. One thing that's great about being white: The rest of my sophomore year I never could figure out the words to hurt Dianna as much as she'd hurt me. Fact is, I still don't think I could.

When I get back Kelly's so hot I'm surprised his little paper hat hasn't burst into flames. "What is it you people want?" he says.

Dominion over nature, time, and the bodies and minds of the white race, I think, but I say, "What'd he say?" and he waves his hairy hands in little circles like he's lost his balance while standing on a log.

"Man that guy burns my ass."

I don't say nothing. I just start collecting silverware and fighting flies, scraping plates, wiping sweat from my forehead, pulling the seam from the crack of my behind. Hell with these jerks, I say to myself. Hell with spooks, ofays, spicks, gooks, flies, cadets, paychecks, heat, necks . . .

"So," says Kelly, and I'm about two seconds from sticking a fork in his neck. I don't care. I just don't care, but the best thing I can do is let him finish his crap and then blow him away with all this stuff inside me, all this crap I been thinking. "So," he says, "I figure the guy's crazy, and I don't say nothing to him or even look at him when him and Whitaker leave the room. If the United States Marine Corps wants to give welfare to a goddamn lazy hophead that's OK. I'm a short-timer, and I don't care. I was in long enough to retire, even though I'd always wanted to do a full twenty-five years. But I just forgot about him. Just went about my business, you see. Least everybody was awake. That was that. I figured I just wouldn't deal with the kid no more.

"But one morning the first sergeant ast a bunch of Marines to redo the squadbay. Seems it was a pretty bad mess. You know it gets like that sometimes. The lads get in a hurry to get to morning chow and miss a spot or two with the swabs and brooms—Will you look at this. Sloppy sons a bitches. Look at this. Some idiot spilled a whole container a milk all over a tray of succotash."

"So fucken what, Kelly, it's not like we're gonna put it in a Tupperware container and stick it in—"

"So I don't know why I went up there, but for some reason I had to go see somebody in the company office. I don't know, but in order to get to the HQ, you gotta go through the squadbay, see? So I'm going up the stairwell, and I hear all this yelling and cussing, so I run up the rest of the way and Barney's got some little boot private pinned up against up the wall. Got his forearm jammed in the kid's windpipe and four other Marines are trying to pull Barney back, but like I told you, Barney's one stout little fella and they're having a pretty tough time getting him to let the little kid loose.

"Well, shit, what was I supposed to do? I help grab Barney's leg, then his arms, and finally we get him off the kid. This kid's name was Hernandez, Mexican fella, and big old Whitaker was there, and then there was this Samoan fella, Tapua, and another Mexican fella, a guy from Comm Platoon I didn't know, and this white fella name of Grice, a radio tech, I think he was. Looked like the goddamn United Nations, I was thinking. Sure wasn't like the Corps I joined. Not that I got anything against you people being in the service. Just never got used to it."

"Roll me the beverage cart, Kelly," I say, and then I tell him to go ahead.

Kelly walks the cart to me and says, "Well, I don't know why we did this. Maybe it was the way Barney relaxed so sudden, the way he just stared out the window like we wasn't even there. Made everybody else relax, too. We all just let him go. And I whispered to Grice to go get the police, and was just getting ready to walk Barney over to the office. I said, "All right, leatherneck, let's go." But he just stood there, staring out the window. Then in this real quiet voice he goes, 'I got something for you ass. I got something for all of you.' He was at his locker so fast nobody could do nothing. Besides, who the hell knew he'd come back with a pistol? But there he was, waving a silver-plated snub nose thirty-eight in all our faces.

"Next thing you know, Hernandez is on his knees, begging for his life. Whitaker's looking sick and pissed off. He sits down on a rack and just starts cussing kinda quiet like, saying how hard he's tried to be a good Marine and how every time he turns around it's some new bullshit. And the Samoan's waving his hands and backing up to the wall, speaking Samoan like he ain't never heard a the United States. The other Mexican kid's just standing there looking white, sweaty, and scared. And then there's me. After looking at all these scared young boys I closed my eyes and lowered my head, see, and it's like I got two brains. One brain's going, 'Now what the fuck am I supposed to say to this hophead to get him to put the stinking gun down.' The other brain's going, 'I don't give a rolling fuck what he does. I've had it. I've had it. Don't even care anymore— You better get that mop and broom. I'll get these carts."

"We got time, just finish."

"Well, he shot me."

"I thought you said he didn't."

"No, that's not what I said. I just told you I didn't say that. Hell yeah he shot me. Right in the thigh, splintered my femur bone like it was rotten bamboo. But the way Hernandez started screaming you'd a thought that Indian bastard'd shot him. But I was the onliest one he shot, and even though Whitaker was on top a Barney before he could get off another round, I knew he was only gonna pump em off into me if he'd had the chance."

"So you think he shot you cause you're white."

Salazar walks by before Kelly answers, and he tells us he'll be passing out the checks at the end of the shift. Kelly glares at Salazar. "Man," says Kelly, "I got no respect for that little prick."

"A guy who wears patent leather shoes is too lazy to shine."

"Kelly."

"Huh?"

"Is that your point? What's your point?"

"That's another reason I retired from the Corps. Lot of lazy goddamn boot officers'd wear patent leather cause they were just too damn lazy to put a good spit shine on their shoes. Why, do you know that some a them bastards were getting away with wearing patent leather combat boots? Where's the tradition? Where's the pride? You think I'd wanna be part a that after twenty-one years? No sir, I don't think so. No thank you . . . Look here, I'll swab this time. You sweep, and then let's get outta here. We're getting our pay, Scotty boy."

That's exactly what I did. I swept. It was like sweeping up a four-foot stack of broken dishes. Big pieces with razor sharp edges, little pieces with needle points, tinier pieces, like little daggers, pieces fine as moon dust. After I finished sweeping, I grabbed my check, went to the locker room and doffed the monkey suit, slipped into my jeans, sneakers, and t-shirt, and broke camp. But all the way home I still felt like I was sweeping broken china, from under tables, under chairs, from corners and cracks, and across wide polished floors, military clean and quiet as the mountains.

QUILTING ON THE REBOUND

F IVE YEARS AGO, I did something I swore I'd never do—went out with some-one I worked with. We worked for a large insurance company in L.A. Richard was a senior examiner and I was a chief underwriter. The first year, we kept it a secret, and not because we were afraid of jeopardizing our jobs. Richard was twenty-six and I was thirty-four. By the second year, everybody knew it anyway and nobody seemed to care. We'd been going out for three years when I realized that this rela-tionship was going nowhere. I probably could've dated him for the rest of my life and he'd have been satisfied. Richard had had a long reputation for being a Don Juan of sorts, until he met me. I cooled his heels. His name was also rather ironic, because he looked like a black Richard Gere. The fact that I was older than he was made him feel powerful in a sense, and he believed that he could do for me what men my own age apparently couldn't. But that wasn't true. He was a challenge. I wanted to see if I could make his head and heart turn 360 degrees, and I did. I blew his young mind in bed, but he also charmed me into loving him until I didn't care how old he was.

Richard thought I was exotic because I have slanted eyes, high cheekbones, and full lips. Even though my mother is Japanese and my dad is black, I inherited most of his traits. My complexion is dark, my hair is nappy, and I'm five-six. I explained to Richard that I was proud of both of my heritages, but he has insisted on think-ing of me as being mostly Japanese. Why, I don't know. I grew up in a black neigh-borhood in L.A., went to Dorsey High School—which was predominantly black, Asian, and Hispanic—and most of my friends are black. I've never even consid-ered going out with anyone other than black men.

My mother, I'm glad to say, is not the stereotypical passive Japanese wife either. She's been the head nurse in Kaiser's cardiovascular unit for over twenty years, and my dad has his own landscaping business, even though he should've retired years ago. My mother liked Richard and his age didn't bother her, but she believed that if a man loved you he should marry you. Simple as that. On the other hand, my dad didn't care who I married just as long as it was soon. I'll be the first to admit that I was a spoiled-rotten brat because my mother had had three miscarriages before she finally had me and I was used to getting everything I wanted. Richard was no exception. "Give him the ultimatum," my mother had said, if he didn't propose by my thirty-eighth birthday.

But I didn't have to. I got pregnant.

We were having dinner at an Italian restaurant when I told him. "You want to get married, don't you?" he'd said.

"Do you?" I asked.

He was picking through his salad and then he jabbed his fork into a tomato. "Why not, we were headed in that direction anyway, weren't we?" He did not eat his tomato but laid his fork down on the side of the plate.

I swallowed a spoonful of my clam chowder, then asked, "Were we?"

"You know the answer to that. But hell, now's as good a time as any. We're both making good money, and sometimes all a man needs is a little incentive." He didn't look at me when he said this, and his voice was strained. "Look," he said, "I've had a pretty shitty day, haggling with one of the adjusters, so forgive me if I don't appear to be boiling over with excitement. I am happy about this. Believe me, I am," he said, and picked up a single piece of lettuce with a different fork and put it into his mouth.

My parents were thrilled when I told them, but my mother was nevertheless suspicious. "Funny how this baby pop up, isn't it?" she'd said.

"What . . . (to come)

"You know exactly what I mean. I hope baby doesn't backfire."

I ignored what she'd just said. "Will you help me make my dress?" I asked.

"Yes," she said. "But we must hurry."

My parents—who are far from well off—went all out for this wedding. My mother didn't want anyone to know I was pregnant, and to be honest, I didn't either. The age difference was enough to handle as it was. Close to three hundred people had been invited, and my parents had spent an astronomical amount of money to rent a country club in Marina Del Rey. "At your age," my dad had said, "I hope you'll only be doing this once." Richard's parents insisted on taking care of the caterer and the liquor, and my parents didn't object. I paid for the cake.

About a month before the Big Day, I was meeting Richard at the jeweler because he'd picked out my ring and wanted to make sure I liked it. He was so excited, he sounded like a little boy. It was beautiful, but I told him he didn't have to spend four thousand dollars on my wedding ring. "You're worth it," he'd said and kissed me on the cheek. When we got to the parking lot, he opened my door and stood there staring at me. "Four more weeks," he said, "and you'll be my wife." He didn't smile when he said it, but closed the door and walked around to the driver's side and got in. He'd driven four whole blocks without saying a word and his knuckles were almost white because of how tight he was holding the steering wheel.

"Is something wrong, Richard?" I asked him.

"What would make you think that?" he said. Then he laid on the horn because someone in front of us hadn't moved and the light had just barely turned green.

"Richard, we don't have to go through with this, you know."

"I know we don't *have* to, but it's the right thing to do, and I'm going to do it. So don't worry, we'll be happy."

But I *was* worried.

I'd been doing some shopping at the Beverly Center when I started getting these stomach cramps while I was going up the escalator, so I decided to sit down. I walked over to one of the little outside cafés and I felt something lock inside my stomach, so I pulled out a chair. Moments later my skirt felt like it was wet. I got up and looked at the chair and saw a small red puddle. I sat back down and started crying. I didn't know what to do. Then a punkish-looking girl came over and asked if I was okay. "I'm pregnant, and I've just bled all over this chair," I said.

"Can I do something for you? Do you want me to call an ambulance?" She was popping chewing gum and I wanted to snatch it out of her mouth.

By this time at least four other women had gathered around me. The punkish-looking girl told them about my condition. One of the women said, "Look, let's get her to the rest room. She's probably having a miscarriage."

Two of the women helped me up and all four of them formed a circle around me, then slowly led me to the ladies' room. I told them that I wasn't in any pain, but they were still worried. I closed the stall door, pulled down two toilet seat covers, and sat down. I felt as if I had to go, so I pushed. Something plopped out of me and it made a splash. I was afraid to get up but I got up and looked at this large dark mass that looked like liver. I put my hand over my mouth because I knew that was my baby.

"Are you okay in there?"

I went to open my mouth, but the joint in my jawbone clicked and my mouth wouldn't move.

"Are you okay in there, miss?"

I wanted to answer, but I couldn't.

"Miss." I heard her banging on the door.

I felt my mouth loosen. "It's gone," I said. "It's gone."

"Honey, open the door," someone said, but I couldn't move. Then I heard myself say, "I think I need a sanitary pad." I was staring into the toilet when I felt a hand hit my leg. "Here, are you sure you're okay in there?"

"Yes," I said. Then I flushed the toilet with my foot and watched my future disappear. I put the pad on and reached inside my shopping bag, pulled out a Raiders sweatshirt I'd bought for Richard, and tied it around my waist. When I came out, all of the women were waiting for me. "Would you like us to call your husband? Where are you parked? Do you feel light-headed, dizzy?"

"No, I'm fine, really, and thank you so much for your concern. I appreciate it, but I feel okay."

I drove home in a daze and when I opened the door to my condo, I was glad I lived alone. I sat on the couch from one o'clock to four o'clock without moving. When I finally got up, it felt as if I'd only been there for five minutes.

I didn't tell Richard. I didn't tell anybody. I bled for three days before I went to see my doctor. He scolded me because I'd gotten some kind of an infection and had to be prescribed antibiotics, then he sent me to the outpatient clinic, where I had to have a D & C.

Two weeks later, I had a surprise shower and got enough gifts to fill the housewares department at Bullock's. One of my old girlfriends, Gloria, came all the way from Phoenix, and I hadn't seen her in three years. I hardly recognized her, she was as big as a house. "You don't know how lucky you are, girl," she'd said to me. "I wish I could be here for the wedding but Tarik is having his sixteenth birthday party and I am not leaving a bunch of teenagers alone in my house. Besides, I'd probably have a heart attack watching you or anybody else walk down an aisle in white. Come to think of it, I can't even remember the last time I went to a wedding."

"Me either," I said.

"I know you're gonna try to get pregnant in a hurry, right?" she asked, holding out her wrist with the watch on it.

I tried to smile. "I'm going to work on it," I said.

"Well, who knows?" Gloria said, laughing. "Maybe one day you'll be coming to my wedding. We may both be in wheelchairs, but you never know."

"I'll be there," I said.

All Richard said when he saw the gifts was, "What are we going to do with all this stuff? Where are we going to put it?"

"It depends on where we're going to live," I said, which we hadn't even talked about. My condo was big enough and so was his apartment.

"It doesn't matter to me, but I think we should wait a while before buying a house. A house is a big investment, you know. Thirty years." He gave me a quick look.

"Are you getting cold feet?" I blurted out.

"No, I'm not getting cold feet. It's just that in two weeks we're going to be man and wife, and it takes a little getting used to the idea, that's all."

"Are you having doubts about the idea of it?"

"No."

"Are you sure?"

"I'm sure," he said.

I didn't stop bleeding, so I took some vacation time to relax and finish my dress. I worked on it day and night and was doing all the beadwork by hand. My mother was spending all her free time at my place trying to make sure everything was happening on schedule. A week before the Big Day I was trying on my gown for the hundredth time when the phone rang. I thought it might be Richard, since he hadn't called me in almost forty-eight hours, and when I finally called him and left a message, he still hadn't returned my call. My father said this was normal.

"Hello," I said.

"I think you should talk to Richard." It was his mother.

"About what?" I asked.

"He's not feeling very well," was all she said.

"What's wrong with him?"

"I don't know for sure. I think it's his stomach."

"Is he sick?"

"I don't know. Call him."

"I did call him but he hasn't returned my call."

"Keep trying," she said.

So I called him at work, but his secretary said he wasn't there. I called him at home and he wasn't there either, so I left another message and for the next three hours I was a wreck, waiting to hear from him. I knew something was wrong.

I gave myself a facial, a manicure, and a pedicure and watched Oprah Winfrey while I waited by the phone. It didn't ring. My mother was downstairs hemming one of the bridesmaid's dresses. I went down to get myself a glass of wine. "How you feeling, Marilyn Monroe?" she asked.

"What do you mean, how am I feeling? I'm feeling fine."

"All I meant was you awful lucky with no morning sickness or anything, but I must say, hormones changing because you getting awfully irritating."

"I'm sorry, Ma."

"It's okay. I had jitters too."

I went back upstairs and closed my bedroom door, then went into my bathroom. I put the wineglass on the side of the bathtub and decided to take a bubble bath in spite of the bleeding. I must have poured half a bottle of Secreti in. The water was too hot but I got in anyway. Call, dammit, call. Just then the phone rang and scared me half to death. I was hyperventilating and couldn't say much except, "Hold on a minute," while I caught my breath.

"Marilyn?" Richard was saying. "Marilyn?" But before I had a chance to answer he blurted out what must have been on his mind all along. "Please don't be mad at me, but I can't do this. I'm not ready. I wanted to do the right thing, but I'm only twenty-nine years old. I've got my whole life ahead of me. I'm not ready to be a father yet. I'm not ready to be anybody's husband either, and I'm scared. Everything is happening too fast. I know you think I'm being a coward, and you're probably right. But I've been having nightmares, Marilyn. Do you hear me, nightmares about being imprisoned. I haven't been able to sleep through the night. I doze off and wake up dripping wet. And my stomach. It's in knots. Believe me, Marilyn, it's not that I don't love you because I do. It's not that I don't care about the baby, because I do. I just can't do this right now. I can't make this kind of commitment right now. I'm sorry. Marilyn? Marilyn, are you still there?"

I dropped the portable phone in the bathtub and got out.

My mother heard me screaming and came tearing into the room. "What happened?"

I was dripping wet and ripping the pearls off my dress but somehow I managed to tell her.

"He come to his senses," she said. "This happen a lot. He just got cold feet, but give him day or two. He not mean it."

Three days went by and he didn't call. My mother stayed with me and did everything she could to console me, but by that time I'd already flushed the ring down the toilet.

"I hope you don't lose baby behind this," she said.

"I've already lost the baby," I said.

"What?"

"A month ago."

Her mouth was wide open. She found the sofa with her hand and sat down. "Marilyn," she said and let out an exasperated sigh.

"I couldn't tell anybody."

"Why not tell somebody? Why not me, your mother?"

"Because I was too scared."

"Scared of what?"

"That Richard might change his mind."

"Man love you, dead baby not change his mind."

"I was going to tell him after we got married."

"I not raise you to be dishonest."

"I know."

"No man in the world worth lying about something like this. How could you?"

"I don't know."

"I told you it backfire, didn't I?"

For weeks I couldn't eat or sleep. At first, all I did was think about what was wrong with me. I was too old. For him. No. He didn't care about my age. It was the gap in my teeth, or my slight overbite, from all those years I used to suck my thumb. But he never mentioned anything about it and I was really the only one who seemed to notice. I was flat-chested. I had cellulite. My ass was square instead of round. I wasn't exciting as I used to be in bed. No. I was still good in bed, that much I did know. I couldn't cook. I was a terrible housekeeper. That was it. If you couldn't cook and keep a clean house, what kind of wife would you make?

I had to make myself stop thinking about my infinite flaws, so I started quilting again. I was astonished at how radiant the colors were that I was choosing, how unconventional and wild the patterns were. Without even realizing it, I was fusing Japanese and African motifs and was quite excited by the results. My mother was worried about me, even though I had actually stopped bleeding for two whole weeks. Under the circumstances, she thought that my obsession with quilting was not normal, so she forced me to go to the doctor. He gave me some kind of an antidepressant, which I refused to take. I told him I was not depressed, I was simply hurt. Besides, a pill wasn't any antidote or consolation for heartache.

I began to patronize just about every fabric store in downtown Los Angeles, and while I listened to the humming of my machine, and concentrated on designs that I couldn't believe I was creating, it occurred to me that I wasn't suffering from heartache at all. I actually felt this incredible sense of relief. As if I didn't have to anticipate anything else happening that was outside of my control. And when I did grieve, it was always because I had lost a child, not a future husband.

I also heard my mother all day long on my phone, lying about some tragedy that had happened and apologizing for any inconvenience it may have caused. And I watched her, bent over at the dining room table, writing hundreds of thank-you notes to the people she was returning gifts to. She even signed my name. My father wanted to kill Richard. "He was too young, and he wasn't good enough for you anyway," he said. "This is really a blessing in disguise."

I took a leave of absence from my job because there was no way in hell I could face those people, and the thought of looking at Richard infuriated me. I was not angry at him for not marrying me, I was angry at him for not being honest, for the way he handled it all. He even had the nerve to come over without calling. I had opened the door but wouldn't let him inside. He was nothing but a little pipsqueak. A handsome, five-foot-seven-inch pipsqueak.

"Marilyn, look, we need to talk."

"About what?"

"Us. The baby."

"There is no baby."

"What do you mean, there's no baby?"

"It died."

"You mean you got rid of it?"

"No, I lost it."

"I'm sorry, Marilyn," he said and put his head down. How touching, I thought. "This is all my fault."

"It's not your fault, Richard."

"Look. Can I come in?"

"For what?"

"I want to talk. I need to talk to you."

"About what?"

"About us."

"Us?"

"Yes, us. I don't want it to be over between us. I just need more time, that's all."

"Time for what?"

"To make sure this is what I want to do."

"Take all the time you need," I said and slammed the door in his face. He rang the buzzer again, but I just told him to get lost and leave me alone.

I went upstairs and sat at my sewing machine. I turned the light on, then picked up a piece of purple and terra-cotta cloth. I slid it under the pressure foot and dropped it. I pressed down on the pedal and watched the needle zigzag. The stitches were too loose so I tightened the tension. Richard is going to be the last in a series of mistakes I've made when it comes to picking a man. I've picked the wrong one too many times, like a bad habit that's too hard to break. I haven't had the best of luck when it comes to keeping them either, and to be honest, Richard was the one who lasted the longest.

When I got to the end of the fabric, I pulled the top and bobbin threads together and cut them on the thread cutter. Then I bent down and picked up two different pieces. They were black and purple: I always want what I can't have or what I'm not supposed to have. So what did I do? Created a pattern of choosing men that I knew would be a challenge. Richard's was his age. But the others—all of them from Alex to William—were all afraid of something: namely, committing to one woman. All I wanted to do was seduce them hard enough—emotionally, mentally, and physically—so they wouldn't even be aware that they were committing to anything. I just wanted them to crave me, and no one else but me. I wanted to be their healthiest addiction. But it was a lot harder to do than I thought. What I found out was that men are a hard nut to crack.

But some of them weren't. When I was in my late twenties, early thirties— before I got serious and realized I wanted a long-term relationship—I'd had at least twenty different men fall in love with me, but of course these were the ones I didn't want. They were the ones who after a few dates or one rousing night in bed, ordained themselves my "man" or were too quick to want to marry me, and even some considered me their "property." When it was clear that I was dealing with a different species of man, a hungry element, before I got in too deep, I'd tell them almost immediately that I hope they wouldn't mind my being bisexual or my being unfaithful because I was in no hurry to settle down with one man, or that I had a tendency of always falling for my man's friends. Could they tolerate that? I even went so far as to tell them that I hoped having herpes wouldn't cause a problem, that I wasn't really all that trustworthy because I was a habitual liar, and that if they wanted the whole truth they should find themselves another woman. I told them that I didn't even think I was good enough for them, and they should do themselves a favor, find a woman who's truly worthy of having such a terrific man.

I had it down to a science, but by the time I met Richard, I was tired of lying and conniving. I was sick of the games. I was whipped, really, and allowed myself to relax and be vulnerable because I knew I was getting old.

When Gloria called to see how my honeymoon went, I told her the truth about everything. She couldn't believe it. "Well, I thought I'd heard 'em all, but this one takes the cake. How you holding up?"

"I'm hanging in there."

"This is what makes you want to castrate a man."

"Not really, Gloria."

"I know. But you know what I mean. Some of them have a lot of nerve, I swear they do. But really, Marilyn, how are you feeling for real, baby?"

"I'm getting my period every other week, but I'm quilting again, which is a good sign."

"First of all, take your behind back to that doctor and find out why you're still bleeding like this. And, honey, making quilts is no consolation for a broken heart. It sounds like you could use some R and R. Why don't you come visit me for a few days?"

I looked around my room, which had piles and piles of cloth and half-sewn quilts, from where I'd changed my mind. Hundreds of different-colored threads were all over the carpet, and the satin stitch I was trying out wasn't giving me the effect I thought it would. I could use a break, I thought I could. "You know what?" I said. "I think I will."

"Good, and bring me one of those tacky quilts. I don't have anything to snuggle up with in the winter, and contrary to popular belief, it does get cold here come December."

I liked Phoenix and Tempe, but I fell in love with Scottsdale. Not only was it beautiful but I couldn't believe how inexpensive it was to live in the entire area, which was all referred to as the Valley. I have to thank Gloria for being such a lifesaver. She took me to her beauty salon and gave me a whole new look. She chopped off my hair, and one of the guys in her shop showed me how to put on my makeup in a way that would further enhance what assets he insisted I had.

We drove to Tucson, to Canyon Ranch for what started out as a simple Spa Renewal Day. But we ended up spending three glorious days and had the works. I had an herbal wrap, where they wrapped my entire body in hot thin linen that had been steamed. Then they rolled me up in flannel blankets and put a cold washcloth on my forehead. I sweated in the dark for a half hour. Gloria didn't do this because she said she was claustrophobic and didn't want to be wrapped up in anything where she couldn't move. I had a deep-muscle and shiatsu massage on two different days. We steamed. We Jacuzzied. We both had a mud facial, and then this thing called aromatherapy—where they put distilled essences from flowers and herbs on your face and you look like a different person when they finish. On the last day, we got this Persian Body Polish where they actually buffed our skin with crushed pearl creams, sprayed us with some kind of herbal spray, then used an electric brush to make us tingle. We had our hands and feet moisturized and put in heated gloves and booties, and by the time we left, we couldn't believe we were the same women.

In Phoenix, Gloria took me to yet another resort where we listened to live music. We went to see a stupid movie and I actually laughed. Then we went on a two-day shopping spree and I charged whatever I felt like. I even bought her son a pair of eighty-dollar sneakers, and I'd only seen him twice in my life.

I felt like I'd gotten my spirit back, so when I got home, I told my parents I'd had it with the smog, the traffic, the gangs, and L.A. in general. My mother said, "You cannot run from heartache," but I told her I wasn't running from anything. I put my condo on the market, and in less than a month it sold for four times what I paid for it. I moved in with my mother and father, asked for a job transfer for health reasons, and when it came through, three months later, I moved to Scottsdale.

The town house I bought feels like a house. It's twice the size of the one I had and cost less than half of what I originally spent. My complex is pretty standard for Scottsdale. It has two pools and four tennis courts. It also has vaulted ceilings, wall-to-wall carpet, two fireplaces, and a garden bathtub with a Jacuzzi in it. The kitchen has an island in the center and I've got a 180-degree view of Phoenix and mountains. It also has three bedrooms. One I sleep in, one I use for sewing, and the other is for guests.

I made close to forty thousand dollars after I sold my condo, so I sent four to my parents because the money they'd put down for the wedding was nonrefundable. They really couldn't afford that kind of loss. The rest I put in an IRA and CDs until I could figure out something better to do with it.

I hated my new job. I had to accept a lower-level position and less money, which didn't bother me all that much at first. The office, however, was much smaller and full of rednecks who couldn't stand the thought of a black woman working over them. I was combing the classifieds, looking for a comparable job, but the job market in Phoenix is nothing close to what it is in L.A.

But thank God Gloria's got a big mouth. She'd been boasting to all of her clients about my quilts, had even hung the one I'd given her on the wall at the shop, and the next thing I know I'm getting so many orders I couldn't keep up with them. That's when she asked me why didn't I consider opening my own shop? That never would've occurred to me, but what did I have to lose?

She introduced me to Bernadine, a friend of hers who was an accountant. Bernadine in turn introduced me to a good lawyer, and he helped me draw up all the papers. Over the next four months, she helped me devise what turned out to be a strong marketing and advertising plan. I rented an 800-square-foot space in the same shopping center where Gloria's shop is, and opened Quiltworks, Etc.

It wasn't long before I realized I needed to get some help, so I hired two seamstresses. They took a lot of the strain off of me, and I was able to take some jewelry-making classes and even started selling small pieces in the shop. Gloria gave me this tacky T-shirt for my thirty-ninth birthday, which gave me the idea to experiment with making them. Because I go overboard in everything I do, I went out and spent a fortune on every color of metallic and acrylic fabric paint they made. I bought one hundred 100-percent cotton heavy-duty men's T-shirts and discovered other uses for sponges, plastic, spray bottles, rolling pins, lace, and even old envelopes. I was having a great time because I'd never felt this kind of excitement and gratification doing anything until now.

I'd been living here a year when I found out that Richard had married another woman who worked in our office. I wanted to hate him, but I didn't. I wanted to be angry, but I wasn't. I didn't feel anything toward him, but I sent him a quilt and a wedding card to congratulate him, just because.

To be honest, I've been so busy with my shop, I haven't even thought about men. I don't even miss having sex unless I really just *think* about it. My libido must be evaporating, because when I *do* think about it, I just make quilts or jewelry or paint T-shirts and the feeling goes away. Some of my best ideas come at these moments.

Basically, I'm doing everything I can to make Marilyn feel good. And at thirty-nine years old my body needs tightening, so I joined a health club and started working out three to four times a week. Once in a while, I babysit for Bernadine, and it breaks my heart when I think about the fact that I don't have a child of my own. Sometimes, Gloria and I go out to hear some music. I frequent most of the major art galleries, go to just about every football and basketball game at Arizona State, and see at *least* one movie a week.

I am rarely bored. Which is why I've decided that at this point in my life, I really don't care if I ever get married. I've learned that I don't need a man in order to survive, that a man is nothing but an intrusion, and they require too much energy. I don't think they're worth it. Besides, they have too much power, and from what I've seen, they always seem to abuse it. The one thing I *do* have is power over my own life. I like it this way, and I'm not about to give it up for something that may not last.

The one thing I do want is to have a baby. Someone I could love who would love me back with no strings attached. But at thirty-nine, I know my days are numbered. I'd be willing to do it alone, if that's the only way I can have one. But right now, my life is almost full. It's fun, it's secure, and it's safe. About the only thing I'm concerned about these days is whether or not it's time to branch out into leather.

MARK MCMORRIS

BLACK PIECES

The colors of the bushes
And of the fallen leaves,
Repeating themselves,
Turned in the room,
Like the leaves themselves
Turning in the wind.

—Wallace Stevens
"Domination of Black"

FLOOD

Clearer now, in this state of darkness, the several pieces in the one, that across the intervening years, I owe to each what I have become. There is no news of the self. In the power station, huge turbines sit silent as the water drips. In my name, St. John, the lights have been put out. The island lies reft of gladness, sodden the roots of crotons, gardens awash in rivers of stalk, petal, and wrack. The flood never ceases. At Queen's Street, at Matilda's Corner, along the Old Hope Road, a trickle of hand carts: a kettle, a photograph of Christ, a broadnosed ax, a lignum vitae bed, a cotton smock, a chest of drawers, an old man's hat, a grandmother's clock, a mermaid of glass, a pair of workboots. The questions fall, they fizzle and go out. Parliament deserted, water babbles in the aisle, left bench and right bench empty of thunder. The empty seats, e pluribus unum, a curse. Women flee to the airport; a child stops, drinks from the puddle left by a donkey's hoof. No planes will kiss the sky, no bird will carry them to land. We are stuck, like a tree, I shout. Shade of Denzil,

385

shade of Tanya and Charles, and the blank shadow of myself. We dance like the fates. Time passes, and clouds gather, and skies leak. Why not go in? A merciless whip, the lash of rain on my back. Where is the nurse, Martha the angellos, paraclete too pure for love? Her insides are bitter. Will she be appeased? Who can read this riddle for us? What man is not a riddle himself? Do we aim too high? Why is the wrath unleashed? Why shall I die and not live? Why shall my race be extinct? Why shall I eat dust? Why go on my belly like a dog? Why do I stare at a blizzard? Why do I scratch at my face? Why do I shriek at Danielle? Why do I hate what I love? The stones talk only to plan our death. Day in day out, the workmen hammer nails, fit joints, saw wood, talk with a loud scrape, and they sing. Chisel and lathe sing to us asleep, doing our tasks, making love, eating soup, waiting for the day of god. Thus we are children to the last. We hunt pigeons by guile and set them loose. We wait for our flight. An old woman thumps her chest and looks grim. Her room smells of lilac or death. Charles has trouble breathing. He'll have to wait for the next bell. Danielle grows thin, stalk of celery. She'll have to wait. She will not again be the girl who followed me home. The next world, where is it? A long time in the oven. Earth is behind us; it rode upon the flood and sank before the flood. No land. Bah! "Let it be done quickly!" "Not yet," the poet said. Once, the lichen clouds, great boulders in the sky, swept over Riverside park. A morning of the trees, cool air, and pale blue light, she will come. Only let it stop. Pax vobiscum sit, undique verba tamquam imbres in me decidunt. Heu! a a. Creeping things take refuge in the house, ant with snake, centipede, galliwasp. Black men die and deepen at the roots of cotton. Shrieks of the cockfight spill from my eyes, mouth, nose. This could take some time, I murmur. Liver? OK. Heart? OK. Kidneys? OK. Lungs? OK. Everything in place and working round the clock. The old cock. What a sight! The bird of Zeus caws for some more liver. It bites, it draws, it feeds. The Titan lies open to the heavens. Eye of a red lid. Sunlight, rain, envy, ash, madness, skin, fire, death. The inner body seeps and quails, quakes, collapses on itself, and the dam of acid bursts. Sabotage, and the bird jabs. Terror, and the frame cracks. Frenzy, and the red eye of the moon searches out the One; her blade lies on my neck. Stars falter. Black sky, grey dirty morning, scream and cower of afternoon, dialtone days, rock of Sisyphus.

ASPECTS OF BLACK

: 1

I make seats for the arena, and on them, the *raison* for the building, the target, the colors that distinguish its areas, the black men, the blue girls, the red boys, the green women, the arrows (stuck into them) which create the hubbub that you no doubt perceive. The letters of the alphabet decide to fight it out. There is A for Antoine, B for Basil, and C for Carol—the latter androgynous and confused. They face forward like buddhas in a museum; they sit like rocks, like lizards in the sun, and hold colloquy with their own desires. This is how the fight goes. They share one hat, and I feel that my time would be better spent among individuals, Denzil, my friend, or Charles, or alone. The colloquy peters out, and then they leave. Each takes a different hat from the one he came in with. Only then does it become clear that three hats cannot occur in this scheme. Only then does it become clear that the letters stand for pieces of the host, wafer-thin mutations put gently on my tongue by a man in black. Antoine, Basil, and Carol build a scaffold for themselves and put a stop to the fight. Yes, for then I will be in remission; then I will have some peace.

: 2

We come to the intersection at Avenue de Clichy. The road is clear. We cross to the metro stop and go underground. I think of a crack in the river tunnel that widens out of sight. As our train dips to the river, the fissure opens to a gash, and waters flood the compartment where Danielle and I sit. Our names float in the wreckage. Beside our names float the extra yellow *billets* Danielle keeps for an emergency. They go to the mouth of the river and are lost. Afterwards, an exchange takes place:

"Where are we now?"
"Where we were then."
"Who sits beside you Now?"
"Who wanted to sit with me."
"Am I the person beside you in the dream?"
"You were asleep."
"Who is Madame N?"
"She was my confidence."
"Who is Tanya?"
"She was my infancy."
"And who is Charles?"
"He is my comfort. He takes the seat next to me."
"And who am I?"
"You were my sin, my anger, and my collapse. Unknown to yourself."

BEING NATURAL

AND APT TO BECOME DRY

Danielle reclines beside me on the pool deck. The loudspeaker tied to a coconut tree announces the event, namely, the performance of a man who makes hats for a living. He himself wears one hat of thatched green with stiff ends poking out; he carries a bundle of thin leaves to his stool, drops them on the concrete, and takes up the microphone. The weaver talks as he weaves. Danielle listens. She is long and sleek on the stripes of the recliner. Both of us enjoy the lazy afternoon. Danielle says that a man who makes hats for a living has never left Paradise. He weaves a hat exactly to the size of his head and avoids the slippage or vice so often found in our efforts. He draws his thatch from coconut trees in the yard; nothing enters or leaves this yard, it is a place, and meaning accrues from a fresh integration of parts: a frond, and its joining with other fronds, makes a natural cover for the head. Danielle says:

"Each hat fits into the former hat and drops from its belly like a foal."

Mellows the Hat Weaver. He builds himself as he builds a hat. He never gets weary. Being natural and apt to become dry, a hat can peel and wear out and fall from his head. The weaver's skin can peel and become dry and fall from his body. But the supply never ends, and as Mellows weaves a hat, so a hat keeps the sun from his scalp. To defend himself, he does what he is, flourishes and entertains, and so makes his living. Pleasure ensues.

Mellows wraps up his demonstration with a freshly made hat. It holds our attention. "Anyone might want such a hat or such an art for himself." I agree with her. Elements of meaning still lie raw and unconnected between us, manifold, implying a finished self. There they must stay until an epithet sticks, and we do what it tells us with the ruminating sherds.

Dialogue stops. Dialogue begins.

A dash of color from the violets. Rough brick. Other shapes come into view.
(People must be nearby.)

A sparrow from the mist. Goes into the mist.

No place to stand; no base for the figure.

One sees with the mouth. I see.

A butterfly, a bumblebee: Cannot settle into the shape that it had.

Shape of horror   an egg yolk   a body   what I fill.

The I stops short. logos.
Seed of perishing or self.

"I am black, like night," I said.
"All the threads enter and lose heart.
They thicken, and drag me to nothing."

"Write on the surface," he said.
"And read yourself in the spaces below them."

"I am too young to read. Too old
to learn how to write, too shadowy
for any seed to sprout in me.

"I eat space like a fire eats paper.
I consume myself.
This is the nature of my ash."

SATURDAYS (DANIELLE)

". . . He just sat down beside me. I thought—I can't be bothered. He began to talk. Of course I didn't. You'd have to see him. We had coffee once or twice. OK. When the weather's warmer. Yes. I put down the paper. I did. He said it was fine with him, he'd like to go out for coffee and talk. Central Park? OK. Because he looked interesting. People have these weird lives in their apartments and you don't know about them. I was curious. The things that you hear. Tanya told me of a guy who raised pit bulls inside his apartment over on Madison Avenue. He snuck them past the doorman in his attaché case and when they were about a year old, he sold them for the extra income. His neighbors believed that he had the same dog for years. Tanya thought that he wanted to go to bed with her and was making up an amusing story about himself. He became very serious, and invited her over to see. The oldest trick in the book, I don't know why she went. Anyway, the guy opens the door and it hits her smack in the face, dogs everywhere—in the front closet, the bathroom, under the kitchen counter, and the smell! He worked for Dean Witter and did not need the money. 'Good day Mr de Angelis,' and Mr de Angelis would go home to his pit bulls and truck load of Alpo. It's strange how the weirdos stick to us like glue. Thadeus—yes. Don't be dumb. He was a fat motorman from Queens. He drove the subway for a living and went home to write his novel. No, he did not circle round for me in his train. We took the bus. About 35. Will you let me finish? I know, but it was in the day and he looked harmless. You can tell. He was wearing an orange jacket with pink stripes—it was his day off—and dark glasses on the #2 Express. No, I did not do it to spite you. Charles is different—we are friends. No. I told you no. I got tired of him and didn't call him back. You get tired of someone who needs you all the time. I mean—I'm not sure how to say this—when we went out he'd tell me things, but I kept thinking, This sure is weird, boy. He liked that I had been in France and wanted me to tell him about Paris. Martha? If I say anything about her you will be upset. It was before we were together, I didn't even know you then. Of course it is! You were Tanya's friend. I knew you through Tanya. I didn't know that you knew her until we had come back. I told you. No. Charles and I are friends. It's not the same. We get along when we are together. In Greece. We were traveling and it, I can't talk about this, it doesn't really have to do with you. I won't talk about this anymore. You never even told me about her. You call me Martha and I don't say anything. You know how that feels? . . ."

PARK

It was rush hour, and my spectacles
broke under impatient feet
and night fell down on Riverside Drive
and entered the elms

And then I saw such light!
Have I told you about light in the park?
How the wind dashes it, and all the leaves
in confusion overhead

and the street lamps like hoses blazing
out orange on the benches
the nozzle of light from stooping trees.

REPLY

I sit on the wicker sofa reading a magazine. Danielle comes from the kitchen. Her cheerful face tells me that she will transmit cheer. Some activity—a film, a request for dinner—lurks. Danielle comes from the kitchen. Her nervous face tells me that she will transmit unease. Some activity—a film, a request for dinner—lurks. Our years together were like this: she moved in, I moved back, she took hold of my hand, I shook it off. On the bar stool, cognac and vodka, bouncing labels from the mirror, Danielle pleads with me: *Let's go.* You go ahead. *It's late.* But I want to relax. Danielle takes herself home. Tomorrow: I walk with myself by the Hudson River. I go along. Danielle goes along. We go along the avenue past the elderly doorman. He waves at us. I am pleased to orbit this village. Too young, both of us, to stop the free fall. I took employment—Angela's breasts poking ahead of her— hauled crates of beer from the cellar, fending off Danielle, not in love. Once, beside her who was still asleep, I stayed in bed to think of Martha's skin. Dogged by memory, the taking of that girl to the shed till she cried for humiliation—still no deflowering took place. Contact needs two poles. She choked on her need for touch. She stomped and stomped as if to kill herself at the root. She tore off her blouse and beat me with her fists. Still no deflowering took place. The cistern packed with green coils of hose. A pitchfork, a rake, a pair of hedge clippers, the smell of overalls and gardener's sweat: crowded by them, we forced the issue. The years well up. Danielle tears at her hair and her face. I walk faster from her. She follows me naked from the waist up and shouts. If I stop, what then? *Why do you hate me so much?* I hate myself. *What have I done to make you despise me?* I despise you. The light falls on us, on tables of the café in the main square. Holiday in ruins. She choked on my need to push her off. Martha believed that conduct shapes personality. I that it should. Contact occurs; we drift apart—the stereo turning out Billie Holiday—on the arras of Danielle's couch. "Whether you care about things, people other than yourself." I agree with her. Interest does not send its tentacles out. Fear builds a scaffold with no one to catch me if I drop. That was Danielle, behind me with her welcome, though I vowed not to go back. Under an attack from all parts of my body now that she has left. Her letters arrived once a week with newspaper clippings, chocolate kisses, for Easter, a care package with a bottle of scotch; once a letter with a reply envelope stamped and addressed that I still have. Then the communications stopped. Events that interfere and interrupt. I can see very little ahead of myself except for what has been done. This is the labyrinth.

FIGHT

Three dice (darts) rattle for my sum;
they orbit the same piece of rock.
Three darts (dice) spoil for my seal.

Antoine Basil Carol
sit in different rooms of my sleep.
Chiefly I serve them.

(ATROPOS)

Danielle tosses the balloons from her seat. I sit beside the Indonesian tiger and bat them back at her. The balloons jostle one another; a few glide to the piano where Charles sits with his wine glass and legs crossed. One balloon goes from Danielle's hand to my hand to Charles's leg, and he kicks it. Suddenly it bursts. Danielle says, "Heavens!" (Danielle is the only person I know who says, "Heavens!") Charles opens another bottle of wine. Denzil comes in with Tanya, and the fun begins. Tanya puts on "Trench Town Rock." We dance like the fates. But Atropos is quiet, and the threads that tie us to her spindle slacken and allow us to choose. We are almost free from character, in between the bars of music. We slip from the bars, into a meadow of wine and desire, Danielle, Charles, Tanya, me, and Denzil. The talking has stopped. Careful not to trample and destroy them, careful not to expel, before we have had our fill, Danielle's breath that makes them expand, we step among her balloons. "This will not come again." Tongue like a gargoyle's, Charles wags his head to the music. But the music has stopped, and he waves his body to the silence. That is where I am. That's where Danielle sits and holds the spindle.

THE STORY OF A SCAR

Since Dr. Wayland was late and there were no recent newsmagazines in the waiting room, I turned to the other patient and said: "As a concerned person, and as your brother, I ask you, without meaning to offend, how did you get that scar on the side of your face?"

The woman seemed insulted. Her brown eyes, which before had been wandering vacuously about the room, narrowed suddenly and sparked humbling reprimands at me. She took a draw on her cigarette, puckered her lips, and blew a healthy stream of smoke toward my face. It was a mean action, deliberately irreverent and cold. The long curving scar on the left side of her face darkened. "I ask *you,*" she said, "as a nosy person with no connections in your family, how come your nose is all bandaged up?"

It was a fair question, considering the possible returns on its answer. Dr. Wayland would remove the bandages as soon as he came in. I would not be asked again. A man lacking permanence must advertise. "An accident of passion," I told her. "I smashed it against the headboard of my bed while engaged in the act of love."

Here she laughed, but not without intimating, through heavy, broken chuckles, some respect for my candor and the delicate cause of my affliction. This I could tell from the way the hardness mellowed in her voice. Her appetites were whetted. She looked me up and down, almost approvingly, and laughed some more. This was a robust woman, with firm round legs and considerable chest. I am small. She laughed her appreciation. Finally, she lifted a brown palm to her face, wiping away tears. "You *cain't* be no married man," she observed. "A wife ain't worth *that* much."

I nodded.

"I knowed it," she said. "The best mens don't git married. They do they fishin' in goldfish bowls."

"I am no adulterer," I cautioned her. "I find companionship wherever I can."

She quieted me by throwing out her arm in a suggestion of offended modesty. She scraped the cigarette on the white tile beneath her foot. "You don't have to tell me a thing," she said. "I know mens goin' and comin'. There ain't a-one of you I'd trust to take my grandmama to Sunday school." Here she paused, seemingly lost in some morbid reflection, her eyes wandering across the room to Dr. Wayland's frosted glass door. The solemnity of the waiting room reclaimed us. We inhaled the antiseptic fumes that wafted from the inner office. We breathed deeply together, watching the door, waiting. "Not a-one," my companion said softly, her dark eyes wet.

The scar still fascinated me. It was a wicked black mark that ran from her brow down over her left eyelid, skirting her nose but curving over and through both lips before ending almost exactly in the center of her chin. The scar was thick and black and crisscrossed with a network of old stitch patterns, as if some meticulous madman had first attempted to carve a perfect half-circle in her flesh, and then decided to embellish his handiwork. It was so grotesque a mark that one had the feeling it was the art of no human hand and could be peeled off like so much soiled putty. But this was a surgeon's office and the scar was real. It was as real as the honey-blond wig she wore, as real as her purple pantsuit. I studied her approvingly. Such women have a natural leaning toward the abstract expression of themselves. Their styles have private meanings, advertise secret distillations of their souls. Their figures, and their disfigurations, make meaningful statements. Subjectively, this woman was the true sister of the man who knows how to look while driving a purple Cadillac. Such craftsmen must be approached with subtlety if they are to be deciphered. "I've never seen a scar quite like that one," I began, glancing at my watch. Any minute Dr. Wayland would arrive and take off my bandages, removing me permanently from access to her sympathies. "Do you mind talking about what happened?"

"I *knowed* you'd git back around to that," she answered, her brown eyes cruel and level with mine. "Black guys like you with them funny eyeglasses are a real trip. You got to know everything. You sit in corners and watch people." She brushed her face, then wiped her palm on the leg of her pantsuit. "I read you the minute you walk in here."

"As your brother . . ." I began.

"How can you be my brother when yor mama's a man?" she said.

We both laughed.

"I was pretty once," she began, sniffing heavily. "When I was sixteen my mama's preacher was set to leave his wife and his pulpit and run off with me to *Dee*troit City. Even with this scar and all the weight I done put on, you can still see what I had." She paused. "*Cain't* you?" she asked significantly.

I nodded quickly, looking into her big body for the miniature of what she was.

From this gesture she took assurance. "I was twenty when it happen," she went on. "I had me a good job in the post office, down to the Tenth Street branch. I was a sharp dresser, too, and I had me my choice of mens: big ones, puny ones, old mens, married mens, even D. B. Ferris, my shift supervisor, was after me on the sly—don't let these white mens fool you. He offered to take me off the primaries and turn me on to a desk job in hand-stampin' or damaged mail. But I had my pride. I told him I rather work the facin' table, *every shift,* than put myself in his debt. I shook my finger in his face and said, 'You ain't foolin' me, with your *sly self!* I know where the *wild goose went;* and if you don't start havin' some *respect* for black women, he go'n come *back!*' So then he turn red in the face and put me on the facin' table. Every shift. What could I do? You ain't got no rights in the post office, no matter what lies the government tries to tell you. But I was makin' good money, dressin' bad, and I didn't want to start no trouble for myself. Besides, in them days there was a bunch of good people workin' my shift: Leroy Boggs, Red Bone, 'Big Boy' Tyson, Freddy May . . ."

"What about that scar?" I interrupted her tiresome ramblings. "Which one of them cut you?"

Her face flashed a wall of brown fire. "This here's *my* story!" she muttered, eyeing me up and down with suspicion. "You dudes cain't stand to hear the whole of anything. You want everything broke down in little pieces." And she waved a knowing brown finger. "That's how come you got your nose all busted up. There's some things you have to take your time about."

Again I glanced at my watch, but was careful to nod silent agreement with her wisdom. "It was my boyfriend that caused it," she continued in a slower, more cautious tone. "And the more I look at you the more I can see you just like him. He had that same way of sittin' with his legs crossed, squeezin' his sex juices up to his brains. His name was Billy Crawford, and he worked the parcel-post window down to the Tenth Street branch. He was nine years older than me and was goin' to school nights on the GI Bill. I was twenty when I met him durin' lunch break down in the swing room. He was sittin' at a table against the wall, by hisself, eatin' a cheese sandwich with his nose in a goddamn book. I didn't know any better then. I sat down by him. He looked up at me and say, 'Water seeks its own level, and people do, too. You are not one of the riffraff or else you would of sit with them good-timers and bullshitters 'cross the room. Welcome to my table.' By riffraff he meant all them other dudes and girls from the back room, who believed in havin' a little fun playin' cards and such durin' lunch hour. I thought what he said was kind of funny, and so I laughed. But I should of knowed better. He give me a cheese sandwich and started right off preachin' at me about the lowlife in the back room. Billy couldn't stand none of 'em. He hated the way they dressed, the way they talked, and the way they carried on durin' work hours. He said if all them tried to be like him and advanced themselfs, the Negro wouldn't have no problems. He'd point out Eugene Wells or Red Bone or Crazy Sammy Michaels and tell me, 'People like them think they can homestead in the post office. They think these primaries will need human hands for another twenty years. But you just watch the Jews and Puerto Ricans that pass through here. *They* know what's goin' on. I bet you don't see none of them settin' up their beds under these tables. They tryin' to improve themselfs and get out of here, just like me.' Then he smile and held out his hand. 'And since I see you're a smart girl that keeps a cold eye and some distance on these bums, welcome to the club. My name's Billy Crawford.'

"To tell you the truth, I liked him. He was different from all the jive-talkers and finger-poppers I knew. I liked him because he wasn't ashamed to wear a white shirt and a black tie. I liked the way he always knew just what he was gonna do next. I liked him because none of the other dudes could stand him, and he didn't seem to care. On our first date he took me out to a place where the white waiters didn't git mad when they saw us comin'. That's the kind of style he had. He knew how to order wine with funny names, the kind you don't never see on billboards. He held open doors for me, told me not to order rice with gravy over it or soda water with my meal. I didn't mind him helpin' me. He was a funny dude in a lot of ways: his left leg was shot up in the war and he limped sometimes, but it looked like he was struttin'. He would stare down anybody that watched him walkin'. He told me he had cut his wife loose after he got out of the army, and he told me about some of the games she had run on him. Billy didn't trust women. He said they all was after a workin' man's money, but he said that I was different. He said he could tell I was a God-fearin' woman and my mama had raised me right, and he was gonna improve my mind. In those days I didn't have no objections. Billy was fond of sayin', 'You met me at the right time in your life.'

"But Red Bone, my co-worker, saw what was goin' down and began to take a strong interest in the affair. Red was the kind of strong-minded sister that mens just like to give in to. She was one of them big yellow gals, with red hair and a loud rap that could put a man in his place by just soundin' on him. She like to wade through the mail room, elbowin' dudes aside and sayin', 'You don't wanna mess with *me*, fool! I'll *destroy* you! Anyway, you ain't nothin' but a dirty thought I had when I was three years old!' But if she liked you she could be warm and soft, like a mama. 'Listen,' she kept tellin' me, 'that Billy Crawford is a potential punk. The more I watch him, the less man I see. Every time we downstairs havin' fun I catch his eyeballs rollin' over us from behind them goddamn books! There ain't a rhythm in his body, and the only muscles he exercises is in his eyes.'

"That kind of talk hurt me some, especially comin' from her. But I know it's the way of some women to bad-mouth a man they want for themselfs. And what woman don't want a steady man and a good provider?—which is what Billy was. Usually, when they start downgradin' a steady man, you can be sure they up to somethin' else besides lookin' out after you. So I told her, 'Billy don't have no bad habits.' I told her, 'He's a hard worker, he don't drink, smoke, nor run around, and he's gonna git a *college* degree.' But that didn't impress Red. I was never able to figure it out, but she had something in for Billy. Maybe it was his attitude; maybe it was the little ways he let everybody know that he was just passin' through; maybe it was because Red had broke every man she ever had and had never seen a man with no handholes on him. Because that Billy Crawford was a strong man. He worked the day shift, and could of been a supervisor in three or four years if he wanted to crawl a little and grease a few palms; but he did his work, quiet-like, pulled what overtime he could, and went to class three nights a week. On his day off he'd study and maybe take me out for a drink after I got off. Once or twice a week he might let me stay over at his place, but most of the time he'd take me home to my Aunt Alvene's, where I was roomin' in those days, before twelve o'clock.

"To tell the truth, I didn't really miss the partyin' and the dancin' and the good-timin' until Red and some of the others started avoidin' me. Down in the swing room durin' lunch hour, for example, they wouldn't wave for me to come over and join a card game. Or when Leroy Boggs went around to the folks on the floor of the mail room, collectin' money for a party, he wouldn't even ask me to put a few dollars in the pot. He'd just smile at me in a cold way and say to somebody loud enough for me to hear, 'No, sir; ain't no way you can git quality folk to come out to a Saturday night fish fry.'

"Red squared with me when I asked her what was goin' down. She told me, 'People sayin' you been wearin' a high hat since you started goin' with the professor. The talk is you been throwin' around big words and developin' a strut just like his. Now I don't believe these reports, being your friend and sister, but I do think you oughta watch your step. I remember what my grandmama used to tell me: "It don't make no difference how well you fox-trot if everybody else is dancin' the two-step." Besides, that Billy Crawford is a potential punk, and you gonna be one lonely girl when somebody finally turns him out. Use your mind, girl, and stop bein' silly. Everybody is watchin' you!'

"I didn't say nothin', but what Red said started me to thinkin' harder than I had ever thought before. Billy had been droppin' strong hints that we might git married after he got his degree, in two or three years. He was plannin' on being a high school teacher. But outside of being married to a teacher, what was I go'n git out of it? Even if we did git married, I was likely to be stuck right there in the post office with no friends. And if he didn't marry me, or if he was a punk like Red believed, then I was a real dummy for givin' up my good times and my best days for a dude that wasn't go'n do nothin' for me. I didn't make up my mind right then, but I begin to watch Billy Crawford with a different kind of eye. I'd just turn around at certain times and catch him in his routines: readin', workin', eatin', runnin' his mouth about the same things all the time. Pretty soon I didn't have to watch him to know what he was doin'. He was more regular than Monday mornings. That's when a woman begins to tip. It ain't never a decision, but somethin' in you starts to lean over and practice what you gonna say whenever another man bumps into you at the right time. Some women, especially married ones, like to tell lies to their new boyfriends; if the husband is a hard worker and a good provider, they'll tell the boyfriend that he's mean to them and ain't no good when it comes to sex; and if he's good with sex, they'll say he's a cold dude that's not concerned with the problems of the world like she is, or that they got married too

young. Me, I believe in tellin' the truth: that Billy Crawford was too good for most
of the women in this world, me included. He deserved better, so I started lookin'
round for somebody on my own level.

"About this time a sweet-talkin' young dude was transferred to our branch from
the 39th Street substation. The grapevine said it was because he was makin'
woman-trouble over there and caused too many fights. I could see why. He
dressed like he was settin' fashions every day; wore special-made bell-bottoms
with so much flare they looked like they was starched. He wore two diamond rings
on the little finger of his left hand that flashed while he was throwin' mail, and a
gold tooth that sparkled all the time. His name was Teddy Johnson, but they called
him 'Eldorado' because that was the kind of hog he drove. He was involved in
numbers and other hustles and used the post office job for a front. He was a strong
talker, a easy walker, that dude was a *woman* stalker! I have to give him credit. He
was the last *true* son of the Great McDaddy—"

"Sister," I said quickly, overwhelmed suddenly by the burden of insight. "I *know*
the man of whom you speak. There is no time for this gutter-patter and indirec-
tion. Please, for my sake and for your own, avoid stuffing the shoes of the small
with mythic homilies. This man was a bum, a hustler and a small-time punk. He
broke up your romance with Billy, then he lived off you, cheated on you, and cut
you when you confronted him." So pathetic and gross seemed her elevation of the
fellow that I abandoned all sense of caution. "Is your mind so *dead,*" I continued,
"did his switchblade slice so *deep,* do you have so little *respect* for yourself, or at
least for the idea of *proportion* in this sad world, that you'd sit here and *praise* this
brute!?"

She lit a second cigarette. Then, dropping the match to the floor, she seemed to
shudder, to struggle in contention with herself. I sat straight on the blue plastic
couch, waiting. Across the room the frosted glass door creaked, as if about to
open; but when I looked, I saw no telling shadow behind it. My companion
crossed her legs and held back her head, blowing two thoughtful streams of smoke
from her broad nose. I watched her nervously, recognizing the evidence of past
destructiveness, yet fearing the imminent occurrence of more. But it was not her
temper or the potential strength of her fleshy arms that I feared. Finally she
sighed, her face relaxed, and she wet her lips with the tip of her tongue. "You know
everything," she said in a soft tone, much unlike her own. "A black mama birthed
you, let you suck her titty, cleaned your dirty drawers, and you still look at us
through paper and movie plots." She paused, then continued in an even softer and
more controlled voice. "Would you believe me if I said that Teddy Johnson loved
me, that this scar is to him what a weddin' ring is to another man? Would you
believe that he was a better man than Billy?"

I shook my head in firm disbelief.

She seemed to smile to herself, although the scar, when she grimaced, made the
expression more like a painful frown. "Then would you believe that I was the
cause of Billy Crawford goin' crazy and not gettin' his college degree?"

I nodded affirmation.

"Why?" she asked.

"Because," I answered, "from all I know already, that would seem to be the most likely consequence. I would expect the man to have been destroyed by the pressures placed on him. And, although you are my sister and a woman who has already suffered greatly, I must condemn you and your roughneck friends for this destruction of a man's ambitions."

Her hardened eyes measured my face. She breathed heavily, seeming to grow larger and rounder on the red chair. "My brother," she began in an icy tone, "is as far from what you are as I am from being patient." Now her voice became deep and full, as if aided suddenly by some intricately controlled wellspring of pain. Something aristocratic and old and frighteningly wise seemed to have awakened in her face. "Now this is the way it happened," she fired at me, her eyes wide and rolling. I want you to *write* it on whatever part of your brain that ain't already covered with page print. I want you to *remember* it every time you stare at a scarred-up sister on the street, and *choke* on it before you can work up spit to condemn her. I was *faithful* to that Billy Crawford. As faithful as a woman could be to a man that don't ever let up or lean back and stop worryin' about where he's gonna be ten years from last week. Life is to be *lived,* not traded on like *dollars!* . . . All that time I was goin' with him, my feets itched to dance, my ears hollered to hear somethin' besides that whine in his voice, my body wanted to press up against somethin' besides that facin' table. I was young and pretty; and what woman don't want to enjoy what she got while she got it? Look around sometime: there ain't *no mens,* young nor old, chasin' *no older womens,* no matter how pretty they *used to be!* But Billy Crawford couldn't see nothin' besides them *goddamn books* in front of his face. And what the Jews and Puerto Ricans was doin'. Whatever else Teddy Johnson was, he was a dude that knowed how to live. He wasn't out to *destroy* life, you can believe *that!* Sure I listened to his rap. Sure I give him the come-on. With Billy workin' right up front and watchin' everything. Teddy was the only dude on the floor that would talk to me. Teddy would say, 'A girl that's got what you got needs a man that have what I have.' And that ain't all he said, either!

"Red Bone tried to push me closer to him, but I am not a sneaky person and didn't pay her no mind. She'd say, 'Girl, I think you and Eldorado ought to git it on. There ain't a better lookin' dude workin' in the post office. Besides, you ain't goin' *nowheres* with that professor Billy Crawford. And if *you* scared to tell him to lean up off you, I'll do it *myself,* bein' as I am your sister and the one with your interest in mind.' But I said to her, 'Don't do me no favors. No matter what you think of Billy, I am no sneaky woman. I'll handle my own affairs.' Red just grin and look me straight in the eye and grin some more. I already told you she was the kind of strong-minded sister that could look right down into you. Nobody but a woman would understand what she was lookin' at.

"Now Billy wasn't no dummy durin' all this time. Though he worked the parcel-post window up front, from time to time durin' the day he'd walk back in the mail room and check out what was goin' down. Or else he'd sit back and listen to the gossip durin' lunch hour, down in the swing room. He must of seen Teddy Johnson hangin' round me, and I know he seen Teddy give me the glad-eye a few times. Billy didn't say nothin' for a long time, but one day he pointed to Teddy and told me, 'See that fellow over there? He's a bloodletter. There's some people with a talent for stoppin' bleedin' by just being around, and there's others that start it the same way. When you see that greasy smile of his you can bet it's soon gonna be a bad day for somebody, if they ain't careful. That kind of fellow's been walkin' free for too long.' He looked at me with that tight mouth and them cold brown eyes of his. He said, 'You know what I mean?' I said I didn't. He said, 'I hope you don't ever have to find out.'

"It was D. B. Ferris, my shift supervisor, that set up things. He's the same dude I told you about, the one that was gonna give me the happy hand. We never saw much of him in the mail room, although he was kinda friendly with Red Bone. D. B. Ferris was always up on the ramps behind one of the wall slits, checkin' out everything that went down on the floor and tryin' to catch somebody snitchin' a letter. There ain't no tellin' how much he knew about private things goin' on. About this time he up and transferred three or four of us, the ones with no seniority, to the night shift. There was me, Red, and Leroy Boggs. When Billy found out he tried to talk D. B. Ferris into keepin' me on the same shift as his, but Ferris come to me and I told him I didn't mind. And I didn't. I told him I was tired of bein' watched by him and everybody else. D. B. Ferris looked up toward the front where Billy was workin' and smiled that old smile of his. Later, when Billy asked me what I said, I told him there wasn't no use tryin' to fight the government. 'That's true,' he told me—and I thought I saw some meanness in his eyes—'but there are some other things you can fight,' he said. At that time my head was kinda light, and I didn't catch what he meant.

"About my second day on the night shift, Teddy Johnson began workin' overtime. He didn't need the money and didn't like to work nohow, but some nights around ten or eleven, when we clocked out for lunch and sat around in the swing room, in would strut Teddy. Billy would be in school or at home. Usually, I'd be sittin' with Red and she'd tell me things while Teddy was walkin' over. 'Girl, it *must* be love to make a dude like Eldorado work overtime. *He* needs to work like *I* need to be a Catholic.' Then Teddy would sit down and she'd commence to play over us like her life depended on gittin' us together. She'd say, 'Let's go over to my place this mornin' when we clock out. I got some bacon and eggs and a bottle of Scotch.' Teddy would laugh and look in my eyes and say, 'Red, we don't wanna cause no trouble for this here fine young thing, who I hear is engaged to a college man.' Then I'd laugh with them and look at Teddy and wouldn't say nothin' much to nobody.

"Word must of gotten back to Billy soon after that. He didn't say nothin' at first, but I could see a change in his attitude. All this time I was tryin' to git up the guts to tell Billy I was thinkin' about breaking off, but I just couldn't. It wasn't that I thought he needed me; I just knew he was the kind of dude that doesn't let a girl decide when somethin' is over. Bein' as much like Billy as you are, you must understand what I'm tryin' to say. On one of my nights off, when we went out to a movie, he asked, 'What time did you get in this mornin'?' I said, 'Five-thirty, same as always.' But I was lyin'. Red and me had stopped for breakfast on the way home. Billy said, 'I called you at six-thirty this morning, and your Aunt Alvene said you was still out.' I told him, 'She must of been too sleepy to look in my room.' He didn't say more on the subject, but later that evenin', after the movie, he said, 'I was in the war for two years. It made me a disciplined man, and I hope I don't ever have to lose my temper.' I didn't say nothin', but the cold way he said it was like a window shade flappin' up from in front of his true nature, and I was scared.

"It was three years ago this September twenty-second that the thing happened. It was five-thirty in the mornin'. We had clocked out at four-forty-five, but Red had brought a bottle of Scotch to work, and we was down in the swing room drinkin' a little with our coffee, just to relax. I'll tell you the truth: Teddy Johnson was there, too. He had come down just to give us a ride home. I'll never forget that day as long as I live. Teddy was dressed in a pink silk shirt with black ruffles on the sleeves, the kind that was so popular a few years ago. He was wearin' shiny black bell-bottoms that hugged his little hips like a second coat of skin, and looked like pure silk when he walked. He sat across from me, flashin' those diamond rings every time he poured more Scotch in our cups. Red was sittin' back with a smile on her face, watchin' us like a cat that had just ate.

"I was sittin' with my back to the door and didn't know anything, until I saw something change in Red's face. I still see it in my sleep at night. Her face seemed to light up and git scared and happy at the same time. She was lookin' behind me, over my shoulder, with all the smartness in the world burnin' in her eyes. I turned around. Billy Crawford was standin' right behind me with his hands close to his sides. He wore a white shirt and a thin black tie, and his mouth was tight like a little slit. He said, 'It's time for you to go home,' with that voice of his that was too cold to be called just mean. I sat there lookin' up at him. Red's voice was even colder. She said to me, 'You gonna let him order you around like that?' I didn't say nothin'. Red said to Teddy, 'Ain't *you* got something to say about this?' Teddy stood up slow and swelled out his chest. He said, 'Yeah, I got somethin' to say,' looking hard at Billy. But Billy just kept lookin' down at me. 'Let's go,' he said. 'What you got to say?' Red Bone said to Teddy. Teddy said to me, 'Why don't *you* tell the dude, baby?' But I didn't say nothin'. Billy shifted his eyes to Teddy and said, 'I got nothing against you. You ain't real, so you don't matter. You been strutting the streets too long, but that ain't my business. So keep out of this.' Then he looked down at me again. 'Let's go,' he said. I looked up at the way his lips curled and wanted to cry and hit him at the same time. I felt like a trigger bein' pulled. Then I heard Red sayin', 'Why don't you go back to bed with them *goddamn books, punk!* And leave decent folks *alone!*' For the first time Billy glanced over at her. His mouth twitched. But then he looked down at me again. 'This here's the *last time* I'm asking,' he said. That's when I exploded and started to jump up. 'I ain't goin' *nowhere!*'

I screamed. The last plain thing I remember was tryin' to git to his face, but it seemed to turn all bright and silvery and hot, and then I couldn't see nothin' no more.

"They told me later that he sliced me so fast there wasn't time for nobody to act. By the time Teddy jumped across the table I was down, and Billy had stabbed me again in the side. Then him and Teddy tussled over the knife, while me and Red screamed and screamed. Then Teddy went down holdin' his belly, and Billy was comin' after me again, when some of the dudes from the freight dock ran in and grabbed him. They say it took three of them to drag him off me, and all the time they was pullin' him away he kept slashin' out at me with that knife. It seemed like all the walls was screamin' and I was floatin' in water, and I thought I was dead and in hell, because I felt hot and prickly all over, and I could hear some woman's voice that might of been mine screamin' over and over, 'You devil! . . . You *devil!*'"

She lit a third cigarette. She blew a relieving cloud of smoke downward. The thin white haze billowed about her purple legs, dissipated, and vanished. A terrifying fog of silence and sickness crept into the small room, and there was no longer the smell of medicine. I dared not steal a glance at my watch, although by this time Dr. Wayland was agonizingly late. I had heard it all, and now I waited. Finally her eyes fixed on the frosted glass door. She wet her lips again and, in a much slower and pained voice, said, "This here's the third doctor I been to see. The first one stitched me up like a turkey and left this scar. The second one refused to touch me." She paused and wet her lips again. "This man fixed your nose for you," she said softly. "Do you think he could do somethin' about this scar?"

I searched the end table next to my couch for a newsmagazine, carefully avoiding her face. "Dr. Wayland is a skilled man," I told her. "Whenever he's not late. I think he may be able to do something for you."

She sighed heavily and seemed to tremble. "I don't expect no miracle or nothin'," she said. "If he could just fix the part around my eye I wouldn't expect nothin' else. People say the rest don't look too bad."

I clutched a random magazine and did not answer. Nor did I look at her. The flesh around my nose began to itch, and I looked toward the inner office door with the most extreme irritation building in me. At that moment it seemed a shadow began to form behind the frosted glass, signaling perhaps the approach of someone. I resolved to put aside all notions of civility and go into the office before her, as was my right. The shadow behind the door darkened, but vanished just as suddenly. And then I remembered the most important question, without which the entire exchange would have been wasted. I turned to the woman, now drawn together in the red plastic chair, as if struggling to sleep in a cold bed. "Sister," I said, careful to maintain a casual air. "Sister . . . what is your name?"

I DO NOT TAKE MESSAGES
FROM DEAD PEOPLE

Sʜᴀᴋᴇꜱᴘᴇᴀʀᴇ McNᴀʙ ᴡᴀɪᴛᴇᴅ in the outer office of the Ministry of Home Affairs. His appointment with the Vice-President of the Republic had been for eleven o'clock. It was now half past. He had no idea why he had been summoned. The secretary had been unable or unwilling to enlighten him. Shakespeare smiled ingratiatingly whenever she looked up from her typewriter and she ignored him. He took some papers from the briefcase on his knee and pretended to study them. The rambling, wooden building in which he waited was one of the old, colonial houses built by the plantocracy and now converted into government offices and ministries. Outside, the gracious width of the street was divided along its length by a stagnant canal. At intervals of fifty yards or so, giant royal palms sported mangy and yellowing foliage. Shakespeare decided that secretaries to public officials ought to be given a course in charm. He would not reprimand her for being ungracious. He would simply shame her with the exquisiteness of his own manners. She paused from her typing and looked up. Shakespeare gave his most delightful smile. She resumed typing with some ferocity. He fanned himself with his papers. It was hot and he was thirsty.

"The Comrade Vice-President will see you shortly." The secretary did not raise her eyes as she spoke. Shakespeare experienced a flicker of anxiety. Could it be that someone at the broadcasting station where he worked had reported him for not using the term "Comrade" frequently enough when addressing his colleagues? He prepared his defense. He was a broadcaster. It befitted him to be accurate in his use of words. His dictionary had informed him that the word "comrade" was supposed to refer to "a close companion" or "an intimate associate", not any old Tom, Dick or Harry as was the custom nowadays. Besides, the Vice-President would hardly be summoning him for a personal interview on such a trivial matter. No, it was bound to be something of more weight. Perhaps the Vice-President was looking for someone to write his official biography. That would be a more appropriate reason for the summons. Shakespeare worried over how he would deal with the widespread and malicious rumour that the Vice-President had been responsible for the death of his own wife, by poison, at a state banquet after she had threatened to reveal certain delicate facts about his financial acquisitions during the current term of government. One moment, apparently, she had been toasting the Republic and the next she was slumped, face down, in a silver dish of curried shrimps. Shakespeare frowned. We allow too much scandal and gossip to interfere with our politics, he thought. It is because we are a relatively young nation. We will mature in time. Although, he recollected, she had been cremated, which was unusual. And with surprising haste.

Shakespeare shifted along the bench to the part that was shaded from the window. If he were truly to be offered the post of Comrade Biographer to the Comrade Vice-President, no doubt he would be required to give some details about his literary accomplishments:

"Of course, there are my two volumes of poetry. The muse does visit me occasionally, usually at night . . ." Shakespeare paused in his thoughts. The enormous hulk of the Vice-President did not seem to be the sort of shape whose owner would be interested in verse. He was puzzled. Why should the Vice-President be interested in what he, Shakespeare, was best known for—the collecting of folklore? Each morning, after the nine o'clock news, Shakespeare came on the air with a proverb or saying from one of the cultural traditions of the nation: African, Asian, Chinese, Amerindian, Portuguese or Dutch. On Thursdays, he had a ten-minute slot and told a longer folk story. Today was Friday. He had just finished a short proverb when Horace Tinling, his boss, put his head round the door of the small cubicle that passed for a studio and informed him that he was wanted immediately at the Ministry of Home Affairs. Shakespeare disliked Horace Tinling. In his opinion, a man who wore a bow tie with his camouflage jacket was a special sort of hypocrite. It occurred to him now that he was possibly going to be asked to replace Horace Tinling as Head of Home Programs. Satisfaction bloomed inside him. He began to rehearse in his head the expansive, man-to-man chat he thought would take place as he was granted this new status. Hopefully, over a cool drink:

"How did I come to be called Shakespeare? Well, Comrade Vice-President, the story is that when I was born, my father came home from work, looked at me and said: 'Well, he don' look so bright. 'E ain' pretty either. We better do something to help him make his way in the world. We goin' name 'im Shakespeare.' And, in fact, I did turn out to have some small literary talent." Shakespeare liked to end this anecdote with a self-deprecating chuckle. He imagined the Vice-President chuckling with him as they sipped their drinks—drinks served by the secretary who would be forced to alter her aloof demeanor to one of friendly respect when she witnessed the intimate camaraderie between the two men. On the other hand, perhaps it would be wiser not to mention names. The Vice-President's name was Hogg. Shakespeare had attended the same school as Hogg, who was a few years his senior. His most distinct memory of the Comrade Vice-President was of him leading the school choir on Empire Day in a lusty rendition of "Here's a Health unto His Majesty. Fal la la la la Fa la la la." It would not be tactful to remind him of that either. But he must remember to congratulate him on his recent appointment to the prestigious post of Vice-President, the only other serious contender for the post having been found shot dead in Camp Street.

"The Comrade Vice-President will see you now." The secretary was holding the door open.

Shakespeare stood in the center of the room, a deferential smile firmly in place on his impish features. The smile was not returned by the Vice-President, a heavily-built black man whose overpowering sullenness held the gravitational density of an imploding star. He remained behind the desk and stared at Shakespeare. Behind his head, on the wall, a formal portrait of the President himself, with pursed mouth and coptic eyes, smirked down at Shakespeare. The Vice-President rose to his feet and came round from behind the desk. Despite his weight, his hips swivelled freely, like those of a spoilt schoolgirl. He came unhesitatingly forward and delivered a resounding slap to the left side of Shakespeare's face:

"Be more careful what stories you broadcast in future, Comrade McNab. That's all. Good morning."

Green with fright, Shakespeare McNab left the office.

Shakespeare made his way past the secretary to the door, his features frozen in a paralyzed, lop-sided rictus, exactly as the slap had left them. He hoped the secretary would mistake the immobile gawp on his face for some sort of farewell smile. Speech was beyond him. He stumbled down the wooden stairs into the street. It was mid-day and there were not many passersby but Shakespeare had the distinct impression that each one of them knew what had just happened to him, as if someone was riding alongside him on a bicycle with a megaphone, announcing: "THIS MAN HAS JUST BEEN SLAPPED ROUND THE FACE BY THE VICE-PRESIDENT OF THE REPUBLIC." His trembling legs moved forward along the grass verge without seeming to make progress, like a mime-walker. "What did I do? What did I do?" he repeated over and over. Usually, the heat and the spaciousness of the street conspired to reduce the most hurried pace to a stroll, but fear and the desire to put as much distance as possible between himself and the Vice-President propelled Shakespeare across one of the small canal bridges, towards the center of town. His khaki shirt tail flapped behind him. "What did I do? What did I do?" he asked himself, over and over again.

Instinctively, he headed for home. By the time he reached the ancient iron structure of the old Dutch slave market, a dreadful realization had begun to dawn on him of a blunder that he might have made, a bloomer of such horrific enormity that the edges of his mind began to tingle. He attached himself to a group of people who had gathered under the pitiless sun, encouraged by the rumor of a bus, but agitation made him incapable of standing still for more than a minute or two and soon he continued, walking briskly away from the heart of the city. What had occurred to him was this:

Yesterday had been a Thursday, the day he regularly broadcast one of his longer folk stories. General laziness had prevented him from preparing the program in advance. The studio clock was already pointing at ten to nine when he burst into the recording cabin, treading over the chaotic jumble of spools, reel-to-reel tapes and story-books. In this sort of emergency, he usually resorted to telling an Anancy story—Anancy, the regional folk-hero, the magic spider with the cleft palate and the speech defect, the tricksy creature of unprepossessing proportions who continually outwitted the great and savage beasts of the jungle. He grabbed a book of Anancy stories from the shelf and flicked through the pages to find one that he had not already read. Unfortunately for him, the one he plumped for was entitled "Anancy and Hog."

"Good morning, Guyana. And it is another beauuuuuuutiful day in our co-operative socialist republic, so I goin' tell you the story of Anancy and Hog.

'One day Anancy and 'im grandmamma go to a ground fi provision. Anancy left him guitar there. When 'im comin' home togedder wid him grandmamma, he said: "Grandmumma, you know I did leave my guitar at groun'." Him grandmamma say: "Me son, you is a very bad boy. Go for it but don' play it."

'When Anancy comin' home he play:

> *When you see a hugly man,*
> *When you see a hugly man*
> *When you see a hugly man*
> *Never mek him marry you sister.*

Then him hear footstep. Him lift up one of 'im legs an' listen. Along come Hog. Hog say: "Brother, you a play de sweet, sweet tune." Anancy say: "No, Bro'er." Hog say: "Play, mek me hear." Anancy play Bap, Twee, Twee, Twee, all wrong note. Hog suck 'im teeth and say: "Tcho! You caan play." Hog pass by. As 'im walk pon de road 'im hear Anancy playing the tune. Hog come back: "Brother Anancy, I think you a play, you beggar. I goin' kill you." An' Hog carry home Anancy an' goin' do him up for him dinner because that night he plan one big feast wid plenty big-wig hog comin' fi supper. But inside de house, Anancy pop off de rope an' dress up in Hog wife clothes. An' 'im say to Hog wife: "If you waan look pretty put on me lickle black suit an' shut up you mouth!" An' then Hog come in an' kill 'im own wife. An' when Hog think 'im done up Anancy, 'im done up 'im own wife and serve her for supper. And that is what make Hog a nasty feeder up to this day.

"Well, that's all from me for today. This is Shakespeare McNab signing off until tomorrow."

As Shakespeare remembered precisely what he had broadcast the day before and the implication for his good health, he came to a halt on the corner of Howard and Queen Street. Some warm slops, thrown by a woman from the verandah of her house, spattered him. He barely noticed. Vice-President Hogg, he thought, believes that I have announced to the nation the fact that he murdered his wife. Shakespeare licked dry lips and put on a final spurt for home.

Safely inside his one-story house on stilts, Shakespeare moved quickly round lowering the jalousie slats on all the windows. It made the place intolerably hot but he felt less vulnerable that way. In near darkness, he made his way to the table and poured himself a stiff rum. Then he sat on the sofa alternately sipping the rum and biting his nails. Just as he was planning to make his next morning's broadcast a fulsome eulogy, extolling the virtues of Vice-President Hogg, the telephone rang. It was the smarmy voice of Horace Tinling giving him the sack:

"So sorry, Comrade . . . unforeseen circumstances . . . replacing you with a recipe program . . . if you could clear out your belongings before nine o'clock on Monday night, when the Vice-President is due to give a ministerial broadcast."

Shakespeare was too stunned to object. He went to the window and peered through one of the slats. His heart gave a flip. Parked on the other side of the street, opposite his house, was an unmarked car. Lolling up against it were three bulky Afro-Guyanese men, all wearing dark glasses. At the same time, he saw his friend, Denzil Bennet, bounding up the wooden steps to his front door:

"Why you sittin' in the dark?" enquired Denzil, helping himself to a glass of rum. Paranoia prevented Shakespeare telling Denzil what had happened:

"I got a headache . . . The light hurtin' me eyes." Denzil flopped onto the sofa and ran his hands through his manic bush of frizzy, greying hair:

"You hear the latest story about Hogg?" he asked.

Shakespeare eyed him suspiciously:

"What story?" Had Denzil heard something, already? He came and sat on the sofa.

"Remember how we laugh at the Cuffy statue?" Denzil continued.

Shakespeare did indeed remember how they had laughed when the statue of the great slave leader had been unveiled. The statue was grasping a scroll in his hand, held at the hip, pointing upwards, but at such an angle that when the covering flag was pulled off, it appeared to a section of the crowd that Cuffy was holding himself with an enormous erection. Shakespeare recalled how he and Denzil had joined in the rippling titter that swept through the onlookers. Just now, however, he was unwilling to admit ever having laughed at anything organized by the government.

"Well," Denzil went on, "the story go so. One night Hogg's personal aide was contemplating the statue when the statue start to speak: 'Get me a horse,' says Cuffy. 'You can't speak—you're a statue!' says the aide. 'Get me a horse. In Berbice in 1763, I used to ride a horse.' Well, the aide is so frighten, he run all the way to Hogg private residence. 'Cuffy speakin',' he says. 'The statue speakin'. Come look.' Now, as you know, Hogg is an extremely superstitious man. He consult an obeah woman and all that foolishness. Apparently, she give him a special ring whose stone change color when 'e life in danger. So now Hogg think 'e bein' given a special sign an' 'e pull on his pants an' come back with the aide to the statue. 'Fool,' says Cuffy to the aide. 'I said I wanted a horse, not a jackass.'"

Denzil let out a screech of laughter. Shakespeare remained silent. He felt sure that Denzil had been sent to trap him. Laughter in the present circumstances could be interpreted as a form of high treason.

"You don' think that funny?" Denzil stared at Shakespeare in disbelief, "What's the matter with you, man? That headache eat out you brain or what?"

"I goin' to my bed," announced Shakespeare, abruptly. "My head is hurtin' me." Denzil shrugged and swallowed the last of his rum.

"Tell me what you see in the street," demanded Shakespeare as Denzil opened the door.

"There ain' nothin' in the street. Street empty. Go to bed, man. You sick."

The door banged shut behind him, leaving Shakespeare in the gloom.

That night, Shakespeare tossed and turned under his single sheet like a cat in a sack. He suffered the most horrible nightmare. He dreamed he was standing on the sea wall. All around him he smelled the detritus of crab and shellfish left there by fishermen. As he gazed out over the waters of the Atlantic, a black shape began to emerge from the sea. It grew larger and larger, laughing in a sinister manner as it became gigantic. Then it sank back down in the sea and he saw the letters H O G G written in the sky. Shakespeare woke sweating from the dream. Too frightened to go back to sleep, he spent the rest of the night hugging up his knees with his arms, fretting over what to do.

The next morning, Shakespeare miserably cleared out his office, scooping his tapes and books into a large canvas bag. Horace Tinling watched him with an expression somewhere between mock sympathy and outright superciliousness. Replacing him in the recording studio was a smartly dressed, young black woman, leaning towards the microphone as she gave out a recipe for Yam Foo-Foo. On his way home, he called at his grandmother's house in Albuoystown. Nibbling at breadfruit cooked in coconut milk, he told her the whole sequence of events, including the dream of the night before. She was a woman of few words:

"Leave the country," she said.

News travels fast in a country without the benefit of advanced communications technology. The whole of that Saturday and the following day, nobody came to call on Shakespeare. None of his friends appeared. The telephone remained mute. It was as if, overnight, he had become a leper. Taking advantage of the unaccustomed solitude, Shakespeare pored over his dilemma. He went over every detail of what had happened to him. He recalled Denzil's scorn of Hogg's superstitious cast of mind. He recalled Hogg's appointment at the radio station. Late on Sunday evening, the first faint inkling of an idea came to him, an idea for his deliverance so wild and fantastical that he put his hand over his mouth and shook his head. "No, I couldn't," he thought. "Yes, I could. No, it's outrageous . . . Yes, I will."

As the Monday morning vendors laid out their pyramids of scarlet wiri-wiri peppers and green watermelons for the day's sale, Shakespeare was already knocking at the door of his grandmother's house.

"You wan' coffee-tea, cocoa-tea or tea-tea? I ain' got milk." She shuffled round the tiny kitchen.

"Tea-tea," said Shakespeare. It was his next request that she balked at. She jutted out her jaw and looked at him askance:

"Why you want to borrow me clothes?" she asked, suspiciously.

Shakespeare avoided an explanation. He cajoled and begged his grandmother until finally she gave in and let him depart with one longish skirt, an old blouse with puffed sleeves, a headwrap and a pair of high-heeled shoes her daughter had abandoned there the year before.

On his way home, Shakespeare bought an old coconut. Once inside the house, he allowed the jalousies to remain shut and moved around in semi-darkness. Every now and then he checked through a slat to see if the unmarked car with its ominous occupants had reappeared. No sign of them. He emptied the tapes and books from his bag onto the sofa and replaced them with the clothes his grandmother had lent him. Then he chopped the coconut in half and cut out the white flesh with a small knife. After that, he spent some time banging the two halves of the shells together until they produced a sound that satisfied him. Then he placed those too inside the bag. He fetched an axe and that also went in the bag. "Now comes the difficult bit," he said to himself, and went over to the telephone. Several times he lifted the receiver and replaced it on the hook. Each time he put it back, he would walk round the room rehearsing a slightly different version of what he planned to say. Finally, he picked up the phone and dialed the number of Vice-President Hogg's office. The secretary answered.

"Good morning." The tone of Shakespeare's voice was fawning. "This is Comrade Shakespeare McNab speakin'. I am so sorry to trouble you—I would not dream of troublin' you if it was not a matter of extreme urgency. I have had a warning dream concerning the Vice-President. My dead mother appeared to me in a dream last night warning me that he is in imminent danger and I felt it my duty to pass the message on."

There was a moment's hesitation on the other end of the line, then came the snappy reply:

"I do not take messages from dead people."

Shakespeare's brain raced. His entire plan would totter if the message did not get through:

"No. The message is from ME," he said, hastily. And to ensure that the Vice-President did, indeed, receive the information, he added, "I shall, of course, be writing to confirm what has happened, but I thought I should pass it on as quickly as possible, lest anything should occur before the letter reaches him. I should not like to be the one responsible for withholding that sort of information." That should fix her, thought Shakespeare, who discovered to his surprise that he was on his knees in front of the telephone.

"All right." The voice was reluctant. "I shall inform the Comrade Vice-President if you think it is really necessary."

"Thank you," said Shakespeare. "I think it is." His scalp was tingling all over as he hung up.

More than once, during the rest of the afternoon, Shakespeare decided to abandon his plan altogether. It was too risky. Too much was at stake. It would be wiser to do what his grandmother suggested and flee the country. Nobody would offer him a decent job if he could not get his old one back, and if this scheme failed, he could say goodbye to the broadcasting world forever. All the same, perhaps it was worth one last attempt.

As dusk fell, a shortish man could be observed sizing up and examining the trees that bordered a narrow stretch of road some distance from the city. To his right, the road led to the entrance gates of Vice-President Hogg's private residence. The house itself remained out of sight at the end of a long drive. To his left, the road extended for a hundred yards or so until it met the main highway. Nothing but a tangle of trees and shrubs stood on either side of it. Overhead, a host of bats sewed up the great opal and silver clouds with their flitting, looping trajectories. Halfway between the gates and the end of the road, Shakespeare spotted the tree that he wanted. It was a young, slender casuarina tree. He took the axe from the bag and began to chop at the base of the trunk. With the sound of each chop, his heart leapt with fear and he glanced up and down the road. No one came. When the trunk was half severed, Shakespeare looked at his watch and decided to wait. He hid out of sight, in the bushes. The tree stayed upright. At about the time he had estimated, a chauffeur-driven limousine turned off the main road and made its stately way up the rutted earth track towards the entrance to Hogg's estate. The driver stopped to unlock the gates and then the car disappeared up the drive. It was nearly dark.

"Quick. Quick. Is now or never," whispered Shakespeare to himself, his face set in a wild grimace. With all his might, he pushed at the trunk of the casuarina tree until it fell in a graceful faint, blocking the road. Shakespeare dissolved back into the bushes, then remembered he had left his bag by the tree, ran to retrieve it and slipped on some wild tamarind pods. He cursed, but the pods gave him an idea. He picked one up and shook it. It rattled. He slipped it under his arm and melted once more into the trees. The sky had turned from silver to grey to black.

Vice-President Hogg gazed moodily from the open back window of his limousine as the driver came to a halt, the branches of the toppled casuarina tree waving in his headlights:

'I have to get some help to move this obstruction,' apologized the driver after inspecting the offending tree. Hogg grunted his assent and waited while the chauffeur sped off towards the main road.

It was then that Hogg began to hear things. First of all he heard the sound of soft, ploppy bangs on the roof of the car which he dismissed as something falling from the trees. Then, what appeared to be the piercing whistle of a bird assailed his ears, a whistle that ended in an unearthly rattle. Two minutes later, from his right, he heard a loud munching sound from the bushes. Almost immediately, from his left he heard a high-pitched voice calling:

"Hello, daalin'."

Silence followed. Hogg's small eyes shifted from side to side. Nothing happened. Hogg permitted himself to relax a fraction when the silence was broken by the clip-clop of hooves along the dried earth road. Hogg thrust his head out of the car window. What he saw appalled him. Beyond the section of road, illuminated by the car headlights, he could just make out the figure of a woman. She wore some kind of headwrap and a whitish dress with puffed sleeves. She was approaching slowly with a lolloping, uneven gait. Worst of all, she was beckoning him with the crook of her first finger, beckoning him to follow her into the bushes. Hogg gave a little moan and fell on his knees in the back of the car. No sooner had he assumed this position than all hell seemed to break loose in the trees at the side of the car. He could hear shouts, the crashing of branches and the snapping of twigs, as if some enormous creature was threshing about. Then Hogg heard a familiar voice yelling:

"Go way! Leave him alone, I tell you." More silence.

Fearfully, Hogg raised his face to the window where it confronted the equally tense face of Shakespeare McNab.

"Praise the Lord. You safe." Shakespeare panted. "Did you get my message? I came to warn you in case the message din reach."

Hogg wiped a film of sweat from his face with a handkerchief. The breast of his khaki jacket rose and fell as he stared, mesmerized, at Shakespeare, his jaw slack.

"Might I get in the car? I think it would be safer for both of us." Shakespeare tried to control his breathing rate. Hogg shifted to the far side of the back seat and Shakespeare slipped in beside him:

"Lord a mercy. All these years I bin tellin' stories about these things an' I never really believe them. Now I know it all true. Lucky I was here. I fought her off. You know who that was?"

Hogg's eyes swivelled towards Shakespeare. They seemed to contain some sort of warning, but Shakespeare could not stop:

"La Diablesse."

"Who?" asked Hogg, confused.

"La Diablesse." Shakespeare lowered his voice to a whisper. "That must have been the warning my mother was trying to give you in the dream. Did you get the message I left?"

Hogg nodded.

"La Diablesse. You know. She got one straight foot and one cloven hoof. She lure people to their death in the forest."

A rumbling laugh emerged from Hogg's nether regions. Shakespeare quailed. The plan was not working. Hogg didn't appreciate the seriousness of an encounter with La Diablesse. Shakespeare's own heroism would go for naught. He shot a worried glance at Hogg's enormous, shaking bulk.

"Jesus God," said Hogg. "I thought it was my wife."

The strength oozed out of Shakespeare's limbs. Never had it occured to him that Hogg would mistake the apparition for the ghost of his wife. He attempted to put the matter right:

"If you will forgive me for contradicting you, Comrade Vice-President, I am sure that what I saw was La Diablesse. When I shouted and shake the branches, she jus' fade back into the trees."

Hogg frowned. "What brought you here?" He sounded suspicious.

"A feelin'. A powerful feelin'," said Shakespeare.

Shakespeare peered timorously at the corpulent figure beside him. Hogg appeared preoccupied. He was scowling as he fingered the ring on his right hand, twisting it this way and that. Suddenly, he pulled the ring off and flung it through the car window. Just then, the car headlights picked out the anxious face of the chauffeur. He was with another man and together they set about removing the tree from the path of the car. Shakespeare knew that if he was to seize the opportunity before it vanished he would have to make his move fast:

"Well, sir . . . Comrade sir, I can see that you are safe now. I must be gettin' home. Sadly, I have been made redundant from the broadcasting station and I have got to get up early and look for other work."

Hogg turned slowly and scrutinized Shakespeare. Shakespeare wilted a little under the penetrating stare.

"I have an idea," said Hogg, thoughtfully, "I think I might be able to help you on this."

Shakespeare batted his eyelids and started to thank him effusively, hoping for an immediate return to the broadcasting station, but Hogg continued: "I am going to offer you a position as my personal adviser."

In his grandmother's kitchen the next day, Shakespeare strutted from the window to the table, laughing and boasting as he related, in full detail, the success of his ruse:

"So, what you think grandmumma. I clever? You grandson clever? I am now Personal Adviser to Comrade Vice-President Hogg," he crowed.

She stirred some casreep into the pepper-pot.

"Leave the country," she said.

A HAPPY STORY

WHAT'S THIS STORY ABOUT?" Everett leans over my shoulder. He really wants to ask "when will dinner be ready?" But he will not have it spread about that he is a traditionalist.

"It's about a woman," I say as he inspects the contents of pots with an air of disapproval. I continue. "Intelligent. Attractive. Educated. A career is possible if she plays her cards right." Everett has thrown open the refrigerator door, is standing, feet apart, fists on hips, as if silently demanding that certain foods present themselves for his until-dinner-gets-ready snacking. I continue. "But one morning she wakes up to realize that despite her efforts, she is living the same life her mother led. She feels desperate at this idea—"

Everett is desperately opening up foil wrappers. Finds one cold pork chop.

"—and in that moment, she begins to plan her own suicide."

"Why?" mumbles Everett around a mouthful of pork chop. "I thought she was so intelligent."

"Maybe she's intelligent enough—" I say to his back as he returns to his armchair enclave, "—intelligent enough to wonder if surviving is worth the trouble."

Everett rattles his newspaper. The TV drones. I sweep up crumbs from the table and deposit the abandoned pork chop foil wrapper in the trash can. Slowly I recover my thoughts, make a few scribbles on my yellow pad.

"Why don't you ever write a *happy* story?" Everett says, moments later, newspaper crumpling in his lap. I pretend I don't hear him, wish that I hadn't.

"Angel? Didja hear me? Why can't you write a *happy* story for a change?" I don't even look up.

"You know one?" I say. "Tell me a happy story and I'll use it," I say. When I do look up, his eyes are waiting. We look at each other. I smile, feeling some triumph. "Tell me," I say, "and I'll write it."

Everett is a determined optimist; I call it self-delusion. I am a realist; he calls it "bad disposition." I say that he pretties up life with pretense. He says that I don't consider the cloud's silver lining. I say you're liable to be struck by lightning standing in a thunderstorm looking for a silver lining. He says I live for bad news. "Tell me a happy story," I persist. "I can't wait to write it."

His tongue is working inside of one cheek; maybe he's thinking . . . or maybe he's just after a sliver of pork chop caught between his teeth. He seems to regard me with infinite patience and pity. But now, his unflagging optimism comes to rescue his face from furrows of doubt. I see firm determination light his eyes. He will, now as ever, rescue me from myself. I am caught off guard by my own laughter; it comes snorting unladylike from my nose.

"Come on," I say, "Lay this fairy tale on me."

It has to be a fairy tale. All stories with nice happy endings are—either that, or gothic romance. But I prefer fairy tales. At least they don't pretend to be in any way real—just morality tales cloaked in an entertainment. Snow White bites the poison apple but does not die—she lives happily ever after (and the bad queen dies a horrible death). An ancient wish for moral justice, but certainly no reflection of life, where victims don't sleep but die, and bad queens suffer fame and millions made on the Vegas circuit.

The problem with fairy tales is that they end just where true stories begin. What if the story of Snow White continued beyond the grand wedding, and her prince carried her to a land called Newark, to a tenement castle subdivided for multiple family dwelling? And what if his princely income waned, and his ardor, as her body sagged with childbearing, and the mirror chanted a different tune, and Prince Charming—whipping up his trusty steed—stumbled across a younger damsel in distress upon the urban glade? And the matronly Snow White became the poison toting neglected wife. . . .

It would not take much to convince me that happiness *is* the darker side of life: suburban housewife pushing husband and kiddies off to work and day care just to crawl back into illicit daydreaming; the unrequited lover tasting the most profound ecstasy at the lip of the poison cup. . . . I try to return to my *own* thoughts, abandon this tired academic problem of art vs. life. But Everett has been pondering.

"You could write a story about my mother," he says.

"Your mother's story is not happy," I say.

"My mother is a saint," he says.

"Saints do not happy stories make. Saints are tragic," I point out. "In order to even qualify for sainthood, one must suffer inordinately and die pathetically for the purpose of inspiring pity, guilt, and other behavior inhibiting emotions. Not a prescription for a truly happy story."

"But it's their triumph over suffering," he says, "That's the happy part."

"The happy part is that it was *their* suffering and not *yours.*" I think this, but I don't say it. Everett can't stand being *always* wrong. So I nod at his last protest even if I don't agree. Because nobody overcomes hardships: we merely survive them, like car wrecks, to haul the scars around with us until we die. But I nod as if the saintly mother story is a possibility to consider. Heartened by this, Everett continues:

". . . And mama has spent her whole life trying to help other people. As hard as her life has been, she could always find something to give. Isn't that happy?" Everett pauses. Studies my face which I make sure is giving away nothing. He waits for my acquiescence on his last point; I can't give it. So I tell him flat out, "That's the saddest story there is. Along with being the oldest." Everett's face tightens. The words sound harsh. Maybe the truth will go better with a musical accompaniment. So I toss aside my writing, flip through albums for something mellow—something sad.

I wouldn't object to writing his mother's story if, in her old age, she had put hard times behind her and was now enjoying some ease and peace of mind. But Everett's mother is living in the same two-story walkup of her childhood—the same, but different, because it's older, more decrepit. The beams are termite riddled, the front porch is a hazard, and her new neighbors are young acid heads who don't know the difference between sleep and death. It is not triumph but the height of tragedy—the final kick: sacrifice rewarded with pain. Maybe it is irreverent to say that her story is the oldest story on record, but it is: a mother sacrificing body and mind for children who will eventually spurn her (or idealize her) but never recognize what was traded for their lives. It is old. It is sad. . . . It is true. It is not happy. And now I hope that Everett can realize the magnitude of the thing he has so frivolously proposed. It's easy to *say* "write a happy story," but when you get down to the brass tacks of it, the task is formidable.

Of course I could manufacture happy tales unending if I made them out of wish instead of life: flawlessly beautiful men and women living lives full of satisfaction; modern episodes of Ozzie and Harriet; heroic tales of John Wayne justice, Right prevailing over Wrong; evil creatures disarmed with a fortuitous bucket of water—

The stove hisses vehemently.

"Your pot is boiled over," says Everett cocking one eye to the stove, then to me. I cross the kitchen, deliberately slow, watching the foaming white water smear down the sides of the saucepan, sizzle into the hot recesses of the stove where it will congeal into an impossible to remove glue.

"What about Alice?" says Everett.

I think about my friend Alice, now a very big costume jewelry magnate on the East coast. She *is* a success story.

"Is Alice happy?"

"She made more money last year than most people ever see—outside a Monopoly game," Everett says.

I swab the stove top with a soppy dishcloth. "Is she happy, you think?" Everett doesn't answer. I stir pots.

€€   €€   €€

"What's *this* story about?"

"Alice's happy story fragment. It's not finished."

"How much've you got?"

"I've got:

"At seven, Alice was a pretty girl. Everyone always said so. Especially her uncle, her mother's step-brother, who had Sunday dinner with them every week without fail.

"But they were poor, so Alice's mother had no chicken for Sunday pots, but depended on her step-brother to bring fish that he caught at the lake. He always brought an extra fish for Alice who hated fish but was always made to thank her uncle for her extra portion with a kiss.

"'You see Alice, a pretty girl will always get more,' he whispered to her every Sunday without fail, and endlessly, like the smell of fish that she came to associate, not with a meal, but with her uncle. With his breath, his shirt, his fingers that squeezed her quick and rough whenever she had to kiss him.

"Men told Alice she was pretty. Alice's mother said, 'You must think you're cute, or somethin','"and slapped her when she was angry. But Alice loved her mother. She knew the slaps were not from lack of love, but because her mother hated fish also. So Alice gathered pretty trash, lost buttons, bright chips of glass, and strung them for her mother who wore them on 'chicken days'—Christmases and Easters—to make Alice smile."

"That's happy?" Everett asks incredulous.

"Well . . . ," I say, "She never went hungry."

"The uncle is a lech."

"She overcomes that hardship," I say. But Everett has heard enough.

"Alice never had any uncles like that," he says.

"How do you know?"

"And she was never poor."

"This is fiction, not biography," I say. "Besides, a story should be universal. Every girl has an uncle, or *some*body, like that."

"Did you?"

"This is fiction, not autobiography," I say.

Everett takes a deep exaggerated breath. "Alice's family was well-off, she went to college, majored in Business Administration. She married, had two sons, and in her spare time, she blasted her way into the costume jewelry market and made a killing." The world according to Everett.

I amend. "Alice was a neglected child who hung around college campuses, married a rich man's son, had two sons right quick, divorced the rich man's son, sued for humongous alimony, bought herself a nanny, and a costume jewelry business," and reality reigns once again.

"You don't have to put it like that. You could emphasize the success part," says Everett.

I sweep gleaming vegetables from the chopping board into the skillet. The hot butter gives a long sigh. "So," I say. "A happy story is a story with the sad parts snipped away. And writing is an aberrant form of—cosmetology?"

I don't agree with this dishonesty, but I have to admire Everett's clear vision, a man for whom happiness is attainable through good sound planning—or a good pearl eraser. Later, as I clear and wash up from dinner, I wonder if he isn't right about Alice. With one son in jail, the other a part-time hairdresser, and her series of interesting but impermanent men, she was surely, I had thought, in pure agony. I scrub pots. Ironic that Everett would be the one to suggest that a woman's happiness could exist despite the failures of children and men.

      ❧   ❧   ❧

Everett seems to have lost interest in this quest for the happy story, but I am tortured by it. The problem is the thing itself—happiness. What is it? The attainment of what I *think* I want, or just the absence of grief? Who has it? How did they get hold of it? Hang onto it? Or is it just mind control—looking for the bright side while constantly living in the dark? Is it the predictable routine of Everett's mother's last years, whose whole life was spent in flux? Is her happiness the mere absence of the awful unexpected, the knowledge that there are no new disasters? That her own death is no longer frightening—that it is a not altogether unpleasant prospect? The idea that every eventuality can be met? The reason that she can refuse to be rescued from the dilapidation of life, finally insist upon having some things her own way and not worry about the consequences? There might be a certain satisfaction in this.

Still, how sad if happiness boiled down to a kind of good-natured fatalism. I wanted my happiness to be more perfect, even if that made it impossible to obtain. Even if it had to remain the property of childhood ignorance, or of memory.

"Are you trying to say you've never been happy?" says Everett.

"I would never say that."

"What was the happiest time of your life?"

"Happiest?" I repeat, balancing a stack of plates to a high shelf. "It's so hard to speak in degrees. . . ."

"Give me one time," he says. "When?"

"When?" I repeat.

When. Everett's voice is like the crossed arms of my old piano teacher, Mrs. Poindexter. One hand always gripping a ruler. "Give me the time," she would say, smacking the ruler against her narrow backside for the tempo. And I played, struggling to meet the demand. Everett waits. I rifle through my life, days, and years, in search of a single convincing moment. I think it must be something wholly selfish and completely satisfying—

Like the time two nickels bought me two whole Big Time candy bars to eat all by myself and *not* share. It had taken me all day to shake little sisters and supervision. The city air had smelled sweet to me as I ran, full tilt, without stopping, to the basement store. The agony, sweet, of impossible choices: candy necklaces or candy mint juleps or "wine" candy sours. But I had already known I wanted the Big Times that were hurt-yourself good and never enough when you had to split one two ways, or three, or four. But I had two nickels and a little bit of time. . . . Except I remember the candy didn't taste as good as I had expected. Maybe they were stale. Or maybe it was because I ate them so fast, afraid of being discovered, afraid of the sudden cry of: "dibs dibs!" our unrefusable demand to share. Or worse, some unexpected adult demanding to know "—and where'd you get the money for that?" Because a nickel for candy was unusual, and two was rare if not completely unheard of. And the nickels were "borrowed" from my grandmother's mantel. No, this was not a happy memory. The selfish moment is always spoiled by guilt.

A happy moment would, evidently, have to be some occasion of selfless generosity or sacrifice. When I was oh, maybe ten years old, my sisters and I had saved a wool sock full of money. A collection of nickels, quarters and even some dollar bills. We counted it constantly, thoroughly excited at our thrift. We discussed what to do with the money, but could think of no purchase exciting or satisfying enough to justify spending all of that money, close to thirteen dollars. It must have been Palm Sunday, or some other special occasion. It could not have been an ordinary Sunday when we carried our treasure in its black wool "bank" to Sunday school, and we decided to give a whole dollar in offering. Our Sunday School master must have smelled our excitement, or our money, because she kept on begging and prodding, saying: "Oh, our class has never won the distinction of best offering. A little bit more, and we might earn a special blessing." (One more dollar). "Oh! wouldn't it be something if the children of the Sunday School outshined the adults in their offering to God?" (*Two* more dollars). And: "I just checked and we're still five dollars lower than the Elders' collection plate." In defeat, we emptied the entire remains of our sock savings into the plate. . . . And, in a moment, a great cry rose up in the church. Three daughters had given thirteen dollars to the collection plate. Wasn't that a wonderment! Wasn't that the spirit of God at work! But there was jealousy in the House of God because a rally cry went up. The adults reached into their deep pockets and came forth with dollar after dollar. Even so, we almost earned our special blessing, which was little enough reward I thought, when my own father came forward with five dollars in his hand. The adults grinned. I wept. No. Selfless generosity was, and always had been, for the birds. How could I have forgotten that even joyful giving *must* offer *some* small reward.

The last possibility: happiness must be some simple uncomplicated moment when your purposes—no matter how unambitious—go unthwarted.

Like I had my own house once. And once, I had a certain recognition for particular kinds of Saturday afternoons, early dusk, mild uneventful days. Yes, summer Saturdays, early dusk, just as the worst of the midday heat has dissipated, and every window is thrown open to the deepening air, the beginning breeze; rooms stretch out infinite in growing shadows. I am part of the shadows, sweaty, rank. But every surface is scrubbed, rubbed to gleaning. Leisurely, slow, I lean in to every doorway and everything is perfect order: perfumed linen, gleaming glass, dark scent of wax and incense burning into dusk. And jazz saxophone mellow on the box—Standing sour and damp, old clothes sticking to me, scalp pricking sweat, lifting my shirtfront to the breath of a breeze, knowing I am the only imperfection within this small perfection made by me. And I, for the moment, am my own creation. It is not the weekly grind of housework that satisfies, but purposes being met without interference. Completion. The signature on the painting. The flourish at the end of the performance.

"Climbing into the wonderful world of Calgon is bliss," I say to Everett. "I have been happy."

"Taking a bath is happiness for you?" he says, voice cracking. His look is scorching. I guess I have missed a beat somewhere. I suppose I ought to include *him* in it somehow.

I return to myself in an incredibly hot bath, so hot I am floating up like the mist, so perfect my thoughts burst open like the bubbles I nudge with my toe. I can dissolve into the sweat of mirrors that multiply me, disappear into the yellow brilliance of saxophone straining toward the treble—a single superb note the horn blower discovers at the top of the riff. He blows, bending at the knees until his chest caves—holding it . . . holding on. . . . It is the uncertainty of the moment that inspires absorption: knowing the sweetness of the bath can't last, knowing how hot dissipates to tepid, knowing that the record will end. That the silence will be broken . . . by a faint sound—the deadbolt sliding back under the key. Joy is the prior regret for the sweet ending of an irretrievable moment. I tell Everett that his returning home from an absence and I'm brand new in the bathtub is an intensely exquisite experience.

Everett considers this—tongue busy. But I'm dissatisfied. What is this feeling I'm looking for, so fleet, like a bubble I burst with my toe? Why should it be that I can recall injuries and slights no end, have at my disposal infinite evidence of the world's injustice, malice, casual cruelty. And disappointments: like discovering that there *is* no magic—no benevolent and timely fairy godmother to rescue us from the daily cinders and rubble; that the bread crumbs strewn to show us the way are *al*ways food for birds, or the hustling industrious ants, leaving us all standing, faces tipped, staring up into a knit of blankness. Where are the matching memories of joy so powerful, so engulfing, enough to muffle the continuous pummeling of life?

This is a happy story with a dole of sadness, like the surplus bread handed out to the poor. Like the rich man whose joy in his richness is tainted with a worry that the poor might get too much. . . .

My neighborhood church is a dispensary to the poor. I volunteer to hand out surplus food to the needy. Sometimes cheese, sometimes bread. The Reverend Lester hands out religion. "Jesus fed the multitude with five loaves and two fish," he preaches a popular sermon.

"You givin' out fish too, Rev'rend?" a young woman asks.

"They given out fish," someone passes it on.

"*Some* folks got fish," another says, dissatisfied. "They run out."

The people stand in lines. I think of fish dinners, back yard fish fries, slapping mosquitoes on summer nights, pungent hot sauces, cold beer and lemonade. Mountains of catfish, perch, fried golden, crisp, the hot steam trapped inside the skin. How it would take all day to get ready with errands and cleaning the fish, and sweeping stray children from underfoot. The air full of expectation and no one too impatient.

A woman stands in front of me, her hands held forth for her portion. Her expression is sour. She looks at the smooth blocks of cheese thinking of fish. She takes the cheese, hands the large weight of it to her small child standing beside her. The child wobbles with the burden.

"There never was any fish," I say to her.

"Sure," she says.

"It was just a rumor," I say, but she stalks off. She wants to know who is in charge. My eyes are met by the direct stare of the woman standing behind her. She is elderly; her skin is smooth like rubbed, cured wood. After a moment, she smiles.

"The good Lord didn't need fish nor bread to do what he done. Don't never call *that* no rumor," she tells me, mocking-stern. "God bless," she says, receiving the cheese into her arms carefully. "I gives some of this to my nephew," she says. "He don't qualify. He earns $10.00 over the limit." Her smile is full of yellow gold, a bright chip drawing the vague light of the dim room to a single brilliant mite. She leaves me with my own smile.

"The happiest day of my life was the day we were married," Everett confesses to me, then waits. Then he says, "What about you?"

"I'm still working on it," I say.

"You weren't happy on our wedding day?" he says.

"Well," I say, "I didn't want to take *your* happiest day."

"But it *was* the happiest? So far? Right?"

Everett no longer asks me about my stories. Now I *make* him listen.

"This is a story about happiness," I say. "It's not finished." Everett says nothing. "This is what I have so far," I say.

"Alice always loved weddings. So, as a young girl, she resolved to have several. Each one would be more beautiful than the last, each husband more beautiful than his predecessor. Therefore, the spareness of her first wedding and the sparsity of beauty in the face and form of her first husband did not disturb her excessively. When the aged preacher misread a few of the vows, it was not devastating to Alice who, later, had to console her new husband's anger regarding the matter.

"'You didn't plan to keep all those promises anyway,' she chided him, laughing, teasing. The accusation shocked him at first, as he did not expect her to know this, and he protested the fidelity of his heart. But, a day later, when Alice found her husband's eyes wandering behind an unfamiliar woman, he smiled, licked his lips and resolved to be more careful.

"His name was Cheever. Cheever did not have good looks but knew 'how to make him some money.' He said this often and Alice, who was always agreeable, agreed.

"But Alice did not despise Cheever for his lack of handsomeness. She felt genuinely grateful to him—he'd been her escape route from home, from her uncle's fish smell. She was satisfied with her marriage and learned how to keep house out of magazines, cooked out of books, and drew designs with colored pencils which she pinned all over her walls until they lived inside a montage of faint scribbly color. She even pinned the light designs to the bedboard above their heads. And sunny mornings when she woke to Cheever thrusting love at her from behind, matter-of-factly like a drowsy bear rubbing an itch against a slender bark, she had only to lift her eyes to study the outlines of dreams, outside the sudden odor of private lust.

"One day, when Cheever had gone, Alice crawled back into the spoiled sheets that held her daydreams. And behind her lids grew a tree supple and bending beneath the jewels that budded on the tips of its branches. She plucked one red fruit and made it disappear inside the warm dark of her palm."

"She's living in a dream world," says Everett. "Her husband is selfish and inconsiderate. *And* ugly. Where does the happy part come in?"

"It's coming," I say.

I am still writing the story of the woman—intelligent, ambitious, attractive, educated. Did I say intelligent? Because she is no longer planning her suicide, realizing it was a waste of her time since death is already scripted and requires no additional preparation. Realizing that her mother's life contained some moments of joy because she was a woman who worked towards the completion of tasks small and large and always spoke of her life without excluding any of its parts.

RECITATIF

M Y MOTHER DANCED ALL NIGHT and Roberta's was sick. That's why we were taken to St. Bonny's. People want to put their arms around you when you tell them you were in a shelter, but it really wasn't bad. No big long room with one hundred beds like Bellevue. There were four to a room, and when Roberta and me came, there was a shortage of state kids, so we were the only ones assigned to 406 and could go from bed to bed if we wanted to. And we wanted to, too. We changed beds every night and for the whole four months we were there we never picked one out as our own permanent bed.

It didn't start out that way. The minute I walked in and the Big Bozo introduced us, I got sick to my stomach. It was one thing to be taken out of your own bed early in the morning—it was something else to be stuck in a strange place with a girl from a whole other race. And Mary, that's my mother, she was right. Every now and then she would stop dancing long enough to tell me something important and one of the things she said was that they never washed their hair and they smelled funny. Roberta sure did. Smell funny, I mean. So when the Big Bozo (nobody ever called her Mrs. Itkin, just like nobody ever said St. Bonaventure)—when she said, "Twyla, this is Roberta. Roberta, this is Twyla. Make each other welcome," I said, "My mother won't like you putting me in here."

"Good," said Bozo. "Maybe then she'll come and take you home."

How's that for mean? If Roberta had laughed I would have killed her, but she didn't. She just walked over to the window and stood with her back to us.

"Turn around," said Bozo. "Don't be rude. Now Twyla. Roberta. When you hear a loud buzzer, that's the call for dinner. Come down to the first floor. Any fights and no movie." And then, just to make sure we knew what we would be missing, "*The Wizard of Oz.*"

Roberta must have thought I meant that my mother would be mad about my being put in the shelter. Not about rooming with her, because as soon as Bozo left she came over to me and said, "Is your mother sick too?"

"No," I said. "She just likes to dance all night."

"Oh." She nodded her head and I liked the way she understood things so fast. So for the moment it didn't matter that we looked like salt and pepper standing there and that's what the other kids called us sometimes. We were eight years old and got F's all the time. Me because I couldn't remember what I read or what the teacher said. And Roberta because she couldn't read at all and didn't even listen to the teacher. She wasn't good at anything except jacks, at which she was a killer: pow scoop pow scoop pow scoop.

We didn't like each other all that much at first, but nobody else wanted to play with us because we weren't real orphans with beautiful dead parents in the sky. We were dumped. Even the New York City Puerto Ricans and the upstate Indians ignored us. All kinds of kids were in there, black ones, white ones, even two Koreans. The food was good, though. At least I thought so. Roberta hated it and left whole pieces of things on her plate: Spam, Salisbury steak—even Jell-O with fruit cocktail in it, and she didn't care if I ate what she wouldn't. Mary's idea of supper was popcorn and a can of Yoo-Hoo. Hot mashed potatoes and two weenies was like Thanksgiving for me.

It really wasn't bad, St. Bonny's. The big girls on the second floor pushed us around now and then. But that was all. They wore lipstick and eyebrow pencil and wobbled their knees while they watched TV. Fifteen, sixteen, even, some of them were. They were put-out girls, scared runaways most of them. Poor little girls who fought their uncles off but looked tough to us, and mean. God, did they look mean. The staff tried to keep them separate from the younger children, but sometimes they caught us watching them in the orchard where they played radios and danced with each other. They'd light out after us and pull our hair or twist our arms. We were scared of them, Roberta and me, but neither of us wanted the other one to know it. So we got a good list of dirty names we could shout back when we ran from them through the orchard. I used to dream a lot and almost always the orchard was there. Two acres, four maybe, of these little apple trees. Hundreds of them. Empty and crooked like beggar women when I first came to St. Bonny's but fat with flowers when I left. I don't know why I dreamt about that orchard so much. Nothing really happened there. Nothing all that important, I mean. Just the big girls dancing and playing the radio. Roberta and me watching. Maggie fell down there once. The kitchen woman with legs like parentheses. And the big girls laughed at her. We should have helped her up, I know, but we were scared of those girls with lipstick and eyebrow pencil. Maggie couldn't talk. The kids said she had her tongue cut out, but I think she was just born that way: mute. She was old and sandy-colored and she worked in the kitchen. I don't know if she was nice or not. I just remember her legs like parentheses and how she rocked when she walked.

She worked from early in the morning till two o'clock, and if she was late, if she had too much cleaning and didn't get out till two-fifteen or so, she'd cut through the orchard so she wouldn't miss her bus and have to wait another hour. She wore this really stupid little hat—a kid's hat with ear flaps—and she wasn't much taller than we were. A really awful little hat. Even for a mute, it was dumb—dressing like a kid and never saying anything at all.

"But what about if somebody tries to kill her?" I used to wonder about that. "Or what if she wants to cry? Can she cry?"

"Sure," Roberta said. "But just tears. No sounds come out."

"She can't scream?"

"Nope. Nothing."

"Can she hear?"

"I guess."

"Let's call her," I said. And we did.

"Dummy! Dummy!" She never turned her head.

"Bow legs! Bow legs!" Nothing. She just rocked on, the chin straps of her baby-boy hat swaying from side to side. I think we were wrong. I think she could hear and didn't let on. And it shames me even now to think there was somebody in there after all who heard us call her those names and couldn't tell on us.

We got along all right, Roberta and me. Changed beds every night, got F's in civics and communication skills and gym. The Bozo was disappointed in us, she said. Out of 130 of us state cases, 90 were under twelve. Almost all were real orphans with beautiful dead parents in the sky. We were the only ones dumped and the only ones with F's in three classes including gym. So we got along—what with her leaving whole pieces of things on her plate and being nice about not asking questions.

I think it was the day before Maggie fell down that we found out our mothers were coming to visit us on the same Sunday. We had been at the shelter twenty-eight days (Roberta twenty-eight and a half) and this was their first visit with us. Our mothers would come at ten o'clock in time for chapel, then lunch with us in the teachers' lounge. I thought if my dancing mother met her sick mother it might be good for her. And Roberta thought her sick mother would get a big bang out of a dancing one. We got excited about it and curled each other's hair. After breakfast we sat on the bed watching the road from the window. Roberta's socks were still wet. She washed them the night before and put them on the radiator to dry. They hadn't, but she put them on anyway because their tops were so pretty—scalloped in pink. Each of us had a purple construction-paper basket that we had made in craft class. Mine had a yellow crayon rabbit on it. Roberta's had eggs with wiggly lines of color. Inside were cellophane grass and just the jelly beans because I'd eaten the two marshmallow eggs they gave us. The Big Bozo came herself to get us. Smiling she told us we looked very nice and to come downstairs. We were so surprised by the smile we'd never seen before, neither of us moved.

"Don't you want to see your mommies?"

I stood up first and spilled the jelly beans all over the floor. Bozo's smile disappeared while we scrambled to get the candy up off the floor and put it back in the grass.

She escorted us downstairs to the first floor, where the other girls were lining up to file into the chapel. A bunch of grown-ups stood to one side. Viewers mostly. The old biddies who wanted servants and the fags who wanted company looking for children they might want to adopt. Once in a while a grandmother. Almost never anybody young or anybody whose face wouldn't scare you in the night. Because if any of the real orphans had young relatives they wouldn't be real orphans. I saw Mary right away. She had on those green slacks I hated and hated even more now because didn't she know we were going to chapel? And that fur jacket with the pocket linings so ripped she had to pull to get her hands out of them. But her face was pretty—like always—and she smiled and waved like she was the little girl looking for her mother, not me.

I walked slowly, trying not to drop the jelly beans and hoping the paper handle would hold. I had to use my last Chiclet because by the time I finished cutting everything out, all the Elmer's was gone. I am left-handed and the scissors never worked for me. It didn't matter, though; I might just as well have chewed the gum. Mary dropped to her knees and grabbed me, mashing the basket, the jelly beans, and the grass into her ratty fur jacket.

"Twyla, baby. Twyla, baby!"

I could have killed her. Already I heard the big girls in the orchard the next time saying, "Twyyyyyla, baby!" But I couldn't stay mad at Mary while she was smiling and hugging me and smelling of Lady Esther dusting powder. I wanted to stay buried in her fur all day.

To tell the truth I forgot about Roberta. Mary and I got in line for the traipse into chapel and I was feeling proud because she looked so beautiful even in those ugly green slacks that made her behind stick out. A pretty mother on earth is better than a beautiful dead one in the sky even if she did leave you all alone to go dancing.

I felt a tap on my shoulder, turned, and saw Roberta smiling. I smiled back, but not too much lest somebody think this visit was the biggest thing that ever happened in my life. Then Roberta said, "Mother, I want you to meet my roommate, Twyla. And that's Twyla's mother."

I looked up it seemed for miles. She was big. Bigger than any man and on her chest was the biggest cross I'd ever seen. I swear it was six inches long each way. And in the crook of her arm was the biggest Bible ever made.

Mary, simpleminded as ever, grinned and tried to yank her hand out of the pocket with the raggedy lining—to shake hands, I guess. Roberta's mother looked down at me and then looked down at Mary too. She didn't say anything, just grabbed Roberta with her Bible-free hand and stepped out of line, walking quickly to the rear of it. Mary was still grinning because she's not too swift when it comes to what's really going on. Then this light bulb goes off in her head and she says "That bitch!" really loud and us almost in the chapel now. Organ music whining;

the Bonny Angels singing sweetly. Everybody in the world turned around to look. And Mary would have kept it up—kept calling names if I hadn't squeezed her hands as hard as I could. That helped a little, but she still twitched and crossed and uncrossed her legs all through service. Even groaned a couple of times. Why did I think she would come there and act right? Slacks. No hat like the grandmothers and viewers, and groaning all the while. When we stood for hymns she kept her mouth shut. Wouldn't even look at the words on the page. She actually reached in her purse for a mirror to check her lipstick. All I could think of was that she really needed to be killed. The sermon lasted a year, and I knew the real orphans were looking smug again.

We were supposed to have lunch in the teachers' lounge, but Mary didn't bring anything, so we picked fur and cellophane grass off the mashed jelly beans and ate them. I could have killed her. I sneaked a look at Roberta. Her mother had brought chicken legs and ham sandwiches and oranges and a whole box of chocolate-covered grahams. Roberta drank milk from a thermos while her mother read the Bible to her.

Things are not right. The wrong food is always with the wrong people. Maybe that's why I got into waitress work later—to match up the right people with the right food. Roberta just let those chicken legs sit there, but she did bring a stack of grahams up to me later when the visit was over. I think she was sorry that her mother would not shake my mother's hand. And I liked that and I liked the fact that she didn't say a word about Mary groaning all the way through the service and not bringing any lunch.

Roberta left in May when the apple trees were heavy and white. On her last day we went to the orchard to watch the big girls smoke and dance by the radio. It didn't matter that they said, "Twyyyyyla, baby." We sat on the ground and breathed. Lady Esther. Apple blossoms. I still go soft when I smell one or the other. Roberta was going home. The big cross and the big Bible was coming to get her and she seemed sort of glad and sort of not. I thought I would die in that room of four beds without her and I knew Bozo had plans to move some other dumped kid in there with me. Roberta promised to write every day, which was really sweet of her because she couldn't read a lick so how could she write anybody? I would have drawn pictures and sent them to her but she never gave me her address. Little by little she faded. Her wet socks with the pink scalloped tops and her big serious-looking eyes—that's all I could catch when I tried to bring her to mind.

I was working behind the counter at the Howard Johnson's on the Thruway just before the Kingston exit. Not a bad job. Kind of a long ride from Newburgh, but okay once I got there. Mine was the second night shift, eleven to seven. Very light until a Greyhound checked in for breakfast around six-thirty. At that hour the sun was all the way clear of the hills behind the restaurant. The place looked better at night—more like shelter—but I loved it when the sun broke in, even if it did show all the cracks in the vinyl and the speckled floor looked dirty no matter what the mop boy did.

It was August and a bus crowd was just unloading. They would stand around a long while: going to the john, and looking at gifts and junk-for-sale machines, reluctant to sit down so soon. Even to eat. I was trying to fill the coffeepots and get them all situated on the electric burners when I saw her. She was sitting in a booth smoking a cigarette with two guys smothered in head and facial hair. Her own hair was so big and wild I could hardly see her face. But the eyes. I would know them anywhere. She had on a powder-blue halter and shorts outfit and earrings the size of bracelets. Talk about lipstick and eyebrow pencil. She made the big girls look like nuns. I couldn't get off the counter until seven o'clock but I kept watching the booth in case they got up to leave before that. My replacement was on time for a change, so I counted and stacked my receipts as fast as I could and signed off. I walked over to the booth, smiling and wondering if she would remember me. Or even if she wanted to remember me. Maybe she didn't want to be reminded of St. Bonny's or to have anybody know she was ever there. I know I never talked about it to anybody.

I put my hands in my apron pockets and leaned against the back of the booth facing them.

"Roberta? Roberta Fisk?"

She looked up. "Yeah?"

"Twyla."

She squinted for a second and then said, "Wow."

"Remember me?"

"Sure. Hey. Wow."

"It's been awhile," I said, and gave a smile to the two hairy guys.

"Yeah. Wow. You work here?"

"Yeah," I said. "I live in Newburgh."

"Newburgh? No kidding?" She laughed then, a private laugh that included the guys but only the guys, and they laughed with her. What could I do but laugh too and wonder why I was standing there with my knees showing out from under that uniform. Without looking I could see the blue-and-white triangle on my head, my hair shapeless in a net, my ankles thick in white oxfords. Nothing could have been less sheer than my stockings. There was this silence that came down right after I laughed. A silence it was her turn to fill up. With introductions, maybe, to her boyfriends or an invitation to sit down and have a Coke. Instead she lit a cigarette off the one she'd just finished and said, "We're on our way to the Coast. He's got an appointment with Hendrix." She gestured casually toward the boy next to her.

"Hendrix? Fantastic," I said. "Really fantastic. What's she doing now?"

Roberta coughed on her cigarette and the two guys rolled their eyes up at the ceiling.

"Hendrix. Jimi Hendrix, asshole. He's only the biggest—Oh, wow. Forget it."

I was dismissed without anyone saying good-bye, so I thought I would do it for her.

"How's your mother?" I asked. Her grin cracked her whole face. She swallowed. "Fine," she said. "How's yours?"

"Pretty as a picture," I said and turned away. The backs of my knees were damp. Howard Johnson's really was a dump in the sunlight.

James is as comfortable as a house slipper. He liked my cooking and I liked his big loud family. They have lived in Newburgh all of their lives and talk about it the way people do who have always known a home. His grandmother has a porch swing older than his father and when they talk about streets and avenues and buildings they call them names they no longer have. They still call the A&P Rico's because it stands on property once a mom-and-pop store owned by Mr. Rico. And they call the new community college Town Hall because it once was. My mother-in-law puts up jelly and cucumbers and buys butter wrapped in cloth from a dairy. James and his father talk about fishing and baseball and I can see them all together on the Hudson in a raggedy skiff. Half the population of Newburgh is on welfare now, but to my husband's family it was still some upstate paradise of a time long past. A time of ice houses and vegetable wagons, coal furnaces and children weeding gardens. When our son was born my mother-in-law gave me the crib blanket that had been hers.

But the town they remembered had changed. Something quick was in the air. Magnificent old houses, so ruined they had become shelter for squatters and rent risks, were bought and renovated. Smart IBM people moved out of their suburbs back into the city and put shutters up and herb gardens in their backyards. A brochure came in the mail announcing the opening of a Food Emporium. Gourmet food, it said—and listed items the rich IBM crowd would want. It was located in a new mall at the edge of town and I drove out to shop there one day—just to see. It was late in June. After the tulips were gone and the Queen Elizabeth roses were open everywhere. I trailed my cart along the aisle tossing in smoked oysters and Robert's sauce and things I knew would sit in my cupboard for years. Only when I found some Klondike ice cream bars did I feel less guilty about spending James's fireman's salary so foolishly. My father-in-law ate them with the same gusto little Joseph did.

Waiting in the checkout line I heard a voice say, "Twyla!"

The classical music piped over the aisles had affected me and the woman leaning toward me was dressed to kill. Diamonds on her hand, a smart white summer dress. "I'm Mrs. Benson," I said.

"Ho. Ho. The Big Bozo," she sang.

For a split second I didn't know what she was talking about. She had a bunch of asparagus and two cartons of fancy water.

"Roberta!"

"Right."

"For heaven's sake. Roberta."

"You look great," she said.

"So do you. Where are you? Here? In Newburgh?"

"Yes. Over in Annandale."

I was opening my mouth to say more when the cashier called my attention to her empty counter.

"Meet you outside." Roberta pointed her finger and went into the express line.

I placed the groceries and kept myself from glancing around to check Roberta's progress. I remembered Howard Johnson's and looking for a chance to speak only to be greeted with a stingy "wow." But she was waiting for me and her huge hair was sleek now, smooth around a small, nicely shaped head. Shoes, dress, everything lovely and summery and rich. I was dying to know what happened to her, how she got from Jimi Hendrix to Annandale, a neighborhood full of doctors and IBM executives. Easy, I thought. Everything is so easy for them. They think they own the world.

"How long," I asked her. "How long have you been here?"

"A year. I got married to a man who lives here. And you, you're married too, right? Benson, you said."

"Yeah. James Benson."

"And is he nice?"

"Oh, is he nice?"

"Well, is he?" Roberta's eyes were steady as though she really meant the question and wanted an answer.

"He's wonderful, Roberta. Wonderful."

"So you're happy."

"Very."

"That's good," she said and nodded her head. "I always hoped you'd be happy. Any kids? I know you have kids."

"One. A boy. How about you?"

"Four."

"Four?"

She laughed. "Step kids. He's a widower."

"Oh."

"Got a minute? Let's have a coffee."

I thought about the Klondikes melting and the inconvenience of going all the way to my car and putting the bags in the trunk. Served me right for buying all that stuff I didn't need. Roberta was ahead of me.

"Put them in my car. It's right here."

And then I saw the dark blue limousine.

"You married a Chinaman?"

"No." She laughed. "He's the driver."

"Oh, my. If the Big Bozo could see you now."

We both giggled. Really giggled. Suddenly, in just a pulse beat, twenty years disappeared and all of it came rushing back. The big girls (whom we called gar girls—Roberta's misheard word for the evil stone faces described in a civics class) there dancing in the orchard, the ploppy mashed potatoes, the double weenies, the Spam with pineapple. We went into the coffee shop holding on to one another and I tried to think why we were glad to see each other this time and not before. Once, twelve years ago, we passed like strangers. A black girl and a white girl meeting in a Howard Johnson's on the road and having nothing to say. One in a blue-and-white triangle waitress hat, the other on her way to see Hendrix. Now we were behaving like sisters separated for much too long. Those four short months were nothing in time. Maybe it was the thing itself. Just being there, together. Two little girls who knew what nobody else in the world knew—how not to ask questions. How to believe what had to be believed. There was politeness in that reluctance and generosity as well. Is your mother sick too? No, she dances all night. Oh—and an understanding nod.

We sat in a booth by the window and fell into recollection like veterans.

"Did you ever learn to read?"

"Watch." She picked up the menu. "Special of the day. Cream of corn soup. Entrées. Two dots and a wriggly line. Quiche. Chef salad, scallops. . . ."

I was laughing and applauding when the waitress came up.

"Remember the Easter baskets?"

"And how we tried to *introduce* them?"

"Your mother with that cross like two telephone poles."

"And yours with those tight slacks."

We laughed so loudly heads turned and made the laughter hard to suppress.

"What happened to the Jimi Hendrix date?"

Roberta made a blow-out sound with her lips.

"When he died I thought about you."

"Oh, you heard about him finally?"

"Finally. Come on. I was a small-town country waitress."

"And I was a small-town country dropout. God, were we wild. I still don't know how I got out of there alive."

"But you did."

"I did. I really did. Now I'm Mrs. Kenneth Norton."

"Sounds like a mouthful."

"It is."

"Servants and all?"

Roberta held up two fingers.

"Ow! What does he do?"

"Computers and stuff. What do I know?"

"I don't remember a hell of a lot from those days, but Lord, St. Bonny's is as clear as daylight. Remember Maggie? The day she fell down and those gar girls laughed at her?"

Roberta looked up from her salad and stared at me. "Maggie didn't fall," she said.

"Yes, she did. You remember."

"No, Twyla. They knocked her down. Those girls pushed her down and tore her clothes. In the orchard."

"I don't—that's not what happened."

"Sure it is. In the orchard. Remember how scared we were?"

"Wait a minute. I don't remember any of that."

"And Bozo was fired."

"You're crazy. She was there when I left. You left before me."

"I went back. You weren't there when they fired Bozo."

"What?"

"Twice. Once for a year when I was about ten, another for two months when I was fourteen. That's when I ran away."

"You ran away from St. Bonny's?"

"I had to. What do you want? Me dancing in that orchard?"

"Are you sure about Maggie?"

"Of course I'm sure. You've blocked it, Twyla. It happened. Those girls had behavior problems, you know."

"Didn't they, though. But why can't I remember the Maggie thing?"

"Believe me. It happened. And we were there."

"Who did you room with when you went back?" I asked her as if I would know her. The Maggie thing was troubling me.

"Creeps. They tickled themselves in the night."

My ears were itching and I wanted to go home suddenly. This was all very well but she couldn't just comb her hair, wash her face, and pretend everything was hunky-dory. After the Howard Johnson's snub. And no apology. Nothing.

"Were you on dope or what that time at Howard Johnson's?" I tried to make my voice sound friendlier than I felt.

"Maybe, a little. I never did drugs much. Why?"

"I don't know, you acted sort of like you didn't want to know me then."

"Oh, Twyla, you know how it was in those days: black—white. You know how everything was."

But I didn't know. I thought it was just the opposite. Busloads of blacks and whites came into Howard Johnson's together. They roamed together then: students, musicians, lovers, protesters. You got to see everything at Howard Johnson's, and blacks were very friendly with whites in those days. But sitting there with nothing on my plate but two hard tomato wedges wondering about the melting Klondikes it seemed childish remembering the slight. We went to her car and, with the help of the driver, got my stuff into my station wagon.

"We'll keep in touch this time," she said.

"Sure," I said. "Sure. Give me a call."

"I will," she said, and then, just as I was sliding behind the wheel, she leaned into the window. "By the way. Your mother. Did she ever stop dancing?"

I shook my head. "No. Never."

Roberta nodded.

"And yours? Did she ever get well?"

She smiled a tiny sad smile. "No. She never did. Look, call me, okay?"

"Okay," I said, but I knew I wouldn't. Roberta had messed up my past somehow with that business about Maggie. I wouldn't forget a thing like that. Would I?

Strife came to us that fall. At least that's what the paper called it. Strife. Racial strife. The word made me think of a bird—a big shrieking bird out of 1,000,000,000 B.C. Flapping its wings and cawing. Its eye with no lid always bearing down on you. All day it screeched and at night it slept on the rooftops. It woke you in the morning, and from the *Today* show to the eleven o'clock news it kept you an awful company. I couldn't figure it out from one day to the next. I knew I was supposed to feel something strong, but I didn't know what, and James wasn't any help. Joseph was on the list of kids to be transferred from the junior high school to another one at some far-out-of-the-way place and I thought it was a good thing until I heard it was a bad thing. I mean I didn't know. All the schools seemed dumps to me, and the fact that one was nicer looking didn't hold much weight. But the papers were full of it and then the kids began to get jumpy. In August, mind you. Schools weren't even open yet. I thought Joseph might be frightened to go over there, but he didn't seem scared so I forgot about it, until I found myself driving along Hudson Street out there by the school they were trying to integrate and saw a line of women marching. And who do you suppose was in line, big as life, holding a sign in front of her bigger than her mother's cross? MOTHERS HAVE RIGHTS TOO! it said.

I drove on and then changed my mind. I circled the block, slowed down, and honked my horn.

Roberta looked over and when she saw me she waved. I didn't wave back, but I didn't move either. She handed her sign to another woman and came over to where I was parked.

"Hi."

"What are you doing?"

"Picketing. What's it look like?"

"What for?"

"What do you mean, 'What for?' They want to take my kids and send them out of the neighborhood. They don't want to go."

"So what if they go to another school? My boy's being bussed too, and I don't mind. Why should you?"

"It's not about us, Twyla. Me and you. It's about our kids."

"What's more *us* than that?"

"Well, it is a free country."

"Not yet, but it will be."

"What the hell does that mean? I'm not doing anything to you."

"You really think that?"

"I know it."

"I wonder what made me think you were different."

"I wonder what made me think you were different."

"Look at them," I said. "Just look. Who do they think they are? Swarming all over the place like they own it. And now they think they can decide where my child goes to school. Look at them, Roberta. They're Bozos."

Roberta turned around and looked at the women. Almost all of them were standing still now, waiting. Some were even edging toward us. Roberta looked at me out of some refrigerator behind her eyes. "No, they're not. They're just mothers."

"And what am I? Swiss cheese?"

"I used to curl your hair."

"I hated your hands in my hair."

The women were moving. Our faces looked mean to them of course and they looked as though they could not wait to throw themselves in front of a police car or, better yet, into my car and drag me away by my ankles. Now they surrounded my car and gently, gently began to rock it. I swayed back and forth like a sideways yo-yo. Automatically I reached for Roberta, like the old days in the orchard when they saw us watching them and we had to get out of there, and if one of us fell the other pulled her up and if one of us was caught the other stayed to kick and scratch, and neither would leave the other behind. My arm shot out of the car window but no receiving hand was there. Roberta was looking at me sway from side to side in the car and her face was still. My purse slid from the car seat down under the dashboard. The four policemen who had been drinking Tab in their car finally got the message and strolled over, forcing their way through the women. Quietly, firmly they spoke, "Okay, ladies. Back in line or off the streets."

Some of them went away willingly; others had to be urged away from the car doors and the hood. Roberta didn't move. She was looking steadily at me. I was fumbling to turn on the ignition, which wouldn't catch because the gearshift was still in drive. The seats of the car were a mess because the swaying had thrown my grocery coupons all over and my purse was sprawled on the floor.

"Maybe I am different now, Twyla. But you're not. You're the same little state kid who kicked a poor old black lady when she was down on the ground. You kicked a black lady and you have the nerve to call me a bigot."

The coupons were everywhere and the guts of my purse were bunched under the dashboard. What was she saying? Black? Maggie wasn't black.

"She wasn't black," I said.

"Like hell she wasn't, and you kicked her. We both did. You kicked a black lady who couldn't even scream."

"Liar!"

"You're the liar! Why don't you just go on home and leave us alone, huh?"

She turned away and I skidded away from the curb.

The next morning I went into the garage and cut the side out of the carton our portable TV had come in. It wasn't nearly big enough, but after a while I had a decent sign: red spray-painted letters on a white background—AND SO DO CHIL-DREN****. I meant just to go down to the school and tack it up somewhere so those cows on the picket line across the street could see it, but when I got there, some ten or so others had already assembled—protesting the cows across the street. Police permits and everything. I got in line and we strutted in time on our side while Roberta's group strutted on theirs. That first day we were all dignified, pretending the other side didn't exist. The second day there was name calling and finger gestures. But that was about all. People changed signs from time to time, but Roberta never did and neither did I. Actually my sign didn't make sense without Roberta's. "And so do children what?" one of the women on my side asked me. Have rights, I said, as though it was obvious.

Roberta didn't acknowledge my presence in any way, and I got to thinking maybe she didn't know I was there. I began to pace myself in the line, jostling people one minute and lagging behind the next, so Roberta and I could reach the end of our respective lines at the same time and there would be a moment in our turn when we would face each other. Still, I couldn't tell whether she saw me and knew my sign was for her. The next day I went early before we were scheduled to assemble. I waited until she got there before I exposed my new creation. As soon as she hoisted her MOTHERS HAVE RIGHTS TOO I began to wave my new one, which said, HOW WOULD YOU KNOW? I know she saw that one, but I had gotten addicted now. My signs got crazier each day, and the women on my side decided that I was a kook. They couldn't make heads or tails out of my brilliant screaming posters.

I brought a painted sign in queenly red with huge black letters that said, IS YOUR MOTHER WELL? Roberta took her lunch break and didn't come back for the rest of the day or any day after. Two days later I stopped going too and couldn't have been missed because nobody understood my signs anyway.

It was a nasty six weeks. Classes were suspended and Joseph didn't go to anybody's school until October. The children—everybody's children—soon got bored with that extended vacation they thought was going to be so great. They looked at TV until their eyes flattened. I spent a couple of mornings tutoring my son, as the other mothers said we should. Twice I opened a text from last year that he had never turned in. Twice he yawned in my face. Other mothers organized living room sessions so the kids would keep up. None of the kids could concentrate, so they drifted back to *The Price Is Right* and *The Brady Bunch*. When the school finally opened there were fights once or twice and some sirens roared through the streets every once in a while. There were a lot of photographers from Albany. And just when ABC was about to send up a news crew, the kids settled down like nothing in the world had happened. Joseph hung my HOW WOULD YOU KNOW? sign in his bedroom. I don't know what became of AND SO DO CHILDREN****. I think my father-in-law cleaned some fish on it. He was always puttering around in our garage. Each of his five children lived in Newburgh, and he acted as though he had five extra homes.

I couldn't help looking for Roberta when Joseph graduated from high school, but I didn't see her. It didn't trouble me much what she had said to me in the car. I mean the kicking part. I know I didn't do that, I couldn't do that. But I was puzzled by her telling me Maggie was black. When I thought about it I actually couldn't be certain. She wasn't pitch-black, I knew, or I would have remembered that. What I remember was the kiddie hat and the semicircle legs. I tried to reassure myself about the race thing for a long time until it dawned on me that the truth was already there, and Roberta knew it. I didn't kick her; I didn't join in with the gar girls and kick that lady, but I sure did want to. We watched and never tried to help her and never called for help. Maggie was my dancing mother. Deaf, I thought, and dumb. Nobody inside. Nobody who would hear you if you cried in the night. Nobody who could tell you anything important that you could use. Rocking, dancing, swaying as she walked. And when the gar girls pushed her down and started roughhousing, I knew she wouldn't scream, couldn't—just like me— and I was glad about that.

We decided not to have a tree, because Christmas would be at my mother-in-law's house, so why have a tree at both places? Joseph was at SUNY New Paltz and we had to economize, we said. But at the last minute, I changed my mind. Nothing could be that bad. So I rushed around town looking for a tree, something small but wide. By the time I found a place, it was snowing and very late. I dawdled like it was the most important purchase in the world and the tree man was fed up with me. Finally I chose one and had it tied onto the trunk of the car. I drove away slowly because the sand trucks were not out yet and the streets could be murder at the beginning of a snowfall. Downtown the streets were wide and rather empty except for a cluster of people coming out of the Newburgh Hotel. The one hotel in town that wasn't built out of cardboard and Plexiglas. A party, probably. The men huddled in the snow were dressed in tails and the women had on furs. Shiny things glittered from underneath their coats. It made me tired to look at them. Tired, tired, tired. On the next corner was a small diner with loops and loops of paper bells in the window. I stopped the car and went in. Just for a cup of coffee and twenty minutes of peace before I went home and tried to finish everything before Christmas Eve.
"Twyla?"
There she was. In a silvery evening gown and dark fur coat. A man and another woman were with her, the man fumbling for change to put in the cigarette machine. The woman was humming and tapping on the counter with her fingernails. They all looked a little bit drunk.
"Well. It's you."
"How are you?"
I shrugged. "Pretty good. Frazzled. Christmas and all."
"Regular?" called the woman from the counter.
"Fine," Roberta called back and then, "Wait for me in the car."
She slipped into the booth beside me. "I have to tell you something, Twyla. I made up my mind if I ever saw you again, I'd tell you."
"I'd just as soon not hear anything, Roberta. It doesn't matter now, anyway."
"No," she said. "Not about that."
"Don't be long," said the woman. She carried two regulars to go and the man peeled his cigarette pack as they left.
"It's about St. Bonny's and Maggie."
"Oh, please."
"Listen to me. I really did think she was black. I didn't make that up. I really thought so. But now I can't be sure. I just remember her as old, so old. And because she couldn't talk—well, you know, I thought she was crazy. She'd been

brought up in an institution like my mother was and like I thought I would be too. And you were right. We didn't kick her. It was the gar girls. Only them. But, well, I wanted to. I really wanted them to hurt her. I said we did it, too. You and me, but that's not true. And I don't want you to carry that around. It was just that I wanted to do it so bad that day—wanting to is doing it."

Her eyes were watery from the drinks she'd had, I guess. I know it's that way with me. One glass of wine and I start bawling over the littlest thing.

"We were kids, Roberta."

"Yeah. Yeah. I know, just kids."

"Eight."

"Eight."

"And lonely."

"Scared, too."

She wiped her cheeks with the heel of her hand and smiled. "Well, that's all I wanted to say."

I nodded and couldn't think of any way to fill the silence that went from the diner past the paper bells on out into the snow. It was heavy now. I thought I'd better wait for the sand trucks before starting home.

"Thanks, Roberta."

"Sure."

"Did I tell you? My mother, she never did stop dancing."

"Yes. You told me. And mine, she never got well." Roberta lifted her hands from the tabletop and covered her face with her palms. When she took them away she really was crying. "Oh, shit, Twyla. Shit, shit, shit. What the hell happened to Maggie?"

A PLAY

I STAND IN A LARGE CUBE. A bare wooden cube, which rises at least twice my height above me and is open in front of me. There are no chairs in the cube, nothing to sit on except the floor. So I stand. In a back corner, the darkest place I can find, trying to look out to see if my audience has been seated.

The wood of the cube, greenish in color, as if the trees were too young to cut, too moist to burn, brings out the Cherokee red in my skin, the Scottish red in my hair, the black red of Mississippi dirt, all over me. But the planks are wide—my nose, wide—so this must be an illusion of my set designer.

This is my stage and I feel like a lone doll standing on a shelf in a child's room, the only toy that isn't on the floor or kept by the bed, dirty and worn.

I wish it was dark, I wish no one could see me up here on this stage. There are three silhouettes in the middle of the orchestra seats. I'm not ready. I don't want to perform my life over again. This show can't last two weeks. Waiting. I wish I could die quickly, quietly, in my own bed, and not have to be here.

Everything is going black. The house lights are going down. I can see orange and violet spheres separate from the blackness. My mind can wander, my toes uncurl; I can fly in this blackness to a place where my mind can be free from these muscles and bones, this skin, my own blood. Fly away and play in the closet with Donna, my little imaginary sister. We used to crawl in the closet and close the door behind us. Disappear. Donna would ask me to tell her stories, but I would only tell her the truth. I would listen to her whimpers in the blackness, between the silences I needed to remember the exact words, events. After a while I wouldn't be able to hear her and I would think my words were being absorbed by clothes, blocked by hangers, and I would crawl across the blackness and touch her chest to be sure she was still breathing, still there.

A CHILDHOOD MEMORY

Momma said that Grandma likes me more than you, likes me more than her and
Daddy. She said Grandma called today and told her so. She said Grandma said
when she dies she's going to leave me everything, her house in Meridian, her jewelry, all her money. I don't want the money. I told Momma I didn't want the
money, but she said I had been telling Grandma secrets and she wanted to know
my secrets, too. I didn't tell Grandma anything, but Momma said I did and if I told
her she would give me a special treat, make me some cookies and I wouldn't have
to eat any vegetables with dinner. But I didn't have any secrets to tell and I only
tell my secrets to you. And you better not tell or else I'm going to turn into a monster, too.

Then Momma said I could stay home because my jaw was swelling fast. She
made me some juice and said I could sit in the kitchen and watch her make cookies all day while I kept an ice pack on my jaw. She said I was good at keeping
secrets. And I am. Do you want to know a secret? I know a secret about Perry. Do
you want to know? Well, maybe I shouldn't tell you because you'll want to see it,
too.

Donna? Donna? Are you listening?

Well, Perry's got a magic flower at the end of his pee pee. He showed it to me.
Momma let me go outside after the cookies and she told me to tell everyone I had
a toothache and the swelling was going to go down after the new tooth comes in.
Perry was home, too. He didn't go to school either and he told me his flower was
soft and it could disappear. He showed it to me. It wasn't like mine. And when I
touched it, the petals started disappearing and then his was just like mine. And he
smelled mine and said his smelled better than mine. And I smelled his. I wish I
smelled like him.

No one's clapping. The stage lights are up and no one's clapping. There wasn't
any music either. There should have been music before the lights. Dueling guitars,
drums beating, never settling in one time signature. Or, a single male voice, moaning and droning. No words. Lonely music, blue music in the blackness, before the
lights. The music should have taken the audience back to no specific time, even
though a piano would have been playing in a strutting style, joined by brushed
cymbals rushing out to tickle ears. A sax should have mirrored the moans, rising
and rising, blowing the hair inside of ears, then suddenly breaking from the voice
to a deafening low note, a tone so low no one would ever imagine a tenor sax
reaching so low. Then the lights should have slowly risen.

The lights are hurting my eyes. They're too bright. Squinting doesn't help.
Putting my hands up doesn't help. I can see the red of blood in the tips of my fingers, along the edges, outlining my hands as if they were on fire. I'm sweating.
Mel-ting, mel-ting. How long have I been up here? How long did I say this show
was going to last? Two weeks. And I will measure time by the dripping of sweat,
down my face, down my cheeks, neck. I feel like an iron skillet, heating up, ready

for frying when the sweat crackles in the grease. I shouldn't have worn black. And my make-up job is melting. Foundation? Rouge? Am I a clown or a sickly drag queen? Diana Ross or Dolly Parton? I should have practiced lip-synching. There's no music anyway. I could be Shirley Bassie in a slinky sequined dress, low-cut in the front, and deep cut in the back, all the way down to the crack, doing my jazzy rendition of "Cry Me A River" or "Blue Velvet" while cradling up to the microphone, using it as my male member. Up, down. Caressing it lovingly. Exaggerating my pronunciations, curling my ruby lips, extending my arms out at the end of each refrain.

What am I doing? What if my father's in the audience? Daddy could be out there with Momma. She probably told him there was a bar in the lobby to get him here, and he's probably well on his way—if he wasn't before he got here. All the way from the Midwest; they left their middle-class home, in their middle-class suburb in Ohio, just to annoy me when I don't need it. And Momma, she's probably wearing those silver, handcrafted earrings I got her for her birthday in a little shop on Fifth Avenue, and that French perfume I bought her for this year's Mother's Day, at Barney's, and one of her fancy dresses she claims she never gets to wear anywhere.

THE MYTH

My mother is a superwoman. Black. Light-skinned with freckles and natural, dark auburn, relaxed hair. All of my family on my mother's side show their Southern ancestry. But that's just an illusion. Momma's black. She makes the best fried chicken, greens and cornbread north of the Ohio River. Her nose is thick. Her lips are full. And she's got a heavy, heavy hand. When she turned on the lights in my room in the morning, I didn't wait for her to tell me to get up. And stop talking to yourself, boy. She would fix breakfast before leaving for work. Pancakes popping in bacon grease. Oatmeal and cinnamon toast. Or grits and eggs. Then she'd drop me off at Aunt Cora's house so I could leave for school from there. And don't bring that doll, boy; I don't know what's gotten into your grandma, sending you a doll. Every morning, six o'clock in the morning. Dad would just be getting in from the night shift and Momma worked the day. In a factory, sewing Cadillac seat covers at Fisher Body. On an assembly line. Doing piece work, avoiding five-inch needles on industrial-size power sewing machines. She would pick me up from Aunt Cora's at five, do the little shopping she had to do. Don't you show off in this store, boy; And I won't forget it when we get home, Donald Jefferson McIntire. We would eat dinner then go to choir practice. She was in the Senior Choir and I was in the Youth and Young Adult Choir. St. Paul's A.M.E. Church. Choir practice on Tuesdays, bible study on Thursdays, Sunday school in the morning and church service all day on Sundays. Your imaginary friend's got to stay home with Daddy on Sundays; You hear me, boy?; And you better not act up. Momma was the treasurer of the Finance Committee and she was the most successful fund-raiser in the church. Every year she led the Ebony Drive, selling subscriptions to everyone at Fisher Body. *Ebony, Jet,* and *Ebony Junior.* Even to the whites. Momma made all of our church clothes when I was young. We were the sharpest family in the whole congregation. Double-breasted, double-knit suits for me and midi- or maxi-dresses for her. The Ebony Showcase Family. Except Daddy stayed at home. Donald's always banging that hard head of his on something; Look at that boy!; There is not a day in the week he doesn't get another hicky on that hard head of his. We always had a nice car to ride to church in, seeing that Momma worked for GM and got an employee discount. Cutlass Supreme. Buick Regal. Ninety-Eight Regency Brougham. We lived in the suburbs and drove in our new cars to church in the city. We lived on a tree-lined street with more and more black neighbors every year. I don't know how Mary's affording to move way out there to Chagrin Falls; Maybe she'll start looking rich, too; She told me you been telling everyone you have a baby sister, boy; Don't be embarrassing me like that in front of white people. Momma always made sure our house looked the best on the street. Inside and out. We plastered and painted walls. We wallpapered. Laid down wall-to-wall carpeting, retiled the bathroom, put up new kitchen cabinet fronts, stripped wallpaper, sanded walls, repainted walls, pulled up carpeting, sanded, stained and polyurethaned our oak floors. Momma subscribed to the Time/Life Do-It-Yourself Home Improvement Series. She knew how to use all of Dad's power tools better than he did. If she couldn't get Daddy to do the outside ladder work, she contracted it out. Aluminum siding with fake aluminum shutters on the upstairs front windows. On Saturdays we worked in the yard. I would cut the grass and Momma would work in the garden. Roses in the front of the house and a vegetable garden in the back. She planted tulip bulbs for the spring and petunias and gladiolas in the summer. Momma's favorite were her potted geraniums on the porch which bloomed from June to October. You better get those leaves up and get in here and practice your piano; I ain't paying all that money for lessons and that big old piano to take up all the space in my living room for you not to play on it; If you don't want to play it I can just give it to Aunt Cora for Louise; You can't be going down the street if we're going to sing our duet on Sunday; We've got to practice and I'm tired; That's what I got you here for—take out the garbage and let me get a little rest without complaining; I declare, you are one hardheaded boy; Donald, stop all that racket in there; I don't care if you are talking in your sleep; Donna's not real, she's imaginary; No you can't go to the movies and I don't want that fast girl calling here at all hours, raising my phone bill; I can't get you to do as I say anymore; You will not be driving my car; You will not be driving my car to the prom; If you want to waste all that money you better spend it with your old imaginary friend; And when you get your pictures taken, get the five poses, everyone's going to want one of your senior pictures; I don't know why on earth you would want to go to college in New York City, the filthiest of all places; Why you want to study art history?; Why can't you become an architect or an engineer?; When you come home this summer I have an internship lined up for you at my job; When you coming for a visit, boy?; I want you to give a talk to the children at church on Thanksgiving; You always come home when it's cold and snowing; I'll send you a ticket for Easter; The upstairs will need some paint by then, and I can't do it myself anymore.

Momma? Are you out there? Dad? If you are, forget the drag queen stuff. Say? What's a drag queen? Oh, that's a guy who thinks he's royalty. You know, like Ivana Trump. See, it doesn't have to be real royalty, it could be a disco queen, like Thelma Houston or Sylvester, Barbra Streisand, of course, or Vicky Sue Robinson. You know what I mean? Diana Ross-like. I know how much you hate fake Diana, but she's like royalty. It's sorta like Flip Wilson doing Geraldine. Remember that show? They call it transvestitism. Some of them are good. You should see the outfits. These boys can sew. I've never even worn a dress, Momma. Although I did use to play with Barbie dolls and dress them up. But all kids do that kind of stuff. I'm not into it now. I like to watch, go to shows and see the outfits, see the boys.

I told you I was gay. Remember and you got all upset because the news was scaring everybody about the gay plague in New York and San Francisco and I told you it was all over and anybody could get it. Remember? 'Cause we still don't talk about it. I had just broken up with my first longtime boyfriend, six months, and I just wanted you to know I was upset. And you sent me that letter with the scary article out of the *Plain Dealer* about AIDS and how it was this homosexual disease. Or druggies. Or people from Haiti. I wanted to call you and assure you that I wasn't sick or anything—I'm still not sick; I just had unsafe sex once, Ma, once. I wanted you to come around. And you did call and you told me you wished I hadn't told you and that I should never tell Dad.

Oh Daddy. Oh Father.

Then when I came home for Christmas, we didn't talk about it. And then Dad drove me back to the airport and you came too, and this guy cut Dad off and Dad called him a faggot. Fucking faggot's probably what he said. But he said it with such hate, like a bad taste in his mouth. Think about that one, Momma.

Momma are you out there? I can't see a fucking thing.

A JOURNEY

We're on our way to Mississippi. Momma and Dad are in the front and Donna and I are in the back. There's lots of room in Dad's new car, but he won't let me play much in the back seat. He won't let me use trucks or cars on his leather seats, so Donna and I sit on the floor most of the time. There's that much room in Dad's new car. He only told me once not to play on the seats. He didn't have to say it again. Momma kept looking back on me anyway, with her warning eyes. We liked sitting on the floor. You could hear the wheels and the road go by underneath. And there was a hump in the middle of the floor, a side for me, a side for Donna. I could feel Momma patting her foot as she listened to the eight-track tapes she had brought with us. She talked a lot, too. She pointed out road signs to Dad and read some to me. Sometimes she would test me on billboards and I would crane my neck up to the window and read the signs before we went by. It didn't count if I said it after we passed. She liked that game and she kept telling Dad that I was going to be a genius. Gets The Dirt Out Fast. Have a Kool One. Rest Stop 4½ Miles. Sometimes Donna and I would just sit in our seats and look out the window at the old barns, empty, doors closed, not like the red ones that I liked to color, rusty barns with big silver silos on the side, domed on top. Ditches by the side of the road. Checkered green hills with perfectly straight rows of bushes and trees. Feather-topped fields of corn. Purple and yellow flowers. Sometimes cows and horses.

Then Momma kept saying that we were almost there and we stopped one last time. She said I better go to the bathroom now, 'cause we ain't going to stop anymore. We were almost there. We had started out when it was dark, early in the morning. Donna and I had bathed and gotten dressed before we went to bed. We slept in our clothes and dreamed ourselves into the car when Momma turned on our bedroom light. Now it was almost dark again and Momma kept saying we were almost there. And I thought I could hold it in, but I think she was lying. I didn't say anything at first and Donna and I played cards to pass the time. I couldn't wait to get to Grandma's house.

I don't know how it happened. Momma started yelling at me and she told me I was going to have to explain everything to Grandma when we got there, that I was a stinky. She called me stinky at first and then she called me other names. And then she took her clog off and threw it in the back seat at me.

It didn't hurt, Donna. Don't get mad. Donna, don't cry. See, I'm not crying. Don't let Dad see me crying, he won't like me or Momma anymore.

Momma told me not to get blood on the leather, and, think about how was I going to tell Grandma about my black eye. Dad didn't stop until we got there.

I'm on a roll now. A little soft shoe, and they'll be mine.
They like it. They're laughing. They're clapping.
Take a bow.
I can't believe it; they really like the soft shoe. Listen to them laugh.
Did I hear Daddy's laugh? I think I hear Daddy's laugh: it's just like mine, similar to the sound a car makes when it's already on and you start it again and you feel embarrassed, the way I feel now.

I don't like being noticed, the center of attention. I love being close enough to a person to see my reflection in their eyes. They talk, I listen, nod at the right moments, respond at the right times, turn the conversation till it's just about to reach a resolution, then change the subject. My reflection in their eyes tells me that I'm a good listener. And they thank me.

Why the music now? I've got to talk to someone about this show. Long, vibratoless, violin notes rising in a twelve-tone scale. I hate this music.

The lights are softer now, reddish. A trap in the floor is opening. A small tree is rising up out of the stage: a birch sapling, not potted, but standing in a mound of dirt, which is sliding from around the roots. I've got to pack the dirt down, keep it alive. Cool and moist. It's like making mud pies after it rains and the dirt smells so good.

Something struck me. Fucking tree. I've got a cut and I feel like crying. Hold it in. I can't let them see me crying. I knocked the tree over, crawled up to the exposed roots, rubbed my head against the tangled knots. Hide. And cry, just a little.

A ROMANCE

It wasn't our first date. We had been seeing each other for more than a month, but each time we ended the night together something strange occurred. We would go to his apartment and he would have to cover my mouth to keep me quiet, stop me from giggling. He didn't want his upstairs neighbors to hear. Instead he preferred to keep everything visual, with the lights on and eyes open. He was an artist, making a living assisting photographers when he thought their work was important enough for him to lower himself to setting up lights, painting backdrops, making sure the music playing was to the model and photographer's liking. Instead of moaning I would listen to the sounds from outside. I became certain that the wind knew exactly when to rise, when to calm down, when to shake branches violently from side to side. He was always the wind.

I love the way you laugh, he said.

You do?

Yeah. Why do you always cover your mouth when you laugh? It's so funny, like you don't want it to come out.

I do?

You have such beautiful teeth, too, big and white. I guess your skin color makes them look whiter. Mine makes my teeth look gray.

Your teeth aren't gray. I wish mine were as straight as yours. I wanted to get braces when I was younger, but my mother told me I shouldn't, they're part of my personality. See? This one canine tooth sticks out in front of the other ones.

I never noticed that. It's cute, too.

Everything was all right for a while, I guess. William didn't work much and he spent most of his time painting. A few collectors had been over and liked his work. They only bought drawings, though, and they suggested that William start preparing for a show of larger paintings, use large canvases that wouldn't confine his work within a frame. He started immediately, working on six-by-eight foot canvases that took up all the wall space in his apartment, working on three paintings at a time, blocking in armless figures topped with tiny heads in confining cubical spaces. I didn't like the images, they scared me. The cubicles were made of jagged wooden planks, distorted in perspective, and unable to accommodate the figures.

So what do you think? he asked me.

Give me a chance to change my clothes and get comfortable first. I love the smell. Turpentine and linseed oil.

You don't like them. I can tell . . . Before I start putting on the flowers I need to know, because I won't be able to go back. You see, all of this hyper-anatomy will be in opposition to stencils of flowers in bright colors. So what do you think?

Flowers sound nice.

Yeah, but what do you think of the base? Is it strong enough to still be seen behind the flowers or do you think it'll be too loud and confusing?

Well . . . Ahh . . .

I know you don't like them. Why?

They sort of remind me of . . . They scare me. Why don't they have arms? It seems like you're making fun of that guy who paints with his toes. You know that guy, he doesn't have any arms and he paints with his toes on the sidewalk in front of museums. You shouldn't make fun of him. He's a nice guy.

That's not where this comes from. I like the silhouette and the arms would get confused with the lines of the flowers.

But they're scary. Like all these big dicks with no brains.

What are you talking about?

They look like me.

I thought you would like it. It's the one I know the best. Better than my own.

You made them look too . . .

So?

So they're big dicks with small brains. That's what you think of me.

He tried comforting me and I soon gave in to his kisses but there was something in what I was saying. I knew. Something he was unconscious of and I knew he was holding it against me. He was always talking about his wealthy family in Wisconsin and how unaware they were of how much power they had. His father was the head of a division of Derek Pharmaceuticals and he had a company jet at his disposal whenever he wanted it. They lived on the largest estate in his town and the whole town was built around it. His father was very conservative and thought that blacks were all right as long as they lived together and never gained power in the city of Chicago. He flipped his lid when a black mayor was elected and wanted to move his company offices to Wisconsin.

William told me all of this and I forgave him.

THE TRUTH

Truth. The truth is I'm blue and orange and purple. I'm the night within the night. The blackness that hides everything. The truth is I'm all colors and I have two mouths and my dick is always hard. I limp because of the weight. I don't understand words and I put them together for others to decipher. When I try to explain them sometimes I have patience, but most of the time they don't get it. I hate that and I hate myself because I'm inadequate. I'm invisible, in my room listening to Momma and Dad drink. Everywhere. I close my eyes often, but I still see everything. In my room listening to Momma and Dad argue. My eyes avoid all ugliness, but then I look in the mirror and I see myself.

I can turn from a solid to gel and back again. At the will of others. Get out of here, back in your room, back in bed, stop crying, what if the neighbors hear.

Tears don't scare me. Why should I make them stop? Blood doesn't scare me. Only my own. William doesn't scare me, only his come. I liked his taste too much. I liked it too hard, too often. And now he's dead.

William grew up with wealth and he expected his life to continue that way. He shopped at Balducci's once a week and restored antique chairs when he wasn't working or painting. Whenever we went out together, he always pointed out the gentlemen with the look of money, the ones wearing Armani slacks or perfectly *coiffed* hair, although he hid behind his paint-splattered jeans and worn hightop sneakers. A friend of mine told me he didn't like William and I should be careful and protect myself. He said he thought William eyed him too much and made subtle advances towards him. I didn't pay much attention to his warning. This was my first big relationship and I wanted it to work.

You look so sad sitting here by yourself, he said.

I'm fine.

I hate looking out windows. It makes you look so sad.

I love looking out windows, seeing the world go by without being seen.

He kissed me gently on the lips and walked out the door. I watched him striding down the street with his new suit on and then suddenly he turned around, looked up to the sky and grabbed his crotch with both hands. A big smile came across his face and I could hear him laughing in my mind. He raised his hands up and wiggled his fingers like he was doing the hokey pokey, then he turned himself around and walked away.

All the lights were off in his apartment, but the street lights made it seem as if it were day inside. I walked around the apartment looking at William's paintings. They really weren't bad, good in fact, technique-wise: good colors, nice compositions, and so on. They reminded me of stills from a movie, a German expressionist film or a Godard movie. Everything looked so common, natural, but skewed just enough to make me dizzy. It was in the details of the distorted perspective of the settings, the use of orchid for the back painting and orange or red for the flower stencils that made the images jump out at me and imprison me, at the same time.

One of the paintings didn't have the stencil over it yet and I could see that he had even added the dark birthmark on my hip to the figure, making it look more like a petunia or a tulip than it really does. He made my erect penis curve more to the right than it really does, made my butt perfectly round. But what did the cut off arms mean? Don't get a hold on me? You'll strangle me so I'll cut off your arms? You are not whole or real and I can dismantle you, accentuate your positives and shrink your weaknesses till they are unrecognizable?

I had a hard time falling asleep by myself. Someone in the neighborhood was having a party or very loud get-together. Voices were raised and I kept recognizing the songs, singing along and thinking about what a good time they must be having.

William got in late and he kept bumping into things as he was taking off his clothes. I turned over on my back to look at the strip show. He was beautiful, an ex-swimmer and cross-country runner. He still ran five miles a day. His legs were thin but hard, his waist small and expanded into a perfect triangle to his broad shoulders. His stomach was losing its definition but it made him look more human. He liked to keep his hair long and combed back so it fell into natural waves down the sides without a part. His eyes were my favorite, transparent brown eyes with flecks of green and orange. They were a bit lopsided, too, just enough so that you noticed them, looked into them and melted. He sank into the bed slowly, and kissed me before saying a word.

How are you?

Fine. I can't sleep.

No wonder, it's so noisy in this neighborhood. Why can't those porch monkeys keep it down? Hanging out all day and all night.

What did you say?

What?

Porch monkeys?

I don't know. Just . . .

You don't know? Porch Monkey. William, how could you say that? I've never heard of it, but you're speaking with someone who could be described as a porch monkey if I was sitting on a porch.

I don't mean you, Honey. Not you.

Get off me. William, this is really sick. I never thought you would say something like that. Where did you get this?

I don't know. I didn't mean anything.

Stop that.

Don't do this. I'm sorry.

If you don't want to see house monkeys, . . . porch monkeys, maybe you shouldn't live in this neighborhood, or sleep with one.

You're not like them.

Why not?

You're not . . . Oh, I don't know. I told you my father is a racist capitalist pig who refused to sit next to a black person on an airplane once. I'm sorry. That was dumb. But if my dad did say things like that, I wouldn't know it existed until it comes out of me. Like just then. I'm sorry. I didn't want to hurt you.

Then who did you want to hurt?

No one, nobody. I just want some peace, it's late.

Then why give a name to a group of people sitting on their porch, in front of their house, in their neighborhood?

You're right. I'm sorry, he said.

And I tried to forget him.

As I uncurled myself from the tree, I noticed that I was naked, my clothes had disappeared. This is no illusion. I'm not wearing a flesh-toned body suit. I'm nude.

My dick, a small bulb sticking out of my pubic hairs. I'm searching my body looking for a sign. The skin on my arms is uneven in color, spotted. Chicken skin. I have a pimple, red and itchy. It's bleeding. My feet are tired and there are strange freckles on my ankle. Are they freckles? Are they purple? Do they hurt? Do I have diarrhea? I'm tired and I want this show to be over. Am I always tired?

I want to scream. Scream. But there's no sound. My mouth opens and I feel the sound trying to escape but it won't; it's trapped somewhere like constipated shit: you grunt and try to force it out, but there's nothing. Just my dick getting heavy and hard again. Why now? This is embarrassing. I can't hide it.

There's a commotion in the audience, muted voices, squabble, like two trumpets competing for the final solo. Two trumpets. One, my father stuttering the same phrase over and over again: Fucking faggot. Fucking faggot. Fucking faggot. The other, my mother shushing, her teeth together, her fingers to her lips, puckered. Shushing as she stands to Dad's command, his one hand on her elbow, the other holding an empty glass. She's fumbling for her coat and purse, trying not to let her eyes leave the stage. I can feel her eyes on me. Smack some sense into me. Knock the color off my skin. One more time. Don't see me, Dad, one more time, the bruises, the black eyes, the nose bleeds. Fucking faggot is all that he sees on this stage and he isn't turning around as he pushes Momma out the door.

I can see them clearly in the light of the theater's outer lobby, framed in the doorway. I'm not a part of them anymore. I'm not myself anymore. For two weeks, the time it takes to get my test results back, I will be on this stage, I will be a number, #000, triple naught. Negative, I hope. Going over every aspect of my life, every sexual encounter, every slap across my face, every heartbreak, every freckle on my skin.

VOODOO

MARTIN WATCHED THE BEE hover between lemon blossoms. It swayed back and forth in the breeze until it finally lit on a waxy white flower and buried its hind legs deep in yellow pollen. That's when Martin snapped out, catching the insect by its papery wings.

"I got it!"

He held the bee up to his snaggletoothed grin and watched its backside swivel with the stinger pushed out. Martin stopped smiling when he saw how close the stinger was to getting him. He jumped back and held the bee as far away from his face as he could. The older boys, Albert and Lawrence, had made it seem like fun, but Martin was too afraid to throw the bee down and stomp it.

He danced from one bare foot to the other, crying.

When he danced completely around he saw his father squatting on the back stair.

"Help daddy!" Martin yelled.

"I tole you not t'be messin' wit' them bees," Mr. LeRoy's voice was clear across the back yard, but not loud.

"I sorry daddy! I won't do it no mo!"

"I know you won't."

Martin started toward his father; he moved slowly because he couldn't take his eyes off his hand. The bee struggled so hard that it pulled one wing completely off and stuck its stinger deep into Martin's thumb.

"Oooowww!" Martin jumped up and down holding his hand. Then he let himself fall to the lawn and buried his face in St. Augustine grass.

"Stop that hollerin!" Mr. LeRoy yelled. "Comon ovah here an les see what you fallin down bout." He was still squatting on the stairs.

Martin got up slowly and walked to his father. He cupped his thumb in both hands holding it like a hurt animal in a basket.

"Looks like she got you." His father pulled a cigarette from his shirt pocket and tore it open. He rubbed the tobacco into Martin's hurt finger. "This suck the poison out."

"Oww!" Martin cried, trying to pull his hand away, but his father held on.

"You shouldda thought bout that fo' you went messin round them bees. Don you know some people is allergic to bee stings and dies?"

Martin stopped crying and stared at his fingers. Mr. LeRoy caressed the boy's shoulder with a big black hand.

"I don wanna die, daddy."

"Nobody want that Marty . . . Les they crazy that is."

"But I'm scared . . ."

"Jes you leave them bees alone an you don need t'be scare't."

Martin started panting and put his good hand against Mr. LeRoy's chest. "But wha bout this time?"

"Wellllll, I guess if you ain't fell down in a coma yet then you gonna live this time. Anyway it's the next time you get stung that you find out if you allergic."

"Whas a coma daddy?" Martin kicked the loose paint on the stair.

"It's like when you go to sleep but can't no one wake you up."

"Like when you be dead?"

"Close to it I guess."

Martin turned around, sat between his father's legs and looked out on their back yard.

The strong Los Angeles sun beat down on the thick green grass and the fruit trees. There was kumquat, avocado, pomegranate and lemon in Martin's back yard. In the far corner, next to the high pine fence, stood a dwarf banana tree that never bore fruit and a rubber tree that Martin hated because it reminded him of weeds.

Martin squeezed his finger to see how much it hurt and he listened to Mr. LeRoy light a cigarette. There was the loud scratch of the match striking and the deep sucking sound of the first drag. Then a cloud of cool white smoke came down over Martin's head and curled around his bare feet.

"Whas it like bein' dead daddy?"

"I ain't never been dead."

"But whas it like?" Martin insisted.

"You gotta ask somebody who knows boy. All I know is how t'stay alive."

"Well, who can I ask if *you* don know?"

"Preacher say he know sumpin' bout it. But I ain't never met no preacher been dead, so I don know what he can say."

The sun was hot. Insects were flitting between the bushes and sparrows chased them. Martin started to feel drowsy and laid his head against his father's knee.

"But daddy I wanna know what it's like!"

"Don you be yellin out here boy."

"Bu' god . . . I wanna know . . ."

Martin felt the hand on his shoulder and heard his father take a deep drag on his cigarette. "I cain't tell you Marty cuz I don know. An it's bes when grownups don lie t'chirren. . . . When I'as boy down Louisiana they was always fillin kids with ghost stories. They talk bout voodoo an zombies, like on the TV on'y they believed that stuff. They say anything come into they heads . . ."

Martin leaned back as Mr. LeRoy wrapped his arm around his chest. "We had a woman stay with me an my little cousin when my daddy went up north loggin. She was called Luvia, an ignorant folks said that she was a witch."

"Was she?" Martin asked. His stomach began to rumble. He knew when his father was going to scare him but there was nothing he could do.

"On'y fo people who believe in that stuff. If you believe in it they could cas' a spell an you'd wither an die . . . I seen it happen."

"I don't believe in it. . . . do you daddy?"

For a long time Mr. LeRoy was quiet. Martin's stomach made whining noises. The heat grew in the damp yard and the boy's thumb ached. But in spite of his pains Martin started to doze.

He was almost asleep when his father began to speak. "One time my lil cousin was sleep an Luvia took me in her lap, jus like I got you, an she said she was gonna tell me a story. Then she said that if I learned a lesson from her that I be lucky all the time. She tole me that an then she tole me how t'sell my soul to the devil. Can you beat that?"

Martin knew his father was trying to make a joke out of it, but he wasn't laughing in his voice.

"I gotta go bafroom, daddy."

"I still remember it," Mr. LeRoy's voice had a far away sound. "She said how you get a all black cat an strangulate it, that mean choke it dead," he touched Martin's neck lightly to show him what he meant. Martin stopped breathing. "Then you wait for the full moon an you throw the cat in water, fur an all, an then you boils it and boils it until all the meat come offa the bones. Then you stand in front of a mirror, wit a candle in fronta you, an you rub the thigh bone between yo teeth, so light that it tickles you, and then you say, 'Come foward Satan, come forward to meet . . .' then you say you name. After a long time the bone in the mirror cover yo whole face and Satan becomes you in the mirror . . . That's when you make yo deal with the devil. . . .''

Suddenly he grabbed Martin by both shoulders, turned him around and shouted, "Boo!" Then he laughed loud with his big yellow teeth and his deep red tongue showing. He laughed so hard that he began to wheeze and tears squeezed out of his eyes.

Martin's heart beat fast and his eyes were wide open.

Mr. LeRoy fell over on his side and laughed in great gulps of air. He was holding his side and he brought Martin falling with him because the boy was caught between his legs.

Finally the man began to get control of himself. He let out a high pitched sigh and said, "I ain't thought bout that in thirty years. . . . Stupid woman."

Martin pulled loose from the tangle of his father's legs and made it up the stairs to the door. His stomach was hurting and he had to go to the toilet. He was just about to run into the house when his father called him again.

"Martin," he said. Martin looked down at his father lying on the stair. He was lying on his side with his legs tucked up like a baby. There were still tears in his eyes when he said, "I love you, boy."

ADALBERTO ORTIZ

BEWITCHED

WHEN MY COUSIN Numancia turned fourteen, the Tunda carried her off. Just like that. The Tunda is an infamous beast. . . . The Tunda is a spook. . . . The Tunda is the devil himself. . . . The Tunda is the restless soul of a widow who killed her son. . . . The Tunda is filthy. . . . No one knows for sure. . . . No one knows. . . .

Be it as it may, the Tunda likes to carry children off deep into the jungle by changing itself into the pleasing figures of those they love. It attracts them deftly with various guiles and it bewitches them. That's the word. There's no other.

Numancia glowed with a beautiful and unusual caramel color and was quite grown, but since she wasn't very bright and lacked the gift of observation, she let the Tunda ensnare her. In the twilight she didn't catch sight of its peg leg, neither did she realize that that figure couldn't be her mother who also mysteriously disappeared years back. . . . She saw nothing. Numancia went out to look for some turkeys that had not come back to the coop for the night, nor had they perched themselves on the hog plum tree out behind the house. Everyone knows that turkeys are stragglers and feather-brained and one always has to round them up to guide them home.

Yes, Numancia was a beautiful girl, but sometimes it seemed to me she was very much like a peahen.

I was three years younger than she and we always played together. There came a time when she was no longer interested in our games and that made me feel sad, though not as sad as that afternoon when the Tunda ran off with her.

We all went looking for her, bringing five hound dogs to trail her. Her father carried a carbine and a machete. Our only farmhand, one-eyed Pedro, carried an

Translated by Teresa Labarta de Chaves.

452

ax. My cousin Rodrigo brought an old double barrel shot gun and I took along a club, a slingshot, and a multipurpose penknife. Stunned by the blow, we all took an extra change of clothes and something to eat. We had no idea how long we would have to stay in the hills, chasing the damned Tunda who, according to those who know the secrets of the jungle, makes its den among thorny bushes and tall bamboos.

We first set out for the houses of the neighbors in other farms along the river: "Have you seen Numancia around here?"

In the dim light of our oil lamps the black men, biting on their big pipes and perplexed by the news of the Tunda's latest exploit, said no by shaking their heads. The women, alarmed, counseled prudence and good behavior to their children, setting Numancia up as an example.

Around midnight, when we were very tired, we finally asked the river itself, which answered, murmuring and shimmering, that the Tunda shies away from the deep waters, that it prefers the creeks where it can catch shrimp and tiny fish with its hairy paws and that it forces its victims to eat them raw until the children become pale and very weak. The river told us, too, that the Tunda has the filthy habit of farting in the children's faces to daze them and make them lose their memories.

When the river spoke to us this way I got very scared and we opted for going home.

The next day we started our search again. This time we set out with more people and better equipped with ropes, hammocks, and trail clothes, in addition to what we had the night before.

Ahead of us the dogs yelped, filling us with vague hopes.

We asked the vigilant owls: "Have you seen Numancia and the Tunda around here?"

The owls sleepily said no, staring at us with their round chestnut eyes.

We asked the chattering parrots and they just repeated our question like an echo: "Have you seen Numancia and the Tunda around here?"

When we inquired from the howler monkeys, who were perched high on the guamo trees, they laughed at us and scratched their behinds.

All the animals answered in unison complicitly: "No, no, no."

But I wasn't giving up, so I went on my own to ask the plants: the stinging gualanga nettle, the black hearted guaiacum tree, the sheltering rampira palm, the miraculous ribwort, the docile hollyhock, the balsa, the ringed guarumos, the blooming acacias, and they all answered affirmatively that they had heard Numancia go by in the company of the horrendous Tunda. . . .

When I told the others of the results of my inquiries, they laughed at me and went another way.

"Crazy kid," they said to me, "plants don't talk."

That night we slept perched on and tied to the trees, because we were afraid of the beasts that don't answer questions unless one of us offers himself as a sacrifice to their gods. Our love for Numancia didn't go that far.

At day break, we started again on our search and, unknowingly, the men took the way that my friends the plants had pointed out to me. It made me very happy and proud.

When my uncle inquired of the sayama serpent, she whistled that yes, she had seen Numancia. She was swimming naked in a pond two miles away, like the goddess Oshun—who is crazy about water and love—but she was always guarded by the mysterious Tunda.

With our machetes we cut a narrow path through the brush and the vines and in the late afternoon, exhausted and filthy, we reached the shores of an unknown, shallow lake of crystal clear waters. After diving in the waters and searching all around the shores, we came up with a small piece of Numancia's lilac dress, but that was all. Her father burst into tears like a child and it broke our hearts.

There was still some hope . . . For many days we kept searching the underbrush, caves, and hiding places, asking the plants and creatures of the jungle, not just around here, but all over. . . . But the Tunda is sharper than the men and the dogs. Hardly do they ever catch it. Once we chanced to arrive at a distant village. The villagers were frightened by our looks, but finally decided to help. Just in case, foolishly we asked them: "Have you seen Numancia and the Tunda around here?" Then, they too told us stories about children captured by the wicked Tunda.

Finally convinced of how vain our search was, we returned to the farm by another route, minus two dogs and with bruised bodies and heavy hearts. Poor one-eyed Peter left his one good eye in the brush forever.

Time cured our bruises, but the memory of my nubile cousin Numancia never left our home, nor our hearts.

After several months, on a clear night, Numancia appeared coming down the river in a canoe. She came up slowly. Nobody heard her but me. I recognized her steps, although they seemed heavier than before. She stole into my mother's room which was also my room. My mother was startled to see her and she started to call my uncle but something she noticed made her change her mind.

I couldn't believe my eyes. I didn't know what to say. I just looked at Numancia. She was barefoot and shabbily dressed. Her long caramel hair hung lank and damp. She had grown taller and her face shone with new beauty that I had never known before. Although the expression on her face was still naive and silly, there was also a trace of suffering. She was not the same. And what I noticed the most was the swelling of her belly, like those of kids with worms. "Surely," I thought to myself, "that was from eating all those raw shrimp and fish."

"My dear girl," my mother cried as she hugged Numancia to her breaking heart.

It must have been our whispering that woke my uncle, asleep in the next room, because suddenly we saw him standing in the doorway dimly lit by the kerosene lamp in our room. He seemed a ghost. He stared at us in amazement and looked so harshly at his prodigal daughter that chills went down our spines.

"Where have you been?" he asked her drily. She looked down and gave no answer. No one seemed to be glad that she was back and this distressed me so much that I was indignant at the insensitivity of the grownups. Ignoring it, I joyously embraced her and asked: "Is it true that the Tunda took you?" She nodded her head. "Did it hurt you a lot?" She shook her head no.

Her father kept staring at her resentfully and contemptuously. It seemed as if he were on the verge of jumping and beating her to death. . . . Then we were all silent and the tension was building when suddenly my uncle shouted at her in a terrible voice.

"Just like your mother! Go back to your filthy Tunda!"

Leaving the house, Numancia went toward the river, which shimmered in the moonlight, and then she disappeared into the June night.

Blind Peter followed her with his dead oyster eyes. Then all I remember is the rhythmic sound of her paddling in the dark. . . .

STANLEY PÉAN

THE DEVIL'S MAW

In plain daylight, under the most radiant of suns, Devils' maws could open up anywhere and snatch me.

—Jean-Paul Sartre, *Words*

H E IS IN THE PROCESS of shaving when it happens and he is so surprised that he cuts himself. With a moan like that of a woman in labor, the swollen lips open up halfway between the mirror and his face, exhaling a putrid breath and spitting a sticky red stream toward him. Struggling against the terror that paralyzes him every time, in spite of himself, he shuts his eyes tightly, wrinkling his eyelids and making a concentrated effort to close up the abyss that is trying to suck him in. The devil's maw disappears without leaving the slightest trace. As usual.

With a sigh, he dabs at the cut and finishes shaving with the distracted thought that he should go by the home today after the session in court.

Translated by Carrol F. Coates.

Péan's title, "Le bouche d'ombre" is apparently suggested by the epigraph quoted from Jean-Paul Sartre's autobiographical essay, *Les Mots* (Words). Sartre got the term, and to all appearances, the idea of a virtually infernal phenomenon that can strike in broad daylight, from Victor Hugo's poem, "Ce que dit la Bouche d'ombre" (What the Shade's Mouth Said), from his volume, *Les Contemplations* (Contemplations). J.-B. Barrère suggested that Hugo may have been inspired by an actual gorge on the coast of Jersey, in the Channel where he was living in exile and where he underwent some mystical experiences. True or not, the name of that gorge, "The Devil's Maw," fits the spirit of Péan's story admirably (translator's note).

456

The courthouse is about a kilometer from his place. As always, he eats lunch in the little Haitian restaurant, *Manje Lakay*,[1] before taking the 12:30 bus. Setting in front of him a plate of ground corn and beans topped by a nauseating quantity of sauce, the friendly waitress, Marie-Marthe, asks for news of his mother. He answers automatically, almost without thinking. Somewhere, someone says, "Son sèl manman yon nèg genyen."[2] But he is . . . already . . . somewhere else.

A little house with its back to the mountain, overlooking a large coffee plantation, somewhere south of Jérémie.

The light shimmers, everything vacillates: He is afraid that the thing may happen again here, among all of these people who are ready to judge him. To condemn him.

Absentmindedly and with beating temples, he manages to get up and run to the toilet. There, at least, he can confront his bête noire face to face, alone.

Curiously, it does not show up.

       🙐   🙐   🙐

". . . the meeting of the organizing committee for the benefit concert of the Haitian Aid Cooperative. Remember, I mentioned it to you the other evening . . . ?"

"Yes, Nadine. But I promised Mom I'd stop and see her."

"Excuses! Excuses! You always find a way to escape every time that somebody tries to get a commitment from you to help your own people. Why can't you be serious?"

"That's not fair! You're exaggerating, love. I attended your last meeting, right?"

"Yes, but how long?"

Pause.

"Alright, listen. I don't promise, but I'll try to stop by your meeting when I return from the home."

There is an acid silence at the other end of the line.

"You won't be able to spend your entire life avoiding responsibility. One day or the other . . ."

"Oh, come on, Nadine!"

Sighs.

"I'm sorry. For you, I mean. Anyway, give your mother a kiss for me."

"I will," but his answer comes after she hung up.

He remains motionless an instant, staring at the buzzing receiver in his hand and trying to discover the source of the groan swelling in his head.

---

1. Home cooking.

2. "A man has only one mother." Especially important in this Creole proverb is the importance of the mother and the non-specificity of the father (translator's note).

Sitting in her corner, the old woman remains gray and silent. Like a charcoal sketch blurred by oblivion. At such a distance from one another, the two of them commune by means of a drab love, no longer finding anything to say. He had placed her in the home because they were too crowded in the two-room apartment that he was living in at the time. Until he located something better, he had said. And yet, nearly eight years later with business growing, he still has not found room for her; not even in the spacious studio apartment that he finally rented. Tired of excuses, the old woman has grown used to biding her time patiently in the home, from which all sunlight is banished.

Once in a while, they exchange a few words or meaningless sentences in order to cover their malaise. Stamp out time. For example, he asks her what she thought about some exhibit that she had visited one day. She asks him how his relationship with Nadine is going. Inevitably, they fall back into the bottomless silence, for which they have acquired a taste.

Today, they are speaking about his father for the first time in years. With a certain equanimity. All he had ever known about the dead man were some old black and white photographs with tattered corners and one or two anecdotes. As a young woman, she had arrived with her widowhood and her only son in this frozen country, hoping for a new beginning. Today, she murmurs her desire to return to her native soil to die and be buried beside her beloved. He is indignant at such lugubrious thoughts. No will to live. To tell the truth, he knows very well that she is right, that it would be better for both of them if she died soon.

Later, stretched out on his large, desolate bed, he reaches the conclusion that it would be best if he returned to her bosom, and that she would die then.

He has to use all his powers of concentration to fend off the enormous mouth that this thought inevitably recalls.

Before the hearings start again, he tries to call Nadine to apologize for forgetting their date last night, but there is no answer. Perhaps she deliberately took the receiver off the hook. Nadine and he have never defined the exact nature of their relationship, but he never conceived the possibility that it could be love. For the first time since they have been going together, however, the question has been needling him a lot. Even back in the courtroom, he cannot get the idea out of his head.

This morning, he is defending a huge brute accused of having beaten his wife. With images of Nadine and his mother filling his head, he relentlessly interrogates the victim, when, suddenly, his colleague, the Crown prosecutor, raises an objection . . .

. . . that he does not even hear.

The familiar groaning swells like a balloon and fills the courtroom with an agonized suffering that he alone hears. The devil's maw, awakened, exhales a humid, hot puff that shakes him from head to toe.

He closes his eyes and tries to stop listening, but he knows that the evil comes from inside. In anticipation of the inevitable, he threads his way through the questions and expressions of concern and runs out of the courtroom, out of the Palace of Justice, out of his mind.

In fact, his running is futile since, even at top speed, death still beats him by a length.

There is a brief ceremony, which, in keeping with the character of the deceased, is discreet and unspectacular. Since she was timid, she made very few friends after she arrived in Canada. Consequently, few people have come to pay their respects. Among those present, there is a distant cousin, a half-brother, and a few of the people who lived with her at the home. In keeping with the rites and customs of such events, they mutter a few banalities and limply shake the murderer's hand.

He is fully aware that it is not an improbable heart attack that carried off his mother, as the director of the home alleges from fear of terrifying the other residents. It is not even the barbituates that his mother had managed to steal from the nurse. Although he would proclaim his innocence, the smell of blood on his hands would never permit him to believe these pretexts.

Fortunately, there were not too many complications with the management of the home and, in keeping with the wishes of the deceased, there was no viewing of the body. Of course, she had repeatedly expressed her desire to be buried in Haiti, as one of the older residents with whom she used to play chess reminded him, but he could never make up his mind to that. Was it egotism or the simple whim of a spoiled child? He did not dare answer the question. He would especially like to have Nadine with him so that he could discuss the whole affair with her and maybe even cry on her shoulder. Like his mother, she has always understood him better than he does himself. Isn't that the reason that he always hesitated to create a closer relationship with her? But for two days he has not been able to contact her, and the messages he left on her answering machine have gone unanswered.

For some time, maybe even hours, he has been picking at his plate indifferently . . . , in a desperate search for the tears that are pent up in some obscure part of himself and that refuse to flow.

When he comes in, Ferdinand, the manager of *Manje Lakay*, has heard the news, which has engulfed him with a flood of regrets and condolences stickier than the okra sauce on all his dishes. Marie-Marthe is more discreet and understanding. She simply expresses sympathy with her eyes.

He does not remember at what time a couple of police officers came in to speak with Ferdinand. Although the snatches of conversation that he overheard had to do with some break-in in the neighborhood, he could not get rid of the impression that one of the policemen kept looking at him with suspicion. Even now, long after they left, he still wonders whether their interrogation was not a pretext to come in and keep him under surveillance.

Lost in thought, he does not even notice that the restaurant is about to close until Marie-Marthe timidly comes over to tell him. With a strained smile that is more pitiful than he would like, he lets her take away the nearly untouched plate. He finally manages to get up and go to the cash register, where the manager is waiting with loathsome compassion.

With a hesitant pace, he goes toward the shelter at the nearest bus stop. He distractedly interrogates himself about his absurd reluctance to buy his own car, especially now that he could afford it, and even about his insistence on consuming a repulsive meal in that mediocre restaurant every day. "Son sèl manman yon nèg genyen," comes a mocking voice in the wind, but he sees nobody in the dark around him. Leaning on the glass wall of the shelter, he takes several deep breaths, trying to control the rhythm of his heartbeat, which has become erratic for no reason.

"You may wait a long time. The last bus passed quite a while ago."

He turns toward the young woman at the wheel of the Renault 5 that has stopped in front of him. There is something in her voice and in her smile that tames the beast thrashing wildly inside. He had almost decided to take a taxi or walk when Marie-Marthe offered to take him home. And, perhaps because the silence of the night has frightened him for the first time in his life, he accepts the *roulib*.[3] He gets in the little car.

One night, when he had been in bed with Nadine, he had made fun of his mother's campaign to find a wife for him before she died, as if she thought him incapable of existing without a feminine presence in his life.

"She was right, wasn't she?" Nadine had asked. Her smile strictly forbade any fairy tales and he had not dared answer. He had never been able to lie to Nadine or to his mother, only to himself.

This particular night, snuggled against that tender, warm body, he finally admitted that, since he does not belong to Nadine, he realized the total futility of the string of words and gestures that he had not had the decency to break off. It was a comedy of solitude and sadness to be joined. A ritual exchange of inanimate smiles, automatic kisses, lifeless caresses that made no sense here.

---

3. Lift.

He looks at the face of Marie-Marthe, who went to sleep a short time ago, and finds her pretty—not as stunning as Nadine, but outright beautiful, radiant with an inner beauty that goes beyond flesh and that he can only compare to that of his late mother. And he aches, for God's sake! He aches at his inability to feel guilty toward his mother and Nadine, both of whom he has betrayed in this cold bed.

Then he begins to laugh, quietly, the monotone, maniacally musical laughter of the psychopath about to strangle his victim.

"I hate it when somebody feels sorry for me," he mutters, as if talking to himself.

"Mmmmmmmmmmmmmmmmmm?"

"I hate it when somebody feels sorry for me," he repeats, abruptly waking her from the arms of Morpheus.

Speechless, Marie-Marthe stares at him from between sleepy eyelids. They can exchange nothing more, only silence.

At noon, he is still sleeping in the fetal position at the edge of the bed where Marie-Marthe's warmth had trapped him.

Gradually, he senses that she has left, feeling at the same time relief at not having to say goodbye this morning and shame at his boorish conduct. In a rested frame of mind, he suddenly recognizes that pity had nothing to do with his presence in her bed last night. He had never suspected that all of the waitress's little services and glances had hidden anything other than professional politeness.

On the telephone, he barely pays attention to the recriminations of his client, who has been trying fruitlessly to reach him since he left the courtroom in a whirlwind yesterday. Insults and threats assail his indifferent ear.

"Fout san-manman,"[4] yells the disincarnate voice at the other end of the line, unaware that he has hit right on target.

With the telephone still in his hand, he instinctively dials Nadine's number and lets it ring four times. At the instant when he is about to hang up, somebody answers. Nadine's apartment mate gives him the message she left for him three days ago, just before her hasty departure for Haiti. It sounds like a definitive goodbye. She goes into some conventional expressions of sympathy. He hangs up before she has finished. In confusion, he thinks about calling Marie-Marthe back to apologize, get rid of the misunderstanding, and, maybe (who knows?), redeem himself. But he does not have the energy to do it.

The sound of his steps on the floor of his oversized apartment echoes in the void of his chest. He goes to the bathroom, hoping that a little fresh water on his face will bring him out of the zombi's daze. He is surprised to see no trace of the smiling boy that he used to be in the mirror.

---

4. Motherless bastard.

"Son sèl manman yon nèg genyen," repeats the faceless voice that he has to recognize as his own.

"The day when you let yourself break down in front of me, I'll be convinced that you trust me and really love me," Nadine had declared one day. He felt that tears had always seemed to lack subtlety. What he would give to cry now, even one little tear!

"A man has only one mother."

The phrase keeps echoing in his head like a Vodun incantation chanted in unison by the voices of a hundred celebrants, and that is all it takes to recall the Devil's maw.

This time, the apparition causes neither surprise nor fear. He has understood. With the usual moan, the enormous swollen lips open halfway between the image that he has never accepted and himself, spraying him with thick blood and overwhelming him with the breath of eternity.

Resigning himself, he takes a step toward the yawning, shadowy maw of oblivion that is calling him.

JUBY'S MORNING

W HEN JUBY FEEL THE EYES, he think it that fine Puerto Rican mama checking him out, but when he look up, trying to be cute, it's old woman staring in his face. She turn away, like she wasn't looking at him no how, so Juby take a minute to watch her. She little, got that curve to the back that make old folks be shorter, but he can tell what she used to look like by her hands. They slender, fingers dancing, folding towels in halves, then thirds, a deft quartet of corners.

Now Juby scope her underthings. The drawers white cotton, ample in the bottom, built for comfort. Girdle must weigh a couple pounds. He imagine her at twenty-five, a heat red garter belt, black nothings, a room of green plants and hardwood floors, bed rich with sunlight and her body. In the corner a record player spin a muted trumpet, and her young man's love come sliding down.

Juby thinking maybe he let the trumpet be a saxophone, when he catch himself just before old woman look up and nail him for being underneath her clothes. He know just what she say, too. What wrong with him; he some kind of sick? Didn't he have no training?

The other two ladies talking Spanish, smoking filter cigarettes. The bony one got a earring in her nose. Her home girl wearing $100 sneakers, fine as she want to be, with a mouth Juby known the time he'd have got in line to talk to.

Juby look at the book in his lap. He read a little and feel it again; old woman sneaking looks his way. He check his watch. The Puerto Rican women leaving, pulling singing carts. They say so long to the attendant: a lanky boy got his hat on backwards, a gold tooth in his mouth. The boy go into the back room, and it's just old woman and Juby now, and he know why she looking. He tell himself she can look all she want; he don't want to be bothered. She got all that laundry *here* by herself, and he got to meet Mabel on 125th Street and Eighth Avenue at twelve o'clock, and he don't want to be bothered.

He read a paragraph. He read it again. Words make the same no sense they did the first time. It's like the steam from the dryers done seep into his head, and he shake his head to clear it. He glance at old woman. She not looking, just putting clothes away, hands careful like she packing eggs. Got a oatmeal colored coat on, button missing. Gray hair in braids, face the tone and texture of a walnut, single-minded as a clock. Juby think it cold outside, she ought to have a hat. She finished now, three big shopping bags, brown ones from Shoprite, the white from Bloomingdale's, and she take them one at a time to the door, coat round her ankles, new pair of desert boots deer-colored on her feet. She stand there, look Juby dead in his eye and settle in to wait. Just be there, like she first cousin to Job or something, like she the one schooled Job bout hanging on.

Juby look back. He grown. He don't look hard, though. He don't mess with old folks. And he ain't superstitious, neither. He was twenty-seven in August. Got a good job in the Post Office and a nice place on the Drive; he can watch the river wash New Jersey from his bedroom. He put three years in the Army, seen Paris in springtime, and R and R'd in Casablanca. He go to night school, and he ain't nobody's fool. But he don't mess with old folks.

He look at his book, then up again. Ain't no minute hand on the wall clock. Little hand point to seven. Outside the fogged window a woman's shape go by, tall, Juby think of Mabel. Old woman standing by the door, just keep looking. Juby thinking how a war going on here in this laundry. Ain't no guns or dead folks, so it won't make the evening news, but it's fighting just the same. And he live long enough to know who win it; already his resistance start to seep. Old woman ain't *hardly* going to move, and he got to pass her to get out the door. No way he can just walk by, pretend she don't exist; he was raised too good. Besides, helping be the proper thing to do, despite the bother. Mabel always say one thing wrong with the world is folks don't look out for each other.

Juby don't dispute that. He just wonder why he always asked to be the lookout. In Morocco, every time he go outside, seem like a hundred kids be gathering with they hands spread. In New York he be walking down the street, minding his business, maybe checking out some world class sister, when a homeless man run over ten folks in Cadillacs to get to him for a dime. At work, he the one called to take up collections for the sick, the dead, the soon-to-marry. Probably have to pass his own hat when him and Mabel tied the knot.

When he study on why folks all the time turn to him for help, Juby figure he give off a scent, or look a certain way. Then he go stand in the mirror, staring. His face the same face, eyes big like he is, balanced by his nose. His color please him: black, one shade short of blue, and he got good lips; Mabel always say so. But if something in his face call out to folks in need, "Over here, I'll help," Juby swear he never see it. And the only smell he catch is Zest soap, which he started using years ago when he found out Ivory made his skin dry.

Then he smiling at something he can tell to Mabel. What he think was his number ain't hit, but old woman had it, and it was up. This tickle Juby even though he don't play no numbers. Then he surrender, sue for peace. He ask old woman if he can help. She look down like she discovering three bags at her feet.

"You sho can, honey. But what about your clothes?"

"I got ten minutes left. Nobody won't bother them."

"I sho appreciate this. My neighbor help me over here, but he had to go to work."

"Well, I'm off today," Juby say.

Now that he helping, he feel good about himself. He put his book in his back pocket. He put on his black ski cap and ask where she live. She say around the corner on 138th Street.

Juby close to her now. He smell her, smell he know, but can't place. She say the Lord going to bless Juby. Juby don't put much stake in the Lord. He figure the Lord got his hands full, most of it with white folks' foolishness. But he don't tell her that.

"Yes, ma'am," he say, and they step out the toasty laundromat and meet a chilled Broadway.

She live above Juan's bodega. Juan in the doorway wearing a purple shirt, face the color of a hard banana. He look at Juby with his eyebrows up. Juby don't pay him no mind. He look at the building. He go past here all the time, it's up the hill from where he live, but he never see it. Fire escape zig-zag rusty across its face. Two milk containers sitting outside a fourth floor window.

Old woman say she got to catch her breath. Lean against the stoop, blowing white at the mouth. Juby think she need something on her head. He wait. On the sidewalk people pass not looking. A skinny woman with a big belly come out Juan's store, go up the block with a heavy, graceful swing. Juby like the way a pregnant woman look. He think about Mabel. In the spring they be married. He look at breath coming from his mouth, white, like a ghost, then it vanish. He look at the sky. Early on, the sun come out, but now the clouds won't let it. The day gray, late in the morning, but still it feel like night.

"Look like snow," Juby say, making conversation.

Old woman grunt. "Maybe I play snow. Lord know I could use a hit. What you like today?"

Juby say he don't play no numbers. A coal colored man with his head conked come out her building scratching at his self. Old woman watch him up the hill.

"You take dope?"

"I does not."

"Chase women though, don't you?"

Juby don't like that kind of talk. Chasing days behind him. He responsible now. "No need to chase. I gots a good woman."

Old woman look at his face, she look at his feet. "Really," she say, and look at his face again.

Juby don't back down. "Really."

"If she all that good, how come you washing your clothes?"

"We ain't married yet," Juby huff. "Be time enough for her to wash my clothes."

She look at Juby, hard, as if she thinking if *she* the mother of this fresh mouth child, she *been* gone up side his head. "Let me know if I'm wrong," she say, righteouslike, "but I don't believe I said what to get hot about. Leastways not as I recall."

Juby say excuse him. He getting chilly. He scuff his foot on the ground and cough. He look at the sky.

"You ready yet?" she ask.

"Yes, ma'am."

Juby hold the dark green door. Old woman go past into the hallway. Again he smell her. Now he know. Basic Training at Fort Dix, Mabel came to visit. She brought chicken and potato salad. They sat beneath the tree and leaves fell slow red past Juby's face and lit up his shoulder, and he held one to his nose. "Leaves smell like dust," he said, and Mabel said, "Well, I declare," and kissed him.

Old woman at the stairs now, in the shadow. "You go first, you younger'n I am. I'm on the third floor."

Juby go. Somebody frying meat. The walls crack green paint, show the white beneath. Ain't no light on the steps and the window boarded with some cardboard. He climb past the meat into a smell of damp. The warm feeling from the thought of Mabel up and leave. He feel cool about the neck, as if a breeze behind him. One minute he feeling good, helping someone who need it, then he spooked. He reach the third floor, look behind him. Old woman still on the stairway, face squinched from climbing.

"Here. Take the key. My door eleven."

Juby go back down and get the key and come back to the landing. He open the door. He see a bathroom where the hall end. A toilet with a box up over it, on the floor a face basin full of kitty litter. Old woman come past him, tell Juby where to put the clothes. The room small and neat and smell like lemons. A color television, white doily on top, a vase of yellow flowers, dying. Past that a purple sheet hide another room. On the wall in front of Juby, a picture: old man and woman, black, arms locked. They look past Juby. He don't turn, ain't nothing but a wall behind him, but he swear something back there looking back at them.

"Them's my ma and pa." Old woman sitting on the couch, knees wide, getting back her breath. "Where you from?"

Juby say right here, New York City. Bronx born, but Harlem raised.

"Reason I ask 'cause you sho favor my child. Why I was looking so hard. Be something if we was related, huh?"

"Yes, ma'am."

"This his children."

She reach in her pocket, hand Juby a Polaroid. They look like anybody's children to him. The boy lightskinned. He look at the girl again. She dark and very pretty.

"That's him over there."

A big photograph by itself on a table. Just a face. Juby feel cold, then he feel hot. Ain't *this* a trip? He want to sit down. It's like looking at his own self.

"Ya'll sho do favor, don't you? Even sound the same. You a bit fuller in the face, though. Buried him last month. In with them gangsters. I *told* him. . . ." Old woman's voice drift, stay out a while, ride the next wave back. "Put a bullet in him over neath the Triboro. You read about it in the Amsterdam? He was my onliest. Kids was crazy about him. Specially the gal."

Juby feel sorry for her. It's one reason he don't play no numbers. Cards or craps neither. Only use he got for a horse is to ride it, which he only do when he take Mabel to the Poconos. He look at picture of old woman's son. Damn! It's like looking at his own self.

"My hope is this," old woman say. "I know that my Redeemer liveth."

Uh oh, Juby think. He turn to where she looking. Picture of a white Jesus on the wall, fat heart running dry. Goo-gobs of blood, but the good Lord keep on living. Blood don't even stain his clothes. Just hang there at the bottom of his heart.

"Sit down," old woman say. "You hungry?"

Juby say, "No, Ma'am, I got to be going," and she say, "Sit for a while. Don't get much company."

Juby sit, fussing to his self. He understand where old woman coming from. He know she lonely. He hope he never be this way, his only child a month in the ground and nothing but a TV set to talk to. He look at his watch. His clothes *been* ready.

"Want something hot to drink?"

"No, ma'am. I got to be going."

A phone start ringing in another room. Old woman point a finger, raise out her chair, go past Juby and pull the sheet that hide the bedroom.

"Ella? Where you been, girl? How the kids? Huh? You know you ain't got to ask me that. Sho . . . Her don't? Put her on. Let me talk to her."

Her voice change, careful, like she coming up on something will fly off if her tone not right.

"Hello, honey. Don't you want to come see your grandma? Got a surprise. Somebody here to see you."

She stick her head out and wave. Juby say, "Me?" He say he got to go. Old woman say just a minute, come to the phone, young man like him *got* to have a minute.

Juby shake his head. He don't go into no strange woman's bedroom, old or not. "No, ma'am."

She say, "Come on. Please? Just do me a favor. I know you got to go."

Juby think what he got himself into. Something go bad, he end up *under* the jail. Be all over the *Daily News*. Folks sucking they tongues and head shaking, talking how bad black men be.

"Please," old woman say.

Juby cross his fingers. Just this once he take a chance, trust this ain't a setup. He walk over. Old woman grab his arm and pull him to her. The room small. A black cat on the bed. Juby never seen a cat so big. Cat look up and yawn and lick his self. Juby don't like no cats.

Old woman got one hand covering the phone. "It's my grandbaby. Tell her you here and want to see her."

"What?"

"Tell her you here and want to see her. She come if you say that. She keep me company."

Juby start to tell her, no, ma'am, he can't say that, beside, he got to be going, and old woman get stiff around the shoulders, and her eyes begin to roll.

"Say it!"

Juby shook. He don't want to lie to no child. He don't want to be here. Cat stand up and stretch and stare at Juby. Why cat eyes look like that? He take the phone.

"Her name Tanya," old woman say.

Juby talk into the phone. "Tanya?"

"Huh?" She got a sweet voice.

"Tanya . . ." He look at old woman. She praying, eyes open, rocking back and forth. On the wall behind her, a three-foot crucifix. Look like her head where Jesus' would of been.

Juby don't think what he doing. "Tanya, I like to see you."

"Who this?"

He say he a friend.

"What you say?"

Juby wonder why she sound so funny. He say he a friend again and wonder. When it come to him, he hear the sound his heart make: BOOMP. He cover up the phone mouth. He shaking. He hot.

"See what you done? See? Why you do that?"

Old woman stop saying hallelujah. "Do what?"

"You got this child thinking I'm her daddy. Why you do that?"

"I ain't done no such thing."

"You did."

"I didn't."

"You *did.*"

Old woman swell up. "Don't make *me* no lie, mister. That what you think, tell her you ain't. That's all you got to do."

Juby stare right back. "I ain't your child," he say. "My mama live in Louisville, Kentucky, 14 Grand Avenue."

Old woman say, "That so?" Her face move like her nose itch. She fold her arms, doing another Job.

Shit, Juby think, but he don't say it. He put the phone to his ear. Tanya crying, "Who is you? What your name?"

"Honey-baby," Juby say, "let me speak to your mama."

Girl just keep crying. Old woman praying, "In the name of *Je*-sus, in the name of *Je*-sus."

Juby say, "Honey, please stop crying."

"*Who is you?*"

Juby don't know what to do. Somebody need to tell this child the truth. He ain't her daddy, her uncle neither. He ain't responsible for this mess.

"Listen," he say. "Tanya? Listen. My name is Juby Alexander Scott. You don't know me. When you get here you see that. You hear? Come on now, hush. I wait right here and buy you some ice cream. I wait right here. Okay?"

She stop crying when Juby tell her that. "Okay," she say.

Juby give old woman back her phone.

"Her like chocolate ice cream," she say.

Juby just look at her. She smiling and he serious as a stroke. He thinking if she be a man, he be in her chest, old or not. She keep watching Juby, smiling. Juby touch his face. He think of the picture of old woman's son. He feel sick. He can't stay.

"You old enough to know better. You . . ." It don't sound like his voice. Sound like gravel in his throat and his stomach funny. He start for the door. Old woman holler, "Where you going? Wait. *Wait.*"

Juby don't answer. He go, half running, out the door, down steps past frying meat, the peeling paint, the tacked up cardboard window. Outside, air slap cold against his face. Juan in the store door shivering in his purple shirt, looking to get in his business.

"Hey, baby, what's happening?"

"Same old same old." Juby say it quick, let Juan know he don't want to be bothered. He hear all this clanging and hollering, and he stop and look up. Old woman leaning out the window with a pot, beating on the fire escape.

"How you go leave? What I tell that child?"

Juan got a grin on his banana face, like he know what going down.

"Tell her anything you want," Juby holler.

Old woman start clanging that pot again. "You come back here."

Juan bat his eyes. "You ain't robbed nobody? Ain't lost your job or nothing."

"She crazy," Juby say. "All I did was help her with her clothes."

"She ain't been right," Juan tell him. "Ever since her son got . . ."

When Juan say "son," his mouth drop open. "Ay, *caramba,*" he say, pointing to Juby. "You look just like him."

Juby face so fed up Juan take a step back. Old woman still clanging. Folks stop in the street, poke their heads out windows. They look at old woman, and they look at Juby.

"Shit," Juby say. He feel like kicking something. He turn, head for the corner.

Old blind man standing there, waiting for someone to say when the light change. Juby walk right past him. Twelve o'clock whistle blow. Woman walking toward Juby look up like the sound come from the sky. Juby think about that child, who's going to answer her questions. Not him. He ain't responsible for this mess. For a scary moment the street tilt, and he stop, fight the fear of losing his balance. He blink and the sun jump out, put a pretty shine on Broadway. Then it slip behind a cloud, and the day go gray again.

M . N O U R B E S E   P H I L I P

STOP FRAME

Is 1958. On a hot, dry island. Somewhere. In the Caribbean. Is 1958 and I hearing the screams of Dr. Ratfinger's patients—the whole village of Bethlehem hearing the screams of Dr. Ratfinger's patients and knowing them as their own. Everybody screaming like this at least once before on a visit to Dr. Ratfinger's office.

Ratfinger not really his name, but Ratzinger, and is me, Gitfa, and Sara who christening him Ratfinger. We writing his new name on a piece of paper and burning it under the big chenette tree in my yard as we repeating an obeah spell we making up. After that he was always Dr. Ratfinger to us—it suiting him better.

He always there—in the village—Dr. Ratfinger. (It seems like that now.) He coming during the war. *The* War. That is how everybody calling World War II— *the* War. My mother saying one morning they getting up and brip brap just like that there he be—Dr. Ratzinger—high and dry in his house—one of the biggest in the town of Bethlehem. And is from the rooms he calling his surgery—at the front and side of his house—that the screams of friends and neighbors coming.

War babies—me, Gitfa, and Sara—is how our mothers calling us. All born at the same hospital in town, within a day of each other at the end of *the* War, so we not really war babies, but we feeling really important when people calling us "the war babies." I couldn't be remembering any of the things I talking about, my mother saying, since I was born after the war: "You too young to remember the screams of Dr. Ratzinger's patients," she telling me, but I knowing otherwise.

And why should I be trusting her memories any more than I trusting mine? My own crick-crack-monkey-break-he-back stories . . .

My own fictions . . .

I could—if I wanted—make Dr. Ratfinger tall and lean . . . give him the pale skin, thin nose, and fair coloring of the Aryan. Blue eyes! I could. If I wanted. Make Dr. Ratfinger six feet six inches tall, make him thin, make him fair, make him blond. I could give him all those "things" *and* a Doberman, as well as a large and perfect specimen of an Aryan wife, all blond hair, fair-complexioned, and reddening in our sun. I could. Or, if I wanted, I could make him short—five feet one inch, perhaps—and fat, with one of his eyes—his pale blue eyes—slightly unfocused, lending him an eerie air of malice, disease, and mystery . . . and *if* I were to give him a monocle, that would make the whole episode even more strange to a young girl on a tiny Caribbean island—far away from events like "the final solution," panzer divisions, and the Desert Fox. Many, many years later she would read of those—she could, if she then wanted, fill in the gaps with whatever fictions (or memories) she chose.

The reality of the fiction is me—Miranda—hanging round Man Fat store, the only store in Bethlehem, listening to the singing and songing of his voice: "Ahtinahmilk, ahpoundahrice," as the neighbors filing in with their ration cards and filing out—"Ahtinahmilk, ahpoundahrice," and the line hot, the line sweaty and winding its way in and out of the store to the refrain.

Sometimes on a Saturday, I finishing my work quick quick, avoiding my mother and going to Man Fat store and buying Kazer Balls that redding-up your tongue and teeth and filling up your cheek so you looking like you having a toothache, and I playing with Mikey, Man Fat little son, who just learning to talk.

"Mikey," I saying to him, "what's that?" and I pointing to the tins of condensed milk that Man Fat handing over the counter.

"Milk-ah."

"What's that, Mikey?" and I pointing to the sugar.

Mikey smiling at me and saying, "Sugar-ah." And I laughing, and all the people in the store laughing, and Mikey laughing and liking how everybody looking at him as he adding 'ah' to everything he saying—"milk-ah, sugar-ah, bread-ah, salt-ah."

And when nighttime falling, I hearing the bombs dropping on London over the wireless, except my mother telling me, in the flat voice she using when she don't want me arguing with her, that bombs stop falling *before* I born. But I hearing them all the same. I hearing them *and* seeing Cousin Lottie too, who living with us since she having a stroke and not walking, lying high high up in her four-poster brass bed that I polishing plenty Saturdays. Everytime a bomb falling Cousin Lottie farting. Long and loud. "Take dat, Hitler, take dat," she saying as she letting go each blast. And sometimes when I creeping into her room and crawling into bed with her, she whispering and telling me that each one of us have to do something. "That is me own war effort," she laughing and telling me, "me-one own." Is so that whenever me, Gitfa, and Sara playing and one of us farting out loud, all of us saying together, "Take dat, Hitler, take dat!" and we laughing out big and loud and hard like we already big women.

"So, Miranda," my mother saying to me one day as we sitting down at the kitchen table for the evening meal, "is why you biting the man hand?" I watching the hot water pouring out from the spout of the old black kettle she holding, into the yellow and blue enamel bowl, and the steam rising and the kitchen filling up with the smell of coconut oil the cassava farine parch in.

"I telling you, Ma, I not liking the way he touching my tongue and telling me how it not going to hurt." My mother spooning some of the farine on to my plate and covering it with fish and gravy. "Hear him, Ma—'Dis vill not hurt—you vill not feel any pain—only ze pressure.'" I talking like Dr. Ratfinger now and I seeing the laughing running all over her face, but she holding it in.

"Eat," is all she saying to me.

"And I remembering how he making people scream, Ma, so I biting him, Ma—hard hard."

And is Dr. Ratfinger turn: is he who screaming and yelling at me and I thinking he hitting me. But he not doing so. Instead, he refusing to fill my tooth, so I suffering weeks and weeks of the tooth hurting. And my mother packing the rotting hole with cloves that smelling sweet and sharp at the same time.

One morning she getting up, setting her face like when she and my father having a quarrel, putting on her good print dress and going to Dr. Ratfinger and "please-sir" apologizing for me, begging for him to fill my tooth and even promising I not biting him again; my mother not "please-sir-ing" anybody, especially somebody white like Dr. Ratfinger, and that morning when she combing it, she pulling and tugging my hair and showing how she angry with me, but it hurting her seeing me hurting so she "please-sir-ing," but he not having anything to do with me and that is just fine, because I hating Dr. Ratfinger and his hands—his white puffy hands with fingers like fat white worms. And I not caring at all I looking like I have a Kazer Ball in my mouth all the time.

"Dis vill not hurt—you vill only feel ze pressure—only ze pressure." First me. Then Gitfa. Then Sara—each of us saying this slow slow and we sticking pins in the figure we making of Dr. Ratfinger. The dough white and soft and I praying my mother not missing it from the bowl she covering with a red-checked towel and leaving to rise in the sun on the sill of the kitchen window. Sara making the body, Gitfa the legs and arms, and me the head, since I was the one biting him. I taking some straw from where the chickens nesting and putting it on the soft white ball of his head, and then with my finger I poking in two holes for his eyes where his face supposed to be. When I putting the two marbles in these holes Sara saying:

"How come you giving him one green and one blue eye?"

"Because," is all I saying as very slowly I pushing his eyes deeper and deeper in his face and the dough not stopping me. I not telling them that these marbles chipped and I not giving my good marbles to Ratfinger, even though "Is for a greater good" as my mother always saying when she doing something she not liking.

"Is why you pushing them in so far?—you can't even see them."

"Leave me alone—I not telling you how to make his body."

I smashing a piece of coal into little black bits and putting two for his noseholes, and with the other little bits making a straight line across for his mouth.

Gitfa putting a stick in one of his hands for the drill and we all laughing at that, but is when we seeing what Sara doing that me and Gitfa sucking in our breath and looking at each other and feeling a little frighten: Sara making a little totie and two little balls and sticking them below the black piece of coal she marking Ratfinger navel with. None of us saying anything—we just stooping down looking at the separate parts of Ratfinger—then still not talking we putting it together—head to body, and we pinching the dough together—hard; body to arm, arm to hand, pinch the dough, leg to foot—hard. Then we trying to sew clothes on him but the dough so soft we leaving him naked. Is then we start sticking pins in him and we putting him on a long piece of stick. Without saying anything we knowing we having to move to where nobody seeing us.

Way down the back of the garden we moving, to where the dasheen—"the best dasheen bush in Bethlehem" my mother saying—growing in a wet sticky patch of black mud, almost to where the forest starting. First we lighting the fire, then we tying our heads with pieces of cloth like we thinking the obeah women doing, and each one of us taking turns holding Ratfinger on the stick and chanting "Dis vill not hurt—only ze pressure you vill feel," while the others stamping the ground and making sounds like a drum—"boom de boom—dis vill not hurt—boom de boom—only ze pressure," as the flames licking him and crinkling his hair right away. "Dis vill not hurt" and the bits of coal glowing bright bright in his face along his smile; "only ze pressure" and we seeing him turning light brown, then dark brown and now the coal in his navel glowing like the ones on his face, "Dis vill not hurt, only ze pressure" and we dancing round the fire and trying to catch the power. Then we stopping and watching Ratfinger burn in the hell we hearing about in Sunday school, as the stick catching fire too and falling in the fire with him.

"I wonder how he liking ze pressure now," I saying, and gentle gentle I probing my rotten tooth with the tip of my tongue and still feeling the pressure and pain.

"Look how black he getting," Gitfa whispering as we watching Ratfinger cooking in the fire.

"Just like Nurse Pamela," Sara saying.

"Nurse Pamela Blantyre!" my mother using the voice that telling me and anybody who listening that she knowing plenty plenty histories about her. "Yes, Nurse Blantyre—but look at she nuh," and she curling her lips round the words in a way that saying she not lowering herself and telling you everything she knowing, but the tone saying what she knowing filling up hours and hours of talking. "She with her pouter pigeon chest."

Me, Gitfa, and Sara agreeing with my mother, because Nurse Blantyre not looking like she having two breasts like our mothers and other women in the village, but her whole front area round, smooth and corset right up to her neck and her bottom cocking out.

Nurse Blantyre black like Dr. Ratfinger white, a black so deep that when you looking at her you feeling you losing yourself in it and not wanting to come out, and people saying she loving with the dentist. But people in the village of Bethlehem also saying she is a zamiist and loving women, and me, Gitfa, and Sara talking and whispering about this and wondering what it is people meaning when they saying Nurse Blantyre loving men and women and I just knowing is not something I asking my mother about.

One day me, Gitfa, and Sara peeping through the window of Ratfinger office and we seeing Nurse Blantyre speeching off Mrs. Standall who believing herself plenty cuts above everybody else in the village, especially somebody like Nurse Blantyre who having a black skin, because she, Mrs. Standall, tracing her ancestry "right back to a white sailor who settled on the island a long time go." "Huh," is what my mother saying whenever she hearing this and adding that that was nothing to be proud of, since anybody with an ounce of sense knowing sailors having syphilis and gonorrhea *and* the morals of a dog. "And not just any old dog either, but a dog in heat." Then she biting down on her mouth which telling me I not to be asking her what syphilis or gonorrhea is. But I knowing what dogs doing in heat, so I know she not thinking much of sailors. Furthermore, my mother adding, she herself tracing her own ancestry right back to African royalty that "de damn white people tiefing and bringing to work for them on the island," and Mrs. Standall ought to be knowing, she adding, that the only thing a red skin meaning is that you have a crook, robber, or rapist in your family, and she could be putting that in her pipe and smoking it.

What me, Gitfa, and Sara seeing when we looking through the window is Nurse Blantyre pushing out her chest even more and telling Mrs. Standall that Dr. Ratfinger was very *very* busy and that she having one of four choices: she could stand and wait, or she could sit and wait; as she saying this Nurse Blantyre puffing herself up even more, then she going on, "You can leave *and* come back," and Nurse Blantyre stopping now, and me, Gitfa, and Sara holding our breath for what coming, "or, you can leave and *not* come back."

I nudging Gitfa in the side, Gitfa nudging Sara and we laughing fit to burst outside the window. Me, Gitfa, and Sara holding our breath and watching how Mrs. Standall's red skin getting even redder, and she flaring her nose-holes wide wide and turning on her heel, walking out, and slamming the door behind her. We not knowing who we laughing at more—because we not liking Nurse Blantyre or Mrs. Standall.

When a patient screaming, is Nurse Blantyre who holding his arms to the side of the chair while Dr. Ratfinger carrying out his worse. *I* know. He touching my tongue and if I not biting him, he doing the same thing to me. Me, Gitfa, and Sara hearing that big big men who working hard splitting rocks in the road, putting up a fight and is Nurse Blantyre who sitting on them or holding them in place easy easy. We frighten for so by Dr. Ratfinger and his nurse.

Nothing we doing getting rid of him though. We waiting and waiting for something to happen to him after our obeah ceremony, but he only getting fatter. And I waiting and waiting with my toothache. *The* War. And my stubbornness. Until the visiting dentist coming to the island. And that was a long long time. The word in the village of Bethlehem was that Dr. Ratfinger meeting with "important collar-and-tie big shots" and sending people to the mad house, and this frightening us even more than the pain sometimes. People saying he also putting electrical wires to your head and shocking you until you begging for mercy. He and Nurse Pamela, people saying "tight as po and bottom" and having "a ting going." Neither me, Gitfa, nor Sara knowing what "a ting going" meaning, but we just knowing it having to do with man and woman business. We hearing the talking and arguing all round us and we listening when we not supposed to be: "I telling you de man is a Nazi, and if he is a Nazi, dere is no way he doing it with her." My father voice coming into the bedroom where I lying quiet quiet.

"But Nurse Pam not black," my mother answering back. "You know what I mean—her skin might be black, but de family mixup . . ."

"Me don't care how mix-up she is—as far as those Nazis go she is a member of an *inferior* face. Me read about it—they even killing Jews and they have white skins!"

"All I know is that when it come to that thing between man and woman, man does say he have all kind of principles, but is like what Cousin Lottie say—a standing prick knows no mercy in a widow's house at night, or any woman house for that matter. And not only at nighttime either. And *I* am going to bed."

I telling all this to Gitfa and Sara and we laughing like big people and nodding our heads as if we understanding what our parents talking about. But what me, Gitfa, and Sara knowing is that we hating Ratfinger and nothing too evil for him to do. And when we behaving bad is threaten our parents threatening us with him and so we wanting to put an end to Ratfinger.

Is so we starting the mango wars. Ratfinger liking mangoes plenty plenty; he priding himself on his Julie mangoes which everybody knowing is the queen of mangoes. Late late one night, when is only duppy and sucouyant about, me, Gitfa, and Sara meeting outside Ratfinger house, slipping the latch on his gate and going into his back garden.

"Is a good thing he not having Long mango or Starch mango eh," I whispering to Gitfa and Sara, and we all laughing because the Julie mango trees not much bigger than us, so I shining my torch and easy easy we reading in between the branches and pulling off every single mango, even the young green ones no bigger than marble and lime. Me, Gitfa, and Sara stripping every single mango tree in Ratfinger yard that night, and we leaving all the green mangoes in a pile outside his front door. For days after, up and down the village, inside and outside our houses, even in the school yard where the other children skipping and clapping hands to the singing about how Ratfinger "mad and bad" and "somebody tiefing he mango and leaving he trees naked," we hearing how Ratfinger don't have no more mangoes for the season, how he angry and wanting to know who "committing this predial larceny." Everybody laughing and saying nobody tiefing nothing since he still having he mangoes, and the market women happy because they only seeing him coming and quick quick they doubling their price. But nothing stopping Ratfinger and Nurse Pamela—we still hearing screams coming from his surgery.

That is how we deciding on another plan. When Sara first whispering it to me as we sitting up in the plum tree in her yard, my eyes opening wide wide and I putting my hand to my mouth and laughing out loud, and even more when I seeing Gitfa doing the same thing when Sara telling her. Is Sara who getting the cow-itch grass, and one day when he making somebody scream, I sneaking into Ratfinger car—after I greasing my hands with lard—and I rubbing the grass all over the car seat. We hiding behind the hedge then, and when we seeing him coming out and getting into his car we holding our breath, and then laughing and laughing when he getting out fast fast and running back into the office scratching his behind. We sitting behind the hedge and peeing ourselves we laughing so hard, as we watching Nurse Pamela trying to scratch it for him.

That night when everybody sleeping we getting up and meeting outside Ratfinger house again. Is Gitfa turn this time and she climbing through the window in his surgery and rubbing Nurse Pamela chair with the cow-itch grass. And we laughing as we thinking what happening the next day when Nurse Pamela coming into the office and sitting down in her stocious way and starting to scratch what my mother calling her "cockmollify behind."

"Is the same Mrs. Standall self," my mother saying the next day. "The one who she speech off only a few days ago, who passing by and taking her home and putting some medicine on her behind." We all sitting round the kitchen table eating supper; the laughing running round and round inside me as I listening to my mother, and when I hearing how Nurse Pamela rushing out the surgery scratching and screaming it breaking out and I hiding it behind my hand and my enamel cup. My mother fixing me with her eyes as if she suspecting me but she not asking anything. I giving my best marble—the big one that is part blue and part clear glass, the same one I winning off my cousin, Theo—to anybody if I could be seeing Nurse Pamela that day.

The next day me, Gitfa, and Sara celebrating and since is Saturday we running around town like we owning it, and in we own way we was owning it. When the woman who selling tickets not looking, we sneaking under the curtains and into the Strand, the only cinema in Bethlehem and watching *King Kong Meets Tarzan*.

"Is not Jane that that King Kong holding—where Tarzan?" Gitfa whispering to me and I whispering to Sara. And we feeling frighten as the ape waving and waving the little, tiny white woman over the big tall building with a spike.

King Kong looming big big in my memory: he stands eighteen inches tall behind the glass display case—"A jointed steel frame, rubber muscles, and a coat of rabbit fur. Stop frame animation moves the model slightly . . ."

It is 1988. On a damp, cold island—a long long way away from 1958. On a hot, dry island. Somewhere. ". . . expose a frame of film, move the model again . . ."

Stop frame: me, Gitfa, and Sara sneaking under the curtain, over the Empire State Building, into the dark dark theater, finding seats, grabbing each other, and screaming for so as King Kong and Tarzan coming up big big on the screen.

Stop frame: ". . . use miniatures . . . glass shots . . . real and model aircraft" as King Kong waving Jane—"No, is Fay Wray that!"

Stop frame: Dr. Ratzinger. Ratfinger—was he a Nazi? It was a long time—a very long time—after he had left us and the screams had died down, that I learnt what the word meant, although it didn't matter that I didn't know—the way my mother saying the word "Nazi," holding in it everything that evil, and I believing Ratfinger was a Nazi who fleeing Germany, and carrying out experiments on the people of Bethlehem. But bad teeth not caring about politics and despite all the mango wars and the cow-itching, Ratfinger still having patients.

Stop frame: move the model slightly—did Sara know about Nazis? She was Jewish. If she did, she and I never talked about them, running round the town of Bethlehem as if we owning it.

Stop frame! Me, Gitfa, and Sara sneaking under the curtain, into the darkened cinema, finding seats and grabbing each other for comfort in the scary parts of the Tarzan movie.

Stop frame! Tarzan—what did I know about Africa? Nothing except "me Tarzan, you Jane."

Stop frame: Tarzan, Nazis, Africa.

Stop frame! you von't feel ze pain, just ze pressure—the weight of memories—a tooth impacted, pushing, pressing against gum against bone—the hard white bone of history, and I remembering the tooth black and rotting—the white memory eating and eating away at the creeping black which making the hard white soft, crumbly, and Ma packing it again and again with the dark brown powder she making from cloves, and it stopping the aching—the memory—

Stop frame: my mother lying; stop frame: my mother lying on the floor; stop frame: (move the model slightly) my mother lying on the floor screaming; stop frame: my mother lying on the floor screaming that she drinking poison; stop frame: my mother lying on the floor screaming that she drinking poison and she killing herself.

Stop frame.

Move the model slightly:

"So, Ma, is why you doing it?"

"Doing what, chile?" She watching me pour the water—steam rising, but no smell of coconut oil. Only the slightly acrid smell of tea.

"You know, Ma—pretending you killing yourself?"

The bowl of tea nestling in her cupped hands; the fingers, gnarled by arthritis and work into a network of roots, tremble ever so slightly and the rheumy eyes lift to look at me—once—before returning to the tea. As if wanting to veil the past, the present—the world itself! from her gaze, age pulling a blue cast over the brown eyes—blue, like my best marble! and I remembering how she packing my rotting tooth with cloves. "Huh—that Ratzinger!" is all she saying for a while. "He was really something, that man—just refuse to take out your tooth."

"That was because I bit him, Ma—remember?"

"Just refuse to take out your tooth! . . . Uh uh." The surprise and anger still there in her voice.

"Why, Ma? Why did you do it?"

The smile she smiling just like the tone of voice that telling me "thus far and no further" and is like the veil over her eyes getting darker—more blue. "You know what I always saying, chile, a memory just like a rotten tooth—if it hurting too bad, you must be taking it out."

"And what if you can't take it out, Ma?" I challenging her right back with my tone.

"Then you pack it with a little cloves, chile." Is like her eyes looking through the blue curtain to another place: "And some forgetting," she adding quietly.

"And wait for the dentist?" Anger and remembered pain roughening the edges of my voice. My tongue tip gently touches the spot where once the tooth ached, exploring old areas of pain, seeking some life where a long time ago ache had splintered into throb and lance and stab—each nerve with its own hurting life—and come together again in a roar as loud, as red as the dye of the Kazer Ball coating my mouth. The cold white porcelain gave nothing back to my questioning tongue. All feeling had gone with the rotting tooth.

"Yes, you wait, chile. You wait for the visiting dentist."

ALIX RENAUD

YAWETIR

I

"I think it's serious, Doctor," he said as he sat down.

The judge of the matter was not Max, however, but rather the owner of those squinting, inquisitive eyes observing him from behind the glasses in delicate, metal frames. That impassive look, the total absence of expression on the face of his interlocutor put him ill at ease. He repeated compulsively.

"It's serious, Doctor."

Since the doctor seemed to be waiting for what would follow, Max warned him.

"It's absolutely incredible . . . , completely! Even I can hardly believe it."

"I'm listening," said the neutral voice.

"Well, here goes," Max began. "There's Martine, first of all. That's not exactly the beginning, but . . . Maybe I should begin with the young woman, Emily. Or maybe with the drunk. . . . I don't know."

The psychiatrist was waiting patiently. He had seen scores of bizarre patients parade by. Each one had an unlikely little tale, and believed it. Why should this one be an exception to the rule?

"Onion soup," Max muttered, blushing.

"What?" The psychiatrist gave a start.

"If I said, 'onion soup,' would that shock you?"

"No, why?"

"Because, my problem is really serious. I've been infected, Doctor. By words! By words, do you understand?"

Translated by Carrol F. Coates.

He seemed to be on the point of breaking down. He managed to stammer something.

"I've got to . . . , I have to get my head together. . . ."

Then he fell silent, as breathless as if he had just finished a long speech. He closed his eyes for a moment. Opening them, he took a deep breath and began.

I I

I have been going with Martine for three years. She lives in Saint-Irisé, five hundred kilometers from here. You probably wonder why I should choose a woman so far away, but you'll tell yourself that it's none of your business, of course. Every time we have a quarrel on the telephone, Martine has such a fit of tears and hysteria that I feel guilty, mean, inhuman, cruel. . . . Then I jump in the car and head straight for her place. I'm crazy. For Martine. The last time that we let each other have it was day before yesterday. I was beginning to get fed up with her mood shifts. I headed off toward Saint-Irisé anyway. Have you ever gone to Saint-Irisé? You've got to try it, believe me! A thousand kilometers round trip! At the rate of an argument every two weeks, that makes a modest record of around twenty-six million meters per year. That means that I know the road by heart. Anyway, it's always the heart that takes a beating. . . .

So, we had at it again day before yesterday. I hop in the car—off to Saint-Irisé. I smoke like a steam engine during half the trip. Then I begin getting pissed off at Martine. All of a sudden, I see a familiar spot ahead. I know that by heart, too. It's a sign. A big yellow sign that points to YAWETIR on the left and SAINT-IRISÉ on the right. I'm driving fast. The sign looms larger, in a manner of speaking, since you can't see with your ears. Do you understand? I have always taken the right fork, toward Saint-Irisé, toward my sweet Martine. . . . Sweet? Now I'm raving mad. To make a long story short, this time, to teach Martine a lesson and punish her, I decided to go left. Curiosity was undoubtedly a factor, too. For three years the name, YAWETIR, had been intriguing me, but I had never thought to tell Martine about it. . . . You know how reconciliations go!

In short, I went left. Notice that it was because of Martine that I took that fork—so, everything is her fault. You've got to tell her that if I ever really go crazy. . . .

I said "road," but that's not quite it. It was full of bumps and chuckholes. A real motocross trail. I've got nothing against motocross, mind you, but there are limits. On both sides of this trail, there were shriveled trees and dried grass. Phantoms of the fields were waiting for a scorcher to set off a quiet little forest fire. From time to time there were animated figures that were actually dead—scarecrows on the alert. At one point, a cow with vacant eyes nodded her head as I passed. A little farther, I saw a hen flattened in the middle of the road. Then, all of a sudden, the countryside changed. The trees were even green. I ought to have been relieved, but I felt empty and tired. I cursed Martine for lack of anything better to say. And then, all of a sudden . . . , the miracle!

"Miracle" is a big word, I know, but put yourself in my place! First, a scene out of a horror movie, then the green countryside, and, bang! Right in front of me, there was a young woman with a knapsack on her back headed in my direction.

She turned her head at the sound of the car, raised her right arm and pointed her thumb toward YAWETIR. I was already braking. I leaned over and opened the door.

"What about a lift?" she asked.

She got in beside me and put her sack at her feet. She was good-looking and smelled good. Twenty-four or twenty-five. And really well built! She had breasts that would make you want to be a baby again.

I started up slowly, vaguely relieved from the solitude that was becoming oppressive. I asked my passenger if that road really led to a city or town called YAWETIR. She laughed.

"YAWETIR's neither a city nor a town. It's a principality."

"A country?" I exclaimed.

"A principality," she insisted.

I found out that YAWETIR[1] had around two million inhabitants scattered through three cities and five villages. I had never heard of it.

"*Outsiders* are jealous of YAWETIR. They refuse to talk about it."

I remained perplexed for quite a while. Finally . . . , or maybe I should say, "To begin with . . . ," because that was when things began to go wrong. In any case, I finally asked the young woman what she was doing alone on a deserted road.

"I was coming back from an orgy," she said in an unconcerned tone.

My heart skipped a beat and I felt my pockets for a cigarette. My passenger had already stuck one in my mouth and was lighting it for me. Something stuck in my throat. I gripped the steering wheel, suspecting that I had misunderstood. I summoned up courage to ask her to repeat.

"You want the whole story? Well, my name is Emily. I'm just coming back from an orgy that our parish priest arranged."

She seemed to reflect nostalgically.

"Only two of my lovers were there. No luck. I had been counting on Gerard being there. But he got beat up in a fight. We had a good time anyway, even without Gerard . . ."

She left her sentence unfinished, but from her smile, I could guess the rest. And the rest intrigued me. I told her so.

"Come on to my place," she said.

"To your place?" I was really surprised by the rapid succession of events.

"We can even do it in your car if you can't wait."

---

1. Translator's hint: The reader will soon discover that everything in YAWETIR is reversed. In the original French text, the name of the principality was SNESNOB ("bon sens," or common sense, spelled backward); The opposite of YAWETIR is RITEWAY.

She was about to unbutton her blouse. I was sweating like a damned fool. I put my hand on hers and swore that I could wait. The air cleared; for me, that is, since Emily never showed the least sign of embarrassment. The conversation continued a bit along indifferent lines, and then she started on the orgy again—she wasn't about to forget it. A little rumbling in my stomach reminded me that I had not eaten anything that morning. Without thinking I spoke.

"I hope that we can find some little restaurant along the way. . . ."

She gave a violent start. She turned toward me, with bulging eyes, and dared me to repeat what I had just said.

"Aren't you ashamed? What a jerk!"

"Ashamed of what?" I persisted. "I'm hungry!"

At this, she turned purple. Her lips were trembling and lightning was flashing from her eyes. She was clenching and unclenching her fists on the sack at her feet. I stopped and turned toward her. Then, she gave a shrill, deafening yell. She slapped my cheek and, a second later, she tumbled out of the car, still yelling.

"You bastard! Louse! Filthy pervert! You gastric maniac!"

I didn't hear any more, because I had taken off. I was surprised, speechless, disoriented, out of my mind, whatever! "Gastric maniac," she had said. Talk about an expression! What about her orgies! Some crazy woman, apparently! Chuckholes or no, I sped up. I was really hungry.

III

A pitiful little hut sheltered the border guards. The officer bombarded me with questions that I answered more or less. No, I did not have a visa, since I had not realized that YAWETIR was a principality. No, I had no intention of engaging in revolutionary activities on Yawetirian territory. When he finally decided to let me pass, he yelled after me.

"If you're here to have fun, I recommend the Clitorama in particular. It's the best place in town!"

I went about a kilometer without thinking about anything. Or, rather, trying to think about anything except that crazy Emily or the deranged officer at the border. If I had realized, I would have gone to Martine's. I could have had something to eat and drink there. I would have taken a good shower and rested. Clitorama, Clitorama! I must have been in some kind of mild delirium.

All of a sudden, on the right, a green sign caught my attention. I almost went off the road! Could I believe my eyes? I slowed down. My clothes were sweaty. I was hungry. A second green sign loomed ahead. "I have to take a careful look," I told myself. I got out of the car and walked over to the sign. I was absolutely stunned. My first impression had been right. The town logo of YAWETIR was a naked ass covered by a hand attached to a hairy forearm. A purple haze blurred my vision. I clasped my arms over my belly and bent double to heave at the side of the road. I was no Puritan, but I was becoming more uneasy as I approached the first houses. Besides, I had not seen a single restaurant on the way and I was hungrier than ever.

I drove another half hour before reaching LATIPAC. The road sign stated that the population of this city was one million. Like all cities, it had its elegant sections and its slums. I drove around it ten or twelve times without finding a single restaurant. It was driving me mad. I was hesitant to ask for directions, without knowing why. Finally, I stopped, got out of the car, and looked around. I had the sudden impression that I was being watched. I turned around. In fact, on the other side of the street, somebody had pulled the curtains back a bit and was watching me. I sort of waved at the person and he did the same. Resolutely, I crossed the road. An old, pinkish door opened on creaking hinges and a bald man spoke.

"You're not from here?"

"No," I said. "And I'm starving!"

The man made a quick sign to lower my voice and glanced around.

"My name is Gerard. Follow me."

He closed the door and motioned for me to follow him. We crossed a large room filled with change machines, then we took a wooden staircase. About ten couples were sitting there, eating and eating at an incredible speed. Here and there, several single men were scooping up soup with the appetite of bears just coming out of hibernation. I wobbled as I sat down at the table that Gerard indicated.

"Carrot soup and beef brisket," announced my clandestine chef.

"Anything! Give me a double serving!"

"That's thirty dollars a plate," stated Gerard.

Seeing my look of consternation, he gave me some story about fines and threat of imprisonment, which I did not understand. The money I had with me would be just enough for one portion.

There was slurping all around me as if the world might fall apart at any second. A lightning-fast waiter was picking up the empty bowls while another one was distributing steaming bowls that smelled of herb broth with equal rapidity. A bowl of soup landed in front of me. I picked it up steaming hot and drank it clear down to whatever the solid contents were. I had barely finished when a hand grabbed it and another put a large plate heaped with the brisket and some purée of suspicious color. I began eating without formalities. I had accelerated to very nearly the speed of the other diners when the restaurant keeper dashed out of the kitchen yelling.

"The cops! The cops! The cops are here!"

The plates and bowls disappeared in nothing flat.

"Quick, quiiiicccck!" Gerard stamped angrily.

Like magic, a metal curtain fell in front of the door leading to the kitchen. Items of clothing flew across the room and the couples began to caress each other and groan with passion. I watched all of this speechless and with my stomach tied in knots. A hand grabbed my place setting.

"Do something quick," Gerard yelled at me.

Steps thundered on the floor above us. I was wondering what I was supposed to do when I saw a single guy close to me wiggling around on his chair with his hands in his pockets, emitting little groans with his head thrown backward. I followed his lead, just as a squad of policemen burst into the room with clubs in their hands. The one who appeared to be the chief sniffed around the room and then yelled.

"It smells like food here!"

"No, it doesn't," said Gerard obsequiously. "It's just a new drug that I was trying out. Unfortunately, I don't have any more of it. . . ."

"New drug, my eye!" said the cop, smacking him.

One couple was having at it on the table with such conviction that a couple of cops sidled over to them. When they were convinced that the couple was not faking, the policemen went away. They prowled into every nook and cranny. To take revenge for the false alarm, the chief gave Gerard another surprise blow. He doubled up, swearing.

"Oof!! Holy barbecue beef with bearnaise sauce!"

And the police took off as suddenly as they had appeared.

"Pay and get the hell out!" Gerard bawled a second later.

I paid. But, as I was leaving, something sweetish rose in my stomach, and I bent over vomiting. I'd had it but that wasn't the end.

When I was certain that I could stand, I went out and tried to stretch my legs a bit. The people passing by seemed to be sullen and uptight. Men and women were parading around not wearing much. Some of the old women, wearing outrageously exaggerated makeup, smiled enticingly at the men as they passed. The houses were discouragingly alike in appearance. Everywhere, signs sporting the logo of YAWETIR proclaimed, "Life is enjoyment!" or "Live to enjoy and enjoy to deserve living!"

I turned into a side street and stopped when I saw a boy of about ten who was writing with a piece of charcoal on a large white wall: "STEAK."

"You little thug!" a voice howled across the street.

The boy burst out laughing. I looked at the person who had yelled. It was a white-bearded old man, leaning out the window of the first floor.

He spoke to me: "Hasn't our young generation gone to the dogs, Sir?"

I picked up the piece of charcoal that the boy had dropped and went over to the wall.

"If you write anything on that wall, I'll call the vice squad," he said in a quavering voice.

Right after the word "steak" I made a plus sign and wrote in large capital letters: "FRENCH FRIES." There was a deathlike gasp behind me and a denture broke on the pavement.

"Help! Help!" the old man howled.

I went on, cursing every type of puritanism on the globe. Finally, I was beginning to understand Emily's reaction at my declaration of hunger. Her insult came back to mind: "Gastric maniac!" What nerve! Obviously, everybody in YAWETIR was wolfing down food, but nobody would admit it in public. Here, apparently, eating was a mortal sin, an offense to public morality or something along those lines. They bragged about the quality of the Clitorama, but they organized raids on clandestine restaurants. I'd had enough, too much! My bowl had already run over twice.

I saw a sign on a hotel. I went in for no particular reason. Maybe because I'd had it. Or from lack of imagination. It was eight dollars a room, with bath, pornographic films and magazines in abundance, shower and massage, and so on. "They're all loony," I told myself as I followed the porter to my room.

It was a clean little room. There was a television set next to the magazine rack, overflowing with naked couples. I put a tip in the attendant's hand as he leaned over to whisper.

"I've got sandwiches."

"Where?" I asked, curious.

"Here," he said, dipping his hand into his pocket.

He pulled out two bent sandwiches in cellophane wrapping. They didn't look fresh. I couldn't take it—I burst out laughing. Eight dollars for a luxury room, and shriveled sandwiches for twelve! Something had gone wrong somewhere.

I V

I slept all afternoon and part of the evening. I dreamed that I was a happy, harnessed donkey. Martine was sitting on my back and dangling a big ham at the end of a stick in front of my nose. I was ambling ahead and braying. I woke up with a shudder. It took me a good five minutes to realize where I was and what I was doing there. I got dressed and left in a hurry.

There were many couples in the street. Each person was hanging onto a partner as if afraid of being left alone at the next street. Without rushing, I headed for the street where Gerard's little restaurant was located. I had left my car there. As I passed the white wall, I noticed that, just below my "FRENCH FRIES," some hateful person had scrawled, "EAT IT, IDIOT!"

I got in the car and drove around town two or three times. At one point, I noticed a giant red neon sign, proclaiming the "CLITORAMA." A long line of eager customers stretched out along the street. Every person was impatiently waiting to go make his offering to Venus, by deed, thought, or simply sight. "The gods and the rites we invent for ourselves," I thought. The worst aberrations can become sacred. It just depends on the brain that harbors them. I was beginning to get hungry and I was ashamed. A new kind of modesty had sprung up in me, to replace the anxiety that had been plaguing me up to that time. I felt a kind of mindless and boundless tranquility.

I got out of the car and went up to the front of the Clitorama. There were only beaming faces going through the temple entrance. Another rumble shook my stomach. I walked away quickly, cursing my stomach. No, I wouldn't give up to temptation. I had no right to profane this sacred ground. I wouldn't allow my guts to blaspheme on Yawetirian territory.

I realized that I was crying. A uniformed doorman was pacing now in front of Clitorama. I went up to him, embarrassed.

"I am a great sinner, Sir. I'm hungry."

"Holy prunes in sticky caramel! Why are you telling me that?"

"I'm just one big alimentary sack!"

"Do you think I'm one of the customers?" protested the man.

"No," I sobbed. "I'm an innkeeper, a restaurateur, a glutton, and a diner."

"You poor ratatouille!" he spit out scornfully and turned his back on me.

I felt ashamed, small, miserable. I wasn't just crying now, I was sobbing. As I got back into my car, I heard some obscenities intoned by a thick voice. A crazy man was invoking sardines, coq au vin, and jelly. I turned around. He came staggering up with a bottle in his hand.

"The bastard," I thought.

He came up to me quickly and nodded his head several times. He saw that I was crying and he smiled.

"Come on, old potato, let's make some broth?"

"You salsify aspic!" I answered, waving my fist at him.

"You're not the restaurateur type, by any chance? Maybe you're the ratatouille or cassoulet type," he muttered.

"You're beginning to squash my prunes," I yelled. "Go get your eggs cooked, you cauliflower!"

He burst out in a demential laugh as he walked away.

"Salad!" he chuckled. "Everything you've said is a bunch of salad."

I felt guilty because I had always liked salad. The drunk, off in the distance, was still talking to the stars.

"Just one big restaurant down here! Carrots, chopped steak, beef filets! Everyone wolfs it down, in giant mouthfuls. Colossal digestion, belches, mastication!"

I was on the verge of hysteria. These obscenities were getting the best of me.

The crazy man's last words . . . "We're all a bunch of eggplants sneaking velvety snacks in the lunch boxes we call houses. . . ."

I couldn't take it any more. I stumbled and fell on the ground, heaving again. The minute I was over my indisposition, I hopped in my car and headed directly home. Right after crossing the border, I saw an animal devouring something and almost had another attack. I drove faster. Roaring through the thick darkness like a madman, I made a superhuman effort to cleanse myself of all the filthy expressions that were dancing through my head. I would go to confession when I got back. Raw vegetables, goodies, banquets, cream of asparagus, cream of sausage, gullets, love feasts, gastronomy, lunches, provisions, blasts, grub, grub, grub . . .

V

Max had finished his confession and grown quiet. Without flinching, the psychiatrist watched him cry through half-closed eyelids. His medical mind was not idle. On the contrary! Precise terms, rigorously defined, were flooding into his head. His patient was victim to multiple problems: Lysophobia, the fear of going insane. Dipsophobia, the morbid fear of drinking. Phagophobia, the morbid fear of eating, as well. There was reason to diagnose a certain form of hamartophobia—the fear of sinning. And the psychiatrist himself did not feel totally devoid of some symptoms of molysmophobia, the obsessive fear of contagion. The best would be to get rid of this patient as quickly as possible.

"You're a real gastric maniac," he said.

Max started, and hunched down.

"What should I do?" he asked.

"Eat!" said the psychiatrist. "Eat everything, anything, but eat!"

His voice went up an octave.

"Try stew, roast lamb, pizza!"

"What?" Max crumpled.

"Everything!" howled the psychiatrist, on his feet and pointing an accusing finger at his patient. "Everything! Everything! Everything!"

"Are you crazy?" sobbed Max.

"I said everything," yelled the psychiatrist. "Intellectual mastication isn't enough! Eat! Stuff yourself with fricassee, lentils, truffles, cheese-topped dishes, flan, spaghetti, caviar, cod, even crayfish!!"

Max backed toward the door, frightened, shocked, red as a tomato, and quivering like a bowl of jello.

The psychiatrist kept yelling. "I gobble up raw veggies, fruit preserves, candies! Sustenance, weddings, feasts! Gullet, tongue, palate—everything's good, nourishing, nutritiously delectable! Heavenly sauces dripping delectably from my chops! Love feasts from the paradisiacal days at my mother's breast!"

Max virtually jumped down the flight of stairs with a torrent of obscene expressions flooding after him: raw veggies, candies, stews, corn, roasts, cheeses, aspics, leeks, celery, beets, lunch, sandwich, vittles, gullets, feasts, weddings, caramel, truffles, caviar, blasts, orgies, grub, grub . . .

ENOUGH RIDES

IT HAD BEEN MONTHS since she'd seen Pop. Now he looked like a man she had never known. There was a tenseness about him—a horrible tautness like cat's gut dried in the California sunshine. His brown skin was blotched red; he smelled of too many beers and of dirt; slight tremors shook his body.

Her Pop had come to take her to Pacific Ocean Park—an amusement resort designed, as it advertised, "to call forth the joy in everyone's heart." Underneath her left armpit, Jackie carried a new bikini bathing suit; after the rides, Pop said, "they would dip into the sea."

But the day conspired against them. The sky was overcast; billowy, gray clouds hung low like a blanket; usually the sun made her eyes want to plop out of their sockets.

The family too conspired against any happiness.

Hadn't Tonie hid in the closet, buried beneath piles of dirty clothing, when Pop drove up?

"What are you afraid of?" Jackie asked; but she knew the answer.

Tonie was terrified Pop would turn on her and foam like a dog. Jackie wished he would. For, months ago, hadn't sister Tonie cowered behind their mother as she brandished a butcher knife screaming "out?" While she had stood with her legs spaced well apart, behind her Pop. Later she stood alone on the porch (fireflies buzzing about) watching Pop drive away.

Now Mother and Pop were both standing on the porch. Mother was screeching like a hoot owl, warning Pop to have her back by five and the support payments mailed on time. She was sitting in the car waiting to be taken away.

Pop's back was to her but in the car's side mirror she could see Mother well enough—hair swept into a bun; gold bracelets jangling about her wrists. It was her face which astounded Jackie. How many times had her mother clasped her in front of a mirror and pressed their faces side to side (like a Siamese monster Jackie always felt)? How many times had she shifted her eyes back and forth from her mother's features to her own? While Mother said:

"Look. Same eyes. Same nose. Same mouth. You look just like me." Then, Mother, if Pop wasn't around, would draw her lips into a thin line; but if he was around, she would add silkily, "Who's my pretty baby?" and Jackie would duti- fully reply, "Me."

The resemblance was amazing, Jackie thought while sitting in the car, cradling her bathing suit.

She stared ahead at the asphalt road but not before she saw Pop's reflection caress Mother's shoulders and Mother shrugging his hands away.

Ocean mist coated the amusement park and pressed Jackie's clothes closer to her body. Cluttered in separate groups were teenage toughs and chanting hare krishnas. She could see young mothers tugging toddlers and a few old men with glazed eyes, playing the penny arcade and sipping wine. Occasionally, too, she could hear a barker crying with gusto to encourage someone to shoot the mark, to hit the bell, or to mystify the "guesser" with your age, weight, or occupation. But few took advantage of the offers.

The only sound of fun in the park could be heard in the yelps of roller coaster riders whose trip swung them out over the ocean. Jackie remembered hearing once that the roller coaster train had jumped its tracks and sent screaming, flail- ing people into the sea.

"Want some cotton candy?" Pop asked.

"Yes, please."

A pimpled and freckled-faced young man spun sweet-pink cotton candy around a pretzel.

Jackie sat on the bench and watched seagulls pluck splattered popcorn while she plucked threads of colored sugar.

"Are you happy?" Pop asked.

She shrugged. "Are you?" She stared at his hands, scarred from when his butcher knife slipped. "It happens," he'd said once, "when I let my mind wander at work." It was amazing how his skin healed cut after cut, but the new skin was never like the old.

"I miss you and your sister."

"Do you miss her?"

"Some."

Jackie twisted her face into a grimace.

"Would you want me to lie and say that I don't?"

"Say what you want." She shoved cotton candy at him. "Here. I don't want any more."

"Not even the pretzel? It's your favorite part."

"Naw."

He scraped the sugar off the stick, broke the pretzel into pieces, and threw them at the birds. "Come on. Let's go for a ride."

It moved like a ferris wheel, backwards and forwards, but it had ten little cages that spun around and upside down as the larger wheel turned.

"It's too scary."

"That's part of the fun, baby girl."

"I'll get dizzy."

Pop bought the tickets. Then, a man in a white shirt and black pants placed them in a green metal cage, snapped a bar across their waists and closed the metal door.

"What if the bar comes undone?"

"Nothing's going to happen. Relax."

Away they went, along with another couple in a cage not far behind. They went spinning in two circles. The smaller wheel kept them twirling around and upside down, and the larger wheel kept pushing the momentum forward.

Jackie pressed her body closer to her Pop's as snatches of images of the barker, the arcade, and the green expanse of sea became jumbled in her vision. She closed her eyes.

"Isn't this fun?" Pop asked.

The larger wheel slowed and then shifted its direction backwards. Soon the cages, one by one, began to spin double-time. Her feet were pushing up towards the sky; her head was trailing afterwards.

"Pop, make it stop."

"It'll be over in a minute. Relax. Take deep breaths."

She tried to relax, but the whipping air made it difficult to breathe. She wondered if the cages wouldn't spin themselves off their spokes, hurling them into the ocean.

Gradually the wheel slowed and came to a halt. She and Pop were positioned at the very top, their cage and bodies, upside down.

"What's wrong?" Her knuckles whitened as she gripped the bar before her.

"They're just letting those kids out. It'll be our turn in a sec."

Jackie could see a couple with their heads thrown back in laughter, stepping out of the cage and onto the platform. She relaxed, knowing she and her Pop were next. But neither the cage nor the wheel moved. The boy in black and white down below hollered for help, and soon a small crowd of people were craning their necks upwards, watching the motionless wheel, the upside down cage and the people hanging over slim metal.

"Try not to put so much weight on the bar."

Jackie watched as Pop tried to press his body back against gravity. Sweat careened down his forehead and onto his chest. Staring at Pop's frightened eyes, she knew he was imagining the bar coming unlatched and he, then Jackie (upside down) hurtling through space.

Caught up in Pop's terror, she became less afraid. Never before had she known him to want to peel himself outside of his skin. Even when Mother turned his cleaver on him.

The wheel jerked and then, with a metallic groan, their cage eased downwards amid the applause of the crowd.

Pop laughed nervously. "You weren't frightened, were you?"

She didn't answer.

"You've had enough rides, don't you think?"

"Suppose."

"Then how about going to the beach?"

He grabbed her hand and began walking quickly towards the lockers. She double skipped in order to keep up with him.

"You sure are getting big," Pop whistled.

Blushing, she wrapped her beach towel closely about her shoulders. Over the summer, because her breasts had begun to bud, Mother had bought her a bra. Her waist and hips had also begun to curve. But she wished Pop hadn't mentioned it. He should have known she'd be uncomfortable in her first two-piece.

And she was already uncomfortable, since Pop seemed to flaunt himself. He strutted as bold as you please in his small, tight black trunks, and for the first time, she noticed his chest was covered with balls of kinky hair.

On the almost deserted beach, two blond-topped kids were digging for shells and over to their left, a couple was stretched full-length with their arms twisted about one another.

Jackie burrowed her body into heat-absorbing sand. She placed her towel beneath her head and closed her eyes against the clouds.

Pop began blowing up a rubber mattress. "You know," he said, "I kinda like living alone." He filled his lungs with air and blew. "Before you were even thought of, I lived with my mother, then your mother and your grandmother, and then with your mother and you kids." He blew again. "Never had the opportunity to be by myself."

Jackie thought how she'd rather be alone than live with Mother and Tonie.

"I really like living alone. No one interrupts when you're trying to get something done or just trying to be quiet." He inhaled again, then expelled the air right back out. "Don't misunderstand me. I enjoyed having you kids around."

And my Mother, thought Jackie.

"And your Mother."

He pushed out one last gust of air. Next, he snapped the rubber closure. "Come on." Pop began whisking away the particles of sand.

Layer after layer, she could feel Pop's hands drawing nearer to her body. Her eyes closed, she kept still. Then, his coarse hands rubbed away the last bits of sand from her legs, stomach, and chest. As she stood, a fine shower of sand fell around her feet. Some sand remained caught between the hair on her upper thighs just beneath her crotch. Wiping it away, she noticed Pop moving his hands to cover the front of his trunks.

Grabbing the mattress rope, she dragged it down to the sea and then shuddered as she dove into the salty water. She laughed aloud as Pop's face twisted and his skin prickled with the cold.

"Why didn't you warn me it was cold?" he asked, splashing foam over her face and hair.

She flipped onto her back and started backpaddling and sending a series of small waves to crash against him.

"I'll get you for that."

Crawl stroking and fluttering her legs as fast as possible, she heard the whoosh of Pop's arms cutting through the water.

"Stop. It hurts."

"Give?" Pop cried, pushing her head underneath the water again.

"Yes. Give." She wiped her face and squeezed the excess moisture from her hair. "I can hardly . . . breathe."

"Serves you right." He swam towards the fluorescent orange mattress. "Here. Lie on this awhile."

She climbed aboard, laid flat, and tucked her arms underneath her chin. The bathing suit bottom clung neatly to her rounded behind.

Pop dogpaddled at her side. "Mind if I come aboard, sailor?"

Pulling himself onto the mattress, his hand curved along the hollow of her behind. He layered his body on top of hers, and like some strange oceanic sandwich, they floated further away from the beach and the dots of people on the shore.

She could feel Pop's chest abnormally expanding and contracting against her back. His hands slid up her sides and cupped themselves beneath her breasts. She tightened the muscles extending outwards from her spine. He began rubbing his trunk up and down the length of her body. His movements quickened and she felt a lump between his thighs. She whimpered.

Pop's head snapped up and he flipped his body into the ocean to swim further away from her and away from the coast.

Fearful that Pop would leave her stranded on the sea, she hollered after a time, "Sun's going down."

"Yes." Without looking at her, he caught hold of the rope and began pulling her and the mattress back to shore.

Once she could feel the sand bar with her hands, she jumped off the mattress and ran to their picnic spot and knotted the beach towel about herself.

Pop limped like an old man as he came dragging, sliding the rubber against the sand. He let the air escape and still not looking at his daughter, said, "Get dressed. I'm taking you home."

They rode in silence.

Pop's touching was wrong, but Jackie wasn't sure why. She could see the guilt lining his eyes. She wanted to touch him and tell him it was all right. But she feared she would only make things worse.

Pop was surely different; the person she knew had been scraped and scarred away.

A beam of light reflected off the side mirror and the image of Pop's hands moving along her body, juxtaposed with the image of him caressing Mother. It wasn't simply, as Pop's eyes had raced over her body, that "she was getting big." No, she was growing more like her mother.

"Look. Same eyes. Same nose. Same mouth."

In the dusk and the glow of the dashboard, she could see her father's legs shifting from time to time as he pumped gas and brakes. She could see the opening between his thighs, the recess of *his* secrets just as when he touched her breasts, she'd felt secrets of her own stirring. She was just like her mother. She pressed her head against the window and tried not to be sick. Watching the sun streak a dying red through the clouds, seeing the pale flicker of the headlights on the road, she doubted whether she would see her father again.

"Did you two have a good time?"

"Great." Pop put his arm about Jackie, squeezing her off-balance. "Yeah, great," she said, stumbling up the porch steps, wanting to hide herself in her room, and curl herself on the edge of the bed, facing the wall.

"We really had a good time," Pop echoed boisterously, bobbing, Jackie thought, like a Jack-in-the-box.

Twilight and screen wire made Mother appear like a pock-marked witch. Jackie could see Mother biting her lip at Pop's bright smile and at his hands as they clutched Jackie's shoulder, pulling her body into his chest.

"Yes, well, some of us had to work. We can't all go to the beach."

Jackie waited impatiently for her mother to snap the screen door lock and let her in. Moths were hovering about the light.

"Jackie, I thought you were supposed to clean your room before you went."

"I did. Didn't I?" Jackie remembered making her bed, stuffing her clothes in a closet corner, arranging her stuffed animals—sea lion, chipmunk, and bear on her dresser and making a straight line with her tennis shoes and patent leathers underneath her bed. Tonie must've dirtied her side of the room—torn her sheets back, littered her clothes, and tossed her animals against the wall. Tonie didn't like her any more than Mother did.

"Let her be, Barbara. We had a real fine time. Don't spoil it." Pop kissed the top of Jackie's head. "I missed my favorite girl. I miss my kids."

Jackie squirmed, feeling more uncomfortable with the way Mother looked at her than with Pop's scarred hands stroking her arms, massaging her neck. Jackie hated how Mother treated her and Tonie as rivals. If a man was around, Mother wanted his attention. It didn't matter if the man was their father. Mother made it impossible to tickle him, cuddle him or kiss his cheek; whenever they got close, Mother would lure Pop away. Or, maybe, too, Mother was remembering five months ago when Jackie had begged to live with Pop. When Mother had hollered, "No," she'd flown out the door, wailing, intent on running all the way to Pittsburgh to live with her Grandma—to the edge of the Earth, if she couldn't live with her Pop. She'd made it two blocks before Pop tackled her on slippery grass, rasping furiously, "Daughters belong with their mothers." She'd screamed, "I hate her. I hate her" and beat at him with her fists as he dragged, half carried her back to the house at 2:00 A.M. while neighbors cursed, poking their heads out windows. Mother didn't forget.

"You look sunburned, Jim." Mother was smiling. "You want a drink before you go? I've even got beer." She unhooked the latch. Jackie ducked inside, asking, "Where's Tonie?"

"Out." Mother sashayed towards the kitchen.

"Tonie could've waited to see me. She could've stayed and said hello." Pop was whining, feeling sorry for himself.

"Here's your beer."

"She could've at least gone to the beach. She could show some respect. Good thing Jackie loves me." Pop was gripping Jackie's hand, pulling her back beside him. Words slurring, his legs off-balance, it was as if he were already drunk.

"Yes. It is, isn't it."

Jackie trembled. Pop's face was pressed nose to nose with hers.

"You know, Barbara. Jackie looks just like you. Only younger. It's amazing, isn't it?"

"Amazing." Mother sipped her beer. "Jackie, I think you should clean your room."

Jackie cocked her head. Hair down, wearing black stretch pants, a white blouse with a scooped neck, gold hoop earrings and Chanel No. 5, Mother was beautiful. But to Jackie, it was a disguise. Mother dressed pretty to get things.

"Stay awhile, Jim. We can talk. About whatever you want." She laid a hand on his shoulder. Beer on his chin, Pop beamed. Slicking down his hair, slapping his chest, he felt proud because his soon-to-be-ex-wife had invited him in.

"I'll stay here. I'll clean my room after Pop's gone." Jackie plopped down on the sofa, her wet bathing suit soaking through her towel and onto her lap.

Mother warned, "Suit yourself," then, brilliantly smiled, "Have another beer, Jim."

"Sure, Barbara. Fine." His hands were tightening on another bottle, holding it reverently like it was a peace offering between them.

"The ferris wheel was nice." Jackie chattered. "It wasn't a ferris wheel. Not really. It spun up and down as well as around and round. But still it was nice."

"How exciting, Jim," whispered Mother.

Jackie felt trapped. Mother was going to do something terrible. It was black outside and in the artificial light, Mother overwhelmed the room, dwarfing Pop. Mother was touching Pop's fingers, murmuring how hard things had been, encouraging him to drink his beer.

Jackie winced at Pop's breathing. It was the same cracked, rasping sound she'd heard when he'd tumbled her on the grass after she tried to run away, when he laid full-length on top of her, rubbing his body against hers while floating on the ocean.

"There hasn't been anyone else, Barbara. No one else." Pop had forgotten she was there. He was swelling between his legs again, the mound jerking sporadically upwards. Jackie was disgusted. Did Pop think Mother wanted him back—the same woman who'd jabbed at him with a butcher knife, yelling "bastard," "fucker," "shit?" The same woman he'd called "slut" and threatened with his fist? Jackie, curled on this very same couch, had heard and seen them arguing. Now Mother was caressing Pop's hair, leaning close and murmuring.

Pop grabbed Mother's arms. His mouth covered hers. Jackie could tell Mother didn't like it. Her head was angled slightly back, her feet didn't step toward him, and her hands remained at her sides.

"We need to talk, Barbara."

"Yes." Her smile was dazzling. "In private." She pulled at his hand, leading him toward their old bedroom door.

"Jackie," Mother called sweetly. "Your dinner's on the stove."

Jackie lifted her head and tried to look blank. Pop was looking at Mother's chest. Mother was looking at her.

"She looks just like me. Doesn't she?"

"Yes," said Pop, leading, tugging Mother into the bedroom.

Jackie stepped onto the porch. It was cool and hazy. Street lamps were on. She couldn't see any stars. She barely saw the moon's slim arc. She imagined having wings, flying high until she could rest in the cradle of the moon. Feet dangling, she'd revel in silence. Like a carnival ride, she'd watch the Earth circle and spin, and count if anybody fell. She suspected people fell all the time but nobody saw. She turned off the porch light and the glow from the fireflies grew brighter. The moths flew away.

She touched her breasts. Did it matter if they felt ticklish or if she felt tremors while rubbing her hand hard between her thighs? Sitting on the step, she collapsed her torso over her knees. She could feel her chest expanding, her breath streaming around her calves. She gripped her ankles. Four and a half more years, she'd be eighteen. She wouldn't look like Barbara. She'd look like Jackie.

Twisting her head to the left, she saw upside-down houses. Dull, yellow lights flooded out of windows. If she stilled her breathing, her senses seemed more alive. She could smell boiling potatoes, chicken cackling in oil, and melted Velveeta over greens. She could hear talk—parents complaining about work, not enough money, and kids lamenting the end of summer. Everyone had plans for the Labor Day vacation. Next door she could hear Charles jabbering about fishing and his mother's joyful talk about harvesting her garden. Across the street, framed by a gingerbread window, the Jacksons were sitting down to dinner. Mother, Father, two little kids. They were holding hands and saying grace. Jackie expelled air, uncurling her body until she sat tall.

She was hungry. She should go inside and eat. But Jackie didn't move. A firefly, its wings spread, its ribbed body pulsing, landed on her thigh. It glowed six times, crawling boldly over her skin. Its light was cool. Jackie smiled. The firefly leapt from her knee and caught itself mid-air. Then, it turned, swooping low past her head, then up and up it went, blinking a message. Jackie blew a fine air stream from between pursed lips. The firefly soared.

She knew it was searching for stars.

ESMERALDA RIBEIRO

KEEP A SECRET

Dᴇᴀʀ Mᴀᴅᴀᴍ:

I was surprised to receive your letter asking me about Grandma. How did you get my address? I came here after witnessing that scene. Here no one knows who I am, but, even so, I am stunned. Yes, that is the right word, stunned. Insomnia pursues me. You know, strange things happened while I lived in that house. "The man who asked to come back" was the last thing that Grandma said.

Everything began when I, Papa, and Mama were thrown out of our little apartment in Rio de Janeiro. We used to live on the Rua Major Mascarenhas in the Todos os Santos neighborhood. I must have been about eleven years old at that time. Although Mama was the only daughter of Grandma, the two of them were bad tempered when they were together, and they fought endlessly. Since Papa adored Grandma, they were obligated to live with Papa's brother. Grandma's house was old. Strangely, I never had noticed that detail. I realized this when I went to live there. It was in the morning; a fine rain was falling. That day I walked to her house. I wanted to feel the fine rain falling on my face. I took less than an hour to arrive there. I carried just a school backpack with me and a small bundle of clothes. When I went to open the gate, it was barred and padlocked. I don't remember how many times I called for Grandma. Standing there outside, I observed the architecture of the house. The gate and the outside wall were of wood and quite high. The walls of concrete were also high. The ample windows had curtains. The curtains must have been very heavy since they were all closed. As I circled around the house, I counted the windows. One was for each room. At

---

Translated by Carolyn Richardson Durham.

some moments, I could swear that I heard sounds coming from one of the rooms. Conversations, laughter, and a click, click, click. But I clapped my hands forcefully, called and shouted, and there was no response. I think that my voice was lost among the leaves of that jaboticaba tree, because when I tried to spy through the vent in the gate, the leaves on the tree were shaking ceaselessly. I looked from here to there. Suddenly another woman emerged there on the corner. My joy ended then. It seemed that it wasn't Grandma Olivia. She was the same color, her face also without a wrinkle, thin and short, and hair of cotton. The difference between the two was the eyeglasses. The firmness and assurance in the walk of that woman alleviated a little of my anguish. I was very involved in the slow dance of life and, before I realized it, she was passing before me, muttering something. Perhaps she was talking to herself. My eyes were glued to that woman. From then on strange things began to happen. When I turned around, Grandma Olivia was standing right there. With fright, I fell back with the backpack and the bundle of clothes. I recomposed myself. I didn't manage to speculate because she had delayed so long in attending to me. She smiled and said, "I was waiting for you. Come in." I continued with the backpack and the bundle in my hands. She had said that as if she already knew about our getting thrown out. As if she were always watching us. We walked.

"Can we visit, Grandma?" I asked.

"No. *He* already left," she answered.

"How did *he* leave, if the only exit was through the gate?" I insisted. She gave a pause, made a noise, and retorted, "Look, don't annoy me." I looked with my eyes, but I didn't find him. They had the same temperament. Mama was also firm and authoritarian. And Grandma didn't respond. Silence prevailed at that moment. The kitchen and the bedroom were clean and neat. It seemed that she was always alone. We hardly used the kitchen and the bedroom. Because of the immensity of the rooms, we used to whisper in order to avoid an echo. The other rooms of the house were abandoned. No, not so abandoned. Grandma used to keep some secret, over there by the household goods because they were locked up. She went with the ring of keys in her pocket and didn't put them away even in order to sleep. I thought that this attitude was strange, but if I asked her, with certainty she would say, "Don't annoy me." She always said that sentence. One day we agreed, another day we didn't. I swept and waxed the floors in two rooms and cleaned the bathroom. I didn't clean the backyard because it was always covered by the leaves and flowers of the trees. After cleaning I took care of the garden, picked some mangoes, and played on the seesaw. I played alone. Alone no. A man always appeared for us to play with. He emerged and also vanished suddenly. We seemed old acquaintances. "Who is he?" I thought. Grandma Olivia was sewing a quilt with scraps of cloth. She sewed stitch by stitch. I am not certain, but I never saw the quilt finished.

Once, while cleaning a room, I saw, very high on the wall, a little picture. Despite being covered with dust, I recognized the same hair, face, and jacket as the man who played in the backyard. Grandma was in the bathroom. Then I took advantage of the opportunity and stood on a chair, but when I reached out my hand to take the picture and see it better, I only managed to read the initials L. B. I hit my body on the platter decorated with grapes hanging a little lower. The porcelain smashed on the floor. Grandma cried and fussed at me so much because of the incident. After that I went to take care of my duties and went to play outside as was my custom. I didn't say the window of our room was facing the backyard. Since we slept in the same area, we managed to raise the window half-way. But when I looked in there, in the place where Grandma was sewing on a little table, I saw the same man in the picture that used to play with me. He was typing something hurriedly. I saw through the window, he was conversing and laughing by himself. I went to look through the room and I didn't see her. I went running there. Meanwhile, when I arrived, Grandma Olivia was sewing her scraps. I shouted, I don't know how many times, her name. But her voice came out low and restrained, "What is it, child?" Perhaps it was an impression, but she had the same smile on her face as that man.

"Who is the man in the picture, Grandma?" I asked.

"He was the most important person for me. His name was Lima Barreto," she responded, with a voice loaded with emotion.

I took advantage of her mood and bombarded her with questions. "Why haven't you ever said this before? Why does he still come to our house?"

She was processing a question at a time. She made a noise. When she was going to answer, a telegram arrived saying that Mama had become sick, and we raced to the hospital. The two of us usually didn't go to anyone's house. Despite Papa's having lost his job as a mailman due to the financial crisis, which made him very sick, he appeared once in a while in order to visit us. We found out about Mama through Papa.

The years were passing by, I was seventeen years old, but my body seemed like that of a woman. I was studying in the afternoon at the National High School, and the twilight was coming. Once when I was returning from school, that young man appeared in front of me.

We conversed for hours and hours. After a few days, we began to fall in love. Casey Jones used gel on his hair and he was well dressed. We went to luncheonettes and bars. He lived in a middle-class neighborhood in Rio de Janeiro, however, I didn't believe it when they told me that he didn't like to work. I didn't love him, but I couldn't manage to resist all that charm. There were days and weeks that I didn't attend classes. I didn't comment to Grandma about my romance, but I think that she already knew. One morning she said to me, "How is Casey Jones?" I became scared and I didn't answer her. She also didn't insist. However I still wasn't able to understand it.

I will never forget that day because everything happened so rapidly. It was All Saint's Day. It began in the morning, when we were having tea. Grandma was totally absorbed. She was like that for minutes, a half hour, I don't know. Her body was there without her soul. Her hands slowly turned her cup at her mouth. First her lips gave the impression of pronouncing sentences, very softly, then she opened her mouth in order to swallow the liquid. She had never noticed, she no longer firmly controlled her movements.

"What is wrong with you today, Grandma?" I asked.

"Today is D-Day," she responded.

"What?" I insisted.

"I like death because it is the annihilation of all of us," she said.

She said all these things without looking at me. Trying to understand all that, I was distracted. When I looked, it was time to go to school. I put on my backpack and ran to school. There was a fine, minute rainfall. That day I walked to school. It was nice to feel the drizzle falling on my face. Just that day, there was no school. I took advantage and went to look for some things that Mama had bought for me. I showed up with a bundle of clothes. When I returned to Grandma's house, I was questioned by a fat lady. She looked a lot like Casey Jones. She crossed my path and stood in front of me. She insulted me so much! . . . She said horrible things of this type, "You are the fifth black girl that my son deflowered and you are not going to be with him. At this very moment he is with another girl." In addition to other absurdities, she spit on me, and I spit on her, too. I hated that woman and her beloved son. Everyone knew that I could not see my own family. It couldn't be worse. Then I went to the market and I bought a knife. I didn't take anything, I had more than enough courage. I looked for the unfortunate one like a crazy woman. I found them in the lobby of a little hotel. She fled, but he didn't have time to react. There were so many knife wounds! I stopped when he fell at my feet. I also pulled a golden necklace from his throat. I put the knife in the bundle of clothes and left tranquilly. It took less than an hour to arrive at Grandma's house. It was there that I saw it, I am certain. The living room, before bolted with a key, was open. I heard a click, click, click. I entered through the kitchen, passed through the bedroom, and stopped in front of the living room door. I shouted, called Grandma. I was entering, and I heard Lima Barreto writing at the typewriter. We conversed and laughed a lot. For a moment, I swear I heard him say, "We were waiting for you. Come in." I was thinking, "Everything is happening at the same time."

"You killed Casey Jones," he interrupted my daydream.

"I killed him," I responded. "How did he know about it?" I asked myself.

"Bravo! That was the other end that I wanted for the lowdown Casey Jones."

The writer pulled the paper from the typewriter, tore it up into little pieces, and threw it in the garbage. He looked at Grandma and said, "Thank you. I thank you eternally." Then Grandma Olivia said this, "You have to be like that, my grand-daughter," and continued, "We don't have to accept destiny with resignation." I stood, looking at the two of them. Grandma continued, "It's not my fault, it was he who asked to come back."

"How did he return?" I asked quickly.

She made a noise, muttered to herself. When she was going to answer me, we heard the noise of a siren, pretty far from here. Someone ordered, "Go hide the knife at the foot of the jaboticaba! Hurry up." I was very nervous, but I went.

When I returned, they hadn't found him. I saw a skull near the shelf. A white thing, almost the size of the living room, came above me. I don't know how I managed to escape. There was only time to leave the area and bar the door. I had to leave that house rapidly. I was calling for Grandma; I was shouting, shouting, and she didn't hear me. A voice was singing in the kitchen. Each time that I called, the song got louder. I wasn't sure, but I felt the walls vibrate. I ran, I ran, when I arrived at the corner, I perceived that I had left my backpack and the bundle of clothes there in the living room. After that day, I never returned to that house. I never knew more of Grandma Olivia. I know that the swing and the seesaw still exist, despite the vegetation that has taken over everything.

I am very afraid. Insomnia follows me. Here where I live, no one knows about this. I changed my name.

Thank you for writing. It was better to have told this to someone.

I don't know how you managed to find me. But, please,

keep this secret forever.

A S T R I D   R O E M E R

THE INHERITANCE
OF MY FATHER:
A STORY FOR LISTENING

*O*N A PINE WORKTABLE *lies a yellowed photograph, two wrinkled airplane tickets, several airmail envelopes, letters, and a stamp album. There is also a red Walkman with several cassettes next to it. A black tape recorder is set to record. The child of a mother who will be forty tomorrow begins to speak out loud.*

Before the summer vacation of this year, I had never seen my grandma. Yet I knew exactly what she looked like, from a photograph, of course.

In the picture, she wears a huge, wide skirt almost to her feet, made of very stiff material that stands straight out. Around her head, she wears a scarf with pointed corners made of the same material as the jacket. Her neck is covered with necklaces. Many bracelets decorate her arms. With her glasses and a twig of flowers in her hand, my grandma looks just beautiful—always smiling, in a frame on the television.

I also know my grandma from the letters she writes. Once a month an envelope with beautiful stamps drops onto the floor in our hall. The stamps are for my album, and later, my mother says, I may also have the letter. She always reads the letter out loud. There is always something for me in the letter. Then my grandma wants to know how I am—in grammar school and in Sunday school. And she

Translated by Hilda van Neck-Yoder.

always writes, that, in the picture, I look just like my father, and how much she longs to see me.

That is what she always tells me when my mother calls her: "Bonkoro my half-breed, I would love to see you yet before I die." And then she starts to talk slowly in a language I cannot understand and then she suddenly cries. It always goes like that. Then I give the telephone back to Mama. Then she begins to talk loud and fast. Sometimes Mama cries too.

I think that Grandma does not like it that we live so far away from each other. We live a plane trip of nine hours and almost three thousand guilders per person away from each other. And that is terribly far away, you know.

One night I wake up and hear my father talk real loud in a language he always uses when he is excited. Because I do not hear the voice of my mother, I go to the living room. Papa is on the phone, naked, and Mama is on the couch in her night-shirt, with a cigarette. Quietly, I sit down next to her and together we look at my father. I can see him clearly in the dark even though his skin is almost black. His upper body is long and his legs are bony and thin, just like mine. He has no mustache and no beard, and I know that he has invisible curly hairs on his chest and arms. That is what I was thinking while I sat next to Mama and felt how tightly she pressed me to her.

I do not know why he suddenly threw down the phone and with long strides sat down next to us—in silence. I do not think that he had seen me, for suddenly he looked at me, shocked. I remember that I looked down immediately and became a little afraid. I had never seen him naked and I was embarrassed. He too. He got up, left, and returned in his housecoat and turned on the lights. It was almost three o'clock in the morning.

"My mother is going to be eighty years old this summer and she especially wants to see you."

He talked and he talked, a little rough, and my heart pounded terribly. I believe my body trembled too. Not that I was shocked, but my father had never talked with me about the country of his birth in a way that made me sad.

While he was talking like that, Mama became very quiet as if she were no longer there. First Papa looked only at me, but then he talked, looking at the floor, and suddenly he stood up, with his back to us telling us how much he loved his country. He said: "Every time I see you, my child, I miss my mother in a way that tears my heart apart."

Then Mama began to cry real loud, and I became even more nervous. In the middle of the night they started to quarrel, and it was frightening: Mama kept getting redder and redder, and Papa turned blacker and blacker. I screamed that they should stop: Otherwise I would leave them and never come back. It seemed as if I was the cause of everything—everything.

After that night I began to think about everything, about who my parents were, about my mother, about where my father is from, about what I am, about who we are together. Often it makes me sick. It is as if I have to throw up but cannot. When we three are eating, I look carefully at the people who are my parents and then it starts. Then I hate rice and cauliflower and how Mama talks to Papa and how Papa looks at Mama. Then I hate meat and fish and how they worry about my appetite.

Then I hope that some day I will puke so much that the whole table and their faces will be covered with the mess. In bed, I keep wondering why my father had not just stayed in his own country—then he would never have met my mother; then I would not be there. And I would not have all that fuss from my mother's family, of how brown I am, and how blond I am becoming.

Because those two could not care less about that, their own fights are loaded with the nasty words that people yell at me in the street—honky, nigger, and the whole alphabet of insults. That is why I never complain to them about what happens to me outside; like lumps of oatmeal I keep swallowing all this teasing, bah!

But that night made everything worse. I really understood what my father meant when he said that he has been living here for twenty years and that he has married a woman of this country and that his child is born here but that they still want him to return to the land of his birth—as soon as possible. And after that night I am ashamed to be the child of a woman with blond hair and grey eyes and a voice that sounds just like that of people who are not black. Believe me, I longed for a mother with a scarf on her head and a skin so dark that I never would have to be afraid at night again that the sun would ever burn me.

A musical instrument is taken out of a drawer of the pine worktable, also some pages of sheet music. The volume of the tape recorder is adjusted. The child of the mother who will be forty tomorrow begins to play the flute with her eyes wide open— so that the frightening dreams mask themselves as a fairy tale.

In a country where the sun is so close that everyone can touch it, in a country where everything is green, and the corn constantly waves to the heavens, in a country where pumpkins glitter like clumps of gold on the ground, in a country where the wind awakes the morning with giggles and the rain hums the night to sleep, in a land where clothes are made of pieces of cloud and jewelry of drops of stars, in a country where beetles, donkeys, elephants, lions, rhinoceroses, serpents, hawks, dolphins, and herrings crawl over each other around everywhere and no one, no one knows who all this belongs to and how that all came about—in that country lives a young girl in a place that even the wind cannot reach. She has no name—she has no family—and she was so full of life that even the bees and ants admired her. Boys daydreamed about her. Men stayed in love with her. Girls wanted to know her. Women talked all the time about a voice whose song could destroy unhappiness and happiness—because the girl had a voice! When her songs sounded over the valley, the wind encircled the trees to keep the leaves from moving and the water no longer ran in the rivers—it danced. As soon as a child could not sleep, its mother would hum the song of the girl; as soon as a man and a woman got into a fight over who was boss, their children would begin to sing the song of the girl; even when someone had died, people would sing her song around the grave.

One day, the people of the country were startled by a curious sound. Everyone kept very quiet and although it was incredibly early in the morning, the chickens did not cluck and the birds did not chirp. Everyone listened to the deafening gargle as if hundreds of giants were rinsing their throats.

Just as suddenly as the sound appeared, it disappeared. Children, women, men—they threw themselves again into the bustle of the day with a hug here and a snarl there. Only the girl kept waiting, living in a spot that even the wind could not reach. She knew that that sound was the sorrowful song of the mountains. The earth was about to explode and mudslides would cover everything.

Because the mountains began to bray more threateningly, people became afraid. They knew the earth could suck in their lovely country so that afterwards no one would know what lay under the boiling mud. That is why they went to the girl who could subdue the wind with her voice and keep the waters in check. They took her along and left her alone with her songs at the foot of the mountains. And the girl sang. And the mountains became quiet. And she sang and she sang without noticing that she slowly changed into a mountain. When she realized what had happened, she screamed so loudly that the earth tore open. Hundreds of butterflies burst out, flashing like fireworks. Like shells covering the beach, the butterflies attached themselves to the land.

This dream did not always end so full of color. Sometimes instead of butterflies, loads of mud burst out of the earth. Then my screams would awaken my parents, and my arms would flay about as if wasps were attacking me. Mama would bring me sugar water to drink, and Papa would ask me to cut out the stories about the land of his birth. But I kept on dreaming—the dream became a fairy-tale garden in which I found myself more and more. With every thing I did, I kept thinking of the mountains, of the greenery, the butterflies, and the girl without a name. I was unfriendly, cold, short. I ate poorly and I slept badly.

Slowly it dawned on my parents that I wanted to go to my Grandma for almost three thousand guilders and a nine-hour flight.

The weeks just went by. The airmail became more urgent; more and more the telephone rang in the night.

My mother was the first to give in; I was allowed to go with or without my father to the birthday of my Grandma. She would stay home. She did not want to run the risk of being treated like an undesirable stranger in his country or by his family. There were dreadful discussions between my parents, sometimes even in the car in the middle of a traffic jam. For me the days of insecurity became days of exuberance. Days of pain followed when Mama began to pack my suitcase with much care. Never had I spent a summer without her.

At first it felt weird to be sitting alone with my father in the airplane. He looked truly handsome in his light summer suit. Moreover, he had not dyed his grey hair black because Mama had asked him not to. She had driven us to the airport and had said a friendly goodbye, long before it was time to go to the departure hall. It had hurt to see her walk away alone, not turning around again, disappearing among the people. Goodbye Mom, my eyes said, while my hand grasped my father's—come along Dad! I knew that we were flying away from the country of my mother and—to rid me of my frightening dreams—toward the country of my father. With a head full of plans and all wound up because almost everyone on the plane had plenty of pigment—and because of how they talked and laughed, joked and played—I saw that my father cried when the plane took off. In between sleeping and being awake, I listened to pieces of conversation that I did not understand. Almost everyone spoke in their own language. Only my father's baritone sounded familiar. Moreover, via my Walkman, I heard my mother say: "My darling, whatever you may experience in your fatherland, do not forget that there is also a woman who has given you a motherland!"

I decided to become a pilot—taking off, flying-flying, descending, from country to country, touching the earth and slicing the sky—north, south, east, west.

Next to the pine worktable is a large kit. It has to become a passenger plane. The hands that hold the recorder now pick up the kit. The stop button is being pushed in. Just a few moments for some dreams about the future. Just a moment. Tomorrow a mother is turning forty and her present has to be revealing. The child pushes the stop button back out.

I do not remember much about the first days in the country of my father's birth. It is as if so much happened at the same time that I barely can retain anything—like a dizzying ride in a race car at the fair.

The whole family had come out to get us. And there were so many kinds of faces of so many kinds of races with so many kinds of voices in so many kinds of languages and of all ages and sizes. This welcome took days, and for days I did little but mumble my name and gasp for air whenever I would disappear in an embrace.

But the dream about the earth bursting with butterflies and about mountains spitting mud did not return. And when my mother called Papa and me after one week, we could at least tell her that I did not wake up screaming at night anymore. The opposite: Dead tired, I would fall asleep early in the evening, and my father had trouble getting me out of bed in the morning before breakfast.

We were staying in a large hotel. There was a bar and also a swimming pool. And there was a strange shopping center. There was also an underground garage where the car was that my father had rented. But a day would fly by so quickly that neither the bar nor the swimming pool nor the shopping center would notice us. Already at breakfast Papa would be picked up and we would be driven to different faces once more. And the fun they always had together—my father and his friends and his relatives! But he would never lose sight of me; I always had to sit next to him. And with an arm around my shoulders he would explain to everyone who wanted to hear that he had returned to the country of his birth especially to give me a chance to really learn to know him. Then everyone would be silent for awhile until he would raise his glass and pronounce: "For thirty years my heart has remained in this country, amen!"

One night I awoke bathed in sweat. I had dreamed about mountains that threw up wasps and that I had to run away real fast because they were buzzing after me. It was cool in the room and the sound of the ventilator was irritating. I got up to turn it off and to get a drink of water when I discovered that my father was not in his bed: It was quarter to one in the morning.

I quietly took a shower, got dressed nicely and took the elevator to the bar. Immediately I saw him, sitting there, not on a barstool like most of the men, but at a table—with candlelight. With him was a woman. They were looking at each other, and I believe they did not say anything. They only stared and remained silent.

Frozen, I stopped in my tracks and did not know what to do. To return to my room was impossible because I had accidentally locked the door. And my father and the woman were so incredibly beautiful together that I could not keep my eyes off them—ach, ach. He let her drink from his wine glass, and she took his hands by the wrists, and they got up slowly and started to dance. There were other people dancing by the bar, but everyone turned around when my father put his arms completely around the woman. Silently and passionately, they moved with the music. With my heart throbbing in my throat I watched until they danced away.

Then I ran, first to the swimming pool, then to the bathroom. But because there were too many people I sneaked into the restaurant. I sat down at the table where we always have breakfast. I wanted to call to Mama, really. But when I opened my mouth there was a wave of warmth—puke on the white table cloth, puke on the plates. And suddenly everywhere the voice of my Grandma: "Bonkoro, I want to see you so badly before I die."

My God, when I saw my father again, I was lying in a strange bed. A friend of Papa, who everyone called "datra," stood next to my bed. She was wearing a doctor's coat and wiped my face with something wet.

"I want to go away!" I kept yelling, and I realized that I was crying. My father asked "datra" to leave us alone. Shaking her head, she left. Then I really let my tears come; my body shook with sobs, but I did not dare tell what I had seen that night. I kept looking at my father; I did not mention my mother. I hoped that he would understand that it was he who had to tell me something. But he kept silent-silent and only tried to hold my hand. I kept pulling my hand away; I was beginning to loathe him.

All those quarrels with my mother and all those letters from Grandma were about something that I slowly began to understand. And I knew then for the first time that it certainly had a whole lot to do with me.

When he started to talk he talked to me like a spoiled child. He promised me all kinds of things: airplane trips to Indian villages, boat trips to waterfalls, camping among the Maroons. But that caused me to gag again, and so the doctor had to come again with her wet cloths, and my father had to stand at the end of my bed again—watching. Ach-ach, I could see from his eyes that he did not understand why I begged him not to leave me for a moment.

There I was, as they say, in my father's country, in a hospital bed recuperating from what everyone called "adjustment problems." For the rest of our vacation I was not allowed to drink water from the tap, and of course no lemonade or fruit juices. And what was definitely worse: I was subjected to a tasteless diet. Furious, I listened to all that, and staring straight ahead of me I nodded in agreement. After all, I was almost thirteen—sensible enough to take the opinion of adults into consideration. Moreover, all that throwing up had weakened me considerably. And everything-everything had disturbed the intimacy with which my father and I had begun our journey.

There I was, just lying in a room listening to my Walkman, and he was just sitting there with his nose in a magazine.

But what I am going to say now, I know as well as the nose on my face. It is as if I made it up, but believe me it happened just like that.

Listen—my father falls asleep with his head a little to the right, the paper in his lap, the magazine on the floor, really snoring. I am leaning against some pillows in bed, and I am just rewinding the tape to listen to my mother saying, "My darling, whatever you may experience in your fatherland, do not forget that there is also a woman who has given you a motherland!"

I hear my mother's voice clearly, and I see my father's face clearly, and I wonder why we still have not gone to Grandma. Suddenly the door swings open and there she is—my Grandma. She is dressed just like in the picture on top of the television—only she is leaning on a cane. Her skin color is even blacker than that of my father, and she has dull grey hair, frizzy at the temples.

One step at a time she approaches. Her cane makes a regular ticking sound, but it is as if my heart is throbbing. Beside my father she stands still. She bends a little to have a good look at my father's face; she only does that for a moment while her cheeks are trembling vehemently. Then very softly she calls his name and Papa wakes up, startled. His chair falls, and he lets it lie to look at his mother with the same look, the same trembling cheeks.

That took much too long—really, much too long. Finally he said, "Ma, you could have waited until I was ready to come and see you." But his mother turned around and commanded: "Boy, tell the doctor that the child is going with us—right now."

Above the pine worktable is a bulletin board. The child of the mother who is going to be forty tomorrow looks at the eyes of Michael Jackson, at the breasts of Madonna,

past the clothes of Prince. Suddenly, she rips the poster in the middle from the board.
On this spot she puts a postcard of an Aucaner woman. The woman smiles to the pho-
tographer.

My Grandma does not live in the city. She lives along a kind of country road—
miles and miles outside the capital. The rented car of my father could not even get
to her house. Walking and dragging our suitcases, we reached the house; it is built
on knee-high stone corbels, is made of wood, and on the outside it looks old and
weathered. Around the house everything is real green: trees, bushes, grass. And
dogs—she has too many. A red stairway took us into the living room full of shiny
furniture, copperwork and the air of ripening bananas. I saw them hanging on a
hook in the kitchen—in bunches.

An ancient man who lives with her shook our hand silently; his eyes glittered behind his bushy eyebrows. There were several fat women sitting on their haunches,
and a man with dreadlocks brought our luggage to a bedroom.

My father did not say much; he listened and smiled, nodding from one to the
other. The women wanted to embrace him, and he allowed that, laughing loudly.
I was sitting on his lap; my anger had actually almost disappeared. Nobody talked
to me. They talked about me and looked at me. When Grandma finally sat down
with us she did not wear her scarf. She was dressed like a lot of the women I had
seen—a cotton dress and a small belt. Her legs were very thin, and her feet were
real skinny in her slippers. She had a potion for me to prevent fainting. She fed it
to me one spoon at a time. Willingly, I swallowed this because it did not taste bad
and smelled like her—like fruit. Ach-ach, I immediately loved her, so totally different from my Grandma in my mother's country. And only after a night together with her would the first day in the land of my father's birth begin.

Ouma, as everyone called her, thought that I had the look of somebody wise
enough to know what the adults were discussing. She did away with my father's
objection by saying: "Everything that our eye looks at on this plantation and
everything our ear hears on this plantation and everything our hand touches on
this plantation is my grandchild's, and therefore my grandchild has to learn our
secrets as well."

After she said that, I went for walks early in the morning to survey the estate.
But neither my eye nor my ear nor my hands could reach far enough to know
what Ouma meant. However, I really felt wealthy—a large landowner—and I sent
a postcard to my mother with a noble title in front of my name—as a joke, of
course!

Henri, as she called my father, walked around the whole day in miserable, short
pants—barefoot. He did all kinds of jobs for his mother. After a few days, with his
beard and mustache, he looked as wild as all the other men. Ach, how wonderful
it was to take a bath in the afternoon with buckets full of ice-cold well water, to
eat hot meals with so many people out in the fresh air, to listen to each other's stories, to sleep on the wooden floor.

Far too often I was thinking about my mother and how she would really have enjoyed this—just like me, she was crazy about the wilderness. Finally I realized what had brought her and my father together, even though it remained hard to figure out that they stayed married because of me. But there was not much time to worry. Ouma's eightieth birthday was coming, and that is the reason I had flown to this country. Therefore no one heard me complain about frightening dreams, about feeling sick, and about my parents. Everyone saw me walking around singing loudly, along with my Walkman. Ouma toned down the excitement of the people around her. On the day of her birth, she only wanted to have a church service and some live music. No dancing, no masses of people. The kitchen should be well provided but not overflowing. Also they should prepare for a lawyer to come to the house and for a special medicine man.

Because she was used to having her orders followed precisely, she quietly went around the house doing her own things the week of her birthday—as if there was nothing special happening. As long as they did not bother her, those that loved her were allowed to make preparations, and thus they fixed up the house on the outside and did some painting on the inside. Her girlfriends polished the wooden furniture even more, and the copperwork could compete with the sun.

During that time, my Grandma demanded all my attention. She showed me her koto-dresses, her jewelry, her Bibles, her money, and she said again-and-again that that would be mine—from now on. She noticed that I did not know what to do with my inheritance because she was still very much alive and because my father was her only child. But as soon as I started to talk about her son, she would silence me. I had to wait patiently for the presence of the lawyer and the medicine man. My father told me that the first one would come from the city, but that the medicine man had to travel for days before he would get to Ouma. And he, too, kept silent as soon as I started about the possessions of his mother.

On the pine worktable stands a wooden drum. It is an apinti-drum from a country that is nine-flight-hours and almost three-thousand-guilders-per-person away from here. She pulls the drum out with her legs. The gold-brown fingers of the child of the mother who will be forty tomorrow drum on the tightly drawn animal skin. Dark sounds well up. The recorder shuts off. The tape is being turned over to arouse the memories with fast drumming.

On a Thursday morning, four days before the celebration, the medicine man announced himself. With a following of three people he arrived on the estate of Ouma. His arrival created considerable excitement. The huts in which he and his helpers were going to stay had to be completed in a great hurry. Three of them were being covered with roofs made of palm leaves. One for him, one for his coworkers, and one for his hocus-pocus. My friend with dreadlocks explained that to me patiently and also why it would be better if I would stay away from the huts.

Therefore I took care of the dogs—washing, combing, feeding. And I was so busy doing that that I did not notice that they were constantly talking about me.

Until, Ouma called me one afternoon just after I had bathed. In the hut of the medicine man were my father and also Ouma's ancient friend. It was a strange get-together, but I was not afraid. Papa was there and my grandma, and even though I could not understand them—with them nothing could happen to me. I had to sit on a kind of bench and do exactly as the medicine man told me: Hold a gourd with water in the palm of my hand while my father talked to me and we looked at each other. At that moment I heard from the mouth of my father that he had to hand over his right to his inheritance because he had turned his back on his mother for almost thirty years, because he was married to a woman of another race, because he had no other descendants but me. My father spoke slowly, clearly, and quietly; he kept looking at me and his eyes looked terribly loving. I heard his mother choke back her tears.

That night we four ate a meal that the medicine man had prepared. I ate too much and too fast. Everyone had nodded to me encouragingly. I was even allowed to drink alcohol if I wanted to. My father poured me a little ginger wine. The medicine man constantly mumbled things I could never understand.

This event has attached itself to my memory as a mysterious experience—together with the secret of the plantation that my grandma revealed to me at the end of the dinner, without witnesses. It was a command that changed me from a child into an adult, from one moment to the next.

When the lawyer came on Saturday afternoon, I was therefore less tense. Even though I did not have to sign anything, he showed me the documents and read out loud with a melodious voice what the inheritance meant. My father had to sign for me because I was under age. After the papers had finally disappeared in big envelopes and the lawyer sealed some of these with a red seal, the champagne exploded.

I was being congratulated on my inheritance in all kinds of ways. Ouma and the people who were always with her sang to me about strength and wisdom—it made me so shy. Maybe it was the alcohol that flowed so generously that loosened their tongues. Ouma started to sing with a croaking voice. Giggling, Papa began to talk about his youth: Like in a poem, he began to describe the daughter of the minister whom he had loved so much that he left his mother and his country forever when her parents refused to give their daughter to the son of a common woman. I listened to him and became afraid when he suddenly did not laugh but burst out in tears, when he told how he had danced-and-danced with her, every night in the bar of the hotel. He got up and stood next to his mother and announced that he had wanted to marry a woman of his own people so badly and that he had wanted to give her dozens of heirs if only that miserable father of the woman of his dream had not constantly been waving the Bible at his daughter; after that, his hatred for everything that had to do with the church had only increased; he had missed his mother so much in all these years that all his dreams had been filled with pain.

Amen-Amen-Amen-Amen, everyone called around him and his mother kept singing with her eyes on her son—slowly and full of moaning.

Gulfs of tenderness, warm as blood, pushed through my whole body, when my papa came to me and lifted me up above his head and laid me down at the feet of his mother.

Everyone joined my grandma and the singing became more intense; happiness and sorrow had joined together.

Champagne sprayed on the floor. Glasses were filled. I heard how too many dogs cried.

The man who was going to lead the church service was small and lively. He was dressed in pearl white, just like Ouma who stared intensely in front of her. She was eighty years old now and was still alive—thank God. That was what I heard everyone say. For her that was not enough of a reason to invite guests and to be cheerful, she told me on that Monday morning.

The church service was intended to ask for a blessing on the covenant that was settled between Mrs. Helena, Mr. Henri, and their heir. That is the way the minister put it, and in a full voice he started to read the story of the prodigal son. Although there were more and more people and more and more flowers in the living room, I began to feel more and more alone. My father was sitting there with his head raised. He only looked at his mother and probably was not aware that the tears were running down his nose. He had shaved himself neatly and was very well dressed. I saw that many women could not keep their eyes off him during the service. None of them, however, was the woman with whom I had seen him dancing that night, so full of love.

Ach-ach, even though he does not really love my mother, my father at least loves his own mother and me, I consoled myself blubbering.

While everyone closed their eyes for prayer, I slipped outside. I walked on to the path along the estate that is mine. With every step I repeated the secret of its soil: Only the person who joins someone of the original African race will have a fertile life on this plantation because too much African blood still breathes in her soil.

On the road I met musicians with drums, laughing black men in native dress, and women who were dressed wondrously, carrying flowers to my grandma. Their husbands, in dark suits, were walking along humming.

Further-further I walked, against the stream of people, just to be alone. But I was not alone. In my thoughts an image of a woman grew: thick blond hair and deep-grey eyes—my own sweet-sweet mother. I suddenly longed for the smell of our house—furniture polish—and how Mama laughs, with her mouth open, and how she always-always waits for Papa with our evening dinner, and how she never-never goes visiting without Papa, and how she watches the news—smoking—and how she embroidered my sheets—with clovers. My thoughts of my mother were like crumbs of happiness that I stepped on with my own shoes as if they were firecrackers. Around me they exploded: Even if I had to suffer my whole long life, all my heart and all my body would belong to a black person—just like you Mama, Amen!

Chased by my own words and pursued by doubts, I ran back to the church service. Too many dogs of Ouma had followed me like friends.

On a pine worktable there is a yellowed picture, two wrinkled airplane tickets, several small envelopes, letters, and a stamp album. There is also a red Walkman with some tapes next to it. A black recorder is being turned off. The child of a mother who will be forty tomorrow begins to cry out loud. Luckily the present is finished.

ELIO RUIZ

THE LITTLE WHITE GIRL

for Claudia Chapou

IN THE BEGINNING, there was milk. From the fat and black teats of her milknurse, she sucked the sap that tinted the spirit with the color of the gods who know how to dance. Her ears awakened at the rhythm of the chants that always reflected the longing for the lost homeland. She learned to walk with her feet in contact with the earth, backbone straight and rump raised, as it must be in all women, creatures destined to support the heavy burdens of life.

With the passage of time she began to smell like those who fed her with their special foods: sweet potato; okra; four roll; boiled yucca with garlic, salt, and lemon; corn flour with fried pork skins; smoked root, black beans; fried *malanga*;[1] red jerked beef, burning, stinging; thick onion and garlic sauces, juices from the sugar cane; molasses; mashed *fufú,* made from plantain, neither green nor ripe, in between; guanábana, chayote, watermelon and melon; and other delicious things, carried for the first time to her mouth by hands that were the sum of all the tastes. Perhaps, for this reason, she grew lips that knew how to kiss.

Later she learned how to name things in two languages, without distinguishing any other difference than the odor that emanated from them. Only after smelling them did the words spring from her lips in Castilian or in Lucumí.[2] When she was

Translated by Sandra L. Dixon, who would like to express special thanks to Josélin Tovar.

1. This is a plant found on the island of Cuba. It is similar to a calla lily

2. Language brought to Cuba by slaves and used in Afro-Cuban religious ceremonies.

made aware that it disgusted Father that she spoke like the blacks, she kept their words for her secret dreams.

They used to call her by one name in the big house and another in the slave shanties. She played with the slaves' children as freely as animals while they weren't old enough to go to the plantation. One bad day, they were carried away also. Much later, there came from among them, other faces, looks, and voices: Those who would see her and say, "LITTLE WHITE MISSY,"[3] no longer simply "Missy" like before. And never more did they have the opportunity to play, except on Sundays and religious holidays, when, by Father's order, they were allowed to dance.

At that time, the drums sounded.

Father liked to see the blacks dance and he would get particularly excited watching the slave women. They would move their bellies, breasts, and hips, frenetically contracting the pelvis area to the rhythm of the percussion instruments made of wood, iron, and seeds inside gourds. The slaves played their instruments and danced until after sunset when the overseer took them back inside the shanties.

On those festival days, the father used to get drunk on alcohol and desires. At the peak of the celebrations, he would point out some of the slave girls. The overseers would set them apart to be taken to the stables. In time, their bellies would grow big and would give birth to pale creatures who would have the eyes and hair of albinos. For this reason, they were stigmatized as people without a color. Because of this, they were hated by their own mothers, and they hated one another. These slave girls demonstrated such fertility in bearing bastards, while his lawful wife was incapable of giving him an heir to his properties—a male heir who would carry on his illustrious surname. The father of the little girl bitterly acknowledged this, watching the increasing number of mulatto and quadroon offspring among his slaves.

In the face of her master's lewd amusements and orgies, inasmuch as he had not been a husband to her since Little Girl's birth, Mother closed herself up in her rooms in the big house repeating "Hail Marys," while Iyá, the African wetnurse with whom Little Girl spent the majority of her time, sang and danced to the Orishas, gods who went up into the head of a chosen person, staying there as long as the music played.

According to what Iyá affirmed, the Orishas themselves made the uncontrollable drums, cowbells, and *chequerés* sound. Their horses, as the possessed ones were called, sweated copiously, jumped about, fell on their knees, rolled around in the mud, climbed trees, flew, swallowed burning embers, and spat out truths with sounds from their innermost recesses, capable of passing through the time and distance that separated them from Africa.

It was something else when they had the *maní* dance. Those who were invited arrived from leagues around. They were, like Father, the owners of plantations,

3. In Cuba, this meant "Miss" or "Missy," a title of respect and endearment directed to employers by servants.

sugar mills, and numerous slaves from Trinidad Valley. Dressed in their best clothes and riding on brightly decorated saddles or in carriages, they had their house slaves, dressed in livery with white powdered wigs, accompany them. Behind them came the gladiators, chosen from among the best of their respective work forces; half-naked, shining bodies. Their limbs were tied with strips of cloth. There was hate in their gazes.

When everyone was gathered together and after the exchanges of respect, greetings, and offerings, and once the bets were made, they passed into the arena where the combat would take place. The *maní* was a slave fight, which, like almost all of the things that come from Africa, was carried on to the beat of the drum.

The owner of the farm introduced the mode of fighting to the death in the *maní*. Searching for great excitement, he armed the dancers with gauntlets and sticks. It was his favorite diversion, and he enjoyed the luxury of risking a piece—as they called the blacks—at the end of each harvest. A good *maní* dancer enjoyed the privilege of not going to the plantations. Rather, he would occupy himself with work within the farm itself and with healthily exercising his body. With the promise of freedom, if he won, he would assure that the master would win his own price many times over.

On one Three Kings' Day, Little Girl surprised everyone with her behavior.

By the decision of His Majesty, the King of Spain and the Overseas Viceroyalties, the sixth of January was an obligatory holiday for the Africans. They were permitted to dress in ritual garments and to name themselves after their kings and queens. They could hold council sessions. Early in the morning, they received gifts from their masters, and they were granted permission to play instruments, to dance, to sing, and to perform the stories of their "savage and infantile myths," as the masters, priests, and overseers were accustomed to saying.

On that memorable Three Kings' Day, from the rising of Olorun, the sun, which was magically awaited with chants and ceremonies, the drums sounded. It was almost sunset. From a crevice, Little Girl at certain times saw Father riding above the young chosen slave girl, hitting her with the whip; or counting his money time and time again until he was asleep.

She was nine years old. Following her nurse, she went to the Mount with the Africans. There they would celebrate farewell rites for Olorun. The only slaves who did not attend were those who considered themselves different because they were house slaves and they preferred the white people's Church before that of Ilé or the House of the Orishas; that is, the open country, the mount, or the kingdom of the spirits. There they cleansed their bodies with holy herbs.

Iyá belonged to the important dignified group, since she sang as a soloist and she had bright necklaces hung around her neck with *moforibale*. The necklaces were kept in earthen pitchers taken from the ground under a giant ceiba tree. The drummers, of whom there were three, occupied a distinguished place. They were presented with fruits, whiskey, and dried tobacco leaves that the participants placed before their sacred instruments.

Little Girl made every dance movement her own. The sound of the drums, prayer, and oath, petition in the Yoruba language. Feeling, in turn, outside of herself as well as inside of everything that vibrated, she suddenly suffered an explosion of something uncontrollable that made her move and whistle like the wind.

She ran in every direction and spoke an archaic language of visceral sounds. Only the most ancient one among the slaves recognized in those syllables the forgotten language of the people who arrived from the desert—at the beginning of time—to establish the Yoruba nation there in Africa.

She, woman and man at the same time, danced as had been seen few times before. And she arrived dancing at the big house, where she caused the crashing of a tornado. When Father tried to contain and trap her, she forced him back with her gaze. Mother, ashamed of her own offspring, locked herself in to pray. She said that she would only come out on God's orders.

Iyá immediately understood that Little Girl's being that way marked her as the legitimate descendant of Oyá Yansá, mistress of the cemetery and the great winds; and of Alafi Changó, King of Kings, the most virile of the Orishas, lord of music and fire. And so she found out how to treat her as was proper. She whispered *Lucumí* words and succeeded in calming her, spitting mouthfuls of water and honey into her face. She who was her wetnurse knew that things suddenly appearing not as they were was the way of the gods to say that Omó was endowed with the gift of being able to communicate directly with the dead. If her head was not cooled on time, she could go insane. With the authority of being the only one who understood the girl, Iyá asked the master for permission to carry her far away from the farm, under the pretext of calming her. She said that a walk through the valley, the vision of the blue profiles of the mountains, the leaves of the royal palms in the wind, would do her good. They left the place on a cart that the slave woman drove, calling the burros that were pulling it by name. They recognized her voice, having no need for reins.

They rode a long way and arrived at the cemetery. Three days and nights Little Girl remained there. Her soul filled up with a peace that was unknown before. It was in this way that Iyá confirmed that she was in the presence of a chosen one, born to be queen.

Nevertheless, on the ride back and without apparent reason, she again fell into a convulsive trance for days and weeks. Doctors who were sent for from very far away considered them symptoms of the holy illness, as it was called since Julius Caesar suffered from it. As a consequence, they recommended to the father not to disturb her so that the illness would not grow worse. With the decision, they allowed her to avoid the predetermined future of a white woman, which permitted her to fulfill her life as a black woman. She would dress, walk, laugh, sing and dance. She was as proud as a *Lucumí*. And she spent more time among them than among her own people, who, little by little, forgot her without understanding that they were losing her.

Thus did Doctor Barrera express it. He was brought into the case by a slaveholder from the surrounding areas. Recently arrived from Havana, he brought with him copies of his work about typical illnesses of slaves, thanks to which he enjoyed notoriety among illustrious landowners. That was not the case with the little girl's father. It was he who defined the problem with his daughter as the "sickness of the blacks"—since, in his career, throughout the width and breadth of the island, he saw similar behaviors in black people, without giving much importance to the latitude of their African origins. In his judgment, Little Girl was sick with nostalgia.

Consequently, he preferred to follow the instructions of his colleagues without success, leaving the patient to act and speak freely, while he observed her. His fear was that the said sickness of the blacks, called nostalgia, undermined the will to exist. He knew of slaves with the same symptoms who decided to throw themselves in water wells, convinced that in this way they would return to Africa.

Father listened to him seriously. Worried about his reputation, he promised the doctor of the slaves a large fee if he liberated his daughter from the horrid illness unworthy of her race, religion, and lineage. The doctor meditated a bit before committing himself. Finally, he took a copy of his work titled *Reflections,* turned to the chapter referring to the diagnosed illness, and read from it the prescription for treating the nostalgia.

"We will try to give her vegetable acids mixed with a somewhat small dose of potassium acid or calcinated salt from the lagoon of the fig tree." He stopped, raised his eyes from the page, his pupils sparkling, and continued. "Or of Glauber,[4] with all its students and families, with pure nitrate, the arcanum duplicated, either dissolved in orange juices or in teabags of *chicora, zerrajas, Cardo santo,*[5] and other related substances mixed with tamarind pulp or the spirit of sweet nitrate; and also we can treat her with the burning of vinegar or powder because these are the fumes of very compressed and flexible air, like the wise alchemists found out about, and which the well-versed philosophers in the material confirm."

Father gave the doctor a perplexed look, but after thinking about it for a while, he authorized him to try his remedies. Thus the doctor did it, in the face of the silent disapproval of Iyá, the same woman who had to put the water on to boil for the bad-smelling medicines. During the siesta, Iyá escaped from the big house to the nearby mount. There she began her secret war against the white warlock.

There were four weeks of comings and goings of both people around Little Girl, who far from getting better to the eyes of the author of her days, seemed to grow worse. No matter how much they did for her or didn't do for her, she was delirious. Finally, she did not even wish to put on the expensive dresses that had been brought to her from Europe, but was set on dressing in coarse clothing and going about barefoot like a black woman of the plantation work force.

---

4. Named for the German doctor and chemist who discovered the use of salt sulphate (Glauber salt) as a purgative.

5. A medicinal plant used as a narcotic.

Fearful of allowing comments about the strange case of his daughter that flew to the city of Trinidad and crossed the sea in ships that went to the port of Casilda and that of Veracruz, the city where a newsletter published the news, Father dismissed Dr. Barrera, inadequately paying him for his efforts. Immediately, he decided that the matter was not to be spoken about anymore. If his daughter had gone insane, what was he going to do with her? They were God's designs. The doctor, under Iyá's satisfied gaze, departed as he arrived, riding an old mule with his belongings, replete with books and instruments.

Nevertheless, when a bishop stopped at the plantation on the way from the coast to New Spain, he observed Little Girl and her strange behavior. He asked the owner if he also had white slave girls, going against the Pope's command, to which the owner answered:

"Your Excellency, that is my daughter. She's crazy. We have treated her with eminent doctors from the colony and the peninsula, and she is not improving. Her madness is wanting to be black. I mean that. If you redeem her, Monsignor, I'll give her to the Church to be a nun."

The bishop looked at the little girl one more time. She came from a nearby river. She carried water with the other young black girls, rumps high and incipient breasts, in spite of the tunic or the slave garments. His Excellency imagined the waspish waist under the caftan material, and perceived in the hips, the swing of prohibited dances. He sighed. Then he glided his tongue over his dry lips. The confusion of seeing the white girl with the backside of a black girl, and a black girl with the face of a white one disturbed him exceedingly. He felt once again the anguish of his youth that had led him to commit so many sins, hidden in the toilets, beneath his mother's sheets, and later in the monastery cells, when his father decided to convert him into a holy man. During the night, inside the walls of the big house, resonated the bishop's whip, punishing his flesh.

At dawn he rang the bell with which he called his servants. He ordered them to take out of his trunk his mitre and surplice; the Holy Bible in Old Latin; the wooden crucifix carved with the wood from the table where Christ Our Lord celebrated the Last Supper, a relic inherited from his Crusader ancestors; and also other things that he believed suitable to wear on his person, or to have at hand, in view of the serious circumstances and the strangest case of demonism that surrounded him.

He called for Father and said to him: "Satan possesses your daughter, and it is my duty to exorcise her before I depart. I shall bring the lustful succubus that hides herself behind her innocence to the light. Bring all the slaves here so that they can see the greatness of our faith. This exorcism will serve as a lesson for them. Make the mother leave her rooms where she hides her shame, so that she also will have the opportunity to give peace to her spirit. Let the foremen, overseers, and servants, and as many subjects of the Crown as there are on your properties attend. The Holy Inquisition orders it."

With the last words he stood up, enhancing the pomp of his hierarchy. Father understood that he would not be able to argue, but simply obeyed.

It was in this way that the house servants and muleteers who accompanied the bishop became judges of the Holy Inquisition. They were invested in a brief ceremony and clothed with habits quickly cut into cloth from curtains. In a short time, we saw them coming out with more dignity than if they had come from Rome.

The slaves did not understand what it was about this time. Anyway, they were happy that they didn't have to work and they were willing to see whatever there was. They saw, however, that the masters remained seated, heads lowered and frightened, and this intrigued them. Later they observed the overseers bringing Little Girl by force. In the same way they made her sit before the white men dressed in long tunics. Only then did they comprehend that the matter was going directly against them. A sound of protest went through the blacks gathered in attendance, which made the bishop look at them angrily, speak to them in words that they didn't understand, and threaten them with gestures that included everyone in attendance. Silence was imposed to the point that the monsignor could hear the flight of a bumblebee that hovered around his head.

The one who suffered most was Iyá, but she had to contain herself. Her Eleddá, or Guardian Angel, had to nourish itself from the surrounding spirits, for she needed energy of a very different type from that of hate. She held back the tears that began to show in her eyes at the spectacle of seeing Little Girl being treated like a criminal with the consent of the masters; and she looked at her eyes with the limitless kindness that she always lavished on her. In thankfulness, she perceived the light of a smile of the most clear and serene kindness that Iyá had ever known.

At that immortal instant, the bishop felt that he had never seen such a beautiful creature as that, but far from abandoning himself to the enjoyment of that feeling, he put the cross between himself and Little Girl.

"Kiss the cross, Satan. Don't trick me! Kiss it, demon!"

Mother felt a leap in her entrails. A lump came to Father's throat because his own future depended as much on the monsignor's ability as his daughter's behavior. If the farm was declared the devil's home . . . Suddenly, everything was in suspense.

"Protect me, Lord!" those who were present heard. The bishop heard it behind him, and later, like an echo, face to face, in the voice of the prisoner. He turned and saw a robust slave woman of an intense olive black color with a disturbingly serene face who defied him with her gaze.

Versed in demonology, the monsignor immediately detected in the slave woman's image, another manifestation of the same kind that occupied him; only this time he was able to confront it in addition to the root of sin. He signaled at his rival with the cross.

"Get back, Satan!" to which Iyá responded the same as before, as Little Girl and some other slave stood before the panel.

With the bravery and strength that faith infuses, the bishop raised his voice and the imperative maxim against the devil was heard very far away, for leagues around, rebounding against the mountains of Escambray. It was not louder than the antiphonal chorus of the blacks because Little Girl was also black or the demon that she had within her was black.

Believing that he was being made to look ridiculous, the bishop ordered the overseers to confine Iyá and to make her kneel down at his feet.

Little Girl, in one leap, put herself between them. She carried in her hand the sheath of the flamboyán tree, the distinctive attribute of Oyá-Yansá. Moving it circularly, she held it over her head. At each rotation, those in attendance heard the wind whistle. It did not linger in the form of a whirlwind in front of the big house. It carried with it the dead leaves of the nearby forest, the dust of the slave shanties, the howling of the country dogs, the cackling of broods of hens, the hissing of the jungle reptiles, the chorus of the branded dead, followed by a watery avalanche with strong rain and hail made of snail shells, seahorses, and blind fish, under laser sparks that uncovered the terror of the unbelievers. In order that no doubts remained, in the sky appeared the rainbow with the colors of the feared goddess.

"Protect me, Lord," said a slave chorus upon seeing how the masters fled to protect themselves under close guard. The wind made the bishop turn upon his own feet. He looked like a top, with his cassock upside down, which carried the slaves to a state of frenetic hilarity of happiness almost forgotten. Not even the discharges from the guns fired in the air by the overseers contained them as the bishop turned, turned, and went turning as far as the Camino Real. And there the wind let him fall, heavily on the mud.

Without waiting for droves of beasts and servants disguised as officials of the Holy Inquisition, the monsignor ran toward the sea. The fear showed on his face, as if what occurred was nothing but the beginning of the terrible days of the Apocalypse, with the guffaws of black slaves who were descended from that tribe expelled from the Holy Land instead of with the trumpets of Jericho.

The great disbandment did not wait. Following the masters, the overseers, the majordomos, and the house slaves locked themselves in. They feared the uprising, so many times the subject of their nightmares. But there was only a party that lasted three continuous days, with bells ringing and chants to the Orishas, which infected the slaves of the neighboring farms. Together they decided to go away to the hills to establish a palenque[6] with Little White Girl at its head, as the legitimate manifestation of Omó-Orisha.

Oyá and Changó had demonstrated to all their immense power. With its sacred names, the palenque was known for decades. It was the palenque that the fugitives founded and their descendants maintained in the mountainous region of Escambray.

On the night of the revelation, Mother, smiling, behind a window on the upper floor of the big house, watched as the blacks joyously celebrated. Mechanically, she squeezed her breasts under her sleeveless bodice. She muttered something in a low voice, which could be one more prayer or the continuation of an interminable

---

6. A fugitive slave community.

conversation that lasted during years spent with herself—a rosary of scattered faults since the unknown night when she, having been left an inheritance by a relative, decided to take revenge for the offenses committed against her honor by the man to whom her parents bequeathed her in Spain, before the Church's altar a few days before embarking for America. She vaguely remembered the little girl with the beautiful golden curls whom she once had inside her womb and who came out from between her legs to turn into the main cause of her conjugal unhappiness. Now she would be the age of that most beautiful woman whom the slaves carried in triumph like a queen. Only God would know what happened to her.

DARIECK SCOTT

THIS CITY OF MEN

DEAR DANIELLE,

Descent, and then a series of gates: The stewardess smiled at the gray-haired man in the baseball jacket in front of me, and at a blond woman and a chubby little red-faced boy who followed closely behind. For me she had only a brief look of wan discomfort. She may have been wearing beige, but that is a detail of reconstructed memory. For what assailed me immediately, as I stepped out of the clunky L-shaped connection tube that ran between the plane and the airport terminal, was the profusion of beige: the beige flooring, the darker beige walls, the variation-on-beige uniforms of the terminal attendants, the beige faces, the beige hair, the beige lips.

Kansas City International Airport: Return of the Native—of a sort, for I was (am) no native really, only a past sojourner in these parts, returned after an absence of twelve years for reasons of irony more than anything else. I remembered nothing, really, nothing perhaps but the broadest details—that the terminal was shaped like a rounded horseshoe, and as the automated door slid open and I glanced around for the shuttle to take me to the rental car, I thought the slant of the horizon looked familiar. And though I had forgotten that this part of Missouri is rather hilly, my body did seem to recall the dip down toward the traffic light as I drove through Platte City (a town, actually, very small, and devolved from beige to sullen gray) on the way to the state line, and to Leavenworth.

Except for these physical recollections—which, because they stood in the here and now, made my remembered images even more dim—I could recall little that was specific. The name, the sights of Leavenworth, such as they were and are, had become in my absence mere proxies for misery: two miserable high school years of friendlessness and quiet, nameless dread. But perhaps the problem was that the town itself has changed not at all in the years since I graduated and my family left,

524

that it is a mausoleum, requiring no independent memory to preserve its past. Everything is the same. The army base. The prison.

Eric.

But everything has changed about him.

Or has it?

But just one more gate to traverse, before I get to Eric, just to set the tone (it tantalizes me, too, to procrastinate this way, but you know me, and, hopefully, have learned to be patient):

The Missouri River travels along the border of Kansas and Missouri proper, rounding a bend and rolling serenely through a wide ravine just outside the town's eastern limits. Nothing stands along the banks here, only the bridge, the dirt and the trees. One imagines, looking down upon the water, European explorers in small boats, peering up into the dark and dangerous woods with little spyglasses held to their eyes, while the people for whom Kansas and its many towns would later be named followed along under tree cover, themselves pondering danger and impending darkness. But the river must have been higher, faster—bolder—then. Now, in this season at least, it is slow and sedate, and from a modest height looks like a long shallow pond in movement.

This is where my thoughts wandered, as I drove toward the bridge along the ponderous arc of an empty two-lane highway. And then I felt, just as I reached the bridge and saw clearly the scattered, dark-windowed homes uphill from the river's edge, a small flutter. A twitch. It was—do not recoil—my (the language is best at conveying its meaning in these matters when at its most stark, so:) cock. I didn't—wouldn't—acknowledge it then, though I will now. I can't remember now what I told myself; I likely ascribed the movement to a contraction of abdominal muscles engaged in digestion, perhaps, like Ebenezer Scrooge proposing the undigested food hypothesis to Jacob Marley's ghost. But that was I-then, and this is I-now.

Now I know better.

There: Now it's not my intention to confuse you, Danielle, though I know I have. But remember that evening, at Green's on the Marina, when you said that we tell ourselves stories in order to live? I'm trying to make what's happened one of mine. And I'm hoping that you'll bear with me, and understand.

I am a homosexual. Surely you guessed it, when you read Eric's name? Even if you did, the shock is probably no less; I'm saying it now because I don't want you to dread it as my story unfolds, to know it without consenting to know. I would apologize, but I can't. I didn't choose it. I knew about it (*it*; already I cannot bear to name it, and must rub it away, elide it beneath the most impersonal of pronouns)—I knew when I met you, yes. When I proposed to you, surely. You no less than I can now thank the gods that you turned me down, but did you *know*, the way you knew when you read Eric's name? I don't expect you to write back, but I wonder.

I discovered what I had long refused to know sophomore year in college. My roommate was a football player, a halfback who was never around because he was being courted by professional scouts and preferred the company of his fellow athletes to the rest of us in the dorm. One night I came home late from a screw-your-roommate party and he was there. I think I smelled them before the door was fully open. The light from the hallway fell slantwise across their bodies in the pitch black room. I saw his huge butt, its thick curly black hair bristling in the crack, wildly bouncing up and down, and heard the two of them breathing like running hogs. His asshole—I do apologize for this, but I want to be clear; I don't want to leave you with any illusions—clenched and unclenched with a mesmerizing power. I couldn't see her at all, but I knew I wanted what she was getting.

And just as promptly I shut the door, and left, and decided I wouldn't get what she got, that I wouldn't even seek it. I would be honest with myself, I decided: I would not forget, would not call myself bisexual, would not *slip* on drunken nights as I *happened* to go to a gay bar. I would face it. But I wouldn't do it. You understand, I think; you can guess the reasons—your father was as sternly Catholic as my own. And then there are the sexual standards we black men must meet—because we are not permitted to be men anywhere else, we must at least be men in the bedroom, etc.—though I hardly need tell you that.

And Eric.

I write that, knowing that his name, too, at this place in my story, is a trick of reconstructed memory. He is significant, true, but to what extent, then as now, he was (is) only a trigger, perhaps a vessel in which I bottled a part of myself, I cannot say. I do wonder whether and how things would have been different here, had things been different between us then. I wonder what meaning this town, this wretched little patch of earth that I've held tight-fisted in my memory as the quintessence of what is contemptible in my life and in the world—I wonder what meaning it would have had. And I wonder if Andy Brent assigning me to this case merely hastened a transformation which was inevitable, and I would have had to return here eventually, anyway.

But Eric: It's an effort, I find, to describe him. My words are so spare when I try to *think* of Eric—embellishment, nuance, metaphor, eloquence disappear as into a hungry black vacuum, and my voice becomes as laconic and laden as the air on an August Sunday afternoon. I can describe only what it means not to be able to describe; I describe only the difference between the me without him, and the me that is now. Oh, he takes me, Eric does. He takes me and I am left dry, bland, malleable, like sand on an exile's desert isle. He takes me and I am left: Wanting.

No, this is not a love story. It is a story of evil.

Eric is in prison.

I picked up the phone book in the hotel room the second night that I was in town. I had to send out for it because, as the pale and hopelessly adolescent bellhop explained, the previous occupant (I surveyed the dust on the table rammed into the corner against the shabby window: when had *he* been here? five years ago?) must have made off with the room's copy. He handed me the slim volume, white and yellow pages combined, revealing a spray of red acne blotches on the underside of his arm as he did so. His was not the sort of presence in which I usually become flustered, but I felt the blood rise in my face as the boy smiled apologetically and backed out of my room. I was embarrassed, you see.

I had felt no sense of urgency when I first contemplated returning to Leavenworth, about Eric or anyone. I had no wish to contact any of my former classmates (nor, I am sure, would they have any desire to come into contact with me). Indeed, driving to the offices of White & Weinberg to meet with opposing counsel that very morning, I saw someone on the sidewalk I ran track with; he looked my way and I glared in the opposite direction. But when the bellhop handed me the phonebook, it became clear what I was doing—frighteningly clear, like the sudden resolution of a shapeless shadow into the distinct features of a malformed brute raising a butcher knife above your head. (Melodrama, you'll say. Yet I swear to you that this whole matter has played in precisely that fashion.) I was lonely, I said aloud; there was nothing playing at the town's one movie theater but something I had seen weeks ago; I had finished preparing for the next day's depositions—those were my excuses.

I was calling Eric.

Or his father, rather, who has the same name. The phone book says Eric Reede without a senior or a junior, so the man who answered when I called thought I wanted to speak to him. I told him that I was a friend from high school, that we had been in Spanish class together junior year. I said, "Do you remember me, Haze?" using his nickname. I spoke with a presumptuousness that, as I think of it now, must have been my way of flirting.

"Oh, you mean my son," Eric Sr. said. I was embarrassed, and fell completely silent.

"He's in prison, you know," he said tentatively.

Again, I said nothing.

"You never heard?"

"No"—I tried now to speak in a professional, detached manner—"No, I haven't been in contact since we graduated high school. I live in San Francisco now." As if that explained anything.

"Oh," he said. Evidently it didn't. "Well, you wanna talk to him, you gotta call his lawyer. He don't see nobody but his lawyer these days. Jeff Weinberg, you can look it up. Eric won't see you though. Just wants to see his lawyer."

"I am a lawyer," I said.

"Oh!" This evidently did explain something. I imagined that he sighed—it seemed that his silence became less wary, anyway—and so I asked, "I hope you don't mind my asking, but—where is Eric in prison, and what for?"

"Right here, in the Leavenworth federal pen," he said. "And *why*, well if you ain't heard, they say he *raped* a boy—I don't like to say *boy*; Eric wasn't but two years older—but they say he did that to a young man on the army post, on federal property, see what I'm sayin, which is why he's in the Leavenworth pen. But you know that, you're a lawyer."

It will be odd to you—it is odd to me—but the moment (I describe this conversation to you because of the moment)—it lived in me, Danielle. I felt a pulsing, breathing, kicking space explode into being inside me as Eric Sr. spoke. I didn't reply, or gasp, or tremble. But I twitched; I twitched again, down there.

"Course I don't believe it," Eric Sr. said.

I did.

That's what I mean, when I say this is a story of evil.

Notes on Eric:

As I said, we were in Spanish class together, junior year. We sat at tables rather than in rows—Mrs. Astorbrook maintained the view that students learn languages best in conversation with one another rather than with the teacher. Eric sat next to me. He missed the first two days of class, and arrived late on the third, smelling as if he had just come from gym class without showering. (This was my story for him. He didn't explain, so I didn't find out, nor did he ever return to class in such a deliciously fulsome state. It's likely that I was titillated, rather than revolted as I pretended to be; the girl on my right and I traded wrinkled-nose faces when Eric sat down.) We didn't talk at first. Mostly we listened to Mrs. Astorbrook. But Eric smiled at me when the bell rang, and asked me for the missed assignments. Something about his smile—I ascribe lasciviousness to it now, but surely it was something different. I gave him the assignments, in any case, and was rather happy to do so, and then forgot about him, until that night at the football game.

I had left the bleachers and passed back through the ticket gate on the way to the parking lot. It was half-time, and colder than I'd expected. And since I was new to town, I didn't know anyone, so I was likely despondent, fearing that I would never make friends, never belong—the all too common run of insecurities that comprise the cultural bludgeoning we conceal behind that clinician's term adolescence.

Eric came up to me, and he didn't seem to be feeling any of that. He walked in my direction, smiling again, if not lasciviously then conspiratorially at least, exuding an ease and familiarity with which I would not have been able to greet my best friend, if I had had one. He wore a long-sleeved thermal t-shirt under an open checkered shirt (a look I associated with white boys—and they excited me, too, I must say now), tucked into the town's one pair of button-fly Levi's 501s (everyone else—I swear—wore boot cut zip ups or Wranglers). The billowing shirt gave him a broad-shouldered, narrow waist look. There was a bulge in his right pocket.

"Hey, Jules! You leavin?" He punch-touched my shoulder, as men and boys do.

"Well, yeah," I said—or something in a casual tone, grateful to be swept into his conviviality. "It's cold. And we're losing anyway."

"Don't go away yet, man. Stay with me and hang out. I'll warm you up."

He reached into his pocket and drew out a small copper pipe, short-stemmed and wide-cupped, with a fine wire grating in its mouth. "Why 'on't you come and help me fire this up?" His eyes were seductively hooded.

We got stoned that night, and infrequently over the rest of the year. I never proposed these assignations; I lacked all confidence that anyone would want to spend time with me unless as a last resort, and so waited, impatiently, the junior high school girl with ugly knees and braces in her mouth, for occasions of last resort. For reasons at which I might guess (or, truth be told, which I might wish), Eric kept coming back and during and after stoned stupor he would talk to me, almost confessionally, about matters which concerned him. I was privileged to be only the second person he told about his first experience of sexual intercourse, for example. I remember that my head rolled slowly forward from the soporific cushion of a beaten faded-blue couch in his basement bedroom when he told me. I couldn't speak, as marijuana rendered me dumb rather than chatty like Eric, but my face tried to register the surprise I felt. Eric smiled. "She's a white girl," he told me, and watched with satisfaction as my mouth opened. "She was crazy, she wanted it so bad," he whispered. Several days later I stood in the cafeteria lunch line behind him and her. She remarked that whatever was passing for meat that day didn't look very tasty, to which Eric loudly replied, "Want me to put some sperm on it?" The white guys behind us (not to mention the girl, whose name and face I cannot recall) were as you might imagine, less than amused. But I relished the moment— for reasons which require very little speculation now, but then were cloaked behind Eldridge Cleaver–like exultation about one of *us* having taken one of *their* women.

I saw Eric less frequently senior year. He didn't take Spanish II, or any of the other pre-collegiate track courses where I was often one of two, at most three, black faces. I saw him in the hallway, lined up against the walls with his fellow athletes, and nodded, as men and boys do. He and his new girlfriend had become very close, I was told.

I've said nothing about his looks, in part because I believe it is their meaning rather than their actuality that's important to the story. Yet again, however, in searching for meaning I am reduced to the kind of breathless description one might easily find in a teenage girl's love novel—or in pornography. Eric had a farm boy's lanky physique, I would say, the deceptive power of its modest musculature honed by sweaty tussles on wrestling mats after school. I think you can imagine the rest—how his legs and buttocks looked in his worn 501s, and other such salacious trivia.

About his color I can say more, I fear. His skin was (and is) very dark, poised just at the edge of ebony, finely dusky and suede-smooth even to the eye. You understand, Danielle, don't you? His skin was the kind of skin we say we most admire in our people—though, as we've rather guiltily discussed, we rarely date anyone of that complexion. There is a compelling sensuality to the color, a *physicality*. A sexual potency. I know where such descriptions originate, of course. Remember what you once said, that sometimes you think that the way you're attracted to black men like that is through the worst of racist stereotypes, of you and of them? You as the wanton woman of color who wants it all night, and he as the big, mean, monstrously endowed and insatiable, slavering buck? Eric isn't big, but he's six feet or so, with broad, powerful shoulders.

So you understand, I think, part of the (perniciously conceived and guiltily repressed) meaning Eric has for me.

Eric Reede is in prison for sexually assaulting a male minor, two years his junior, at the boy's home, which was on federal property. So Jeff Weinberg, esquire, echoed Eric, Sr., as we drove from the courthouse downtown to the prison on the town's outskirts. Weinberg, founding partner of White & Weinberg—coincidentally the very firm which represents the plaintiffs suing the corporation my firm is defending—agreed to help me see Eric without further question once I told him that the two of us were old friends. "It's important that Eric not become a one-man freak show," he told me, by way of apology for his initial suspicion. He said that he was Eric's friend, too, though he had only come to know him during the trial, and related to me the tale of Eric's unspeakable deeds with blunt stoicism and occasional, unblinking eye-to-eye contact, as if to say, *man to man, between friends, we both understand how to speak about and react to these untidy matters, right?* He intended quite the opposite, but his presence and comfortably *male* demeanor shamed me.

Eric may have been drunk, Weinberg said, but then again he may not have been. The "boy"—Todd Stoffen, a name which, when Weinberg said it, I felt some dim connection to—was probably a homosexual, but as there was no evidence of prior acts and laws prevented Weinberg from probing the matter too vigorously, and the prosecution managed to present over objection testimony that Todd had dated several girls and had a wonderful time at his junior high prom, etc.—that may not have been true, either. It is undeniable, however, that at approximately four in the afternoon of a Tuesday in July, Eric entered the Stoffen home, apparently at Todd's behest, and, for whatever reason—Weinberg used precisely that phrase and shrugged: "for whatever reason"—punched and kicked and wrestled Todd "into submission," and then dragged him up the stairway and into Mr. and Mrs. Stoffen's bedroom, where he lashed him with twine to the posts of the Stoffens' Victorian antique bed, and anally and orally "sodomized" him.

"The whole thing must have taken about thirty-five, forty minutes," Weinberg said, and stopped.

Weinberg drives a sleek red European convertible, a diamond among the Leavenworth rough of Trans Ams and Firebirds and Ford trucks. A short, Superman curl of brown hair blew back from the top of his forehead in the wind as he talked to me, and I chose to focus upon it, in an effort to appear wholly unconcerned with the rest of the story. The clarity of my memory of his curl—I can see its individual strands, the minuscule S-tail at its end—suggests something of my state: I was experiencing a kind of tunnel vision, like an accident victim's disoriented focus upon the sight of fuzzy dice, dangling behind the windshield of the approaching car just before it strikes her. I was breathless.

Weinberg made no effort to rescue me. "He brought the twine with him," he continued. "So evidence of premeditation was there. The worse part was the, the *ejaculate*," he stumbled, staring up into a green traffic light. "When the general's wife came home—must've been as short as five minutes after Eric left—she found it smeared all over Stoffen's forehead, cheeks, and lips." He shook his head. "Eric must've had a lot to blow!"

I fear this tale must now become truly lurid and macabre, because Weinberg, quite uproariously in fact, laughed. I didn't—but I laugh now, as I write this to you—I twitched.

(There is a scene from an all-male pornographic video I've just received in the mail—its name escapes me; I ordered several—in which the star makes his penis "speak" by contracting his well-exercised abdominal muscles so that it lifts and bounces, in a way which calls to mind the *boiinnnng!* sound that would spring from the panels of Archie comics when Archie or Reggie saw Veronica. This repulses you, I know. But I can't restrain myself now. You have become my mother-confessor, distasteful though it may be to both of us. I am taking you, one step by one and later three by three and then over tall buildings in single bounds into what you might call my particular hell. I don't know if *I* call it hell, or whether one day I will feel justified in doing so. It is, I confess, a place where magazines torn from plastic bags scatter the dust of the hotel room floor beneath my bed. It is, if you will, a place of sin.

And I must walk you there with me now, my dear. You must follow as I recount, because I must, the labor and birth of—*this*, whatever we choose to call it. There are two metaphors here, you see: one of journey, one of birth. The journey is for you, a narrative straight-line path with signposts and sights and historical trivia. The birth is mine, the Rosemary's Baby metaphor for what I feel: a deep and terrifying physical evolution.)

The Fort Leavenworth prison is massive and imposing, as one expects (though I did not remember) a federal prison to be. With its rotunda dome and gleaming white paint, and its position atop a low hill overlooking the ripple of valleys that house the greater part of the town, it looks like a state capitol rather than a penitentiary, or like a patrician palace of ancient Rome, towering above the hovels of the plebeians. Indeed the only other building of such majesty is the courthouse, which pales in comparison. To complete this law and order trinity there is of course the army base itself, Fort Leavenworth, a green and sprawling country club miniature town which is the site for the War College, and where, every year, officers the rank of major arrive to be schooled in Clausewitz and other masters of the art. The open gates of the fort are a two minute drive, west to east, from the gates of the prison. Together, the War College and the penitentiary are the town's distinguishing features (the courthouse fades, like the Holy Ghost), colossi of federal power bestriding the supine and meek local body. No doubt they provide the greater part of local jobs, as well—twin patriarchs, one might say, tall, grim, strong and solidly male. Women here disappear into their vital and invisible helpmeet roles: wife, mother, teacher, nurse, secretary.

It is in this city of men that Eric grew to what we may charitably call his adult-
hood.

(I have enclosed for your perusal a few copies, randomly selected, of homosexual pornographic magazines. They're the kind with fantasy experiences detailed in
letters, so you needn't worry about offensive photographs. Just note one thing: the
frequent reoccurrence of military and prison themes.)

"It's racism that put me in here, man," was the first thing he said to me. The
necessary fiction Weinberg concocted to persuade him to see me was that I was a
criminal lawyer, looking for grounds on which to re-open the appeal of his conviction—preposterous, of course, and I felt guilty about it. Perhaps I mumbled
something or other about constitutional reversible errors and racial selection of
jurors, etc. He was sitting down behind a glass partition when we arrived, so that
I couldn't see his lower body. His shirt, long-sleeved, hung loosely on him, but his
pectoral muscles had a more powerful presence than I remembered.

I interrupted him. "Are you saying that you're innocent?" I asked. "I have to
know," I added quickly, like a television lawyer.

"I fucked him, but I didn't rape him." He was blunt. I caught the faint whiff of
musk in the slot at the bottom of the glass.

"Lotta people, lotta guys, get real nervous when I say that shit. But I fucked
him. I was curious. Lotta guys are curious but don't say nothin. You, too, probably."

He spoke as if in challenge to a duel. I said nothing. I felt heat, though it wasn't
hot.

"You, too," he said again. He hadn't recognized me, it seemed. "But I did what
other guys've done. I'm not worried about it. I'm not a faggot." This cheerfully
enough, but with a force that made the teeth in his smile look feral. "It woudna
mattered if he'd been black, that's what I'm trying to say. It doesn't matter! But he's
a white boy and a general's son and was goin to college so some shit had to happen behind it. He asked for it. And if he'd been black, who cares? Nobody gives a
shit about a black faggot."

I nodded in grave assent. He looked at me more closely. "So what else do you
need to know? I went and read that jury selection case. I don't think it can help
me."

I groped for a lie. "Well there's a Ninth Circuit decision with some language
about how a federal statute about rape doesn't extend to violations of the anatomy
of the sort suffered by a male victim," I burbled. It was all rather comic, as I look
back on it now. The room was intolerably, stiflingly hot, I remember that. Rivulets
of sweat ran down from my underarms along my stomach, which, incongruously,
made me shiver. "But you say—he asked for it?" (You will note again the devolu-
tion of my language as well as my capacity for subtlety: he asked for *it,* I said.)

His eyes flickered upward, toward Weinberg, who stood many feet back, behind
me. I was suddenly struck by his eyes—their size and roundness, the soft brown
color like a child's eyes. His lashes were long and curved.

"I know you," he said.

I introduced myself then, crafting a smile of some kind, and jokingly invoked the memory of Mrs. Astorbrook. His eyes widened. "We were friends," he said, with, perhaps, a measure of incredulity.

"We were," I replied. And then of course I pounced. "And I'll need to know everything in order to help you. From you, not Jeff. As a friend," I said, and swallowed, because I had become thirsty beyond reason. "But . . . I have to go now." It made no sense even to me. But I had to leave. It was an imperative. It had to be different from this, I thought. The setting had to be different, and it couldn't happen now, so quickly.

"We'll schedule it," he said, official but gruff.

He stood then. Eric stood, and Danielle, I've said that I would take you through this by steps, but this moment was not a step; it cannot be imagined or understood as part of a path *to*, as a paving stone in the grass of a park winding toward a garden. It *was*, Danielle. He rose: I watched and felt his torso, the dark valley between his legs, rise slowly, above the horizon of the table, and, to employ the metaphor of the journey, I was *there*. I didn't have to go anywhere, I was there, *it* was there, and *it* was me. Did it puzzle you when I began to describe our conversation, that my story lacked a moment of recognition, a catch in the throat when I first beheld him again, a misty-eyed locking of gazes, a surge of excitement and fear? Perhaps not; this is of course not a romance. It is perversion, pure—unspeakably pure—and simple. In the vacuum created by that lack, by the absence of an acknowledged or acknowledgeable link, romantic or otherwise (this was a meeting of shames, after all: his shameful deed to my shameful desire for him—shame deflects; it does not bond)—in this vacuum I sat at the partition without actually sitting there. I looked through the glass without seeing him, listened without listening. But when he rose.

I beheld him. And he was firm, and full, and strong.

Outside the prison, Weinberg asked me what we had said. He was uneasy with the idea of another attorney talking to his client. I thought of Eric's eyes, and asked Weinberg whether Eric was separated from his fellow prisoners. "He wasn't segregated at first," Weinberg said, seeming to catch my meaning. "But he is now." He said no more, choosing for the first time to be mysterious.

In the convertible, I said that I would be returning to speak to Eric again, and wondered aloud whether there might be some way to see him next time without the glass partition.

That night was the first night I didn't call you. I looked at your number in my address book, because I was unable to remember it, but I didn't call. I sat on the bed instead, held there without will to move. To explain why, or how I felt, I have to tell another story, one that took place twelve years ago, the summer after I graduated from high school. It may not do the trick, but the memory of it moved through my mind that night, and it seems appropriate to tell it now: Two fellow track team members and I had planned to drive up to Chicago for a few days— ostensibly for some concert or another where Stevie Wonder headlined a string of performers like Sister Sledge and Ashford & Simpson. I had dreamt of this trip as others dream of a weekend in Paris. I relished the anticipation of laughing in the car with my teammates, of hearing about their scandalous sexual escapades with girls, of—so I hoped—picking up women under their tutelage (or perhaps the same woman, a fantasy towards which my thoughts often tilted in those days, for reasons which now seem more clear). But one of them, the younger one, Kelvin, who was still a junior, backed out at the last moment. Kelvin was a small, svelte boy, but abundantly hairy, with sideburns and five o'clock shadow and a mass of fine, curly black hair on his trim, chestnut-brown chest. I waited all afternoon by the phone in my mother's house for him to call and tell me whether his parents would let him go on the trip.

A slight and paltry memory, this: But it was with precisely that unnameable longing and unbearable fear that I sat up that night, held upon the bed, poised to make a phone call I never made, until at last I collapsed and slept.

I saw Eric again, two days later. It was relatively easy then, and most times afterward, to be granted an audience, since Eric—quite without my asking—had informed the prison officials that I and Weinberg both were his attorneys.

Each time I visit him I walk through four gates: The first is not a physical construct but an imagined one. The prison building's doors stand atop a wide white stairway that travels up from an innocuous parking lot and a capacious green lawn seemingly open to all. The appearance is almost suburban, as of a great grand house across the street from mother, apple pie and the two-car garage, though I cannot shake the feeling—prisons being prisons, or what we *think* prisons are—of being within a tale more Gothic than Fifties sitcom. Behind the doors is a rotunda hall with polished floors and large, grim paintings; from that reception I am ushered through the first of several metal detectors into a carpeted rectangle that has the ominous air of an interrogation chamber, complete with an impossibly high desk shielded by bulletproof plastic, and stark gray walls bearing a lone square placard which details do's and don'ts in red letters (DO follow the instructions of the corrections officers / DON'T smoke); and from there past another gate into a long, empty hallway with a low ceiling (no paintings or placards, just glowing EXIT signs pointing the opposite direction); then finally outside the building and into a gravelly courtyard, and through a final gate to a row of dilapidated barracks. At the door to the especially forlorn one where I usually meet Eric one might expect to read *Abandon hope*—or, perhaps, *Arbeit macht frei*. On the other hand—to balance fantasized horror with absurdity—I feel like Don Adams at the beginning of *Get Smart*.

The second or third time I saw him he was waiting for me, sitting with his hands quietly clasped on a bare table. Always when I first see him there is a moment of disjunction. He is not towering or imposing or *meaty* there as in my fantasies, but a slight, human figure in gray coveralls—grainy almost, colorless like a figure in a videotaped seventies TV-movie. It is when he speaks that he ascends to his full power.

That day I sat at the opposite end of the table, and laid a briefcase between us. The guard left us alone, without explanation.

"I'll tell ya something else," Eric said. "Todd was always hinting. At first he was subtle, right, like asking me shit about my girlfriends. Stupid shit you don't really ask like I bet you and her have a good time, tell me the dirty details an' shit. And then laugh like it was a joke. I wouldn't answer. But he'd always find a way to bring it up: I saw Angel today and she was walking funny so I knew you'd busted her stuff good last night an' shit. Right? After awhile I just started waiting, you know, waiting to see how he'd do it. And I thought maybe, you know, he's inexperienced and he's two years younger and he wants to live vicariously cause he doesn't get any an' shit. But something didn't feel right. I mean he didn't *touch* me or look at me weird, but I knew something even though I didn't think about it. Maybe it was the way *I* felt around him when he asked that shit. *My* body felt different. And it had to be *him*. You understand that, am I making sense?"

"Yes," I said.

"And that feeling, Jules—you *know* this feeling, man—it got to be *exciting* and shit, right? Yeah." He paused, looked down. I remember clearly, because we both had time to readjust our breathing. "Yeah sometimes that summer I was so bored I looked forward to him coming by. I looked forward to him asking, right, and feelin what was happening when he asked it. I think—well, yeah, that was when I first let him come down to my room."

Something in me wanted to prolong it. "How did you ever start hanging out with Todd?" I asked. "I didn't even know you knew him in school."

Eric laughed, which he doesn't often do. His mouth was enormous. "He was fuckin *weird*, man!" he shouted. His demeanor seemed to me outrageous, distorted and lurid like eerie reflections in an amusement park house of mirrors. I twitched again, but by then, sad to say, that had become a frequent occurrence.

"He was *strange!* I mean, an officer's kid an' shit, a *general's* kid, lookin for jobs doing menial shit off post, in town? He was lookin for trouble, I think. Nobody even knew who he was. He came up to our house in some Japanese truck and asked my dad if he wanted somebody to mow the grass every week, and dad said what the hell, I was workin in Western Sizzlin full time, my brother was too lazy. Dad said he'd get a kick out of having a white boy mow his grass, so. Then he started cuttin, started showin up more than once a week to do the hedges and pull weeds an' shit, for free, he said, but dad paid him anyway. They got to start talkin a lot, and I was there, and so we talked, about school at first, and how he wanted to go out for the wrestling team next year and shit. I guess he was about to be a senior then. We *talked*, like I said. I got used to havin him around, like rich white folks get used to havin the maid around, right?" He stopped and looked at me suspiciously, as if he expected me to think this a lie.

"So you took him down to your room?" I asked.

Eric smirked—wild again, outrageous. "I had a bench and some weights down there. We went down and lifted. He kept askin questions that I didn't really answer. I tried to ask him some shit about his girlfriends—I didn't care, but I just wanted to see what he would say. He just smiled, real stupid, and made some bullshit noise about some girl he liked and he was gonna ask her out and he was a one-woman man. Just shit like that. Pretty soon we'd work out together every other day. He liked comin by, he was always cheerful." He spread his hands on the table and shrugged.

I fumbled, looking at his dark eyes. "But you—did anything unusual happen? You said he *asked* . . ." I couldn't complete the sentence.

He didn't smirk this time, as I expected he might, but he leaned forward. His words and manner, his voice and hands (despite a certain studied dispassion which was his version of the requisite masculine cool) were always intense, taut the way a prisoner needing to do whatever, say whatever in order to achieve freedom likely must be. But below the neck, other than the hands—I rarely saw him below the waist, you recall—his body was generally relaxed, at indolent rest. He leaned forward then and changed that. I confess I very much wished, suddenly, that the guard had not left us.

"One time," he said in a lower voice, his gaze focused away from my face, "he fucked up and put too much weight on the barbell. He was too weak and couldn't handle it. I'd already warned him, but he was too busy tryin to be like me an' shit. So the barbell got unbalanced when he was doin a press and one whole side of it crashed down on the floor. I got real pissed. My dad was right upstairs in the living room tryin to sleep, and here he was making all this noise, right? I was pissed. I got up in his face. What the fuck, mothafuck, I told your skinny ass not to do that shit. Shit like that. He got scared. White boys like him get scared when you go off on em. So you know this little son of a bitch started to *cry?* Not hollerin and shit, but his eyes got wet, and he was holdin his stomach in like he wasn't gon breathe. I was about to just throw his ass outta my house. But somethin—I mean it was a turning point. Curiosity took over me, like I told you. He had his back to me and I grabbed up under his arms like I was doin a nelson on him, and just started wrestling him. At first he was scared, saying don't hurt me and whiney shit, but then he figured it out and started wrestling back. I played cat and mouse with him till I got tired—cause he couldn't even *think* about whippin *my* ass—but then finally I pinned him down. On the floor. We were both real funky. I held him down on his back, both shoulders down, you know, for a pin, and my face was right over his. He just laid there, pantin hard an' shit. He looked up at me, right? It was like—when you wrestle, and you pin somebody, they don't look at you like that, most people don't *look* at you, period. He looked, and it was like, like total fuckin *submission.* Which is a fuckin weird feelin, man."

He looked sharply at me. "But he liked that shit."

I was by this time insatiable, Danielle, insatiable.

"So you took this to be—an invitation?" Laughable, but I actually said it, and with a straight face. I often found myself, in conversations with Eric, saying such things, playing an odd and utterly fallacious part: my detachment to his passion, my subtlety to his melodrama, psychiatrist to patient, lawyer to criminal. It was, as you can see, quite a farce.

Eric, as he occasionally did, usually at precisely such moments, put on the air of one entirely unimpressed—of someone with power. "What's all this got to do with that Ninth Circuit decision—which I looked up and read?"

"I need to know everything, every detail," I snapped, slipping easily into the television lawyer role.

He stared for a moment, grim, then rose and walked to the door. I looked straight ahead as he passed out of my peripheral vision. My flesh felt horrifyingly—but titillatingly, Danielle—exposed. There was a knock, and the guard entered.

"See you a couple of days?" he said, turning his head back over his shoulder as I turned mine. He smiled.

Back in the hotel room I cried, and then masturbated until my sweat spread out in a dark pool on the white, pressed sheets.

Later I remembered Todd. I remembered the thick, pale blond hair on top of his head. I remembered this because sometimes he rode the school bus from post with me, and he always looked down, reading, maybe, so that you would see the top of his head if you sat in front of him and looked back. I hated him then—a casual hate, without fire, as one hates the fat kid in third grade who smells like spoiled milk. No one paid attention to Todd, which seemed to me quite proper, since no one paid much attention to me, either. But occasionally when some of the others were laughing and clowning and I, aloof and excluded, was watching them, I saw Todd watching them, too. The expression on his pasty, plain freckled face was ingenuous, and dumb with terrible, terrible need.

I tormented myself, Danielle, as I now no doubt torment you. You know this in me—the compulsion to hold satisfaction at bay, to dangle it out of reach, and suffer trials to reach the place where I myself have set the prize. I visited Eric, many times. The depositions which I had originally been sent to conduct were concluded. You phoned, and I left oblique messages on your machine when I knew you would be out. Weinberg grew testy, but could do nothing. Eric insisted that he would continue to see me. Whether he knows my purpose, my passion, he has not said. But he must. I daresay he may know better than I.

What follows, then, is the climax, as it were, the journey's end. That is for you. For me there is no climax, no end. Perhaps I do not seek one. My obsession is in the details, in the slow, exquisite nursing and labor of this birth which has already occurred, and will never be complete. Eric understands this. But he has given you, Danielle, something as well: An explanation. I do not subscribe to it, but neither do I deny its power.

"It's about power, man," Eric said. He turned his head and blew smoke from his mouth. I brought him, with official permission, a package of cigarettes. We sat at a table again, but two guards stood in the room's far corners. "I thought a lot about this. Read some of that New Wave, New Age shit. Everybody's got power. Everybody. Some got more, some got less, but they got it. And some—*most*, prob'ly—are afraid of it, see what I'm sayin. They want somebody else to do it for them. Nothin new about that, right? I mean that's like Nietzsche an' shit—oh yea, I read some of that, I read some of everything. It's just plain psychology. Passive-aggressive, puttin themselves someplace where somebody else can accomplish for em what they want. It can be extreme, or not extreme. Todd, he was extreme. Little white soldier boy—he was in ROTC, did I say that? He wanted authority in his life. Liked to bend over, right. That day—I don't remember what day, you have to look it up—somethin made me think about him. I meditated on him. I don't remember exactly—but about his little body, little weak ass, half-flabby body, and that goofy golly-gee-you-my-big-brother shit. And then he called me at work. Right when I thought about it. And he said come over, I got a new weight set. And I got mad, man. He was so fuckin *goofy*, just thinking about him *wantin* me, you know, but he couldn't say it because he was so *weak*. So I said yeah I'll be over. I had some rope in the car, so I could move a book shelf and tie down the hatch. And when I got to his house I'd brought the rope up from the back to the front seat."

He stopped and calmly tapped cigarette ashes into a tray. This was the kind of detail which, evidently, I had somehow communicated to him that I wished to hear. Patiently he allowed me to contemplate the movement of the twine, while he tranquilly blew smoke into the air above our heads.

"And then?" I said thickly.

He nodded, satisfied. "Todd answered the door and looked proud of himself. Because he got the weight set, I guess. Which made me a little more mad, kinda. I grabbed him from behind after he shut the door, in a full nelson, as he was walkin up the stairs, and he laughed an' shit, said let's wait until we get upstairs, we'll fuck up my mom's shit. I said yeah we'll go upstairs all right, and dragged him up, hard, right, with his face down, over the steps. The steps weren't carpeted, they were just bare wood. He was gigglin, though, like a little kid. He kept laughin and jokin around an' shit till I tied one of his wrists up. He started squirming then. Which I have to admit was kinda nice. I was gettin into it. Made me even more curious. But mad, too, a good kind've mad. That energy, that power, right. He still didn't know what was up. All right, that's enough, let's stop, he said. I tied up his last ankle and he said, stop, Eric! Which was funny. That was his moment of power. Stop! Like he was a general. I ripped his pants down to his spread-out ankles and his breath caught. I heard it. He didn't say anything, which was *very* nice. I got hard, man, real hard. You ever feel a bone like that and you'll know how it makes you feel. I pulled it out and it never felt bigger. He said he was gon scream, so I slapped him and said if you do I'll kill you. Which he should've known was a lie! But he shut up! Abandoned his power, just like that. He coulda stopped it then, but he wanted it, Jules. He wanted it bad. I dipped my dick in his mouth to get it wet. He slurped it good when I pushed his head down on it. Then I went around and porked him. You ever see that movie *Deliverance?* I almost laughed when I remembered that. Blood got all over his ass and I had him lick everything off my dick before I fucked him again. I did it as hard or as soft as it felt good, but I tried to do it hard mostly, because that's what he wanted.

"You know that whole time he breathed hard and whimpered an' shit, but he didn't cry out? What a little wimp. I bent over close to him and held his shoulders down while I screwed him, because I wanted to keep my face right in front of his and look at him, eye to eye. He couldn't hold it, though. After awhile he looked away. He closed his eyes. I felt sorry for him. I guess it'd started to hurt by then. And see, he didn't expect that."

He grinned, with frightening and hypnotic charm.

I slumped in my hard chair. I must say—and this will be the last of these per-versities—that my bottom felt tinglingly raw as it slid forward in the smooth depression of the chair. And I had gone quite beyond twitching. I couldn't bring myself to speak.

Finally, Eric did.

I could do it to you, too. Would you like that?

They grabbed him then—I suppose they had heard him—a veined, straining hand laid hold of his arm just below the shoulder and pulled at him, like the crook of a cane from offstage at a burlesque show. He rose from the chair without resis-tance. He must have known, as he was pulled away backward, that I would follow his eyes.

I did. They were gentle.

I have been told that he is in "isolation," and that I won't be able to see him for some time.

I am sitting now, at a little round table, writing in dim light. The view from the window of my hotel room is of a dirty, empty street, parking meters unattended except by a few lone, dusty cars. It is early evening in August, twilight.

I wish that I had an ending for you. I've been writing for hours. At the very least, it seems, I should leave you with some image—something metaphoric, something haunting, if possible.

Something poignant or lyrical, some fantasy construct by which we—we, as in you and I, separately—might assimilate changes, by which we might pretend to conclude one way of living or thinking or loving for another, or reverence what we have known as if it had truly passed, when, in truth, everything continues even as everything disintegrates. The obvious symbols of descent and ascent and gates, of heaven and hell, of prisons both physical and psychological; the unrelenting frenzy and insatiable appetite of desire deferred—these, perhaps, will have occurred to you. They have, no doubt, inspired images of your own, stronger and more true for you than any I might devise.

But you will ignore such considerations. You will want an image. To have com-municated the matter to you as a story, with plot and quotes, demands it.

A note, then:

The Leavenworth streets at night are caliginous passageways, as dark as a back-woods country road. Barely illuminated by feeble streetlamps, they meander away into the distance under droopy tree branches to become tunnels of gloom, a habitat for skulkers and prowlers, for ghosts, perhaps, and presences.

I have begun to drive these dark ways, with the windows up and the radio off. So far I've seen only pot-bellied white men in baseball caps, staggering over rocky driveways toward their trucks. But a thrill, fierce and expectant, returns me to the streets, night after night . . .

I will disclaim this image, whether adequate for your purposes or not. I have no need of images or metaphor, having lived, in this instance, what they purport to represent. But if I chose an image for myself, it would be starker. Like, perhaps, the card I hold in my hand now. I purchased it along with the magazines. On its face is a white man—I could not find many cards of this variety that boast black men, which is both an outrage and a blessing (the latter because I frankly think I would be a bit undone if I encountered a menagerie of Erics, parading themselves in row upon row of pornographic splendor on cardshelves).

But, the card: The model is white, rather slight and not particularly well-built, moderately hairy, with large hands. His undistinguished morphology serves to accentuate a single feature: He has no face, you see; the picture cuts off above his bare shoulders. What he does have, what he *sports,* is a thick and prominent erection, clad—if that is the word—in damp white bikini briefs. At a rightward lean, it laughably resembles a coke bottle with a ballooned cap, nestled in a man's crotch.

I say *laughable.* I'm not laughing at it. I fear—I know; I don't fear—that this is the image which adorns the altar at which I shall be worshipping for some time.

That is, if one needs images—or stories, for that matter.

Yours,
Julius

OLIVE SENIOR

YOU THINK I MAD, MISS?

YOU THINK I MAD, MISS? You see me here with my full head of hair and my notebook and pencil, never go out a street without my stockings straight and shoes shine good, for is so my mother did grow me. Beg you a smalls nuh? Then why your face mek up so? Don't I look like somebody pickney? Don't I look like teacher? Say what? Say why I living on street then? Then is who tell you I living on street? See here, is Sheraton I live. All them box and carochies there on the road-side? Well, I have to whisper and tell you this for I don't want the breeze to catch it. You see the wappen-bappen on the streetside there? Is one old lady ask me to watch it for her till she come back. And cause mi heart so good, me say yes. I watching it day and night though is Sheraton I live. For the old lady don't come back yet. Quick, before the light change for I don't eat nutten from morning. I don't know is what sweet you so. But thank you all the same. Drive good, you hear.

&.&.&.

I hope you don't hear already, Sar, what that foolish Doctor Bartholomew saying about me all over town? Is him should lock up in Bellevue, and all the people inside there set free, you know. But he couldn't keep me lock up for I smarter than all of them. That's what Teacher used to tell me. I come brighter than all the other pickney around. And tree never grow in my face neither. Beg you a little food money there nuh before the light turn green. A who you calling dutty? A why you a wind up yu window and mek up yu face? You know say is Isabella Francina Myrtella Jones this you a talk to? And since when dutty bwoy like you think you can eggs-up so talk to Miss Catherine daughter that studying to turn teacher? Why you a turn yu head a gwan seh you no see me? I know you see me all right for, though I don't behave as if I notice, I know all you young men sitting on the bridge every day there eyeing me as I pass. Would like to drag me down, drag me right down to your level. Have my name outa road like how you all have Canepiece Icilda. And that is why I hold up my head and wear two slip under my skirt. And I don't pay you all no mind. For what I would want with any of you? Then wait, you not even giving me a two cents there and I don't eat from morning? Gwan, you ol' red nayga you. From I see you drive up I shoulda know seh is that Bartholomew send you. Send you to torment me. You ugly just like him, to rah. Go weh!

Hello, my sweet little darling. What you have to give me today? I don't eat a thing from morning, Mother. I wouldn't tell you lie in front of your little girl. Is same so my little one did look, you know? Seven pound, six and a half ounce she did weigh, and pretty like a picture. Is bad-minded people make them take her away. Thank you, Mother. God bless you and the little darling. Say who take her? Well me have to whisper it for me don't want the breeze to catch it. But is that Elfraida Campbell, that's who. The one that did say me did grudge her Jimmy Watson. Then you nuh remember her? Is she and her mother burn bad candle for me mek me buck mi foot and fall. For I never had those intentions. No such intentions. Is two slip I wear under my skirt for I was studying to be teacher. Is Miss Catherine my mother, you know. Say the light changing? You gone? God bless you, my precious daughter.

Young girl, I see you courting. But don't mek that young man behind steering wheel have business with you before you married, you hear? For once he know you he drag you down, drag you down to nutten. Then is pure ashes you eat. Pure dutty fe yu bed. The two of you a laugh! You better mind is nuh laugh today, cry tomorrow. But what a way you resemble Jimmy Watson ee. Him was handsome just like you. Thank you, mi darling, the two of you drive good, you hear. Say who is Jimmy Watson? Then you never know him? The same Jimmy Watson that did come as the assistant teacher and all the girls did love him off. Well, not me. For I didn't have no intention to take on young man before I get certification. Is Shortwood Teacher Training College I was going to, you know. Eh-eh, then you just wind up yu window and drive off so? What a bad-mannered set of children ee.

Like I was saying, Sar, I was busy with my studying and that is why that Elfraida Campbell did get her hooks into Jimmy Watson. For what Jimmy would really want with girl that can barely sign her name, nuh matter she walk and fling her hips about? So I just study and bide my time. Oh, God bless you, Sar, I could kiss yu hand. Is from morning I don't eat, you know. But that Elfraida is such a wicked girl, Sar, she and her mammy. If you ever see her, please call the constable for me, for is plenty things she have to answer for. Courthouse business, sar. If she and her mammy didn't work negromancy on me, Doctor Bartholomew wouldn't be looking for me all now. But he will never never find me. You want to know why? You see that big box there a roadside? Is there I hide, you know. Once I get inside my box, not a living soul can find me. They could send out one million policeman to search for me. Two million soldier. The whole of Salvation Army. They could look into the box till they turn fool. They could shine they torch, bring searchlight and X-ray and TV and atomic bomb. Not one of them could ever find me. Aright, Sar. You gone? God bless you.

&. &. &.

Look at my darling lady in the white car who always give me something. God bless you and keep you, my dear. Mine how you travel, you hear? Satan set plenty snares in the world for the innocent. Take me now. Is not me did go after Jimmy Watson. As God is mi judge. Him and Elfraida Campbell was getting on good-good there. It was a disgrace that a girl should act so common and make people carry her name all over the district like that. Even the breeze did tek it. And he was man of education too. What about his reputation? So when he first put question to me I didn't business, for I never want people have anything to say about me and I don't get my certificate yet. But it was just as I thought. Jimmy Watson wanted a woman that wouldn't shame him, a decent woman with broughtupcy and plenty book-learning. That is how he put it to me. And I resist and I resist but, after a while, that Jimmy Watson so handsome and have sweet-mout so, him confabulation just wear down mi resistance. Never mind bout certification and teacher college—eh-eh, you gone already. God bless you, sweetheart.

&. &. &.

Sar, you see that police fellow there from morning? The constable that is like a thorn in mi side? Can't get a good night rest from him beating on mi bedroom with him stick. Is what do him ee? Is Satan send him to torment me, you know. You know who Satan is? Beg you a dollar, nuh? A hungry, you see. A don't eat a thing from morning. Satan and Bartholomew is one and the same. Then you never know? And you look so bright? Look as if is university you come from. Don't is so? Well thank you, Sar. The good Lord will bless you. And if you see Bartholomew there up at U.C., tell him is lie. Is lie he telling about the baby. Say it was all in mi mind. You ever hear a piece of madness like that? Is Bartholomew they suppose to lock up and the child weigh eight and three-quarter pound? A spanking baby boy. Is that cause Elfraida Campbell to burn bad candle for me. Jealousy just drive her crazy. Eh-hm. Drive good, ya. And beg you tell government what Bartholomew going on with, you hear?

&. &. &.

From I born and grow I never know man could lie like that Jimmy Watson. Is only Bartholomew lie good like him, you know, my lady and gentleman. Thank you for a smalls, Sar, for a cup of tea. Nothing pass my lips from morning. Thank you, Sar. God bless. You did know Jimmy Watson swear to my mother he never touch me? Never have a thing to do with me? Fancy that! So is who was lying with me every night there? Who was plunging into me like St. George with his sword? He cry the living eye-water the day my mother ask if he business with me, for that time the baby already on the way. I could feel it kicking inside me. And that lying Jimmy Watson say he never lay hands on me. Same thing the lying Bartholomew did tell my mother. That no man ever touch me. How man can lie so, ee? So is how the baby did come then, answer me that? How baby can born so, without father? Ten and a half pound it weigh. Say what, Sar? Say why if I have children I living on street? Then is why unno red nayga so faas and facety ee? Answer me that? You see me asking you question bout fe yu pickney? Unno gwan! Think because you see me look so I don't come from nowhere? Ever see me without my paper and pencil yet? Ever see me without my shoes and stocking and two slip under my dress? Think I wear them little clingy-clingy frock without slip like that Elfraida Campbell so every man could see my backside swing when I walk? Unno gwan!

&. &. &.

So is what sweet you so, you little facety bwoy? You never see stone fling after car yet? You want me bus one in yu head? Say somebody shoulda call police? So why you don't do it, since you so shurance and force-ripe. Mek that constable bwoy come near me today. Mek them send that Bartholomew. Send for them. Do. I want them to arrest me at Lady Musgrave Road traffic light here today. I want them to take me down to courthouse. I want to have my day in court. I want to stand up in front of judge and jury. I want to say "Justice" and beg him to ask them certain question. He-hey. Don't mek I laugh here today. You want to know something, sweet boy. Them not going to do a thing about me, you know. Say wha mek? Well, me have to whisper it, for me nuh want no breeze catch hold of it. But the reason is because they fraid. Fraid to give me my day in court. Fraid to have me ask my question there. All of them fraid. Even the judge. Even Massa God himself. For nobody want to take responsibility to answer me. Gwan, you little dutty bwoy. Yu face favour!

&. &. &.

Good day, Missis. You did say you want to hear my question? Well, beg you a money there nuh, please. I don't get a thing to eat from morning. Thank you, Miss. You want to hear my question, please? So why you winding up yu glass? Why you unmannersable so? Well, whether you want to hear or not, you stupid bitch,

I, Isabella Francina Myrtella Jones, am going to tell you. So you can ease down all you want. I going to shout it from Lady Musgrave Road traffic light. I going to make the breeze take it to the four corners of everywhere. First: Is who take away my child? Second: Why Jimmy Watson lie so and say he never lie with me? Third: Why they let that Elfraida Campbell and her mother tie Jimmy Watson so I never even have a chance with him? Fourth: Why my mother Miss Catherine never believe anything I say again? Why she let me down so? Is obeah them obeah her too why she hand me over to that Bartholomew? Fifth: Why that Bartholomew madder than mad and he walking bout free as a bird? Who give him the right to lock up people in Bellevue and burn bright light all night and ask them all sort of foolish question? Sixth: What is the government going to do about these things? Seventh: If there is still Massa God up above is what I do why him have to tek everybody side against me?

MAKEDA SILVERA

HER HEAD A VILLAGE

for Nan

Her head was a noisy village, one filled with people, active and full of life, with many concerns and opinions. Children, including her own, ran about. Cousins twice removed bickered. A distant aunt, Maddie, decked out in two printed cotton dresses, a patched-up pair of pants and an old fuzzy sweater marched up and down the right side of her forehead. Soon she would have a migraine. On the other side, a pack of idlers lounged around a heated domino game, slapping the pieces hard against her left forehead. Close to her neck sat the gossiping crew, passing around bad news and samples of malicious and scandalous tales. The top of her head was quiet. Come evening this would change, with the arrival of schoolchildren; when the workers left their factories and offices, the pots, banging dishes and televisions blaring would add to the noisy village.

The Black woman writer had been trying all month to write an essay for presentation at an international forum for Third World women. She was to address the topic "Writing As a Dangerous Profession." This was proving to be more difficult as the weeks passed. She pleaded for quiet, but could silence only the children.

The villagers did not like her style of writing, her focus and the new name she called herself—feminist. They did not like her choice of lovers, her spending too many hours behind her desk or propped up in her bed with paper and pen or book. The workers complained that she should be in the factories and offices with them; the idlers said she didn't spend much time playing with them and the gossiping crew told so many tales that the woman writer had trouble keeping her essay separate from their stories. Some of the villagers kept quiet, going about their business, but they were too few to shut out the noise. Maddie did not often

546

side with the writer, but neither did she poke at her. She listened and sometimes smiled at the various expressions that surfaced on the woman writer's face. Maddie stood six feet tall with a long, stern face and eyes like well-used marbles. The villagers said Maddie was a woman of the spirits, a mystic woman who carried a sharpened pencil behind her ear. She walked about the village all day, sometimes marching loudly, and other times quietly. Some days she was seen talking to herself.

"When I first come to this country, I use to wear one dress at a time. But times too hard, now you don't know if you coming or going, so I wear all my clothes. You can't be too sure of anything but yourself. So I sure of me, and I wear all my clothes on my back. And I talk to meself, for you have to know yourself in this time."

The villagers didn't know what to make of her. Some feared her, others respected her. The gossipers jeered behind her back.

Plugging her ears against spirit-woman Maddie, the Black woman writer sat in the different places she thought would be good to her. She first sat behind her desk, but no words came. It was not so much that there were no words to write down—there were many—but the villagers were talking all at once and in so many tongues that it was hard for her to hold onto their words. Each group wanted her to feature it in the essay.

Early in the morning, after her own children left for school, she tried to write in her bed. It was a large queen-size pine bed with five pillows in a small room on the second floor. The room was a pale green and the ceilings a darker shade of green—her favourite colour. She was comfortable there and had produced many essays and poems from that bed. Its double mattress almost reached the ceiling. She felt at peace under the patchwork blanket. It took her back to her grandparents' wooden house a mile from the sea, in another village, the tropical one where she was born. Easter lilies, powder-puff trees, dandelions and other wild flowers circled the house. She saw a red-billed Streamertail, then a yellow-crowned night heron and a white bellied Caribbean dove. Their familiar voices filled her head: "Quaart, Tlee-oo-ee, cruuuuuuuuuuu," and other short repeated calls.

She wrote only lists of "To do's."
washing
cleaning
cooking
laundry
telephone calls
appointments.
At the edge of the paper birds took flight.

Nothing to do with writing, she thought. On days like these, convinced that she would get no writing done, she left the village and lunched with friends. She did not tell her friends about the village in her head. They would think her crazy, like Maddie. When she was alone, after lunch, scores of questions flooded her head.

What conditions are necessary for one to write?
What role do children play in a writer's creativity?
Is seclusion a necessary ingredient?
Questions she had no answers for.

Sometimes, she holed up in the garden shed at the edge of the backyard. She had cleared out a space and brought in a kerosene heater. The shed faced south. Old dirty windows ran the length of it and the ceiling's cracked blue paint threatened to fall. There she worked on an oversize ill-kept antique desk, a gift from a former lover. She had furnished the space with two chairs, a wooden crate stacked with a dictionary and a few books, a big armchair dragged from the neighbour's garbage, postcards pasted on the walls to remind her of Africa. There were a few things from her village: coconut husks, ackee seeds, photographs of birds, flowers and her grandparents' house near the sea.

One afternoon, however, the villagers discovered the shed and moved in. The idlers set up their gambling table. Gossip-mongers sat in a large area and Maddie walked around quietly and read everything written on every piece of paper. Soon they all wanted to read her essay. The idlers made fun of her words. The gossip-mongers said they had known all along what she would write. Offices and factories closed early, as the others hurried into the shed to hear what all the shouting was about.

They were all talking at once, with varying opinions.

"Writing is not a dangerous profession, writing is a luxury!" shouted one of the workers.

"Many of us would like to write but can't. We have to work, find food to support our families. Put that in your essay."

"Look here, read here, something about woman as a lover and the danger of writing about that."

The Black woman writer's head tore in half as the villagers snatched at the paper. She shouted as loud as she could that there was more to the paper than that.

"See for yourselves—here, read it, I am also writing about the economics of writing, problems of women writers who have families." Almost out of breath, she continued, "See, I also wrote about cultural biases."

"Cultural biases," snarled a cold, grating voice. "Why not just plain old racism? What's wrong with that word?" Before she could answer, another villager who was jumping up and down silenced the rest of them. "This woman thing can't go into the paper. It wouldn't look right to talk about that at a Third World conference." They all shouted in agreement.

She felt dizzy. Her ears ached. Her mouth and tongue were heavy. But she would not give in. She tried to block them out by calling up faces of the women she had loved. But she saw only the faces of the villagers and heard only the sounds of their loud chatter.

"No one will write about women lovers. These are not national concerns in Third World countries. These issues are not relevant. These," they shouted, "are white bourgeois concerns!"

Exhausted, the Black woman writer tried again. "All I want to do is to write something about being a Black lesbian in a North American city. One where white racism is cloaked in liberalism and where Black homophobia . . ." They were not listening. They bombarded her with more questions.

"What about the danger of your writing being the definitive word for all Black women? What about the danger of writing in a liberal white bourgeois society and of selling out? Why don't you write about these things?"

She screamed at them to shut up and give her a voice, but they ignored her and talked even louder.

"Make it clear that you, as a Black woman writer, are privileged to be speaking on a panel like this."

"And what about the danger of singular achievement?" asked a worker.

"Woman lover," sniggered another. "What about the danger of writing about racism? Police harassment? Murders of our villagers?"

Many times during the month the Black woman writer would scream at them to shut up. And when she succeeded in muting their voices she was tired because they refused to speak one at a time.

On days like these the Black woman writer escaped from the garden shed to play songs by her favourite blues singer, drink bottles of warm beer and curl up in her queen-size pine bed. She held onto the faces of her lovers and tried to forget the great difficulty in writing the essay.

The writer spent many days and nights staring at the blank white paper in front of her. The villagers did not ease up. They criticized the blank white paper. It was only a few days before the conference. "You have to start writing," they pressured her. "Who is going to represent us?"

Words swarmed around her head like wasps. There was so much she wanted to say about "Writing As a Dangerous Profession," about dangers to *her* as a Black woman, writer, lesbian. At times she felt that writing the paper was hopeless. Once she broke down and cried in front of the villagers. On this particular day, as the hour grew close, she felt desperate—suicidal, in fact. The villagers had no sympathy for her.

"Suicide? You madder than Maddie!" they jeered. "Give Maddie the paper and let her use her pencil," they heckled.

"I'm not mad," she protested with anger. "Get out of my head. Here"—she threw the blank paper on the ground—"write, write, you all write."

"But you are the writer," they pestered her. They were becoming hostile and vicious. The woman writer felt as if her head would burst.

She thought of Virginia Woolf's *A Room of One's Own*. She wondered if Woolf had had a village in her head.

She took to spending more time in bed with a crate of warm beer at the side. Her eyes were red from worry, not enough sleep and too much drink. She studied her face in a small handmirror, examining the lines on her forehead. They were deep and pronounced, lines she had not earned, even with the raising of children, writing several essays and poetry books, cleaning, cooking and caring for lovers. She gazed at all the books around her and became even more depressed.

Interrupted by the angry voices of the villagers, overwhelmed by the force of their voices, she surrendered her thoughts to them.

"Well, what are you going to write? We have ideas to give you." The Black woman writer knew their ideas. They were not new, but she listened.

"Write about women in houses without electricity."

"Write about the dangers of living in a police state."

"Write about Third World issues."

"Write about . . . about . . ."

"Stick to the real issues that face Black women writers."

"Your sexuality is your personal business. We don't want to hear about it, and the forum doesn't want to know."

They accused her of enjoying the luxury of being a lesbian in a decaying society, of forgetting about their problems.

She tried to negotiate with them. "Listen, all I want is a clear head. I promise to write about your concerns." But they disagreed. "We gave you more than enough time, and you've produced nothing." They insisted that they all write the paper. She was disturbed by their criticism. She would never complete the paper with so many demands. The Black woman writer was full of despair; she wanted to explain to the villagers, once again, that what made writing dangerous for her was who she was—Black/woman/lesbian/mother/worker. . . . But they would not let her continue. In angry, harsh voices they pounded her head. "You want to talk about sexuality as a political issue? Villagers are murdered every time they go out, our young people jailed and thrown out of schools." Without success, she explained that she wanted to talk about all the dangers of writing. "Have you ever heard of, read about lesbians in the Third World? They don't have the luxury of sitting down at an international forum and discussing this issue, so why should you?"

Her head blazed; her tiny, tight braids were like coals on fire. The villagers stayed in her head, shouting and laughing. She tried closing her eyes and massaging her forehead. With her eyes still closed, she eased her body onto the couch. Familiar footsteps sounded at the side of her head. Maddie appeared. "All this shouting and hollering won't solve anything—it will only make us tired and enemies. We all have to live together in this village." Not one villager joked about her two dresses, pants and sweater. Not one villager had anything to say about the pencil stuck in her hair, a pencil she never used. Maddie spoke for a long time, putting the villagers to sleep.

The Black woman writer slept late, dreaming first of her grandparents' village and then of her lovers. Now Maddie's face came. She took Maddie's hand and they set out down the village streets, through the fields of wild flowers, dandelions, Easter lilies. Maddie took the pencil from her head and began to write. With Maddie beside her, she awoke in a bed of wild flowers, refreshed.

CARLOS ARTURO TRUQUE

SONATINA FOR TWO DRUMS

It was impossible to sleep that night. There, in the very room, a few paces away, maybe closer, lay Damiana, wheezing. Her lungs sounded like old bellows. And to make it worse, that old character Mr. Sterns had wasted three days stumbling drunkenly from here to there, from one bank of the river to the other, getting more and more sucked into the mesmerizing beat. Nothing but the music mattered to him when he heard an infectious song; his feet just started right up dancing.

The celebrations for the patron saint of the town, Santa Barbara del Rayo, happened to fall at the very worst time, right when la Damiana's lungs were giving out.

It was painful for the woman to breathe; she slowly drew air in through her nose, then let it escape her wind-bag lungs with a quivering sound, much like the high trill of the small "conuno" drums. Damn it all! This problem had gone on for three years now!

"I can't breathe, Santiago . . . I can't breathe!"

And then there was the cold. She was always cold, though our Lord had blessed the town of Santa Barbara of Timbiquí with a burning sun. And she was cold, even at night.

She shivered, while he twisted and turned in bed, sweating so much that he felt like *melcocha*—brown, sticky molasses taffy. Unable to sleep, he touched his giant, naked body, longing for a woman. Sometimes he would go to the roof and stretch

Translated by Elizabeth M. Allen. Translator's Note: I wish to thank Dr. Margaret Peden, for her editing and suggestions, and Ricardo Restrepo Pinilla, whose knowledge of Colombian and Panamanian coastal dialect was an invaluable help.

out on the cool surface, facing the star-filled sky, to count, star by star, until his eyes ached. Or until he heard her, from inside, gasping: "I can't breathe, Santiago . . . I can't breathe!"

Then, he would enter and stand there, beside his wife's bed, unable to figure out what he should do. Her eyes shone at him out of the darkness, and he could hear the rasping, labored rise and fall of her lungs as the air escaped them, with a sound that echoed inside his ears. The thing he could never understand was why she said she was cold. She always complained of being cold, but when he touched her body it was covered with beads of sweat, and was as hot as the sun-baked stones along the river at siesta time.

Mr. Sterns, when he discussed the matter of the chills, would shake his head from side to side and exclaim "Very bad." This struck Santiago as strange, because he thought Mr. Sterns always said "Very good." To clear up any doubts, Mr. Sterns added, "*Mucho malo, carajo!,*" and then promised to take Damiana down to Buenaventura by boat. If he hadn't shown up at so many parties and drunk his fill of *biche* and *tapestura* that flowed like streams through the streets of Timbiquí this time of year, he would have done it for sure, because he was a man of his word.

"I can't breathe, Santiago, I can't breathe. . . ."

He heard her. He couldn't help hearing her, but there was nothing he could do. And she called out for him, only for Santiago, who was probably the last person who knew what to do in this situation.

For three long years now he had heard the same words moaned in the same rasping tone, sounding like *conuno* and bass drums reverberating inside his head—three times three hundred and sixty-five days of the damned noise!

For too long he had spent his nights fitfully awake and asleep, tossing and turning, contemplating a sliver of moonlight shining through an opening in the woven palm leaf thatching.

He spent many a night thinking about the firm breasts and supple body of the other Damiana, the one who danced her *Patacorés, Jugas* and *Currulaos* so well during fiestas in years past in honor of "Our Little Protectress Against Lightning."[1]

Maybe it was just as well that Damiana's lungs were finally giving out. Many nights, he couldn't deny it, he wished that it could all be over with, especially when he entertained thoughts of cornering la Guillermina, an ebony woman who was

---

1. The *Currulao* is a Colombian coastal dance of African origin in which a woman pretends to pursue, then flee from her partner, tantalizing him by flitting a handkerchief or her skirt at him. The man eventually begins to lean over the woman, who dances bending backwards. It becomes a contest to see how far he can make her go without falling. The *Juga* and the *Patacoré* are both variations of the *Currulao,* only differing in tempo. The chorus "she's going to fall" and "it's coming down" is sung during the part of the dance when the man is trying to make the woman fall. The same refrain is heard throughout the Caribbean in modern *salsa* and *merengue* tunes, probably all echoes of this original African dance. Possibly, North American popular music shares this heritage; lines such as "it's coming down," "get down," and "catch me I'm falling," can be heard in many top 40 tunes.

constantly laughing and who little by little was getting under his skin. The whole thing was sheer torture! Even though he had never given her so much as a kiss, she got him so worked up his heart beat faster than the fiesta day drums.

"Hey you, Guillermina, . . . yeah, you, Guillermina. . . ."

And she, with her saucy body, her breasts like smooth dark custard, slipped from his hands, leaving his desires frustrated, his male lust unfulfilled, and his throat feeling like a metal tube, all tense and dry.

"Get your hot hands away from me! . . . You'd better just cool on down, or I'll go tell la Damiana! . . ."

"Nah, you're not going to tell her nothing . . ."

There he was again, making his moves. Once again he was "that slick, black gigolo, Santiago . . .", with his mouth all dry because of what these women did to him, looking for something Damiana could no longer give him, her lungs all tattered to shreds.

"Damn those *conuno* drums, *carajo!*" Santiago said to himself again, hearing the constant beat from the other side of the river, where his *patrón,* Mr. Sterns, had to be pretty drunk by now, even though he had promised to take la Damiana down to Buenaventura so they could do something for her wheezing before it was too late.

"Damn it—those drums!"

Sleeping was out of the question. It was hardest of all for Santiago, whose whole body throbbed to the beat of the drums. Right there in bed, his body was itching to dance. The beat seemed to take hold of him, welling up inside of him.

"I can't take that damned racket anymore!"

He just couldn't sleep with that noise. It wasn't just la Damiana's rhythmic gurgling that kept him from sleeping. Now he could hear clearly the drums being played at the dance honoring Santa Barbara, Protectress Against Lightning. The air was reverberating with the sound of drums, marimbas and maracas. That damned *Patacoré* was filling his ears and seducing his feet; he just couldn't keep them still. He found his lips forming the dance refrain, "The *Patacoré* is coming down . . . she's going to fall . . . going to fall . . ." His body was prickling and restless, infected by the rhythm wafting from across the river.

"Those damned *conuno* drums, *carajo!*," he said to himself, just to say something, wondering if Mr. Sterns, the landowner, would be at the fiesta or not, and if he'd be able to wake up in any shape to take Damiana by boat down to Buenaventura. He wondered whether Mr. Sterns might already be so drunk that his English had gone the way of his broken Spanish. "I'm sure he's pretty far gone by now," he thought. "Tomorrow he'll wake up and he won't even know where his head is. It will never occur to him that he was going to take the woman down to the port, to get rid of that damned wheezing. It sure would be nice if he would remember that. . . ."

Santiago wanted to go across to the other side of the river, but not to say anything to Mr. Sterns. It was because he knew that he would find la Guillermina over there, in her starched skirt, with pointed breasts showing beneath her blouse. That old sensation was coming over him again; he was possessed by an uncontrollable desire to watch her dance the *Juga* and the *Patacoré,* to get that tickly feeling at the sight of her large quivering breasts. The same thing had happened when he first started winking at la Damiana. No one ever knew, but as a result, she had some very jolting, unsettling dreams. She felt a fluttering as if *guatiné* birds were inside her chest, and her breasts tingled even in their tightly bound nightclothes.

"Hey, you, Damiana. . . . yeah, you! . . . ."

Her body would counter his advances, as she flicked her petticoat to tantalize him, like a bullfighter provoking a bull. He would duck and lunge at her, then extend his arms out like wings, his nose filling with the delicious smell of sweating woman.

"Hey, you, Santiago! . . . yeah, you, Santiago!"

He couldn't take it any longer; the sheer passion in the sound of the drums enveloped him. Even there in bed, he felt stricken as if by a fever. He itched from head to toe.

"*Carajo*—those drums are driving me crazy!"

There was no way to sleep with that incessant din. La Damiana's rhythmic wheezing was getting louder, but the beat of the drums outside had gone absolutely crazy. They had reached a frenzied, continuous beat. Maybe he'd be better off on the terrace, sprawled out on the thatching damp from the night dew, where he could be free from the sticky, honey sensation he felt in bed. It was worse when he thought about la Guillermina, and of how long it had been since he had slept in the same bed as Damiana. He wasn't sure if it was before or after Damiana's illness that the other woman caught his eye. It must have been afterwards, because la Damiana had been quite a woman before she withered into big, sunken eyes and skin hanging on bones. She had been one fine looking black woman, a beautiful female specimen from head to toe. She was a devil when it came to withstanding her dance partner's advances, making her body completely taut, then moving only her curved hips and her ample, rounded breasts. When he looked at her, he was completely beside himself. He would tease her by fanning her with a handkerchief, resolutely lunge at her head-on, then stand perfectly still, while the bass drums, the maracas, and the women's voices reached an ever more frantic pitch. As they sang "The *Patacoré,* it's coming down, she's going to fall . . . ," old Pola's voice could be made out above it all, singing the last "she's going to fall" as serene as a kite blowing in the peaceful winds of childhood summers. And from far away, the beautiful verse could be made out, from under the beat of the tempered drum skins: "Even if the sea turned black and the fish could write poetry, it could never say how much I love you. . . ."

And Mr. Sterns, with a bottle of homemade liquor in his hand, went from couple to couple, saying over and over in his atrocious Spanish: "*Mucho bonito, carajo, much bonito!*"

It was that old feeling again, the feeling that never left him in peace or with any hope of peace. It had flowed through his veins for as long as he could remember. It was tempting him again, and he, Santiago, the slick, shameless woman chaser, couldn't take it anymore; he could never resist the allure of Guillermina's enticing, saucy laughter, as she slipped away from his charms like a slithering fish when he had almost gotten to her.

"Hey, that's enough! I know what you're up to—get your shameless black self the hell away from me!" And just like that she turned him down. He stood there, strangely shaky, feeling a dizziness surge up in his head, and his mouth filled with saliva, thick as shoemaker's paste.

"Hey you Damiana, yeah, you, Damiana!"

But no, it wasn't Damiana! He could no longer expect anything from her, stretched out there in the same room, fighting the air, her lungs like the flag Coronel García brought back from the battle of the river Telembí.

"That damned beat, *carajo!,*" he said under his breath, wondering why his wife hadn't called out to him in that way she always did when she had to gasp for air: "I can't breathe, Santiago . . . , I can't breathe! . . ."

He felt as desperate and hopeless as she did. And that's why he wished it could all just be over with, quickly. Yes, if only her breathing could gently cease, then her yellowed countenance with its sunken eyes might finally find peace, with those eyes hidden in the depths of a bottomless abyss. He wished it would finally happen, and then he wouldn't have to spend all night long tossing and turning in a sweat, or peering at the sky through openings in the thatch roof, while his animal desperation reared up, begging for the woman whose lungs had been eaten away before he had gotten all that he desired from her.

At that, he realized that what he desperately needed was outside, across the river, and that Damiana's gurgling noises were going to drive him absolutely crazy. His body kept on with its trembling, kept on with its hungry longing: like the night when he couldn't take it any longer and he went over to his wife's bed and thrust his hands inside her gown, only to find two withered sacklike breasts that just slipped from his hands.

On that occasion he had thought, without knowing exactly why, that this woman wasn't the real Damiana, or that it was Damiana without her body, without any of the fiery attributes that used to make his eyes sparkle like little candles. "Hey you, Guillermina . . . yeah, you . . . over here, Guillermina! . . ." He always thought of Damiana when he called out to la Guillermina; he confused her with the other Damiana, with the Damiana who embodied all that a woman could be, whom countless evenings he had held and made love to after dancing the night away to a *Juga,* drunk on *tapestusa,* their bodies burning up to the refrain of the *Patacoré:* "she's going to fall . . . going to fall . . ." How they would dance, shooting each other inviting looks, then mockingly rejecting flirtatious advances, their feet swollen from endlessly pounding out the rhythm of the drums.

He heard the drums start up again across the river.

At first they purred softly, as if the drummer were afraid of hurting the drumskin. Then, the sound got louder as the bass drum started up, joined by the marimba and then the thrashing sound of the maracas—Damn! how could he possibly sleep with all that sound pounding in his ears!

It was getting to him more and more. There was no way he could lie still in the darkness inside, hearing, but not really knowing exactly what was going on. It was a thousand times better to be sprawled out in the cool of the roof, with his ear fully exposed to the sound of the *Patacorés*.

From afar, the voice of old Pola, accompanied by the marimba, rang out, compelling him to go to the door and open it silently.

And, at last, there he was, alive, enveloped in the rasping rhythm of the maracas, once again swaying in circles as if on top of a drum, his blood flowing, completely out of himself, better than even in his memories.

Finally he was there, doing what he wanted to do, that devil, Mandingo Santiago, his hot breath singing the words "The *Patacoré*. . . . she's going to fall. . . .", finally feeling some relief.

And off in the shadows, la Damiana suffered with her breathing and her lungs that couldn't go on anymore, gurgling for air, making one last attempt to fill her two flacid lungs, barely emitting one last rhythmic wheeze, before reaching a final unconscious peace. Now they were like two old drumskins, completely out of air, and probably finally out of their pain.

Maybe no one realized what had happened. Perhaps it occurred just when the rooster crowed at the break of dawn, or when old Pola's voice rang out on high, as serene as a kite in the skies of summers past. Maybe it happened when the chorus could be heard during a lull between the beat of the throbbing drums.

Who will ever know?

ANA LYDIA VEGA

KEMBÉ
(CHRONICLE-GOSPEL
FOR A CERTAIN DECEMBER 19TH)

We have evidence of a Haitian agent named Chaulette, who arrived in
Puerto Rico in November, 1805 . . . Chaulette was part of a general conspir-
acy of all the slaves of the Caribbean, coordinated from Haiti . . .

—**Guillermo Baralt**, *Esclavos rebeldes*

YOU'RE CRAZY," they say Cubelo told Paul Pierrot the night the stars danced
over Fort Allen like the pips on some evil domino. "You're crazy," and laughing in
his face and telling him in the bloodless tongue of every coward on earth that con-
finement was messing up his mind—that was Cubelo's mistake. But they'd had all
they could take. Reality is a hired killer, you know that all too well. And there was
that other one, carrying on in his halting Creole Spanish, and Cubelo with his
knees shaking, trying to smile his way out.

Fine, so they were milling around stone soul naked in that Vietnam-in-Puerto-
Rico tent camp, but they weren't crazy, not those men. They might play with the
guards' burnt matches, fight over the undersized pants they got from the Juana

---

Translated by Mark McCaffrey.
On December 19, 1981, the Haitian prisoners at Fort Allan (Puerto Rico) collectively confronted
U.S. authorities in what the U.S. press called "a riot." (Author's note)

Diaz charities, paint trees and barbed wire on grocery bags, and bang on cookie tins to summon the throat cutter. But they weren't crazy. Never mind the daily lies, the searchlights, and the insomnia. Never mind the constantly busy pay phone, and no one to call anyway. Never mind the loudspeaker and its paternal, good-Joe deportation sermon, every hour on the hour.

"We were the crazy ones," says Lucas Marrero whenever asked, and his friends laugh to hide their agreement. Our hands were sweating and we could feel our insides crawl. No one wanted to say a goddamn thing anymore, so we passed around the rum to brace ourselves for guard duty on F-Block when it came time for it. Here Juan Merced enters the relay in his desire to get his say in: "No one ever found out what Innocent died of, did they? The autopsy and all that were a waste of time. I only know that from the time they found him dead on that cot with his hands crossed and his eyes rolled back, some pretty strange things began to happen."

Marcos Xiorro steals into the conversation.

"Things didn't just happen, they sort of spooked this way, and that was worse. The Haitians said they were seeing spirits. They'd wake up at night shaking and complaining about a weight on their chests. Something was sitting on them and wouldn't let them breathe. And they'd hear asses braying and dogs howling and I mean there was nothing like that around the camp."

Mateo Suarez, who has kept to himself all along, makes the most of the unexpected pause.

"Listen, man, I don't even believe in electricity, know what I mean, but whenever one of those cold, early morning breezes would come through, and there you were, all alone, dust kickin' up between the huts like in an Ay-rab movie . . . I swear on my mother's grave, there's not a macho here whose knees wouldn't turn to jelly."

"Well, I was pretty cool," rejoins Juan Merced, "until that old man and the other six Haitians got together and broke into their song and dance and started pouring out the Coke and scribbling on the ground with toothpaste and singing and dancing and talking weird and smoking and then blowing the smoke out through their mouths a certain way . . . Jesus, Mary, and Joseph, just thinking about it makes my hair stand up. All of a sudden the old man has this fit and starts jumpin' around and rollin' on the ground like doña Meri's daughter when one of her spirits gets into her. I mean I'm an outright officially baptized Catholic, seven sacraments and amen, but I've got a certain respect for things like that."

The ex-guards from the fort smile now, mumbling under their breath as though remembering boyhood pranks. And I'm still bent on reading in their eyes a clue to my own trap doors.

So, a bad spirit was making the rounds among the cots in F-Block. That is what the Loas said, who are the powers sought in a ritual somewhat affected by the ordeals of exile. Up on the hill, the misters in the jeep that never seemed to stop its daily run found out. And Bwana Jim declared that voodootion is revolution and ordered vigilance doubled in F-Block. Mas'r Congressman don't believe in ghosts.

Everybody else—prisoners and guards—was walking around with their soul in a tin can and their pockets full of amulets. No one was sleeping a wink in the F-Block. You had to do something to chase sleep away, though, so staying awake became a job in itself.

From Octela, Marcos Xiorro learned to make a closed circle of gravel around his feet when he had to go on watch and to call Legba with a simple rhyme.

"He told me that Legba was the traveler's saint, the one who keeps you company at the crossroads. So I prayed, what the hell. I figure what have you got to lose?"

Juan Merced patiently nudged Joseph's fist to make him sign his initials on a piece of windblown newspaper.

"I taught him to sign like I do so he wouldn't have to write that garbled name of his."

Lucas Marrero lent Jean-Marie a transistor radio that picked up Haiti in the early morning.

"Christ, he'd get so happy when they'd start speaking in their language. And if there was music on they'd get the boogaloo goin' anytime of day."

Mateo Suarez passed them his bottle of Don Q whenever he could.

Far off somewhere, aloof in his natural shyness, what was Cubelo thinking? Probably about the wandering zombie, goddamn his unwelcome soul. Or maybe about his three kids, their little bellies bloated with hunger. Was that why he could only answer "you're crazy" when Paul Pierrot said what he said the night the moon took to tumbling its wakebreaking barbedwirelight over death-struck Fort Allen?

As for who first heard the voice, no one recalls. But someone heard it. It came punching through the loudspeaker's broken litany in perfect Creole, so that even Cubelo understood:

Kembé rèd!	[Stand together!
Chaulette ap vini pou aidé nou:	Chaulette is coming to help us:
Kembé	Stand firm!]

And the guedé[1] had a name. And the guedé was. And its name was Chaulette. And it was not a guedé but a kanzo.[2] And the men heard. And the women, confined in the farthest blocks of the fort, also heard. With each sleepless night there grew here and there a pasty song that began, ended, and kept going in Kembé.

Kembé rèd!
Chaulette ap vini pou aidé nou:
Kembé!

---

1. Guedé: hostile or evil spirit in voodoo.
2. Kanzo: a good soul; a pure soul going through initiation into voodoo.

Juan Merced could whistle it. Marcos Xiorro could da-da-dum his way through it. With Jean-Marie's help, Lucas stammered through it with a Rican accent. Mateo learned it by heart. But he could never bring himself to sing it lest he call forth something he feared seeing. Finding out what it meant only made things worse for him:

"It means that this Cholet, or whoever, is coming to get them out of here. They have to hold out until he gets here, no two ways about it."

Meanwhile Cubelo is playing dumb and calling Paul Pierrot crazy. And the song mushrooming and spreading through the camp, snaking through the cracks in that hellish maze of cages, reaching Juana Diaz at night, crossing mountains and pounding the distant North like a storm mistaking its island.

Still they were awake, still they woke through sleep. And now Marcos had a saint, for Octela had initiated him into voodoo:

"When I put the necklace on, the saint came into me kind of strange and easy."

Now Joseph could sign his name with ease.

"He has a better hand than I did," confesses Juan Merced, both proud and embarrassed.

And Lucas Marrero could understand Creole.

"The radio's a good teacher, you know."

And Jean-Marie could read his own request for asylum.

"And it was in English," says Mateo Suarez, speaking from ten years' experience in the Bronx.

The braying donkey ceased to appear. The milk-thirsty serpent ceased to burden their breathing. The all-night song ceased to be heard. What had become a familiar refrain wasted away to an undernourished kembé, a kembé with diarrhea and miasma, sunken cheeks and hollow eyesockets. A rasping rag of a kembé.

"The truth is, a jail will kill anybody's appetite."

"Chaulette's not coming," the old medium told them, the houngan that knew all. And the light in every eye failed. Every hope grew weak.

"We told them that the people outside were protesting, marching with picket signs. I don't know if they understood us."

In the distance the marchers' torches went by like sails on forgotten boats. Every brow looked troubled.

The arrival of the jeep was to blame, or so everyone said. It came at dawn. And behind it, a busload of men in uniform.

"They brought the Texas guard in because they didn't trust us," says Lucas, lowering his voice just in case.

One: In came twelve men with weapons.

Two: they cleared out the inside aisle connecting the separate blocks.

Three: they brought a new wire fence out of the dark to block the doorways that opened out into the aisle.

"Then," says Marcos, his hands racing ahead of his words, "everyone started to sing . . ."

Kembé rèd!
Chaulette ap vini pou aidé nou:
Kembé!

The paltry kembé starts filling out, grows more solemn, deeper, like real skins on a real soundbox, gets raw, gets tambou, gets more tumbadora, more bomba, more tambora, more batá. The voices peal through the black hills, find their weight and return, redoubling the rulé, blowing the true asotos harmony, serving the night its explosion.

"Then," says Juan, "the women gathered on that side of the camp and the men on this side. And everyone pitched in at once with the thrust of eight hundred bodies, God help them, and they lunged together to force that fence down between the two blocks and the aisle. And they heaved and pushed and heaved until it's sure enough down and then you had that mass of raging men and women mixing it up, and God, it got really frightening."

And what about you four?

"We had orders not to intervene until told to," says Mateo, wetting his dried lips. "So we stepped back and kept quiet just in case. It was gonna come down hard now and it was sad to see, but hey, you know . . ."

When the Americans in the jeep that never seemed to stop gave the orders to spray the morning rosary, so to speak, Cubelo saw the Texas guardsmen grab the hoses and gas. He saw Mateo, Juan, Lucas, and Marcos, too, watching it all from way back. And though he alone knows this for sure, he probably saw the boy in white with the red bandana around his head, making signs from atop the rusty barbed wire fangs, serene, smiling, standing on seven feet of air.

"That Cubelo's crazy. He didn't have to do anything."

He tore the night stick off of his belt.

"It was out of our hands entirely. I don't know what got into the man's head."

He threw his pistol on the ground and joined the long scream that woke the children, out in Juana Diaz, from the dream of their father's death.

NINETEEN FIFTY-FIVE

1955

The car is a brandnew red Thunderbird convertible, and it's passed the house more than once. It slows down real slow now, and stops at the curb. An older gentleman dressed like a Baptist deacon gets out on the side near the house, and a young fellow who looks about sixteen gets out on the driver's side. They are white, and I wonder what in the world they doing in this neighborhood.

Well, I say to J. T., put your shirt on, anyway, and let me clean these glasses offa the table.

We had been watching the ballgame on TV. I wasn't actually watching, I was sort of daydreaming, with my foots up in J. T.'s lap.

I seen 'em coming on up the walk, brisk, like they coming to sell something, and then they rung the bell, and J. T. declined to put on a shirt but instead disappeared into the bedroom where the other television is. I turned down the one in the living room; I figured I'd be rid of these two double quick and J. T. could come back out again.

Are you Gracie Mae Still? asked the old guy, when I opened the door and put my hand on the lock inside the screen.

And I don't need to buy a thing, said I.

What makes you think we're sellin'? he asks, in that hearty Southern way that makes my eyeballs ache.

Well, one way or another and they're inside the house and the first thing the young fellow does is raise the TV a couple of decibels. He's about five feet nine, sort of womanish looking, with real dark white skin and a red pouting mouth. His hair is black and curly and he looks like a Loosianna creole.

About one of your songs, says the deacon. He is maybe sixty, with white hair and beard, white silk shirt, black linen suit, black tie and black shoes. His cold gray eyes look like they're sweating.

One of my songs?

Traynor here just *loves* your songs. Don't you Traynor? He nudges Traynor with his elbow. Traynor blinks, says something I can't catch in a pitch I don't register.

The boy learned to sing and dance livin' round you people out in the country. Practically cut his teeth on you.

Traynor looks up at me and bites his thumbnail.

I laugh.

Well, one way or another they leave with my agreement that they can record one of my songs. The deacon writes me a check for five hundred dollars, the boy grunts his awareness of the transaction, and I am laughing all over myself by the time I rejoin J. T.

Just as I am snuggling down beside him though I hear the front door bell going off again.

Forgit his hat? asks J. T.

I hope not, I say.

The deacon stands there leaning on the door frame and once again I'm thinking of those sweaty-looking eyeballs of his. I wonder if sweat makes your eyeballs pink because his are sure pink. Pink and gray and it strikes me that nobody I'd care to know is behind them.

I forgot one little thing, he says pleasantly. I forgot to tell you Traynor and I would like to buy up all of those records you made of the song. I tell you we sure do love it.

Well, love it or not, I'm not so stupid as to let them do that without making 'em pay. So I says, Well, that's gonna cost you. Because, really, that song never did sell all that good, so I was glad they was going to buy it up. But on the other hand, them two listening to my song by themselves, and nobody else getting to hear me sing it, give me a pause.

Well, one way or another the deacon showed me where I would come out ahead on any deal he had proposed so far. Didn't I give you five hundred dollars? he asked. What white man—and don't even need to mention colored—would give you more? We buy up all your records of that particular song: first, you git royalties. Let me ask you, how much you sell that song for in the first place? Fifty dollars? A hundred, I say. And no royalties from it yet, right? Right. Well, when we buy up all of them records you gonna git royalties. And that's gonna make all them race record shops sit up and take notice of Gracie Mae Still. And they gonna push all them other records of yourn they got. And you no doubt will become one of the big name colored recording artists. And then we can offer you another five hundred dollars for letting us do all this for you. And by God you'll be sittin' pretty! You can go out and buy you the kind of outfit a star should have. Plenty sequins and yards of red satin.

I had done unlocked the screen when I saw I could get some more money out of him. Now I held it wide open while he squeezed through the opening between me and the door. He whipped out another piece of paper and I signed it.

He sort of trotted out to the car and slid in beside Traynor, whose head was back against the seat. They swung around in a u-turn in front of the house and then they was gone.

J. T. was putting his shirt on when I got back to the bedroom. Yankees beat the Orioles 10–6, he said. I believe I'll drive out to Paschal's pond and go fishing. Wanta go?

While I was putting on my pants J. T. was holding the two checks.

I'm real proud of a woman that can make cash money without leavin' home, he said. And I said *Umph*. Because we met on the road with me singing in first one little low-life jook after another, making ten dollars a night for myself if I was lucky, and sometimes bringin' home nothing but my life. And J. T. just loved them times. The way I was fast and flashy and always on the go from one town to another. He loved the way my singin' made the dirt farmers cry like babies and the womens shout Honey, hush! But that's mens. They loves any style to which you can get 'em accustomed.

1956

My little grandbaby called me one night on the phone: Little Mama, Little Mama, there's a white man on the television singing one of your songs! Turn on channel 5.

Lord, if it wasn't Traynor. Still looking half asleep from the neck up, but kind of awake in a nasty way from the waist down. He wasn't doing too bad with my song either, but it wasn't just the song the people in the audience was screeching and screaming over, it was that nasty little jerk he was doing from the waist down.

Well, Lord have mercy, I said, listening to him. If I'da closed my eyes, it could have been me. He had followed every turning of my voice, side streets, avenues, red lights, train crossings and all. It give me a chill.

Everywhere I went I heard Traynor singing my song, and all the little white girls just eating it up. I never had so many ponytails switched across my line of vision in my life. They was so *proud*. He was a *genius*.

Well, all that year I was trying to lose weight anyway and that and high blood pressure and sugar kept me pretty well occupied. Traynor had made a smash from a song of mine, I still had seven hundred dollars of the original one thousand dollars in the bank, and I felt if I could just bring my weight down, life would be sweet.

1957

I lost ten pounds in 1956. That's what I give myself for Christmas. And J. T. and me and the children and their friends and grandkids of all description had just finished dinner—over which I had put on nine and a half of my lost ten—when who should appear at the front door but Traynor. Little Mama, Little Mama! It's that white man who sings —— ——. The children didn't call it my song anymore. Nobody did. It was funny how that happened. Traynor and the deacon had bought up all my records, true, but on his record he had put "written by Gracie Mae Still." But that was just another name on the label, like "produced by Apex Records."

On the TV he was inclined to dress like the deacon told him. But now he looked presentable.

Merry Christmas, said he.

And same to you, Son.

I don't know why I called him Son. Well, one way or another they're all our sons. The only requirement is that they be younger than us. But then again, Traynor seemed to be aging by the minute.

You looks tired, I said. Come on in and have a glass of Christmas cheer.

J. T. ain't never in his life been able to act decent to a white man he wasn't working for, but he poured Traynor a glass of bourbon and water, then he took all the children and grandkids and friends and whatnot out to the den. After while I heard Traynor's voice singing the song, coming from the stereo console. It was just the kind of Christmas present my kids would consider cute.

I looked at Traynor, complicit. But he looked like it was the last thing in the world he wanted to hear. His head was pitched forward over his lap, his hands holding his glass and his elbows on his knees.

I done sung that song seem like a million times this year, he said. I sung it on the Grand Ole Opry, I sung it on the Ed Sullivan show. I sung it on Mike Douglas, I sung it at the Cotton Bowl, the Orange Bowl. I sung it at Festivals. I sung it at Fairs. I sung it overseas in Rome, Italy, and once in a submarine *underseas.* I've sung it and sung it, and I'm making forty thousand dollars a day offa it, and you know what, I don't have the faintest notion what that song means.

Whatchumean, what do it mean? It mean what it says. All I could think was: These suckers is making forty thousand a *day* offa my song and now they gonna come back and try to swindle me out of the original thousand.

It's just a song, I said. Cagey. When you fool around with a lot of no count mens you sing a bunch of 'em. I shrugged.

Oh, he said. Well. He started brightening up. I just come by to tell you I think you are a great singer.

He didn't blush, saying that. Just said it straight out.

And I brought you a little Christmas present too. Now you take this little box and you hold it until I drive off. Then you take it outside under that first streetlight back up the street aways in front of that green house. Then you open the box and see . . . Well, just *see.* What had come over this boy, I wondered, holding the box. I looked out the window in time to see another white man come up and get in the car with him and then two more cars full of white mens start out behind him. They was all in long black cars that looked like a funeral procession.

Little Mama, Little Mama, what it is? One of my grandkids come running up and started pulling at the box. It was wrapped in gay Christmas paper—the thick, rich kind that it's hard to picture folks making just to throw away.

J. T. and the rest of the crowd followed me out the house, up the street to the streetlight and in front of the green house. Nothing was there but somebody's gold-grilled white Cadillac. Brandnew and most distracting. We got to looking at it so till I almost forgot the little box in my hand. While the others were busy making 'miration I carefully took off the paper and ribbon and folded them up and put them in my pants pocket. What should I see but a pair of genuine solid gold caddy keys.

Dangling the keys in front of everybody's nose, I unlocked the caddy, motioned for J. T. to git in on the other side, and us didn't come back home for two days.

1 9 6 0

Well, the boy was sure nuff famous by now. He was still a mite shy of twenty but already they was calling him the Emperor of Rock and Roll.

Then what should happen but the draft.

Well, says J. T. There goes all this Emperor of Rock and Roll business.

But even in the army the womens was on him like white on rice. We watched it on the News.

Dear Gracie Mae [he wrote from Germany],

How you? Fine I hope as this leaves me doing real well. Before I come in the army I was gaining a lot of weight and gitting jittery from making all them dumb movies. But now I exercise and eat right and get plenty of rest. I'm more awake than I been in ten years.

I wonder if you are writing any more songs?

Sincerely,
   Traynor

I wrote him back:

Dear Son,

We is all fine in the Lord's good grace and hope this finds you the same. J. T. and me be out all times of the day and night in that car you give me—which you know you didn't have to do. Oh, and I do appreciate the mink and the new self-cleaning oven. But if you send anymore stuff to eat from Germany I'm going to have to open up a store in the neighborhood just to get rid of it. Really, we have more than enough of everything. The Lord is good to us and we don't know Want.

Glad to here you is well and gitting your right rest. There ain't nothing like exercising to help that along. J. T. and me work some part of every day that we don't go fishing in the garden.

Well, so long Soldier.

Sincerely,
   Gracie Mae

He wrote:

Dear Gracie Mae,

I hope you and J. T. like that automatic power tiller I had one of the stores back home send you. I went through a mountain of catalogs looking for it—I wanted something that even a woman could use.

I've been thinking about writing some songs of my own but every time I finish one it don't seem to be about nothing I've actually lived myself. My agent keeps sending me other people's songs but they just sound mooney. I can hardly git through 'em without gagging.

Everybody still loves that song of yours. They ask me all the time what do I think it means, really. I mean, they want to know just what I want to know. Where out of your life did it come from?

Sincerely,
Traynor

1968

I didn't see the boy for seven years. No. Eight. Because just about everybody was dead when I saw him again. Malcolm X, King, the president and his brother, and even J. T. J. T. died of a head cold. It just settled in his head like a block of ice, he said, and nothing we did moved it until one day he just leaned out the bed and died.

His good friend Horace helped me put him away, and then about a year later Horace and me started going together. We was sitting out on the front porch swing one summer night, dusk-dark, and I saw this great procession of lights winding to a stop.

Holy Toledo! said Horace. (He's got a real sexy voice like Ray Charles.) Look *at* it. He meant the long line of flashy cars and the white men in white summer suits jumping out on the drivers' sides and standing at attention. With wings they could pass for angels, with hoods they could be the Klan.

Traynor comes waddling up the walk.

And suddenly I know what it is he could pass for. An Arab like the ones you see in storybooks. Plump and soft and with never a care about weight. Because with so much money, who cares? Traynor is almost dressed like someone from a story-book too. He has on, I swear, about ten necklaces. Two set of bracelets on his arms, at least one ring on every finger, and some kind of shining buckles on his shoes, so that when he walks you get quite a few twinkling lights.

Gracie Mae, he says, coming up to give me a hug. J. T.

I explain that J. T. passed. That this is Horace.

Horace, he says, puzzled but polite, sort of rocking back on his heels, Horace.

That's it for Horace. He goes in the house and don't come back.

Looks like you and me is gained a few, I say.

He laughs. The first time I ever heard him laugh. It don't sound much like a laugh and I can't swear that it's better than no laugh a'tall.

He's gitting fat for sure, but he's still slim compared to me. I'll never see three hundred pounds again and I've just about said (excuse me) fuck it. I got to thinking about it one day an' I thought: aside from the fact that they say it's unhealthy, my fat ain't never been no trouble. Mens always have loved me. My kids ain't never complained. Plus they's fat. And fat like I is I looks distinguished. You see me coming and know somebody's *there*.

Gracie Mae, he says, I've come with a personal invitation to you to my house tomorrow for dinner. He laughed. What did it sound like? I couldn't place it. See them men out there? he asked me. I'm sick and tired of eating with them. They don't never have nothing to talk about. That's why I eat so much. But if you come to dinner tomorrow we can talk about the old days. You can tell me about that farm I bought you.

I sold it, I said.

You did?

Yeah, I said, I did. Just cause I said I liked to exercise by working in a garden didn't mean I wanted five hundred acres! Anyhow, I'm a city girl now. Raised in the country it's true. Dirt poor—the whole bit—but that's all behind me now.

Oh well, he said, I didn't mean to offend you.

We sat a few minutes listening to the crickets.

Then he said: You wrote that song while you was still on the farm, didn't you, or was it right after you left?

You had somebody spying on me? I asked.

You and Bessie Smith got into a fight over it once, he said.

You *is* been spying on me!

But I don't know what the fight was about, he said. Just like I don't know what happened to your second husband. Your first one died in the Texas electric chair. Did you know that? Your third one beat you up, stole your touring costumes and your car and retired with a chorine to Tuskegee. He laughed. He's still there.

I had been mad, but suddenly I calmed down. Traynor was talking very dreamily. It was dark but seems like I could tell his eyes weren't right. It was like something was sitting there talking to me but not necessarily with a person behind it.

You gave up on marrying and seem happier for it. He laughed again. I married but it never went like it was supposed to. I never could squeeze any of my own life either into it or out of it. It was like singing somebody else's record. I copied the way it was sposed to be *exactly* but I never had a clue what marriage meant.

I bought her a diamond ring big as your fist. I bought her clothes. I built her a mansion. But right away she didn't want the boys to stay there. Said they smoked up the bottom floor. Hell, there were *five* floors.

No need to grieve, I said. No need to. Plenty more where she come from.

He perked up. That's part of what that song means, ain't it? No need to grieve. Whatever it is, there's plenty more down the line.

I never really believed that way back when I wrote that song, I said. It was all bluffing then. The trick is to live long enough to put your young bluffs to use. Now if I was to sing that song today I'd tear it up. 'Cause I done lived long enough to know it's *true*. Them words could hold me up.

I ain't lived that long, he said.

Look like you on your way, I said. I don't know why, but the boy seemed to need some encouraging. And I don't know, seem like one way or another you talk to rich white folks and you end up reassuring *them*. But what the hell, by now I feel something for the boy. I wouldn't be in his bed all alone in the middle of the night for nothing. Couldn't be nothing worse than being famous the world over for something you don't even understand. That's what I tried to tell Bessie. She wanted that same song. Overheard me practicing it one day, said, with her hands on her hips: Gracie Mae, I'ma sing your song tonight. I *likes* it.

Your lips be too swole to sing, I said. She was mean and she was strong, but I trounced her.

Ain't you famous enough with your own stuff? I said. Leave mine alone. Later on, she thanked me. By then she was Miss Bessie Smith to the World, and I was still Miss Gracie Mae Nobody from Notasulga.

The next day all these limousines arrived to pick me up. Five cars and twelve bodyguards. Horace picked that morning to start painting the kitchen.

Don't paint the kitchen, fool, I said. The only reason that dumb boy of ours is going to show me his mansion is because he intends to present us with a new house.

What you gonna do with it? he asked me, standing there in his shirtsleeves stirring the paint.

Sell it. Give it to the children. Live in it on weekends. It don't matter what I do. He sure don't care.

Horace just stood there shaking his head. Mama you sure looks *good*, he says. Wake me up when you git back.

Fool, I say, and pat my wig in front of the mirror.

The boy's house is something else. First you come to this mountain, and then you commence to drive and drive up this road that's lined with magnolias. Do magnolias grow on mountains? I was wondering. And you come to lakes and you come to ponds and you come to deer and you come up on some sheep. And I figure these two is sposed to represent England and Wales. Or something out of Europe. And you just keep on coming to stuff. And it's all pretty. Only the man driving my car don't look at nothing but the road. Fool. And then *finally*, after all this time, you begin to go up the driveway. And there's more magnolias—only they're not in such good shape. It's sort of cool up this high and I don't think they're gonna make it. And then I see this building that looks like if it had a name it would be The Tara Hotel. Columns and steps and outdoor chandeliers and rocking chairs. Rocking chairs? Well, and there's the boy on the steps dressed in a dark green satin jacket like you see folks wearing on TV late at night, and he looks sort of like a fat dracula with all that house rising behind him, and standing beside him there's this little white vision of loveliness that he introduces as his wife.

He's nervous when he introduces us and he says to her: This is Gracie Mae Still, I want you to know me. I mean . . . and she gives him a look that would fry meat.

Won't you come in, Gracie Mae, she says, and that's the last I see of her.

He fishes around for something to say or do and decides to escort me to the kitchen. We go through the entry and the parlor and the breakfast room and the dining room and the servants' passage and finally get there. The first thing I notice is that, altogether, there are five stoves. He looks about to introduce me to one.

Wait a minute, I say. Kitchens don't do nothing for me. Let's go sit on the front porch.

Well, we hike back and we sit in the rocking chairs rocking until dinner.

Gracie Mae, he says down the table, taking a piece of fried chicken from the woman standing over him, I got a little surprise for you.

It's a house, ain't it? I ask, spearing a chitlin.

You're getting *spoiled,* he says. And the way he says *spoiled* sounds funny. He slurs it. It sounds like his tongue is too thick for his mouth. Just that quick he's finished the chicken and is now eating chitlins *and* a pork chop. *Me* spoiled, I'm thinking.

I already got a house. Horace is right this minute painting the kitchen. I bought that house. My kids feel comfortable in that house.

But this one I bought you is just like mine. Only a little smaller.

I still don't need no house. And anyway who would clean it?

He looks surprised.

Really, I think, some peoples advance *so* slowly.

I hadn't thought of that. But what the hell, I'll get you somebody to live in.

I don't want other folks living 'round me. Makes me nervous.

You *don't?* It *do?*

What I want to wake up and see folks I don't even know for?

He just sits there downtable staring at me. Some of that feeling is in the song, ain't it? Not the words, the *feeling.* What I want to wake up and see folks I don't even know for? But I see twenty folks a day I don't even know, including my wife.

This food wouldn't be bad to wake up to though, I said. The boy had found the genius of corn bread.

He looked at me real hard. He laughed. Short. They want what you got but they don't want you. They want what I got only it ain't mine. That's what makes 'em so hungry for me when I sing. They getting the flavor of something but they ain't getting the thing itself. They like a pack of hound dogs trying to gobble up a scent.

You talking 'bout your fans?

Right. Right. He says.

Don't worry 'bout your fans, I say. They don't know their asses from a hole in the ground. I doubt there's a honest one in the bunch.

That's the point. Dammit, that's the point! He hits the table with his fist. It's so solid it don't even quiver. You need a honest audience! You can't have folks that's just gonna lie right back to you.

Yeah, I say, it was small compared to yours, but I had one. It would have been worth my life to try to sing 'em somebody else's stuff that I didn't know nothing about.

He must have pressed a buzzer under the table. One of his flunkies zombies up.

Git Johnny Carson, he says.

On the phone? asks the zombie.

On the phone, says Traynor, what you think I mean, git him offa the front porch? Move your ass.

So two weeks later we's on the Johnny Carson show.

Traynor is all corseted down nice and looks a little bit fat but mostly good. And all the women that grew up on him and my song squeal and squeal. Traynor says: The lady who wrote my first hit record is here with us tonight, and she's agreed to sing it for all of us, just like she sung it forty-five years ago. Ladies and Gentlemen, the great Gracie Mae Still!

Well, I had tried to lose a couple of pounds my own self, but failing that I had me a very big dress made. So I sort of rolls over next to Traynor, who is dwarfted by me, so that when he puts his arm around back of me to try to hug me it looks funny to the audience and they laugh.

I can see this pisses him off. But I smile out there at 'em. Imagine squealing for twenty years and not knowing why you're squealing? No more sense of endings and beginnings than hogs.

It don't matter, Son, I say. Don't fret none over me.

I commence to sing. And I sound—wonderful. Being able to sing good ain't all about having a good singing voice a'tall. A good singing voice helps. But when you come up in the Hard Shell Baptist church like I did you understand early that the fellow that sings is the singer. Them that waits for programs and arrangements and letters from home is just good voices occupying body space.

So there I am singing my own song, my own way. And I give it all I got and enjoy every minute of it. When I finish Traynor is standing up clapping and clapping and beaming at first me and then the audience like I'm his mama for true. The audience claps politely for about two seconds.

Traynor looks disgusted.

He comes over and tries to hug me again. The audience laughs.

Johnny Carson looks at us like we both weird.

Traynor is mad as hell. He's supposed to sing something called a love ballad. But instead he takes the mike, turns to me and says: Now see if my imitation still holds up. He goes into the same song, *our* song, I think, looking out at his flaky audience. And he sings it just the way he always did. My voice, my tone, my inflection, everything. But he forgets a couple of lines. Even before he's finished the matronly squeals begin.

He sits down next to me looking whipped.

It don't matter, Son, I say, patting his hand. You don't even know those people. Try to make the people you know happy.

Is that in the song? he asks.

Maybe. I say.

1977

For a few years I hear from him, then nothing. But trying to lose weight takes all the attention I got to spare. I finally faced up to the fact that my fat is the hurt I don't admit, not even to myself, and that I been trying to bury it from the day I was born. But also when you git real old, to tell the truth, it ain't as pleasant. It gits lumpy and slack. Yuck. So one day I said to Horace, I'ma git this shit offa me.

And he fell in with the program like he always try to do and Lord such a procession of salads and cottage cheese and fruit juice!

One night I dreamed Traynor had split up with his fifteenth wife. He said: *You meet 'em for no reason. You date 'em for no reason. You marry 'em for no reason. I do it all but I swear it's just like somebody else doing it. I feel like I can't remember Life.*

The boy's in trouble, I said to Horace.

You've always said that, he said.

I have?

Yeah. You always said he looked asleep. You can't sleep through life if you wants to live it.

You not such a fool after all, I said, pushing myself up with my cane and hobbling over to where he was. Let me sit down on your lap, I said, while this salad I ate takes effect.

In the morning we heard Traynor was dead. Some said fat, some said heart, some said alcohol, some said drugs. One of the children called from Detroit. Them dumb fans of his is on a crying rampage, she said. You just ought to turn on the TV.

But I didn't want to see 'em. They was crying and crying and didn't even know what they was crying for. One day this is going to be a pitiful country, I thought.

JOHN EDGAR WIDEMAN

FEVER

To Matthew Carey, Esq., who fled Philadelphia in its hour of need and upon his return published a libelous account of the behavior of black nurses and undertakers, thereby injuring all people of my race and especially those with-out whose unselfish, courageous labours the city could not have survived the late calamity.

Consider Philadelphia from its centrical situation, the extent of its commerce, the number of its artificers, manufacturers and other circumstances, to be to the United States what the heart is to the human body in circulating the blood.

        —Robert Morris, 1777

H<small>E STOOD STARING</small> through a tall window at the last days of November. The trees were barren women starved for love and they'd stripped off all their clothes, but nobody cared. And not one of them gave a fuck about him, sifting among them, weightless and naked, knowing just as well as they did, no hands would come to touch them, warm them, pick leaves off the frozen ground and stick them back in place. Before he'd gone to bed a flutter of insects had stirred in the dark outside his study. Motion worrying the corner of his eye till he turned and focused where light pooled on the deck, a cone in which he could trap slants of snow so they materialized into wet, gray feathers that blotted against the glass, the planks of the deck. If he stood seven hours, dark would come again. At some point his reflection would hang in the glass, a ship from the other side of the world, docked in the ether. Days were shorter now. A whole one spent wondering what goes wrong would fly away, fly in the blink of an eye.

Perhaps, *perhaps it may be acceptable to the reader to know how we found the sick affected by the sickness; our opportunities of hearing and seeing them have been very great. They were taken with a chill, a headache, a sick stomach, with pains in their limbs and back, this was the way the sickness in general began, but all were not affected alike, some appeared but slightly affected with some of these symptoms, what confirmed us in the opinion of a person being smitten was the colour of their eyes.*

Victims in this low-lying city perished every year, and some years were worse than others, but the worst by far was the long hot dry summer of '93, when the dead and dying wrested control of the city from the living. Most who were able, fled. The rich to their rural retreats, others to relatives and friends in the countryside or neighboring towns. Some simply left, with no fixed destination, the prospect of privation or starvation on the road preferable to cowering in their homes awaiting the fever's fatal scratching at their door. Busy streets deserted, commerce halted, members of families shunning one another, the sick abandoned to suffer and die alone. Fear ruled. From August when the first cases of fever appeared below Water Street, to November when merciful frosts ended the infestation, the city slowly deteriorated, as if it, too, could suffer the terrible progress of the disease; fever, enfeeblement, violent vomiting and diarrhea, helplessness, delirium, settled dejection when patients *concluded they must go (so the phrase for dying was), and therefore in a kind of fixed determined state of mind went off.*

In some it raged more furiously than in others—some have languished for seven and ten days, and appeared to get better the day, or some hours before they died, while others were cut off in one, two or three days, but their complaints were similar. Some lost their reason and raged with all the fury madness could produce, and died in strong convulsions. Others retained their reason to the last, and seemed rather to fall asleep than die.

Yellow fever: an acute infectious disease of subtropical and tropical New World areas, caused by a filterable virus transmitted by a mosquito of the genus *Aëdes* and characterized by jaundice and dark colored vomit resulting from hemorrhages. Also called *yellow jack.*

Dengue: an infectious, virulent tropical and subtropical disease transmitted by mosquitos and characterized by fever, rash and severe pains in the joints. Also called *breakbone fever, dandy.* [Spanish, of African origin, akin to Swahili *kin-dinga.*]

Curled in the black hold of the ship he wonders why his life on solid green earth had to end, why the gods had chosen this new habitation for him, floating, chained to other captives, no air, no light, the wooden walls shuddering, battered, as if some madman is determined to destroy even this last pitiful refuge where he skids in foul puddles of waste, bumping other bodies, skinning himself on splintery beams and planks, always moving, shaken and spilled like palm nuts in the diviner's fist, and Esu casts his fate, constant motion, tethered to an iron ring.

In the darkness he can't see her, barely feels her light touch on his fevered skin. Sweat thick as oil but she doesn't mind, straddles him, settles down to do her work. She enters him and draws his blood up into her belly. When she's full, she pauses, dreamy, heavy. He could kill her then; she wouldn't care. But he doesn't. Listens to the whine of her wings lifting till the whimper is lost in the roar and crash of waves, creaking wood, prisoners groaning. If she returns tomorrow and carries away another drop of him, and the next day and the next, a drop each day, enough days, he'll be gone. Shrink to nothing, slip out of this iron noose and disappear.

Aëdes aegypti: a mosquito of the family *Culicidae,* genus *Aëdes* in which the female is distinguished by a long proboscis for sucking blood. This winged insect is a vector (an organism that carries pathogens from one host to another) of yellow fever and dengue. [New Latin *Aëdes,* from Greek *aedes,* unpleasant: *a* –, not + *edos,* pleasant . . .]

All things arrive in the waters and waters carry all things away. So there is no beginning or end, only the waters' flow, ebb, flood, trickle, tides emptying and returning, salt seas and rivers and rain and mist and blood, the sun drowning in an ocean of night, wet sheen of dawn washing darkness from our eyes. This city is held in the water's palm. A captive as surely as I am captive. Long fingers of river, Schuylkill, Delaware, the rest of the hand invisible; underground streams and channels feed the soggy flesh of marsh, clay pit, sink, gutter, stagnant pool. What's not seen is heard in the suck of footsteps through spring mud of unpaved streets. Noxious vapors that sting your eyes, cause you to gag, spit and wince are evidence of a presence, the dead hand cupping this city, the poisons that circulate through it, the sweat on its rotting flesh.

No one has asked my opinion. No one will. Yet I have seen this fever before, and though I can prescribe no cure, I could tell stories of other visitations, how it came and stayed and left us, the progress of disaster, its several stages, its horrors and mitigations. My words would not save one life, but those mortally affrighted by the fever, by the prospect of universal doom, might find solace in knowing there are limits to the power of this scourge that has befallen us, that some, yea, most will survive, that this condition is temporary, a season, that the fever must disappear with the first deep frosts and its disappearance is as certain as the fact it will come again.

They say the rat's-nest ships from Santo Domingo brought the fever. Frenchmen and their black slaves fleeing black insurrection. Those who've seen Barbados's distemper say our fever is its twin born in the tropical climate of the hellish Indies. I know better. I hear the drum, the forest's heartbeat, pulse of the sea that chains the moon's wandering, the spirit's journey. Its throb is source and promise of all things being connected, a mirror storing everything, forgetting nothing. To explain the fever we need no boatloads of refugees, ragged and wracked with killing fevers, bringing death to our shores. We have bred the affliction within our breasts. Each solitary heart contains all the world's tribes, and its precarious dance echoes the drum's thunder. We are our ancestors and our children, neighbors and strangers to ourselves. Fever descends when the waters that connect us are clogged with filth. When our seas are garbage. The waters cannot come and go when we are shut off one from the other, each in his frock coat, wig, bonnet, apron, shop, shoes, skin, behind locks, doors, sealed faces, our blood grows thick and sluggish. Our bodies void infected fluids. Then we are dry and cracked as a desert country, vital parts wither, all dust and dry bones inside. Fever is a drought consuming us from within. Discolored skin caves in upon itself, we burn, expire.

I regret there is so little comfort in this explanation. It takes into account neither climatists nor contagionists, flies in the face of logic and reason, the good doctors of the College of Physicians who would bleed us, purge us, quarantine, plunge us in icy baths, starve us, feed us elixirs of bark and wine, sprinkle us with gunpowder, drown us in vinegar according to the dictates of their various healing sciences. Who, then, is this foolish, old man who receives his wisdom from pagan drums in pagan forests? Are these the delusions of one whose brain the fever has already begun to gnaw? Not quite. True, I have survived other visitations of the fever, but while it prowls this city, I'm in jeopardy again as you are, because I claim no immunity, no magic. The messenger who bears the news of my death will reach me precisely at the stroke determined when it was determined I should tumble from the void and taste air the first time. Nothing is an accident. Fever grows in the secret places of our hearts, planted there when one of us decided to sell one of us to another. The drum must pound ten thousand thousand years to drive that evil away.

Fires burn on street corners. Gunshots explode inside wooden houses. Behind him a carter's breath expelled in low, labored pants warns him to edge closer to housefronts forming one wall of a dark, narrow, twisting lane. Thick wheels furrow the unpaved street. In the fire glow the cart stirs a shimmer of dust, faint as a halo, a breath smear on a mirror. Had the man locked in the traces of the cart cursed him or was it just a wheeze of exertion, a complaint addressed to the unforgiving weight of his burden? Creaking wheels, groaning wood, plodding footsteps, the cough of dust, bulky silhouette blackened as it lurches into brightness at the block's end. All gone in a moment. Sounds, motion, sight extinguished. What remained, as if trapped by a lid clamped over the lane, was the stench of dead bodies. A stench cutting through the ubiquitous pall of vinegar and gunpowder. Two, three, four corpses being hauled to Potter's Field, trailed by the unmistakable wake of decaying flesh. He'd heard they raced their carts to the burial ground. Two or three entering Potter's Field from different directions would acknowledge one another with challenges, raised fists, gather their strength for a last dash to the open trenches where they tip their cargoes. Their brethren would wager, cheer, toast the victor with tots of rum. He could hear the rumble of coffins crashing into a common grave, see the comical chariots bouncing, the men's legs pumping, faces contorted by fires that blazed all night at the burial ground. Shouting and curses would hang in the torpid night air, one more nightmare troubling the city's sleep.

He knew this warren of streets as well as anyone. Night or day he could negotiate the twists and turnings, avoid cul-de-sacs, find the river even if his vision was obscured in tunnel-like alleys. He anticipated when to duck a jutting signpost, knew how to find doorways where he was welcome, wooden steps down to a cobbled terrace overlooking the water where his shod foot must never trespass. Once beyond the grand houses lining one end of Water Street, in this quarter of hovels, beneath these wooden sheds leaning shoulder to shoulder were cellars and caves dug into the earth, poorer men's dwellings under these houses of the poor, an invisible region where his people burrow, pull earth like blanket and quilt round themselves to shut out cold and dampness, sleeping multitudes to a room, stacked and crosshatched and spoon fashion, themselves the only fuel, heat of one body passed to others and passed back from all to one. Can he blame the lucky ones who are strong enough to pull the death carts, who celebrate and leap and roar all night around the bonfires? Why should they return here? Where living and dead, sick and well must lie face to face, shivering or sweltering on the same dank floor.

Below Water Street the alleys proliferate. Named and nameless. He knows where he's going but fever has transformed even the familiar. He'd been waiting in Dr. Rush's entrance hall. An English mirror, oval framed in scalloped brass, drew him. He watched himself glide closer, a shadow, a blur, then the shape of his face materialized from silken depths. A mask he did not recognize. He took the thing he saw and murmured to it. Had he once been in control? Could he tame it again? Like a garden ruined overnight, pillaged, overgrown, trampled by marauding beasts. He stares at the chaos until he can recall familiar contours of earth, seasons of planting, harvesting, green shoots, nodding blossoms, scraping, digging, watering. Once upon a time he'd cultivated this thing, this plot of flesh and blood and bone, but what had it become? Who owned it now? He'd stepped away. His eyes constructed another face and set it there, between him and the wizened old man in the glass. He's aged twenty years in a glance and the fever possessed the same power to alter suddenly what it touched. This city had grown ancient and fallen into ruin in two months since early August, when the first cases of fever appeared. Something in the bricks, mortar, beams and stones had gone soft, had lost its permanence. When he entered sickrooms, walls fluttered, floors buckled. He could feel roofs pressing down. Putrid heat expanding. In the bodies of victims. In rooms, buildings, streets, neighborhoods. Membranes that preserved the integrity of substances and shapes, kept each in its proper place, were worn thin. He could poke his finger through yellowed skin. A stone wall. The eggshell of his skull. What should be separated was running together. Threatened to burst. Nothing contained the way it was supposed to be. No clear lines of demarcation. A mongrel city. Traffic where there shouldn't be traffic. An awful void opening around him, preparing itself to hold explosions of bile, vomit, gushing bowels, ooze, sludge, seepage.

Earlier in the summer, on a July afternoon, he'd tried to escape the heat by walking along the Delaware. The water was unnaturally calm, isolated into stagnant pools by outcroppings of wharf and jetty. A shelf of rotting matter paralleled the river edge. As if someone had attempted to sweep what was unclean and dead from the water. Bones, skins, entrails, torn carcasses, unrecognizable tatters and remnants broomed into a neat ridge. No sigh of the breeze he'd sought, yet fumes from the rim of garbage battered him in nauseating waves, a palpable medium intimate as wind. Beyond the tidal line of refuse, a pale margin lapped clean by receding waters. Then the iron river itself, flat, dark, speckled by sores of foam that puckered and swirled, worrying the stillness with a life of their own.

Spilled. Spoiled. Those words repeated themselves endlessly as he made his rounds. Dr. Rush had written out his portion, his day's share from the list of dead and dying. He'd purged, bled, comforted and buried victims of the fever. In and out of homes that had become tombs, prisons, charnel houses. Dazed children wandering the streets, searching for their parents. How can he explain to a girl, barely more than an infant, that the father and mother she sobs for are gone from this earth? Departed. Expired. They are resting, child. Asleep forever. In a far, far better place, my sweet, dear, suffering one. In God's bosom. Wrapped in His incorruptible arms. A dead mother with a dead baby at her breast. Piteous cries of the helpless offering all they own for a drink of water. How does he console the delirious boy who pummels him, fastens himself on his leg because he's put the boy's mother in a box and now must nail shut the lid?

Though light-headed from exhaustion, he's determined to spend a few hours here, among his own people. But were these lost ones really his people? The doors of his church were open to them, yet these were the ones who stayed away, wasting their lives in vicious pastimes of the idle, the unsaved, the ignorant. His benighted brethren who'd struggled to reach this city of refuge and then, once inside the gates, had fallen, prisoners again, trapped by chains of dissolute living as they'd formerly been snared in the bonds of slavery. He'd come here and preached to them. Thieves, beggars, loose women, debtors, fugitives, drunkards, gamblers, the weak, crippled and outcast with nowhere else to go. They spurned his church so he'd brought church to them, preaching in gin mills, whoring dens, on street corners. He'd been jeered and hooted, spat upon, clods of unnameable filth had spattered his coat. But a love for them, as deep and unfathomable as his sorrow, his pity, brought him back again and again, exhorting them, setting the gospel before them so they might partake of its bounty, the infinite goodness, blessed sustenance therein. Jesus had toiled among the wretched, the outcast, that flotsam and jetsam deposited like a ledge of filth on the banks of the city. He understood what had brought the dark faces of his brethren north, to the Quaker promise of this town, this cradle and capital of a New World, knew the misery they were fleeing, the bright star in the Gourd's handle that guided them, the joy leaping in their hearts when at last, at last the opportunity to be viewed as men instead of things was theirs. He'd dreamed such dreams himself, oh yes, and prayed that the light of hope would never be extinguished. He'd been praying for deliverance, for peace and understanding when God had granted him a vision, hordes of sable bondsmen throwing off their chains, marching, singing, a path opening in the sea, the sea shaking its shaggy shoulders, resplendent with light and power. A radiance sparkling in this walkway through the water, pearls, diamonds, spears of light. This was the glistening way home. Waters parting, glory blinking and winking. Too intense to stare at, a promise shimmering, a rainbow arching over the end of the path. A hand tapped him. He'd waited for it to blend into the vision, for its meaning to shine forth in the language neither word nor thought. God was speaking in His visitation. Tapping became a grip. Someone was shoving him. He was being pushed off his knees, hauled to his feet. Someone was snatching him from the honeyed dream of salvation. When his eyes popped open he knew the name of each church elder manhandling him. Pale faces above a wall of black cloth belonged to his fellow communicants. He knew without looking the names of the men whose hands touched him gently, steering, coaxing, and those whose hands dug into his flesh, the impatient, imperious, rough hands that shunned any contact with him except as overseer or master.

Allen, Allen. Do you hear me? You and your people must not kneel at the front of the gallery. On your feet. Come. Come. Now. On your feet.

Behind the last row of pews. There ye may fall down on your knees and give praise.

And so we built our African house of worship. But its walls could not imprison the Lord's word. Go forth. Go forth. And he did so. To this sinful quarter. Tunnels, cellars and caves. Where no sunlight penetrates. Where wind off the river cuts like a knife. Chill of icy spray channeled here from the ocean's wintry depths. Where each summer the brackish sea that is mouth and maw and bowel deposits its waste in puddles stinking to high heaven.

Water Street becomes what it's named, rises round his ankles, soaks his boots, threatens to drag him down. Patrolling these murky depths he's predator, scavenger, the prey of some dagger-toothed creature whose shadow closes over him like a net.

When the first settlers arrived here they'd scratched caves into the soft earth of the riverbank. Like ants. Rats. Gradually they'd pushed inland, laying out a geometrical grid of streets, perpendicular, true angled and straight edged, the mirror of their rectitude. Black Quaker coats and dour visages were remembrances of mud, darkness, the place of their lying in, cocooned like worms, propagating dreams of a holy city. The latest comers must always start here, on this dotted line, in this riot of alleys, lanes, tunnels. Wave after wave of immigrants unloaded here, winnowed here, dying in these shanties, grieving in strange languages. But white faces move on, bury their dead, bear their children, negotiate the invisible reef between this broken place and the foursquare town. Learn enough of their new tongue to say to the blacks they've left behind, *thou shalt not pass.*

I watched him bring the scalding liquid to his lips and thought to myself that's where his color comes from. The black brew he drinks every morning. Coloring him, changing him. A hue I had not considered until that instant as other than absence, something nonwhite and therefore its opposite, what light would be if extinguished, sky or sea drained of the color blue when the sun disappears, the blackness of cinders. As he sips, steam rises. I peer into the cup that's become mine, at the moon in its center, waxing, waning. A light burning in another part of the room caught there, as my face would be if I leaned over the cup's hot mouth. But I have no wish to see my face. His is what I study as I stare into my cup and see not absence, but the presence of wood darkly stained, wet plowed earth, a boulder rising from a lake, blackly glistening as it sheds crowns and beards and necklaces of water. His color neither neglect nor abstention, nor mystery, but a swelling tide in his skin of this bitter morning beverage it is my habit to imbibe.

We were losing, clearly losing the fight. One day in mid-September fifty-seven were buried before noon.

He'd begun with no preamble. Our conversation taken up again directly as if the months since our last meeting were no more than a cobweb his first words lightly brush away. I say conversation but a better word would be soliloquy because I was only a listener, a witness learning his story, a story buried so deeply he couldn't recall it, but dreamed pieces, a conversation with himself, a reverie with the power to sink us both into its unreality. So his first words did not begin the story where I remembered him ending it in our last session, but picked up midstream the ceaseless play of voices only he heard, always, summoning him, possessing him, enabling him to speak, to be.

Despair was in my heart. The fiction of our immunity had been exposed for the vicious lie it was, a not so subtle device for wresting us from our homes, our loved ones, the afflicted among us, and sending us to aid strangers. First they blamed us, called the sickness Barbados fever, a contagion from those blood-soaked islands, brought to these shores by refugees from the fighting in Santo Domingo. We were not welcome anywhere. A dark skin was seen not only as a badge of shame for its wearer. Now we were evil incarnate, the mask of long agony and violent death. Black servants were discharged. The draymen, carters, barbers, caterers, oyster sellers, street vendors could find no custom. It mattered not that some of us were born here and spoke no language but the English language, second-, even third-generation African Americans who knew no other country, who laughed at the antics of newly landed immigrants, Dutchmen, Welshmen, Scots, Irish, Frenchmen who had turned our marketplaces into Babel, stomping along in their clodhopper shoes, strange costumes, haughty airs, Lowlander gibberish that sounded like men coughing or dogs barking. My fellow countrymen searching everywhere but in their own hearts, the foulness upon which this city is erected, to lay blame on others for the killing fever, pointed their fingers at foreigners and called it Palatine fever, a pestilence imported from those low countries in Europe where, I have been told, war for control of the sea-lanes, the human cargoes transported thereupon, has raged for a hundred years.

But I am losing the thread, the ironical knot I wished to untangle for you. How the knife was plunged in our hearts, then cruelly twisted. We were proclaimed carriers of the fever and treated as pariahs, but when it became expedient to command our services to nurse the sick and bury the dead, the previous allegations were no longer mentioned. Urged on by desperate counselors, the mayor granted us a blessed immunity. We were ordered to save the city.

I swear to you, and the bills of mortality, published by the otherwise unreliable Mr. Carey, support my contention, that the fever dealt with us severely. Among the city's poor and destitute the fever's ravages were most deadly and we are always the poorest of the poor. If an ordinance forbidding ringing of bells to mourn the dead had not been passed, that awful tolling would have marked our days, the watches of the night in our African American community, as it did in those environs of the city we were forbidden to inhabit. Every morning before I commenced my labors for the sick and dying, I would hear moaning, screams of pain, fearful cries and supplications, a chorus of lamentations scarring daybreak, my people awakening to a nightmare that was devouring their will to live.

The small strength I was able to muster each morning was sorely tried the moment my eyes and ears opened upon the sufferings of my people, the reality that gave the lie to the fiction of our immunity. When my duties among the whites were concluded, how many nights did I return and struggle till dawn with victims here, my friends, parishioners, wandering sons of Africa whose faces I could not look upon without seeing my own. I was commandeered to rise and go forth to the general task of saving the city, forced to leave this neighborhood where my skills were sorely needed. I nursed those who hated me, deserted the ones I loved, who loved me.

I recite the story many, many times to myself, let many voices speak to me till one begins to sound like the sea or rain or my feet those mornings shuffling through thick dust.

We arrived at Bush Hill early. To spare ourselves a long trek in the oppressive heat of the day. Yellow haze hung over the city. Plumes of smoke from blazes in Potter's Field, from fires on street corners curled above the rooftops, lending the dismal aspect of a town sacked and burned. I've listened to the Santo Domingans tell of the burning of Cap François. How the capital city was engulfed by fires set in cane fields by the rebelling slaves. Horizon in flames all night as they huddled offshore in ships, terrified, wondering where next they'd go, if any port would permit them to land, empty-handed slaves, masters whose only wealth now was naked black bodies locked in the hold, wide-eyed witnesses of an empire's downfall, chanting, moaning, uncertain as the sea rocked them, whether or not anything on earth could survive the fearful conflagration consuming the great city of Cap François.

Dawn breaking on a smoldering landscape, writhing columns of smoke, a general cloud of haze the color of a fever victim's eyes. I turn and stare at it a moment, then fall in again with my brother's footsteps trudging through untended fields girding Bush Hill.

From a prisoner-of-war ship in New York harbor where the British had interned him he'd seen that city shed its grave-clothes of fog. Morning after morning it would paint itself damp and gray, a flat sketch on the canvas of sky, a tentative, shivering screen of housefronts, sheds, sprawling warehouses floating above the river. Then shadows and hollows darkened. A jumble of masts, spars, sails began to sway, little boats plied lanes between ships, tiny figures inched along wharves and docks, doors opened, windows slid up or down, lending an illusion of depth and animation to the portrait. This city infinitely beyond his reach, this charade other men staged to mock him, to mark the distance he could not travel, the shore he'd never reach, the city, so to speak, came to life and with its birth each morning dropped the palpable weight of his despair. His loneliness and exile. Moored in pewter water, on an island that never stopped moving but never arrived anywhere. The city a mirage of light and air, chimera of paint, brush and paper, mattered naught except that it was denied him. It shimmered. Tolled. Unsettled the watery place where he was sentenced to dwell. Conveyed to him each morning the same doleful tidings: *The dead are legion, the living a froth on dark, layered depths. But you are neither, and less than both.* Each night he dreamed it burning, razed the city till nothing remained but a dry, black crust, crackline, crunching under his boots as he strides, king of the nothing he surveys. We passed holes dug into the earth where the sick are interred. Some died in these shallow pits, awash in their own vomited and voided filth, before a bed in the hospital could be made ready for them. Others believed they were being buried alive, and unable to crawl out, howled till reason or strength deserted them. A few, past caring, slept soundly in these ditches, resisted the attendants sent to rouse them and transport them inside, once they realized they were being resurrected to do battle again with the fever. I'd watched the red-bearded French doctor from Santo Domingo with his charts and assistants inspecting this zone, his *salle d'attente* he called it, greeting and reassuring new arrivals, interrogating them, nodding and bowing, hurrying from pit to pit, peering down at his invisible patients like a gardener tending seeds.

An introduction to the grave, a way into the hospital that prefigured the way most would leave it. That's what this bizarre rite of admission had seemed at first. But through this and other peculiar stratagems, Deveze, with his French practice, had transformed Bush Hill from lazarium to a clinic where victims of the fever, if not too weak upon arrival, stood a chance of surviving.

The cartman employed by Bush Hill had suddenly fallen sick. Faithful Wilcox had never missed a day, ferrying back and forth from town to hospital, hospital to Potter's Field. Bush Hill had its own cemetery now. Daily rations of dead could be disposed of less conspicuously in a plot on the grounds of the estate, screened from the horror-struck eyes of the city. No one had trusted the hospital. Tales of bloody chaos reigning there had filtered back to the city. Citizens believed it was a place where the doomed were stored until they died. Fever victims would have to be dragged from their beds into Bush Hill's cart. They'd struggle and scream, pitch themselves from the rolling cart, beg for help when the cart passed a rare pedestrian daring or foolish enough to be abroad in the deadly streets.

I wondered for the thousandth time why some were stricken, some not. Dr. Rush and this Deveze dipped their hands into the entrails of corpses, stirred the black, corrupted blood, breathed infected vapors exhaled from mortified remains. I'd observed both men steeped in noxious fluids expelled by their patients, yet neither had fallen prey to the fever. Stolid, dim Wilcox maintained daily concourse with the sick and buried the dead for two months before he was infected. They say a woman, undiscovered until boiling stench drove her neighbors into the street crying for aid, was the cause of Wilcox's downfall. A large woman, bloated into an even more cumbersome package by gases and liquids seething inside her body, had slipped from his grasp as he and another had hoisted her up into the cart. Catching against a rail, her body had slammed down and burst, spraying Wilcox like a fountain. Wilcox did not pride himself on being the tidiest of men, nor did his job demand one who was overfastidious, but the reeking stench from that accident was too much even for him and he departed in a huff to change his polluted garments. He never returned. So there I was at Bush Hill, where Rush had assigned me with my brother, to bury the flow of dead that did not ebb just because the Charon who was their familiar could no longer attend them.

The doctors believe they can find the secret of the fever in the victims' dead bodies. They cut, saw, extract, weigh, measure. The dead are carved into smaller and smaller bits and the butchered parts studied but they do not speak. What I know of the fever I've learned from the words of those I've treated, from stories of the living that are ignored by the good doctors. When lancet and fleam bleed the victims, they offer up stories like prayers.

It as a jaunty day. We served our white guests and after they'd eaten, they served us at the long, linen-draped tables. A sumptuous feast in the oak grove prepared by many and willing hands. All the world's eyes seemed to be watching us. The city's leading men, black and white, were in attendance to celebrate laying the cornerstone of St. Thomas Episcopal African Church. In spite of the heat and clouds of mettlesome insects, spirits were high. A gathering of whites and blacks in good Christian fellowship to commemorate the fruit of shared labor. Perhaps a new day was dawning. The picnic occurred in July. In less than a month the fever burst upon us.

When you open the dead, black or white, you find: the dura mater covering the brain is white and fibrous in appearance. The leptomeninges covering the brain are clear and without opacifications. The brain weighs 1450 grams and is formed symmetrically. Cut sections of the cerebral hemispheres reveal normal-appearing gray matter throughout. The white matter of the corups callosum is intact and bears no lesions. The basal banglia are in their normal locations and grossly appear to be without lesions. The ventricles are symmetrical and filled with crystal-clear cerebrospinal fluid.

The cerebellum is formed symmetrically. The nuclei of the cerebellum are unremarkable. Multiple sections through the pons, medulla oblongata and upper brain stem reveal normal gross anatomy. The cranial nerves are in their normal locations and unremarkable.

The muscles of the neck are in their normal locations. The cartilages of the larynx and the hyoid bone are intact. The thyroid and parathyroid glands are normal on their external surface. The mucosa of the larynx is shiny, smooth and without lesions. The vocal cords are unremarkable. A small amount of bloody material is present in the upper trachea.

The heart weighs 380 grams. The epicardial surface is smooth, glistening and without lesions. The myocardium of the left ventricle and septum are of a uniform meaty-red, firm appearance. The endocardial surfaces are smooth, glistening and without lesions. The auricular appendages are free from thrombi. The valve leaflets are thin and delicate, and show no evidence of vegetation.

The right lung weighs 400 grams. The left lung 510 grams. The pleural surfaces of the lungs are smooth and glistening.

The esophageal mucosa is glistening, white and folded. The stomach contains a large amount of black, noxious bile. A veriform appendix is present. The ascending, transverse and descending colon reveal hemorrhaging, striations, disturbance of normal mucosa patterns throughout. A small amount of bloody, liquid feces is present in the ano-rectal canal.

The liver weighs 1720 grams. The spleen weighs 150 grams. The right kidney weighs 190 grams. The left kidney weighs 180 grams. The testes show a glistening white tunica albuginea. Sections are unremarkable.

Dr. Rush and his assistants examined as many corpses as possible in spite of the hurry and tumult of never-ending attendance on the sick. Rush hoped to prove his remedy, his analysis of the cause and course of the fever correct. Attacked on all sides by his medical brethren for purging and bleeding patients already in a drastically weakened state, Rush lashed back at his detractors, wrote pamphlets, broadsides, brandished the stinking evidence of his postmortems to demonstrate conclusively how the sick drowned in their own poisoned fluids. The putrefaction, the black excess, he proclaimed, must be drained away, else the victim inevitably succumbs.

Dearest:

I shall not return home again until this business of the fever is terminated. I fear bringing the dread contagion into our home. My life is in the hands of God and as long as He sees fit to

spare me I will persist in my labors on behalf of the sick, dying and dead. We are losing the
battle. Eighty-eight were buried this past Thursday. I tremble for your safety. Wish the lie of
immunity were true. Please let me know by way of a note sent to the residence of Dr. Rush
that you and our dear Martha are well. I pray every hour that God will preserve you both. As
difficult as it is to rise each morning and go with Thomas to perform our duties, the task
would be unbearable if I did not hold in my heart a vision of these horrors ending, a blessed
shining day when I return to you and drop this weary head upon your sweet bosom.

Allen, Allen, he called to me. Observe how even after death, the body rejects this
bloody matter from nose and bowel and mouth. Verily, the patient who had
expired at least an hour before, continued to stain the cloth I'd wrapped round
him. We'd searched the rooms of a regal mansion, discovering six members of a
family, patriarch, son, son's wife and three children, either dead or in the last
frightful stages of the disease. Upon the advice of one of Dr. Rush's most outspo-
ken critics, they had refused mercury purges and bleeding until now, when it was
too late for any earthly remedy to preserve them. In the rich furnishings of this
opulent mansion, attended by one remaining servant whom fear had not driven
away, three generations had withered simultaneously, this proud family's link to
past and future cut off absolutely, the great circle broken. In the first bedroom
we'd entered, we'd found William Spurgeon, merchant, son and father, present
manager of the family fortune, so weak he could not speak, except with pained
blinks of his terrible golden eyes. Did he welcome us? Was he apologizing to good
Dr. Rush for doubting his cure? Did he fear the dark faces of my brother and
myself? Quick, too quickly, he was gone. Answering no questions. Revealing nothing of his state of mind. A savaged face frozen above the blanket. Ancient beyond
years. Jaundiced eyes not fooled by our busy ministrations, but staring through us,
fixed on the eternal stillness soon to come. And I believe I learned in that yellow
cast of his eyes, the exact hue of the sky, if sky it should be called, hanging over the
next world where we abide.

Allen, Allen. He lasted only moments and then I wrapped him in a sheet from
the chest at the foot of his canopied bed. We lifted him into a humbler litter,
crudely nailed together, the lumber still green. Allen, look. Stench from the coffin
cut through the oppressive odors permeating this doomed household. See. Like an
infant the master of the house had soiled his swaddling clothes. Seepage formed a
dark river and dropped between roughly jointed boards. We found his wife where
she'd fallen, naked, yellow above the waist, black below. As always the smell pre-
saged what we'd discover behind a closed door. This woman had possessed clos-
ets of finery, slaves who dressed, fed, bathed and painted her, and yet here she lay,
no one to cover her modesty, to lift her from the floor. Dr. Rush guessed from the
discoloration she'd been dead two days, a guess confirmed by the loyal black maid,
sick herself, who'd elected to stay when all others had deserted her masters. The
demands of the living too much for her. She'd simply shut the door on her dead
mistress. No breath, no heartbeat, Sir. I could not rouse her, Sir. I intended to

return, Sir, but I was too weak to move her, too exhausted by my labors, Sir. Tears rolled down her creased black face and I wondered in my heart how this abused and despised old creature in her filthy apron and turban, this frail, worn woman, had survived the general calamity while the strong and pampered toppled round her.

I wanted to demand of her why she did not fly out the door now, finally freed of her burden, her lifelong enslavement to the whims of white people. Yet I asked her nothing. Considered instead myself, a man who'd worked years to purchase his wife's freedom, then his own, a so-called freeman, and here I was following in the train of Rush and his assistants, a functionary, a lackey, insulted daily by those I risked my life to heal.

Why did I not fly? Why was I not dancing in the streets, celebrating God's judgment on this wicked city? Fever made me freer than I'd ever been. Municipal government had collapsed. Anarchy ruled. As long as fever did not strike me I could come and go anywhere I pleased. Fortunes could be amassed in the streets. I could sell myself to the highest bidder, as nurse or undertaker, as surgeon trained by the famous Dr. Rush to apply his lifesaving cure. Anyone who would enter houses where fever was abroad could demand outrageous sums for negligible services. To be spared the fever was a chance for anyone, black or white, to be a king.

So why do you follow him like a loyal puppy, you confounded black fool? He wagged his finger. *You* ... His finger a gaunt, swollen-jointed, cracked-bone, chewed thing. Like the nose on his face. The nose I'd thought looked more like finger than nose. *Fool. Fool.* Finger wagging, then the cackle. The barnyard braying. Berserk chickens cackling in his skinny, goiterknobbed throat. You are a fool, you black son of Ham. You slack-witted, Nubian ape. You progeny of Peeping Toms and orangutans. Who forces you to accompany that madman Rush on his murderous tours? He kills a hundred for every one he helps with his lamebrain, nonsensical, unnatural, Sangrado cures. Why do you tuck your monkey tail between your legs and skip after that butcher? Are you his shadow, a mindless, spineless black puddle of slime with no will of its own?

You are a good man, Allen. You worry about the souls of your people in this soulless wilderness. You love your family and your God. You are a beacon and steadfast. Your fatal flaw is narrowness of vision. You cannot see beyond these shores. The river, that stinking gutter into which the city shovels its shit and extracts its drinking water, that long-suffering string of spittle winds to an ocean. A hundred miles downstream the foamy mouth of the land sucks on the Atlantic's teat, trade winds saunter and a whole wide world awaits the voyager. I know, Allen. I've been everywhere. Buying and selling everywhere.

If you would dare be Moses to your people and lead them out of this land, you'd find fair fields for your talent. Not lapdogging or doggy-trotting behind or fetch doggy or lie doggy or doggy open your legs or doggy stay still while I beat you.

Follow the wound that is a river back to the sea. Be gone, be gone. While there's still time. If there is time, *mon frère*. If the pestilence has not settled in you already, breathed from my foul guts into yours, even as we speak.

Here's a master for you. A real master, Allen. The fever that's supping on my innards. I am more slave than you've ever been. I do its bidding absolutely. Cough up my lungs. Shit hunks of my bowel. When I die, they say my skin will turn as black as yours, Allen.

Return to your family. Do not leave them again. Whatever the Rushes promise, whatever they threaten.

Once, ten thousand years ago I had a wife and children. I was like you, Allen, proud, innocent, forward looking, well-spoken, well-mannered, a beacon and steadfast. I began to believe the whispered promise that I could have more. More of what, I didn't ask. Didn't know, but I took my eyes off what I loved in order to obtain this more. Left my wife and children and when I returned they were gone. Forever lost to me. The details are not significant. Suffice to say the circumstances of my leaving were much like yours. Very much like yours, Allen. And I lost everything. Became a wanderer among men. Bad news people see coming from miles away. A pariah. A joke. I'm not black like you, Allen. But I will be soon. Sooner than you'll be white. And if you're ever white, you'll be as dead as I'll be when I'm black.

Why do you desert your loved ones? What impels you to do what you find so painful, so unjust? Are you not a man? And free?

Her sleepy eyes, your lips on her warm cheek, each time may be the last meeting on this earth. The circumstances are similar, my brother. My shadow. My dirty face.

The dead are legion, the living a froth on dark, layered depths.

Master Abraham. There's a gentleman to see you, Sir. The golden-haired lad bound to me for seven years was carted across the seas, like you, Allen, in the bowels of a leaky tub. A son to replace my son his fathers had clubbed to death when they razed the ghetto of Antwerp. But I could not tame the inveterate hate, his aversion and contempt for me. From my aerie, at my desk secluded among barrels, bolts, crates and trunks of the shop's attic, I watched him steal, drink, fornicate. I overheard him denounce me to a delegate sent round to collect a tithe during the emergency. 'Tis well known in the old country that Jews bring the fever. Palatine fever that slays whole cities. They carry it under dirty fingernails, in the wimples of lizardy private parts. Pass it on with the evil eye. That's why we hound them from our towns, exterminate them. Beware of Master Abraham's glare. And the blackcoated vulture listened intently. I could see him toting up the account in his small brain. Kill the Jew. Gain a shop and sturdy prentice, too. But I survived till fever laid me low and the cart brought me here to Bush Hill. For years he robbed and betrayed me and all my revenge was to treat him better. Allow him to pilfer, lie, embezzle. Let him grow fat and careless as I knew he would. With a father's boundless kindness I destroyed him. The last sorry laugh coming when I learned he died in agony, fever shriven, following by a day his Water Street French whore my indulgence allowed him to keep.

In Amsterdam I sold diamonds, Allen. In Barcelona they plucked hairs from my beard to fashion charms that brought ill fortune to their enemies. There were nights in dungeons when the mantle of my suffering was all I possessed to wrap round me and keep off mortal cold. I cursed God for choosing me, choosing my people to cuckold and slaughter. Have you heard of the Lamed-Vov, the Thirty Just Men set apart to suffer the reality humankind cannot bear? Saviors. But not Gods like your Christ. Not magicians, not sorcerers with bags of tricks, Allen. No divine immunities. Flesh and blood saviors. Men like we are, Allen. If man you are beneath your sable hide. Men who cough and scratch their sores and bleed and stink. Whose teeth rot. Whose wives and children are torn from them. Who wander the earth unable to die, but men always, men till God plucks them up and returns them to His side where they must thaw ten centuries to melt the crust of earthly grief and misery they've taken upon themselves. Ice men. Snowmen. I thought for many years I might be one of them. In my vanity. My self-pity. My foolishness. But no. One lifetime of sorrows enough for me. I'm just another customer. One more in the crowd lined up at his stall to purchase his wares.

You do know, don't you, Allen, that God is a bookseller? He publishes one book—the text of suffering—over and over again. He disguises it between new boards, in different shapes and sizes, prints on varying papers, in many fonts, adds prefaces and postscripts to deceive the buyer, but it's always the same book.

You say you do not return to your family because you don't want to infect them. Perhaps your fear is well-founded. But perhaps it also masks a greater fear. Can you imagine yourself, Allen, as other than you are? A free man with no charlatan Rush to blame. The weight of your life in your hands.

You've told me tales of citizens paralyzed by fear, of slaves on shipboard who turn to stone in their chains, their eyes boiled in the sun. Is it not possible that you suffer the converse of this immobility? You, sir, unable to stop an endless round of duty and obligation. Turning pages as if the next one or the next will let you finish the story and return to your life.

Your life, man. Tell me what sacred destiny, what nigger errand keeps you standing here at my filthy pallet? Fly, fly, fly away home. Your hose is on fire, your children burning.

I have lived to see the slaves free. My people frolic in the streets. Black and white. The ones who believe they are either or both or neither. I am too old for dancing. Too old for foolishness. But this full moon makes me wish for two good legs. For three. Straddled a broomstick when I was a boy. Giddy-up, Giddy-up. Galloping m'lord, m'lady, around the yard I should be sweeping. Dust in my wake. Chickens squawking. My eyes everywhere at once so I would not be caught out by mistress or master in the sin of idleness. Of dreaming. Of following a child's inclination. My broom steed snatched away. Become a rod across my back. Ever cautious. Dreaming with one eye open. The eye I am now, old and gimpy limbed, watching while my people celebrate the rumor of Old Pharaoh's capitulation.

I've shed this city like a skin, wiggling out of it tenscore and more years, by miles and els, fretting, twisting. Many days I did not know whether I'd wrenched freer or crawled deeper into the sinuous pit. Somewhere a child stood, someplace green, keeping track, waiting for me. Hoping I'd meet him again, hoping my struggle was not in vain. I search that child's face for clues to my blurred features. Flesh drifted and banked, eroded by wind and water, the landscape of this city fitting me like a skin. Pray for me, child. For my unborn parents I carry in this orphan's potbelly. For this ancient face that slips like water through my fingers.

Night now. Bitter cold night. Fires in the hearths of lucky ones. Many of us still abide in dark cellars, caves dug into the earth below poor men's houses. For we are poorer still, burrow there, pull earth like blanket and quilt round us to shut out cold, sleep multitudes to a room, stacked and crosshatched and spoon fashion, ourselves the fuel, heat of one body passed to others and passed back from all to one. No wonder then the celebration does not end as a blazing chill sweeps off the Delaware. Those who leap and roar round the bonfires are better off where they are. They have no place else to go.

Given the derivation of the words, you could call the deadly, winged visitors an *unpleasantness from Egypt.*

Putrid stink rattles in his nostrils. He must stoop to enter the cellar. No answer as he shouts his name, his mission of mercy. Earthen floor, ceiling and walls buttressed by occasional beams, slabs of wood. Faint bobbing glow from his lantern. He sees himself looming and shivering on the walls, a shadowy presence with more substance than he feels he possesses at this late hour. After a long day of visits, this hovel his last stop before returning to his brother's house for a few hours of rest. He has learned that exhaustion is a swamp he can wade through and on the far side another region where a thin trembling version of himself toils while he observes, bemused, slipping in and out of sleep, amazed at the likeness, the skill with which that other mounts and sustains him. Mimicry. Puppetry. Whatever controls this other, he allows the impostor to continue, depends upon it to work when he no longer can. After days in the city proper with Rush, he returns to these twisting streets beside the river that are infected veins and arteries he must bleed.

At the rear of the cave, so deep in shadow he stumbles against it before he sees it, is a mound of rags. When he leans over it, speaking down into the darkness, he knows instantly this is the source of the terrible smell, that something once alive is rotting under the rags. He thinks of autumn leaves blown into mountainous, crisp heaps, the north wind cleansing itself and the city of summer. He thinks of anything, any image that will rescue him momentarily from the nauseating stench, postpone what he must do next. He screams no, no to himself as he blinks away his wife's face, the face of his daughter. His neighbors had promised to check on them, he hears news almost daily. There is no rhyme or reason in whom the fever takes, whom it spares, but he's in the city every day, exposed to its victims, breathing fetid air, touching corrupted flesh. Surely if someone in his family must die, it will be him. His clothes are drenched in vinegar, he sniffs the nostrum of gunpowder, bark and asafetida in a bag pinned to his coat. He's prepared to purge and bleed himself, he's also ready and quite willing to forgo these precautions and cures if he thought surrendering his life might save theirs. He thinks and unthinks a picture of her hair, soft against his cheek, the wet warmth of his daughter's backside in the crook of his arm as he carries her to her mother's side where she'll be changed and fed. No. Like a choking mist, the smell of decaying flesh stifles him, forces him to turn away, once, twice, before he watches himself bend down into the brunt of it and uncover the sleepers.

Two Santo Domingan refugees, slave or free, no one knew for sure, inhabited this cellar. They had moved in less than a week before, the mother huge with child, man and woman both wracked by fever. No one knows how long the couple's been unattended. There was shame in the eyes and voices of the few from whom he'd gleaned bits and pieces of the Santo Domingans' history. Since no one really knew them and few nearby spoke their language, no one was willing to risk, et cetera. Except for screams one night, no one had seen or heard signs of life. If he'd been told nothing about them, his nose would have led him here.

He winces when he sees the dead man and woman, husband and wife, not entwined as in some balled of love eternal, but turned back to back, distance between them, as if the horror were too visible, too great to bear, doubled in the other's eyes. What had they seen before they flung away from each other? If he could, he would rearrange them, spare the undertakers this vision.

Rat feet and rat squeak in the shadows. He'd stomped his feet, shooed them before they entered, hollered as he threw back the covers, but already they were accustomed to his presence, back at work. They'd bite indiscriminately, dead flesh, his flesh. He curses and flails his staff against the rags, strikes the earthen floor to keep the scavengers at bay. Those sounds are what precipitate the high-pitched cries that first frighten him, then shame him, then propel him to a tall packing crate turned on its end, atop which another crate is balanced. Inside the second wicker container, which had imported some item from some distant place into this land, twin brown babies hoot and wail.

We are passing over the Dismal Swamp. On the right is the Appalachian range, some of the oldest mountains on earth. Once there were steep ridges and valleys all through here but erosion off the mountains created landfill several miles deep in places. This accounts for the rich loamy soil of the region. Over the centuries several southern states were formed from this gradual erosion. The cash crops of cotton and tobacco so vital to southern prosperity were ideally suited to the fertile soil.

Yeah, I nurse these old funky motherfuckers, all right. White people, specially old white people, lemme tell you, boy, them peckerwoods stink. Stone dead fishy wet stink. Talking all the time bout niggers got BO. Well, white folks got the stink and gone, man. Don't be putting my hands on them, neither. Never. Huh uh. If I touch them, be wit gloves. They some nasty people, boy. And they don't be paying me enough to take no chances wit my health. Matter of fact they ain't paying me enough to really be expecting me to work. Yeah. Starvation wages. So I ain't hardly touching them. Or doing much else either. Got to smoke a cigarette to get close to some of them. Piss and shit theyselves like babies. They don't need much taking care anyway. Most of them three-quarters dead already. Ones that ain't is crazy. Nobody don't want them round, that's why they here. Talking to theyselves. Acting like they speaking to a roomful of people and not one soul in the ward paying attention. There's one old black dude, must be a hundred, he be muttering away to hisself nonstop everyday. Pitiful, man. Hope I don't never get that old. Shoot me, bro, if I start to getting old and fucked up in body and mind like them. Don't want no fools like me hanging over me when I can't do nothing no more for my ownself. Shit. They ain't paying me nothing so that's what I do. Nothing. Least I don't punch em or tease em or steal they shit like some the staff. And I don't pretend I'm God like these so-called professionals and doctors flittin round here drawing down that long bread. Naw, I just mind my own business, do my time. Cop a little TV, sneak me a joint when nobody's around. It ain't all that bad, really. Long as I ain't got no ole lady and crumb crushers. Don't know how the married cats make it on the little bit of chump change they pay us. But me, I'm free. It ain't that bad, really.

By the time his brother brought him the news of their deaths . . .

Almost an afterthought. The worst, he believed, had been overcome. Only a handful of deaths the last weeks of November. The city was recovering. Commerce thriving. Philadelphia must be revictualed, refueled, rebuilt, reconnected to the countryside, to markets foreign and domestic, to products, pleasures and appetites denied during the quarantine months of the fever. A new century would soon be dawning. We must forget the horrors. The Mayor proclaims a new day. Says let's put the past behind us. Of the eleven who died in the fire he said extreme measures were necessary as we cleansed ourselves of disruptive influences. The cost could have been much greater, he said I regret the loss of life, especially the half dozen kids, but I commend all city officials, all volunteers who helped return the city to the arc of glory that is its proper destiny.

When they cut him open, the one who decided to stay, to be a beacon and stead-fast, they will find: liver (1720 grams), spleen (150 grams), right kidney (190 grams), left kidney (180 grams), brain (1450 grams), heart (380 grams) and right next to his heart, the miniature hand of a child, frozen in a grasping gesture, fin-gers like hard tongues of flame, still reaching for the marvel of the beating heart, fascinated still, though the heart is cold, beats not, the hand as curious about this infinite stillness as it was about thump and heat and quickness.

About the Book and Editor

Ancestral House is the only short story anthology in existence that acknowledges the richness and diversity of writers from the African Diaspora. The collection is stunning and comprehensive, laying open in one sumptuous stroke the fascinating and complex tradition of black life throughout the Americas and Europe. Within this ancestral house reside José Alcántara Almánzar of the Dominican Republic, Luiz Silva "Cuti" of Brazil, René Depestre of Haiti, Suzanne Dracius-Pinalie of Martinique, Adalberto Ortiz of Ecuador, Astrid Roemer of Surinam/Holland, Elio Ruiz of Cuba, Ann Lydia Vega of Puerto Rico, and a plethora of U.S. citizens, including Toni Cade Bambara, Amiri Baraka, Rita Dove, Ernest J. Gaines, Charles Johnson, Jamaica Kincaid, Toni Morrison, Alice Walker, and John Edgar Wideman. The 70 uncut stories in this collection comprise 36 writers from the United States and 34 writers from Europe and the Americas.

For the student, the general reader, and the scholar alike, what better introduction to the black short story can there be? As the editor and founder in 1976 of *Callaloo,* Charles H. Rowell has been the unwavering prism through which new talent and established artists have cast their considerable light; his choices have been exquisite and his influence profound. With the authority of this experience, Rowell has given us in this carefully selected anthology of short fiction abundant proof of the fact of African continuities; of the cultural exchange among Africa, Europe, and the Americas; and of the shared literary and oral traditions among countries, continents, and epochs. It is a brilliant achievement and a joy—and by the mere fact of its inclusiveness, a scholarly contribution.

Charles H. Rowell is professor of English at the University of Virginia in Charlottesville and editor of *Callaloo: A Journal of African-American and African Arts and Letters.*

Notes on Contributors

AI is author of one novel and five books of poems, *Cruelty, Killing Floor, Sin, Fate,* and *Greed.* She lives in Tempe, Arizona.

JOSÉ ALCÁNTARA ALMÁNZAR was born in Santo Domingo. In his native Dominican Republic, he is widely known for his short stories (e.g., *Viaje al otro mundo* and *Callejón sin Salida*) and literary criticism, *Estudios de poesia Dominicana. The Masks of Seduction* won the 1984 National Prize for Short Stories in the Dominican Republic.

TINA MCELROY ANSA, who lives on St. Simons Island in Georgia, is author of two novels, *Baby of the Family* and *Ugly Ways.*

TONI CADE BAMBARA is author of two collections of short stories, *Gorilla, My Love* and *The Seabirds Are Still Alive,* and a novel, *The Salt Eaters.* In 1970, she edited an anthology entitled *The Black Woman.* She lives in Philadelphia.

AMIRI BARAKA (LeRoi Jones) is author of several books, including *Tales, The System of Dante's Hell, Dutchman, The Autobiography of LeRoi Jones/Amiri Baraka, Blues People, Black Magic Poetry, 1961–1967,* and *Daggers and Javelins.* He lives in Newark, New Jersey.

HAL BENNETT is a native of Virginia, living in Mexico. His numerous books of fiction include *Insanity Runs in Our Family: Short Stories, Lord of Dark Places,* and *Seventh Heaven.*

DIONNE BRAND, who lives in Canada, is author of *Primitive Offensive, Chronicles of the Hostile Sun, Winter Epigrams and Epigrams to Ernesto Cardenal in Defense of Claudia, Sans Souci and Other Stories, No Language Is Neutral,* and many other texts. She was born in Trinidad.

OCTAVIA E. BUTLER, winner of the 1985 Nebula Award, lives in Los Angeles. Her books of fiction include *Patternmaster, Kindred, Clay's Ark, Dawn,* and *Imago.*

OSWALDO DE CAMARGO, a native of Brazil, is a poet, fiction writer, journalist, and literary critic. His publications include *Um homen tenta ser anjo, O carro do [ecircum]xito, O estranho,* and *O negro escrito.* He is one of the co-founders (with Luiz Silva "Cuti" and Paulo Colina) of the Quilombhoje writers group of São Paulo.

AÍDA CARTAGENA PORTALATÍN (d. 1994) was known as a writer and intellectual throughout the Santo Domingo, where she founded the press Brigadas Dominicanas. Her books of poetry, fiction, and cultural criticism include *Una mujer está sola, Visparas del Sueño, La voz desatada, Escalera para Electra, José Vela Zanetti,* and *El culto sincrético en villa mell, música, canto y danzas de los indio de española.* She was born in 1918 in Moca, Dominican Republic.

MAXINE CLAIR teaches English at George Washington University in Washington, D.C. She is author of *Rattlebone,* a collection of short stories.

AUSTIN C. CLARKE is a native of Barbados. *When He Was Free and Young and He Used to Wear Silk* (short stories), *Survivors of the Crossing, Storm of Fortune, The Bigger Light, When He Was Free and Young and Used to Wear Silks*, and *The Meeting Point* are among his many books. He lives in Canada, where he is also well known as a broadcaster.

MICHELLE CLIFF, who was born in Jamaica, is author of *No Telephone to Heaven, Claiming an Identity They Taught Me to Despise, The Land of Look Behind, Abeng*, and *Bodies of Water*. She lives in California.

MERLE COLLINS grew up in Grenada and spent a major portion of her adult life in England. Her publications include *Because the Dawn Breaks, Angel*, and *Rain Darling*. She recently moved to the United States.

CHRISTINE CRAIG is author of *Mint Tea* (short stories) and *Quadrille for Tigers* (poems). She lives in her native Jamaica.

LUIZ SILVA "CUTI" was born in São Paulo, Brazil, where he (with Oswaldo de Camargo and Paulo Colina) co-founded the Quilombhoje writers group. *Poemas da carapinha, Suspensão, Quizila, Batuque de Tocaia*, and *Reflexões sobre literatura Afro-Brasileira* are some of his numerous books of fiction, poetry, drama, and literary criticism.

SAMUEL R. DELANY, who began his writing career at the age of twenty, is author of several books of fiction, including *The Fall of Towers, Nova, Babel–17, The Einstein Intersection, Dhalgren*, and *The Mad Man*. A four-time winner of Nebula Awards from the Science Fiction Writers of America, he teaches comparative literature at the University of Massachusetts in Amherst.

RENÉ DEPESTRE was born in Jacmel, Haiti, from which he has been exiled since 1946. He is author of *Aléluia pour une femme-jardin, récits d'amour solaire, Poète à Cuba, Un Arc-en-ciel four l'occident chrétien* (transl. as *A Rainbow for the Christian West* by Joan Dayan), *Le M[acircum]t de cocagne* (transl. as *The Festival of the Creasy Pole* by Carrol F. Coates), *Journal d'un animal marin*, and numerous other books. He lives in France.

RITA DOVE, Poet Laureate of the United States and Consultant in Poetry at the Library of Congress (1993–1995), is Commonwealth Professor of English at the University of Virginia in Charlottesville. She is author of two books of fiction, *Fifth Sunday* (short stories) and *Through the Ivory Gate* (a novel), a play, *The Darker Face of the Earth*, and six books of poems, *The Yellow House on the Corner, Museum, Thomas and Beulah* (winner of the 1987 Pulitzer Prize), *Selected Poems, Grace Notes*, and *Mother Love*.

SUZANNE DRACIUS-PINALIE, a native of Martinique, is author of two novels, *L'Autre qui danse* and *La mangeuse de lotus* (forthcoming). She is a professor of classical studies at Université des Antilles-Guyane.

HENRY DUMAS, who was murdered by white policemen in a New York subway in 1968, was born in Sweet Home, Arkansas, in 1934. *Jonoah and the Green Stone*, a novel, *Goodbye, Sweetwater*, a collection of short fiction, *Knees of a Natural Man*, a volume of poems—these are his posthumous books, variously edited by Eugene Redmond.

QUINCE DUNCAN was born in San Jose, Costa Rica. His numerous publications include a collection of short stories, *Una cancion madrugada*, a novel, *Final de calle*, and a study (with Carlos Melendez), *El negro en Costa Rica*.

NELSON ESTUPIÑÁN BASS lives in Quito, Ecuador. His numerous publications include *Canto negro por la luz poemas para negros y blancos, El último río, Cuando los guayacanes slorecían,* and *Senderos brillantes.* In recognition of his literary production, the Ecuadorian government has given him a lifelong pension.

PERCIVAL EVERETT, a native of South Carolina, is author of nine books of fiction, including *Walk Me to the Distance, For Her Dark Skin, Zulus,* and *God's Country.* He is chair of the Department of Creative Writing at the University of California at Riverside.

GUY-MARK FOSTER is currently doing graduate work in English at Brown University. His work has appeared in *The Portable Lower East Side, The Road Before Us, Brother to Brother,* and *Shadows of Love.*

ERNEST J. GAINES is a MacArthur Foundation Fellow and author of *Bloodline* (short stories), *The Autobiography of Miss Jane Pittman, Of Love and Dust, A Gathering of Old Men,* and *A Lesson Before Dying.* He lives in his native southern Louisiana.

THOMAS GLAVE, a Jamaican by birth, lives in New York. He has published in a variety of periodicals and anthologies, including *Sojourner, Callaloo, The James White Review, The Best Short Stories by Black Writers, II,* and *The Kenyon Review.* During the 1980s, he performed with The Dance Theatre of Harlem.

LORNA GOODISON was born in Jamaica. She is author of *Tamarind Season, Baby Mother and the King of Swords,* and *Heartease.* She was awarded the Commonwealth Poetry Prize for *I Am Becoming My Mother.*

CLAIRE HARRIS moved from her native Trinidad to Canada in 1966. In 1984, she won the Commonwealth Prize for her *Fables from the Women's Quarters. Travelling to Find a Remedy, The Conception of Winter, Translation into Fiction, Drawing Down a Daughter,* and *My Sister's Child* are some of her other publications.

WILSON HARRIS is author of numerous books of fiction and nonfiction prose, including *The Guyana Quartet, Carnival, Infinite Rehearsal, The Four Banks of the River of Space, Resurrection at Sorrow Hill, The Radical Imagination, Tradition, the Writer and Society,* and *The Womb of Space: The Cross-Cultural Imagination.* This native of Guyana lives in England.

JOHN HOLMAN, a native of North Carolina, is author of *Squabble and Other Stories.* He teaches at the University of South Florida in Tampa.

KELVIN CHRISTOPHER JAMES was born in Trinidad. He is author of a collection of short stories, *Jumping Ship and Other Stories,* and a novel, *Secrets.* He lives in Harlem, New York.

CHARLES JOHNSON is author of *Middle Passage, Faith in the Good Thing, Oxherding Tale, The Sorcerer's Apprentice,* and *Being and Race: Black Writing Since 1970.* He also writes screenplays. He teaches at the University of Washington, Seattle.

EDWARD P. JONES won the Pen/Hemingway Award for his first book, *Lost in the City,* a collection of short stories. He lives in Arlington, Virginia.

GAYL JONES is a native of Lexington, Kentucky. She is author of three books of fiction and two volumes of poems, including *White Rat* (short stories), *Eva's Man,* and *Corrigadora,* and *Song for Anninho. Liberating Voices: Oral Tradition in African American Literature,* her first book of literary criticism, was published by Harvard University Press in 1991.

JOHN R. KEENE was born in St. Louis, Missouri. His work has been published in *Brother to Brother, Kenyon Review, Callaloo,* and other anthologies and periodicals.

WILLIAM MELVIN KELLEY lives in New York. His books of fiction include *A Different Drummer, dem, A Drop of Patience, Dancers on the Shore,* and *Dunfords Travels Everywheres.*

RANDALL KENAN, winner of a Whiting-Giles Award in 1994, is author of *A Visitation of Sprits* (a novel), *Let the Dead Bury the Dead,* and *James Baldwin: Author, Activist, Visionary* (a biography for young adults). This North Carolina native lives in New York City.

JAMAICA KINCAID, a frequent contributor to *The New Yorker* magazine, was born in Antigua. *At the Bottom of the River, Annie John, A Small Place* (nonfiction), and *Lucy* are some of her publications. She lives in Vermont.

YANICK LAHENS lives in Haiti, where she serves as an editor for Editions Henri Deschamps. She is author of *L'Exil: en pre l'ancrage et la fuite—l'écrivain haiti[euml]n* (nonfiction) and *Tante resia* (short stories).

HELEN ELAINE LEE, a graduate of the Harvard University Law School, lives in Washington, D.C. *The Serpent's Gift* is her first novel.

EARL LOVELACE lives in his native Trinidad. His books of fiction include *While Gods Are Falling, The Schoolmaster, The Wine of Astonishment, The Dragon Can't Dance,* and *A Brief Conversation and Other Stories.*

CLARENCE MAJOR is director of the creative writing program at the University of California (Davis). *My Ambutations, All Night Visitors, Such Was the Season, Painted Turtle: Woman with Guitar, The Syncopated Cake Walk, Surfaces and Masks, The Dictionary of Afro-American Slang,* and *The Dark and Feeling: Black American Writers and Their Work* are some of the numerous books of poetry, fiction, and nonfiction prose he has authored.

PAULE MARSHALL, a MacArthur Foundation Fellow, is author of four novels, *Brown Girl, Brownstones, Daughters, The Chosen Place, The Timeless People,* and *Praisesong for the Widow;* and three books of short fiction, *Soul Clap Hands and Sing, Reena and Other Stories,* and *Merle and Other Stories.*

JOHN McCLUSKEY JR. teaches English and African American studies at Indiana University in Bloomington. *Look What They Done to My Song* and *Mr. America's Last Season Blues* are his two novels. He is editor of *City of Refuge: Collected Stories of Rudolph Fisher.*

REGINALD McKNIGHT is author of a book of nonfiction prose, *African American Wisdom,* and three books of fiction, *Moustapha's Eclipse, I Get on the Bus,* and *The Kind ofLight That Shines on Texas.* He is professor of English at the University of Maryland, where he teaches courses in creative writing.

TERRY McMILLAN is author of three novels, *Mama, Disappearing Acts,* and *Waiting to Exhale.* She edited *Breaking Ice: An Anthology of Contemporary African-American Fiction.* She lives in San Francisco.

MARK McMORRIS, editor of the Caribbean section of *Exact Change Yearbook, I,* was born in Kingston, Jamaica, where he received his early education. His work has appeared in *Apex of the M, Callaloo, Conjunction, Hambone,* and *The Kenyon Review.* He is currently studying for a Ph.D. in comparative literature at Brown University.

JAMES ALAN McPHERSON, one of the first MacArthur Foundation Fellows (1981), is author of two collections of short stories, *Hue and Cry* and *Elbow Room* (winner of the 1978 Pulitzer Prize for Fiction). He teaches creative writing at the University of Iowa.

PAULINE MELVILLE, a native of Guyana, is an actress and author of *Shape-Shifter,* which won the Commonwealth Writers Prize. She lives in England.

OPAL MOORE teaches at Radford University in Virginia. Her short stories have appeared in numerous anthologies and periodicals, including *American Voice* and *Callaloo.* She lives in Richmond, Virginia.

TONI MORRISON won the 1993 Nobel Prize for Literature. Her most recent publications include *Tar Baby, Beloved* (winner of the 1988 Pulitzer Prize for Fiction), *Jazz,* and *Playing in the Dark: Whiteness and the Literary Imagination.* She is Robert F. Goheen Professor, Council of the Humanities, Princeton University.

BRUCE MORROW is associate director of the Teachers and Writers Collaborative in New York. His work has appeared in *Callaloo, New York Times,* and *Speak My Name: An Anthology of Writings About Black Men's Identity and Legacy.* With Charles H. Rowell, he is co-editing *Signing Myself,* an international anthology of short fiction by gay men of African descent.

WALTER MOSLEY is author of *Black Betty, Devil in a Blue Dress, A Red Death,* and *White Butterfly.* He lives in New York.

ADALBERTO ORTIZ is author of *Juyungo* (novel) and *Tierra, son y tambor: cantares negros y mulatos* (poems). In 1964, he was awarded the Ecuadorian National Prize for Literature for his novel *El espejo y la ventana.* He lives in Quito.

STANLEY PÉAN was born in Port-au-Prince, Haiti. His publications include *La Plage des songes et autre récits d'exil* (short stories) and *Le Tumulte de mon sang* (novel). He lives in Canada.

RICHARD PERRY is author of two novels, *Changes* and *Montgomery's Children.* He lives in New York and teaches at Pratt Institute.

M. NOURBESE PHILIP, a lecturer and lawyer living in Canada, was born in Tobago. She is author of a novel, *Harriet's Daughter,* and three books of poetry, *Salmon Courage, Thorns,* and *As She Tries Her Tone Her Silence Softly Breaks.* She won the 1988 Casa de las Americas Prize for Poetry.

ALIX RENAUD, a native of Haiti, lives in Canada. He is author of several volumes of fiction, drama, and poetry, including *Car[ecircum]me, Merdiland, Le troc mystérieux, Snesnob, A corps joie,* and *M. de Vastey.*

JEWELL PARKER RHODES is author of the novel *Voodoo Dreams.* Her work has also been published in *Callaloo, Calyx, Ms.,* and *Seattle Review.* She teaches creative writing at California State University in Northridge.

ESMERALDA RIBEIRO, a poet, fiction writer, and poststructuralist critic, was born in São Paulo, Brazil, where she is a member of the Quilombhoje writers group. She is author of the novella *Malungos e milongas.*

ASTRID ROEMER, who was born in Surinam, lives in The Hague, Holland. *Levenslang gedicht, Sasa, Nergens Ergens, Noordzeeblues,* and *Over de gekte van een vrouw* are four of her many books of fiction and poetry. She has also written numerous plays for stage and radio.

ELIO RUIZ, writer, journalist, and filmmaker, was born in Cuba. His documentaries "Los Que Llegaron Despues" (1989) and "¿Quien Baila Aqui? La Rumba Sin Lente Juelas" (1990) have won awards in Cuba, Puerto Rico, and Mexico. He lives in Mexico City.

DARIECK SCOTT, a candidate for the Ph.D. degree in Modern Thought and Literature at Stanford University, is author of *Traitor to the Race,* a novel. He co-founded and edited the *Yale Journal of Law and Liberation* in 1989 and has previously published his fiction in *Christopher Street.*

OLIVE SENIOR won the 1987 Commonwealth Writers Prize for *Summer Lightning,* her first collection of short stories. This native of Jamaica is also author of *Talking of Trees* (poems), *The Arrival of the Snake Woman, Gardening in the Tropics,* and *The Discerner of Hearts.*

MAKEDA SILVERA, co-founder of Sister Vision: Black Men and Women of Colour Press, is author of *Remembering G and Other Stories* and *Silenced: Oral Histories of Caribbean Domestic Workers in Canada.* She has edited numerous anthologies, including *Piece of My Heart* and *The Other Woman: Women of Colour in Canadian Literature.* She was born in Kingston, Jamaica.

CARLOS ARTURO TRUQUE was born in El Choco, Colombia. His collection of short stories, *Granizada y otros cuentos,* won the 1953 Premio Spiral. His short stories have been widely translated.

ANA LYDIA VEGA is author of a screenplay, *La Gran fiesta,* as well as books of fiction—e.g., *Encancaranublado y otros cuentos de naufragio* and *Falsas cronicas del sur*—for which she has won the Puerto Rico PEN Club Award, Juan Rulfo International Prize (Paris), and the Casa de las Americas Prize.

ALICE WALKER, whose novel *The Color Purple* won the Pulitzer Prize, is author of numerous books of fiction, poetry, and nonfiction prose, including *Possessing the Secret of Joy, The Third Life of Grange Copeland, The Temple of My Familiar, In Love and Trouble, You Can't Keep a Good Woman Down, Her Blue Body Everything We Know: Earthling Poems 1965–1990 Complete, In Search of Our Mothers' Gardens,* and *Living by the Word: Selected Writings 1973–1987.*

JOHN EDGAR WIDEMAN, a MacArthur Foundation Fellow, is author of numerous award-winning books of fiction and nonfiction prose, including *Fever, Philadelphia Fire, Reuben, Damballah, Hiding Place, Sent for You Yesterday, Brothers and Keepers,* and *Father Along.* He teaches at the University of Massachusetts (Amherst).

DATE DUE
